Australianuak: Basques in the Antipodes

Australianuak:
Basques in the Antipodes

by

William A. Douglass

Center for Basque Studies
University of Nevada, Reno
2019

This book was published with the generous
financial assistance of the Basque Government.

Basque Diaspora and Migration Series
No. 16
Series editor: Xabier Irujo
Copyright © 2019 Center for Basque Studies
Translation © 2019 William A. Douglass
Cover design copyright © David Ter-Avanesyan

LIBRARY OF CONGRESS CATALOGING-IN-PUBLICATION DATA

CIP to come

To Miren and Mary
Josu and Joe
and may there always be
Australian Nekanes and Aitors.

Contents

	Preface	ix
	Introduction: Basque Background	1
1.	Conclusion as Introduction	13
2.	Australia Beckons	40
3.	Basques in Nineteenth-Century Australia	69
4.	From the Fraire Expedition (1891) to the Ferry Exposition (1925)	103
5.	Controversy and Confrontation (1925–1945)	165
6.	Rehabilitation and Renewal	235
7.	The Spanish Alternative	271
8.	Basques in the Antipodes	305
9.	Coming Together	334
10.	Basques in the New Australia	381
11.	Voices	391
12.	The Facilitator	591
13.	Becoming a Basque Entrepreneur	611
14.	The Wandering Basque	627
	Conclusion (Bis)	679
	Appendix I: European Residence of Basque Adult Males Recruited for Queensland, 1958–1960	691
	Appendix II: Queensland Basques Entering Australia Who Became Naturalized Citizens	699
	Appendix III: Australian Poem in Basque	703
	Appendix IV: Original Membership List of the Spanish Society of North Queensland	709
	Coda	711
	Bibliography	759
	Index	771

Preface

This book has its own rather peculiar history. It began as anthropological field research that I conducted in Australia (and North Queensland in particular) in the spring of 1977 and then between February and November of 1980 (and with subsequent shorter return visits). During the 1980 stint, my new bride, Jan, my recently married younger brother, David, and his spouse Mary came along. They were all excited to sample the fieldwork aspect of my chosen profession and certainly shared a romanticized notion of it. So the four of us were off on our rather exotic working honeymoons.

During our first week in Sydney, I purchased a flamboyantly yellow, well-used station wagon that had served as a taxicab before being retired from active duty. We promptly christened it "La Bamba." It was just capacious enough to accommodate our several suitcases and squished bodies—we were pretty reminiscent of the proverbial sardines in a can or maybe the classic clown act in which a dozen pop out of some tiny vehicle. Anyway, the car dealer had filled our tank, no doubt to assuage his conscience whenever he contemplated our foreordained car trouble. It was a good thing, too, since New South Wales was embroiled in a gasoline dealers' strike and there was no fuel on offer. So, we crossed our fingers and just managed to cross into Queensland on the vapors of our depleted reserve. It then took us several days of marathon driving to reach the "Far North," the Australian counterpart to our own American "Deep South."

Along the way, we crossed the Tropic of Capricorn and experienced the gradual transition of a changing landscape that evolved from temperate zone foliage to semitropical and then the real deal. By journey's end in the small country town of Ingham (about a hundred kilometers north of Townsville) we were practically adjacent to New Guinea, a point that was underscored when the remnants of a cyclone dropped thirty inches of rain during our first twenty four hours—isolating us from the outside world for several days. We knew we were no longer in Nevada when we saw beleaguered wallabies wandering about the downtown and heard about the twelve-foot sea crocodile perched on our main bridge!

We rented a house and I began interviewing informants while my three companions spent their days in the archive of the local newspaper, the *Herbert River Express*, taking notes for me regarding the history of the local sugar industry and recruitment of labor for it. After a few months, we completed the Ingham phase of the research—David and Mary were ready to go home to the States and Jan and I prepared to move to our second field site in the town of Ayr in the Burdekin.

La Bamba then became our home on wheels as we tracked down former canecutters who had resettled elsewhere in Australia. The odyssey took us from the Atherton Tablelands in the extreme north to Sales on the border of South Australia. Along the way we spent time in the agricultural district of Griffith and with relocated urbanites in Brisbane, Sydney, and Melbourne. Then there was the two-week stint in Canberra poring through official immigration records and bonding with colleagues at the Australian National University.

And what was the point? I was engaged in a controlled comparative study of Spanish Basque and Italian Abruzzese immigrants recruited in the late 1950s as manual canecutters for one of the world's most extensive sugar industries stretching along nearly two thousand miles of the eastern Australian littoral. But then, in the 1960s, the harvesting had been mechanized and the newcomers suddenly faced unemployment. It was my intention to interview a cohort of each ethnic group that remained in the sugar districts (but with new economic strategies), another of each that resettled and began a new life elsewhere in Australia, and, finally, a sample of those that returned to their European homeland. As a social anthropologist, I was trying to determine if I could "explain" (at least in part) variation in the formulation of specific new life strategies in terms of the cultural differences between Old World Basque and Abruzzese society.

The "controlled comparison" dimension of the research derived from the fact that I had conducted prior social anthropological fieldwork on the causes and consequences of emigration in the village of Aulesti

(Murélaga), Bizkaia,[1] in the Basque Country; and the town of Agnone, Isernia, in the Abruzzo-Molise region of southern Italy.[2] In both I had interviewed returnees who had cut sugar cane in North Queensland. Indeed, some of my informants from Aulesti and Agnone had actually met one another while in the sugar districts. Small world, indeed!

In addition to the field and archival research in Australia, I applied questionnaires to samples of twenty-five Basques and twenty-five Abruzzesi who had remained in the cane districts after mechanization of the harvest, twenty-five of each group who had resettled elsewhere in Australia pursuing new economic strategies, and finally two cohorts of twenty-five of each who had given up on Australia and returned to Europe with their savings.[3] The results of this comparative research project were published in 1996 (in Spanish) by the University of the Basque Country Press.[4]

There was also a sense in which I was engaged in a study of the respective immigration histories of the two groups. Indeed, I subsequently published a book with Queensland University Press that is limited to the Italians.[5] I have also published some of my impressions of Basque-Australian history.[6] On balance, however, to date I have written far more about Italians than Basques in Australia. That is ironic, given my career history as founder and first director (for thirty-three years) of the Basque Studies Program of the University of Nevada System.

I had always intended to write a book about "Basques in the Antipodes," a work that would transcend their history as canecutters in Australia by including the extensive Basque contribution to Spanish exploration of the South Pacific. Other professional commitments and personal challenges (particularly years of caregiving after Jan became critically ill) bogged down the project. In 2002, she and I returned to Australia—presumably to update my data and to give her the opportunity to visit and take her leave of our many Australian friends.

The intense caregiving absorbed most of my energy until Jan's death in 2005. I was then distracted by other writing projects, as well as new challenges in my personal and business life. It was not until 2013 that I returned to this work. I envisioned a first part that would deal with Basque precursors to the recent canecutters, but then that grew into a book of its own.[7] So, here I am in 2019, finally completing the present *Australianuak: Basques in the Antipodes.* Better very late than never!

Notes

1. William A. Douglass, *Echalar and Murelaga: Opportunity and Rural Depopulation in Two Spanish Basque Villages* (London: C. Hurst and Co.; New York: St. Martin's Press, 1975). [*Echalar and Murelaga*].
2. William A. Douglass, *Emigration in a South Italian Town: An Anthropological History* (New Brunswick: Rutgers University Press, 1984).
3. The European questionnaires were administered by two assistants who had worked with me previously. Iban Bilbao completed the Basque ones, while Angelo de Vita was my Italian interviewer. I am deeply grateful to both.
4. William A. Douglass, *Azúcar amargo: vida y fortuna de los cortadores de caña italianos y vascos en la Australia tropical* (Bilbao: Servicio Editorial de la Universidad del País Vasco, 1996). [*Azúcar*].
5. William A. Douglass, *From Italy to Ingham: Italians in North Queensland* (Brisbane: University of Queensland Press, 1995). [*From Italy*].
6. William A. Douglass, "Sheep Ranchers and Sugar Growers: Property Transmission in the Basque Immigrant Family of the American West and Australia," in *Households: Comparative and Historical Studies of the Domestic Group*, ed. Robert M. Netting, Richard R. Wilk, and Eric J. Arnould (Berkeley and Los Angeles: University of California Press, 1984), 109–29. ["Sheep Ranchers"]; William A. Douglass, "Basques," in *The Australian People: An Encyclopedia of the Nation, Its People and Their Origins*, ed. James Jupp (North Ryde, N.SW.: Angus and Robertson, 1988), 282–84; William A. Douglass, "The Basques of North Queensland, Australia," in *Homenaje a Francisco de Abrisketa/Frantzisko Abrisketa'ri Omenaldia*, ed. Román Basurto Larrañaga (Bolibar, Bizkaia: Sociedad Bolivariana del País Vasco, 1993), 443–66; William A. Douglass, "Los vascos de North Queensland, Australia," in *Los otros vascos. Las migraciones vascas en el s. XX*, ed. F. Xavier Medina (Madrid: Editorial Fundamentos, 1997), 189–219.
7. William A. Douglass, *Basque Explorers in the Pacific Ocean* (Reno: Center for Basque Studies, University of Nevada, Reno, 2015). [*Basque Explorers*].

INTRODUCTION

Basque Background

Within Europe's ethnic spectrum, the Basques' claim to distinctiveness is strong, particularly as evidenced by their language Euskara (which to date most linguists regard to be unrelated to any other known human tongue). The Basque homeland, or Euskalherria (El País Vasco; Le Pays Basque),[1] straddles what would eventually become the Spanish-French border during the sixteenth century. The contemporary geopolitical expression of Iparralde, or the Northern Area, known to many as the French Basque Country, includes Lapurdi (Labourd), Behe Nafarroa (Basse Navarre), and Xiberoa (Soule). Hegoalde, or the Southern Area (the Spanish Basque Country), encompasses the four provinces of Bizkaia (Vizcaya), Araba (Álava), Gipuzkoa (Guipúzcoa), and Nafarroa (Navarra).

Euskalherria is quite small. From Baiona (Bayonne) in the north to Tutera (Tudela) in the extreme south of Navarra is 160 kilometers and the distance from Bilbo (Bilbao) on the extreme western fringe to Maule-Lextarre (Mauleón-Licharre) near the eastern one is 170 kilometers. Of the total 20,000 square kilometers of Euskalherria, about nine-tenths is in Hegoalde. Its population is about 2.5 million inhabitants; that of Iparralde is only around 220,000.

The component units of Hegoalde retain their historical personalities down to the present day—in part due to a "foral" tradition. Reference is to the *fueros* of each of the constituent entities. The emblematic example is that of Bizkaia. Its *fuero*, or "Old Law," was first written down in 1451. For Basque nationalists, this was merely formal codification of consuetudinary practices dating from centuries earlier, ones that take precedence over the whims and wishes of external rulers including absolutist royal

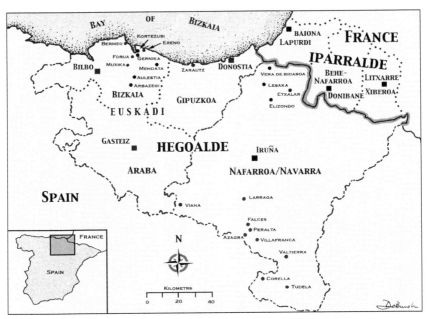

MAP 1. Basque Country/Euskalherria. Drawing by Patricia DeBunch.

ones. Indeed, until the nineteenth century, upon acceding to the throne, first the Castilian and subsequently the Spanish monarch either traveled to Bizkaia or sent a representative to swear to respect Bizkaia's foral order. It was also recognition that Bizkaians were in contractual agreement to be part of a larger political order, an arrangement that can only be modified by mutual agreement but abrogated by either party. The monarch's vow was taken in Gernika (Guernica) beneath the oak tree where the elected representatives from throughout Bizkaia met periodically to legislate. To this day, the tree of Gernika has sacred overtones for many Basques and is the visible symbol of their political independence and aspirations. Spanish nationalists have a different interpretation of foral history, whereby the *fuero* is a grant of privilege that may only be altered or even rescinded by the monarch (or state). After their defeat in the last Carlist War of the late nineteenth century, the Basques were essentially stripped of their foral privileges.

Today, Spain is a federalist state composed by seventeen autonomous regions. There is an Autonomous Basque Community (Euskadi) that includes Bizkaia, Araba, and Gipuzkoa. It has its own president and parliament and (along with Galicia and Catalunya) has the status of historical territory under the constitution forged in the late 1970s after the death of dictator Francisco Franco. The designation of "historical territory" is recognition of the greater ethnic and linguistic uniqueness and historical personality of the three regions in question—yet within the framework of a unified Spanish state. Although also "Basque," Navarra has pursued an independent course and now has its own autonomous community status and regional political infrastructure within a federated Spain. There is a modern Basque nationalist movement (dating from the late nineteenth century) that garners roughly half of Euskadi's vote in regional elections. Its radical left, aligned formerly with the terrorist organization ETA, receives about one-tenth to one-fifth of the vote depending upon the issues of the day. While all Basque nationalists may be regarded as foralists, ETA[2] and the radical left advocate full independence (or at least self-determination) for all of Euskalherria—an agenda that receives its greatest support in Euskadi, considerably less in Navarra, and practically none in Iparralde.

Situated at the point where the western Pyrenees meet the Cantabrian Sea, Euskalherria is characterized by a long coastline indented with several natural harbors. Consequently, the area has an extensive fishing complex and a longstanding maritime tradition. Basques may well have been Europe's earliest whalers and Basque cod fishermen have plied the North Atlantic since at least the early 1500s and possibly before.[3] During much of the sixteenth century, 80 percent of the sea traffic between Spain and its New World territories was controlled by Basque interests and manned by Basque sailors.[4] This extensive involvement with the sea continues down to the present.

Another characteristic of the Basque economy is industrialization. Iron ore deposits have made it a locus of mining activity since antiquity.[5] In the nineteenth century, local entrepreneurs and British interests developed an iron ore export trade between Bizkaia and England. During the same period an indigenous industrial complex emerged, primarily in the largest Basque city of Bilbo and a number of Bizkaian and Gipuzkoan towns such as Gernika, Durango, Eibar, and Tolosa. In the mid-twentieth century, tax incentives (during the Franco dictatorship) created extensive manufacturing complexes around Gasteiz (Vitoria) and Iruñea (Pamplona) as well. As a consequence, Hegoalde emerged as one of Iberia's two most industrialized regions (Catalunya being the other) that, until recently, enjoyed the highest *per capita* income in Spain.[6]

As one of Spain's most prosperous regions during the twentieth century, Hegoalde has attracted massive numbers of migrants from elsewhere within the country.[7] Its pronounced population growth since the middle of the nineteenth century was concentrated in urban centers and satellite manufacturing towns. Throughout the period, the countryside experienced a rural exodus, as ethnic Basques themselves joined the search for employment in the local burgeoning industrial complex or emigrated abroad.[8]

In contrast to Hegoalde, Iparralde is devoid of industry and is one of the least prosperous regions of France. It receives more funds in government subsidies than it sends in taxes to Paris. While it has a robust emigration history, practically none of its leavers went to Australia. Consequently, Iparralde falls largely outside the purview of this text.

With the exception of a number of Navarrans (derived mainly from central and southern Navarra where the Basque language and culture are largely absent at present) and a handful of Arabans and Gipuzkoans, Australia's Basque immigrants came from Bizkaia—and particularly a few foci in its rural districts. Certainly, some were mariners from coastal villages like Bermeo and Lekeitio, but the majority came from the interior rural districts such as greater Markina-Aulesti-Arbazegi and Gernika-Mungia-Muxika. There are also notable foci in northern Navarra (Bera/Vera de Bidasoa to Elizondo) and in its south (Larraga to Valtierra).

The Australian emigrants from Euskadi were, in the main, Basque-speaking agriculturalists with limited formal educations. Their terrain was extremely mountainous. Only the narrow river bottoms contain reasonably level land. The majority of farmsteads (*baserriak*)[9] are located in hilly areas where even the arable patches have some degree of slope. Working them requires enormous effort and defies mechanization. The soil was literally turned over by hand or with animal-drawn single-bladed plowshares. On the plus side, the maritime Cantabrian climate is mild and predictable; winter snow and summer drought being unusual.

The typical *baserri* encompassed about a hectare of arable, two or three hectares of meadowland, and about five to six hectares of forest—roughly ten hectares in all. Furthermore, the vast majority conformed to this mean, underscoring the essentially egalitarian nature of rural Basque life.

Ideally, each *baserri* maintained a family engaged in what was largely subsistence agriculture—producing its own fruits and vegetables, pork from its few pigs, mutton from its small flock of sheep, and milk from its four or five dairy cows. The fairly minimal need for cash was covered by the sale of a little timber, a few piglets, lambs, calves, and sheep's cheese and cow's milk.[10] The farmstead was either a social isolate situated roughly in the center of its combined private property, and possibly removed by as much as a half kilometer from its closest neighbor, or part of a hamlet of a dozen or fewer households surrounded by their collective landholdings. In both cases, the residents enjoyed access to the village commons where they pastured livestock on both grass and nuts from the deciduous oaks and chestnuts and obtained the ferns that were mixed with manure to fertilize their private plow land and meadow. Such use of the commons by one and all further underscored the egalitarian ethos.[11]

The *baserri* formed part of an *auzo*, or neighborhood, constituted either by ten or twelve scattered *baserriak* or the hamlet. Within the *auzo* each household was obligated to send a member to engage in periodic communal work projects called *auzolan* ("neighborhood work")—such as maintenance of roads, streams and springs, and possibly a chapel. The *auzo* would also provide mutual aid to families suffering the crippling effects of the severe illness of a member or the sudden death of a cow (a big deal). Neighbors gathered together to rebuild a member's dwelling lost to fire.[12] It might be argued that such corporate sentiments underscored a Basque propensity to organize the world-famous industrial cooperatives of Arrasate (Mondragón)[13]—not to mention the cane-cutting gangs of North Queensland.

The *auzoak* of a particular village were located at distances ranging from a kilometer to several from a nucleus that contained the school, church and graveyard, the mayoralty, the police, essential professionals like the doctor and blacksmith, taverns, dry goods stores, a bakery and grocery shop, a restaurant or two, and possibly a soccer field and a *frontón* (court) for handball and/or *jai alai*. In sum, like the *auzo* and *baserri*, the Basque village, or *herri*, displayed a considerable degree of autonomy and self-sufficiency.

The French sociologist Frédéric Le Play singled out the *baserri* Basque household as the archetypical example of the *famille souche* or stem family. He extolled its virtues as a bastion of social stability in contrast to the chaotic deterioration observable in the modern urban-industrial nuclear family milieu.[14] The moralistic and political implications in such thinking notwithstanding, Le Play was correct about the structural nature of the rural Basque family and its capacity for continuity and stasis.

The stem family is reproduced through the practice of naming a single married heir to the farmstead in each generation who then co-resides with his/her parents. Ideally, legal transfer of *baserri* ownership is consummated at the marriage of the selected successor. The heir's siblings are expected to leave the household, although they retain a right of residence insofar as they remain single and are willing to be subordinated to the authority of the active married couple. Most leave, however, possibly marrying the heir or heiress of a neighboring farmstead, professing religious vows or migrating to a nearby urban area or abroad. The status of a stayer is underscored by the terminology of *mutil zahar* ("old boy") for a bachelor and *neska zahar* ("old girl") for a spinster.

The criterion for selecting the heir/heiress varies throughout the Basque Country, ranging from prescribed male primogeniture in Bizkaia (the region of origin of most of the Australian emigrants) to unfettered competition for the inheritance among all offspring of a given generation irrespective of age, order, or gender.[15]

Within the stem family household the twin authority figures are the active male or *etxekojaun* ("lord of the house") and female *etxekoandre* ("lady of the house"). The terminology is reflective of the unique contention of Basque peasants, dating from the Middle Ages when they enjoyed not only the status as freemen (when most of their European counterparts were entailed serfs) but also claimed universal nobility. While the "spectacle" of rustic bumpkins flaunting noble titles was the object of ridicule by "true" aristocratic Spaniards, and lampooned by writers such as Cervantes,[16] in point of fact universal *hidalguía* provided Basques with access to administrative and ecclesiastical posts within the Hispanic world that would have otherwise been off bounds.

Jurally, within Basque rural society, the marriage of the heir/heiress signals the retirement of his/her progenitors, albeit in practice the latter tended to remain active until death according to their physical capacity.

There is a strong sense of egalitarianism between the *etxekojaun* and *etxekoandre* regarding the critical decisions affecting family and farmstead. Basque women retained personal property rights even when they were withheld from most of their counterparts under the European feudal order. This sense of equality carries over to the work sphere in which women engage in the heaviest agricultural tasks alongside their menfolk.[17]

Until recently, for rural Basques, the *baserri* represented the epitome of the good life. To be an *etxekojaun* or *etxekoandre* were the two most prestigious roles to which a man or woman could aspire. *Baseritarrak* ("*baserri* people") were deemed to be morally superior to *kaletarrak* ("street people")—urbanites. City dwellers and even residents of the village nucleus were somewhat disdained. Life on the *baserri* was extolled in oral literature and music as embodying freedom and rugged individualism. The first stanza of a popular nineteenth-century folksong reflects this attitude:

Ikusten dozu goizean	[Look up at the break of day
argia asten denean,	when sunlight begins to bathe everything
menditxo baten gainean.	upon the small rise.
Etxe txikitxo, aintzin zuri bat,	There appears a small white house,
lau aitz ondoren artean,	surrounded by four oaks,
txakur txiki bat atean,	a small dog on the doorstep,
iturriño bat aldean.	a fresh spring nearby.
An bizi naiz ni, pakean.	There I live in peace.]

For the rural Basque, then, there was love of the land. Each generation was expected to serve as custodian of an agricultural heritage received from the ancestors to be passed on to descendants. It should be noted that land ownership, while extensive, was not ubiquitous. Many families were renters, inhabitants of a *baserri* owned by an absentee landlord. Nevertheless, custom (and some legislation) dictated that the renter families had similar rights to the *baserri* as did those who owned one. This included the right to will tenancy of it to their selected heir. So ownership per se did not create a social class division within the ranks of the *baserritarrak*.

Paralleling the reverential attitude toward land is the perception that hard, physical labor upon it is both the means to economic security and a validation of self-worth. There is the concept of *indarra* that embraces several semantic domains such as "strength," "fortitude," "perseverance," and "power." It is a pervasive value in rural Basque culture. Devotion to task, a capacity for endurance, and physical strength all confer *indarra* upon the individual.[18] Even standards of physical beauty are reflective of *indarra*, since it is the man or woman who is large, muscular, and therefore in possession of stamina and strength who is esteemed rather than the slighter person.

Throughout much of the nineteenth and twentieth centuries (or until the death of Francisco Franco), there was little emphasis upon formal education in rural Basque society. The children were kept at home to help with agricultural chores, particularly during the fall harvest. Anti-intellectualism was reinforced by the friction between teachers who instructed in Spanish and denigrated the Basque language, on the one hand, and the pupils who arrived at school age as monolingual Basque speakers, on the other. Students were regularly punished for speaking their maternal language. For some parents, this was a daily reminder of the detested Spanish imperialism with respect to the Basque language and culture, particularly during the Franco era. The priesthood was the only scholastic occupation esteemed by rural Basques.

The foregoing description of rural life captures the Old World background of a majority of the Basque emigrants to Australia. There was, however, a smaller focus in southern and central Navarra that resulted from a formal recruitment there in the late 1950s of canecutters for Queensland. It was a region of agro-towns in which the rural workforce was landless and salaried to farm wheat, olives, and vines in the surrounding countryside, traveling daily from their households in the nucleus to work the fields. Historically, it was an area of large Roman estates or latifundiums. To this day, many large properties in this region are owned by absentee landlords.

This book regards but one tiny chapter in the lengthy book of the history of Basque emigration. The rural poverty endemic in farming difficult terrain, along with the relatively small size of the typical *baserri*, the longstanding maritime tradition that exposed Basques to other lands, the endemic and frequent Iberian military conflicts, and, above all, the inheritance system that produced many leavers in each generation combined to make rural Basque society one of the most pronounced European seedbeds of candidates for emigration. Furthermore, the three territories constituting present-day Euskadi were a part of the Castilian orbit for the last millennium and the Kingdom of Navarra was conquered and incorporated into an emerging "Spain" in 1512, or but two decades after Columbus's first voyage under the patronage of the Catholic monarchs. As early as 1511, when the monarchs needed to recruit colonists for the New World, King Ferdinand issued an edict to his administrators: "I order them to publicize [this notice] in the mountains of Guipúzcoa where there are many inhabitants and few recourses, so that workers will go out to those parts."[19]

As one of Iberia's prime maritime and shipbuilding centers, Basques played a prominent role in the transatlantic voyages of discovery. It was a Basque, Elkano, who completed Magellan's voyage, taking command of the expedition after his admiral was killed in the Philippines, and thereby becoming the first man to circumnavigate the globe. For the next two and a half centuries there was considerable Basque involvement in the exploration of the Pacific Ocean.[20]

So, Basques were intricately involved in the New World endeavor from its infancy—not to mention in practically every capacity from manual laborers through merchants and mercenaries to missionaries and elite administrators.[21] Furthermore, at different times and in different places, they formed ethnic enclaves. Their group success sometimes evoked the envy of other Iberians and the fear that the colonial enterprise was being subverted into a Basque undertaking.

The New World independence movements of the early nineteenth century interdicted elitist Basque emigration. However, there were new developments within Spain, notably the Napoleonic invasions and a series of Carlist Wars (fought primarily in the Basque homeland), that stimulated renewed emigration—particularly to the established Basque diasporic enclaves of Latin America. This was facilitated by the tendency of several nascent Latin American countries to foment Iberian (and other European) immigration as a nation-building strategy to supplant "barbarian" Native Americans from vast potential agricultural lands—notably, albeit not exclusively, in the so-called "southern cone" of Uruguay, Argentina, and Chile.

By the 1830s and 1840s, Basques were firmly established as sheepmen on the pampas. When gold was discovered in California, some South American Basques joined the ranks of the fortune-seeking Argonauts. Quickly disillusioned with prospecting, many saw the opportunity to acquire sheep bands and run them on the largely unoccupied public lands of southern and central California. Over the next half century they expanded throughout the region, and particularly into the high desert of eastern Oregon, northern Nevada, and southern Idaho. Consequently, by century's end, Basques had become the stereotypic sheepmen of the American West, an identification that persisted until about the late 1970s. In short, several Latin American host societies and the American West were often viable alternatives to Australia as a young intending-emigrant Basque chose his/her destination.

Much of the emigration of rural Basques to New World destinations was coterminous with the industrialization of the Basque economy. While some Basques migrated to the new factory districts along with even more job seekers from other impoverished parts of Iberia, it is somewhat ironic that the majority emigrated abroad in search of opportunity. The two migration patterns were so pronounced that today ethnic Basques are in a minority in their Hegoalde homeland.

It is equally true, however, that the majority of Basque emigrants left with the intention of returning. The leaver was typically a young male in search of the opportunity to accumulate a stake with which to purchase a *baserri* or pay off the mortgage on the family one, or possibly establish a small business somewhere back in the Basque Country. Of course, along the way many changed their minds and became established with families and businesses in their New World host country.

Such households formed the basis for what are today the Basque diasporas in dozens of countries around the world. Wherever there are significant concentrations of Basques and persons of hyphenated Basque descent (Basque-Argentinians, Basque-Chileans, etc.), there tends to be considerable ethnic group consciousness that underpins ethnic associations, dance groups, and festival celebrations. In short, whether in the European homeland or one of the diasporas, there is a marked tendency for many persons to define themselves as Basques rather than in terms of their nationality as Spaniards or Frenchmen. In both venues there is tension, as well, between Basques, a "nation without a state," and the dominating Spanish and French cultures.

The particular Australian expression of all of these themes and conflicts are the subject of the following narrative.

Notes

1. I follow current Basque etymological usage for place names, rather than the Spanish or French (which I place in parentheses). I will use Navarra for that territory, since it is employed by that region's autonomous government.
2. In 2011, ETA declared a unilateral ceasefire truce and willingness to forsake violence for political protagonism. While issues such as the destruction of its arms, the fate of incarcerated ETA operatives, reinsertion of its fugitives back into society, and compensation of the victims of terrorism after more than a half century of violence remain, the truce has held. See Teresa Whitfield, *Endgame for ETA: Elusive Peace in the Basque Country* (Oxford and New York: Oxford University Press, 2014). On May 2, 2018, ETA declared unilaterally its own dissolution.
3. William A. Douglass and Jon Bilbao, *Amerikanuak: Basques in the New World* (Reno: University of Nevada Press, 1975), 51–57. (*Amerikanuak*).
4. John Lynch, *Spain under the Hapsburgs*, vol. 1, *Empire and Absolutism (1516–1598)* (Oxford and New York: Oxford University Press, 1964), 165.
5. Douglass and Bilbao, *Amerikanuk*, 49–51.
6. Stanley G. Payne, *Basque Nationalism* (Reno: University of Nevada Press, 1975), 230–31.
7. Francisco Javier Gómez-Piñeiro et al., *Geografía de Euskal Herria*, vol. 7, *Euskal Herria* (San Sebastián/Donostia: Luis Haranburu, 1979), 136.
8. Douglass, *Echalar and Murelaga*, passim.
9. In Basque the suffix –a serves as the definite article and the suffix –k is the pluralizer. Thus, *baserri* (literally "forest settlement") is the root for "farmstead," *baserria* means "the farmstead," and *baserriak* "the farmsteads."
10. William A. Douglass, *Death in Murelaga: The Social Significance of Funerary Ritual in a Spanish Basque Village*, American Ethnological Society Monograph No. 49 (Seattle: University of Washington Press, 1969), 83–144. [*Death*]. For more anthropological treatments of the *baserri* and rural Basque family, among many others, see Joseba Zulaika, *Basque Violence: Metaphor and Sacrament* (Reno and Las Vegas: University of Nevada Press, 1988), 105–20 [*Basque Violence*]; Sandra Ott, *The Circle of Mountains: A Basque Shepherding Community* (Reno and Las Vegas: University of Nevada Press, 1993); Davydd Greenwood, *Unrewarding Wealth: The Commercialization and Collapse of Agriculture in a Spanish Basque Town* (Cambridge, London, New York, Melbourne: Cambridge University Press, 1976), 7–12; Julio Caro Baroja, *The Basques*, trans. Kristin Addis, intro. William A. Douglass (Reno: Center for Basque Studies, University of Nevada, Reno, 2009), 241–47; Philippe Veyrin, *The Basques of Lapurdi, Zuberoa, and Lower Navarre: Their*

History and Their Traditions, trans. Andrew Brown and intro. Sandra Ott (Reno: Center for Basque Studies, University of Nevada, Reno, 2011), 37–77; William A. Douglass, "The Basque Stem Family Household: Myth or Reality?" *Journal of Family History* 13, no. 1 (1988), 75–90; William A. Douglass, "The Famille Souche and Its Interpreters," *Continuity and Change* 8, no. 1 (1993), 87–102; William A. Douglass and Joseba Zulaika, *Basque Culture: Anthropological Perspectives* (Reno: Center for Basque Studies, University of Nevada, Reno, 2007), 213–28. [*Basque Culture*]; Douglass, *Echalar and Murelaga*, 18–50.

11. Ibid, 71–84.
12. Douglass, *Death*, 145–65; Douglass, *Echalar and Murelaga*, 50–70.
13. Baleren Bakaikoa and Eneka Albizu, eds., *Basque Cooperativism* (Reno: Center for Basque Studies, University of Nevada, Reno, 2012); Zulaika, *Basque Violence*, 137–50; Douglass and Zulaika, *Basque Culture*, 326–39.
14. Frédéric Le Play, *L'Organisation de la famille selon le vrai modèle signalé par l'histoire de toutes les races et de tous les temps* (Paris: Téqui, 1871).
15. William A. Douglass, "Rural Exodus in Two Spanish Basque Villages: A Cultural Explanation," *American Anthropologist* 73 (1971), 1100–14.
16. Miguel de Cervantes Saavedra, *The Adventures of Don Quixote*, trans. J. M. Cohen (Harmondsworth, Middlesex: Penguin Books, 1950), 73.
17. Douglass, *Echalar and Murelaga*, 40–43.
18. Douglass and Bilbao, *Amerikanuak*, 407–10; Sandra Ott, "*Indarra*: Some Reflections on a Basque Concept," in *Honour and Grace in Anthropology*, ed. J. G. Peristiany and Julian Pitt Rivers (Cambridge, New York, and Melbourne: Cambridge University Press, 1992), 193–214.
19. Segundo de Ispizua, *Historia de los vascos en el descubrimiento, conquista y civilización de América*, vol. 3 (Bilbao: J. A. Lerchundi, 1917), 39.
20. Douglass, *Basque Explorers*, passim.
21. Douglass and Bilbao, *Amerikanuak*, passim.

CHAPTER 1

Conclusion as Introduction

Amaia da hasera, atzekoz aurrera
("The end is the beginning, from back to front")¹

When John Ugalde, secretary of the directive committee of Melbourne's *Gure Txoko* (Our Corner) Basque club, called to discuss my impending 2002 visit, his pronounced Aussie accent and impeccably correct English suggested that he must be Australian-born. Could Jan and I change our plane tickets to stay over the Sunday that the club planned to celebrate *Aberri Eguna* (Day of the Basque Fatherland)? Prior commitments made it impossible, so John promised to arrange a midweek dinner. As it happened, Australia's ANZAC² holiday fell on the Thursday of my stay, and the club simply moved the *Aberri Eguna* celebration to it.

My first morning in Melbourne I met Juan Antonio Ugalde at the Park Hyatt Hotel. He would later note that its lobby's impressive red granite was quarried in Ereño and its black and white marble in Aulesti (both in Bizkaia). The stone had been transported to Italy for polishing and then exported to Australia. John was not an Australian native. Born on the *baserri* Anbekoetxea, near Gernika (Bizkaia), and son of a skilled machinist, he had immigrated in 1956, at age eighteen, accompanied by his twenty-seven-year-old sister, and assisted (with the required sponsorship papers and a loan to cover passage) by their two brothers. After cutting sugar cane in Ingham (North Queensland) for several seasons, siblings Juan Antonio and Tomás had relocated to Melbourne where they were both truck drivers for a scrap-metal firm.

The day after his arrival in Australia, John went to work in the same company thanks to his brothers' intercession. He was an aspiring boxer and was befriended by another, the Basque Agustín Argote (who was once world-ranked). Agustín reckoned that employment in the scrapyard was too physically demanding to allow the young aspirant energy for proper training. He therefore secured John easier work with his own employer, Consolidated Pneumatic Tool, an air compressor manufacturer.

John stayed with Consolidated for four years. But then a brother-in-law, Tomás Ormaechea, arrived from Gernika about the same time that some North Queensland sugar farmers put out a call for cutters among Melbourne's Basques. John decided to accompany Tomás there, and, for the next two seasons, they cut cane in Innisfail for Australian farmers. They then spent two years as timber contractors in Gippsland, Victoria, initiated by other Basques in the "art" of the chainsaw. John then added construction laborer and waiter (two years) to his increasingly varied vita, before becoming a waterside worker and union activist on Melbourne's docks.

In 1973, John obtained a year's leave of absence from his waterside workers' job and returned to the Basque Country—possibly to stay. He worked for several months for Talleres Echevarria (manufacturer of marine engines) in Bermeo, Bizkaia, as an English interpreter, but was content neither with a desk job nor office politics. Juan Antonio and Tomás moved back to Bizkaia and purchased a commercial fishing vessel working out of Ondarroa. While their hired crew went to sea, the brothers ran a fish processing plant.

John was attracted to an *abertzale* (Basque patriotic) circle of friends and was far too outspoken in his Basque nationalist and leftist views, feeding maternal anxiety in the ominous and uncertain final phase of the Franco dictatorship. She urged her son to return to Australia for his own good. John did so and resumed his job on the Melbourne docks. Shortly thereafter he went to work at a branch of the State Bank of Victoria as a janitor; some twenty years later he would retire as its general custodian.

At age forty-two, John married Lidia Masino, a forty-two-year-old immigrant from Marsicovedere (Potenza), Italy. They have one daughter, aged twenty-one, and still living at home, but serious about a first-generation young man of Italian descent (Venetian father, Calabrian mother).

John spells his name with an "h" and pronounces his surname "Ewe-gald." "After all, we *are* in Australia," he remarked. Would my wife Jan and I accompany him home for lunch? Lidia was on standby. Yes? Daughter Amaia would come by car to collect the three of us.

Like the stone in the Park Hyatt, despite her Basque-Italian genesis, Amaia was now thoroughly Australian. She was studying pathology at a local college. We rode to their small bungalow in a nearby suburb and were greeted by Gorri ("Red" in Basque), the gregarious family dog. "I love to take him on walks because he is so friendly with people and when they ask after his name it gives me an excuse to talk about the Basques," John commented.

Unlike her husband, Lidia spoke sparingly and with a heavy Italian accent as she served *al dente* spaghetti graced with tomato sauce from the family's extensive, home-preserved supply stored in the shop of a made-over garage out of which for years Lidia has sewn professionally. We were seated in a dining room reminiscent of the *sala*, or parlor, in any Old World Basque or South Italian home. There were the ubiquitous family portraits, with Italy holding a slight advantage over Euskadi in the competition for wall space—the many photographs of Amaia's childhood providing the compromise. A carved *pelotari* (ballplayer) and two sets of *mutil/neska* (boy/girl) dolls in Basque costume seemed lost on the shelves of Lidia's cornucopian Italian bric-a-brac. John spoke to her in Italian, and both parents code-switched between it and English when addressing Amaia. He noted that almost weekly they frequented the *Federazione Lucana*, a Basilicatan-Italian regional club with its own fine premises.

The next day, Victoria San Gil, daughter of a Navarrese father (from Azagra) and a Gipuzkoan mother (from Eibar), picked Jan and me up at the Park Hyatt for the trip to Gumbuya Park, the preferred venue for the club's events. It is situated about halfway to Traralgon (eighty miles distant), where several of *Gure Txoko*'s members reside. Gumbuya is also an amusement park and zoological garden. On fair weather days (which this wasn't), the children could go on the rides and view the dingoes, emus, and kangaroos. Sack races and the smashing of a candy-filled *piñata* were regular events at *Txoko* get-togethers. It was all part of the attempt to hold the children's interest.

Victoria works for the Australian government in human disability services, has a masters' degree in education, and is quite computer literate. She is on *Gure Txoko*'s directorate and generates the newsletter sent out in advance of a club event. It features "hatches, matches and dispatches" (births, marriages, and deaths), and other personal details (particularly the travels of members and the visits to Melbourne of relevant outsiders). There is considerable news from the Basque Country, as well as other clubs throughout the Basque emigrant diaspora, gleaned through the miracle of the Internet.

Victoria was pessimistic about the future. The forces of assimilation seemed so overwhelming. She referred to her "B and B" kids, Basque and Bosnian, since her husband Eddie was first-generation Bosnian-Australian. He would be at today's festivities—more out of respect for her work on the committee than personal enthusiasm. Next year they planned to travel to Europe, dividing their time equally between Euskadi and Bosnia so that the children "could get to know all of their cousins." As long as her now retired mother and father were here in Melbourne there was the cultural influence of a Basque extended family—but later?

When we arrived at Gumbuya Park, Victoria expressed her nervousness over the possible attendance. Despite it being ANZAC Day, she knew that several members either had to work or were committed to previous engagements. Actually, her concern was perennial, since the entire membership list was comprised of fewer than one hundred persons (counting children) in the greater Melbourne/Traralgon area.

Gure Txoko meets four times annually: *Aberri Eguna* (usually the Sunday after Easter), Saint Ignatius's Day (July 31, or rather a Sunday close to it), in early December for a Christmas party for the children complete with an *Olentzero* (or the Basque Santa Claus figure), and in May to elect the committee. Given the thinness of the ranks, an inordinately poor turnout was always possible.

Such had not always been the state of affairs. For a decade after its founding, *Gure Txoko*'s membership numbered in the low hundreds, stimulated by spin-off from Basque settlement in North Queensland. Between about 1910 and the late 1960s (when harvesting of the area's sugar crop was mechanized), cane cutting in tropical Australia had provided employment, indeed the main opportunity, for Basque immigrants. The work was well compensated but seasonal (lasting about seven months). During the "slack," the men gravitated to nomadic fruit and vegetable picking in the agricultural districts of New South Wales and Victoria, or to temporary employment in Sydney or Melbourne. Each year some of the latter became established in urban Australia and failed to return to the "Far North." With the advent of the mechanical harvesters, the entire cane-cutting labor force was displaced within a few years. Many of its Basques simply returned to Europe, but the hated Franco dictatorship remained in power and Australian wages were still more attractive than those of the homeland, so others relocated within Australia—particularly in greater Sydney and Melbourne.

By the mid-1960s, there was sufficient Basque critical mass in both cities to stimulate associative initiatives. A *Gure Txoko* club was founded in Melbourne in 1964 and another in Sydney in 1966. The Sydney club coalesced around the purchase of a property on Liverpool Street; the Melbourne one leased premises and began saving toward an eventual real-estate purchase.

The difference in their respective edifice complexes eventuated into significantly different historical destinies for the two clubs. The infusion of Basques into both cities proved ephemeral, and, by the early 1970s, both clubs were hemorrhaging as founding member families decided to return to the Basque Country. By the mid-1970s, the Sydney *Txoko* was, if not moribund, at least agonizing. Nevertheless, the Liverpool Street premises provided it with tangible anchorage. In 1975, faced with a rent increase and waning enthusiasm, the Melbourne *Txoko* closed its doors.

As a bachelor with time on his hands, John Ugalde had been one of the most diligent volunteers at the old *Txoko*, and he was most chagrined to find it closed (its quarters converted to an Argentinean immigrants' club) upon his return to Melbourne in the mid-1970s. He was skeptical of the optimistic view that *Gure Txoko* could somehow survive as an occasional barbecue in some member's backyard. It was only during the late 1980s, when the situation seemed truly critical, that he renewed his commitment to the reorganizational effort that culminated in the club's present configuration.

If the new *Txoko* has its regular calendar of events and even a set of statutes, membership is largely informal and consists of simply being on the mailing list. There is, however, one statute that delineates eligibility and permits up to ten percent of non-Basque "friends" to belong. There are no dues; rather, at each function the hat is passed (suggested minimum donation A$2 per person, though most give more) and tickets are sold for a raffle (today's prize was a basket with wine, cheeses, and fruit). In this fashion, *Gure Txoko* meets its immediate needs and general expenses (when I asked about the club's principal expenditure, one member answered, only half-jokingly, "paying for funeral wreaths").

We arrived at Gumbuya Park, and the wall of our rented space was already adorned with political symbols. There was a major poster outlining the geography of the Basque homeland, its caption proclaiming *Aberri Eguna*. A similar map, in funereal black, demanded *Euskal Presoak Etxera* ("Basque Prisoners to the Homeland"). There was a Basque flag as well, balanced precariously in its makeshift stand. I was introduced to the grand old man of the Melbourne Basques ("our honorary *lehendakari*[3] for life"). He was wearing a tricolored hat (the national red-white-green) and I asked him to pose for a photo with the matching Basque flag. He was delighted and lovingly lifted one of its folds to his pursed lips. "I'm going to Durango in five months' time," he beamed, an exclamation that would become his mantra by day's end. When I casually mentioned the hat, it was instantly transferred to my head as a welcoming present.

"You can see that we are all very Basque here," John Ugalde noted. "Most of us believe in an independent Basque Country. We wrote to Ibarretxe[4] recently urging him to hold out for sovereignty. We received a very nice letter back, but, of course, there was no mention of sovereignty." The "most-of-us" in John's comment underscored that all was not peace and light in Melbourne Basquelandia. Indeed, even within *Gure Txoko* there are varying degrees of concern with Old World Basque politics. A few members hold membership in the city's Spanish Club as well, and there are Melbourne Basques (particularly Navarrans) who do not belong to *Gure Txoko*. For ultranationalists like John, *Eusko Jaurlaritza* is itself problematic, an unacceptable acquiescence in regional autonomy *within* Spain when the goal ought to be full independence. Throughout the day, ETA was mentioned seldom, but never criticized, and on several occasions Batasuna[5] came up approvingly. During lunch, a petition proclaiming *Gure Txoko*'s solidarity with the recent proclamation of the Idaho State Legislature[6] was circulated and signed by all.

Partly reflecting ambivalence toward *Eusko Jaurlaritza* and partly internal factionalism, two years ago there had been serious friction within *Gure Txoko*. In 1999, *Eusko Jaurlaritza* held its Third International Congress of Basque Collectivities in Gasteiz, attended by delegates from Basque clubs in seventeen countries, including the (former) president and secretary of the Melbourne one. I had given the inaugural address at the Congress, in which I emphasized the potential importance of the Internet in the effort to maintain contact with both the homeland and other diasporic communities around the world.[7] I therefore felt at least moderately complicit, and even culpable, as I now learned of the Melbourne club's troubles.

After a week of workshops at the Congress, a prime recommendation of the assembled delegations to *Eusko Jaurlaritza* was the need to provision each diasporic Basque center with computer technology. This resulted in an offer to fund 80 percent of the cost if the recipient would bear 20 percent of the burden. For most clubs this was a generous and reasonable plan, but for Melbourne, with its tiny membership and lacking a locale at which to provide computer access, the prospect raised concern. In the aftermath of the membership's overwhelming rejection in a formal vote on the directive's recommendation to proceed with computerization, the former leadership resigned. I was therefore delighted and relieved when the Melbourne delegates that I had met at the 1999 Congress appeared. The best of faces was put on by all.

A distinguished elderly man wearing formal attire (in contrast to everyone else's casual dress) and a black beret approached me on a mission. Pablo Oribe had written his personal memoirs and he wanted to give me both a Spanish and English version. His Australian immigration odyssey had culminated in formal university studies and he was a recently retired schoolteacher.

We were interrupted by Andoni Elordieta. He is an enthusiastic bachelor in his late thirties who serves as *Gure Txoko*'s treasurer. Andoni remarked,

You interviewed my father, Jesús Elordieta, in Sales [South Australia] twenty years ago. I went to Euskadi with him twice before he died. Here he was always cranky, but there he was happy. He loved the vitality. He was pretty sick by then, and I remember him saying "One day of life here is worth a year in Australia." Towards the end he lost his English and his Spanish. He was born hearing Basque and died speaking it.

Andoni had been to the Basque Country five times and now struggled with the decision over possible relocation there. "I love the social scene. There's so much going on. They have so many different kinds of rock music!" He was in daily contact with Euskadi through the Internet, reading the press and frequenting chat rooms.

A familiar figure grinned coyly at me. Excepting the snow on his mountain, Javier Iriondo was the same timber contractor who, two decades earlier, took me into the eucalyptus forests near Traralgon. We slipped into our private reverie and he recounted his ten years working on an Esso drilling-rig platform in Bass Strait, and then his semi-retirement on a 30-acre property with its twenty cows. He had been back to the Basque Country and was about to go again. He and Basque wife, María, didn't entirely rule out moving there.

At one point, John Ugalde asked me to address the crowd regarding my work. He began his introduction in Basque, and then passed quickly to Spanish before finishing up in English. Since there were several non-Basque spouses, and a fair smattering of seemingly monolingual young children in attendance, I spoke in my maternal tongue.

Before the afternoon was over, I was taping an interview in the backseat of a van with José Antonio Azkue, a middle-aged man from Sopela (Sopelana), Bizkaia, who had worked in specialized construction for the last twenty years. He had come to Australia as a merchant mariner on an ore transporter, jumped ship in Mackay, Queensland, and then made his way to a (surprised) second cousin in Melbourne. As we talked, Maite, his strikingly beautiful Eurasian daughter, regarded us from the front seat. José Antonio had met his wife, a refugee from mainland China, in an evening class in which both were studying English.

Each family had brought its own food, and after lunch there was both a men's and women's *soka tira* (tug of war) followed by the children's games. Someone produced a copy of Mark Kurlansky's recent book, *A Basque History of the World*,[8] and I was questioned intensely about it. I expressed my admiration of the work's elegant style and candor and pronounced it to be the single most successful effort to explain the Basque viewpoint to an uninstructed Anglo audience. Did I think that Kurlansky had purposely avoided using the term Euskadi? I didn't, since the work is unabashedly pro-Basque. And what about Saint Ignatius? "We thought he was the Basque saint and we celebrate his feast day!" From Kurlansky they had learned, to their perplexity, that their patron was wounded while fighting as a soldier in Castile's service during the (1512) siege of Pamplona that terminated the Kingdom of Navarra's independence.

My previous research had focused primarily upon the thoroughly male world of the canecutters. I wanted to interview women, particularly those few intrepid ones who had emigrated to Australia on their own. Arrangements were made for me to meet with Susana Irisarri. Susana, aka Susie, had not attended *Aberri Eguna* because of her deceased husband, a veteran in the Australian Armed Forces. Every year she participated in the ANZAC patriotic commemoration.

The next day Susie (from Beasain, Gipuzkoa) shared her recollections of the single-female immigrants' uncertainty, vulnerability, and loneliness. She recounted with disgust the sexual advances of the Australian Catholic priest who was her first contact in the country (she had immigrated with the assistance of the Catholic Action organization). Then there were the serving and factory jobs in which she felt very much alone and exposed. We were sitting in the lobby of the Park Hyatt. Her companion, José, who was a Castilian from Valladolid, sat quietly and nodded in agreement whenever she underscored the immigrant's plight.

As we concluded the interview, two exuberant young men arrived. Johnny Ugalde (Tomás's son) is John's nephew. His employment in parking lot security at Melbourne's airport had prevented him from attending *Aberri Eguna*, even though he is on *Gure Txoko*'s five-person directorate. He was curious to meet me and had learned about the scheduled interview with Susie from her son, Robert Harris. Both were dressed in the boosters' uniform of the St. Kilda football (Australian rules) team. In an hour's time, their heroes were to engage Sydney at a nearby stadium.

Johnny, a bachelor in his mid-forties, was born in Australia but went back to Euskadi with his parents at thirteen years of age. He finished his schooling there, and then, as a young adult, returned to Melbourne. He now moves back and forth—a total of nine times and counting. "When I'm there I appreciate Australia and when I'm here I miss Euskadi." Unlike the classic immigrant who laments giving up his homeland without ever fully integrating into his adopted one, Johnny, being fully fluent in English, Spanish, and Basque, possesses full facility in the two cultures—its own dilemma. His widowed mother (from Sevilla) who lives near Gernika is urging him to move to Euskadi. He is (perpetually) undecided. "It's the footie," Robert opined only half-jokingly. "He can't give up on the St. Kilda team."

Johnny's enthusiasm for Euskadi had not been diminished by his encounter, in 1974, with the police. He and some friends had attended a political demonstration in Ondarroa and were arrested by the authorities. "We were just expressing our opinion; we weren't in ETA or anything." He was almost jocular as he described being beaten by four policemen each evening. "They would make you lean against the wall with two fingers and then just one. You couldn't do it for long and when you fell they bashed you. There was nothing to tell them; we knew nothing." His Australian citizenship was the key in springing him from prison after a week. Johnny is now a hard-line Batasuna supporter. "As long as there is a breath in a single Basque the cause for freedom is never lost."

In contrast to Johnny's dark hair and chiseled features, blond Robert seemed a "fair dinkum Aussie."[9] He was married to a Greek girl and spoke more of her ethnic world than his own. They had been to Euskadi as tourists and he was keen to go again. However, his failed attempt to learn much Spanish ("I can understand some of it"), and his total lack of Basque, underscored his outsider status. Susie noted that Robert at least had an interest in his heritage, her other son had none. Their Anglo-Australian[10] father had been against any expression of multiculturalism, and it was only after his death that she had joined *Gure Txoko*.

Carlos Orue, president of the other *Gure Txoko*, met us at the Sydney airport. It was Sunday and he had taken a break from his (volunteer) cooking duties at the club, leaving his wife Miren to carry on there. By mid-afternoon we were at *Gure Txoko*, as were about forty other regulars, for the weekly members' dinner.

After lunch, Carlos asked me to address the gathering about my project. He introduced me in Spanish, the *Txoko's lingua franca*, so I followed his lead. Several of the "old-timers" nodded in assent as I recollected my previous visits to the club, the first in the late 1970s. After my talk, Rafael Alegría, one of the former presidents, gave me a few tantalizing leads. There was the list of names of the crew on the ill-fated French expedition that visited Botany Bay in the late eighteenth century displayed at the La Perouse museum.[11] Also, somewhere in New South Wales there was the place name "Hernani," which must have some sort of connection with the Gipuzkoan town.[12] Rafael had once photographed the highway sign.

It was then Eusebio Illarmendi's turn. Another former president of the *Txoko*, Eusebio wanted to correct the negative impression of its future that he had given me two decades earlier. "In 1981, I didn't anticipate the future new immigration," he explained. Reference was to the window that opened in the late 1970s and early 1980s when, for a few years, the Australian government recruited immigrants actively in Spain. Of particular interest were skilled tradesmen and mechanics. Carlos and Miren had entered the country as a part of that program, as did about ten other members of *Gure Txoko*. Indeed, it became clear that there had been a passing of the leadership baton at the *Txoko* from the founding generation to this newer cohort, as well as to one first-generation Australian member (Josu).

Eusebio added that the other factor that had reinvigorated *Gure Txoko* was the current support of the Basque government. He claimed that it transpired quite by accident, through a casual exchange on a plane flight. A member of the *Txoko* was traveling in Spain and happened to be seated next to a Basque politician. When the conversation turned to Basques in Australia, the senator was dumbfounded—it was all new to him. He urged the *Gure Txoko* to contact *Eusko Jaurlaritza*, and the rest is history.

Treasurer Josu (Joe) Goicoechea, a software programmer and born here in Sydney, described his humorous attempts to understand the many moods and faces of his Greek wife's fellow ethnics and their ethnic association. He also recounted his wonderment at entering a Basque chat room while surfing the internet and finding a comment from Andoni Elordieta, self-identified as the treasurer of Melbourne's *Gure*

Txoko. It was Goicoechea's first knowledge of the Melbourne club's existence, and he now maintains a "treasurer to treasurer" email correspondence with his counterpart. He met another Basque in Amsterdam in the same fashion, and now maintains a "virtual friendship" with her.

Despite all the apparent Sunday afternoon's vitality, Carlos commented that all was not well at the *Txoko*. There had been tension over Old World Basque politics. From its inception, the club had included a number of Navarran members who were generally indifferent, and, in some cases, downright hostile toward Basque nationalism. The bylaws also permitted up to 20 percent of the membership to be non-Basque. This quota was fully subscribed, entirely by Spanish nationals (an attempt to expand this category to 25 percent had been rejected in general assembly as too threatening to *Gure Txoko*'s "identity"). Nearly two-thirds (63 of 99) of the persons on the *Txoko*'s existing membership list are, or have been, members of the much larger (about 2,000 person) and more prestigious nearby *Club Español*. Indeed, during the meal a flyer was circulated announcing the Spanish Club's upcoming Spanish film festival.

There is an unwritten rule that *Gure Txoko* itself walks a politically neutral line, yet, in practice, the middle ground is highly charged. Basque politics matters prove at times to be a razor's edge that cuts right through the collective shoe leather. Carlos favors Batasuna's political goals while rejecting ETA's violence. When, in 1999, ETA killed Miguel Angel Blanco, a town councilor from the ruling Popular Party, triggering massive protest demonstrations throughout Spain, including the Basque Country, some of its members demanded that the *Txoko* take an official stance against the distant violence. Carlos refused on the ground of the club's tradition of political neutrality (as well as nervousness over the Australian public's irritation with the importation of "foreign" problems), while respecting their right to express their personal opinion. About a dozen *Txoko* members engaged in a silent protest in downtown Sydney that went largely unnoticed and unremarked upon in the press.

However, about a year ago, the shoe shifted to the other foot. "We removed a broken air-conditioner which left an ugly hole in the inside wall. Before I could fix it, someone covered it over with an *Euskal Presoak Etxera* poster" (identical to the one displayed during the Melbourne *Aberri Eguna*), Carlos remarked. The leader of the "Blanco dissidents," now a strong PNV (Partido Nacionalista Vasco or Basque Nationalist Party)[13] advocate, demanded its removal. He refused on the grounds that *Eusko Jaurlaritza* was on record as approving the transfer of all Basque political prisoners to their homeland, so display of the poster was not "doing politics" in his view, but merely a reflection of Basque official policy. Undaunted, the dissidents collected signatures and forced the issue. At a general assembly, by a close vote, Carlos was directed to remove the offending message. I now understood the significance of Miren's tee-shirt that proclaimed, "*Euskal Presoak Etxera.*"

Of more sweeping concern for Carlos was burnout. He noted that for years he and Miren had given up most of their Sundays to cook at the *Txoko*. Recently, another key volunteer had dropped out when new employment required her to work on weekends. In short, the volunteer ranks were paper thin and tattering. "As long as the old members keep coming around to play *mus*,[14] I'll try to keep it going." But he saw no replacements on the horizon. As Josu Goicoechea had underscored, "It's hard for many members to come to the *Txoko*. Sydney's a hundred kilometers across in all directions."

Like in Melbourne, then, urban sprawl frustrated the efforts of a precariously tiny and fragile membership to meet regularly. In Sydney the problem was exacerbated by the *Txoko*'s location next to King's Cross, a somewhat seedy central district where many immigrants had resided when the *Txoko* was founded. After financial success and family formation, Sydney's Basques had moved to the suburbs, some quite distant from the downtown.

On the other hand, Sydney was itself a sufficient magnet to attract international visitors, including Basque tourists, professionals, and businessmen, some of whom appeared at *Gure Txoko* (the 2000 Olympics and Special Olympics produced bursts of visitations). However, such influence was fleeting and ephemeral. It scarcely contributed a foundation upon which to found, and then sustain, an organization.

Carlos gave me a tour of the *Txoko*'s premises—what he called his "little museum." The walls were festooned with photographs, posters, and plaques depicting both Basque and *Txoko* traditions. In particular evidence were memorabilia of Basque soccer teams—Bilbo's *Athletic*, Donostia's *Real Sociedad*, and Pamplona's *Osasuna*—as well as the *Vasconia* professional basketball team from Gasteiz. Famed Basque *pelotariak* (handball players), both vintage and recent, were prominent. The *Txoko*'s own soccer team from the 1970s (liberally laced with non-Basques) was also in evidence. There was the autographed photo of mountaineer Koke Lasa displaying the Basque flag on the summit of Hidden Peak in the Himalayas. Another framed Basque flag had been left in Sydney by Manuel Garizoai (from Pamplona) during his one-man, small-craft voyage around the world. A saw blade and an axe both bore dedicatory inscriptions from their Australian makers, and there was a cane knife donated to the *Txoko* by sugar farmer Agustín Arrate during Carlos's recent trip to North Queensland.

Then there was the work of David Mendieta, a skilled woodcarver who was born in North Queensland, raised in Euskadi, and now residing in Sydney. He had made a distinctive frame for the *Txoko*'s map of the Basque Country and a truly impressive, finely detailed carving of the Basque *Zazpiak Bat*[15] escutcheon. Also under glass was a damaged *Gure Txoko* tee-shirt. Mark Schlink, an Aussie, belongs to the "No-Bull-Shit-Monkey" *peña*, or one of the many fan clubs that attend the running of the bulls during Pamplona's famed annual *San Fermín* festival. A few years ago he had been hooked by a bull, though not gored, and the rent tee-shirt was a remembrance. Mark is an honorary member of the *Txoko*.

The only part of the wall display that was truly active (and interactive) regarded *mus*. Since 1986, the *Txoko* has fielded a team (two-person) in the annual world championship competition that moves around the planet. Contestants pay a A$100 entry fee at the *Txoko* level to enter an elimination round that determines the club's representatives. Their way is then paid to the finals. This year seven teams were signed up (the high-water mark was fourteen), and their progress in the Sydney eliminations was noted on a large chart. There was also a plaque bearing the names of Sydney's representatives to former world championships. A display case was filled with the memorabilia (souvenirs and trophies) from Europe, and North and South America, brought back by the *Txoko*'s *muslariak* (*mus* players) ambassadors and clearly regarded as the common property of the club's membership.

During our tour, Carlos was apologetic about the condition of the tiny *frontón* that served as the *Txoko*'s backyard. It was in disrepair and was obviously being used as a storage area rather than for competition.

Twenty years earlier it had been the main focal point of any Sunday's activity. "We are all too old now to play, but we really should fix it up." The other pregnant moment was when we visited the second floor. One wall was lined with shelving that housed a small library of Basque books and videos. However, a jumble of intervening tables, chairs, and other objects made access all but impossible. "No one really uses them," Carlos admitted. He then added sheepishly, "those who criticize the *Txoko* as just a place to play *mus* don't understand that we couldn't have survived without those few members who came often and bought their drinks here. You can't pay the bills by just selling bargain A$15 meals on Sundays."

Actually, the club's finances were in pretty good shape. The building had long since been paid for and there was money in the bank. "We get something from the Basque government every year. It makes a big difference." Carlos noted that the Melbourne club's rejection of the support for computerization from *Eusko Jaurlaritza* was wrong-headed. "Some of their members think that it would be taking money from the PNV. But *Eusko Jaurlaritza* is more than just the PNV. It is our Basque government, too. The subsidies aren't from the PNV, they come from the Basque people."

I asked about the *Txoko*'s two computers. They had been purchased several years ago with *Eusko Jaurlaritza* support. One was at the treasurer's home for keeping the accounts and the other used to stay at the *Txoko*. Access to the latter was somewhat restricted because it was adjacent to the quarters of the live-in custodial family. Consequently, after 10 p.m. it had been off-limits. But, in fact, there had been only one dedicated regular and he liked to enter the chat room debates emanating from the Basque Country. Given the time difference between Australia and Europe, he was prone to hang around until the wee hours of the morning. After the Blanco affair, he sent what he thought to be an anonymous message challenging one of the prisoners-rights' groups in Euskadi to organize a demonstration in support of the victims of terrorism. The communication was disseminated as if it were the stance of Sydney's *Gure Txoko*. At that point, Carlos exercised a president's prerogative and simply took the computer home to be able to answer *Txoko* correspondence. However, it was antiquated and unreliable. He now uses his own computer for *Txoko* business.

Jon Patrick, professor of Communications in the Department of Language Policy at the University of Sydney and the other honorary member of *Gure Txoko*, was overwhelmed by emotion during his speech at the book launch. He had just coauthored the work *A Student Grammar of Euskara* with Ilari Zubiri Ibarrondo, and the accomplishment was being celebrated at a campus reception cosponsored by Jon's colleagues and the *Gure Txoko*. There were about twenty members of the latter in attendance. The Spanish consul put in an appearance, spoke first, promised to communicate the significance of the event to Madrid, and then split. The French consul had failed to even reply to his invitation. A spokesperson from the *Txoko* then explained the significance of Jon's project to Sydney Basques, and particularly their children. Josu Goicoechea read a congratulatory letter from Miren Azkarate, *Eusko Jaurlaritza*'s minister of culture.

Carlos is the Australian point person in the Urazandi project.[16] He had already conducted about a hundred interviews in Sydney, Melbourne, and North Queensland, and was amassing an impressive photo archive as well. He and my former colleague at the University of Nevada, Gloria Totoricagüena, planned to collaborate on the Australian volume. We were sharing our research materials and Carlos was delighted when I identified three individuals of interest to me that he had yet to interview. He had taken time off from his work as a line inspector for the local power company to accompany me.

The logistics proved challenging. Pedro Altuna lives in a distant suburb, so we met him after dark at a public soccer field nearer the city where his son's team was practicing. Pedro was from the Basque-speaking Ulzama Valley of northern Navarra. He recounted how his entire family had migrated to Toronto in 1966, where Pedro worked in a factory and met his future wife, a first-generation Australian of Italian ancestry. In 1976, she convinced him to give Australia a go (facilitated by the ease of movement among British Commonwealth countries). He did so (after first acquiring Canadian citizenship "just in case") and has been here in Sydney ever since, now working in a polyurethane plant.

My second interviewee, Juan Uribe, had one thing in common with Pedro Altuna. They both met and married an Australian woman before coming here. Juan (originally from Gernika) had been a professional *jai alai* player, a career that had taken him to Madrid, Benidorm, Florida, and Djakarta. It was while in Indonesia that he met his bride. Again, we were conducting an afterhours interview, this time at the Sydney headquarters of Australia's major video game distributor and arcade operator—Leisure and Allied Industries. Juan was its harried general manager as the company fought for survival in the rapidly evolving world of electronic and computer amusement games. Consequently, while a former president of the *Txoko*, he was apologetic about seldom having time for it these days.

Juan's whole demeanor softened noticeably when he and Carlos reminisced about their efforts to retain the children's interest. He still oversees their games on the occasions when the *Txoko* holds outdoor picnics at Sydney's Centennial Park. When president, Juan would bring the kids to Leisure's showroom and organize competition in which there were so many contestant categories that nearly everyone was a champion and got a prize. "It was really market research," he tried to dissimulate. They then laughed about the "MacTxoko." It seems that the MacDonald's fad hit Sydney during Juan's presidential tenure. The kids complained about the Sunday fare at the club, usually built around steaks. So, he sliced them up, put the meat in a hamburger bun, and drowned it in catsup. "Some of our young adult members still miss the MacTxoko," Carlos added.

We met Xavier Ugarte and his Chilean wife, Rebecca, at the Cathay Pacific desk in Sydney's airport. In two hours' time they were off to Manila, his birthplace, for both business and pleasure. We sought out a corner where the ubiquitous Muzak was somewhat muted and commenced the interview. He had brought along a book, published in Manila in 1998, that details the history of one of his family lines—the Aboitiz clan. "It is only a small exaggeration to say that they own half of the Philippines." Xavier is a partner in a Sydney accounting firm. He described his many difficulties in gaining access to Australia (he had gone back to school for several years in Manila to become a certified public accountant after Australian immigration officials declined to qualify his business degree from New York's Manhattan College as "professional"). Xavier had been largely oblivious to the existence of Sydney's Basques (though a member of the Spanish Club) until called in to redesign the *Txoko*'s corporate structure, while ameliorating some serious tax issues. Carlos spoke reverentially of Xavier's (entirely *pro bono*) efforts on their behalf.

I rendezvoused with Christine Challis at the Mitchell Library, the outstanding Australiana special collection of the State Library of New South Wales. Christine had conducted genealogical research on her ancestor, Jean Baptiste Lehimas de Arrieta, possibly a native of Gipuzkoa, and an early free settler in New South Wales. She had graciously shared several leads with me. As we sipped our drinks in the coffee shop, I was given a graphic demonstration of Sydney's status as international crossroad. The out-of-context, yet familiar, face of the excited young woman rushed toward me from across the room. Blanca and I embraced and then melted into our shared "small-world-isn't it" delight. The preceding November, at her dinner table in Gasteiz, she had whimsically mulled over the possibility of going to Australia to learn English. Now she had been living here for two months and happened to be in the library this morning to attend a film festival. In addition to pursuing Lehimas de Arrieta, at the Mitchell I conducted a fruitful search for Australian resources regarding Spanish activity (with its Basque dimensions) in the South Pacific.

Carlos and Miren invited Jan and me home to dinner. A fairly extensive collection of Basque books occupied about half of the space in his library. "I learned about the Basques while here in Australia—from these," he pointed with pride. Basque motifs dominated the wall decorations. We were to share our repast with two regular visitors.

Irati Garaizar, a young student from Gernika, had been studying biology for more than a year at a Sydney University. She was staying with her uncle, Juan Uribe, the video-game impresario. They lived nearby and she liked to hang out with Carlos and Miren. She was particularly prone to use his computer for contacts with the Basque Country. She downloaded a cartoon from there and passed it around.

David Mendieta, the woodcarver and another open-ended repeat visitor at the Orues, was also Carlos's partner in a "tinny," a small aluminum fishing craft. The dinner conversation was dominated by hilarious descriptions of their fishing forays in the local waters—particularly targeting a bottom species called flatheads.

Our last night in Sydney we hosted Carlos and Miren for dinner and a performance of Lerner and Loeb show tunes by the Australian Pops Orchestra at the Sydney Opera House. Carlos chuckled at such an

"American" conclusion to our Sydney sojourn. During intermission he pointed to a block of seats above the orchestra pit. "When the Odinetz choir from Tolosa (Gipuzkoa) performed here, about fifty of us Basques reserved that section. We had a Basque flag and cheered them on. We made quite a spectacle."

If there are two places in Australia seemingly virtually untouched by a Basque presence, they are Tasmania and the Northern Territory. So, it was incongruous to be deplaning in Hobart in order to visit a retired Darwin Basque. Somewhere along the line, on one of my many trips Down Under, I had heard of Frank Alcorta, a genuine media personality. He was the editor of the *Sunday Territorian*, political pundit, and a regular columnist in the most prestigious national newspaper, *The Australian*. In the early nineties I wrote to him at the newspaper, a missive that had either gone unreceived or unheeded.

In 1994, I passed through Darwin on a barramundi fishing trip to the nearby Coburg Peninsula. I had but a few hours in the city and a couple of phone calls failed to establish contact with Frank. Then a year later I was awakened at night by a call from Geoff Hawkins, my Coburg fishing guide. "That bloke Alcorta is on a radio talk show right now. What shall I do?" Call him, of course.

Frank retired in 1996 and moved with his wife, Arantxa, to Bicheno, a coastal town two hours' drive north of Hobart. We had initiated lively correspondence and had even met in Donostia for a day in 1997. By then we were "mates," and over lunch at his mother's house we vowed to get together in the future in both Reno and Bicheno.

We turned off the country road at the "*Ongi Etorri*[17] Bill and Jan" sign. With evident pride, Frank showed us the cute house and grounds of his new seaside retreat, carved recently out of the Tasmanian bush. We lingered over the splendid view of the water and rocky shoreline. "I love to watch the storms come in from Antarctica, sometimes the waves are five meters high. There is nothing like it in the tropics." Frank's daily ritual is a swim in his Antipodean Bay of Biscay.

Frank's life story is indeed singular (cf. Chapter 14). He had prospected successfully for diamonds in Venezuela and opals in the Australian Outback. After joining the Australian army, he served with distinction for six years in Malaysia and Vietnam. He also initiated correspondence study from the University of Queensland (and later that of New England) that would culminate in a bachelor's degree in history and political science, and an MA in education. After his military service they lived in Papua, New Guinea, where he was a patrol officer and high school teacher before accepting a similar teaching position in Darwin. Frank became a community college instructor before opting to become a speechwriter for the sitting premier of the Northern Territory. Subsequently, rather than returning to academia, he turned to journalism, becoming the editor-in-chief of the *Sunday Territorian* and then the daily *Northern Territorian News*. Along the way, he authored the text for a photo book of the many natural wonders of the Northern Territory, a history of the defense of Darwin during World War II, and a work on the outrages perpetrated against Australian Aborigines.

"We love it here, but who knows how much longer we can stay." In 1977, and again 1979, Frank and Arantxa had purchased land in the Basque Country for eventual retirement. But then, in 1996, they sold both parcels convinced that, with a daughter in Alice Springs, another in Darwin, and grandchildren in both, it was simply unrealistic to move back to Europe. However, with Arantxa in delicate health, both aging, and now a continent away from family support, it was also questionable that they could manage to live a two-hour drive from the nearest decent hospital. "Maybe we'll end up in one of those assisted living units on the Gold Coast."[18]

They were planning a trip to the Basque Country next year to see Frank's ninety-one-year-old mother. From Australia they nourished their atavistic Basque interests by watching *Telediario*, the Spanish national newscast broadcast from Spain, provided daily over Australia's multicultural television channel. Frank's extensive library included a Basque section. He produced his copy of the Kurlansky book. "I didn't like it much," he opined. "I think it elevates too much myth to history." Frank uses the Internet regularly to access information about Basque topics and planned to study Basque. He asked me to put him in touch with the instructor of the Internet university course offered by my university's Center for Basque Studies.

Both Frank and Arantxa were critical of the present political situation in Euskadi. Frank noted,

We Basques have external and internal enemies. Aznar is a traditional Spanish centralist and he just wants to take back all of the power for Madrid. And ETA murders people for their opinions. Where's the democracy? I would vote in favor of a referendum for independence, but I'm not sure we need it. You can't make a people by just redrawing borders. If you are a people, which we are, maybe borders don't matter. In San Sebastián I get into a lot of arguments over politics.

When Jan and I lived in North Queensland in 1980, the four Mendiolea boys ranged from toddler Stephen to teenager Johnny. Now we were sharing a welcoming dinner with three of the four grown young adults (Tommy lives in Sydney and is a globetrotting airline attendant with Qantas). Allison, Johnny's Tasmanian wife, kept an eye on her infant Ethan and Michael's Queenslander spouse, Tricia, watched after her Adan. Johnny and Michael were both schoolteachers here in Townsville. Stephen, still a bachelor but in a serious relationship with an Aussie lass currently teaching in Mount Isa, works locally as the service manager for a Townsville auto agency.

In 1980, our frequent get-togethers were at the Mendiolea sugar farm in Ingham. About ten years ago, with John nearing sixty and in poor health, he and his wife Conchi sold the property and moved to Townsville. She then studied art at James Cook University and is now a promising painter. For a few years he worked for the government as an interpreter for monolingual Spanish-speaking immigrants. It was particularly appropriate employment, since the Mendiolea family (in particular, John's mother, Teresa) was legendary for having assisted literally dozens, if not hundreds, of Basques (and Spaniards) to enter Australia.

Whenever Allison, Tricia, and Jan were present we used English, otherwise we code-switched between Spanish and Basque. All of the boys were pretty fluent in the former; Johnny and Tommy were by far the best polyglots. They had studied Spanish and Basque for a semester in the San Sebastián USAC study-abroad program initiated by the University of Nevada.[19]

The Mendioleas had been my first contacts in Australia, when, in 1977, I made an exploratory visit to ascertain the feasibility of conducting a study of North Queensland's immigrant canecutters. I still recall John's initial reserve as we talked in the courtyard of *Villa Milano*, his Ingham sugar property. But as I outlined the improbable sequence of circumstances that had brought me to his doorstep, all reticence had evaporated, and I was seated in the kitchen ensconced forever within the family circle.

My quest had begun with another kitchen table conversation in 1962 in Goitiandia, a *baserri* in the *auzo* Zubero of the small Bizkaian town of Aulesti, where, for a year, I conducted anthropological field research on the causes and consequences of farm abandonment (including emigration). I was taping Josu Zabala, a former sugar canecutter recently returned from North Queensland. He was courting Beatriz, the youngest daughter in our household. Josu plied me with wondrous tales—the many joys and sorrows of incredibly hard work wielding a cane knife under the tropical sun, the good wages and the bad snakes, the youthful exuberance of the bachelor life, the camaraderie of the cane barracks during the season, the camps of the itinerant fruit-picker in the slack, and the struggle to learn English while immersed in a world whose *lingua franca* was Italian.

Goitiandia was but a few meters distant from the only ruined farmhouse in Zubero. Gojeascoa had been abandoned sometime in the 1920s by a young couple after the somewhat mysterious illnesses and deaths of their first two children. The symptoms suggested tuberculosis, and the village doctor advised the family to leave for a warmer climate. So, Tomás Mendiolea and his wife, Teresa, departed for Ingham in North Queensland in search of a new beginning.

The prospects of North Queensland's Basques were not encouraging. There had been practically no new immigration for many years, a few families had recently returned to Spain or relocated in urban Australia, and the grim reaper was alive and well. John opined, "There aren't any Basques left in Ingham," which was only a slight exaggeration. From Townsville to Cairns the situation was equally bleak, and the same could be said for the Atherton Tablelands—all formerly endowed with a larger Basque presence. The heartland of North Queensland's Basque community had shifted to the Burdekin, with its three dozen or so remaining families.

For the next several days, Aulesti was the *leitmotiv* of our deliberations. We reminisced over the Aulesti-Ingham connection whereby at one time or another the Mendioleas had sponsored the Australian immigration of Félix and José María Jayo, José and José Domingo Lecuona, José Antonio Longarte, Juanito Unamuno, and Cornelio Careaga. The Jayo brothers still lived in Trebonne near Ingham, the others were either deceased or had returned to Europe.

The christening party of the infant Patxi Phillips was at Idoia's house in the (improbably named) suburb of Nome located near Townsville and behind the Billabong roadside attraction (Australian wildlife). About sixty people, including a big part of the Burdekin's Basque contingent, were in attendance, including the proud grandparents—Agustín Arrate and Mary Bengoa. We were to continue on to Ayr after the ceremony, where Jan and I would spend the night at their house.

Agustín and Mary had recently moved into town from their sugar farm in Clare. Their son John was now in charge there, assisted sporadically by his semiretired father. Daughter Idoia was a medical technician in Townsville, and her sister Amaia taught elementary school in that city. Amaia was particularly conversant in Spanish and Basque since she had attended the USAC program in Donostia along with Tommy and Johnny Mendiolea. She was married to Mark Kelly from Sydney and was expecting their first child. To Mary's consternation, Mark had just interviewed for a job in distant Perth.

Agustín and Mary had refurbished her deceased mother's townhouse. Mary pointed with pride to the chestnut plank adorning the entry and etched with the name "Goikola." "That was my father's *baserri* in Aulesti. The wood is from a large tree that grew there." She had commissioned the carving in nearby Markina, Agustín's hometown.

Gloria Lazzarini, treasurer of the North Queensland Spanish Society, brought me a current membership list. We reviewed the forty-eight names on it one by one. Conceived originally by Benito Droguet, a Burdekin Catalan, the Ayr association had fused in 1970 with a Townsville initiative and then, in the late 1980s, resumed its independent course. Today, the Society holds two dinners annually to celebrate the feast day of the Virgin of Montserrat and that of Saint Ignatius of Loyola. If the Burdekin's Basque community was small, its Catalan contingent was now miniscule. The Society's roster included but nine Catalans sharing four surnames. Perhaps the most graphic evidence of the assimilatory effect of the passage of time was the cryptic notation that twenty-eight of the forty-eight letters of invitation to Society functions should be in English (the remaining twenty are sent in Spanish).

Joe Goicoechea is a prominent man in Townsville. He once lost the mayor's race by 300 votes. He is president of the Mendi Construction Company (*mendi* means "mountain" in Basque). Although raised in Australia since early childhood, Joe makes frequent pilgrimages to the Basque Country. He also attended the last Basque *Jaialdi* celebration in Boise, Idaho.[20] His Australian wife, Jenny, greeted us at the door of their impressive home on a hill overlooking Townsville. Once again, we were contemplating an entryway plaque, this time with "Etxetxu" etched in stone, evoking a specific house in a land half a world away. Joe observed, "Etxetxu was my parent's farm in Aulesti. The marble was quarried in Markina."

Agustín Adarraga has an equally sound claim for prominence in both Euskadi and Queensland, but of a more sporting nature. Born in Hernani, Gipuzkoa, and son and sibling of several cycling champions, Agustín was himself the provincial handball champion before emigrating to Australia. He is a trained veterinarian, a graduate of the University of Zaragoza (where he met his Catalan wife, María). They came out to Australia as part of the first of three contingents of Basques (and Spaniards) recruited in the late 1950s and early 1960s to cut sugar cane. Agustín noted, "They looked at my hands and didn't want me. They were too soft so I showed them a picture of me holding a shovel. It took some talking to convince them."

In Australia he found employment in hospital work, first as an orderly in the Bonegilla Migrants Centre Hospital, then as a lab assistant in Melbourne, and finally as a biochemist with the Red Cross Blood Bank in Brisbane. The Australian system refused to recognize his veterinarian credentials, so he decided to attend the University of Queensland—this time to obtain a science degree in chemistry and biochemistry. Upon graduation, he applied for an opening at a Townsville hospital and has been there ever since.

Agustín's notoriety, though, flows from his athletic prowess. In Australia he was exposed for the first time to the game of squash (Australia is one of the sport's leading nations). "I had played every kind of ball game in Euskadi, but this was a little different. At first, I kept hitting the ceiling, but it just took a slight adjustment and then I could hardly find an opponent. I was playing the club's pro."

Agustín became known as "Mr. Squash"[21] in North Queensland, winning championships at several competitive levels, and capping his illustrious career by triumphing in the 50–54 age category of the world masters' championship held in 1985 in Toronto. Agustín's son, Austin, followed the paternal lead and became a squash professional. At one time, he was the eleventh-ranked player in the world.

Now retired, Agustín tries to go to Europe every year. There he divides his time between his beloved Hernani and Madrid (where he has two other sons—Xavier and Ignacio[22]). He showed me his collection of the Basque language local paper (*Hernani Kronika*) that he downloads regularly from the Internet. "I try to read Basque for a least an hour every day." He then showed me a photograph of a dolmen in Hernani to which he makes an annual pilgrimage in order to place a rose on the spot. "I have three priorities, three *txapelas*[23] that I wear," he said. "The first is the Basque Country where I was born. The second is Spain. I have relatives in many parts of it. The third is humanity. We are all people."

Jan and I flew out of Brisbane and into her brief and star-crossed future. We had made the trip so that she could say goodbye to our many Basque-Australian and Italo-Australian friends. Her decade-old breast cancer had returned and metastasized as bone cancer.

—July 10, 2002

Notes

1. This is the organizational and philosophical tenet of the Basque oral poetic form of *bertsolaritza*. The performer, or *bertsolari*, is expected to improvise spontaneously on any topic, expressing his or her thoughts in rhyme that is then performed as a song. It is commonplace to begin formulating the verse by composing its last line and subsequently conceiving the beginning. For further description of this art form see Gorka Aulestia, *Improvisational Poetry from the Basque Country* (Reno and Las Vegas: University of Nevada Press, 1995).
2. ANZAC (Australia and New Zealand Army Corps) Day is arguably Australia's most important national holiday. It commemorates the sacrifices of Australian and New Zealand troops killed at Gallipoli in World War I. In many regards, it was the defining moment for the new Australian nation.
3. Basque word for "president."

4. The then *lehendakari* of Euskadi.
5. The party of the Basque radical left, Batasuna (Union), is the successor of HB (Herri Batasuna) that was outlawed by the Spanish government for its pro-ETA sentiments and actions. Batasuna would in turn be disqualified from the electoral process, as would all future parties believed to be in sympathy with ETA's political violence.
6. Introduced by a legislator of Basque-American descent, it calls upon the Spanish state to respect the Basques' right to self-determination.
7. "Speech Delivered by Professor William A. Douglass," in *Euskadi munduan eraikitzen. World Congress on Basque Communities, 1999* (Vitoria-Gasteiz: Servicio Editorial del Gobierno Vasco, 2000), 15–17.
8. Mark Kurlansky, *The Basque History of the World* (New York: Penguin Publishing Company, 1999).
9. Slang for a "true Australian."
10. For the sake of brevity, I will use "Anglo" throughout this manuscript when depicting the dominant "non-ethnic" Australian society. In invoking the nation's "British" heritage, it would be more accurate to label it "Anglo-Celtic."
11. I later went there and discerned no Basque surnames on the list.
12. Given our Basque concern in this book, it is interesting to note that the first recorded discovery of gold in Australia was made in the early 1840s in the Pyrenees Mountains of Victoria. They were so-named by the explorer and surveyor Thomas Mitchell, who was the first European to pass through the area (in 1836). The landscape reminded him of the Gipuzkoan countryside that he experienced while serving as a military officer during the Napoleonic War. Another veteran of the Napoleonic Wars, Major Edward Parke, christened a settlement that he founded "Hernani" after the Gipuzkoan town of that name.
13. The largest and most centrist party within the Basque nationalist movement. While it has never garnered an absolute majority, the PNV is the largest single party within the electorate of Hegoalde. From Franco's death until the election of 2009, the PNV always formed a part of the ruling coalition and held the post of *lehendakari* within the government of the Basque Autonomous Community. There was a brief four-year interlude under Socialist *Lehendakari* Patxi Lopez (2009–2012), but in 2012 the head of the PNV, Iñigo Urkullu, became president and still occupies the position as of 2019.
14. A popular Basque card game that is not unlike poker.
15. *Zazpiak bat* means "Seven in One." Reference is to the political unity (and desired unification) of Lapurdi, Behe Nafarroa, and Xiberoa (or Zuberoa) in present-day France and Bizkaia, Gipuzkoa, Araba, and Nafarroa (Navarra) in Spain.
16. A book series (more than twenty titles to date) published by the Basque government with the purpose of conserving the history of individual Basque diasporas around the world.
17. "Welcome" in Basque.
18. A resort area near Brisbane favored by many retirees and therefore well appointed with senior-care options.

19. Today, USAC, or the University Studies Abroad Consortium, is a top-rated study-abroad organization with 33 consortium universities in the United States and sends students to 54 campuses in 28 countries around the world. USAC began as an initiative of the Basque Studies Program of the University of Nevada, Reno, and included Boise State University and the University of Nevada, Las Vegas. Its purpose was to expose Basque-American students to their ancestral homeland (as well as other interested persons) by means of a structured academic program. The Donostia campus of the University of the Basque Country (UPV) provided the initial venue and continues to host a USAC foreign-student contingent to this day. USAC maintains a second Basque Country program at the UPV's Bilbao campus. To date, USAC has sent more than 9,000 foreign students to the Basque Country.
20. Jaialdi is the world's largest Basque cultural festival outside of the homeland. Held over a weekend every five years in the late summer, Jaialdi attracts 30,000–40,000 visitors. They include persons from the Basque Country itself, as well as Basque-Americans from throughout the American West. There are also participants from the various Basque diasporas around the world, notably several Latin American ones.
21. It is a nickname that he dislikes. Nor is it the only one. He remarked that instead of calling him Agustín, Australians invariably shortened it to "Gus." He therefore anglicized his personal name to "Austin," and then christened his son with it as well.
22. Named after the two Basque saints, Saint Francis Xavier and Saint Ignatius of Loyola. "It was the call of the Mother Country."
23. *Txapela* is the Basque term for beret.

CHAPTER 2

Australia Beckons

One of the most salient themes of modern world history is human migration, a movement that has been both massive and multifaceted. Among its many guises are the voluntary relocation of colonizers from their metropoles to the homelands of the colonized (e.g., the temporary spread of European hegemony to much of the globe), the involuntary transport of subject populations from one part of a colony or country to another (e.g, the Latin American *encomienda* system, Stalinist population relocations within Soviet society), or from one part of the planet to another (e.g., the African slave trade). Then there are the international wanderings of displaced persons (e.g., economic and political refugees, war victims). The expansion of monolithic political hegemonies to far-flung corners of the globe itself created conditions which facilitated population transfers that might otherwise seem if not "unnatural" then at least unlikely. A prime example is the dispersion of East Indians to places as disparate as Trinidad, Fiji, Kenya, and England because both the sending and receiving areas were parts of the British Empire. The emergence of politically integrated modern states with national markets likewise stimulated internal migration, whether from the countryside to the city or between regions, a process that is discernible to some degree in virtually every country of the world.

Within the foregoing panorama we may discern a pattern that is of particular relevance to the present work. Reference is to population transfers from "overpopulated," "developed" areas of the planet to its less-populated "frontiers."[1] The latter were vast in geographic extent and sparsely inhabited by native populations that, both in terms of sheer numbers and social (hence military) organization, were ill-equipped to defend their territories against modern invaders. Such "natives" posed a brief, if at times thorny, impediment to the juggernaut of new settlement. Once neutralized, their memory might become a part of the new nation's mythology and imagery; their shattered remnants a source of real, albeit tolerable, national guilt. National purpose, however, turned less upon the issue of subjugating, and then accommodating, autochthonous peoples than of replacing them through immigration. This pattern is characteristic of southern South America (particularly Chile, Argentina, Uruguay, and southern Brazil), South Africa, parts of North America (the United States and Canada), and Oceania (Australia and New Zealand).

Inherent in the migratory process was a degree of choice. When speaking of choice in this context we must underscore the qualifying "degree of," since the immigrants were not a monolithic category or group but rather displayed a considerable range of social class, racial, confessional, political, and even civil-status distinctions. Thus, the transportation of convicts to Australia and debtors to North America was not a matter of individual choice; the transatlantic crossing of persecuted religious groups to perceived New World havens was only slightly more so. Indeed, the decision of an impoverished European or Asian peasant to seek a better future on some developing frontier contains as much the elements of coercion and constraint as of choice. However, there is a sense in which many of those who emigrated did so with an optimism born of hope that the act of emigration itself portended a better future. Furthermore, most were able to exercise control over at least some aspects of the process, choosing from a range of possible destinations and occupations.

Another source of choice was the freedom, relative in some cases and absolute in others, of the receiving nations to determine their own immigration policies. In the early nineteenth century the United States and the several Latin American nations shed their former colonial status. By the mid-nineteenth century Canada, part of South Africa, New Zealand, and the several Australian colonies, though still under British sovereignty, were pursuing their own immigration policies. A characteristic of all the areas under consideration, then, was their ability to stimulate or discourage immigration according to their perceived national needs in any given period. To the extent that each was a potential recruiter of new population it competed with the others; to the extent that each was capable of discouraging potential immigrants it affected the prospects and policies of the others.

At the very least, when one of the receiving nations closed its doors to newcomers it increased the flow of emigrants to those countries still accepting immigration. While the relationship was not of a direct or mechanical nature, in general terms it seems evident from a perusal of comparative immigration statistics correlated with changing national immigration policies. What this would suggest is that, once the decision to emigrate was taken, the individual was likely to carry it out, selecting a secondary destination if, for whatever reason, his/her destination of choice proved inaccessible. Nor were intending emigrants prone to engage in "deferred departure," predicated upon the longer-range view of history that policy changes in the receiving nations were cyclical. Whether escaping misfortune or pursuing fortune, intending emigrants were unlikely to manifest patience.

While the "New World" receiving areas had much in common, they also had their differences. Parts of the same book, each constituted an individual chapter. All were the creations of European conquest, and, in their present guises, constitute the undeniable outposts of European civilization in a postcolonial world. Indeed, today when we speak of "western" civilization we are referring to the combined cultural, economic, political, and religious expression of the European colonizers *and* their colonized. The sanctity of the European connection is reflected in the immigration policies of all of these New World nations, policies that were designed to preserve their European character. In fact, until the post–World War II period, to the extent that nonwhites were admitted at all, they entered under highly circumscribed arrangements. That is, menial or "coolie" laborers might be deemed necessary for a particular project or denigrated occupation but were treated more as sojourners than settlers. Discriminatory legislation curtailed their geographic and occupational mobility, while anti-miscegenation laws and male-only immigration policies precluded their establishing family ties, and hence firm *pieds-a-terre* in the host country.[2]

Consequently, not to mention ironically, as all of the new New World nations in question sought to populate vast frontier areas they turned to Europe for potential immigrants. In the process they created what

Donald Denoon has called "settler societies," predicated upon settler capitalism.³ However, there were certain differences among them. Conditioned by their respective colonial experiences, Canada, Australia, South Africa, New Zealand, and the United States manifested a British orientation, epitomized by the use of English as the national language, whereas Argentina, Chile, Uruguay, and Brazil propounded a Latin worldview expressed through the medium of Spanish (or Portuguese). For an intending emigrant, the prospect of entering a familiar culture with full fluency in its language was compelling. From the standpoint of the receiving country, the immigrant with full facility (or nearly so) in the national culture and language was equally attractive. Such persons posed a minimum of potential adjustment problems and could be assimilated readily into the mainstream.

The ex-colonies therefore targeted their former metropoles when recruiting potential immigrants, thereby ensuring the influx of "kith and kin." When such sources of immigrants proved inadequate to meet the demands, other considerations came into play. The Anglo-oriented receiving countries shared the British view that the best human stock on the European continent inhabited the northern climes. Consequently, Germans and Scandinavians were regarded as the best "compromise" immigrants in the United States, Canada, South Africa, New Zealand, and Australia. In Latin America, the extension of the notion of kith and kin extended eastward through the northern reaches of the Mediterranean Basin, particularly to Italy.

Thus, by 1890, of the foreign-born population of the United States 33.76 percent were from the British Isles, 33.73 percent from the Germanic nations, and 10.09 percent from Scandinavian ones.⁴ The non-French population of Canada (total population 8,787,949) in 1921 included 4,868,738 persons descended from British stock, with the 294,635 Germans and 167,359 Scandinavians occupying the second and third places respectively.⁵ In Australia, of the total population of 4,455,000 in 1911, the foreign-born persons from the British Isles (591,729) constituted an overwhelming majority. Those from Germanic nations (38,245) and Scandinavia (14,700) were again second and third respectively.⁶

In the South American nations, there is a discernible Latin bias. In Argentina, with a total population of 3,954,911 in 1895, 198,685 of the foreign-born were from Spain. They occupied, however, second place behind the Italians numbering 492,676 persons.[7] In Uruguay, the statistics are murkier. However, in 1889, of the 100,739 inhabitants of Montevideo, 46.8 percent were foreign born, and of these 47 percent were from Italy while 32 percent were from Spain.[8] Conversely, in Chile, with a total population 2,357,052 in 1907, of the European foreign-born population, the largest contingent was from Spain (18,755), followed by Italians (13,023).[9] Finally, in Brazil, of 1,823,286 immigrants between 1872 and 1899, 1,012,956 were Italians, followed respectively by 379,070 Portuguese and 197,751 Spaniards.[10]

If the tendencies are clear, they are far from absolute. Germany and Italy, themselves new nations in the late nineteenth century, had large populations and insignificant colonies. Parts of the Austro-Hungarian and Russian empires of Central and Eastern Europe also proved to be seedbeds of candidates for transatlantic emigration. Conversely, Great Britain, Spain, and Portugal possessed insufficient population to service the entire immigrant demand of their robust former colonies. Furthermore, there was a kind of "grass is greener" effect discernible in the immigration statistics as well. Reference is to the significant number of British, Germans, and Scandinavians who viewed Argentina as a land of greater opportunity than either Canada or Australia. Conversely, some Spanish and Portuguese nationals sought entry to Britain's former colonies, as did Italians by the hundreds of thousands.

Such countertrends may be appreciated by considering that in 1890 there were 182,580 Italian-born persons in the United States (compared with 1,871,509 from Ireland and 2,784,894 from Germany).[11] The ethnic origins of Canadians in 1921 included 66,769 persons of Italian descent. It also included 106,721 Ukrainians, 100,064 Russians, and 53,403 Poles.[12] In the 1911 census for Australia, there were 6,719 Italian-born persons, making them the largest contingent of non-British Europeans after Germans and Scandinavians.[13] Conversely, in Argentina, of the foreign-born in 1895, 21,788 were British.[14] In Uruguay, by the 1920s, immigration from Central and Eastern Europe had surpassed that from the Mediterranean.[15] Of Chile's European-born population in 1907, Germans (10,724) occupied third place followed closely by the British (9,845).[16] Meanwhile, 50,310 Germans entered Brazil between 1872 and 1899.[17]

For all of the receiving areas in question, the accommodation and assimilation of the compromise immigrants posed a challenge. In Argentina, the preferred Spanish immigrant was practically an instant citizen; the Italian was quick to learn Spanish and generally comfortable with the country's Euro/Latin culture. It was the Englishman and German (not to mention the Swiss, Pole, Jew, etc.) who was prone to establish ethnic enclaves dominated by alien cultures and languages. The same scenario and fears obtained in Australia, but in reverse order. Thus, for Australians, the British immigrant posed a minimal challenge and Nordic continentals were perceived as sharing similar, if not the same, cultural values, while displaying a willingness and ability to learn English. The Italian, Greek, and Slav, on the other hand, were culturally exotic and slow to assimilate.

Australia's European Presence—Australia's early history as an English penal colony is well known to scholars and the general reading public alike.[18] In 1770, Captain James Cook landed at Botany Bay and claimed for Great Britain what turned out to be a vast continent. By then, North America was the established dumping ground of British prisoners, but the American Revolution created an immediate crisis in that system. By the mid-1770s, English prisons had overflowed and thousands of convicts were incarcerated in ships' hulks on the Thames awaiting transportation to somewhere.

In 1787, or during the reign of King George III, the first fleet of British intending colonists sailed for Australia. On January 26, 1788, the eleven vessels, carrying 1,030 persons in all, arrived at the future Sydney Harbor. More than half of the contingent—548 males and 188 females—was comprised of convicts. At least 160,000 prisoners were subsequently transported to the colony. Robert Hughes notes,

> The late eighteenth century abounded in schemes of social goodness thrown off by its burgeoning sense of revolution. But here, the process was to be reversed: not Utopia, but Dystopia; not Rousseau's natural man moving in moral grace and free social contracts, but man coerced, exiled, deracinated, in chains. Other parts of the Pacific, especially Tahiti, might seem to confirm Rousseau. But the intellectual patrons of Australia, in its first colonial years, were Hobbes and Sade.[19]

It might be noted that there was both ethnic and religious discrimination inherent in the transportation system. Irishmen residing in England were more likely than Englishmen to be incarcerated for real and alleged crimes. English prisons were also filled with Irish political prisoners detained for their patriotism regarding the independence of their island from British rule. Consequently, there were disproportionate numbers of Irish prisoners among the ranks of the transported convicts. They were Roman Catholics as opposed to their Protestant wardens. The subsequent religious tension throughout Australian history between Catholic and Protestant is rooted in this beginning. As we shall see, it would influence the debates and policies regarding the subsequent settlement of Roman Catholic Southern European immigrants in a Protestant-dominated Australia.[20] Today, Italians are Australia's largest non-British ethnic group.[21] That this should be so was not inevitable. Indeed, Italian immigrants had to overcome considerable opposition, both in order to enter the country and to prosper there. Most of the influx postdates World War II, a movement that in terms of chronology, magnitude with respect to the national population, and issues posed shares much in common with that of the entry of Hispanics into the United States. It might be argued that each served as the similar litmus test of its respective host society's immigration policy.

Basques constitute a tiny tile in the mosaic of Australian immigration. Like in the American West, where the vast majority of Basque immigrants were identified with a single occupation (that of sheepherder), for more than half of the twentieth century the typical Basque immigrant entered Australia to cut sugar cane. There was a salient difference, however, in the Basque immigrant's experience in these two Anglo-dominated societies. The Basque sheepherder had an ethnic support system in the guise of an established Basque-American community of some magnitude, but once he stepped outside of its confines he was confronted with the Anglo world. Conversely, by the time that Basques began to emigrate to Australia as intending canecutters, the sugar industry was becoming dominated by Italians. It was more important for the "new-chum"[22] Basque to learn Italian than English if he was to function within the fields and farm barracks of the cane districts. Furthermore, for Anglo-Australians it was the Italian who incarnated the Southern European.

Consequently, the Basque experience in Australia was configured and constrained by several unique factors. Compared with Basque immigration in such settler societies as the United States and several southern South American countries (Chile, Argentina, Uruguay, southern Brazil), Basque Australians remained few in number and largely without ethnic critical mass. Their Australian circumstances were influenced mightily by both the Italian immigration that preceded them and the massive ongoing twentieth-century influx of Italians into the country. As we shall see, the majority of Basque immigrants in Australia also passed through the occupational filter of first cutting sugar cane and doing so in North Queensland. Consequently, before we can analyze Basque immigration in Australia in its own terms, we must first examine its many influences—the historical formation of Australian attitudes toward immigrants in general, the Italian immigration that determined the Australian views of all Southern Europeans, and the history of the sugar industry—and particularly in its North Queensland venue. Australian Basques would live both the few joys and many sorrows of this "Mediterranean" stereotype.[23]

From the outset, genuine administration of Australia was of little concern to London. The convicts were simply banished with no thought of their rehabilitation. The new colony was no more than a convenient dumping ground a world away for criminal and political problems. During the initial years, Australia, or in reality New South Wales, was governed by military officers. Over the next few decades, adventuresome agriculturalists (some from Great Britain, others drawn from the ranks of the soldier-administrators, and even ex-convicts who had served out their sentences) secured land grants and settled parts of the country, and counted upon assigned (and essentially uncompensated) convicts for agricultural workers. It all leant itself to corrupt cronyism; close collusion between self-interested colonists and complicit jailers.

Meanwhile, beginning in 1793 with the War of the First Coalition against the French Revolution and nearly continuously until the Battle of Waterloo that defeated Napoleon in 1815, Europe was ablaze. Neither Spain nor Great Britain was in much of a position to provision, let alone administer, its colonies. Of particular relevance to New South Wales were the Peninsular (Iberian) campaigns of the British army. Upon their successful conclusion, and the subsequent final victory over Napoleon at Waterloo, Great Britain faced serious economic difficulties that limited the opportunity for returning veterans. At the same time, the demobilized constituted a cadre of trained individuals with considerable management skills. This was particularly true of those from the British Commissariat (the civilian corps charged with the logistics of supplying the army). After 1815, a portion of these veterans applied for administrative posts and/or land grants in New South Wales. Their involvement represents a watershed in Australian history; a critical step in the professionalization and normalization of Australian Governmental affairs.[24]

The history of human settlement in Australia is rife with ambiguities and seeming contradictions. Stark depictions of the harshness of the land, which made it suitable only for one of the planet's most primitive peoples in Aboriginal times and for convict settlements during the first phases of European colonization, contrast with the more recent image of a vast continent rich in natural resources, free from population pressure, and enjoying one of the highest standards of living in the world.

The accounts of European exploration of the Australian continent are largely a litany of failure and disappointment. Most attempts to penetrate the interior verified the overriding geographical fact that the coastal districts and their hinterlands were the most habitable.[25] To be sure, some settlers tested their mettle against the interior, prospering through a few wet years before succumbing to one of the periodic great droughts. However, true advancement of the agricultural frontier had to await the modern-day massive inversion of capital and technology represented by such undertakings as the Snowy Mountains Project in New South Wales and similar irrigation schemes in Western Australia. Even today, the economy of interior Australia is more characterized by mining than agriculture, and the latter is dominated primarily by extensive animal husbandry. The population of the interior remains sparse, and, in point of fact, the country's human settlement is largely urban and restricted to the littoral. As of 2003, 91 percent[26] of the national population resided in cities and their suburbs, making Australia demographically one of the most urbanized nations in the world.

Another strong theme running through Australian history is what historian Geoffrey Blainey phrased "the tyranny of distance."[27] A vast, if inhospitable, continent, settled by a handful of Englishmen and Celts, perched next to Asia's teeming millions and ever fearful of the possible consequences, a world away from "the mother country," and for that fact among her most loyal sons, Australia developed a variety of dependencies and complexes. From an economic standpoint, to this day the emphasis is upon the extraction or production and export of raw materials rather than their processing into finished goods. In this respect, the country continues a nineteenth-century tradition in which clothing and even many foodstuffs were imported from England, while raw materials were sent around the world in exchange. Consequently, Australia has an underdeveloped industrial infrastructure, and the penetration of the economy by foreign capital (today more American, Chinese, and Japanese than British) is a major national issue.[28]

There is an accompanying psychological dependence that permeates Australian worldview. One cannot help but be impressed by the extent to which Australians have reproduced a European lifestyle in even the tropical reaches of the nation. While the propensity to follow Britain's lead has certainly diminished somewhat in recent years, it might be argued that today there is strong orientation to an American substitute. On balance, then, Australians have been more consumers than producers of western culture.[29]

Of particular relevance to the subsequent treatment of immigration and immigrant adaptation in Australia are the related questions of labor history, political egalitarianism, and the concept of mateship. Conceived as a "prison-without-walls," Australia, from the outset, was a two-class society of free settlers and emancipated former convicts who would develop the land by utilizing transported prisoners as laborers. The distribution of the better agricultural land among the settlers and colonial administrators proceeded apace, and the best districts were claimed early on. The more marginal lands came to be controlled by another group of freemen (both emancipists and new immigrants) known as squatters, persons who owned cattle and sheep and moved them about the Crown (i.e., public) lands.

By 1830, both the settlers and squatters on the expanding Australian frontier required more labor than transported convicts could provide. Consequently, a "bounty" system was instituted in which proceeds from the sale of Crown lands in Australia were employed to encourage workers from the British Isles to emigrate "down under." This established an assisted passage and settlement scheme that, under various guises, would characterize Australian immigration policy throughout much of the nation's history.

During the first twenty years of its operation (1831–1850), some 200,000 persons entered Australia as immigrants. Their arrival, however, proved a mixed blessing, since many were of poor quality and unwilling to endure the privations of the bush.[30] When gold was discovered in California, Australia's paltry corps of Europeans proved fragile. Despite the efforts of officialdom and the media to prevent it, California lured away many of the settlers.[31] Ironically, the world's next major bonanza was found in Victoria (1851) and the demographic flow was reversed. Californians constituted a significant contingent among those flocking to Australia from throughout the globe. If Melbourne's population stood at 4,479 persons in 1841, by the early 1850s it was 39,000; growing thereafter to no fewer than 139,916 by decade's end.[32]

As with other mining booms throughout history, the Australian one created a few fortunes and stimulated its own demand for goods and services, while prompting a wage and labor shortage when few accepted salaried employment before first trying their luck in the pursuit of elusive wealth. The transportation of criminals, already under assault in certain circles of both Australian and English society, was quickly terminated in the face of the new developments.[33] Abolition of the penal system, with the emancipation of the existing convict population, did not resolve the labor crisis in the short run. To the contrary, the lure of instant wealth was far more attractive than the stock drover's wages.

The gold rush was short-lived and then, as is the case with any mining frontier, began to sputter into a series of localized booms and busts, relinquishing its dominant role within the national economy. However, during the decade 1851–1861, Australian society had made a quantum leap. The national population almost tripled from 437,665 to 1,168,149 persons.[34] If, for many Australians, the decade of the 1850s was one of physical privation in the goldfields, the common experience was itself a crucible for forging strong democratic values. It was also a period of material progress, as mineral wealth enriched not only the successful prospectors but also underwrote elevated gold camp wages and stimulated commerce.[35]

The successful ex-digger might invest his savings in rural land or an urban enterprise, in either case laying the basis of a nascent middle class. Its economic and political triumph was so complete that one Australian historian was prompted to label the period 1861–1883 as "The Age of the Bourgeoisie,"[36] a time in which business interests expanded the infrastructures of the several Australian colonies. While poverty was far from unknown, it was also generally a period of prosperity for the Australian working class, particularly since the construction industry prospered.[37]

On balance, then, by the latter decades of the nineteenth century Australian society contained a landed elitist aristocracy descended from the original settler (and even convict) families and disdainful of everyone else.[38] However, real economic and political power was vested in an upwardly mobile, recently emerged bourgeoisie and a prosperous, almost pampered, working class. Many a bourgeois and laborer alike had shared the nation's convict and impoverished-immigrant heritage and knew the privations of the bush hut and mining-camp tent. The result was a pervasive spirit of almost fanatical egalitarianism personalized in a system of mateship. A man could rely on his best friend and in return extended unquestioned loyalty and support to his mate. In Donald Horne's words, mateship "...promoted a belief in equality and the habit of judging a man by his performance rather than his inheritance."[39]

If mateship was a kind of spiritual glue holding members of particular classes together and, to a degree, transcending class lines to forge a national democratic ideal, this is not to say that the interests of employers and workers always coincided. Class conflict was as endemic to the Australian colonial scene in the late nineteenth century as it was to the rest of the western world. However, some of the details were unique to the continent and conditioned the nation's posture toward subsequent immigration. At a time when, for example, the Basque peasantry was largely illiterate, disenfranchised, economically ineffective, and incapable of collective action, the Australian working class was better educated and capable of asserting itself through pamphleteering, lobbying, and formal organization. In the 1880s, trade unions emerged to increase working class leverage in the marketplace, and the Australian Labour Party formed to garner political influence.

By the 1890s, the economic bubble had burst and Australia, along with the rest of the world, was plunged into a deep depression. It was a trying period of bank and business failures, acrimonious strikes and political confrontation between *laissez-faire* liberals and social-welfare-minded labourites. It was a time during which the more utopia-oriented preachers of social revolution were replaced in the labour movement by pragmatists dedicated to effecting social change through parliamentary practice. While the details vary from colony to colony,[40] the decade of the 1890s was one of considerable consolidation of Labour's political and economic power. Legislation guaranteed the workers' right to form unions, established minimum wage scales, regulated industrial working conditions, and provided for compulsory arbitration of work disputes. On the political front, Labour successfully espoused the concept of one-man-one-vote and opposed gerrymandering of electoral districts. As a result, by the first decade of the twentieth century, it had captured a majority of seats in all the parliaments of the individual Australian states[41] and assumed the prominent role in Australian national politics that it continues to play down to the present.

In sum, by the late nineteenth century, the nascent Australian labour movement was one of the most influential in the Western world. It protected the Australian worker's interests in the workplace and projected his concerns into the political arena. While its efforts did not always triumph, its string of victories was quite impressive. From a statutory standpoint, the Australian worker was clearly one of the most privileged on the planet. However, to the extent that class solidarity, cemented by mateship, strove to create a worker's utopia, it was highly inward looking. The beneficiaries of the system were

> …morbidly suspicious of the new comer or the intruder who might upset their monopoly of labour, or disturb their way of life. The sentiments of mateship tended to be reserved for the native-born, and the ideals that were the offspring of their loneliness and isolation became in turn forces to strengthen their provincialism and their xenophobia.[42]

It was on this question of control of the labor market that Labour differed (at times sharply) with its foils, the Conservatives and the Liberals. Employers had a vested interest in an abundant and cheap workforce, while the workers' cause was better furthered when labour was scarce and dear. Consequently, throughout Australia's history, immigration policy has always been hotly contested and, at times, equated with the nation's destiny.

An overriding theme throughout Australian immigration history has been the conscious attempt to maintain the continent as a bastion of British culture. When, in 1837, a New South Wales stock raiser requested permission to import Indian coolies to relieve the labor shortage, the move was opposed vehemently on both economic and racist grounds. The coolies were to enter on fixed contracts at a set wage. Critics charged that this would lower the salaries of European workers, establish a system of indenture, and discourage future European emigration to the continent. It would also introduce a colored race doomed to occupy a station of social inferiority.[43] The move was actively opposed and denied by the head of the Colonial Office in London who noted,

> ...introducing the black race there would, in my mind, be one of the most unreasonable preferences of the present to the future... There is not in the globe a social interest more momentous—if we look forward for five or six generations—than that of reserving the continent of New Holland as a place where the English race shall be spread from sea to sea unmixed with any lower caste...we now regret the folly of our ancestors in colonizing North America from Africa.[44]

A few hundred Indians entered Australia before the opponents of the scheme were successful in imposing a ban.

A short time later, or in 1847, another pastoralist familiar with the Pacific Isles took it upon himself to recruit a few Islanders, or Kanakas as they were called. Again, the effort met with praise from certain potential employers and opposition from the proponents of a White Australia.[45]

Between 1848 and 1852, approximately 3,000 coolies were recruited in China and introduced into the stock-raising districts. Predictably, this drew its own measure of by now redundant opposition by those emphasizing racial, religious, and standard-of-living differences between the newcomers and Britishers.[46]

It was on the goldfields that the issue of Asian immigration came to a head. The mining boom was particularly attractive to the Chinese, and their numbers in the Colony of Victoria reached 42,000 by the year 1858. However, anti-Chinese violence and legislation quickly reversed

Map 2. Present state and former colony of Queensland with places referenced in the text. Drawing by Patricia DeBunch.

the trend, and, by 1871, Victoria's Chinese population had been more than halved to 18,000.[47]

While the opponents of non-European immigration won the battle of the mining camps, history and the ecological realities of the continent conspired against such a simplistic policy. From the outset, the attempts of white Australians to settle the northern tropical districts ended in failure. Consequently, as early as 1837, the notion that Europeans were unsuited for physical labor in the tropics was a part of Australian worldview.[48]

Western Australia, South Australia (its Northern Territory), and Queensland all had tropical regions. Queensland's coastal districts, backed by a narrow belt of uplands, were watered, fertile, and amenable to human settlement.[49] More than 2,000 miles of the Queensland coastline were north of the Tropic of Capricorn.

If the future of northern Australia was to be tropical agriculture, the way seemed clear. By the second half of the nineteenth century the plantation system, in which European planters and supervisors directed the activity of nonwhite manual laborers, was *the* pattern of commercial agriculture in most semitropical and tropical areas of the globe.

While the plantation system seemingly provided the obvious (and possibly only) means of settling the northern part of the continent, it was anathema for most white Australians. Imbued with a sense of racial superiority, political egalitarianism, a pronounced disrespect and suspicion of the landed classes, and in the throes of emancipating themselves from a convict heritage, lower- and middle-class Australians were loath to institute a system that stereotypically smacked of near feudal land ownership, an enslaved or indentured workforce, and miscegenation.

The Sugar Initiative—From the outset, Australian agriculture as a whole was dominated by pastoralism and the national economy postured around the export of pastoral products. Wheat production was the second most important emphasis within the agrarian sector. However, for tropical eastern Australia sugar emerged as the dominant cash crop. Currently cultivated discontinuously on alluvial plains along a 2,100-kilometer coastline stretching from Grafton in northern New South Wales to Mossman in extreme north Queensland, Australian

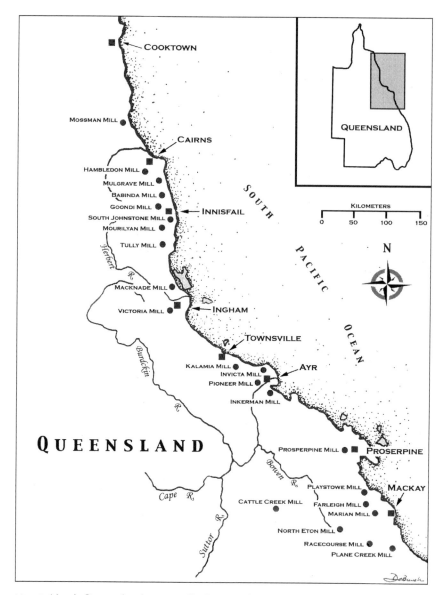

MAP 3. North Queensland sugar mills. Drawing by Patricia DeBunch.

sugar producers meet the national demand and supply Australia's second largest export crop, as well as making the country the world's third largest exporter of sugar. The degree of mechanization and technical efficiency of the Australian sugar industry are second to none.

Sugar cultivation began in Australia as early as 1823 when 70 tons were produced at Port Macquarie in New South Wales.[50] During the next four decades, a small-scale industry emerged in the coastal districts of the northern reaches of the colony. Expansion was fueled by a high local demand. Australians at the time had the highest per capita consumption of sugar in the world.[51]

Many of the initial efforts met with failure. Experience was to demonstrate that sugar could only be grown profitably north of the Clarence River, thereby disqualifying much of New South Wales (today the state produces only about 5 percent of the total crop with the remainder coming from Queensland).[52] The real future of the industry resided in the more tropical districts to the north.

In 1859, Queensland attained its independence from New South Wales, and the economic destiny of the fledgling colony was clearly linked to the development of tropical agriculture—particularly cotton and sugar. From the outset, there were attempts to import nonwhite labor. In 1861, the Queensland Parliament passed enabling legislation to allow Indian coolies into the colony. However, the attempt foundered when London and Indian officials imposed severe restrictions designed to protect them.[53]

It was at this point that the potential agricultural entrepreneurs took matters into their own hands and dispatched "recruiters" to Melanesia. In 1863, the first boatload of Kanakas was introduced into the colony, sixty-seven in all.[54] In 1904, the traffic was abolished. In the intervening forty-one years a total of 61,160 Pacific Islanders had entered Queensland.[55] Throughout its history, the system was controversial, at times pitting Brisbane against Westminster, Queensland against the other Australian colonies, southern Queenslanders against their northern counterparts, and white workers, small farmers, and businessmen against the planters. Recruiting abuses, including kidnapping and debt peonage by the so-called "blackbirders," and intolerable mortality rates due to poor sanitation, diet, and working conditions on some of the plantations posed grave humanitarian questions for the detractors and supporters of the traffic alike.[56] The introduction and eventual abolition of Kanaka labor in Queensland was inexorably intertwined with the development of the colony's sugar industry.

The initial attempts to establish it in Queensland date from the early 1860s. In 1862, John Buhot, a man with West Indian sugar experience, produced the first granulated sugar in the colony and was awarded 500 acres by the Queensland Government in appreciation of his efforts. The following year, another planter had 20 acres under cane near Brisbane and had installed a mill to crush it. He, too, was awarded acreage. By 1865, the Queensland government was offering land to potential planters under very favorable conditions, and a number of entrepreneurs, many lacking the necessary expertise, entered the industry.[57] Between 1865 and 1880, sugar production expanded notably in Queensland. If, in 1867, there were six mills in operation, manufacturing a total of 168 tons, by 1880 there were eighty-three producing 15,564 tons.[58] By this time, there were planters operating as far north as Cairns.

It might also be mentioned that there were attempts to introduce other crops into the Far North. It seems that Chinese settlers pioneered banana cultivation on a commercial scale, particularly in the Innisfail area.[59] We also have evidence of the activity of the (in)famous Henry Wickham, the Englishman who, in 1876, "stole" rubber seeds in Brazil, the germination of which in London's Kew Gardens became the foundation of rubber plantations in British Southeast Asia that sounded the death knell for South America's wild rubber industry. He sojourned in the Hinchinbrook briefly where he planted tobacco. Apparently, he failed because his product was too sweet for the white smokers' tastes, albeit it had chewing appeal for the Kanakas.[60] There is also indication that there were as many as 1,000 Russians in Queensland alone, displaced from their country (and after a sojourn in Manchuria) by the turmoil surrounding the collapse of the Tsarist regime.[61]

Photographs and some written accounts of the period depict a lifestyle highly reminiscent of that of the plantations of the pre-Emancipation American South. Paddle wheelers plied the rivers past ornate mansions with wide verandas, manicured grounds, and an air of leisurely tropical opulence. White supervisors directed the labor of gangs of "darkies" (Kanakas) in the fields and mills. However, in retrospect, such appearances were highly deceiving, as the period was largely one of spectacular economic failure in which several factors conspired to ruin many a settler.

There was the frontier-like quality of the enterprise in which the oftentimes neophyte planter risked his all in a previously unproven area with only a vague notion of whether local climatic conditions and soil types would prove amenable to the growing of cane. In the pioneering days, the plantations were established in the midst of the occasionally hostile Aboriginal groups, and more than one white settler and Kanaka worker ended up on the wrong end of a spear. Tropical diseases, the abundance of some of the planet's deadliest varieties of snakes, and infestations of man-eating crocodiles in the river systems all diminished the settler's sense of personal safety.

Then there was the perennial concern with the labor supply. The felling of virgin forest by hand and preparation of the fields were labor intensive. The initial supposition that whites were unsuited for such work, and the general opposition in Australia to nonwhite immigration, made the planter's insecurity regarding labor endemic. While approval to import Kanakas into Queensland was obtained from the colony's parliament, the plan elicited heated opposition from Labour interests and from the urban Liberals. Further factors undermining the planters' success were distance from markets and the capital requirements of the industry. Sparse settlement of Queensland meant that there was virtually no local demand and the plantations were thousands of miles away from the major Australian, let alone world, markets.[62] Added to this isolation was the fact that a plantation required sufficient capital to survive a lengthy startup period of clearing and field preparation (minimally five years from scrub to finished paddock), as well as considerable investment in a crushing mill. Not surprisingly, many of the plantations were undercapitalized, understaffed, or both.

Adding to the intrinsic problems of the growers was the fact that, in 1875, a rust disease broke out in the fields, and certain districts were found to have a problem with grubs. While the wealthier planters weathered the storm by experimenting with new rust-resistant strains of cane and methods of grub control, financial backers became nervous and the extension of credit to the industry was curtailed.[63] Still, on balance, the period 1875–1882 was a profitable one for many of the plantations.

In 1882, however, the combined production from Queensland and British interests in Fiji met and surpassed Australia's domestic demand for sugar. Shortly thereafter, the rapid emergence of European beet sugar, stimulated by government subsidies, depressed the world market to levels that, by 1885, made all Queensland operations unprofitable. Again, a number of growers failed to survive the crunch.[64]

One might argue that, had the labor- and capital-intensive plantation system continued to dominate, the Queensland sugar industry would not have evolved into the present twentieth-century behemoth, and quite possibly might not have survived at all. However, as early as 1870, there was another development that was to shape its future. In that year the Colonial Sugar Refining (CSR) Company erected three sugar mills in New South Wales. The Company, with established operations in Fiji, brought a new level of expertise and capitalization to the Australian scene. In 1881, the CSR extended its operations to North Queensland, acquiring land and mills in the Mackay and Herbert River districts. Its entry into Queensland was controversial and required special enabling legislation by the parliament. The "Colonial Sugar Refining Company's Bill" of 1881 transferred to the CSR Crown lands held by selectors who had failed to fulfill all of the terms of their conditional purchases. In return, the CSR was required to expend a minimum of £200,000 in capital improvements over a five-year period. It more than met this condition, and, by the end of the decade, was a dominant force on the Queensland scene. It possessed three mills in the colony and had 38,000 acres of land.[65] In the words of one contemporary, "I think we can thank them [CSR] for the fact that there is any sugar being grown in Queensland at the present time. They have made the manufacture of sugar their specialty. They came into the business when it was being conducted in a crude and unscientific manner."[66]

In its New South Wales operations, the Company had pioneered a new concept—the central mill system. Following the lead of certain West Indian sugar interests, the CSR became convinced that it was more profitable to concentrate upon the milling and refining of sugar rather than its actual cultivation. Consequently, it divested itself of its New South Wales land to smallholders under extremely favorable terms, and with purchase provisions for the cane.

When, in 1883, the CSR commenced crushing in North Queensland it was operating its own plantations. The Company's main focus was upon improving output, but via the plantation system. It did, however, become the first milling operation to encourage the growing of cane by small, independent farmers within the orbit of a CSR mill.

Meanwhile, in the mid-1880s, pressure began to build in North Queensland to institute a central-mill system. The greatest interest was centered in Mackay, where a number of independent farmers grew cane for neighboring plantation mills. The plan was supported by the opponents of the Kanaka traffic and opposed by most plantation owners. However, in 1885, with the Liberal government of Sir Samuel Walker Griffith in power in Brisbane, the planters' opposition was overridden and legislation passed to subsidize creation of two central mills in the Mackay district. The farmers themselves were to be the shareholders of the operations. Both the CSR's Homebush Plantation and the nearby Habana Plantation were subdivided into medium-sized farms that were quickly taken up.[67] That same year, the Queensland parliament passed The Pacific Islanders Act, which was to abolish importation of Kanakas by the end of 1890.

It was felt by the planters' opponents that the central-mill system would be a kind of panacea that would ensure white settlement of the tropical north. While this eventually proved to be true, the project encountered many problems. The question of the suitability of white labor under tropical conditions had yet to be resolved. Rather, in the initial years the system fragmented the former social organization of labor without revolutionizing it. According to Harry T. Easterby,

> ...Instead of about fifty planters in a district, 800 small farmers took their place. The overseer of a gang of, say, sixty Kanakas, was replaced by half a dozen farmers employing four Kanakas each. The small men, in many cases labourers, who then entered on canegrowing were raised in the social scale to employers and finding themselves so, improved their opportunities.[68]

Despite their ascent in status, however, these were not men of the leisured class, nor did the scale of their operations permit them the luxury of being mere *dirigistes*. When a number of the former mill hands, mechanics, etc. took up small sugar properties, they therefore initiated a serious experiment in manual laboring by whites under North Queensland conditions.

During the decade of the 1880s, Queensland sugar production increased fourfold, making the crop one of the most important and most promising products in the colony's economy. The scale was becoming more industrial, since, between 1885 and 1888, the number of operating mills actually declined from 166 to 118.[69] However, while the central-mill approach was gaining ground, the industry remained dominated by the larger plantations and the CSR. Although the CSR officials favored the central-mill scheme for its New South Wales and Mackay holdings, they were profoundly skeptical regarding the suitability of white labor under the more tropical conditions of the Far North. The Kanaka question was but one of several contentious issues between the government in Brisbane and its far northern constituents—contentions that spawned serious talk of secession among the latter.[70]

In 1888, Premier Griffith was replaced by the conservative Sir Thomas McIlwraith, a man with personal investments in the sugar industry and a longstanding proponent of the Kanaka traffic.[71] Predictably, he questioned the continued viability of the sugar interests in Queensland were the Kanakas to be removed, and, in 1889, a Government Board of Inquiry held hearings in the sugar districts of North Queensland.

The investigation covered a broad range of issues, but none received fuller treatment than that of the feasibility of using white labor in the fields. Testimony taken in the Johnstone district from the manager of Goondi plantation, a CSR property, was typical. He noted that, in 1888, Goondi employed 120 Europeans, 271 Kanakas, and 44 Chinese. The Kanakas received about £9 yearly; the Chinese earned 15–17 shillings, and the Europeans 20 to 60 shillings weekly. The mill was operated exclusively with Europeans, the Chinese were engaged in clearing scrub, and the Kanakas were the field hands. Particular questions and their answers were as follows:

Q: Have you employed European labour in field work?
A: Yes.
Q: Are Europeans willing and able to do it?
A: I first started Goondi with Europeans. The first piece of scrub fallen was done by Europeans. But they signally failed.
Q: Were they working by contract or by day work?
A: Contract. There was a great deal of dissatisfaction, and they were always changing hands. Last year the mill broke down and I offered to find the men, who had been in the mill, work in the field till it was repaired, but they told me that that was blackfellows'

work, and they would sooner stop on and do nothing till the mill was put right. A few of the men went into the field, but their labour cost too much, and the work was done badly, and they said the heat was so great that they could not stand it.

Q: Could the company afford to grow cane on this plantation with European labour and make a profit?

A: No.

Q: You are aware that according to the law the introduction of Kanakas ceases at the end of 1890?

A: Yes.

Q: What effect is that likely to have on the sugar industry?

A: If I had a plantation of my own I would most decidedly look on it that I should have to expect to shut up if I was prevented from employing Kanakas.[72]

The following year the fate of the plantation system seemed sealed when Griffith was again elected premier. However, Griffith himself toured the sugar districts in early 1892. Returning to Brisbane, he issued a manifesto that stunned his supporters, urging that the Kanaka traffic be extended for another ten years. It is uncertain as to what prompted the decision. Clearly, the premier was treated to a litany of planters' complaints. Some observers felt that pressure was brought to bear by financial institutions with exposure in the sugar industry. Others felt that the CSR forced the outcome, and, in fact, the Company had announced its intention to dismantle its Victoria Mill in the Herbert district for removal to Fiji.[73]

Whatever the reason(s), the plantation system gained a bit of breathing room. However, the controversy from 1885 to 1892 had put the handwriting on the wall, and Griffith's reversal merely postponed the inevitable. Indeed, some planters were already seeking alternative solutions prior to it. Chinese, Japanese, Arabs, and Javanese were all imported in modest numbers under conditions that were much more humane than those surrounding the Kanaka traffic. Still, from a political standpoint, this was a short-term palliative rather than a permanent solution, since it fanned Australian fears of the "yellow peril." The individual colonies were but a decade away from federation into a single nation, one of the cornerstones of which was to be the White Australia Policy.

It was within this economic and political climate that a new initiative emerged. Until the last decade of the nineteenth century, white settlers in tropical Queensland were almost exclusively Britishers, with a small contingent of northern Europeans (Germans and Scandinavians).[74] The climatological arguments underpinning the assumption that whites were incapable of manual labor in the tropics notwithstanding, one possibility had not been explored. Mediterranean Europe had a bronze-skinned peasantry that was accustomed to agricultural work under torrid conditions. While not exactly inured by experience to tropical climes, it was possible that Southern Europeans might provide the backbone of a white laboring force in the tropical north—a swarthy alternative.

Notes

1. Admittedly, these are all subjective terms.
2. See Charles A. Price, *The Great White Walls Are Built: Restrictive Immigration to North America and Australasia 1836–1888* (Canberra: Australian National University Press, 1974). [*Great White Walls*]. Of course, such policies were never completely effective, nor were they applied evenly in all times and places. Consequently, Asian immigrants did establish footholds in these European-dominated redoubts.
3. Donald Denoon, *Settler Capitalism: The Dynamics of Dependent Development in the Southern Hemisphere* (Oxford: Clarendon Press, 1983). Denoon focuses more upon economic issues than immigration history and restricts his treatment to the southern hemisphere. Similarly, the essentially rural frontier context of the settler society is in sharp contrast to the "urban frontier" experienced by European peasants choosing a New World city or industrial town as their destination. See John Bodnar, *The Transplanted: A History of Immigrants in Urban America* (Bloomington: University of Indiana Press, 1985).
4. Stephen B. Thernstrom, ed., *Harvard Encyclopedia of American Ethnic Groups* (Cambridge: Harvard University Press, 1980), 1051. [*Harvard Encyclopdia*].
5. Department of Manpower and Immigration, *Immigration and Population Statistics* (Ottawa: Federal Publications, 1974), 9–10. [*Immigration*]. Given the special near-enclave circumstance of Quebec, the 2,452,743 persons of French descent are left out of account.
6. Commonwealth of Australia, *Census of the Commonwealth of Australia*, vol. 2 (Melbourne: Government Printer, 1911), 134–35. [*Census of the Commonwealth 1911*].
7. José Panettieri, *Inmigración en la Argentina* (Buenos Aires: Ediciones Macchi, 1970), 25–26. [*Inmigración*].
8. M. H. J. Finch, *A Political Economy of Uruguay since 1870* (New York: St. Martin's Press, 1981), 25. [*A Political Economy*].
9. Carl Solberg, *Immigration and Nationalism: Argentina and Chile, 1890–1914* (Austin: University of Texas Press, 1970), 38. [*Immigration and Nationalism*].

10. Thomas W. Merrick and Douglas H. Graham, *Population and Economic Development in Brazil, 1800 to the Present* (Baltimore: The Johns Hopkins University Press, 1979), 91 [*Population*]. Adapted from Table V-I.
11. Thernstrom, *Harvard Encyclopedia*, 1052.
12. Department of Manpower and Immigration, *Immigration*, 10.
13. Commonwealth of Australia, *Census of the Commonwealth*, 1911, 134–35. The number of Spain-born persons was but 658 in the entire country.
14. Panettieri, *Inmigración*, 26.
15. Finch, *A Political Economy*, 25.
16. Solberg, *Immigration and Nationalism*, 38.
17. Merrick and Graham, *Population*, 91. Adapted from Table V-I.
18. Robert Hughes, *The Fatal Shore: The Epic of Australia's Founding* (New York: Vintage Books, 1988). [*The Fatal Shore*].
19. Ibid, 1.
20. Edmond Campion, *Rockchoppers: Growing Up Catholic in Australia* (Blackburn, Vict.: Penguin Books, 1982), 44–58. [*Rockchoppers*].
21. Charles A. Price, "The Ethnic Character of the Australian Population," in *The Australian People: An Encyclopedia of the Nation, Its People and Their Origins*, ed. James Jupp (North Ryde, N.S.W.: Angus and Robertson, 1988), passim. ["Ethnic Character"]. According to Price, an analysis of the birthplaces of all 14,694,861 Australians in 1981, and projected over past generations as well, reflects 10,553,997 persons of British origin. Italians, with 603,241 persons, occupy second place, followed closely by Germans with 578,898. Greeks, with 298,088, are the next largest group.
22. Australian slang for the recently arrived immigrant.
23. For fuller treatment of all of these subjects see William A. Douglass, *From Italy*.
24. They were also prone to name places in the Antipodes after battles of the Peninsular War. It is likely that this is the genesis in Australia of Basque place names such as Hernani in New South Wales and Tolosa Park in Tasmania. Of more recent vintage in New South Wales are Bay of Biscay Swamp (ten kilometers from Mungery) and Estella (a suburb of Wagga Wagga). There is also the Basque Road Reserve, a public park in Auckland, New Zealand.
25. Manning Clark, *A Short History of Australia* (New York: Mentor Books, 1969), 45–46, 62–64, 83, 138–39. [*A Short History*].
26. See http//www.nationmaster.com/country/as-australia/peo-people.
27. Geoffrey Blainey, *The Tyranny of Distance* (Melbourne: Sun Books, 1966). [*Tyranny*].
28. Donald Horne, *The Lucky Country* (Blackburn, Victoria: Penguin Books, 1976), 132 [*Lucky*], notes that, "Of the top 100 Australian firms at least two thirds are overseas controlled. When it is remembered how these firms then dominate their suppliers and clients it would be safe to say that Australian manufacturing is ultimately dependent on overseas enterprise and decision."
29. Ibid, 94–102.
30. Ibid, 85–86.

31. Jay Monaghan, *Australians and the Gold Rush: California and Down Under 1849-1854* (Berkeley and Los Angeles: University of California Press, 1966), passim.
32. Ibid, 218.
33. After 1853, only Western Australia continued to receive convicts, a practice abolished there in 1868.
34. Horne, *Lucky*, 135; Sydney Spanish Consul Antonio Arrom de Ayala (1853–1859) informed Madrid that, in 1855, there were 80,000 residents in the city and it received 2,000 new arrivals monthly. See Carlos M. Fernández-Shaw, *España y Australia. Quinientos años de relaciones* (Madrid: Ministerio de Asuntos Exteriores de Espana, 2000), 200 [*España*]. His successor, Eduardo San Just Torner (1860–1869), sent glowing reports to Madrid regarding the dynamic demographic expansion of Australia. In 1863, the southern continent, including New Zealand, attracted 53,054 immigrants, while the United States welcomed but 18,083 (Ibid, 190). He added that between 1850 and 1865, commerce between Spain and Australia had increased a thousand percent (Ibid, 207).
35. Ibid, 137.
36. Ibid, 140–62.
37. Ibid, 148.
38. Ibid, 146–47.
39. Ibid, 118.
40. It should be noted that throughout the nineteenth century the future Australian "states" were individual British colonies. Each had its own parliament and, as a component within the empire, dealt directly with officialdom in London. It was not until 1901 that the several colonies constituted a federated "Australia" as a united nation-state.
41. Ibid, 169–84.
42. Ibid, 118.
43. Price, *Great White Walls*, 39–42.
44. Clark, *A Short History*, 109.
45. Price, *Great White Walls*, 43.
46. Ibid, 43–47. The term "Britisher" is used by Australians as a surrogate for "Anglos" and refers to both immigrants from the British Isles and their Australian descendants.
47. Ibid, 67–92, 120.
48. Ibid, 51–52; P.P. Courtenay, "The White Man and the Australian Tropics—A Review of Some Opinions and Prejudices of the pre-War Years," in *Lectures on North Queensland History*, Second Series, ed. B.J. Dalton (Townsville: History Department, James Cook University of North Queensland, 1975), 57–65.
49. A. Grenfell Price, "The White Man in the Tropics and the Problem of North Australia," 7–8. Manuscript in the Edward Leo Hayes Collection, Fryer Library, University of Queensland. ["White Man"].
50. Harry T. Easterby, *The Queensland Sugar Industry* (Brisbane: Frederik Phillips, Queensland Government Printer, 1931), 1. [*Queensland Sugar*].
51. Ibid, 8.

52. "From Two to Two Million Tons of Sugar," *Producer's Review* (July 1964), 21. [*From Two to Two*].
53. Grenfell Price, "White Man," 148–49.
54. Raphael Cilento, *Triumph in the Tropics: An Historical Sketch of Queensland* (Brisbane: Smith and Patterson, 1959), 289.
55. P. M. Mercer, "Pacific Islanders in Colonial Queensland 1863–1906," in *Lectures on North Queensland History*, ed. B. J. Dalton (Townsville: History Department, James Cook University of North Queensland, 1974), 101.
56. For fuller treatment of the issue see Peter Corris, *Passage, Port and Plantation: A History of Solomon Islands Labour Migration 1870–1914* (Melbourne: Melbourne University Press, 1973); William T. Wawn, *The South Sea Islanders and the Queensland Labour Trade* (Canberra: Australian National University Press, 1973); and George Palmer, *Kidnapping in the South Seas Being a Narrative of a Three Months' Cruise of the H. M. Ship Rosario* (Edinburgh: Edmonston and Douglas, 1871).
57. Easterby, *Queensland Sugar*, 2.
58. B. B. Levick, "Origin and Development of the Central Mill and Small Farm System in Queensland," ms. [*Origin and Development*]. Copy in Colonial Sugar Refining Company Archive (Sydney). Box n.1.0, Folder 3.
59. When, in 1912, the Australian government was debating an Aliens Restriction Act, it was opposed by the Silkwood correspondent to the *North Queensland Register* on the grounds that its "education test" would have excluded the Chinese pioneers who had done so much for his area (*North Queensland Register*, May 18, 1912, 74). That same year, the newspaper reported that the Ingham police "were having a busy time lately, particularly amongst the Chinese opium smokers" (Ibid, January 22, 1912, 34). In the Burdekin, Mr. Ching Do's application to cut timber on public land was denied by the Ayr Shire Council as it needed the logs for its own purposes (Ibid, May 11, 1912, 26).
60. See Bianka Vidonja Balanzategui's blog: https://interpretinginghamhistory.blogspot.com/search?q=wickham.
61. *North Queensland Register*, April 5, 1912, 11.
62. In 1878, Australian consumption of sugar was 91,500 tons. Queensland produced 12,000 tons of which about half was exported to the southern colonies. New South Wales provided about 3 million tons to the Australian market. The remainder was being imported from Java and Mauritius. Even at this early date, it was anticipated that Queensland would one day meet the national demand. (Easterby, *Queensland Sugar*, 8).
63. G. C. Bolton, *A Thousand Miles Away: A History of North Queensland to 1920* (Canberra: Australian National University Press, 1972), 77–78. [*A Thousand*].
64. Easterby, *Queensland Sugar*, 9.
65. Ibid.
66. Cited in Levick, "Origin and Development," 4.
67. Ibid, 7; Easterby, *Queensland Sugar*, 10.
68. Ibid, 13.
69. Levick, "Origin and Development," 2.

70. Christine Doran, *Separatism in Townsville* (Townsville: History Department, James Cook University of North Queensland, 1981), xi–xx.
71. Bolton, *A Thousand*, 86–87.
72. Queensland Royal Commission, *Minutes of Evidence Taken before the Royal Commission to Inquire into the General Condition of the Sugar Industry of Queensland* (Brisbane: Government Printer, 1889), 75, 76, 78.
73. "From Two to Two," 53; Bolton, *A Thousand*, 201.
74. Rosemary Lawson, "Immigration into Queensland 1870–1890," B.A. thesis, University of Queensland, 1963, passim.

CHAPTER 3

Basques in Nineteenth-Century Australia

Southern European Precursors—Australian demographic historian Charles Price, in his seminal work, analyzed naturalization records and concluded that, by 1891, the entire Southern European population on the Australian continent (excluding Australia-born ethnics) numbered about 6,000 persons. Of these, 3,900 were Italians (2,400 from North Italy). There were 600 Greeks, 200 Maltese, and 300 Slavs. Price assigned 1,000 individuals to the category "Basques, Catalans, other Spanish, Portuguese and Southern French."[1]

According to the 1891 census, there were 184,653 "foreign-born" persons residing in Queensland, of whom 77,117 were from England and Wales, 43,036 from Ireland, and 22,400 from Scotland. These 142,533 Britishers constituted no less than 77 percent of the colony's foreigners. The next largest groups were 14,910 Germans, 9,243 Kanakas (Pacific Islanders), and 8,522 Chinese. Taken together, there were but 1,178 Southern Europeans (438 Italians, 400 French, 80 Spaniards, and 25 Portuguese).[2] The data exclude Australian-born persons of a particular ethnic group. Consequently, they progressively undercount the numbers of individuals who were likely to regard themselves as "Irish" or "Italian."

It is apparent that, through most of the nineteenth century, the emphasis upon British and Northern-European immigration was quite effective in minimizing the entry of Southern European settlers into Australia, as well as Queensland. Despite the sentiment favoring a White Australia Policy, both the Chinese and Kanaka populations of Queensland alone were half again as large as the Southern European population of the entire continent. However, it is equally clear that a reticence to encourage Southern European immigration was not tantamount to a proscription against it. By the last decade of the nineteenth century, there was an established Southern European immigrant presence in the several colonies, and Australians had had sufficient exposure to "Mediterraneans" to hold opinions regarding their suitability as citizens. Of particular relevance to the present work are the histories of the Italian and Spanish immigration experiences. For, as we noted earlier, it was the former that heavily influenced the terms and magnitude of the latter.

It is difficult to document with precision the arrival of the earliest Italians in Australia. Filiopietistic works sometimes emphasize that there was an Italian official on Cook's voyage of discovery and that the navigator Alessandro Malaspina visited the New South Wales coast a short time later in 1793. An oral history suggests that two Italians were transported as prisoners from Dublin to Van Diemen's Land (Tasmania) in 1803.[3] By 1824, there was an Italian superintendent employed by the New South Wales police force.[4] In 1849, eight Italian clergymen (Neapolitans) were among a contingent of Benedictine missionaries departing for Australia.[5]

It was, however, the discovery of gold that triggered the real influx represented by the Italian contingent in the ranks of the fortune seekers. According to Vittorio Briani, the majority of Italians who entered Victoria in the decade of the 1850s was North Italians who, rather than mining themselves, concentrated on supplying the camps with timber. Many settled down, acquiring sawmills and small properties.[6] At the same time, Italians were sometimes depicted in the mining camp press as volatile and truculent.[7] An ex-school teacher named Raffaello Carboni was prominent in the organization of resistance at the Eureka Stockade, and a year later published the first eyewitness account of it.[8]

During the 1860s, events in Europe affected the attitude toward Italy and produced a different kind of emigrant. The unification of Italy under Garibaldi was much admired by many Europeans and London concluded a treaty of friendship with the new Italian state. Australia, and particularly Melbourne, became the destination of a few well-educated veterans of the Garibaldi campaigns, including one of Garibaldi's own sons.[9]

It might be noted that there were many tangible contributions by

Italians to nineteenth-century Australia. In addition to becoming shopkeepers, food vendors, and waiters in urban areas, some became viticulturalists and contributed to the foundation of the country's wine industry. Indeed, in 1888 the government of Victoria appointed a Signor Bragato as its first wine expert. J. Lyng also tells us, "it may be said with a considerable measure of truth that the Italians brought music to Australia."[10] In addition to street musicians, there were several prominent Italian music teachers in Sydney and Melbourne. The political refugee, Count Carandini, established himself in Tasmania during the 1840s as a dance master. From 1860–1880, Italian opera flourished in Australia. Two Italians, Alberto Zelman and Roberto Hazon, exerted enormous influence over the Australian classical music scene. The former's son, Alberto Zelman, became the conductor of the Melbourne Philharmonic Society, and the latter was instrumental from the eighties in organizing the opera scene in Sydney.[11]

By 1869, there were Italian consuls in Melbourne and Sydney, and the former reported to the Italian government that the combined Italian population of Australia and New Zealand was 1,700 persons (of whom 1,000 resided in Victoria). Of these, fully 57 percent were from Lombardy in North Italy. There were between 50 and 70 new arrivals from Italy each year, and between 30 and 50 individuals annually returned to Europe after a sojourn of between five and eight years.[12]

In the same year the Suez Canal was inaugurated, modifying the sea routes between Europe and Australia, in the words of Blainey,

> Once many steamships began to use the Suez Canal in voyaging to Australia, they called at Italian and Mediterranean ports where they sometimes signed on local sailors. Some of those sailors deserted ship in Australian ports, liked the country, sent home for relatives, and set in motion the chain of migration.[13]

Consequently, during the 1870s, the essentially North Italian character of the earlier immigration was diluted with Tuscans and South Italians. Sicilian fishermen became established near Fremantle, and the Italian fruit and fish vendor became common on the streets of Melbourne, Sydney, Perth, and Brisbane.[14]

Meanwhile, in 1878, several Italians in Melbourne founded an Italian Colonial Committee to advise potential immigrants regarding conditions in Australia. One member published a colonization scheme that proposed settling one hundred immigrant families in an agricultural community seventy miles from the capital.[15]

In 1881, Australia received its first colony of Italian settlers, although not through its own desire or design. Reference is to the ill-fated Marquis de Rays' venture in the southwest Pacific.[16] The marquis was an impractical, visionary Frenchman who was determined to establish a colony, to be called "La Nouvelle France," in East New Guinea, New Britain, and New Ireland. He announced the plan in 1879 and appointed a recruiting agent in North Italy. Approximately fifty Venetian peasant families were enlisted for the venture. Both the French and Italian governments denounced it, and the would-be colonists went to Barcelona to embark. In October of 1880 they arrived in New Ireland and found that none of the promised preparations had been made. Provisions ran low and death began to thin their ranks. By February of 1881, the situation was dire and the colonists were able to secure passage to New Caledonia, whence they petitioned the authorities of New South Wales to be allowed to proceed to Australia. The request was granted on humanitarian grounds, and, on April 7, the surviving 217 persons reached Sydney.

There was a great outpouring of public sympathy and charity, and the existing Italian population rallied to the aid of its countrymen. The government was anxious to settle and Anglicize the group as quickly as possible. The Venetians' request to be given a block of land so that they could remain together was denied. Considerable effort went into dispersing individuals and families by placing them with Australian employers.

The following year, however, a young Italian who had befriended the expeditioners found them available land south of the Richmond River in northern New South Wales. Over the next few years, several of the Venetian families gravitated to what became an Italian settlement. Initially, the community was called *La Cella Venezia*, or "The Venetian Cell," but the name was quickly changed to "New Italy."

The enterprise prospered, raising a variety of crops and dairy products, and even experimenting with sericulture. Cane sugar was also grown and sold to nearby Broadwater Mill, and the settlement supplied four gangs of canecutters to the surrounding districts. By the late 1880s, New Italy was being touted in the Australian press as a model

TABLE 1. Foreign-Born Immigrants Residents in Queensland

Birthplace	1861	1871	1881	1891	1901
1. England & Wales	8,670	26,296	37,390	77,117	68,589
2. Scotland	2,493	8,564	9,929	22,400	19,934
3. Ireland	5,537	20,972	28,295	43,036	37,636
4. Germany	2,124	8,317	11,638	14,910	13,163
5. Austria	—	56	188	231	222
6. Belgium	—	—	—	35	35
7. Netherlands	—	—	—	89	62
8. Norway & Sweden	—	—	—	1,955	2,142
9. Denmark	—	136	2,223	3,071	3,158
10. Russia	—	—	—	676	902
11. Canada	—	—	—	381	404
12. United States	93	215	344	427	926
13. China	538	3,305	11,253	8,522	8,448
14. India	119	174	64	425	417
15. Japan	—	—	—	49	2,358
16. Malaya	—	—	—	1,171	659
17. Other Asians	—	—	235	137	823
18. Pacific Islanders	—	2,336	6,396	9,243	8,760
19. France	89	188	840	400	364
20. Spain	—	—	—	80	34
21. Portugal	—	—	—	25	24
22. Italy	—	88	250	438	895
23 Greece	—	—	—	235	147

Source: John A. Moses, "Attitudes to the Questions of New Settlers in Queensland During the Twentieth Century," p. 8a.

enterprise—a visible demonstration of Italian dedication and prowess in agriculture. In 1890, the director of agriculture and forestry of New South Wales visited the area and informed the colonial secretary that the "...pioneers are clearly hard workers, industrious and sober, law-abiding and desirable colonists from every point of view."[17] A comparison of the Price estimates with Table One suggests that, by this time, only about 11 percent of the continent's Italy-born inhabitants resided in Queensland.

Shortly after achieving independence (in 1859) from New South Wales, the new colony established an agent general in London who reported to the colonial secretary in Brisbane. In addition to his responsibility of representing all of the colony's interests, the agent general was charged with personally supervising immigrant recruitment in the British Isles. He filed an annual report regarding his activities in this regard. For its part, the Queensland Parliament legislated immigration laws and provided funding for assisted-passage schemes. While the emphasis was upon recruiting Britishers, there was a willingness to consider continental immigrants as well. To this end, the agent general maintained a recruiting agent in Hamburg who also operated in Scandinavia and explored other possible European sources of emigrants.

From the outset, Italy held a particular fascination. In 1862 (or three years after Queensland's independence and one year after Italian unification), Queensland officials were querying the Italian consul in Sydney regarding the possibility of an Italian immigration scheme. They underscored the fact that the immigrants would be accorded the same rights regarding land ownership as British subjects, and stipulated that, "…It should be distinctly understood that emigrants from Italy should be principally of the laboring class, that is, agricultural laborers and shepherds. Emigrants from the higher and educated classes are not likely to succeed in this Colony. Vine dressers, gardeners, and especially men accustomed to the cultivation of cotton are much wanted here."[18]

The negotiations continued over a three-year period, and, in 1865, the Queensland government approved land grants to potential Italian immigrants, while stipulating that they ought to be either single individuals or married couples with only one or two children. However, there was a reticence to recruit more than two hundred immigrants, since,

> …the Italians to be introduced in the first instance will labor under the disadvantage of being a new class of immigrants, and may fail to procure suitable engagement immediately on their arrival, while they will not, like the Germans at present arriving, find among the colonists many persons of their own nation and language, to whose advice they could have recourse to when in difficulties….[19]

The prospect of introducing Italians into Queensland so fascinated J. C. Asselin, the vice consul of Italy in Sydney, that he personally petitioned the Queensland government for a land grant in order to establish a sericulture enterprise to be staffed with Italians experienced in the art.[20]

It would seem, however, that these early initiatives were stillborn. It was not until the next decade that there would be new official attempts to recruit Italians. In 1873, Queensland's Agent General Daintree published a pamphlet on the colony and arranged for an Italian language edition. In January of 1874, Daintree informed the British government that the colony planned to "…inaugurate an emigration service from an Italian port, probably Genoa, to Queensland, and give free passages to a limited number of Piedmontese silk, olive and vine husbandmen."[21] Before the scheme could be implemented, he received instructions from Brisbane to abandon it in favor of intensification of recruitment in the British Isles.[22]

However, in light of effective competition from Canada and New Zealand, it was proving increasingly difficult to obtain Britishers. Furthermore, the Prussian government was tightening restrictions on emigration to such an extent that, in his 1874 annual report, Daintree advised against continued efforts in that country. He did note that Italians could be obtained, but only if they could be transported directly from Italian ports.[23]

The following year, Daintree's agent in Germany reported, "…I have lately sent some Italians to New Zealand—a very fine class of people from the North of Italy, sober, frugal and industrious and I think they would suit Queensland remarkably well, as they can stand any amount of heat they would do much better in the canefields than Germans."[24]

He recommended that Queensland accept three to four hundred Italians. Daintree passed on the information to Brisbane with the comment, "…it must be from Italy or Scandinavia that Queensland must look for a revival of Continental emigration."[25]

By late 1875, Daintree had been informed of a degree of interest among the plantation owners for indentured (two-year) laborers from Italy.[26] At the same time, he forwarded to Brisbane a colonization scheme whereby twenty-five Tuscan families would pay their own passage in return for a land grant and permission to found an agricultural colony to be called "Toscano."[27]

The following year, A. MacAlister succeeded Daintree as Queensland's agent general in London. He continued the efforts to inaugurate Southern European emigration to the colony. At one point, a Marseilles recruiter requested permission to recruit French, Spanish, and Italian emigrants;[28] and he proposed processing five thousand annually.[29] Similarly, an agent in Italy requested permission to send about three thousand North Italians per year.[30]

Such grandiose proposals notwithstanding, by the 1870s there was only a trickle of Italians to the colony. By 1881, there were fewer than two thousand Italians in all of Australia.[31] In 1877, MacAlister wrote to Brisbane noting that a Count Franceschi had embarked for Queensland intending to purchase land for an agricultural colony, and that other persons of means would soon join him if the prospects were favorable. In March, MacAlister dispatched a contingent of Italians to Rockhampton on the ship *Indus*; however, he noted that the Italian program was too difficult to administer and recommended that it be discontinued. The Italian passengers filed an official complaint concerning their treatment aboard ship, and the agent who recruited them stated that they had not found ready employment in Rockhampton. He suggested that they be relocated, noting "...they are useful colonists, and will, no doubt, stimulate wine-growing in the colony, but to enable them to do so, their operations must be entirely contained to the Southern districts."[32]

In 1884, a Genoese agent proposed recruiting as many as 10,000 North Italian immigrants,[33] but to no avail. Two years later, the Queensland Government was actively pursuing indentured laborers from the European continent for the sugar plantations, since, "...The supply of Pacific Island labour, which is recognised by the Government as a

> merely temporary expedient, is...limited in quantity and uncertain in duration, and it is not proposed to expose the Colony to the dangers which would result from the introduction of Indian coolies."[34]

Recruiting efforts focused upon Germany and Scandinavia, but, as in the past, encountered considerable official opposition. In Germany, the conditions of tropical Queensland were depicted as unfit for Europeans and the terms of the labor contracts likened to slavery;[35] and a Dane residing in Brisbane denounced the scheme in a letter to a Danish newspaper.[36] It was not until 1891 that serious consideration was again given to the Italian alternative.

The Spanish Element—While rarely visited by Europeans and never settled by them until the late nineteenth century, under the terms of the Treaty of Tordesillas (1494) Australia remained a Spanish possession for three centuries. Indeed, Cook's voyage to the area evoked strong protests from the Spanish ambassador in London. However, in 1790, faced with the *fait accompli* of British settlement at Botany Bay, as well as her own declining naval power, Spain concluded a treaty with Great Britain abandoning the exclusive claim to navigation in the Pacific.[37]

From this time forward, the thread of Spanish influence and settlement in Australia is intimately intertwined with its Italian counterpart. In March of 1793, two ships entered Port Jackson (Sydney) and spent nearly two months visiting the tiny prison settlement. They were commanded by Alessandro Malaspina, an Italian nobleman sailing under the Spanish flag. Malaspina was a confidante of François Cabarrús, a French Basque who played a critical role in the launching of the Royal Philippine Company (1785–1882).[38] That venture called for direct trade between Spain and the Philippines, and, in 1786, Malaspina assumed command of the Spanish naval vessel *Astrea* that undertook the Company's maiden voyage from Cadiz to Manila. Among his crewmen was a young Basque officer, Francisco Javier Viana. Another Basque, Manuel Agote, was the supercargo on board as the Company's overseer of its goods. The *Astrea*'s voyage lasted nearly two years and became another circumnavigation of the globe. Four months after landing back in Cadiz, Malaspina and his fellow officer, José Bustamante y Guerra, were petitioning to command a two-vessel scientific expedition to the Americas and Pacific.[39]

Malaspina viewed his mandate in broader terms than simply the command of a vessel carrying cargo. He was supposed to put into Buenos Aires to promote the new Manila enterprise. However, he decided not to do so, since, in his view, the Philippine Company's trade would likely be with the west coast of South America. Rather, he focused upon Chile and was particularly hopeful of selling Company shares in Lima. Along the way, he decided that Manila should also be cut out of the loop, and that Chinese trade with the Americas should be directly between Canton and Lima. In short, he was very insensitive to the political concessions that had made the Philippine Company possible in the first place.[40] It would not be Malaspina's last clumsy foray into Spanish politics.

With his *Astrea* assignment behind him, Malaspina was then engaged in a multiyear (1789–1794) scientific exploration of Spain's holdings, an expedition that, in the Pacific, was quite akin to the recent ones of Cook and France's La Perouse. Tellingly, Malaspina had named his vessels the *Descubierta* (Discovery) and the *Atrevida* (Resolved) after Cook's ships—the *Discovery* and the *Resolution*.

Among the 450 members of the Malaspina expedition, several were Basque-surnamed.[41]

This lends a small, yet striking, ironic coincidence to our story. The earliest historical evidence of a Basque setting foot in the Americas was during the first voyage of Columbus, an expedition commanded by an Italian in the service of Spain. It also represented the birthing of a Spanish global empire. Now, after nearly three centuries in their fruitless search for the southern continent, for the first time Spaniards (and Basques) were visiting it. While Malaspina had no way of knowing so, the Spanish empire was entering upon its final agony. Within three decades Latin America would be ablaze with independence movements that would reduce Spain's transoceanic holdings to footholds in Cuba, Puerto Rico, and the Philippines.

Malaspina's visit to Australia convinced him that the English presence at Port Jackson posed a grave threat to Spanish interests in the Pacific. He raised the specter of "hordes of rapacious convicts, whom he likened to the Huns in Europe, invading Chile and Peru under the leadership of regular troops."[42] Indeed, within the next few years, Spain and Great Britain went to war and there were at least three proposals to use Australia as a naval base for aggression against Spanish possessions in the South Pacific.[43] However, since the west coast of South America was too far from Europe for Spain to defend, he recommended that the Spanish colonies be allowed to trade with Port Jackson to the benefit of both. Dependence upon trade would blunt possible British aggression. But, of course, Spanish mercantilist and monopolist policy with respect to its colonies remained firmly in place, so Malapina's suggestion was both heretical and ignored.⁴⁴

The Benedictine monastery of New Norcia was founded in 1847 by two Spaniards—the Galician Dom Rosendo Salvado and the Catalan José María Serra. Both were among the founders of Catholic mission stations for the Aborigines in Western Australia. In 1849, they returned to Europe and recruited 39 missionaries, 30 of whom were from Spain, primarily Catalunya.⁴⁵

In his memoirs (first published in 1851, or prior to the Australian gold rush) Salvado wrote regarding the 50,000 inhabitants of Sydney, "…all the nations of the world are represented: British, American, German, Spanish, Italian, French, Chinese, Malay—all with their strange and various customs, which give a kind of brilliant kaleidoscopic appearance to the city as a whole."⁴⁶

Salvado would, of course, have been sensitized to the Spanish element; however, there is little supporting evidence to suggest that Spaniards were present in anything approaching significant numbers.

It seems that a few Spaniards entered Australia in 1853 on the *Spartan* and made their way to the Victorian goldfields. In 1854, Peter Gras-i-Fort (or Gras y Fort) sailed on the *Flanders* from Marseille to Melbourne, arriving in Australia with a contingent of ten immigrants from Catalunya destined for the mineral strikes. He was from Vilaseca.⁴⁷

The recent exhibit of Catalans in Melbourne states that its Parers originated in the Rosselló area of southern France [where a dialect of Catalan is spoken]. A General Anton Parer was captured by the Spanish when they invaded France during the Napoleonic War. On his release he married a Catalan woman, Josefa Arenas, and they had a son Pau. The family had a flour milling operation in Alella. Pau married twice and fathered fourteen children in all with the two wives. We are told the following:

> According to the Spanish traditions of inheritance, the eldest son, Antonio, took over the mill and stayed in Alella. Two of the thirteen [sic] children died young, a situation quite common at the time. The first brother to leave Spain was Josep, who decided to migrate to South America in 1851, following his sense of adventure

and eye for business. He left Montevideo (Uruguay) on board of the 'Alabama' and landed in Australia in 1855. A year later, his half brother Francisco joined him and they started a poultry breeding industry in Petersham near Sydney, but the business was not successful. They decided to move to Bendigo looking for gold and finally settled on the banks of the Yarra river, a tent town to cope with the rapid expansion of Melbourne during the gold rush. It was their entrepreneurial character and perseverance, and also a spark of luck which triggered the start of the Parer Empire in Melbourne. Did you know that in less than 40 years they invested in more than 30 hotels and restaurants? Did you know that they are believed to be the first ones to commercialise meat pies in Australia?[48]

Lyng speaks of the arrival of Stephan [Esteban] Parer in 1856, who "commenced selling saveloys and hot potatoes to 'late birds' in the streets of Melbourne."[49] According to J. Cortes,

> ...In 1855 Jose Parer from Alella, Catalunya, arrived in Sydney, having come through South America; with his brothers Francisco and Esteban, who arrived in 1858, he opened the first Spanish restaurant in Bourke Street, Melbourne, in 1860. In 1861 their brothers Felipe and Juan joined them in their business....[50]

According to the great-granddaughter of one of the sisters, Josep [José] brought out many of his siblings so that eventually five brothers and three sisters in all settled in Australia. The Parers came to own five hotels and three restaurants in Bourke Street alone, and other Spanish nationals were proprietors of seven others in Melbourne. A Parer had a restaurant pavilion in the Melbourne Exhibition of 1881.[51]

In 1857, Spain's first consul in Australia, Antonio Arrom, underscored the prime factor that inhibited Spanish immigration in Australia. He noted that Spain itself discouraged emigration to any destinations other than Cuba, Puerto Rico, and the Philippines. Of course, at that time, these were the only three remnants of the vast Spanish empire, and Spain was understandably interested in shoring up its presence in them.[52]

In 1863, the colonial government of Victoria asked the emigration office in London to query the British consuls in Palermo, Marseille, Bayonne (Baiona), Bilbao, Barcelona, and Genoa regarding the possibility of recruiting agriculturalists versed in the cultivation of vines, olives, and tobacco. The replies were scarcely encouraging,

> The Consuls at Bayonne and Bilbao state that no emigrants of the description required could be obtained within their consulates.... The consul at Barcelona is of the opinion that none with any knowledge of the specified cultivations could be obtained, and points out that before he is allowed to emigrate a young man would have to pay £80 for a military substitute.[53]

The following year, the bishop of Brisbane, James Quinn, petitioned the Queensland government for aid to introduce Iberian settlers in the Far North, but to no avail. Consul San Just noted that such interest turned upon the fact that Spaniards, Portuguese, and Italians were familiar with agriculture under conditions similar to those in Australia, but that any attempt to promote immigration from those countries foundered upon the predominant Protestant aversion to Catholics from anywhere.[54]

According to Lyng, by 1871, the Spanish colony in Victoria numbered 136 persons and looked upon Stephan Parer as its father figure. He further noted, "...In the middle of the eighties the then Mayor of Bendigo, desirous of promoting tomato culture, introduced a number of Spanish families, settling them at a place named White Hill. Other Spanish tomato growers have since settled near Echuca."[55]

Probably symptomatic of nineteenth-century Spanish immigration in Australia is the story of Joseph Merrey Vasquez, a native of a coastal community in La Coruña, Galicia. A seaman who jumped ship in Townsville in order to make his way to the Croydon goldfields, Vasquez later worked as a drover and then became a land selector (homesteader) in New South Wales.[56] There was also the case of the father of the musician Luis Pares who moved from the South of Australia to Mareeba in 1893 with his wife and six children.[57] By the year 1891, the Spain-born population of Australia numbered 507 persons, concentrated highly in urban New South Wales and Victoria.[58]

Just as there was a bias in favor of northerners in the contingent of nineteenth-century Italians in Australia, Catalans predominated amongst the Spaniards. Of 133 Spanish nationals who entered between 1852 and 1903,[59] 91, or 69 percent of the total, were from one of the four Catalan provinces. Barcelona alone accounted for fifty-four of the immigrants, while chain migration from the small town of Alella (Barcelona province) accounted for another fourteen. Fifty-nine, or 45 percent of the sample, were residing in Victoria at the time of their naturalization, forty-two in Western Australia, twenty-three in New South Wales, six in Queensland, and three in South Australia. Forty-six resided in greater Melbourne, which meant that that city could claim 35 percent of the entire sample.

In terms of skills, the group was decidedly upscale.[60] Only twelve listed their occupation as manual laborer; farmers and truck gardeners provided for another seventeen individuals. Sixteen were craftsmen and an additional sixteen were small businessmen (cork merchant, fruiterer, grocer, storekeeper, tobacconist). There were five priests, three "gentlemen," one architect, and one medical practitioner. Of particular note was the clustering of Catalans in the restaurant and bar business (waiter, barman, proprietor). Indeed, there were nineteen owners of restaurants or hotels, representing fully 15 percent of the total, as well as sixteen professional cooks. These food service specialists were concentrated in Melbourne, Perth, and Fremantle.

If, in 1891, there were but eighty Spaniards in all of Queensland, by the 1901 census their numbers had been more than halved to thirty-four.[61]

The Spanish presence in Queensland, as reflected in official records, is faint.[62] In 1869, a Spanish national laborer residing in Brisbane was naturalized, as was a Spanish gardener living in the city in 1873. In 1881, two individuals (relatives?) with the same Catalan surname, one a postmaster in Emerald and the other a draftsman in Brisbane, applied for naturalization, as did a sailor in Bowen. Two years later, a Spanish laborer in Hughenden made application; as did a cook in Mackay (1885); a laborer in Maryborough (1886); a stockman in Bowen (1886); a fisherman in Breakfast Creek (1889); a fisherman in Townsville (1891);[63] a carpenter in Normanton (1892); a laborer in South Brisbane (1893); another in Hughenden (1894); and a shipwright (1892) and jeweler residing on Thursday Island (1897).[64]

On November 30, 1892, the Spanish naval clipper, the *Nautilus*, departed El Ferrol for a circumnavigation of the world. It carried 187 officials and crew, many of whom were Basque-surnamed.[65]

The voyage was under the command of Captain Villaamil, and he was a keen observer.[66] Nearly two years later, on August 10, 1894, the *Nautilus* returned to its port of El Ferrol. During its travels in the Antipodes—various ports from Perth to Newcastle, Tasmania and both islands of New Zealand—Villaamil reported on the Spanish presence and the awareness of Spain among non-Spaniards, particularly government officials. In April of 1893, the *Nautilus* was in Victoria and we are told that Melbourne's Catholic Archbishop Carr informed Villaamil that Spaniards were held in high esteem in the city since they were "hard-working citizens." It seems that a Catalan from Tarragona [actually, Alella], Esteban Parer, had arrived somehow in Melbourne in the 1850s, obtained a modest position, and then sent word home. He helped intending immigrants to the extent that by the 1890s there were around three hundred Spanish nationals in the city. Many of them turned out to welcome the crew of the *Nautilus*, and even took some of the mariners on a rabbit-hunting trip into the interior. A relative of Mr. Parer, a Mr. Caroline, the ex-mayor of the gold-mining center of Bendigo, escorted Villaamil to it. He was given a tour of a mine by an Australian familiar with the famous mines in Huelva, Spain. Caroline then took him to the finca where he grew grapes and tomatoes. He had recruited several Catalan farmers two years earlier to help him install "Mediterranean" crops, and the experiment was a great success.[67]

In Christ Church, the expedition was received by the honorary Spanish vice consul, D. Francisco Arenas, an Andalusian from Cadiz. Villaamil was astounded to find a Spanish official in such a remote post.[68]

The Basque Element—I would accord the modest honor of being the first Basque on Australian soil to Francisco Javier Viana. We know it to be the case from the Malaspina expedition's co-commander Bustamente's diary. He tells us that Viana was highly trusted by Malaspina and frequently assigned by him as commander of landing craft. Bustamante goes out of his way to acknowledge the hospitality extended to him and Malaspina by Viana's mother when the ships reached Montevideo—as well as by her Basque-surnamed son-in-law, Juan Pedro Aguirre (who had two brothers among the crew of the expedition) and Melchor de Viana.⁶⁹

Francisco Javier Viana was born in Montevideo and educated in Spain. His father was from Lagran, Araba, and his mother from Lemoa (Lemona), Bizkaia. He was twenty-three years old when he became a ship's officer on Malaspina's two-year circumnavigation on the *Astrea*. One might speculate that he could have been related to Leoncio de Viana, the Araban immigrant in Manila who was one of the precursors of the Philippine Company. In any event, Francisco Javier would go on to have an extraordinary career. After his service on the *Descubierta*, he was placed in command of it on a voyage to southern South America. He later served, from 1798 to 1801, as governor of the Malvinas (Falklands). When the British attacked Uruguay in 1806 and 1807, he was second in command of the fortress of Montevideo, the last bastion to fall. The conquerors offered him the post of the city's chief of police and he refused it. When the revolution broke out in 1811, the Viana family was divided into royalists and revolutionaries. Despite his service in many capacities to the Spanish Crown, Viana joined the revolt. At one point he commanded a force besieging Montevideo. After falling out with his commander, he went to Argentina where he was made governor of Córdoba. He was promoted to colonel and headed the Ministry of War and the Navy in the revolutionary government. He organized the successful siege of Montevideo that led to the final defeat of the Spanish fleet in southern South America. Viana retired as a brigadier general and died in 1820.⁷⁰

If the first Basques to set foot in Australia were part of the Malaspina expedition, they obviously failed to leave much of a footprint. Our earliest evidence of a Basque (and Spanish) inhabitant of the southern continent regards Jean Baptiste Lehimas de Arrieta.⁷¹ His father was of French origin and the son may have been named after him or his paternal grandfather. His mother may have been from Arrieta, a suburb of the Gipuzkoan town of Tolosa near Donostia. While the evidence is not conclusive, Jean Baptiste may have been born in Gipuzkoa and then spent considerable time in France while growing up.⁷² Among his descendants, he is thought to be a Basque count.⁷³

Lehimas de Arrieta was incarcerated for years in an English prison, probably Portchester Castle in Hampshire, after having been captured as a prisoner of war by the British. By about 1808, he was free and supplying the British Commissariat in Iberia with mules and provisions. There is also the claim that he worked for a time as an investigator seeking to document for King George IV the infidelities on the continent of his consort, Queen Caroline.[74]

By 1820, the Basque was seeking to emigrate to Australia, and, on August 16, 1820, William Morton Pitt wrote in a letter of recommendation that Lehimas de Arrieta had,

> ...long resided in England at different times, formerly as a Prisoner of War for many years and latterly for the purposes of recovering monies claimed by him for services to the British Army in Spain...He was a merchant and lost great property during the deplorable wars which the last thirty years have provided. In one instance, above 30,000 pounds.[75]

Pitt extolled the "Spaniard" as being a "worthy and sensible man," of "genius, industry and perseverance," who, "though a Foreigner, is an Enthusiastic Admirer of England." He was knowledgeable in viticulture, olive cultivation, and the production of olive oil. He would introduce into the colony superior Spanish techniques for producing these agricultural products. His only defect was in being "too sanguine" in his "expectation of rapid success."[76] The intending free settler arrived in Australia with another important letter of recommendation; one written by a son to his powerful father, John Macarthur (Lehimas de Arrieta's future neighbor).[77]

On March 17, 1821, the *Sydney Gazette* reported the Basque's arrival via Hobart as a free intending settler on board the *Duchess of York*. In a letter dated August 17, 1821, Lehimas de Arrieta petitioned Governor Macquarie requesting land on which to cultivate wine and olives and raise "fine Wool Sheep." He claimed to have £5,000 working capital and expected to receive more from time to time.[78]

On August 16, 1821, Sir Thomas Brisbane, governor of New South Wales, issued the maximum-sized land grant permissible under the law to Lehimas de Arrieta. It included,

> Two thousand acres of land situate lying and being in the County of Camden and District of Camden. Bounded on the South by a

line bearing west fifteen chains (commencing near the head of Harris Creek). On the West by a line bearing East to the Nepean River, and on all other sides by that River and Harris Creek to be called Morton Park.[79]

He was also assigned six convicts as laborers, to be victualed for six months by the government, and another twenty that he would have to provision himself. He received ten cows that he would have to purchase after three years. In short, he was given substantial and attractive land, the labor to clear and work it, and the foundation of a cattle herd. According to Judith Keene,

> Convicts built a sturdy house on a gentle rise at Morton Park commanding sweeping views over the surrounding country. Clearing parties set about felling timber for cultivation of corn, wheat and tobacco. The latter, a highly prized crop, was one of which De Arrieta was inordinately proud. He began his farming career with high hopes of planting and curing his own tobacco for sale in the colony.[80]

The size of the property, its quality, and its name suggest the involvement and patronage of William Morton Pitt. To this day there is a so-denominated Spaniard's Hill that runs through the property. It is sometimes asserted that Lehimas de Arrieta was Australia's first settler of Spanish origin.[81]

He was welcomed by John Macarthur—a most influential landholder.[82] Ironically, Macarthur had introduced Spanish merino sheep into Australia and would become its most successful pastoralist and viticulturalist. However, he coveted Morton Park and maneuvered to obtain it. The relationship between the two men quickly soured. The Basque began to complain that the Macarthurs allowed their cattle to trespass on his land and destroy its crops.

Beginning in March of 1824, Mr. G.T.W.B. Boyes spent several weeks at Morton Park and subsequently published his letters and diaries. Boyes had known Lehimas de Arrieta in Europe. His account provides our best insight into the character and circumstances of Australia's first Basque settler,

During the greater part of the Peninsular War he [De Arrieta] accompanied Mr. Wilkinson, the Commisary now residing at Portchester—and occasionally dabbled in merchandize—perhaps as a sort of go-between with his patron and the contractors. In that capacity he contrived to pick up a few thousands, but an unfortunate speculation in Commt. laid him low—his demands upon the Government were not presented in time and no interest could be found to get over the difficulty. However that he had a claim upon the British Public seemed to be tacitly acknowledged, for on the representation of Mr. Morton Pitt, Member for Dorsetshire, an early friend of D'A.'s, and some other people of weight with the Ministry, Lord Bathurst gave him an order for two thousand acres of land—in hopes that he would succeed in cultivating the vine and the olive—of which D'A knew as much as G. Boyes [this is a disparaging aside, since Boyes, a treasury-clerk, knew nothing about agriculture].

In the meantime—whether the richness of the soil be considered or the beauty of situation—his farm yields to none in the country. Arrieta began at the wrong end, instead of feeding sheep he put in the plough and what money he had was soon swallowed up and the Estate mortgaged beside for its full value.

In this situation A.'s temper which was naturally good, has become soured by disappointment and pecuniary troubles—an interminable list of mortifications which his embarrassments subject him to—has encreased [sic] the irritability of a temper originally warm and hasty till it is become a disease, and the gay warm, easy open hearted man of thirty is become at forty eight envious, suspicious, gloomy, and irritable. At times a ray of former happiness illumines his mind and while it lasts he is quite a different creature, but the bright beam is soon lost amongst the clouds that usually darken his brow…

He was born at San Sebastian—spent his boyhood in France and his early manhood in England—but of the latter country he has got the language in which he chuses [sic] to converse, though with so little effect that it is sometimes difficult to guess his meaning. French and Spanish he has nearly forgotten.[83]

Boyes reports an accident at Morton Park that illustrated the Basque's insensitivity to his convicts. When his (convict) tobacco horticulturalist blew off his hand with a shotgun while attempting to shoot a hawk,

> De Arrieta in the meantime was running about and exclaiming: "Oh my God—what shall I do without a Gardener. Oh what great loss I meet wid. Nobody shall tell what much I lose. Oh, my Tobacco, who will take care of my Tobacco. Any oder time had no been so great loss to me. Noting can make up to me for so great loss."
>
> Not caring a fig for the poor wretch who had actually sustained an irreparable loss, and thinking only of himself—for while he trusted the poor fellow to the contingencies of a Bullock car and a journey of nine hours, there was a chaise standing in the yard in perfect repair, and a horse idle in the stable which would have transported him to the hospital with ease and safety in three hours! So much for abominable self.[84]

Another visitor, in 1826, reported that, while the Basque was "a happy, good-humoured, hospitable Spanish gentleman," he had a peculiar security arrangement,

> ...take care how you approach his mansion!—for, being of a military turn, he has, 'by way of protection from burglars and bushrangers drawn a regular chain of videttes around it, in the shape of fierce growling devils of dogs, pegged down to the ground at such exact mathematical distances, that two can just meet to lick each other's faces, and pinch a mouthful out of any intruder's hip.'[85]

In 1825, a convict charged Lehimas de Arrieta with separating the man from his wife—the implication being that the Basque was a sexual predator. The colonial secretary found for the plaintiff, reunited the couple, and removed them from Morton Park.

In 1826, the Basque's crops at Morton Park were destroyed in a flood. That same year, or,

> In May 1826 there was a fire at Morton Park that was probably set by convicts in revenge for some previous injury. The newspaper report went so far as to remark on 'the wonder' that despite the

building housing the convicts having been burnt down, none of the men who slept there was injured.[86]

Challis contends that her ancestor once petitioned the government (unsuccessfully) to have a jail constructed on his property.

Again, in 1829, a fire thought to be maliciously set destroyed a barn along with the summer's grain harvest and hay, as well as farm equipment. The government offered a conditional amnesty for information and Lehimas de Arrieta put up a £100 reward to "bring to justice the perfidious wretches that had acted so cruelly towards a man striving to overcome his difficulties by unceasing labour"—all to no avail.[87]

According to Keene,

> As early as the beginning of 1823 the property was mortgaged to the hilt and the delighted Macarthurs were poised to buy De Arrieta out at knock down prices. The loans increased and in 1827 Morton Park and its contents were put up for auction. For reasons which are not clear, the sale did not go ahead but De Arrieta's indebtedness continued.[88]

In any event, by 1825, according to Susan Ballyn, Morton Park had been mortgaged heavily to a wealthy former convict, Samuel Terry, and was eventually sold to him in 1831.[89]

Lehimas de Arrieta was born in 1774[90] and was therefore a bachelor in his late forties when he arrived in Australia. Unlucky in life, he was also unlucky in love. Pitt mentioned that he had a young Welsh fiancée, but she disappears from view before the onset of the Basque's Australian venture. It is only in his fifties, or in February of 1828, that Lehimas de Arrieta marries Sophie Spearing, an eighteen-year-old girl with her own checkered history.[91] He came to know her when Winchester, his British friend in the Peninsular Wars, introduced him to her father, James Spearing, in England. When James and some of his children, including Sophie, migrated to Australia, they resided initially with Lehimas de Arrieta. Sophie bore him a daughter four months after the marriage and a son two years later.

There is also speculation that he had an affair with a young Spanish woman, Adelaide de la Thorezia de la Vega, assigned as a convict servant to his household. In 1831, she bore a child that he might have fathered.[92]

Lehimas de Arrieta died in 1838, and it is not until the 1850s that we have evidence of any other Basque in Australia. Gloria Totoricagüena analyzed immigration documentation in the Public Records Office of Victoria (by the mid-nineteenth century Melbourne was the main port of entry in Australia) and was able to identify thirty-two individuals entering the country during the second half of the nineteenth century who may be Basque.[93] Interestingly, some of these individuals were listed as "merchants" and as "Italian."[94] Eighteen entered during the decade of the 1850s—most likely attracted by the Victorian gold rush. The earliest newcomers in her sample were three solitary men who arrived in 1852—Pedro Artozano, H. L. Bilbao, and John Echalar. Twenty of the thirty-two persons were adult males (probably bachelors in the majority) and none came together. There were but two families. In 1857, Mr. Aresti (age forty) and Mrs. Aresti (age thirty-eight) arrived with their three teen-aged daughters. In 1882, there is a clearly French-Basque family—Henri Echart (thirty) and his wife Bertha (twenty-three) along with their with two toddler daughters.

I was able to examine naturalization records[95] and also turned up a handful of Basques entering the country in the 1850s. These records had the added advantage of listing the profession and Australian residence at the time of an individual's application (usually decades after entering the country). There was a Cedro Arlendi from Bilbo who came in 1854 and was a sixty-year-old farmer in Waanyarra, Victoria. In 1855, Pierre Doltheguy of Baiona (in Iparralde) immigrated at age sixteen and became a miner in Ballarat. Another French Basque, Arnaud Echeberry, entered the same year at age twenty-eight and settled as a miner in Great Western, Victoria. In 1861, sixteen-year-old Eugene Perrot, from Baiona, entered the country and became a fruitgrower in New South Wales by 1890, the year he applied for citizenship. In 1863, the Navarran, Charles Arthur Goby,[96] was thirty-four on entering. When naturalized, he listed his occupation as coppersmith and Melbourne as his residence. In 1866, a thirty-five-year-old widower, Abram Schuette from Bilbo, came to Sydney from Callao, Peru. He spent the next forty-eight years as an itinerant tinker in Victoria and New South Wales. Then there was twenty-one-year-old Manuel Arriola of Bilbo who, in 1874, came from Java to Port Adelaide. Upon application, he had been in Adelaide for thirty-five years and was a carpenter.

In sum, all of these individuals seem to have been errant fortune seekers, many probably attracted by the Victorian gold rush. Some subsequently resettled outside the mining districts and in different occupations—such as the two middle-aged farmers listed above.[97] We also have the intriguing case of José María Lizasoain Echegia. He was Uruguayan, albeit of Basque descent, born on May 15, 1857 in Mercedes, Uruguay. By the 1880s, he was residing in Wagga Wagga, New South Wales (an interior town halfway between Melbourne and Sydney). He was married to the seamstress Mary Morgan. She gave birth to a daughter in 1886 and sons in 1887 and 1888. In 1913, he appears in a record as a "gardener." José died in 1930 and his wife in 1933.[98]

There is also the likelihood that the odd Basque merchant mariner became established in an Australian port. There is the case of Pedro Tellechea (recorded alternatively as Peter Telechi, Telechi, Teilechea) who was from Bermeo, Bizkaia, a major Basque coastal town. He entered Australia in 1873, and worked as a mariner, watchman, and cable rigger in the port of Melbourne. When he was naturalized in 1884, he was residing as a forty-three-year-old laborer in Williamstown, Victoria. Miguel Urquijo worked as a fisherman in Victoria. In 1896, a twenty-two-year-old, Juan Francisco Allica (from Bermeo, Bizkaia), deserted ship in Melbourne. A short time later, he was engaged out of its port as a ship's cook. He would later work as a baker and then had a confectionary and restaurant in Port Philip, Victoria. He was working as a carpenter when conceded Australian citizenship in 1902.[99] Another Basque old-timer in Victoria was Vicente Urquijo of Bilbao. He worked for no fewer than thirty-two years on tugboats and steamships out of Williamstown. He lived on Ann Street near the port. When he was nationalized in 1913, he was employed as a cook in Sydney.

The New South Wales Registers of Seamen 1859–1956 are sprinkled with Basque seamen disembarking in Sydney and in search of new contracts. This likely took months in many cases, during which the men lived in the Australian port.[100] There was the case of the Basque ship's captain Francisco Piñerena who arrived in Sydney in 1857 and applied for citizenship in 1871. In 1866, Juan Ochoa was engaged on the ship *Express*, a barge that plied Sydney harbor. Julián Echabe became a stoker out of Sydney. In 1900, he shipped out from there on the *Lodore*, and, in 1901, on the *St. Mary*.

The sporadic presence of Basques in the ranks of mariners visiting Australia may be appreciated against the backdrop of two developments in their European homeland. First, there was their extensive involvement in whaling. Many Basques served on board "foreign" whalers. Ports such as Noumea in New Caledonia and Dunedin on New Zealand's South Island became important centers for South Pacific whaling activities.

Second, there was the nineteenth-century collapse of the Basque economy—damaged as it was by the Napoleonic wars, the Latin-American struggles for independence. and the nineteenth-century Iberian Carlist conflicts. All disrupted "Spanish" sea traffic, as did the failure of the largely Basque-owned Philippine Company.[101] The Philippines remained a significant Asian *pied-a-terre* for Basques throughout the nineteenth century.[102] Indeed, the Philippines served as a source of secondary Basque migration into Australia.

We might consider the nineteenth-century case of Zolio Ibañez de Aldecoa, born in Aulesti (Murélaga), Bizkaia, in 1834. As a lad, he joined the Bizkaian mercantile company Ibarra and then moved to London to complete his studies. From there, he embarked to Australia, where he spent three difficult years. Nevertheless, he founded a mercantile business (place unspecified) that he sold to Italians. On February 2, 1859, he arrived in Manila (not clear whether from Australia directly or Europe). He quickly established Aldecoa & Co. that came to dominate the abaca industry and inter-island shipping. He became the most prominent merchant in the Philippines and was the general manager of important coal and gold mining companies. He founded the inter-island postal service and served as the mayor of Manila. From 1886 to 1889, he lived in his homeland. It was then that Spain conferred upon him its most prestigious award, the Cross of Isabel the Catholic. He died in 1895. According to his obituary, for the thirty years of his life in the Philippines he helped Iberian immigrants to become established there. Aldecoa & Co. "was the home of all Spaniards, the handkerchief that dried the tears of the needy, there, all, and especially the Basques, found their caring father."[103] De Borja provides a lengthy list of Basque immigrants in the Philippines sponsored by Aldecoa, and details how they came to dominate the Philippine economy during the second half of the nineteenth century.[104]

Basque mariners sought service in foreign merchant marines during the nineteenth century—particularly the French ones. Then, too, during the 1840s, English shipping agencies such as the Ashley Brothers and W & J Tyrer, based primarily out of Liverpool, began contracting with Spanish companies to establish links between Great Britain and both Cuba and the Philippines. They dispatched the odd ship to Australia. For example, on October 20, 1846, the Spanish merchant ship *Preciosa* landed in Melbourne. It remained in that port for three months before continuing its journey. There were likely Basques among the crewmembers—men who received considerable exposure to Australia during the lengthy layover.

During the first half of the nineteenth century, there were several Basque ships' captains and merchant mariners engaged in trade between South America and Alta California.[105] We have evidence that a Basque ship's captain of a Chilean merchant vessel (and married to a Chilean national) landed in the port of San Francisco in 1849. He was from Ea (Bizkaia) and was accompanied by two Basques—"Natxitua" and Senda—the former named for his hometown of Natxitua (Bizkaia) that is located close to Ea. The following year, two Basques arrived in San Francisco on a whaling ship.[106] It seems unlikely that they were the only ones to do so, given that San Francisco was emerging as North America's prime whaling center for Pacific waters.[107]

For nineteenth-century Basque emigrants to English-speaking destinations, Liverpool was key. The city had a growing Basque quarter of its own, and a major figure was the emigration agent Prudencio Clemençot of Elantxobe, Bizkaia. By this time, there were professional schools in the Basque Country, including the *Escuela de Naútica* (Nautical School) founded in Lekeitio by wealthy returned emigrants to train technicians for the region's maritime industry. Clemençot sent them announcements of his services in Liverpool. In fact, that English port also became a key center for training mariners to be machinists, greasers, stokers, etc. on the new steamships plying the planet's oceans. In this regard, it was a magnet for Basque mariners as well. While the majority ended up in New York and Havana, some emigrated to Australia.

There is the intriguing case of Bonifacio Zurbano (1846–1914), of Laukiz, Bizkaia, who resided for a while in St. Thomas in the West Indies. In 1871, at twenty-four years of age, he arrived in Dunedin on the South

Island of New Zealand while serving as a cook on a whaler. In 1874, he married Bridget Donelly, but she died two years later. In 1877, he was remarried to Maude Perry, a member of the Church of England. Bonifacio was working in the "Spanish Restaurant," and, in the same year as his remarriage, purchased the business from its owner, a Catalan surnamed Guardiola. A newspaper article announced the sale of an "old established and popular Restaurant." It had forty rooms that it likely rented out to passing mariners, but also to "visitors from the Provinces."[108]

In 1880, Zurbano closed the Spanish Restaurant.[109] He then moved to the nearby mining town of Lawrence where he became a publican.[110] By 1885, we know that he was back in Dunedin and the licensee of the Prince of Wales Hotel because he pleaded guilty to accepting a stolen watch, two rings, and a purse from the thief in return for room and board.[111]

Soon thereafter, Bonifacio moved his wife and two young daughters to Sydney (they would later have a son as well). Until 1888, he was the proprietor of a boardinghouse at 37 Buckingham Street near the fish market in Sydney harbor. That year, he took over the Sydney and Melbourne Palace Hotel at 233 George St. near the harbor, but, in 1889, sold it to the Catalan, Martín Arenas.[112] Zurbano then acquired the Rose Hotel on the corner of William and Duke Streets. By 1891, he owned the nearby Black Swan Hotel. By 1898, he was a fisherman out of Woolloomooloo Bay, East Sydney. Between 1901 and 1913, Zurbano resided there at 59 Cowper Wharf, and he and Maud rented rooms out of their home to mariners. In 1900, one of his daughters was married in the Church of England, and, in 1904, Zurbano was naturalized. In the last couple of years of his life he worked as a watchman on the wharf of the German-Australasian Steam Company. Bonifacio was buried in 1914 in the Anglican cemetery of Waverley (Sydney), suggesting that he had converted to that religious denomination.[113] His son, Bonnie, was killed in France on October 7, 1917, while fighting for the ANZAC forces.[114]

By century's end there were clearly a few Basque mariners engaged in shipping between southern Europe and Australia who were visiting Melbourne and Sydney regularly. The vessel *Armand Béhie* plied a route between Marseille and Sydney, and then the round-trip from Sydney to Noumea before returning to Europe. In July of 1895, when it arrived in Sydney from New Caledonia, it had on board as crewmen several

Basques, of whom the majority were natives of Iparralde—Gregopire Anchochoury and Andrés Zozaya were listed as carpenters. The mariners included José Zozaya, Antoine Ancibero, Joseph Amonarriyz, Vincent Elisabe, Jean Ugartemendia, Pierre Arandi, José Ugartemendi, François Elosseguy, and Joaquín Leunda.

In July of 1898, ships' carpenters Nicolás Zozaya and Jean Larramendy arrived in Sydney from Noumea on board the *Polynesien*. As late as 1901, the Zozaya and the Ugartemendia brothers were still working on the *Armand Bétie*. Then, too, there were its other four Basque crewmen (the boatswain Tomás Santamaría, the stoker Jean Baptiste Chilibots, and the seamen Clement Lasserre and Jean Baptiste Ugartemendia). Larramendy worked this route for ten years and, like several other Basque mariners, established his family in Sydney. By this time, there were several Basques residing in both Melbourne and Sydney who appear in the records as "workers" or "dockworkers."

Notes

1. Charles A. Price, *Southern Europeans in Australia* (Melbourne: Oxford University Press, 1963), 11. [*Southern Europeans*].
2. John A. Moses, "Attitudes to the Question of New Settlers in Queensland during the Twentieth Century," B.A. thesis, University of Queensland, 1959, 8a.
3. Vittorio Briani, *Il lavoro italiano oltremare* (Roma: N.p., 1975), 271. [*Il lavoro*].
4. L. D. Henderson, "Italians in the Hinchinbrook Shire, 1921–1939," B.A. thesis, James Cook University of North Queensland, 1978, 197. ["Italians"].
5. Dom Rosendo Salvado, *The Salvado Memoirs: Historical Memoirs of Australia and Particularly of the Benedictine Mission of New Norcia and of the Habits and Customs of the Australian Natives*, trans. and ed. E. J. Stormon (Nedlands: University of Western Australia Press, 1977), 104. [*Salvado Memoirs*].
6. Ibid.
7. G. R. Quaife, *Gold and Colonial Society 1851–1870* (Stanmore: Cassel Australia Ltd., 1975). 186.
8. Reference is to a rebellion in late 1854 by miners or "diggers" in protest over increased government license fees and other limits upon their rights to prospect in the goldfields. Carboni was the de facto spokesmen of non-Britisher miners.
9. Briani, *Il lavoro*, 272.
10. J. Lyng, *Non-Britishers in Australia: Influence on Population and Progress* (Melbourne: Macmillan and Co., 1927), 95.
11. Ibid.
12. Ibid, 273.
13. Blainey, *Tyranny*, 287.
14. Briani, *Il lavoro*, 272.

15. C. Melchiore, *Il divinismo ossia la civile convivenza per tutti. Opuscolo progetto per la fondazione de una colonia italiana agraria e industriale in Australia* (Melbourne: N.p., 1878), 97.
16. The following account is based upon Anne-Gabrielle Thompson, *Turmoil—Tragedy to Triumph: The Story of New Italy* (Stanthorpe, Qld.: International Colour Productions, 1980), passim.
17. Cited in Briani, *Il lavoro*, 278.
18. *Queensland Votes and Proceedings* (Brisbane: Government Printer, 1865), 706.
19. Ibid, 707.
20. Ibid, 709–11.
21. "Richard Daintree to the Secretary of State of the Colonies," January 13, 1874, Queensland State Archives, Col. 77.
22. "Richard Daintree to the Colonial Secretary," February 6, 1874, Queensland State Archives, Col. 77.
23. "Annual Report of the Agent General for Emigration, 1874," Queensland State Archives, Col. 78/A, passim.
24. "William Kirchner to the Agent General," August 13, 1875, Queensland State Archives, Col. 78/A.
25. "Richard Daintree to the Colonial Secretary," August 20, 1875, Queensland State Archives, Col. 78/A.
26. "Richard Daintree to the Colonial Secretary," November 13, 1875, Queensland State Archives, Col. 79.
27. "Richard Daintree to the Colonial Secretary," November 7, 1875, Queensland State Archives, Col. 79.
28. "S. E. Depas & Cie to the Agent General," August 26, 1876. Queensland State Archives, Col. 79A.
29. "S. E. Depas and Cie to the Agent General," September 8, 1876. Queensland State Archives, Col. 79A.
30. "Aden to Hough," July 21, 1876." Queensland State Archives, Col. 79A.
31. Lyng, *Non-Britishers*, 94. Furthermore, "In 1891 they had increased to 3890, in 1901 to 5660, and, in 1911 to 6719, thus showing and average [slow] annual growth of about 150..." (Ibid).
32. *Queensland Votes and Proceedings, 1877*, vol. 2 (Brisbane: Government Printer, 1877), 1192.
33. *Queensland Votes and Proceedings, 1884*, vol. 2 (Brisbane: Government Printer, 1884), 608.
34. *Queensland Votes and Proceedings, 1886* (Brisbane: Government Printer, 1886), 907.
35. Ibid, 910, 911.
36. Ibid, 912–14.
37. Al Grassby, *The Spanish in Australia* (Melbourne: AE Press, 1983), 15–24. [*Spanish*].
38. Douglass, *Basque Explorers*, 198–203.
39. John Kendrick, *Alejandro Malaspina: Portrait of a Visionary* (Montreal: McGill-Queen's University Press, 1999), 23–34. [*Alejandro*].
40. Ibid, 27–31.

41. Of the 39 officials listed on the two vessels when they made Australia, the *Atrevida* carried the Basque-surnamed Antonio de Tovar Arredondo, Manuel Ezquerra, and Juan de Inciarte, while Francisco Javier Viana served on the *Descubierta*—see Ricardo Cerezo Martínez, *La Expedición Malaspina 1789–1794*, vol. 1, *Circunstancia Histórica del Viaje* (Madrid: Ministerio de Defensa, Museo Naval, and Lunwerg Editores, 1987), 152.
42. Ibid, 73.
43. Fernández-Shaw, *España*, 110.
44. Upon his return to Europe in 1794, Malaspina managed to get at cross purposes with the Spanish government and ended up, in late 1796, in prison for sedition. He was released after nearly seven years and exiled to his native Italy. The charts and documents from his expeditions were put under lock and key, and it is only during the twentieth century that this extraordinary figure has received his full treatment and due by historians.
45. Salvado, *Salvado Memoirs*, 101, 104–5.
46. Ibid, 238.
47. Robert James David Mason, "Agitators and Patriots: Cultural and Political Identity in Queensland's Spanish Communities, 1900–1975," PhD diss., University of Queensland, 2008, 36. ["Agitators"]. Also google Catalan Footprint in Australia. Exhibition. It refers to a Catalan exhibit at the Melbourne Immigration Museum. [Catalan Footprint Exhibition].
48. Catalan Footprint in Australia Exhibition inaugurated in Melbourne at the Melbourne Immigration Museum on September 11, 2011. [Catalan Footprint].
49. J. Lyng, *Non-Britishers*, 134–35.
50. J. Cortes, "Spanish," in *The Australian People: An Encyclopedia of the Nation, Its People and Their Origins*, ed. James Jupp (North Ryde, N.S.W.: Angus and Robertson, 1988), 803. ["Spanish"].
51. Lola Waring, "Lola's Memories of the Catalans in Melbourne," in *The Spanish Experience in Australia*, ed. Carmen Castelo (Jamison Centre, ACT: The Spanish Heritage Foundation, 2000), 74. ["Lola's Memories"].
52. Fernández-Shaw, *España*, 334.
53. "Murdock to Elliott," January 12, 1863, Queensland State Archives, Col. 77.
54. Fernández-Shaw, *España*, 310; 334.
55. Lyng, *Non-Britishers*, 135.
56. Grassby, *Spanish*, 44–46.
57. Luis Amadeo Pares, *I Fiddled the Years Away* (Brisbane?: N.p., 1943?), 7. [*I Fiddled*].
58. Commonwealth of Australia, *Census of the Commonwealth of Australia: Taken for the Night between the 3rd and the 4th of April, 1921*, vol. 1 (Melbourne: Government Printing Office, 1921), 51.
59. The following analysis was conducted with data graciously provided by Charles A. Price of the Australian National University. He gleaned them from the pre-1903 Colonial Naturalisation Records for New South Wales, Victoria, and South Australia. They exclude Western Australia, Tasmania, and Queensland. The data in no way suggest the magnitude of immigration. It may be assumed that a percentage

of the Spanish immigrants left Australia after a sojourn there and that others who remained permanently never bothered to seek citizenship. I have included Spanish nationals who entered by 1903 and who were naturalized at some later date. In this instance, the sample is Australia-wide (i.e., including Queensland). The fact that so many individuals were residing in Western Australia when applying post-1903 for naturalization suggests a profound end-of-the-century swing in Spanish immigration away from Victoria in favor of Western Australia. (Charles A. Price, Collection of Naturalisation Records, passim. [Collection].

60. It should be noted that the profile of those seeking naturalization is likely not a random sampling of Spanish immigration. Those with property or an established trade were more likely to desire and seek Australian citizenship.
61. Commonwealth of Australia, *Census of the Commonwealth of Australia*, 1911, 127.
62. The Queensland naturalization records fail to specify the Old World regional origins of the applicant.
63. "Return of Aliens Naturalised during the Last Five Years, From August 1880 to August 1885—Numbering 2,320," *Queensland Votes and Proceedings*, vol. 2 (1885), passim.
64. "Oaths of Allegiance Registered at Brisbane, Bowen, Rockhampton and Townsville Courts," Queensland State Archives, SCT/CF 35-9, 919028.
65. Don Fernando Villaamil, *Viaje de circunnavegación de la corbeta Nautilus* (Madrid: Sucesores de Rivadeneyra, 1895), 21–27. The only mariner to perish in the voyage was the Basque Esteban Letamendi Zabala, of Santurtzi (Santurce), Bizkaia, who fell from the rigging while trimming sails during a severe storm (Ibid, 283–84).
66. Ship's captain Villaamil was a Spanish war hero who designed the world's first destroyer, built in 1887 in a British shipyard for the Spanish navy, to countermand the new threat of torpedoes. He had extensive experience in the Philippines and Cuba. Villaamil was killed while commanding the destroyer *Furor* as it sought to run the American naval blockade at Santiago de Cuba in the Spanish-American War, a sea battle that destroyed the entire Spanish fleet.
67. Ibid, 159–60; 162–65.
68. Ibid, 261.
69. *La Expedición Malaspina 1789–1794*, vol. 9, *Diario General del Viaje, Corbeta Atrevida, por José Bustamante y Guerra*, ed. María Dolores Higueras Rodríguez (Madrid: Ministerio de Defensa, Museo Naval and Lunwerg Editores, 1999), 97.
70. Juan Carlos Luzuriaga, "Francisco Xavier de Viana y Alzáybar," *Euskonews & Media* (online journal), 302, at http://www.euskonews.eus/0302zbk/kosmo30201.html.
71. I am particularly indebted to Christine Denshire Challis, one of the subject's descendants and family genealogist, for what follows (http://chris46.tribalpages.com/). Lehimas is not a Basque surname, but has been traced by Challis to Gironne, adjacent to Iparralde.
72. Despite considerable genealogical investigation by several of his Australian descendants, none of the foregoing has been documented conclusively. It might be noted that there were many French residents in coastal Gipuzkoa beginning as early as the late Middle Ages. Indeed, they are accorded special privileges and exceptions in

some early town charters. So the Lehimas surname could be long-standing in some Gipuzkoan coastal communities and our subject could have been descended from it. Furthermore, Arrieta is a common Basque surname and can derive as easily from a house name (meaning "stony place"). As we shall see, one British acquaintance of De Arrieta reports that he was from Donostia/San Sebastián. This may not be precise. It is common for immigrants from any small town or village to claim origin from the nearest large city when communicating with foreigners. It saves a lot of explaining. In this particular case, the Basque and his interlocutor were both in the Peninsular War and its final battles were near Donostia/San Sebastián. If, indeed, Lehimas de Arrieta was claiming a familiar city rather than an insignificant village as his birthplace, it is perhaps indicative that at least he was from Gipuzkoa. In fact, there are Arrieta-named houses in many Basque villages. The contention that Arrieta may be an Asturian surname (see Susan Ballyn, "Jean Baptiste Lehimas de Arrieta, the First Spanish Settler?," *The La Trobe Journal* 68 (Spring 2001), 45 ["Jean Baptiste"]) is simply incorrect.

73. See the Christine Denshire Challis webpage. Here the "de" in his name may be at play. It means "from" and when employed with a Basque house name usually implies claim to Basque collective nobility.

74. James Valentine, *Then and Now: Historic Roads Around Sydney* (Sydney: Angus and Robertson, 1937), 125.

75. Mitchell Library, MSS a/1992, 334–37. According to another account, De Arrieta complained of "The cargo of Irish Pork which O'Callaghans of Cork deceived him in, to which he attributes his present [financial] embarrassment." Peter Chapman, ed., *The Diaries and Letters of G.T.W.B. Boyes. Volume l, 1820–1832* (Melbourne: Oxford University Press, 1985), 180. [*Diaries*].

76. Quoted in Judith Keene, "Surviving the Peninsular War in Australia: Juan D'Arrieta—Spanish Free Settler and Colonial Gentleman," *Journal of the Royal Australian Historical Society* 84, no. 2 (June 1999), 42.

77. Captain John Piper Papers, Mitchell Library A254, vol. 6, 489–91. It is signed simply "MacArthur" and would be from either Edward or James (Ballyn, "Jean Baptiste," 50, fn 34).

78. Memorial (18 July 1821), Reel 6051, 4/1748; Colonial Secretary's Letters Relating to Land 1826–56, SRA (NSW), 392–94.

79. Quoted in Ballyn, "Jean Baptiste," 47.

80. Keene, "Surviving," 42.

81. Cortes, "Spanish," 803.

82. John Macarthur (of Plymouth, England) served as the regimental paymaster and inspector of public works under Francis Grose, commander of the New South Wales Corps that came to dominate the colony's affairs—and particularly the lucrative rum trade. In his official capacity, Macarthur controlled the supply of convict labor. The Corps invested its profits in land and livestock. It became so powerful that, in 1808, it launched a successful coup d'etat, directed by Macarthur from the jail cell in which Governor Bligh had incarcerated him. Bligh was forced to flee and the insurrectionists, under Macarthur, governed the colony for the next two years.

Even after British authority was restored, in 1810, Macarthur and his colleagues prevailed at their trial in London. In the 1830s, Macarthur owned 60,000 acres of land at Camden Park. Hughes describes the Macarthurs as "the doyen of Australian pastoral conservatism." He further notes that they were "the founders and prototypes of the rural gentry" (Hughes, *Fatal Shore*, 109–11, 285, 325).

83. Chapman, *Diaries*, 175–76.
84. Ibid, 179. Boyes further describes the Basque as knowing no more than fifty words of English (an obvious exaggeration) and of being boringly obsessed with his own problems that he discussed *ad nauseum* (Ibid, 180–81).
85. Peter Cunningham, *Two Years in New South Wales* (Sydney: Angus and Robertson, 1966), 61. Perhaps some of this near paranoia derived from an earlier incident. Eighteen months after the Basque arrived in the colony, while escorting a woman to town he was accosted on the road by a bushranger. He fired one shot at the fleeing criminal. On that occasion, Lehimas de Arrieta was said to have had three loaded pistols with him (Chapman, *Diaries*, 176).
86. Ibid, 43.
87. Ibid, 44.
88. Ibid.
89. Ballyn, "Jean Baptiste," 48. In this account, the Basque died on the property in 1838 as Terry's tenant. Keene states that: "Immediately upon his death on 17 March 1838 the heirs were sold up lock, stock and barrel to Samuel Terry, Morton Park's largest creditor." (Keene, "Surviving," 44). Either way, clearly Lehimas de Arrieta had a very hard time in Australia.
90. There is some confusion about Lehimas de Arrieta's age. His death certificate in 1838 lists him as sixty-four, meaning that he was likely born in 1774. However, Keene states that his birth year was 1780 (Ibid, 41). It might also be remembered that Boyes said his host was forty-eight at the time of the 1824 visit to Morton Park—which would render a birthdate of 1776.
91. See the Christine Denshire Challis webpage.
92. Ibid.
93. Gloria Totoricagüena Egurrola, *Australia: Vasconia and the Lucky Country* (Vitoria-Gasteiz: Servicio Central de Publicaciones del Gobierno Vasco, 2008), 447–51. [*Australia*]. The individual's specific birthplace is not listed so her analysis incorporates possible Basques and is based on surnames, some of which are misspelled by the recorder, some (like Mendoza) may or may not regard a culturally Basque person, and a few may be a stretch (e.g., Murillo, Balenzuela, Istorneta). Part of the problem is reflected in the John Echalar entry. While the surname is clearly Basque, in this one case birthplace is listed as "England," citizenship as "British," and his residence before leaving for Australia as "New York." His profession is "gentleman" and he arrived with three steamer trunks. Clearly, he does not fit the profile of the nineteenth-century Basque emigrant to Australia. It would be interesting to know what he subsequently did in the country.
94. Ibid, 448–49. José Arresuvieta, José Decalzara, José Delaraga, Pedro Echevarria, and José Eguia. The last two are clearly Basque-surnamed, the first three are not.

It seems likely that the port official recording the arrivals simply lumped all five of these Southern Europeans together as "Italian."

95. Source: Price, Collection. Price generously shared with me his entire data base.
96. This entry, like many others, reflects the difficulty that Australian officials had with Southern European personal and place names. In this case the applicant likely Anglicized his own name, as well. Thus, the original name of this individual was likely Carlos Arturo Goñi.
97. It should be reiterated that the naturalization process documents only those who stayed in the country for many years and came to embrace an Australian future. They in no way correspond to an accurate count of the number of immigrants. It is highly likely that at least a few dozen Basques entered the country for a sojourn (particularly in the mining rushes) and then left. Others may well have stayed, but never felt the need to seek citizenship.
98. Totoricagüena, *Australia*, 450. Koldo San Sebastián, personal communication, February 10, 2019.
99. In 1901, he married an Australian and had four children with her. Widowed, he remarried and had two more children. He was quite religious, and, in 1912, served as the secretary of The Australian Catholic Federation. His children attended parochial colleges. In 1923, he opened a restaurant, called "The Bermeo," in the suburb of Carrum. It was a community focal point and Allica was extremely popular. The Carrum Progress Association, in which he was quite active, was headquartered in the restaurant. It was an obligatory stopover for any Basque mariner passing through Melbourne. He died in Melbourne on October 2, 1943 (San Sebastián, "Vascos en Australia: los marinos," *Euskonews & Media* 724 (2017), 11, at http://www.euskonews.eus/0724zbk/kosmo72401es.html). Koldo and I were collaborating at this time. He sent me most of the information regarding individual Basque mariners (and early non-mariners) in Australia and I incorporated them into an overview that is much like the one in this *Euskonews* article. He plans to use it in an as-yet-unpublished work on Basque mariners around the world (and particularly their presence in the United States).
100. Ibid.
101. Pablo Fernández Albaladejo, *La Crisis del Antiguo Régimen en Guipúzcoa, 1766–1883: Cambio Económico e Historia* (Madrid: Akal, 1975).
102. Marciano R. de Borja, *Basques in the Philippines* (Reno and Las Vegas: University of Nevada Press, 2005). [*Basques*].
103. Excm. Sr. D. Zoilo Ibañez de Aldecoa, "Apuntes Necrológicos," *Euskal-Erria* 33 (1895), 378–80.
104. De Borja, *Basques*, 93–94.
105. Douglass and Bilbao, *Amerikanuak*, 196–201.
106. Ibid, 203–4.
107. J. T. Jenkins, *A History of the Whale Fisheries from the Basque Fisheries of the Tenth Century to the Hunting of the Finner Whale at the Present Date* (Port Washington, N.Y. and London: Kennikat Press, 1921), 239–43.
108. *New Zealand Tablet*, March 9, 1877.

109. *Otago Daily Times*, September 13, 1880, 3.
110. *Tuapeka Times*, September 29, 1881.
111. *Evening Star*, November 11, 1885.
112. Arenas had arrived in Australia in 1870 from Liverpool with his wife and three children. For several years he ran a restaurant in Melbourne.
113. I am now introducing my first entry derived from the magnificent work of Koldo San Sebastián. He is the compiler of a vast two-volume work *Basques in the United States* (Reno: Center for Basque Studies, University of Nevada, Reno, 2016) with literally tens of thousands of biographical sketches of immigrants from all of the Basque territories. San Sebastián has provided me with similar information in several emails on Basques who emigrated to Australia. They were primarily from the parts of Bizkaia that were the main sending areas of all Basque transoceanic emigrants. He is a native of Lekeitio and has interviewed several of the region's returnees from Australia (Koldo San Sebastián, "Basques in Australia," unpublished document, n.d.). ["Basques"].
114. *Sydney Morning Herald*, November 10, 1917, 11.

CHAPTER 4

From the Fraire Expedition (1891) to the Ferry Exposition (1925)

> *Just consider the staggering consequences of the belief that only black men were suited for labour in tropical climates. As a result of that myth, millions were uprooted, enslaved, degraded. Today, though, there are white men growing sugar cane in places like Queensland. Something ought to be written about it.*[1]

The Italian Alternative—By the last decade of the nineteenth century, Italians, while few in absolute numbers, constituted the largest and most visible contingent of Southern Europeans in Australia. Despite the several schemes to introduce agriculturalists from Italy, most of the Italians had entered Australia as individuals or as members of single households and had gravitated to the mining camps and the cities.

More than the other colonies, Queensland had considered formal proposals for Italian settlement (mostly targeting northern Italians from the Piedmont region). Ironically, the Tuscan-based recruitments of the *Indus* contingent for Rockhampton, and the unfortunate peasants who followed Count Franceschi into the oblivion of *Toscano*, were the only "successful" recruitments. Together they entailed fewer than two hundred settlers and failed to establish perdurable chain migration from Tuscany to Queensland.

Despite their modest numbers and the checkered history of the colonization schemes, and to the extent that the immigration of Southern

Europeans was an issue in nineteenth-century Australia, the parameters were defined by the Italians. Other Mediterranean peoples, and particularly the Greeks and Spaniards, remained so few in numbers as to be incapable of engendering free-standing ethnic stereotypes of their own.

If Anglo-Australians were practically unanimous in subscribing to a White Australian future, secured through the exclusion of Asians and Pacific Islanders, there was greater ambiguity with respect to Southern Europeans. Few quarreled with the notion that Australia ought to remain an ethnically homogeneous bastion of British culture. For some, the swarthy Mediterranean was deemed an unfit settler on biological grounds, while, for others, differences in language and culture sufficed to make him a poor prospect.[2] Proposals to found non-British ethnic communities were particularly suspect. However, at least some Australians had a broader view of the continent's destiny and capacity to absorb non-Britisher Europeans into a single national purpose. Furthermore, a basic penchant for "fair play" predisposed the more open-minded to reserve judgment and to acknowledge laudable achievements when praise was due.

It was against this backdrop that, in 1890, several Queensland planters commissioned a North Italian resident of Townsville, Mr. C. V. Fraire,[3] to return to his home district of North Italy to recruit laborers for the canefields. The plan differed from former ones in that the initiative emanated from North Queensland and its economic interests, rather than from European recruiting agencies or the official machinery of the Queensland government. Indeed, the scheme took the latter somewhat by surprise, since the planters practically presented it as a *fait accompli*. On October 2, 1890, a member of Parliament asked the chief secretary if the government was aware of newspaper reports circulating in the Far North to the effect that Piedmontese Italians were being recruited for the plantations. He asked if appropriate regulations had been framed to deal with this importation. The answer was that, indeed, the government was aware of the scheme, was processing applications for 280 indentured Italian immigrants, and saw no need for special regulations.[4]

This set the stage for an acrimonious parliamentary debate occasioned by consideration of the annual subsidy for the colony's assisted-passage immigration program. The tone and substance of the debate are particularly revelatory of Queenslander attitudes toward Southern

Europeans, which echoed the ambivalence discernible throughout Australia. Opponents of the plan tended to be from the urban South and Labour representatives from the mining camps. The proponents, not surprisingly, represented the sugar districts. Spokesmen for the government, including the chief secretary and the minister of mines, favored the scheme. The chief secretary noted the difficulty of recruiting sufficient numbers of the preferred Britishers, and suggested, "...it would be advantageous if a small number of people could be obtained...from the plains of Lombardy, in the north of Italy—not the south of Italy, as they were a different class of people altogether."[5]

The minister of mines then provided a glowing picture of the agricultural settlement of New Italy, quoting at length from a publication extolling its virtues.[6]

The representative from Ipswich provided the counterarguments, noting,

> ...There was no doubt there had been a considerable amount of doubt and anxiety in the minds of the people of Queensland about Italian colonisation. Life was too short to go into the history of the sugar industry; but those interested in that industry had always demanded different and specific treatment from the other industries in the colony. First of all they required the Kanaka. When they were shut off from the Kanaka they required the Italian, and when they were shut off from the Italian they would want something else. The people of Northern Italy were no more constituted to endure the climate of the North of Queensland... than the immigrants from other parts of Europe—even Scandinavia. They [Italians] would come to the South and swamp the Southern part of the colony, to the detriment of the people already here....[7]

He further noted that one of the mining camps where he had worked in Victoria in 1861 had an unsavory reputation "...on account of the number of Italians congregated there." He doubted that Italians could be successfully "amalgamated" with the existing populace, and hence, "...They were an undesirable class of immigrant."[8] Indeed, "He had no objection to immigration from Great Britain and Ireland, Scandinavia, and Germany, provided the immigrants were agriculturalists; but if his seat depended on it, if it closed his political career, he would not consent to the introduction of such an undesirable people as the Italians."[9]

Other points underscored by the detractors were the excitable nature of Italians and their unfamiliarity with British Parliamentary procedures (hence their lack of civic responsibility). One opponent ascribed the current economic difficulties in Argentina to the presence of a large Italian immigrant population there;[10] while another noted that Italian migrant laborers were regarded as undesirables in other European countries.[11]

Such vilification notwithstanding, the issue came down to the question of whether the scheme would introduce into the colony cheap labor that would undermine existing salaries. Key to the plan was the fact that the Italians were to be offered a *metayer*, or sharecropping, arrangement whereby they would work initially for wages but then acquire land and raise cane for the plantation's mill. In effect, the scheme was designed to introduce the central-mill system to the Far North. As such, it could not be evaluated solely on the grounds of wage scale. If successful, it held out promise of meeting three longstanding goals of the Queensland government—(1) recruitment of immigrants with an agricultural orientation, (2) replacement of the Kanaka labor force, and (3) permanent white settlement of the tropical Far North.

Perhaps one index of the extent to which opinion had changed is reflected in the attitude of the Parliamentarian Macrossan. In 1884, he had denounced the arrival of a handful of Maltese as posing a greater danger to Queensland than coolie labor, since they were the forerunners of a flood of immigrants who would slavishly follow the dictates of their priests while undermining local wage scales.[12] By 1890, Macrossan was a major proponent of the Italian immigration scheme, regarding which he noted,

> ...If the proper selection was made...it would not fail, and... would be the means of preserving and extending the sugar industry of Queensland, and at the same time do no injury whatever to the labourers of the colony.... It would be a means of establishing a large agricultural or yeoman population in different portions of the North, and...in the South also.[13]

So, in 1891, the Townsville resident, Chiaffredo Venerano Fraire, traveled to his native Italy as representative of several sugar planters and with the blessing of the Queensland government. Skeptics of the plan denounced it as delusory, invoking the conventional belief that whites would never prove suitable manual laborers under tropical conditions. Furthermore, a vocal coalition of nativists and unionists opposed it. For the former, the Italians were an inferior people that would flood the colony with undesirables. To the extent that they failed to assimilate, they would form potentially dangerous ethnic enclaves; to the extent that they did assimilate, they would dilute British superiority both by introducing inferior cultural standards and transmitting inferior genes. For unionists, the Fraire experiment represented a direct threat to wages and living standards. The proposed terms of their indenture included a salary considerably below the going rate for white labor. Should the experiment fail, there was the likelihood that the Fraire Italians would gravitate to the towns and compete directly in the labor market, providing employers with an alternative labor supply in their dealings with the Anglo-dominated unions.[14]

The debate raged throughout 1891 in both the Parliament and the popular press. Meanwhile, Fraire proceeded with his recruitment. In early December, 335 Italians (including 273 adult males) arrived in Townsville from Genoa on board the *Jumna*. One hundred and thirteen were sent to the plantations in the Herbert River district, 153 went to the Burdekin, and the remaining 69 continued on to the Bundaberg area. Under the terms of the agreement, the Italians were guaranteed a weekly food ration, housing, free hospitalization, and a salary per man of eleven shillings a week for the first year and twelve for the second. After two years, they were free of all obligations to their sponsors.[15]

In the short term, the Fraire expedition was neither the panacea envisioned by its supporters nor the disaster predicted by its detractors. In fact, there is a sense in which its significance was downgraded almost immediately, when Griffith, after touring the sugar districts in early 1892, reversed his stand on the Kanaka issue. Scarcely two months after the arrival of the *Jumna*, Queensland's premier announced his decision to extend the Pacific Islander traffic, but under tighter conditions and safeguards.

By March, there were clear signs of problems with at least some of the Fraire recruits. The owners of Ripple Creek Plantation wrote as follows to the *North Queensland Herald,*

Sir, —As each Queensland paper taken up to-day, Thursday, contains some account of the sufferings of the guileless Italian and the injustice of the bloated planter, we should feel obliged by your allowing us to place on record the following facts, feeling sure that an outcry will be raised to the effect that the planters "did not give the experiment a fair trial." First: The men engaged in Italy were not suited for the labor they had undertaken; our own small consignment contained a cook, a baker, a barber, three bricklayers, a shoemaker, a navvy, two factory hands (weavers) and a broken down swell, while many of the so-called agricultural labourers are unable to put the harness on a carthorse. Second: That some of the men have made sworn affidavits that the agreement they signed was neither read nor explained to them. Third: That when we summoned two men out of a large number (as a test case) for being absent from work, the Ingham bench dismissed the charge on the ground that the agreement (drawn up and approved by the Queensland Government) was not under the Masters' and Servants' Act, and it was consequently valueless. Fourth: That the men have been grossly tampered with; not only have letters from various parts of the colony reached them offering extravagant wages, but last week a man named Duchi received a communication from Nelson, N.Z. requesting him to go there and bring some of his compatriots with him. As evidence that the planters are not responsible for the desertion of the men we beg to enclose for publication and return a written notice sent to us by a man with a wife and daughter. These latter are employed as cook and housemaid, and the family is earning 25s/- a week and everything found; yet tempted by an offer from a Mr. Tomatis [sic] at Cairns he throws this certainty up and is going to grow rice and pay his landlord a quarter of the crop as rent. We have offered to raise our men's wages a shilling a week on condition of their signing an agreement under the Masters' and Servants' Act of Queensland but this they declined to do…Every morning during the rain the overseer in whose charge they were…went to their quarters and requested them to turn out to work which they refused to do. We are of opinion…that a man who prefers lying in bed to getting his jacket wet, has no claim to payment, but should be thankful he gets his food for nothing. As to their being "honest workers," perhaps the least said about this the better; we are, however, open to admit that they are a quiet civil set of men, neither howling nor quarrelsome, and have probably conducted themselves far better than an equal number of Englishmen of the same standing would have done under similar circumstances....[16]

There was another concern,

A good many of the recently imported Italians on the Burdekin plantations have deserted, tempted, it is said by reports of the ease and rapidity with which a handsome fortune can be acquired at Charters Towers in the wood-cutting industry. Why should they toil for a master at cultivating cane when they might be, "picking up gold and silver?"

...even Italian peasants, bred as agriculturalists, will not work on sugar plantations when tempted by the high rate of wages obtaining on nearby goldfields. Trans-plantation of agriculturalists fails here with Italians, as it failed with English farm-labourers, and for the same reason.[17]

Furthermore,

Three of the Italian immigrants introduced for the sugar planters reached Toowoomba last week and applied for temporary employment at one of the local monumental works, stating they were journeymen stonecutters. They were subsequently interviewed and from them it was gleaned that more than 100 of the Italian immigrants were mechanics and artisans. They gave a very harrowing account of the way they were rushed to come to the colony, and of their treatment on the sugar plantations, and said they were working their way to Sydney. Their countrymen informed them that work in stonecutting and marble sculpture would be found for them.[18]

Subsequently, although the Queensland press documented the travails rather than the triumphs of the Fraire Italians (including litigation over terms of employment, work stoppages, and some defections), by the end of 1892 the Italian issue simply disappeared from public awareness. However, while the Fraire recruitment remained more an isolated event than the beginning of a process, it did create the basis for chain migration from Italy to North Queensland that lasted well into the twentieth century. In the words of *The Queenslander* newspaper,

> We have it from a reliable source that some of the Italians who were brought to Queensland by Signor Fraire, and who are now settled on the sugar plantations in the North, have received letters from friends in Italy expressing a desire to come to Queensland. They state that they will willingly pay their passages provided a guarantee is given that employment will be found them on terms similar to those under which the Italians now on the plantations are working.[19]

Over the long run, the Fraire recruitment proved a watershed event in the history of Italian settlement in North Queensland. Indeed, it established the baseline. This was particularly true of the area north of Townsville, where Italians subsequently emerged as a major element in the ranks of both the canecutters and the sugar farmers. The Herbert River district (centered upon the town of Ingham) became Queensland's strongest bastion of Italian influence. It was partially true of the Burdekin and as far south as Proserpine, where the Italian presence, while not as prominent as in the Townsville-to-Cairns region, remains discernible to this day. Further to the south, shading from Mackay through Bundaberg, the experiment scarcely took at all.

Federation and the Sugar Industry—In 1901, the several colonies federated into the Commonwealth of Australia. A cornerstone of their accord was the White Australia Policy under which there was to be rigid exclusion of all non-whites. As a concession to Queensland and its sugar industry, Kanakas were to be tolerated until December 31, 1906. However, no new Kanakas could be introduced after 1904 and, beginning in 1907, Queensland's resident Kanaka population was to be repatriated to the Pacific Islands. The sugar industry was therefore given a short reprieve, as well as an ultimatum. The policy also contained an incentive, known as the "white bounty." Under its provisions, Australians were to pay an excise tax on sugar which was then transferred to the producers in the form of a £2 (later raised to £3) subsidy for each white-grown ton.

Some of Queensland's sugar growers embraced the policy and pursued the bounty, others simply watched the clock tick, either too skeptical or paralyzed at the prospect of exclusive dependence upon white labor or hopeful that the government would ultimately come to its senses (as with Griffith's earlier reversal). When the deadline approached without any indication of an impending policy change, sugar properties were dumped on the market, depressing land values and hamstringing the industry's credit rating.[20]

While there were many problems, it was at this time that the features of Queensland's modern sugar industry emerged. In order to understand the subsequent history of Southern Europeans in North Queensland, it is necessary to consider the economic dynamics of the post-plantation era, and particularly the interplay between field worker, farmer, and mill owner. It is the convergence and divergence of these three interests that both created and limited economic opportunity for old settlers and newcomers alike.

Despite the skeptics, the provisions of federation and the white-bounty approach to the growing of cane stimulated a genuine experiment with European manual field labor. The new economics of employing dearer labor for what had previously been "black fellow" or "coolie" work forced an immediate adaptation to the seasonal waxing and waning of labor needs. The labor demands of the industry peaked during the five- to seven-month (depending upon the district) period of harvesting. For the remainder of the year, there was a more modest demand for men engaged in plowing, planting, fertilizing, and weeding. During the plantation era, the owners maintained the number of men (indentured non-whites) needed for the harvest, while absorbing the cost of their underemployment during the slack season. Once the cane was cut by salaried white labor, cane cutting became a seasonal activity.

Whites had to be recruited from great distances, some coming from as far away as Sydney and Melbourne, not to mention Europe. Given their travel expenses, the difficult working conditions, and the seasonal nature of the employment, there was considerable upward pressure on wage scales. The men themselves organized gangs of, say, eight to twelve individuals who then contracted with three or four adjacent farms in a particular district. There was a fixed wage scale from the outset.[21] It was favored by farmers and the AWU (Australian Workers Union) that came to represent the canecutters (while obliging them to purchase a union card in order to work).[22] However, veteran cutters preferred to be compensated on a piecework basis.

Many of the men who sought employment as canecutters lacked the strength and/or stamina for the task. The work was brutal, whether under a hot tropical sun or in rain-soaked, muddy fields. Then there were the critters—the snakes and insects in particular. The co-novelists Robert Donaldson and Michael Joseph provide a vivid description of the first day on the job with hands as yet unhardened to the cane knife,

> Like crops of small button mushrooms, the first blister-buds appeared on the hands, grew tight and burst. Sword-edged cane leaves cut into the skin drawing blood in fine beaded lines and a host of muscles began first to throb, then to stiffen and finally to settle to a raw burning torture. As if at a given signal, the flies of Queensland left their dunghills and moved in on the cutters' eyes, ears and noses, and stuck inquisitively to the corners of their mouths and the air, trapped by tall cane, became thick, hot and full of sultry weight.[23]

The system came to depend upon the middleman known as the ganger. Drawn from the ranks of the gang, the ganger negotiated its interests (and complaints) with the farmers, government overseers, mill representatives, and the AWU. It was a thankless task without any additional compensation. The ganger's negotiations could be testy. The per-ton price of harvesting a particular stand of cane was predicated upon its condition. That is, sparse stands or ones in which the ratoons were overly tangled by the wind commanded a greater price than luxuriant ones with straight stalks. Terrain could affect the distance that cane would have to be transported manually for loading on the tramway to the mill.

The gang was paid as the work progressed, but the grower withheld a percentage until the end of the contract. This was known as "retention money" and served to guarantee that the contract be successfully completed. Any canecutter who was discharged by the ganger for failing to perform, or who left the gang of his own volition, forfeited his share of the retention money.

In addition to paying the ganger so much per ton, the farmer had to provide room and board for the men while on his property. Thus, each cane farm came to have a simple barrack, usually within a short distance of the farmer's house. During the slack season, the canecutters might stay in the barracks, with or without sporadic wage employment from its farmer (or others) for odd jobs such as weeding and cane planting. Some went to the city, where they might squander their savings before returning broke for the next harvest. Eventually, it was the practice of some to migrate to the South for seasonal work harvesting the fruit and vegetable crops in New South Wales and Victoria or felling pines in the latter. Given the common living arrangement and the cooperative nature of cutting and loading cane, the cutters developed a strong sense of mateship; their slack-season wanderings gave them a spirit of adventure.[24]

The figure of the canecutter has been immortalized in literature and stone (as in monuments like the one that stands in Innisfail today).[25] As is so often the case with iconic figures, they attract greatest attention at the time of their passing (think of the frontiersman of the American West in books and film). Bianka Vidonja Balanzategui provides a comprehensive summary and analysis of this development in her magisterial *Gentlemen of the Flashing Blade*.[26] The author herself is descended from a Slovenian "displaced person" (DP) who was recruited to cut sugar in Queensland in the immediate aftermath of World War II and is married to a Basque Australian. The book focuses upon the contributions of the DPs to the sugar industry. Vidonja Balanzategui interviewed a number of them and then created a pastiche of the canecutter's lot out of their accounts, augmented by the plethora of literary works and memoirs. Some of the latter treat the canecutter as unsung hero and backbone of the sugar industry; others as vagabond villain and its nemesis—all depict him as practically larger than life.

Below I cite the works in question,[27] while noting that they all give near-ethnographic descriptions of the everyday existence of the canecutter in this twilight period of his very existence. Out of her interviews and her reading, Vidonja Balanzategui created her own fictional protagonist—Branko Domanovicé—who arrives in Australia on the vessel

Mohammedi in May of 1949 and goes to Ingham (the author's natal town) to cut cane during the 1950 season. She states, "In name, Branko Domanovicé never existed; yet he is every displaced person who migrated to Australia."[28] Branko could have been Iñaki, a Basque immigrant arriving on the *Monte Udala* in 1960, as well.

The gangers and gangs enjoyed considerable leverage in their dealings with the farmers and mill owners. The former needed to harvest their crop expeditiously, and the latter required a steady supply of cane in order to operate the mill efficiently. If the cane remained standing in the fields beyond the optimum harvesting point, its sugar content began to drop rapidly. Once cut, the cane had to be milled as quickly as possible or it would lose its value. Consequently, great care had to be exercised in scheduling the harvest on each farm within the aegis of a particular mill. Obviously, the system was perched precariously on the performance of the canecutters and the millworkers and was quite vulnerable to the threat of work stoppages by either group. Vidonja Balanzategui provides a table for the wage scale in the Northern Region between 1948 and 1951. It was, as we shall see, a period in which there was an extreme labor shortage. Unsurprisingly, the compensation of the existing canecutters went through the roof. The fixed wage nearly doubled from £5, 19s to £9, 15s weekly. Piecework cutters were averaging 9 shillings per ton in 1948 to 13 shillings, 3 and one-half pence in 1951. By 1951, the average canecutter was earning about £641 per season.[29]

From the viewpoint of the farmer, several factors merit attention. Over time, the farmers' and canecutters' interests diverged considerably, crystallizing into a full-blown social class difference. However, initially the distinction was blurred. The candidate for leaseholder, purchaser, or homesteader of a small farm was the man with previous experience in the industry. During the plantation era, Europeans worked as supervisors, ploughmen, transporters of cane, and millworkers. These men were the prime candidates to become farmers. The CSR, for instance, gave preference to its former employees when divesting itself of its landholdings.[30] The townspeople in the sugar districts also provided some impetus for the fragmentation of the plantations. More than one storekeeper and professional person took up blocks that they further subdivided to men willing to actually work them.[31] Then, too, there were the canecutters themselves. As we shall see, it became quite common, particularly among Southern Europeans, for members of a gang to pool their savings to allow one and then another to purchase or lease a farm.

Unquestionably, there was considerable demand for level, fertile land in the shadow of the mills. However, as they entered the period of divestiture, the plantations were interested in first ridding themselves of their most marginal holdings, reserving the best until last (or possibly forever). Despite such considerations, it is clear that the small-farm/central-mill concept was taking hold. Between 1903 and 1905, the number of "sugar producers" in Queensland increased from 2,697 to 3,422 (of whom 2,681 had registered for the white bounty).[32] Nearly 15 percent of Queensland sugar was grown with white labor in 1902; by 1908, the figure stood at almost 88 percent.[33]

Many of the first farmers failed. Some were simply unsuited to the challenge through lack of skill or dedication; others cast their lot on hilly, infertile ground too distant from the mill and located beyond the reach of existing tramways. Thinly capitalized and/or consumed by the cost of drayage, many a farmer lost his savings and years of personal toil to boot.

The position of the farmer was, in many respects, unenviable. He was dependent upon transient, potentially unreliable labor and was a captive of one mill. Each mill had its catchment of potential suppliers, and was the focal point of the road and tramway network in the district. The farmer simply did not have the option of marketing elsewhere.

For their part, the mills were interested in ensuring a steady, optimum supply of cane throughout the crushing season. Therefore, they assigned what came to be known as "sugar peaks." That is, mill inspectors calculated the needs of the mill and then allocated the right to grow a fixed amount of cane to each farmer. Since the mill could not deal with an oversupply, the peak for the average farm was less than its total acreage might produce. While the system restricted the farmer's actions by precluding expansion of his sugar acreage, it also prevented unbridled competition. No new acreage could be brought into sugar production without expansion of the mill. This placed a premium on the sugar peak. Over time, the very worth of the farm came to be determined by its peak, with its non-sugar acreage, dwelling, etc. receiving a trivial value.

Under the system, it was in the mill's interest to keep all of its producers financially sound. From the outset, the mill owners played an active role in recruiting canecutters and scheduling the annual sign-ons. They also quickly devised a system of rotated harvesting. That is, each farmer wanted to harvest his cane during the short period when sugar content in the ratoons was at its highest. The mill could only absorb so much sugar on a daily basis, and the mill owners wished to operate for as long as sugar content was sufficient to remain profitable (or about six months). Consequently, the mill inspector allocated the percentage of each farm's crop that could be sent to the mill at different periods throughout the crushing season, thereby equalizing the opportunities and risks among the growers.

Given this arrangement, it was in the farmers' interests to organize themselves into small groups (usually four to ten farms) that then contracted with a single ganger. No one farm could provide a gang with sufficient cane over the season, but the group as a whole could. The gang moved from property to property according to the schedule laid down by the mill inspector. Most groups further spread their risks internally by instituting a rotating schedule from year to year. That is, farm A might be the first farm to harvest its portion at each phase of the cutting cycle in a given year, and the following year it became the last with every other farm in the group moving up one slot.

The mill constituted the primary employer in a sugar district. It maintained permanent supervisory staff and hired a seasonal labor force during the crushing season to operate both the mill and tramway. It also had to arrange to export the raw sugar elsewhere for final processing, since there have never been sugar refineries in North Queensland. The mill owners were initially in a precarious position of unregulated competition vis-à-vis one another, vying individually for contracts.

There was also a sense in which all were arrayed against the Colonial Sugar Refining Company, since its huge market share gave it leverage verging upon monopolistic powers. While most mills were either government-subsidized farmers' cooperatives, or closely held small corporations doing business practically as family concerns,[34] the CSR was the epitome of the professionalized, aloof giant prone to pursue an independent course, except when believing that its interests coincided with those of the smaller operators. Of constant concern to the mill owners was the quality and quantity of cane in their district. With the CSR playing a leadership role, there was experimentation with cane varieties, cultivation, harvesting practices, and milling technology and techniques.

Finally, over time, the government came to play a pivotal role in regulating the sugar industry. Queensland's foray into subsidizing central mills and the Commonwealth's sugar bounty scheme both enhanced the general public's vested interest in the status of sugar production. Experimental stations were established to facilitate basic research into the suitability of cane varieties, control of plant diseases and vermin, etc. Of greatest significance, the Australian government became the ultimate marketer of the nation's sugar crop. That is, it erected tariff barriers that virtually assured a closed national market at a predetermined price. Today, it is the Australian government that negotiates export contracts as part of a worldwide quota system. The government estimates the future demand predicated upon trends in national sugar consumption and its negotiated sugar futures in the world market. This outcome determines how much sugar the individual farmer will be allowed to harvest and each mill to process in a particular year.

Such, then, are the broad outlines of the dynamics of twentieth-century sugar production in Australia.[35] Most of the factors were either determined or anticipated by developments during its first decade as part of the transition from plantation agriculture to the small-farmer/central-mill system.

The Italian Penetration—The foregoing developments created opportunities for the Fraire expeditioners and their successors. While it is unlikely that we shall ever know for certain, it is possible that the first white cane gang was Italian (constituted, in 1892, by desperate defectors from the Fraire indentures).[36] By the late 1890s, there is fragmentary evidence that a handful of Italians were acquiring small sugar properties in the Bundaberg, Burdekin, and Herbert districts.[37] By 1898, 16 percent of the cane-producing acreage for the CSR's Macknade Mill (in the Herbert) was Italian-owned.[38] That same year, in the annual report of the agent general, it was stated,

> It will be remembered that in 1890 [sic] a number of families of the peasant class from Piedmont and Lombardy were taken to the colony by Signor Fraire of Townsville and located in the Wide

Bay district and on the Herbert River. These people have done so well that they have sent for their families and friends and there are forty nominations now in this office waiting for the nominees to get passages from Italy without the expense of coming to London to embark.[39]

By the turn of the century, it is clear that Italians were scattering well beyond the sites of their original introduction in 1891. In 1901, an Italian cane gang was employed briefly in Cairns.[40] By 1903, the Italians had established an ethnic-group reputation as reliable canecutters. It could be reported that, while most of the crop during that season was still being harvested by colored labor, in the Burdekin Italians were the desired canecutters.[41] That same year, Italians had outperformed other white workers at Macknade, prompting the general manager to ask his CSR superiors rhetorically, "…is it that Italians are more fitted for cane cutting in the tropics than whites of other nationalities?"[42] If so, it was lamentable, since the two Italian gangs that worked for him the previous season had disbanded. Some of the men had returned to Europe, some were working in the mines, others had gone off to engage in charcoal-burning, while about a dozen had remained in the district employed on the farms.[43]

Shortly thereafter, it became apparent that the Italians were drifting back together to form gangs for the next season. Macknade's general manager recommended to the CSR's head office that the farmers in the district be encouraged to form a central camp for canecutters during the slack season where the men could be provided room and board and occasional work in the fields. Otherwise, the gangs would continue to disperse to the four winds at the end of each harvest. He noted that the only farmers to respond were a dozen Italian ones who, while not forming a central camp, were carrying individual cutters over the slack season.[44] This is the earliest evidence of a pattern that eventually came to characterize much of the industry.

During the 1904 season, of the thirty-four white cutters at Macknade, eighteen, or a majority, were Italian. Macknade was the only CSR operation employing them, since white cutters at other Company properties were all Anglo-Australian.[45]

In 1906, Macknade's general manager reported to the home office that the cutters recruited from Brisbane and Sydney, "...were rather better than the average although not equal to our Italian gangs."[46] The following year, the other CSR operation in the Herbert, Victoria Mill, reported employing seventeen Italian canecutters.[47] It was at this time that two Spaniards, formerly involved in the tobacco industry in the Philippines, were reportedly cutting cane in Mossman prior to establishing themselves growing tobacco in Queensland.[48]

The circumstances of the Italian canecutters may be appreciated from the following detailed interview with Mario Brigando,

> I began by cutting cane on contract. This is generally done by gangs of eight or ten men, who work on a measured tract of land at so much per ton. The season begins at the end of May or beginning of June, and continues till the end of November, in all about 23 weeks, we ourselves finished in the first week of December. The amount one can earn depends upon the quality of the cane and the condition in which it is found, but on an average one can make from £4 to £5 a week, net. In my gang we made £86 each for 20 weeks' work; others however, have had dividends up to £117 each. But to do this one has to work with a will from 10 to 12 hours a day. After the season proper the rains begin, and last for two or three months. Then labour is not very remunerative. The rest of the year we plant cane and clean up the fields and for this the wages are only 25s. a week and keep. The work, however, is not nearly so hard as when we work for ourselves under contract.[49]

Brigando makes no mention of the difficult conditions—the humidity, the heat, and the snakes. For instance, the *Herbert River Express* reported,

> The prevalence of snakes in the district esp. in the canefields, is causing some concern to field workers as hardly a week passes by without a case of snakebite being recorded. On Tuesday an Italian canecutter named Vescatti while working on Macknade Plantation was bitten in 2 places below the knee by a black snake.[50]

The budding reputation of the Italian canecutter seemed to offer some hope, when, in 1906, no political compromise was forthcoming regarding repatriation of the Kanaka labor force. Some growers and millers sought to invoke an "Italian solution" highly reminiscent of the Fraire recruitment of some fifteen years earlier. One newspaper article captures the climate of opinion as North Queensland entered the final year of the Kanaka,

> A Herbert River sugar authority says that the greatest difficulty facing the growers this year is harvesting. Eighty percent of the sugar areas are registered for the bounty, and although it may be possible to get white men to take off the crops, it is very doubtful if the mills will be kept going as regularly and evenly as under the old labour conditions. The C.S.R. Co. is making endeavors to introduce as many labour-saving appliances as possible, and has already supplied derricks and sledges to relieve workers' manual labour.... Some growers hope to obtain labour in the Southern markets, while a number of Italians, who have settled on the Herbert for many years, are negotiating with their countrymen in Italy to come out and engage in work in the field....[51]

Prompted by its growing concern, the sugar industry lobbied both the Queensland and Commonwealth governments for aggressive recruitment of continental labor. Faced with considerable dillydallying by immigration authorities, the sugar interests took their own initiatives. In Mackay, the Pioneer River Farmers' and Graziers' Association applied for 500 immigrant laborers, as did the Canefarmers' Association of North Queensland. Mossman Central Mill made its own separate application for fifty men, while producers on the Burdekin requested 110 workers.[52]

In its application, dated September 20, 1906, Mossman Central Mill noted that, while half of the district was registered for the sugar bounty, fear of lack of white labor for the following season was prompting some growers to withdraw their registrations. The white canecutters during the 1906 season had failed to perform adequately, sending in only about half of their allotted quota to the mill. The application further noted,

> ...the cane-growers of this district entertain very grave doubts regarding the future of the sugar industry in the far North, unless permission be granted to indent labour from Southern Europe,

the Italian cane-cutters employed at Mossman during the past three years having proved themselves to be good workers and thrifty, peaceable citizens.[53]

In approving the request, the Commonwealth secretary of external affairs, Atlee Hunt, remarked that, while there was no objection to Italians, preference ought to be given to recruitment in the British Isles.[54] The suggestion was ignored, since Mossman Central Mill informed the premier of Queensland of Commonwealth governmental approval, and requested that the immigration agent "... supply any information.... as to the best way of getting out the right class from the most suitable districts of Italy...."[55]

Shortly thereafter, the Colonial Sugar Refining Co. became a reluctant party to the recruitment. Chagrined at the prospect of its suppliers being unable to secure the necessary labor for the 1907 season, the Company quietly drew up a plan for the use of the local farmers' associations. Recognizing the political sensitivity of its position, were it thought that one of Australia's foremost corporations was a prime force in introducing contract labor, General Manager Knox informed his mill managers: "It is essential to the success of any such scheme that we should not be in any way identified with it before the assent of the federal authorities is obtained...."[56]

In mid-December, Victoria Mill's manager informed Knox that there was considerable interest in the CSR scheme among the farmers. Not only were they faced with a labor shortage, they were also fearful that such a state of affairs would translate into strikes and exorbitant wage demands. The Italian recruitment might alleviate the situation.[57]

In late December, the farmers met in Cairns and formed an association, called the Canefarmers' Association of North Queensland, which immediately made application to the Commonwealth authorities to recruit five hundred Southern Europeans for the canefields.[58] Permission was forthcoming quickly, and the CSR agreed to effect and underwrite the operation, requiring eventual repayment of passages. The farmers were to accept a two-year lien against their crops, and in turn would withhold a portion of the recruits' wages until the passage was repaid.[59] Costs were estimated at about £18 per immigrant.

On February 2, 1907, Thomas Hughes, a CSR employee, was dispatched to Europe with orders to focus recruitment upon southern Europe to the exclusion of Scandinavia and the British Isles.[60] While he was still en route, the Queensland government launched a recruitment initiative of its own. Emphasis was to be placed upon obtaining Britishers, passages to be paid by the government and the farmers to pay only £5 per man. This was cause for consternation in CSR circles. Many farmers still preferred British laborers to Southern Europeans, and might not be induced to accept the latter if there were prospects that the former were forthcoming, and at considerably less cost.[61] The CSR was forced to reduce its charge to the sponsors from £18 to £5 in order to compete.

By late March, the Company was considering recalling Hughes. Mulgrave Mill had withdrawn its request for men, and the authorities in London had bogged him down with their insistence that he emphasize recruitment of British subjects. Time was running out (the men were needed by May or June) and Hughes was anxious to get to the continent.[62] When he finally arrived in Italy, there was another unanticipated difficulty. The Italian government refused to approve the contract-labor scheme. Hughes was forced to improvise.

In late February, a concerned Queensland official in London sent an encoded cablegram to Brisbane informing that a Senor [sic] Juan Duch, through an agent of the Schipper Steamship Company, had recruited five hundred emigrants in Barcelona by promising free passage and guaranteed employment on the sugar plantations. This was causing concern in London, as it might affect Queensland's plans to recruit in the British Isles.[63]

In late May, Knox informed his mill managers that eight British and 104 Catalan Spanish nationals had left Genoa for Queensland. The men had been guaranteed free passage and the farmers were to be charged only £5 of the cost, with the remainder of the expenses to be borne by the CSR. This was necessary were the plan to be competitive with the Queensland government's program.[64] When, in late June, a German vessel (the *Bulow*) reached Fremantle, it was erroneously reported in the local press that it carried 117 of an estimated 1,000 contract Spaniards, "principally town-bred," engaged by the CSR. The Company hastened to deny the allegation of having conducted a major Spanish recruiting effort.[65]

Between Fremantle and Melbourne, it was discovered that eight men had left the ship. While it turned out that only three were Catalans (possibly enticed to stay in Perth/Fremantle by contacts in the Catalan community previously established in that area), the *Melbourne Argus* focused upon the Spaniards, noting that some had no intention of honoring their contracts. When Commonwealth secretary of external affairs, Atlee Hunt, was queried about the matter, he disclaimed all interest and responsibility. Since the Immigration Restriction Act did not apply to Europeans, in the secretary's view, "…If these Spaniards like to land in Australia it is no concern of ours. They are under contract to the CSR Co. and if they break that contract it is the business of the CSR Co. It has nothing to do with us."[66]

When the contingent reached Sydney, it was reported regarding the Spaniards,

> Apart from their attire, which was in some cases very curious…, they looked as fine a lot of labourers as could be seen. They appeared mostly to be about 21 to 26 years of age, and without exception all are single men. The men are to sign on for 18 months at 23s 6d to 25s per week. Their passage is paid out to Australia, but no provision has been made for their return.[67]

When the coastal steamer *Marloo* landed the men in Brisbane on July 9, *The Queenslander* newspaper (under the rubric of "The Spanish Invasion") reported,

> Not that of Philip's Armada in the eighties of the sixteenth century, in good Queen Bess's brilliant reign, but that of yesterday, or today, by olive-cheeked Spaniards who came to cut cane in Queensland. Every nationality has something of picturesqueness about it…, and these children, who people the shores of the blue Mediterranean along with Italians, Sicilians, and other old and romantic nationalities, have much in them to commend to the eye of the artist…. The men understand their agreements well, and protest that they will faithfully observe them. Most of the

immigrants speak of going home again when their three years are up. They are very interested in the country, and anxious to learn, and with judicious handling should prove cheery and honest workers.[68]

Nonetheless, the newspaper concluded,

The introduction of a large number of Spanish labourers to replace the departed kanakas on the sugar cane plantations is a step that will be regarded with mingled feelings. It is to be regretted that immigrants of British race could not have been found for this work.... Sceptics...are not wanting who declare that these Spaniards will not easily adapt themselves to our ways, and that the kanaka, with all his faults, was a more suitable man for the condition prevailing in north Queensland. The introduction of labourers from Southern Europe will have one good effect: if the trial proves satisfactory, there should be more inducement for British immigrants to abandon their attitude of aloofness....[69]

Meanwhile, on June 20, 1907, or while the Spaniards were in transit, Hughes sent a second shipment of 74 Britishers, and informed Knox that a third shipment of 31 Britishers, 81 Scandinavians, and 41 Austrians would leave Genoa shortly. Knox advised his mill managers that news of the second and third shipments should remain confidential, since it was necessary to place the (less desirable) Spaniards before alternatives became available.[70]

Such was the fate of the Hughes' mission, which managed to reach only a third of its objective of 1,000 immigrants and without a single Italian in their ranks. It did (like the earlier Fraire expedition), however, establish the baseline of settlement in Queensland of two European groups. The Catalans and "Austrians" were the first foothold of North Queensland's Spanish and Yugoslavian settlers.

In late August, General Manager Knox of the CSR wrote the premier of Queensland requesting reimbursement for the expenses of the Hughes' recruitment, while stating, "Although in our opinion the Catalans are at least as suitable as any of the others for the intended work, in deference to public opinion we are willing thus to bear the entire cost of their introduction...."[71]

The introduction of the Catalans into Queensland proved fraught with difficulties. The CSR planned to distribute one hundred of the men to farmers in their four North Queensland mill areas (twenty-five for Victoria, thirty-three for Macknade, twenty-five for Goondi, and seventeen for Hambledon).[72] When the Catalans arrived at Townsville, there was great confusion and discontent, as many of the men resented separation from friends or fellow villagers, and it was found that several had swapped landing papers to avoid it. Others were in a drunken state, and the CSR representative went to receive them accompanied by two policemen.[73]

The Catalans changed ships in Brisbane and arrived in Townsville July 12 on the *Wakefield*. Despite measures taken to keep them from absconding, five of them did so. They were subsequently apprehended and returned to the cane district. Of course, few of the growers wanted these recalcitrant cutters on their property.[74] The *Brisbane Courier* had already expressed misgivings about the Spaniards' dedication to hard labor.[75] The mills, too, were relieved that fewer Spaniards arrived than was originally anticipated, since they were encountering difficulty in placing them. The AWU was equally opposed, as it feared that the immigrants would become a non-union workforce that would suppress workers' wages. Journalists sympathetic to the AWU parroted the objection, one article gloating over the growers' discomfort, while noting: "...it serves them right, as they refused good steady men work before the arrival of their Spanish pets."[76]

Several farmers refused to accept their assigned Spaniards. One who did so complained that he got a blacksmith, a carpenter, a railway station manager, a town commission clerk, and two fiddlers![77] Furthermore, the first decade of the twentieth century was characterized by the rise of anarcho-syndicalism in Spain, and Barcelona was ground zero for the movement and its industrial protests. According to Robert James David Mason,

> It seems likely that the Spaniards were unaware of the stringent controls employers [in Australia] were permitted to use regarding their indentured labourers. Even in Catalunya, there was no precedent for the ease with which an employer could compel labourers to work, dictate their hours and prosecute them for

failure to comply. Migrants complained to mill managers that they had not understood the contracts they signed in Barcelona....[78]

During the first month, there were clear signs of problems. Three farmers reported that their Spaniards had armed themselves with knives and revolvers and were refusing orders. So, farmers were also carrying weapons when going to the paddocks. There was the illustrative case of the Lacaze farm, where,

> Lacaze reported that his Spanish workers had almost rioted, following his attempt to reinstall a cook against the gang's wishes. The group's spokesperson then rushed at Lacaze with a knife, forcing Lacaze to brandish his revolver. Since Lacaze refused to back down, all of the Spanish gang went on strike and appealed to the mill for mediation. When Lacaze prosecuted the ringleader in court (with the full support of the CSR CO.), the man failed to appear and subsequently was later arrested. The Spaniards in his gang again went on strike until he was released and reinstated.[79]

It was later claimed that the dispute at the Lacaze farm centered around four Spaniards who were anarchists in Spain that the Spanish police had encouraged to sign on with Hughes in order to get them out of the country.[80]

Nevertheless, many of the farmers were said to be satisfied with their Catalans, and it could be added,

> ...The trouble with the Spaniards is unfortunate but it is hoped that both employer and employee will see the foolishness of going about with loaded weapons which in the case of some trifling disagreements are liable to go off by themselves. It was not to be expected that a large number of foreigners absolutely ignorant of the language and ways of the country could be introduced without some friction....[81]

By September, one of the farmers had obtained a judgment against a Catalan who had deserted and the CSR was filing an action against two other absconders.[82] By this time, the Company was worried that it would be stuck with the Spaniards, since some of the farmers wanted to get rid of them even if it meant forfeiting the £5 advanced for recruiting expenses.[83] In October, the Spaniards were becoming a national issue, and the government requested information from the CSR on the number of men who had abandoned their contracts. Some had gone to Cairns and then on to Cloncurry, where they were detained for killing residents' goats.[84]

With news of trouble with the Spaniards filling the pages of the Queensland press (reminiscent of the reporting regarding Italians during the first year after the Fraire expedition), the *Italo-Australiano* newspaper of Sydney noted with glee,

> The Colonial Sugar Refining Company has imported a number of Spaniards and, as was only to be expected, has "fallen in." We understand these Spaniards come principally from the Pyrenees, where they potter about small lots of land, and live on the proverbial "smell of an oil rag," perfectly happy so long as they are not expected to work. Even the better class of Spaniards have [sic] a deep-rooted objection to manual labour.... Spain has deteriorated, but even in her palmy days, in the days of Pizzaro [sic] and Cortez, she was never a coloniser; she was a conqueror, and a harsh and cruel conqueror, but not a coloniser.[85]

By year's end, the Spanish issue was again in the limelight. In December, there were reports of four Spaniards who were traveling mysteriously about the Far North agitating their countrymen. After their visits, some of the Catalans demanded that their original contracts be cancelled and then renegotiated; they went on strike when the CSR refused. All twenty-nine of the Spaniards contracted to cut sugar for the Goondi Mill laid down their tools. The CSR was convinced that the union was behind the whole mess, noting that the four agitators were using language such as "black-fellows agreement" to refer to the Spaniards' contracts informed by the *Masters and Servants Act*, a phrase that would never have been in the Spaniards' vocabulary.[86] According to *The Queenslander*, the Spaniards had been tampered with by the unions. They were told that the terms of their contract were well below standard. To wit, "Although the men could not speak a word of English this result was achieved in about six weeks, the men having become members of the labour unions. Thereupon, it is alleged, they began to shirk work, with the evident intention of breaking the agreements...."[87]

As the harvesting season drew to a close, six Spaniards employed in the Geraldton district went on strike to test the validity of their contracts. The police magistrate fined each £10 plus court costs, while threatening to imprison for four months anyone refusing to return to work. When the defendants rejected the terms, the police attempted to apprehend them. Other Spaniards in attendance rushed the bench, shouting "all together," and seized temporary control of the courthouse. In all, twenty-eight persons were jailed. The incident caused a flap in the Australian Parliament.[88]

Eventually, the men were fined and removed to Townsville to serve jail sentences. By February, some had been released from jail and had returned to the Geraldton area. It was thought that all of the men, upon their release, could be held to the original terms of their contracts. However, "One serious aspect of the disturbance was that threats were made against some of the employers, and revolvers were secured for defensive purposes...."[89]

Clearly disgusted with the whole mess, at the end of the 1907 season the CSR released all of the Spaniards from their contracts, on condition that the men reimburse the farmers the £5 advanced for their passage.[90]

Still and all, in early 1908, a CSR report stated that, of the ninety-five Spaniards originally under contract, thirty-two remained so. Forty-seven of the agreements had, by mutual consent, been cancelled. Five men had been dismissed for habitual drunkenness and eleven had absconded. Many of those who cancelled their agreements remained in the sugar districts and were grubbing or cutting firewood; others had gone South lured by the false promise of better wages. Several of them had written their former employer requesting a cane-cutting job in the following season. Seven of the Spaniards had nominated their wives for immigration into Australia.[91] By the 1909 season, two of the twenty gangs on the Johnstone River were Spanish (during a strike action they began cutting, but quickly ceased out of fear for their lives).[92] Goondi Mill reported a preference for immigrant gangs, including Spaniards and Italians.[93] In short, the Spanish presence in North Queensland had survived its difficult birth.

From Canecutter to Grower—Given the unavailability of Italians and the seeming undesirability of the Spaniards introduced in 1907, by early 1908 not a single CSR farmer had petitioned for the introduction of European laborers, despite the Company's offer to provide a subsidy for each recruit.[94] These were, of course, anxious times for the farmers and mill owners alike. Continued reports of the unsuitability of white labor were ubiquitous in the Queensland press. Some farmers failed; others reduced their acreage in sugar production. However, its problems notwithstanding, the experiment began to take. While hundreds of the men from the Queensland mining districts and the southern states who tried their hand at cutting either found the work unbearable or failed to give satisfaction, a core of cutters met the challenge. Consequently, with each passing season the pool of hardened, experienced Anglo canecutters expanded. Indeed, by 1910, the fear of a labor shortage had abated.

The government was also expanding the land approved for sugar-growing. In 1912, more than 25,000 acres were opened in the Lower Burdekin to supply the projected new Inkerman Mill. The acreage was parceled into 141 farms, 60 to 790 acres each.[95] Most were taken up immediately by applicants from far and wide, and the "Majority of the applicants [were] young men, sons of farmers or farm labourers, though there were a number of men of other callings—teamsters, mining men and tradesmen."[96]

However, there was a new concern in the industry. The Anglo-Australian laborer was imbued with a propensity for confrontational industrial action and the sugar industry was highly vulnerable to its consequences. In the 1909 season, labor organizers were successful in attracting many men to the Australian Sugar Workers' Union, and, by year's end, there had been strikes in the Mulgrave and Mossman districts. On January 8, 1910, worried mill directors and managers met at Cairns to discuss the situation, and the CSR, which had previously pursued an independent course, sent its own representative to help forge a common front.[97]

During the 1910 season, there was a strike by mill hands that was broken by importing extra men from New South Wales. 1911 was another story when a series of work stoppages rocked the entire industry. These coincided with renegotiation of the white-bounty scheme. Consequently, federal arbitrators wielded considerable clout. A Royal

Commission of Inquiry recommended abolishment of the bounty program, establishment of stricter state control of the industry, implementation of working and living standards for the laborers, and creation of a minimum wage that was considerably higher than the prevailing one.[98]

Then, too, there was the question of the Catalans. Mason tells us,

> The Spaniards' arrival in Queensland occurred at a particularly inauspicious moment. The gradual erosion of the Pacific Islanders' presence in the canefields had been matched by the progressive growth of unionism in the industry. During 1906 and 1907 sugar workers' unions were formed at Mossman, Innisfail, Ingham, Ayr, and Proserpine. Largely ineffectual in the improvement of working conditions, the small sugar unions were rapidly consolidated by the much larger AWU the following year. From this position of increased influence, relations between unionised workers, farmers and mill owners became steadily more acrimonious. The first major strike occurred in 1909 and was repeated to great effect in 1911. Importantly for the Spaniards, foreign workers were central to British workers' complaints, and unions blamed them for having caused a perceived decline in conditions. The 1911 strike focused on British labourers' refusal to work under the *Masters and Servants Act* as indentured labour. Much of the social frustration and tension that developed during the strike was expressed through an increased violence towards non-British migrant workers.[99]

The union's preference for an hourly wage scale and a fixed work week was in sharp contrast to the "contract" approach, in which the ganger negotiated piecework rates and the cutters set their own daily and weekly schedules. Under the former system, the worker was essentially a protected, salaried employee, whereas in the latter case he was an at-risk entrepreneur. Cutters oriented to the employee approach sought to professionalize their status through union activism directed at maximizing wages and benefits. This stance introduced a divergence of interests between canecutter and canegrower that was tantamount to a social-class distinction.

The contract system, on the other hand, was preferred by the canecutter aspiring to farm tenancy or ownership. Today's employee was potentially tomorrow's employer. In this approach, cane cutting was not a career but rather a way station, a sort of purgatory that one endured in the process of becoming a canefarmer. While British canecutters were present in both camps, Italians were almost exclusively oriented to contract cutting.

By 1911, there was no longer a labor shortage in the industry; rather, from the owners' standpoint (both farm and mill), the main concerns were the quality of the workers and their attitude. Not surprisingly, the reliable contract cutter was preferred by the industry. Anticipating the 1911 cutting season, the manager of Macknade Mill informed CSR headquarters that competition in the district for cane-cutting contracts was considerable. At the end of the 1910 season, about thirty Italians had departed for Italy, but there had been a steady influx of new-chum ones, and more Italians were said to be on the way, coming from Europe at their own expense. Consequently, farmers in the district were making no special effort to recruit European labor. He also noted that the Australian Sugar Workers' Union had largely failed in the Herbert, "I think owing to the difficulty of getting the Italians to combine...."[100]

As the 1911 season degenerated into a major confrontation with the union, the CSR's General Manager Knox informed one of his mill managers that the Company might consider subsidizing part of the passage costs of two to three hundred Southern Europeans. Knox noted, "...Italians and possibly Spaniards would...be preferred as they would be more difficult for the labour unions to handle than labourers from Great Britain...."[101] Ever sensitive to the political consequences, Knox cautioned secrecy regarding the CSR's role.

The manager of Macknade Mill informed Knox that he was employing twenty-three Italian, five British, and three black gangs. He advised that in the future only Italians be retained "...as the worse gangs we have are Britishers...."[102] Victoria Mill echoed this sentiment, noting that, of its twenty-six gangs, sixteen were Italian and ten British. Regarding the Victoria Mill district's Italians, it could be said,

> ...The local organisers tried hard to persuade them to join them in their demands for eight hours a day on wages but failed miserably. The Italians are out here to make big checks in as short a time as possible regardless of the hours they work and fully

recognize what cane cutting by wages instead of by contract would mean to them....[103]

Testifying in November of 1911 before a Royal Commission charged with assessing the state of the sugar industry, the manager of Victoria Mill answered a query regarding the suitability of white labor in the canefields by noting,

> The hot weather affects most men. When cutting crops they go off very much unless we have the proper class of men, men who come from hot climates and understand agricultural work. For instance, Italians seem to adapt themselves to the circumstances very quickly, much more so than our own people who come from the south, simply because they have been used to hot climates and agricultural work. A new-chum coming from Italy can do a whole season here better than a cane-cutter from the south....[104]

Nevertheless, scientific opinion was shifting on the issue. In 1912, a lecture was given before the Economic Science Section of the Philosophical Society of Glasgow in which it was stated,

> ...it was at one time believed that manual occupation was impossible for white men in the tropics. Recently, however, the opinion had been growing that this view was fallacious. The most daring modern experiment in the cultivation of the tropics by white labour had been made in the sugar plantations of Queensland. Sugar cane cultivation had generally been regarded as the best suitable of all work for white labour. Sugar cane in the tropics of Australia were originally grown by Kanakas, from South Sea Islands.... It was predicted that the abolition of Kanaka labour meant the ruin of the Australian sugar industry. The sugar planters however have not only survived the change but had produced much more sugar since the Kanakas had gone.[105]

This view, however, did not go unchallenged. Under the rubric of "The Proposed Tropical White Man," Professor L. W. Lyde contended,

> ...only by evolving dark skins and other characteristics of the yellow and black races can a white race permanently settled in such

a climate hope to retain its rigour.... [A] white race in the north, unless continually reinforced with fresh white blood would inevitably, in the course of generations, either die out or develop a purely pigmented skin.

Another modification that would have to be developed, in the course of generations, by the white race, is the shape of the nose and in the respiratory organs.... The pureness of a white race varies in inverse ratio to the width of the nose, so that again the projected tropical white man is going to be essentially a black man.[106]

Clearly, then, in the first decade of the twentieth century, the Italian canecutter proliferated in at least some North Queensland districts. In 1907, one Italian farmer passed through Sydney on his way back to North Queensland after a return visit to Italy. In an interview with the *Italo-Australiano*, he noted that, prior to his departure the year before, there had been 150–200 Italians in the Herbert, but there were currently "...considerably over 300."[107] Shortly thereafter, the newspaper ran another interview with a man recently returned from North Queensland, who noted, "Halifax is the chief town of the district, and there very frequently on Saturday evenings there is a reunion of Italians, where you will hear almost every dialect of Italy spoken.... They have a good time and spend money, too."[108]

Nor was the Italian population restricted any longer to North Italians. That there was an awareness of Queensland and its sugar industry in Sicily is evident. In 1907, for instance, when news reached Australia of the failure of the agent sent by the CSR and the farmers to recruit in North Italy, the Socialist Francesco Sceusa of Sydney sent a warning to a Sicilian newspaper. He noted that it was rumored in Australia that the recruiting effort would shift to Sicily. He urged all Sicilians to reject this union-busting plot of Queensland capitalists.[109] That there were already South Italians in the cane fields was apparent. During the 1908 season, the most successful gang of canecutters in Halifax on the Herbert was Sicilian.[110]

Just as the Swiss-Italian hotelkeeper, E. Regazzoli, was a key figure and cultural broker for the influx of North Italians into the Herbert, Felix Reitano played a similar role for southerners. Reitano was born in Naples in 1892 and joined relatives in Sydney at eleven years of age. He worked for his uncle in a fruit shop across the street from Government House. It was said that his natural intelligence attracted the attention of the governor himself, who began to teach the youngster English. It could be stated, "…It was the means of him inculcating the British attitude and he became more British than his own nationality…."[111] Pursuing "the lure of the North," he moved to Mossman where he worked in the cane breaks and the mill. In 1909, he resettled in Halifax where, after working on the Italian-owned Buffa and Antony farms, he became a clerk in the Regazzoli Hotel. He subsequently started a hairdressing salon in the establishment, became a commission agent, and, later, the district auctioneer. He frequently served as interpreter in any dispute involving Italians. Over the years, Reitano assisted many South Italians to come to the Herbert.

In the 1911 census, Queensland had 929 Italy-born and 97 Spain-born residents.[112] While the absolute numbers were small, they mask other realities. First, there were 181 Italy-born and 19 Spain-born women. Their Australia-born offspring were not recorded in the census as ethnics. The same is true of the offspring of the few mixed marriages between Italian and Spanish males and other European or Australian women.

Second, by this time, the Southern European male sojourner (and particularly the Italian) was common in Queensland. Reference is to the individual who spent a few years in Queensland before returning to Europe with his savings. Should that stay fall within an inter-census period, his presence would go unrecorded.

Third, given the seasonal nature of the cane-cutting profession, with subsequent dispersion of the men, it is likely that they were undercounted. It is noteworthy that the 1911 census was conducted on the night between April 2 and 3. This was more than a month before the sign-on of cane gangs in late May. Many of the intending canecutters would not have been present in the sugar centers where they would have been more easily counted. It was common for the unemployed to go timber-felling or prospecting in the bush. Others languished on the fringes of society, biding their time before the next season. It is also likely that some of the men who had cut in the 1910 season, and would do so again in 1911, were in Europe on visits home when the census was taken.

Finally, by 1911, there had been a noticeable shift in the distribution of

Queensland's Southern European population. The three census districts from the Burdekin to Cairns (Kennedy, Cardwell, Cairns) accounted for 42 percent of the state's Italy-born and 52 percent of its Spain-born residents. The Cardwell district alone, which encompassed the Herbert, had 27 percent of Queensland's Italians.[113]

In light of the foregoing, the impact of the Southern European presence upon North Queenslander awareness was considerably greater than the raw census data might suggest. This was particularly true in the Herbert. There, it could be stated by a visiting journalist that,

> ...as one chatted with this one and the other on the way up the line [from Lucinda], the fact was driven home that the Britisher was losing his grip on the Herbert River, giving way to the Italians who owned many of the farms and did 90 percent of the harvesting, and consequently received a proportionate share of the farmer's money. Such a pity! Where the Neames, Woods and Boyds spent so much money and displayed so much enterprise to have their homesteads eventually people [sic] by those who are not in any way allied to the Britisher or Australian. It is not far distant when the Italian, who is already a licensed victualler [E. Regazzoli], will be the principal tradesman in the district—will dominate commercial life as he dominates the harvesting industry.[114]

Furthermore, it could be stated that, in the Herbert,

> A considerable number of farms are changing hands here just now, the buyers in most cases being Italian canecutters. The prices paid are high, but the terms of sale are easy, a small deposit being accepted with the balance payable over a term of years, with the usual rate of interest added.... Farms are becoming hard to buy in this district except at very high prices.[115]

In 1912, the Australian Sugar Producers' Association held its annual conference in Ingham. Newspaper coverage of the event told of the rows of humpies or cottages built along the tramway on elevated ground so as to be above the flood plain of the Herbert River. "...Most of the occupiers,...were Italians or Spaniards, the conditions for some reason apparently not suiting the British or Australian workers...."[116] Equally alarming was the arrival from Italy in Brisbane of the two Gettona brothers. They were investigating the possibility of taking up a block of Crown land in Queensland, to be cleared and settled by Italian farmers. If successful, they planned to publish their impressions in Italian newspapers in order to attract colonists.[117]

In some cases, Italian canecutters were buying the farm of their employer.[118] This was probably exacerbated by the 1911 Sugar Workers Act, with its Leases to Aliens Restriction Act that prohibited leasing land to aliens.[119]

Similarly, there was broadening of the Spanish presence, both in terms of its North Queensland distribution and its Iberian regional origins. In 1913, one disgruntled Johnstone River district observer complained,

> The word "cutting" again brings to my mind the question of the cutters. Last year the majority of the cutting was done by Spaniards. These men don't spend their money in the town like the Australians; they only spend what they can't help, and the balance goes home to Spain to bring out their countrymen. I think this sort of thing should be stopped. We have enough Australians to do the cutting without, perhaps unwittingly, flooding this fair country with hordes of people foreign to us. I think the farmer, providing all things are equal, should have a white gang to cut his cane.[120]

That same year, when the first fifty intending canecutters showed up for the sign-on in Mackay, it could be stated that they "…comprise all nationalities, Germans and Spaniards perhaps predominating."[121] A 1914 article stated,

> The influx of Italians and other Southern Europeans into the industry in the Far North, to which attention was drawn last year, still continues and in given districts such as the Herbert River, the labour employed is almost wholly of this class and they are spoken of by the farmers in the highest terms, being both sober and reliable and giving absolutely no trouble in the field. In addition to this, however, they are acquiring many of the farms. These are usually sold by the Queensland owners at good prices but on

a small deposit and extended terms. In the case of the Italians the modus operandi is for several of them to get together their earnings to pay the deposit and put one of their number in to run the farm. This has been done by several gangs of men each year, the balance of the men going working in the canefields and saving enough to put another fellow citizen in and so on. It is quite safe to say that every farm that has been sold in the Herbert River lately has been sold to Italians and the percentage of Italians owning farms on the River at present is at least 30. Italians with a percentage of Austrians, Russians, Spaniards and Greeks are also buying farms to some extent at Mossman, Cairns, Innisfail and Mourilyan.[122]

There was, then, a budding awareness that aliens were taking over farm ownership. In the event, a few examples were capable of creating an exaggerated perception. For example, if, in the 1915 season, there were a total of combined 81,470.87 acres providing sugar to the two mills in the Hinchinbrook, only 11,407.37 (14 percent) were in Italian ownership and 402.5 were held by Spaniards. Only one of the latter properties was owned by Basques (the Menchaca and Iraegui partnership), with most of the remainder in Catalans' hands.[123]

The increase in Spanish immigration is reflected dramatically in a sample of 259 naturalized Spanish males who entered Australia between the years 1908 and 1916. Thirteen, fourteen, and fifteen individuals arrived in the years 1908, 1909, and 1910 respectively. There is then a quantum leap to thirty-nine, thirty-nine, thirty-six, and thirty-seven in the four years 1911–1914. It then peaked with a total of fifty in 1915, or the first full year of global war, but before shipping lanes were effectively interdicted.[124] While Spain remained neutral throughout the conflict, this could not be anticipated in 1915. Thus, although young Australians as well as young Italians in Europe were conscripted for the military, their Spanish counterparts remained free to emigrate.

The outbreak of World War I polarized Australia along class and ethnic lines. There was considerable Anglo-Australian patriotism and adherence to the Triple Entente effort to defeat the Triple Alliance powers. However, there was also the fear that the conflict would become Great Britain's excuse for squashing the growing Irish Independence movement that resonated in the ranks of Irish Australians. There was also considerable antiwar sentiment among leftist Laborites, imbued as they were with the Socialist view that the workers of the world constituted their own constituency destined to take over the planet. They were convinced that the workers of individual countries were impervious to parochial nationalism and would refuse to kill the supposed enemy workers across the battle line (they would soon receive a tragic lesson in that regard). There were many anti-conscription protests.

The AWU leadership in Queensland backed the war effort, but there was significant dissent among the rank and file. The Australian economy was hammered by the war's interruption of maritime commerce that provoked, by 1915, dramatic inflation combined with eighteen percent unemployment. The government placed several "seditious" groups under surveillance, and there was growing anti-immigrant sentiment. Many Anglo workers were conscripted, and it was believed that the immigrants were taking their jobs. While Italo-Australians came under considerable pressure from Italy to return home to enlist in the armed forces, few did.[125]

The success of Italians and other Southern Europeans in acquiring properties during the war years was facilitated by other factors. In 1916, there was labor strife in the sugar industry. The troop mobilizations had eroded the ranks of the canecutters, and the union's victory in achieving the so-called Dickson award regarding wages and work conditions added as much as 40 percent to the cost of producing and processing the crop. The resulting uncertainty forced many sugar properties on the market that were acquired by Italian syndicates. Since Italians resident in Australia were exempted from the call-up for military service until the final months of the conflict, for most of the war years Italo-Australians were ideally situated to take advantage of the opportunity to acquire both cane-cutting contracts and farms.[126]

Unsurprisingly, the Dickson Award was not embraced by most farmers—Anglos and Italians alike. In 1916, there was a gathering of Italian growers in the Herbert and Felix Reitano served as an interpreter. The consensus was that the award was totally unreasonable and made farming marginal, but that the farmers had to continue just to service their debts and other financial obligations.[127]

One bemused Anglo canecutter summed up the growers' hand-wringing as follows,

> Once more the sugar industry is ruined, this is the third time I have seen it ruined. In the good old days about 14 years ago the farmer lived in a grass hut, had 2 or more Kanakas, and he got about 8s per ton for his cane.... and he was happy. Then the Kanakas had to go—there was weeping and wailing, as the CSR company said the industry could not be carried on by white labour, so the farmer said he would not plant any more cane. But he did, and in 2 years he built a fine house, and he went to town for his rations in a good buckboard buggy and a good horse pulling it. The white storekeepers in town increased by 200%, and then the CSR told him that the Govt was robbing him, and even though he didn't know this before he started to scream that he was being robbed.... The CSR poked him in the ribs and made him scream louder so the Federal Govt handed the industry over to the State and told him he had to pay 1s per hour so he knocked off planting again. But he was getting 16s–19s per ton for his cane so he made up his mind to plant and be robbed by those thieves, the A.W.U. In another 2 years it was a common sight to see the canefarmer taking his family to town in his own car, mind you a six seater, and then came 9s2d per day. Ye Gods, he wanted to sell his land and he was going straight out of the country. But he did not, he bought another 50 acres of land, and a few more horses, and his children were sent south to be educated. The state schools were not good enough for him. Then came the Dickson Award: it requires an abler pen than mine to describe the looks of horror on the faces of the farmers and general managers of the CSR.... and now the same agitators are using the same old pointed stick and telling them that everybody is ruined, and still in spite of everything they will go on planting and in another 2 years the canefarmers will be taking their families to Sydney in their own steam yachts—now the other side, the sugar worker. Let us see what the Dickson Award has done for him. At 9s 2d a day his family was starving.... Now under the present humane award I am

able to put good clothes on my children and give them enough to eat, and every sugar worker and his family blesses [sic] Judge Dickson for giving him the means to live.[128]

Then there is the view of an Italian canecutter who came to Australia after five years in America and cut with a gang that his wife cooked for—between them they cleared £230 in six months. He declared that, "neither in America or [sic] any other country that he had visited were the same splendid opportunities available for a working man as in Queensland."[129]

There was an effort to recruit Italians for Australia's war effort. In 1916, a large gathering of Italians in Ingham was addressed in their language.[130] Certainly the sons of some Italo Australians enlisted voluntarily, but it was not until 1918 that they became eligible for conscription. In September, 137 Italo-Australian reservists were given medical examinations in the Herbert River. Two representatives of the Italian consul-general were present. All but seventeen were declared fit and 70–80 were put on a train to the South. A large crowd of their compatriots, in festive spirit, bid them farewell, and "A large Italian flag, made especially for the occasion, was carried by one of the reservists at the end of the train."[131]

In his 1916 annual report on the status of the sugar industry, Easterby again emphasized the Southern European penetration of it north of Townsville. In the Herbert and Johnstone River districts, of the 451 canefarmers, 145 were non-Anglo, with 107 being Italian. Of the 790 canecutters, 621, or 79 percent, were non-British.[132]

The southern Australian media were prone to underscore the piebald makeup of North Queensland's population. In addition to attention upon the "swarthy" Southern Europeans, there was the "colored" element. An article in the Melbourne *Argus* stated,

> There is no "White Australia" in North Queensland. In the Cairns district 500 aliens are working. They are Chinese, Hindoos and Kanakas. There are also many hundreds of half-castes, who are as a rule excellent workers. The "coloured" canecutters receive the same rates for canecutting as the white man. The white man tolerates him and is not above suggesting to the Hindoo and Chinese

that he should "shout." All these aliens are "permit" men—that is, men allowed to remain, having already become permanent residents, when the deportation took place. In 20 years they will be extinct.[133]

All of these groups, including the Italian canecutters, worked hard and saved their money for a better future, whereas the white Australian cutters drew down his wages, went South, and returned the next season, "with nothing in the world but the clothes on his back."[134]

By 1918, it could be reported,

> ...In the Babinda district some 60 percent of the farmers are Italians. They work largely on what is called the community system. They cut their cane in "bees"—that is all the members of a community cut the cane of each of them. They have implements in common, and thus work economically. Many of them marry—some of them Australian girls, some Italian—and they settle down as prosperous and contented settlers. They are hardly at all affected by strikes as they do nearly all their own work; and to a visitor it would seem that the labour difficulty would disappear if their system of the cooperation of small farmers became general in all sugar districts....[135]

As the war drew to a close and Australia faced the problem of both rewarding and reabsorbing her war veterans, soldier-settler schemes were proposed that would provide the country's heroes with land. In Queensland, this was touted as an antidote to the Southern European "takeover." As the *North Queensland Register* editorialized under the rubric of "Sugar for Soldiers,"

> With sorrow and dismay it has to be acknowledged that Australians are not showing much enthusiasm in the acquirement of sugar farms, and that Italians and Spaniards and other foreigners are supplanting the original settlers. However worthy in other respects those who are not of our own race may be as citizens of the state, however ready we may be to welcome them that they may enjoy the rare privileges of living under our laws, it would

be sheer misappropriation of patriotic funds if even the distant effect were to encourage the friendly aliens in the belief that the lands were theirs.... The sugar lands of the north are of great but not unlimited extent, and must be in some degree conserved for Australians...."[136]

This same letter went on to state,

I admit this vast hemisphere needs population, but for heaven's sake, if we must import it, let it be the right sort, and something we can physically and morally assimilate. The fair-haired, blue-eyed, pure blooded Northern European, no matter of what nationality, I have always found to be a good citizen, but when it comes to the hybrid scum and backwash, the hucksters and beachcombers of the Mediterranean shores and islands, it is up to someone to protest. Some of these people were good men 2,000 years ago, and showed the way the world should go; in fact it was a Greek...who first brought civilisation to John Bull's island. That, however, was in the long ago, before the Moor invaded the southern portion of Europe and tainted the different races with his blood and discoloured their cuticles. It is to these swarthy people that the offensive term of "dago" is applied—not that they can help it.... These men might be tolerated if it were not for their low down cunning—the cunning of a sewer rat—and ways that are dark and deep and despicable.[137]

Another letter to the editor of the same newspaper opined,

...The Australian lad who sailed away to foreign strands and to war will be a very angry individual indeed when he comes back only to find the job he left behind him filled by a strange, dark gentleman from the Mediterranean shores. If things go on as they are it is only a matter of time when the Australian, or any English-speaking man for that matter, will be the foreigner here.[138]

Spain was officially neutral in World War I; most of the Spanish nationals in Queensland kept their distance from the anarcho-syndicalist Italian (and Catalan) protesters and struck a low profile generally throughout the conflict. However, according to Mason:

The situation changed with servicemen's return, when Spaniards became the target of xenophobia. Many Spanish children were taunted as they walked to school, whilst adults were ostracised by the hostile servicemen angry at the Government's reticence to provide them with the farms demanded as recompense for wartime sacrifices.[139]

For some Australians, the Italians were dangerous because they were clannish and did not become citizens. For others, there was the opposite danger, namely, that if too many naturalized and voted they would take control of the Far North through the ballot box. Ergo, "No foreign born immigrant should be granted the franchise [vote] until after a residency of 10 years, and in the case of immigrants from enemy countries (if it should be given to them at all) of 15 years."[140]

It was against the backdrop of such increasingly vocal sentiment that Commonwealth authorities empowered a commission, in 1919, to look into the sugar industry, including the issue of alien penetration of it. During the testimony, various charges were levelled against the Italians. These included the by now familiar litany regarding their willingness to work for less than the award rates, live on the smell of an oily rag, save their money, pool their savings to buy a farm at exorbitant prices, and then assist each other while exploiting their fellow countrymen to make it pay, when a Britisher, demanding a better standard of living and personal independence, would surely fail.[141] The problem was that under persistent questioning by the commissioners the Italians' detractors were unable to prove their charges, stating instead that their contentions were "general knowledge" in their districts.

At the same time, the Italians had their grudging supporters who volunteered observations such as, "…The Italians in this district are proving themselves law-abiding, industrious and sober, and are ambitious, and, but for ousting Britishers, there is no doubt to be found with them…."[142]

Then, too, there are the more positive takes, such as the "Defence of Italians," published in Brisbane's *Daily Mail*. The newspaper's correspondent from Innisfail argues that Anglos were less fit than "swarthy" Italians to resist the climate (not to mention the formers' propensity for alcohol abuse), but that was only a small part of the story. The Italians were inured by their upbringing in Italy to privation, thrift, and investment. Every Italian sugar worker had a bank account. The Italian ignores the politics and industrial actions of the union that buffet the Anglo sugar worker, and, instead, simply works hard to get ahead. The Italian is not doing anything that the Anglo could not, were he so inclined. In sum, "The Italians are thrifty, industrious, and law-abiding, and there is every reason to believe they will become good citizens in every sense of the word, in the same way that the great body of aliens settlers in America have become good Americans."[143]

Consequently, the extreme measures proposed by some critics, such as the nationalization of the sugar industry to preserve its British character, were simply unwarranted.[144] Indeed, when pressed, the detractors could do little more than admit that Britishers could also save their money, pool their resources, and compete with the Italians, but simply did not choose to. At the same time, many British canefarmers and mill owners took the position that the exorbitant demands of the AWU were the prime cause for the alienation of the workforce. In this view, Labour's triumphs, as represented in the Dickson Award, were Pyrrhic victories that priced the British worker out of the market.

Nevertheless, the seemingly resounding Italian socioeconomic mobility from canecutter to canefarmer needed to be qualified as well. Clearly, the successes of some masked the failures of others, as persons acquired a tenuous foothold with a small down payment upon a property with an inflated value, and then farmed in dangerously undercapitalized circumstances.[145] Italian-owned farms changed hands rapidly, partly in response to forfeitures, partly through a pattern in which dedicated farmers traded up, and partly as a cashing out of assets as owners sold out to return to Italy. This latter phenomenon came under scrutiny, since it belied the notion that Italians were truly settlers committed to an Australian future. Clearly, some took over marginal or poorly managed properties with an eye toward improving them in the shortest possible time in order to sell out (probably to an aspiring fellow countryman). There were instances of Italian farmers applying excessive manure and then planting an entire acreage (rather than resting a part of it) to produce an artificially high cutting in the year they intended to sell their property in order to give a false impression of its capacity.[146]

Finally, given the war-imposed restraints upon European emigration, it was impossible in 1919 to demonstrate a Southern European–invasion effect in North Queensland. While many districts north of Townsville reported an increase in non-British farm ownership and canecutter gangs, the overall trend was not particularly startling.[147]

Hence, the upshot of the report of the 1919 Royal Commission on the Sugar Industry was to undermine the contention that North Queensland was in imminent danger of being taken over by undesirable aliens. On balance, to the extent that Italians and others were acquiring a foothold, it was by and large a fair and healthy process.[148]

In fact, during 1921, Queensland authorities officially supported Italian immigration as a means of settling small farmers on the land. The state government published a pamphlet that was circulated among Queensland's Italian residents urging them to encourage their friends and relatives in Italy to immigrate.[149] However, when opponents of Southern European immigration attempted to call out the Commonwealth government, the latter's position was that only British immigrants qualified under the assisted-passage scheme. The Italians were coming of their own volition and expense.

From the perspective of nationwide trends, there was also notable concentration of Southern Europeans in North Queensland by the 1921 census. During the three decades from 1891 to 1921, Australia's Italy-born population had grown from 3,890 to 8,135 persons. We have noted that, in 1891, Queensland's European-born Italian population was 438 persons, or 11 percent of the national total, and that few resided in North Queensland. By 1921, the state's percentage had more than doubled to 22.5 percent, and there was a noticeable shift within Queensland to the northern littoral.[150] Fully 73 percent of the state's Italy-born population resided in the coastal districts from Sarina (Mackay area) to Douglas (Cairns area). Consequently, by this time, one in six of Australia's European-born Italians resided in the North Queensland sugar districts. Similarly, 270, or 29 percent of Australia's total population of 928 Spain-born persons, resided in Queensland, and over half of them were in the sugar districts of the Far North.

The totals for Queensland showed that the state's population of Italy-born persons had doubled (from 929 to 1,838) and its Spain-born residents had nearly tripled (from 97 to 270). The trend, discernible in the 1911 census, for Southern Europeans to concentrate in the sugar districts from the Burdekin to Cairns, had intensified. Fully 79 percent of Queensland's Italy-born (1,457 persons) resided in just four shires (Hinchinbrook, Ayr, Johnstone, and Cairns). Again, the Herbert stood out, since Hinchinbrook Shire alone accounted for more than one-third of the state's entire total (674 individuals).[151] In terms of nationality,[152] the Spanish population of the same four shires encompassed 51 percent of the state's total. The greatest concentration was in Johnstone Shire, which alone contained 36 percent (97 individuals) of Queensland's Spanish nationals.[153]

By 1921, several factors had conspired to increase Italian emigration to Oceania. Beset with economic problems in the postwar period, Europe was wracked with popular discontent, further inflamed by the developments in Russia. In Italy, this was already creating the confrontations and conditions that led to Mussolini's triumph. If economic and political unrest in Italy were producing more candidates for emigration, developments in the traditional receiving countries were far from propitious. Argentina and the United States, the two main destinations for Italian emigration, both restricted their immigration policies. While the United States had received an average of a quarter of a million Italians annually between 1906 and 1915, in 1922 it admitted only 42,057—a figure which, by 1925, was reduced to 3,845! In 1924, the intake of Spanish nationals was but 131.[154]

While Australia did not even begin to feel the full potential impact of such developments, in her own historical terms she faced a quantum leap in Italian immigration. Thus, if, in 1920, 697 Italians immigrated into Australia, by 1922 the figure stood at 4,222—or more than half as many new arrivals as the nation's entire Italy-born population in the 1921 census! The implications of the new reality regarding the Italian presence proved divisive within Australian governmental and public opinion circles and led to renewed debate over the non-Britisher immigration issue.[155]

At the end of 1921, Mr. Gullett, Commonwealth superintendent of immigration, stated,

> Most European countries are overcrowded. I have received information that their Government [sic] would be pleased to co-operate with the Commonwealth for the transfer of large numbers of people to Australia. It is now open to us to recruit

freely from the peasantry. A contingent of a few hundred Italians have [sic] arrived within the last fortnight, and may be regarded as the pioneers of a great growing movement.... The fact that the Lloyd Sabaudo Steamship Company has now established a direct line of vessels between Australia and Italy is certain to lead to the arrival of an increasing number of Italian immigrants.[156]

Mr. Gullett was firmly of the school of thought which believed that one of the lessons of World War I was the national-defense imperative of populating the Australian continent with Europeans, a goal that could not be reached by restricting immigration to Britishers alone.

The reaction in Queensland's sugar districts was mixed. While some reports of the arrival of new contingents of Italians were benign, bemused, and, at times, even laudatory,[157] others raised an alarm. Typical of the language of the detractors were, "Last week...there were over 40 new Italian arrivals. Most of these are prospective settlers. Wake up Queenslanders, why let our most remunerative industry slip from our hands. The writing on the wall is very plain and includes every business in the district."[158]

And again, "...I wonder will [North Queensland's] future advancement rest with the sons of Italy? It looks much as if North Queensland from Lucinda Point northwards in the near future will be really a 'New Italia'."[159]

In the light of such sentiment, Premier Theodore of Queensland tried to strike a neutral pose. When the Returned Soldiers' League, a strongly nativist organization of World War I veterans, practically accused the government of encouraging Italian immigration at the expense of Britishers, the premier responded that Queensland's assisted-passage scheme was reserved for the latter. Italians were coming at their own expense, and their admission into the country was a Commonwealth rather than a state matter.[160] A short time later, the premier declared that Italians made good settlers, thereby setting an example for unemployed Anglo-Australians who apparently preferred a government handout to the challenge of settling the land.[161]

The anti-aliens' constituents enjoyed greater success on the much smaller scale of "colored" residents. Apparently, 200 or 250 Japanese lost their employment in Babinda and other sugar districts and protested that they were permanent residents who were now being denied their fundamental rights.[162] Soon thereafter, the minister for lands admitted that several aliens, mainly Chinese, had been given sub-leases by farmers in the Atherton Tablelands and Cairns. He noted that this was between private individuals, and, therefore, beyond his control. It was in keeping with the longstanding practice in the Far North of short-term leases to Chinese for market-gardening purposes.[163] One canefarmer in the Burdekin reported that he had employed two Malays for grubbing. He noted, "I prefer white workers and gave them a chance on this job some time previously, and they did not carry it out."[164] Then, too, a delegate to the eighth annual R.S.S.I.L.A. conference held in Hobart declared that there were thousands of Japanese in North Queensland, "becoming every week more and more arrogant," and with more on the way. He contended, "In some of the towns a Returned soldier dared not walk down the street with his badge on. Again, in some towns, only Japanese, Greek and Italian was [sic] spoken."[165]

Meanwhile, the Queensland press began to report the arrival on an almost weekly basis of substantial contingents of Italians.[166] It was also noted that the Italians of Cairns had purchased a property for an Italian club and hospital.[167] Those in the Herbert River had purchased a store from its Chinese proprietor and planned to run it as an Italian cooperative.[168] Consequently, as 1922 progressed, the rising concern over the Italian "invasion" became palpable. Under the rubric of "White Australia or White Italia?" one Queenslander wrote,

> ...it is time to protest. It is not the one or two thousand aliens who are already here, it is the thousands who will follow.... We must see that we do not fail in our duty to the coming generations, and that this heritage of the British race shall not be allowed to become a dumping ground for other nations.[169]

At the same time,[170] the notion that such immigration was in Australia's defense interest was refuted with the argument that an "alien" takeover of the coastal districts could actually pose a security threat to the nation in time of war.[171]

Nor was the Italian penetration of North Queensland limited any longer to the coastal districts. A CSR official wrote to Company headquarters that many Italians were now settling in the Atherton Tablelands, that two to three hundred Italians were coming to the Herbert each year assisted by friends and relatives, and that there was a surplus of fifty to sixty unemployed Italians in the district this year (1922). He opined, "Foreigners wandering about from place to place is bound to incite adverse criticisms...."[172] In Innisfail at this time, "Many new arrivals from Italy are stranded in the district, and seem unable to get work. Many of them are not experienced farm hands, there are a few amongst them who have been brought up to make hats. It is said that they are going round begging food."[173]

Similarly, had the figures been public knowledge, the extent of Italian land ownership at Macknade Mill would certainly have added to the controversy. A CSR document shows that, of the 160 suppliers in the 1922 season, 86, or 54 percent, were Italian. They controlled 58 percent of the acreage. Only slightly more than a third of the growers (57) were Britishers, and they controlled slightly less than a third of the acreage (3,819 acres of the 11,650 total). Eight other ethnic groups farmed the rest, including five Spanish nationals cultivating 291 acres.

The terms and amount of land speculation among Italians were astounding,

> ...farms have been sold on deposits as little as £5, with an agreement to make over 60% or more of the crop each year in payment for the property. The result has been that farms have been sold as often as a dozen times over, as each successive buyer failed to comply with the terms.[174]

Growing opposition to Italian immigration was not limited to the complaints of citizens acting as individuals. Rather, various Britisher-dominated organizations began to work in concert against the Southern Europeans. In Townsville, when a branch of the New Settlers' League was formed in 1921, the purpose of which was to facilitate immigrant adaptation, it was stressed that any future immigration must be of "the right sort" (i.e., British).[175] In early 1922, the White Australia Sugar League was formed in Queensland to "do justice to our great national industry that means so much to Queensland and is going to keep Australia white and save it from being cursed with a piebald population."[176]

Between 1922 and 1925, the "Italian invasion" was rarely out of the limelight as Queensland and Commonwealth officials debated the issues. Italian consular authorities cautioned moderation, and Australian unionists and nativists regularly proposed restrictions on Southern European immigration.[177]

Representative of the negative viewpoint is the following excerpt from a letter to a newspaper editor,

> …from a social point of view, after watching the influx of Southern Europeans during recent years, we are watching the mixing of oil and water.
>
> Socially the Southern Europeans we have been getting are irritating the local people. They are industrious, but it is the industry born of greed in trying to dig themselves in and the other fellows out. They are not the fine big sociable and hospitable people of the good Scotch, British, Irish, German, Swedish, Norwegian or Dutch races.
>
> Where there is a number of them in the North—and it is hard to find at present an exception—they tend to keep to themselves and their own language, and drink vile decoctions, and eat imported food. We are nation building. We want the best, or better than what we're getting. We want immigrants who can teach us something new, or better than what we have. If the Italians, Greeks and Maltese can give us anything new we want them, but we do not want them to be rushed out merely to displace our own people.[178]

The next issue of the newspaper published an endorsement of the above that stated that the Lower Burdekin "supports a population of 9,000 people—and to its credit and honour a 98% British population, and may it remain so will be the sentiment of all who love this great land Australia."[179]

Meanwhile, in spring of 1922, an Italian warship berthed in Townsville with Italian Consul-General Grossardi on board. The officers and consul were received by the mayor. In late 1922, Doctor Dell'Oro, the Inspector of Immigration for the Italian government, toured the Far North to assess the situation. He noted that the Australian businessmen, politicians, and professionals he met in the sugar districts were all "eulogistic" of the honesty, industry, and capacity for hard work of the Italian immigrants. He underscored that most Italian immigrants were experienced agriculturalists intending to seek their futures, whether as canecutters or farmers, in Queensland's sugar industry. However, he recognized that the flow needed to be monitored and administered carefully to ensure that the supply of Italian labor met the demand for it.[180]

Such a cautionary note notwithstanding, there were regular reports in the Australian press of the continued arrivals of Italians intending to head for the Far North. The Lloyd Sabaudo Shipping Line was accused of recruiting potential immigrants in southern Italy with exaggerated claims that jobs were awaiting them in North Queensland simply in order to sell passages. This was reported to be but £8 for the journey, the implication being that the Far North was about to be flooded with Italian immigrants. The notion of an £8-fare was debunked as absurdly inaccurate.[181] Nevertheless, it was also claimed that illiterate, unsophisticated immigrants had to pay £42, but in *lire* that the Company then exchanged at such an astoundingly unfavorable rate that the fare became equivalent to £176 8s! Many immigrants used all they had in savings and could borrow to pay that. It was therefore scarcely surprising that they arrived impecunious in Australia, and were in danger of becoming public wards.[182]

Despite the fixation upon the positive and negative issues surrounding Southern European settlement in the Far North, there was also general celebration of "Queensland's Great White Industry,"

> What does the Queensland sugar industry mean to Australia? It means this year a crop of 355,000 tons—a record in the history of the industry! It means a crop worth £9,700,000 which, when refined and ready to distribute will be worth £12,500,000. It means the settlement of the North by an industry to which the soil and the climate are peculiarly suited, and a new race of white people, 90% British stock—the healthiest people in Australia—the placing of 5,000 sugar farmers on the land, and employment of 19,000 workers on the fields and in the factories. It means the development of industries based on utilization of the byproducts of the cane, and the building of secondary industries. Contast the story of north Queensland with that of the adjoining territory within the same parallels of latitude.[183]

Kanakas cut an average of one-and-a-quarter tons of cane daily, whereas the past year the white cutters produced slightly over four tons.[184]

By 1924, Commonwealth Prime Minister Bruce was hard-pressed to salvage his immigration bill (by a 21–18 vote in committee) against the attacks by opponents of continental immigration.[185] Bruce declared,

> The people of Australia should realize that if we are to have the rule of justice under the League of Nations, unless we can get more than 6,000,000 of people into this the greatest uninhabited white man's territory in the world, we shall never be able to hold it. We shall be told that Australia is the only place that can absorb the great surplus populations of the world, and it must be open to them.[186]

Such thinking, however, was neutralized by press coverage of the unsubstantiated report that a fleet of Italian ships was being readied to transport a horde of emigrants to Australia.[187] While the fleet failed to materialize, in early 1925 it was reported that an Italian periodical had published an article amounting to a guidebook on emigration to Australia (Queensland in particular) that contained surprisingly accurate information and extolled Australia as a land of opportunity. The crux of the article was that,

> To-day...is not the moment to give free impulse to our immigration into Australia, but a tomorrow not far distant is approaching, and should not find us unprepared. Already the signs of its imminence are observable, and from now onward we should develop our plan.[188]

In April of 1925, the *North Queensland Register* published an interview with an Italian ship's captain who had just landed ninety-three Italians in Brisbane on their way to the sugar districts. He stated, "...300,000 Italians of the agricultural class are ready to come to Australia," and predicted that 8,000 Italians would enter the country annually.[189] In light of such inflammatory prognostication, Queensland authorities called for a Commission of Inquiry into the question of aliens in the sugar districts. Since Queensland had a Labour government that, nevertheless, urged tolerance regarding continental immigration, and was thereby at odds with the state's increasingly xenophobic unionists, the measure was partly a palliative designed to blunt criticism within Labour's own ranks. However, the resulting investigation was conducted in a serious and constructive fashion.

Thomas A. Ferry and his fellow commissioners toured the sugar districts in late spring of 1925 and held extensive hearings in several key centers. They received input from a number of sources, including canecutters, canefarmers, millworkers, labor organizers, clergymen, etc. Ferry determined that the causes of the recent increase in immigration were fivefold: (1) the recent restrictions posed by the American authorities on entry into the U.S., (2) the propaganda of steamship agents, (3) the present economic and political situation in Europe, (4) the advice and assistance of friends and relations in Australia, and (5) the publicity about the Australian standard of living deriving from Australia's participation in the war.[190]

In paying considerable attention to the experience of the United States, Ferry concluded that Australia was likely to see a dramatic rise in immigration that would in part consist of American rejects. However, it was impractical to initiate a quota system, since Australia lacked its own consular service abroad to administer it.[191]

Ferry took exception with the current nomination system. It seems that persons in Italy were being recruited by recently arrived Italians who themselves were out of work. Some of the nomination forms were being sold in Italy for £1 each. One returnee from Ingham was reported to have distributed several hundred. The £40-landing requirement was equally ineffective, since some simply borrowed the money for presentation to Australian officials, returning it after disembarking or otherwise quickly expending it upon their arrival in the country. However, Ferry conceded that no Italians in Queensland had become public wards because the Italian community cared for its own.[192]

The report noted that the recent influx of aliens had not been absorbed into the labor force. Rather, many were now billeted in barracks throughout the sugar districts awaiting the cutting season. Some of the men were staying with their relatives. In testimony before the Commission, one Ingham Italian, who frequently served as an interpreter and commission agent, stated that his records showed that between April 1924 and March 1925 there were 1,127 Italian arrivals in the Herbert. Of these, 860 were nominated, while the remainder were not. Of the total, only 161 were women and children, so 966 adult males were thrust upon the labor market.[193] There were currently 1,200 unemployed Italians in the district.[194] About 200 had gone south, some to Sydney, some to Newcastle, others to Roma (Queensland) where they were working in the grape vineyards. About 30 Ingham Italians had resettled in Proserpine.[195]

Ferry echoed the charge that foreign farmers exploited their own countrymen and that the foreigners generally engaged in some award-breaking.[196]

The commissioner concluded that the best workers and settlers were the British followed by the North Italians. He stated, "…It is worth noting that these latter hailed originally from the cool mountains of Piedmont and Lombardy and are much superior to Southern Italians and the Mediterranean races generally."[197]

In extolling the virtues of North Italian settlers, Ferry waxed eloquent, harking back to the success of the Marquis de Ray's New Italy settlers in New South Wales and the Fraire expeditioners. He noted that, "one of the original Fraire group was settled in Innisfail and had 52 relatives in the district and all are going well."[198] Sanitizing Queensland's collective memory somewhat, Ferry observed,

> These early arrivals were from Northern Italy and were of a selected peasant class, and generally were life-long cultivators of the soil. For some years many of the Italian immigrants to Northern Queensland were relatives of those brought out by Signor Fraire.
>
> They knew exactly where to go and what to expect on arrival. They quickly conformed to the laws of the State and the British standard of living, and were without friction absorbed in the social and economic life of the country.[199]

Ferry mustered a whole series of statements to the effect that the North Italian was a good unionist and adhered to a high standard of living.[200] He also noted that the AWU was not against Italians *per se*, but rather decried the dumping of any class of worker on the already glutted labor market in North Queensland. In this respect, the settled Italian had as much to fear from an influx of newcomers as did the settled Anglo-Australian.[201]

Finally, Ferry maintained that the North Italians were adapting well, establishing families, and that their children were becoming good Australians. Despite charges to the contrary, they were not transferring significant sums of money back to Italy.[202]

Ferry, however, held a different opinion of other Mediterranean immigrants. The Maltese, Sicilians, and Greeks were all undesirable. The latter group was particularly vilified in the report as town dwellers rather than agriculturalists who "…add nothing to the wealth or security of the country…and who had even displaced the Chinaman from his China Town."[203] Sicilians were described as illiterate, impoverished and "…more inclined to form groups and less likely to be assimilated in to the population of the State."[204] No mention was made of Spaniards.

Ferry recommended that agricultural alternatives to sugar growing and harvesting be developed for the Southern Europeans. In future, there should be better selection of them at their point of origin, and their distribution in Australia should be carefully regulated. In the case of Italians, the nomination system needed improvement, as it was currently being circumvented. Some "racial stocks" should be excluded in favor of immigrants "…that will assist rather than hinder the building up of superior social and economic conditions in the State." Aliens convicted of crimes should be deported. There should be a record kept in each state of its alien population. There should be stricter medical examination of the immigrants. The surplus aliens in any one district should be encouraged and assisted to resettle in another. Formation of foreign clubs should be discouraged as barriers to assimilation.[205] Ferry's concluding remark was to the effect that,

> …at the present time our foreign immigration appears to be largely induced and controlled by selfish and unscrupulous interests entirely outside Australia, and the question for consideration is whether it shall continue to be controlled by such interests or by a responsible Government in Australia.[206]

By exporting the problem abroad (or at least to Canberra), he essentially trivialized Queensland's capacity to deal with it. Consequently, his conclusions were scarcely designed either to fuel the fires of further controversy or ameliorate the current situation. It gave the appearance of action rather than the promise of concrete results. However, on balance, it was a victory of sorts for immigration proponents, and for at least one sector of the Southern European immigrant community—namely, the North Italians.

Notes

1. Shiva Naipaul, *A Hot Country* (London: Hamish Hamilton Ltd., 1983), 9.
2. Price, *Southern Europeans*, Chap. 6.
3. Fraire was a partner in the drapery business in Townsville with another Italian immigrant, P. V. Armati (whose main profession was pharmacist). Both had apparently been influenced through Brisbane's Bishop Quinn to come to Australia. For more extensive biographical details on both men, see Douglass, *From Italy*, 37–38, and Armati's obituary in the *North Queensland Register*, December 10, 1923, 6.
4. *Queensland Votes and Proceedings*, vol. 1 (Brisbane: Government Printer, 1890), 143–44.
5. Ibid, 1558.
6. Ibid, 1585.
7. Ibid, 1562.
8. Ibid, 1563.
9. Ibid, 1564.
10. Ibid, 1573.
11. Ibid, 1571.
12. Bolton, *A Thousand*, 151
13. *Queensland Votes and Proceedings* (1890), 1573.
14. Douglass, *From Italy*, 43–50.
15. Ibid, 51.
16. *North Queensland Herald*, March 9, 1892, 18.
17. *The Townsville Herald*, March 2, 1892, 10–11.
18. Ibid, May 4, 1892, 28.
19. *The Queenslander*, December 3, 1892.
20. Sugar Industry Labour Commission, *Report of the Royal Commission Appointed to Inquire into and Report regarding the Number of Pacific Islanders to be Deported from Queensland at the end of the Current Year, the most efficient manner of Repatriating them, with the probable cost thereof; whether there are in Queensland any Pacific Islanders whose Compulsory Deportation would be inconsistent with humanity or with good faith; and whether sufficient Labour for carrying on the Queensland Sugar Industry is likely to be available when Pacific Islanders can no longer be lawfully employed; and if sufficient labour for such purpose is not likely to be locally obtainable, the best means of supplying the deficiency; together with the Minutes of Proceedings. Minutes of Evidence taken before the Commission, and Appendices* (Brisbane: Government Printer, 1906), passim.
21. Dating from 1901, the cane districts were divided into three districts each with its own standard wage. Since it was hotter, wetter, and stormier, the Northern Region

(north of the 20th parallel) commanded the highest scale; 3 pence per ton more than the Central Region (20th parallel to the Tropic of Capricorn and 6 pence more than the Southern Region (Tropic of Capricorn south). See Bianka Vidonja Balanzategui, *Gentlemen of the Flashing Blade*, 2nd ed. (Brisbane: Boolarong Press, 2015); references here are to the 1st ed. (Townsville: James Cook University, 1990), 78–79. [*Gentlemen*].

22. Cris D'all Osto, Italian consul in Ingham, used to monitor the sign-ons for the canefarmers and told me that the AWU exploited the immigrants. They signed them up for a fee and did little on their behalf. He knows for a fact that some recruits in the 1950s were given union tickets lacking the usual ballot forms for union elections so their vote could be manipulated by the AWU bosses (Douglass field notes).
23. Robert Donaldson and Michael Joseph, *Cane!* (London: Sphere Books Limited, 1967), 72. [*Cane!*].
24. Vidonja Balanzategui, *Gentlemen*, 42.
25. Ibid, facing 41, xiv, 42.
26. Ibid.
27. F. E. Baume, *Burnt Sugar* (Sydney: Macquarie Head Press, 1934). [*Burnt Sugar*]; Jean Devanney, *Sugar Heaven* (Sydney: Modern Publishers, 1936); Jean Devanney, *By Tropic Sea and Jungle* (Sydney: Angus and Robertson, 1944); Ray Lawler, *Summer of the Seventeenth Doll* (Sydney: Currency Press, 1957); John Naish, *The Cruel Field* (London: Hutchinson & Co., 1962); John Naish, *That Men Should Fear* (London: Hutchinson & Co., 1963); Robertson and Joseph, *Cane!*
28. Vidonja Balanzategui, *Gentlemen*, xvi.
29. Ibid, 80–81.
30. "Extract," *The Sugar Journal and Tropical Cultivator* (Mackay), April 15, 1893, 1. Copy in Colonial Sugar Refining Co. Archive (Sydney), Box D.1.0, Folder 4, Document 11.
31. Alan Birch, "The Implementation of the White Australia Policy in the Queensland Sugar Industry 1901–12," *Australian Journal of Politics and History* 11, no. 2 (1965), 207.
32. Ibid.
33. Walter Maxwell, *Sugar Industry of Australia* (Melbourne: Government Printer, 1912).
34. Roy Connolly, *John Drysdale and the Burdekin* (Sydney: Ure Smith, 1964).
35. For more extensive treatment of the foregoing see Bianka Vidonja Balanzategui, *The Tropical Queensland Sugar Cane Industry: A Structural and Material Survey, 1872 to 1955* (Townsville: Material Culture Unit, James Cook University, 1994).
36. *The Queenslander*, May 7, 1892.
37. Douglass, *From Italy*, 71–72.
38. "Actual Yields, Macknade Mill, 1898," Colonial Sugar Refining Co. Archive (Sydney), Box D.3.0, Folder 3, Document 12.
39. Thomas Arthur Ferry, "Report of the Royal Commission Appointed to Inquire into and Report on the Social and Economic Effect of Increase in the Number of Aliens

in Queensland," *Queensland Parliamentary Papers*, vol. 3 (Brisbane: Government Printer, 1925), 14. ["Report"].
40. The Parliament of the Commonwealth of Australia, *Commonwealth Parliamentary Debates, First Parliament, First Session*, vol. 5 (Melbourne: Government Printer of the State of Victoria, 1901), 6913–14.
41. *The Queenslander*, February 8, 1904.
42. March 10, 1904, Colonial Sugar Refining Co. Collection, Archives of Business and Labour, Australian National University, Letter Book, Macknade Out, 142/1511.
43. January 27, 1904, Colonial Sugar Refining Co. Collection, Archives of Business and Labour, Australian National University, Letter File 1, Macknade In, 142/1493.
44. March 17, 1904, Colonial Sugar Refining Co. Collection, Archives of Business and Labour, Australian National University, Letter File 1, Macknade In, 142/1493.
45. "Notes in connection with the Return of Harvesting by White Labour at N. Queensland Mills: Season—1904," Colonial Sugar Refining Co. Collection, Archives of Business and Labour, Australian National University, 142/3438.
46. "Canecutters—Season 1906, Macknade Mill," Colonial Sugar Refining Co. Collection, Archives of Business and Labour, Australian National University, 142/3440.
47. "White Labour Statistics—Victoria Mill—Season 1907," Colonial Sugar Refining Co. Collection, Archives of Business and Labour, Australian National University, 142/3441.
48. *Herbert River Express*, August 6, 1906.
49. *L'Italo-Australiano*, January 18, 1908, 2.
50. *Herbert River Express*, December 17, 1906.
51. *North Queensland Register*, February 24, 1906, 36.
52. "Contract Immigrants, Queensland: Permits to Introduce," broadsheet (Melbourne: The Parliament of the Commonwealth of Australia, 1907).
53. "September 20, 1906," Queensland State Archives, PRE 120.
54. "October 2, 1906," Queensland State Archives, PRE 120.
55. "October 30, 1906," Queensland State Archives, PRE 120.
56. "November 22, 1906," Colonial Sugar Refining Company Collection, Archives of Business and Labour, Australian National University, Letter File 8, Macknade Out, 142/1514, 243–46.
57. "November 29, 1906," Colonial Sugar Refining Co. Collection, Archives of Business and Labour, Australian National University, Letter File 3, Victoria In, 142/1594, Letter 440.
58. "December 19, 1906," Colonial Sugar Refining Co. Collection, Archives of Business and Labour, Australian National University, Letter File 3, Victoria In, 142/1594, Letter 400.
59. "January 24, 1907," Colonial Sugar Refining Co. Collection, Archives of Business and Labour, Australian National University, Letter File 8, Macknade Out, 142/1514, 325–26.
60. "February 7, 1907," Colonial Sugar Refining Co. Collection, Archives of Business and Labour, Australian National University, Letter File 8, Macknade Out, 142/1514, 344.
61. "February 20, 1907," Colonial Sugar Refining Co. Collection, Archives of Business

and Labour, Australian National University, Letter File 8, Macknade Out 142/1514, 396–98.
62. "March 28, 1907," Colonial Sugar Refining Co. Collection, Archives of Business and Labour, Australian National University, Letter File 8, Macknade Out, 142/1514, 430–31.
63. "February 26, 1907," Queensland State Archives, PRE 120.
64. "May 30, 1907," Colonial Sugar Refining Co. Collection, Archives of Business and Labour, Australian National University, Letter File 9, Macknade Out, 142/1515, 12–14.
65. *North Queensland Register*, July 6, 1907, 39.
66. Cited in *North Queensland Register*, July 13, 1907, 34.
67. Ibid, 41.
68. *North Queensland Register*, July 20, 1907, 29.
69. Ibid.
70. "June 20, 1907," Colonial Sugar Refining Co. Collection, Archives of Business and Labour, Australian National University, Letter File 9, Macknade Out, 142/a5a5, 43.
71. "August 31, 1907," Colonial Sugar Refining Co. Archive (Sydney), Box B.2.1, Folder 2, Document 2.
72. "July 6, 1907," Colonial Sugar Refining Co. Collection, Archives of Business and Labour, Australian National University, Letter File 9, Macknade Out, 142/1515.
73. "July 4, 1907," Colonial Sugar Refining Co. Collection, Archives of Business and Labour, Australian National University, Letter File 9, Victoria In, 142/1515; "July 25, 1907," Colonial Sugar Refining Co. Collection, Archives of Business and Labour, Australian National University, Letter File 9, Victoria In, 142/1515; "August 1, 1907," Colonial Sugar Refining Co. Collection, Archives of Business and Labour, Australian National University, Letter File 9, Macknade Out, 142/1515.
74. Mason, "Agitators," 60–61.
75. *Brisbane Courier*, July 10, 1907, 4.
76. *North Queensland Herald*, September 7, 1907, 4.
77. "July 18, 1907," Colonial Sugar Refining Collection, Archives of Business and Labour, Australian National University, Letter File 4, Macknade In, 142/1496.
78. Mason, "Agitators," 63.
79. Ibid, 64.
80. Ibid, 66.
81. "August 22, 1907," Colonial Sugar Refining Co. Collection, Archives of Business and Labour, Australian National University, Letter File 9, Macknade Out, 142/1515.
82. "September 5, 1907," Colonial Sugar Refining Co. Collection, Archives of Business and Labour, Australian National University, Letter File 9, Macknade Out, 142/1515.
83. "September 6, 1907," Colonial Sugar Refining Co. Collection, Archives of Business and Labour, Australian National University, Letter File 4, Victoria In, 142/1595.
84. "October 2, 1907," Colonial Sugar Refining Co. Collection, Archives of Business and Labour, Australian National University, Letter File 4, Victoria In, 142/1595.
85. *L'Italo-Australiano*, October 26, 1907, 2. Reference to Spaniards living "on the smell of an oil rag" is ironic since it was the phrase commonly used by their Australian detractors to denigrate Italians!

86. Mason, "Agitators," 65.
87. *North Queensland Register*, February 22, 1908, 23.
88. Ibid, December 14, 1907, 28.
89. Ibid.
90. "December 12, 1907," Colonial Sugar Refining Co. Collection, Archives of Business and Labour, Australian National University, Letter File 4, Victoria In, 142/1595.
91. "February 27, 1908," Colonial Sugar Refining Co. Collection, Archives of Business and Labour, Australian National University, Letter File 4, Victoria In, 142/1592.
92. *The Australian Sugar Journal*, November 4, 1909, 284.
93. "September 25, 1909," Colonial Sugar Refining Co. Collection, Archives of Business and Labour, Australian National University, Letter File 5, Macknade Out, 142/3444.
94. "February 13, 1908," Colonial Sugar Refining Co. Collection, Archives of Business and Labour, Australian National University, Letter File 4, Victoria In, 142/1595.
95. *North Queensland Register*, January 29, 1912, 5.
96. *North Queensland Register*, January 1, 1912, 67.
97. "Report of Proceedings of Meeting of Directors of Central Mills, and Managers of Northern Mills, held in Cairns, Tuesday, 8th January, 1910," n.d., Copy in Colonial Sugar Refining Co. Archive (Sydney), 142/3447.
98. John Kerr, *Northern Outpost* (Mossman: Mossman Central Mill Company Limited, 1979), 54–56; Easterby, *Queensland Sugar*, 43–44.
99. Mason, "Agitators," 61–62.
100. "February 23, 1911," Colonial Sugar Refining Co. Collection, Archives of Business and Labour, Australian National University, Letter File 5, Victoria In, 142/1596, Letter 686.
101. "August 31, 1911," Colonial Sugar Refining Co. Collection, Archives of Business and Labour, Australian National University, Macknade In, Private 142/3116, 21.
102. "September 14, 1911," Colonial Sugar Refining Co. Collection, Archives of Business and Labour, Australian National University, Macknade In, Private 142/3114, 9.
103. "June 22, 1911," Colonial Sugar Refining Co. Collection, Archives of Business and Labour, Australian National University, Letter File 5, Victoria In, 142/1596, Letter 925.
104. The Parliament of the Commonwealth of Australia, *Report of the Royal Commission on the Sugar Industry Together with Minutes of Evidence and Appendices* (Melbourne: Government Printer for the State of Victoria, 1912), 216. [*Report*].
105. *North Queensland Register*, July 22, 1912, 33.
106. Ibid, December 30, 1912, 65.
107. *L'Italo-Australiano*, November 30, 1907, 2.
108. *L'Italo-Australiano*, January 18, 1908, 2.
109. "June 23, 1907," Translation of Francesco Sceusa letter to *La Battaglia*. Copy in Queensland State Archives, PRE 120.
110. "March 17, 1909," Colonial Sugar Refining Co. Collection, Archives of Business and Labour, Australian National University, Letter File 5, Victoria In, 142/1596, Letter 686.
111. *Herbert River Express*, January 16, 1945, 4.

112. Commonwealth of Australia, *Census of the Commonwealth of Australia*, vol. 2 (Melbourne: Government Printer, 1911), 340.
113. Ibid, 340, 345. On March 22, 1980, I interviewed Robert Shepherd, editor of Ingham's *Herbert River Express*. He was born in Ayr and grew up in the Burdekin. He remarked that Ayr had been settled by Anglo-Australian miners from Charters Towers; persons that relocated after the mines gave out. He also noted that Ayr was elitist and class-conscious compared with the egalitarianism of Ingham. Southern European migrants, and particularly Italians, albeit tolerated, were nevertheless frowned upon in the Burdekin, as opposed to the Herbert where they were accepted and embraced. Assimilation in Ingham has been a two-way street since Anglos here have been "Latinized," particularly in their cuisine. Also, in Ingham, even Protestants are now going in for the elaborate funerary vaults built in the local cemetery by Southern Europeans. There is so much intermarriage here now that you can't stereotype anyone by surname.

    There also seems to have been a kind of "halo" effect within the immigrant communities themselves of the two areas. Cris Dall'Osto remarked to me that Ingham Italians were more egalitarian than Ayr ones. He noted that many of his countrymen in the Burdekin made too much money too easily. Similarly, when I spoke with Francisco Javier Larragan in Ingham he noted that he preferred living in the Herbert to the Burdekin (where he also lived for several years). The Basques in the Burdekin are more reserved and have lots of in-fighting among themselves. Hardly anyone there speaks well of another Basque. When two enter into the same bar, they might not acknowledge one another (Douglass field notes).
114. *North Queensland Register*, August 3, 1914, 42.
115. Ibid, January 12, 1914, 22.
116. Ibid, July 29, 1912, 26–27.
117. Ibid, December 9, 1912, 108.
118. Ibid, January 4, 1915, 25.
119. A correspondent from Silkwood denounced the measure since the criterion for excluding the alien was his failure to pass a dictation test to determine required English-language skills. That would likely have the unintended consequence of excluding the Chinese sub-leasers in his district that had founded North Queensland's banana industry (*North Queensland Register*, March 18, 1912, 74).
120. Ibid, February 3, 1913, 55.
121. Ibid, May 5, 1913, 111.
122. Ibid, October 26, 1914, 23.
123. Colonial Sugar Refining Co. Collection, Archives of Business and Labour, Australian National University, Cane Contracts, 1915, 142/2932.
124. Price, Collection, passim.
125. Mason, "Agitators," 84–85.
126. It was not until early 1918 that Australia required alien males of military age to register under the War Precautions Act.
127. *North Queensland Register*, October 7, 1916, 35.
128. Ibid, February 27, 1917, 53.

129. *North Queensland Register*, May 15, 1916, 7.
130. Ibid, January 24, 1916, 17.
131. Ibid, September 23, 1918, 65.
132. Ibid, November 27, 1916, 7.
133. Reproduced in Ibid, July 18, 1918, 20. "Shout" refers to offering to pay for another's drink in a pub.
134. Ibid.
135. Ibid, July 8, 1918, 21.
136. Ibid, February 18, 1918, 19.
137. Ibid.
138. Ibid, May 12, 1919, 49.
139. Mason, "Agitators," 85.
140. *North Queensland Register*, December 9, 1918, 6.
141. Parliament of the Commonwealth of Australia, *Report*, 185–86.
142. Ibid, 324.
143. Reproduced in *North Queensland Register*, April 7, 1919, 16.
144. Parliament of the Commonwealth of Australia, *Report*, 199.
145. Ibid, 351.
146. Ibid, 24, 181, 295, 353, 354. *North Queensland Register*, April 10, 1922, 7.
147. Parliament of the Commonwealth of Australia, *Report*, 236–37, 281, 282.
148. Ibid, xv.
149. Parliament of the Commonwealth of Australia, *Commonwealth Parliamentary Debates*, vol. 1 (Canberra: Government Printer, 1929), 122, 395.
150. Commonwealth of Australia, *Census, 1921*, 51.
151. Commonwealth of Australia, *Census of the Commonwealth of Australia, Taken for the Night between the 3rd and 4th of April, 1921* (Melbourne: Government Printer, 1921), 828, 830, 834. [*Census, 1921*].
152. The 1921 census failed to discriminate Queensland's Spanish population according to birthplace by shire. However, it does report Spanish nationals retaining a foreign "allegiance" (i.e., nationality) by shires.
153. Ibid, 839, 841, 843, 845. Sugar production expanded rapidly in the Johnstone district during the first two decades of the twentieth century. It seems likely that the relatively late-arriving Spaniards were attracted to it by the opportunities afforded by the frontier atmosphere. Conversely, by this time, Italians were more prone to join established kinsmen in the settled Herbert district. The role of Johnstone Shire as an important center (though not the exclusive focal point) of the Spanish presence is reflected in a 1927 article,

> During the visit to Innisfail of the celebrated violinist Senor Don Luis Pares [kinsman of the two 1882 settlers in southern Queensland mentioned earlier?], the Spanish residents of the community met to welcome this distinguished North Queenslander and to congratulate him on the success he has gained in the musical world. The visitor was also requested to organize a Spanish colony in the state, it being pointed out to him that natives of Spain and their descendants numbered about 500. Senor Pares addressed

the gathering in the Spanish tongue and suggested that all the residents of Queensland should join the *Centro Español de Queensland*, a recently formed Spanish club, of which he had the honor of being president. The Club he pointed out aimed at looking after the Spanish interests in this state, and making known the language, art, literature and music of Spain to sympathetic Queenslanders. The suggestion of the distinguished visitor was immediately acted upon and over 100 names were enrolled in the room. (*North Queensland Register*, January 17, 1927, 39).

154. Francesco Cordasco, *Italian Mass Emigration: The Exodus of A Latin People. Bibliographical Guide to the Bollettino dell'Emigrazione 1902–1927* (Totowa, N.J.: Rowman and Littlefield, 1980), 290–91. [*Italian Mass Emigration*]; U.S. Department of Labor, *Annual Report of the Commissioner General of Immigration to the Secretary of Labor, Fiscal Year Ended June 30, 1925* (Washington, D.C.: Government Printer, 1925), 6. For American discrimination against immigrants from southern and central Europe see Daniel Okrent, *The Guarded Gate: Bigotry, Eugenics and the Law That Kept Two Generations of Jews, Italians, and Other European Immigrants Out of America* (New York: Simon & Shuster, 2019), passim.
155. Cordasco, *Italian Mass Emigration*, 285.
156. *North Queensland Register*, December 26, 1921, 8.
157. Ibid, April 3, 1922, 49; Ibid, May 8, 1922, 79; Ibid, June 12, 1922, 47.
158. Ibid, March 20, 47.
159. Ibid, April 24, 1922, 28.
160. Ibid, April 10, 1922, 7.
161. Ibid, May 1, 1922, 18.
162. Ibid, February 21, 1921, 16. This had been brewing for several years. A 1914 article stated that, in the Herbert River, "Last week the town presented the appearance of having fallen into the hands of the Jap. The street was full of the little yellow men. On making enquiry, it was learnt that they had come in from Victoria Mill to sign a declaration to the effect that they were employed in the sugar industry" (Ibid, March 2, 1914, 19). It seems that they had filed for authorization under the Sugar Cultivation Act years earlier, and their applications still languished.
163. Ibid, April 18, 1921, 12.
164. Ibid, May 23, 1921, 23.
165. Ibid, December 3, 1923, 66.
166. Ibid, May 8, 1922, 34, 79; Ibid, May 22, 1922, 1; Ibid, May 29, 1922, 8; Ibid, June 12, 1922, 14, 37; Ibid, September 11, 1922, 7; Ibid, October 23, 1922, 1; Ibid, November 27, 1922, 71; Ibid, December 4, 1922, 26; Ibid, December 11, 1922, 1.
167. Ibid, June 20, 1921, 75.
168. Ibid, June 27, 1921, 4.
169. Ibid, July 3, 1922, 1.
170. Ibid.
171. "June 29, 1922," Colonial Sugar Refining Co. Collection, Archives of Business and Labour, Australian National University, Letter File 14, Victoria In, 142/1602, Letter 45.

172. "January 25, 1923," Colonial Sugar Refining Co. Collection, Archives of Business and Labour, Australian National University, Letter File 13, Macknade In, 142/1505.
173. *North Queensland Register*, July 31, 1922, 9.
174. *North Queensland Register*, July 28, 1924, 91.
175. Ibid, October 17, 1921, 23.
176. Ibid, January 30, 1922, 17.
177. Douglass, *From Italy*, 168–87.
178. *Home Hill Observer*, December 11, 1924, 4.
179. Ibid, December 24, 1924, 4.
180. *North Queensland Register*, October 23, 1922, 79; Ibid, October 30, 1922, 55.
181. Ibid, December 29, 1924, 24.
182. Ibid, December 18, 1922, 77.
183. Ibid, July 28, 1924, 91.
184. Ibid.
185. Commonwealth of Australia, *Commonwealth Parliamentary Debates* (Canberra: Government Printer, 1924), 4094.
186. Ibid, 4092.
187. *North Queensland Register*, July 5, 1924, 9.
188. Ibid, January 19, 1925, 83.
189. Ibid, April 27, 1925, 13.
190. Ferry, "Report," 28.
191. Ibid, 31.
192. Ibid, 32, 34–35.
193. Ibid, 40.
194. Ibid, 41.
195. Ibid, 40.
196. Ibid, 35–36.
197. Ibid, 36.
198. Ibid, 39–40.
199. Ibid, 41.
200. Ibid.
201. Ibid, 45–46.
202. Ibid, 48–49.
203. Ibid, 38.
204. Ibid, 42.
205. Ibid, 50–52.
206. Ibid, 26.

CHAPTER 5

Controversy and Confrontation
(1925–1945)

The Immigration Debate—Constituting of The Ferry Commission and its conciliatory conclusions were scarcely capable of ameliorating the growing concern in some Queensland and Australia circles regarding Southern European immigration. In 1921, the United States passed the Johnson Act that severely curtailed future immigration. It limited the number of foreign-born allowed into the country to three percent of the resident population of that nationality as reflected in the 1910 census. In 1924, the quota was reduced further to two percent.[1]

That same year, Queensland's sugar production surpassed the Australian demand. Sales of the surplus on the world market were at a reduced price, thereby curtailing the Queensland industry's capacity to absorb additional labor through expansion. Consequently, throughout the remainder of the decade, nativists and unionists pressed their case for what ultimately was glossed under the slogan of "British preference." At the Commonwealth level, this meant a campaign to restrict the entry of non-Anglo or non-Nordic immigrants into the country. At the state level, it implied attempts to ensure employment for Anglo-Australians and to limit "alien" ownership of real property. In point of fact, the state measures were limited almost exclusively to North Queensland—its cane-cutting jobs, on the one hand, and control of the cane farms, on the other.

In June of 1925, Queensland Premier Gillies informed Commonwealth Prime Minister Bruce of the conclusions of the Ferry Commission. He demanded that the Commonwealth deal with the immigration problem immediately, since, in the present year alone, two thousand aliens had passed through Brisbane on their way to the sugar districts where there was no employment to be had.² Gillies urged the prime minister to adopt a system whereby aliens would be distributed among the states and then be required to reside there for a minimum of three years or become subject to deportation.³ He underscored,

> It is also necessary that some further consideration should be given to the racial stock of the migrants. Many of the new arrivals are undesirable from every point of view. It would be impossible for them or their children ever to make good Australian citizens or to be assimilated into the social and economic life of the community. Their continued admission to the country can only result in lowering the standard of living and in creating racial bitterness.⁴

In the federal forum, Mr. Bruce argued against adoption of a quota system. It was one thing for the United States to do so with a population of 115,000,000 people, but a similar policy by an underpopulated Australia would create considerable resentment in Europe.⁵ Rather, the government requested that it be given discretionary power to screen and deny admittance to any class of alien deemed to be undesirable should subsequent events warrant its use.⁶

The Bruce administration did notify Italian consular authorities in Queensland that, henceforth, immigrant nominations would only be accepted from Italian residents holding immovable property in Australia. The nominator would be required to provide the new chum with employment.⁷

In August of 1924, the Anglican ministers and bishops of North Queensland held a synod in Townsville. There was considerable discussion of the Italian immigration issue. Reverend A. H. Adey from Ingham noted that many Italians in his district were good citizens, although some did not want to learn English and also worked on Sundays. The latter should be discouraged. Bishop Lefanu noted that the whole issue was semi-political and "contended that in some places the White Australia policy was apt to be anti-Christian." He preferred that immigrants be from English, Scotch, or Irish stock, but "understood that Italians made good citizens."⁸

At this same time, an Italian Consular Agency was opened in Townsville; its jurisdiction extending from Mackay to Cape York.[9]

There was also input from Spain,

> Senor J de Montero, who has been Consul-in-Chief for Spain in Australia for 13 years, will leave Melbourne at the end of the month to take up a new position in Madrid. In an interview Senor Montero said that Australia could not hope to develop rapidly as it was wished if she did not throw open her doors to European immigrants as the Argentine was doing. He thought that only when Australia had reached a population of 100 million could she afford to limit the influx, and he held the view that Australians would tend, through climatic influences, to develop a darker type more nearly Mediterranean than the Anglo-Saxon race.[10]

Meeting in Brisbane in July of 1925, the Queensland branch of the influential Australian Natives' Association debated a report on the Italian question submitted by its Townsville delegate. Accepted unanimously, the report concluded that: "the large influx of Southern Europeans constituted a menace not only to North Queensland in particular, but to Australia as a nation."[11] The conference called upon the Commonwealth to institute a quota system that would guarantee that five Britishers enter Australia for every other nationality. Italian immigration was particularly worrisome, since it was tantamount to colonization with the colonists retaining their "...national traits, language and outlook," and thus, from an Australian viewpoint, "...they would become a sore on the body politic and in time of National danger may even rank as an enemy."[12] The delegates singled out Neapolitans and Sicilians as particularly undesirable, since they were drawn from Italy's cities, were draft dodgers, went about armed, and were quick to resort to violence. The conference raised the specter that the Old World political disputes rife in Italy (Fascists versus Bolshevists) might be transplanted to Australia. It also opined that the government subsidy of the sugar industry might be endangered should other Australians conclude that it had fallen into the hands of foreigners.

The conference offered a program emphasizing: (1) compulsory attendance in public schools of all alien children, (2) prohibition of the leasing of land to any un-naturalized person or his proxy, (3) enforced employment of two Britishers for every alien employee, and (4) the prohibition of any alien club in which English was not the medium of discourse.[13]

Of course, the Italians and their supporters were concerned. When an Innisfail Anglo besmirched Italians in the interest of settling returned soldiers, the Italian consular general telegraphed a reply. It was one thing for Mr. Egan to refer to the sacrifices of thousands of young Australians in the recent war, but it was another to ignore that of five million Italian soldiers allied with the Australian "Diggers" in the same conflict, albeit fighting under a different flag.[14] Meanwhile, another Innisfailer wrote that the constant preposterous horror stories in the southern press about the town were a prime factor. By depicting its climate as unhealthy and its social life and economy to be dominated by undesirable foreigners, the media discouraged Anglos to settle in Innisfail. He asked the rhetorical question, "Who would like to make a home in a place that has the manufactured reputation of Innisfail?" The upshot was,

> Meanwhile the Italian comes along and discovers that this district is the most fertile in Australia. Amongst his luxuriant cane he can see nothing but visions of prosperity. No doubt he wants his brother out to share in his happiness, also his uncles and his cousins and his aunts. On the other hand, the Britisher, with his foolish stories will frighten all his friends away. And then we wonder why so much of the rich land is slipping into the hands of foreigners.[15]

An Italophile with extensive travel experience in the country wrote,

> …why all this outcry against Italian immigrants? Some years ago this same antagonism was extended towards the Chinese, yet there is only a whispered protest against a far greater menace, the Jap. We are already flooded with the invidious Greek. Our cry is "fill our empty spaces, populate the country." Surely the Italians are proving themselves good men on the land, nor do they hang in the cities like the Greeks; they proved themselves our ally in the last war—the Greeks did not, what is more they are a clean-blooded and clean-living race. Should the Italians make this fair

land of ours, the land of their adoption, they will prove an invaluable asset, from a military standpoint.[16]

At the behest of the apostolic delegate in Australia and Brisbane's Archbishop Duhig, Italy-born Bishop Coppo of Kimberly (Western Australia) traveled to Queensland to conduct missions among its Italian residents. He was also to investigate the work conditions obtaining there, particularly with respect to the Italian question. He planned to seek out newcomers from Italy and organize them into religious and moral societies. He also intended to start a Catholic newspaper and schools for Italians that would facilitate the learning of English. He favored the rapid assimilation and intermarriage of Italians in Australia.[17] Subsequently, Bishop Coppo announced the formation of an Italo-Australian Union, whose object was "...to assist Italians in their material, intellectual, and economic needs and teach them the laws, language and customs of Australia."[18]

Another dimension of the problem was Italy's perception of Australia's public debate over the Italian immigration issue. In 1925, an Italian journalist visited Australia and published a scathing critique in the influential newspaper *Corriere della Sera*,

> And it is for these 4,286 [his figure for Italian immigration in Australia in 1924], for this infinitesimal percentage of Italians—healthy, model workmen who come to offer strong arms and willing hearts—that commissions are set up, congresses are agitated, newspapers are perturbed, it is for this…that the doors are shut in our faces with foul words, as upon another "yellow peril"—the olive peril—shut against the ally of yesterday, the friend of today, the third great European power—Italy!
>
> Brave comrades! Our blood sullies, soils, adulterates their Australian blood. "Pollute, polluted," are the concise and brutal expressions employed.[19]

Such attitudes prompted Fleetwood Chidell to conclude,

> It had probably not occurred to the promoters of meetings convened to warn Australians against the "olive peril"—the politicians, the lady orators, and newspaper editors—that the peril

might conceivably take a more immediate and destructive form than that which was demonstrated on their platforms…. Italy has been thrust into the ranks of those nations…which are ready to join with those who in any part of the world favour a forcible reconstruction of frontiers."[20]

For its part, the Italian government remained cautious. In the 1924/1925 report of the Commissary General of Emigration presented to the Italian prime minister, there was a frank and sage assessment of the situation in Australia.[21] It noted AWU opposition to continued immigration and counseled short-term moderation in sending out emigrants. It claimed that the Australian authorities were pleased with the measures taken by the Commissary to control Italian emigration in the wake of the events of 1924 and 1925. Thus, while the numbers of Italian emigrants had risen from around 4,500 in 1924 to 6,000 in 1925, the latter caused less of a stir since the Commissary had directed the flow away from volatile North Queensland. Apparently, all emigration from the Italian province of Alessandria (source of many North Queensland Italian residents)[22] had been interdicted for four months by Italian authorities. The Commissary had also decided to limit approval of nominations of intending North Queensland emigrants to those made by either close relatives or by a landowner making a firm offer of employment. It was noted that, "With this we shall avoid ordinary irresponsible labourers signing nominations for friends and even strangers immediately on arrival, sometimes for gain, others to please friends, knowing they cannot fulfill the conditions imposed thereby."[23]

In late 1926, Count Di San Marzano arrived in Brisbane accompanied by his family. He had been appointed by Mussolini to the newly created position of Italian consular agent in Queensland. In London, he had become familiar with emigration, as well as trade matters between Italy and Australia. The count declared that the press could do much in removing misconceptions between the two countries and underscored his appreciation of the Commonwealth government in dealing with the immigration issue. Nevertheless, "He was convinced there was a great opportunity for Italian migrants who, when properly selected before leaving the homeland would assist in the development of Australian agriculture in no small way."[24] The Italian consul in Sydney added,

...the Italian consuls in Australia would meet in conference in Melbourne to discuss matters affecting Italian settlers in Australia. He expressed the hope Count Di San Marzano, the new Consul in Queensland would be able to settle satisfactorily any matters of conflict between the Queensland people and Italian settlers. It was the policy of the Italian Government, he said, to do everything possible to create harmony between Australians and Italian immigrants.[25]

It was probably not helpful that the "well known estate agent" Mr. T. M. Burke had just arrived back in Sydney having proposed to the Italian Government that it allocate £2,000,000 for the purchase in Australia of land on which to settle Italian farmers. He had discussed the matter with the Italian minister for emigration, "who proposed to send thousands of Italians to Australia if the scheme was agreed to by the Australian Government."[26]

In 1927, the national debate over Italian immigration continued unabated in Australia. Italian Consul General Grossardi founded an Italian Immigration Office as part of the Melbourne General Consulate. In June of 1927, it was under attack and he wrote Commonwealth Prime Minister Bruce that its purpose was not to foment immigration, but rather to smooth the adaptation of those who were already in the country. Grossardi added that, in light of high unemployment among Australians, he had cabled Italy requesting that the number of passports to intending emigrants be reduced. He had also ordered all Italian consuls, vice-consuls, and consular agents in Australia to tighten the means' requirements of those nominating immigrants. Finally, he had mandated that no nominations be issued for those intending to come to several of Australia's industrial centers.[27]

Meanwhile, Parliamentarian William Hughes declared Italians to be undesirable and observed,

> I do not deny that these people are industrious; but that may be said with even greater truth of the Chinese. No people on earth are more industrious than the Chinese. If the price to be paid for a White Australia is the colonization of the tropical parts of the country by Southern Italians or Sicilians, the price is too high.

> When we are dealing with the Chinese or other eastern races we know exactly where we stand. There is very little probability of the hybridization or mongrelization of our races. I am a stalwart believer in the superiority of homogenous peoples.[28]

Prime Minister Bruce declared that the national population was and would remain 98 percent British under his immigration policy; opponents continued to call for an explicit quota system for alien immigrants. They were tired of being fettered by the provisions of England's forty-one-year-old treaty with Italy[29] and world opinion. They maintained that immigration policy was a domestic matter to be determined by each country.[30]

Government spokesmen retorted that current policy and negotiations with authorities in the sending countries were a sufficient response. An agreement had been concluded with Italy, in August of 1927, that would limit Italian immigration to relatives of Italian residents of Australia and persons with employment contracts prior to embarking in Italy. The measure was likely to reduce Italian immigration by 50 percent.[31]

This did not mollify the opposition, however, since it could be stated that, if the excess of Italian arrivals over departures for the first six months of 1926 was 805 individuals, for the first half of 1927 it had been 2,996.[32] The debate ended on an acrimonious note when one opposition spokesman was called to order for asserting that the average Italian uses a knife to resolve his disputes.[33]

As intractable as the problem posed by the continued influx of Italians seemed, it was about to be resolved largely at the Italian end. In 1927, the Mussolini government placed severe restrictions on emigration from Italy as it prepared to steel the country for its star-crossed drive for national glory. Population was wanted if Italy were to join the ranks of the world's powers. At the same time, heightened Italian national pride dictated repudiation of conditions in Australia that might be perceived as discriminatory. Consequently, by late 1927, Consular Agent Pascale of Townsville noted,

> ...any demands by Italians to return to Italy will be favoured and helped. This measure issued by the Royal Italian Government is due not only to the abuse of the Italian Emigrant but also to the

unfriendly reception given him, to the most regrettable boycott made, and the lack of consideration shown to him in Australia.[34]

The combination of Italian and Australian restrictions on Italian immigration clearly worked effectively, since, in 1928 and 1929, only 2,353 and 1,445 Italians, respectively, emigrated to Oceania.[35] Indeed, by early 1929, it was claimed that during the preceding twelve months in Australia, departures of Italians had exceeded arrivals.[36] In fact, the decline of Italian immigration actually prompted fears in some quarters. In March of 1928, The Brisbane *Courier-Mail* editorialized,

> We talk of a White Australia, and insinuate that Italians are not white, when we know they are.... We cannot claim that the people of Europe are inferior to ourselves or that we possess any exclusive key to the workings of democracy; and we cannot say that we are making full use of this immense continent.... Sooner or later [Australia] will have to justify her policy of restricting migration from white races. Will an overcrowded world tolerate our Closed Door policy, especially when we have not the military power to defend it?[37]

It seems clear that during this period there was incentive for Southern European aliens to seek naturalization as a legal shield against possible discriminatory legislation. Mason notes that, in Innisfail alone, between June of 1923 and June of 1925 five to ten Spaniards were naturalized every six months, and there were commensurate rates among the area's Greek and Italian aliens. In the case of Spanish nationals, however, this declined in the second half of the decade—and particularly after the advent of the Spanish Republic (1931–1936) when a return to Spain became more palatable.[38] The rise of Mussolini in Italy produced the opposite effect for Italians.

As Australia accompanied the rest of the world into the Great Depression, there was renewed debate over the immigration issue. The Commonwealth's immigration policy was tightened considerably in 1930, citing the unemployment problem. The consulates of all represented countries in Australia were informed that, henceforth, only close family members of persons already resident in Australia would be granted entry, and that each case would be judged on its merits.[39] The measures would go into effect immediately for "quota" countries (that by now included Italy), since it was felt that they had already received sufficient advance notice of Australia's intent.

On April 1, 1931, further restrictions were implemented requiring that Australia issue a special permit to each intending immigrant, while reserving the right to deny entry to anyone.[40] Actually, this was a moderate policy, given the fact that jingoistic elements within the nation were calling for much more extreme measures. At its annual conference in 1931, the Australian Natives' Association called for a complete ban for ten years on all Southern European immigration, or until such time as the economy improved.[41]

It is evident that Australia's immigration restrictions, Italy's emigration ones, and the voluntary repatriations of many persons due to the Great Depression meant that the number of Italians entering and leaving Australia during the 1930s remained essentially stable. However, it is equally true that, during the 1920s, the Italo-Australian community had grown and matured to a remarkable degree. If, in the 1921 census, Queensland had a total of 1,838 Italy-born persons, in the 1933 one the figure stood at 7,945 individuals,[42] or an increase on the magnitude of 432 percent! If we consider that, over the same period, the figure for Queensland residents born in Greece increased from 701 to 1,618 individuals and those of Spanish nationality from 174 to but 259,[43] we can appreciate the extent to which the continuing Southern-European controversy remained essentially an Italian one.

The greatest concentration of Italians in Queensland continued to be Hinchinbrook Shire (2,586) in the Herbert and Johnstone Shire (1,576), which, together with Cairns (974), accounted for almost 65 percent of the state's total Italy-born population.[44] There were, however, budding Italian colonies on the Burdekin, particularly Ayr (520), as well as Cardwell (316), Douglas (246), and Proserpine (177) Shires, all of which were North Queensland sugar districts.

In Hinchinbrook, the percentage of Italy-born persons in the total population had increased dramatically from 15.63 percent in 1921 to 25.41 percent in 1933. In Johnstone, it had declined, but only slightly from 13.51 percent in 1921 to 12.33 percent in 1933. However, when we consider that both areas were experiencing an increase in Italo-Italian family formation, the offspring of which were treated in the census as simply Australians, it is clear that there was considerable growth in the magnitude of the Italo-Australian population of these two bastions of the Italian presence in North Queensland. In the Herbert, Italians (defined to include both the Old World–born and Italo-Australians) may well have attained the status of the largest single ethnic group in the shire—Britishers included. There, at least, the vaunted white "triumph" in the tropics could have been spelled *trionfo*!

There were also signs that the Italian colony was increasingly less an alien beachhead and more of a permanent factor in Australian life. In 1933, only 4,483 of Queensland's Italy-born population, or slightly more than half the total, retained Italian citizenship. The remainder had become naturalized Australian citizens.[45] Among the Italy-born populace, the sex ratio favoring males had declined from an imbalance of 3.04-to-one in 1921 to 2.56-to-one in 1933. Clearly, the ratio of females within the Italian community had experienced a faster growth than that of the Italo-Australian ethnic group as a whole.

On balance, then, the decade of the 1920s had been a period of spectacular growth in Queensland's Italian collectivity. While the early years of the Great Depression checked its expansion in absolute numbers, they were a period of consolidation and demographic maturation.

The British Preference Movement—During the 1924 sugar season, the AWU's northern district organizer was alarmed that, of the fifty-eight cane-cutter gangs at Goondi and Mourilyan Mills, all but ten were composed of aliens. Given the many unemployed Britishers in his district, he advocated that there be a fifty-fifty division of the available jobs between the two groups.[46] While this would have modified the labor equation radically, in retrospect it was a moderate proposal.

The opening shot and portend of things to come was fired by the millworkers of the South Johnstone in April of 1925. They informed the local canegrowers' associations that 75 percent of the gangs during the coming season had to be British or they would refuse to process the harvest.[47] Within a few days, the AWU branch at Cairns followed the Innisfail workers' lead and declared that the 75-percent-Britisher quota would apply at the Babinda Mill as well.[48]

This demand was opposed strongly by the farmers of both districts as a violation of the sugar award, as too restrictive of the farmer's right to choose their own employees, and as unfair to tried and tested men who had proven their mettle in previous seasons. The proposal was remanded to the Arbitration Court.[49] In early May, the AWU and farmers' representatives in the South Johnstone met, and the latter proposed that a quota of 40 percent British and 60 percent alien cutters be instituted in the district. This counter-proposal was rejected by the union, but was also remanded to the Arbitration Court in Brisbane.[50] Justice Webb, the presiding magistrate, ruled that, for the 1925 season, throughout Queensland first preference was to be given to men who had worked as cutters in the same area the previous harvest, and second preference to those, irrespective of nationality, who held an AWU ticket the previous year.[51] While this did little to modify the existing ratio of British to alien cutters, it did have the effect of making it difficult for new arrivals from Europe to gain employment in the industry. So, the measure was a modest, if somewhat disappointing, victory for the proponents of British preference. On the other hand, within a short time there was evidence that Italians were buying and selling union tickets and that some counterfeit ones were in circulation.[52]

The first-preference system was tested almost immediately in the Herbert, where, by mid-May, there were many unemployed men, including a contingent of new chums who were awaiting the sign-on. Farmers desirous of contracting them were informed that the existing AWU membership roll would have to be exhausted first. Since the Ingham roll contained seven hundred men, it was likely that no newcomers would be hired.[53]

Meanwhile, the South Johnstone millworkers persisted in their pro-British stance. When ten new British gangs were formed, bringing the number in the district to twenty-three in all, the millworkers demanded that the new gangs be contracted.[54] At first, they resolved to handle only British-cut cane until all Anglo cutters in the district had been employed, prompting one observer to note that the position of the victimized Italian was becoming precarious, but, in the end the millworkers compromised. They agreed to run the mill longer each day in order to process enough surplus cane to accommodate the signing-on of eleven extra British gangs, while still crushing all cane sent in from the other farms as well.[55] However, the AWU membership of South Johnstone passed a resolution asking the government to exclude all Southern Europeans from the sugar industry.[56] Torrents wrote to a friend, "It makes no difference that one is naturalized, has a Union ticket, you are a *Dago* and have no right to live."[57]

Another commentator on the situation stated,

> From the Italian side the position must appear extraordinary. No doubt the Italians were encouraged by every means to come to this country. They were told of free conditions, a hearty welcome, land for settlement, and regaled with tales of the success of their compatriots. They were attracted here by the people of Australia and now it appears that the people of Australia have changed their minds.[58]

At the same time, "During the present year sales of land at thumping prices have taken place in the Banyan district. Most of the purchasers have been foreigners. Intelligent Australians would not look at the prices. But still in time they will wonder how other people got hold of such a quantity of good land."[59]

In early June of 1925, it was reported in the Herbert that 610 men had been engaged as cutters and 79 as cooks. There were only nineteen Anglos in all, with Italians constituting about 85 percent of the total and other aliens the remainder. Despite the lack of jobs, more Italians were coming into the district and could be seen hanging about the streets.[60] The same situation obtained in Innisfail, where a relief fund was being established to prevent unemployed Italians from starving. Bishop Coppo appealed to the Italian consul general in Melbourne to prevent anymore Italians from coming to North Queensland.[61]

Meanwhile, there was a work stoppage by the millworkers at Innisfail over the British preference issue. As June passed, the millworkers demanded that 60 unemployed Britishers be contracted, but the farmers, mainly Italians, refused. More Italians continued to arrive in Innisfail, particularly from South Australia where they had previously found employment in the vineyards.[62]

The mill at Babinda was also shut down briefly over the British preference issue,[63] but, by early June, an accord was reached when the directors agreed to hire forty British cutters and thirty for work on the tramline, and promised that, the following year, 75 percent British preference would be instituted.⁶⁴

As the preferential rule was policed most assiduously in the areas of greatest Italian concentration, the unemployed new chums fanned out to fresh places in hopes of finding work. By June of 1925, there was a hint of labor trouble in the Burdekin. A number had arrived there and been hired. None of them had union tickets, and AWU representatives were going about the district replacing them with Britishers whenever they were found.⁶⁵

On balance, the situation suggested that, despite the stringent dictums from judicial benches and self-interested policing of the award by AWU officials, it was possible for the less scrupulous farmer (Italian or otherwise) to employ clandestine labor and take his chances. Seemingly, were he discovered, the worst that would happen was the forced replacement of his illegals with union members who were likely Britishers. In 1926, it was reported that, for a fee of £1 each, Italians with falsified tickets were being supplied to farmers by agents.⁶⁶ Clearly, then, one result of the so-called Webb ruling was to spread the alien labor issue to districts heretofore largely unaffected and drive it underground. In this respect, the union's partial triumph in the districts of longstanding concern (the Herbert, South Johnstone, Babinda) merely served to generalize the problem to North Queensland as a whole.

In Mackay, the situation was less benign than in the Burdekin. In the former, there was longstanding hostility to Italians. In 1915, P. Fenoglio sent a notice to the local newspaper stating that he was moving his family out of the area, "because of the way that we have been treated. They protect the loafer and won't protect the honest man."⁶⁷ In May of 1925, there was a protest among British workers in Mackay when it was learned that four Italians had been employed in the district. The AWU representative Fallon had them all laid off. They were in desperate circumstances, so Fallon did secure for them rations and train tickets to Brisbane. *The Worker* commented that Fallon's actions were extreme, but understandable, given the frustration in the country.⁶⁸

Mackay continued to be a trouble spot even after agreements had resolved work stoppages further to the north in the South Johnstone and Babinda districts. In August, two farms were sold to Italians, one of which was purchased by a partnership of five men intending to cut their own crop, thereby putting a "white" gang out of work. The Mackay millworkers passed a resolution that "...no cane be accepted by any mill cut by Southern Europeans on and after August 31."[69] The climate of opinion may be appreciated from the following,

> During the meeting it was stated that information had been received from a reliable source that there was a movement to purchase 200 farms for Italians in the Mackay district. There is a general feeling among canecutters that persons behind the alien policy are buying up farms, seeking eventually to capture complete control of the mills of the district.[70]

In August of 1926, the Mackay millworkers were still refusing to process Italian-grown cane, and Mr. W. J. Dunstan, Labour member of the Board of Trade and Arbitration, had been dispatched there to convene a conference of AWU representatives to resolve the problem.[71] At the same time, Italian Consul-General Grossardi traveled to Mackay from Melbourne to obtain firsthand knowledge of the situation. He met with the districts' Italians, of whom there were but about twenty-five.[72] He then called upon Queensland's premier, who assured him that every measure would be taken to safeguard legitimate Italian interests in the state.[73] Premier McCormack denounced the actions as those of a few AWU members at Mackay, whose stand was at variance with that of their union.[74] Meanwhile, news arrived that Dunstan's mission had been a success, and that the millworkers of Mackay, by a small majority, had voted henceforth to make no distinction between Italian- and British-grown cane.[75]

At the same time, there was an interesting sidebar regarding both Italian land sellers and purchasers: "It is understood that one of the Italians, who was purchasing part of Mr. Buffa's land at Mossman, had forfeited his deposit, and gone to Cooktown looking for some of the peanut land at that place."[76]

As if matters were not ticklish enough, it was reported that, "Most of the surrounding farms at Mourilyan are worked by Italians. The name of New Lombardy has been suggested, but the Italians are quite satisfied with the vigorous ring about, 'mourilyan.' A place by any other name would produce only the same density."[77]

Meanwhile, there was the hint that the "'problem" posed by Italian immigration might be self-correcting,

"Within 6 months Italian immigration in Australia will practically cease." That prediction was made today by the chief officer of the Italian liner Palermo, which arrived in Melbourne yesterday with 300 Italian migrants. "A new field of Italian emigration has been opened in northern France. Thousands of Italians have already settled there, and the influx is increasing every day. France has great need of manpower, and Italians are being warmly welcomed to the devastated areas where they are buying farms and building homes. With such a large field of expansion so near home, Italians will not come to Australia.... Within a few months the only Australia bound Italian migrants will be the near relations and friends of people now settled here.[78]

In 1927, industrial strife was limited to the South Johnstone, but attained serious dimensions there. At issue remained the desire to institute some kind of quota system guaranteeing a considerable share of the employment to Britishers. According to *The Worker*, growers in the area continued to prefer alien cutters who were then easily exploited and intimidated.[79] To make matters worse (from the British standpoint), more aliens were securing employment at the mills. The industrial magistrate refused to order that all men employed in the mill the previous year (in the main Britishers) be given preference.[80]

A general strike of millworkers and canecutters was called that quickly turned nasty. One protesting Anglo was killed by an unknown assailant—thought to be Sicilian. The growers tried to import Sicilian cutters from elsewhere, but these scabs were driven away by the strikers. Police raided the Silkwood area and confiscated many firearms from the strikers, and the growers were said to be arming themselves. Unlike previous actions, however, this was not a case of Britishers opposing aliens, but rather of "old chum" Britishers and aliens alike protecting their jobs against a continuing influx of newcomers. Indeed, most of the press ignored the ethnic composition of the confrontation, while *The Worker* noted that the Spaniards were loyal to the union and that the majority of strikers were Italians.[81]

The strike was resolved when it was agreed that, during the 1929 season, there would be 70 percent Britisher preference, up from 50 percent during 1928. It was stated that only 70 percent had been demanded in recognition of the ten foreign gangs that stood by the strikers. The twenty-four gangs that cut during the strike were Maltese and Sicilians. *The Worker* railed against these scabs, "whose general physiognomy betrayed their recent descent not indeed from the organ-grinder man himself but rather from the grotesque simian that shuffled on top of the organ."[82]

Both the 1928 and 1929 sign-ons proceeded without a hitch. In 1928, the 70 percent Britisher preference on the South Johnstone was not attained,[83] but it was by 1929. Its proponents were predicting that the district would soon be 100 percent Britisher.[84] At the same time, it was evident that the workforce of the Far North was becoming polarized along ethnic lines. In 1929, there were 1,083 Britishers and 1,380 foreigners in the gangs north of Townsville. Goondi, Mourilyan, Macknade, and Victoria districts employed aliens exclusively. Conversely, at Tully there were 287 Britishers and only 50 foreigners.[85]

The 1930 harvesting season proved to be pivotal. In retrospect, it initiated a period during which the pro-Britisher worker policy was pushed to its limits, tested, and eventually rejected. The year witnessed formation of a British Preference League agitating for the ultimate removal of all aliens from the workforce, organization of Italians in defense of their rights, and creation of a new Parliamentary Inquiry into the status of the sugar industry (with considerable focus upon the alien labor question).

At issue from the outset was the so-called sugar embargo that was up for its periodic five-year renewal. Legacy of the white bounty paid to growers who had converted from Kanaka to European labor at the turn of the century, the embargo was a tariff against imported sugar that provided domestic producers with a closed market. As such, it was the linchpin of the price structure of Australian-grown sugar and represented a subsidy by southern consumers of the northern growers. Given the world's depressed economic condition, there was considerable opposition in urban Australia to renewal of the embargo.[86]

Opponents of alien labor sought to turn this vulnerability to their advantage, arguing that the Australian citizenry was particularly unlikely to support a subsidy for an industry that was rapidly falling into the hands of foreigners.[87] The timing seemed right for reversing the alien presence within the ranks of the sugar workers.

In April, unemployed British workers in Tully met to protest the fact that the 75 percent Britisher quota promised for the district by 1930 had not been met. The group sent a deputation to the local canegrowers to register its protest.[88] At the same time, there were rumors afloat that Britisher cutters were about to be reintroduced in the Herbert—a district that had become virtually 100 percent alien in the makeup of its canecutters.[89]

In late April, a meeting was held in the Burdekin, attended by delegates of the Australian Workers' Union, the Australian Labour Party, the Brandon Progress Association, and the Returned Soldiers' League, to address the issues posed by the influx of Southern Europeans into the district. Unlike the Herbert, South Johnstone, and Cairns areas, the Burdekin remained largely Anglo in its makeup. However, in the post–World War I period, irrigation schemes had increased significantly in the land under cane cultivation, and this expansion had attracted Southern European cutters and aspiring growers into the district. Consequently, the elements were present for a backlash. The delegates to the April meeting formed a British Preference Committee with the immediate goal of ensuring 90 percent Britisher employment in the paddocks, continued Anglo control of farm ownership, and preferential patronage of Britisher-owned business establishments (a sign that aliens were branching out into other commercial activities such as pubs and stores).[90]

The continued efforts of the Burdekin's British Preference Committee met with a degree of local skepticism. In late May,

> A special general meeting of Kalamia and Pioneer growers was held in the Drill Hall, Ayr, on Sunday 18th of May, when there were about 76 farmers present.... The meeting was called at the request of the British Preference Committee for the purpose of considering the advisability of giving preference to the extent of 90% to British workers in the industry. Mr. Hoey stated the Secretary had supplied him with a list of farms owned by foreigners on the Burdekin and out of 300 only 43 were owned by men of foreign names, and after analyzing this 43, it was found that over 32

were naturalized British subjects. Taking the figure for Queensland there were 1077 farmers of foreign names, no doubt mostly naturalized British subjects out of 8000 growers, and the percentage of foreigners employed throughout the whole industry was 8%. Mr. Hoey drew attention to the fact 6300 workers were employed in the sugar mills in Queensland, all of whom were British, therefore it is apparent there is no need for the anxiety that some bodies would have us believe existed.[91]

The next month, the British Preference League lamented the decision of the Ayr Chamber of Commerce not to send a delegate to the BPL's meetings, questioning the Chamber's "manhood" in failing to protect the country. It added that there were now 120 farms in the Burdekin where "British workers need not apply."[92]

While the British Preference Committee of the Burdekin had difficulty in implementing its program locally, it was not without its admirers elsewhere. Like-minded persons in other districts formed chapters of the British Preference League. The immediate goal was to ensure that all new men signed to cane contracts be Anglos, henceforth new cane assignments be reserved for them, and that the residency requirement to qualify for naturalization be extended from five to ten years (at which time the applicant would also be tested for English-language fluency).[93]

As the 1930 sign-on proceeded, it was clear that the Britishers were making some inroads. The British Preference League was negotiating with farmers in both the Goondi and Mourilyan Mill districts to hire more Britishers, and federal Parliamentarian Martens from the Herbert cabled his sympathies to the League.[94] At Babinda, 76 percent of the cutters were Britishers, at South Johnstone, 50 percent, and at Ayr, 90 percent. In Tully, 250 farmers agreed to hire Britishers only after the 1929 first-preference men were placed.[95]

Meanwhile, in mid-June, there was a conference held in Brisbane with representatives of the Australian Sugar Producers' Association and the Queensland Canegrowers' Association at which an accord, referred to as the "Gentlemen's Agreement," specified that, north of Townsville, wherever the percentage of Britishers was below 75 percent it would be brought up to that figure—except at Macknade, Victoria, and Mourilyan where "a reasonable percentage will be employed."[96] South of Townsville, the figure was to be 90 percent British. Overall, the industry would aspire to 85 percent Britisher employment.[97]

The Australian Workers' Union was under considerable pressure from several sources at this juncture. The depressed economic conditions that were producing farm and other business failures and unemployment weakened the union's ability to use the threat of industrial strife in its negotiations with management. Its caution in this regard was beginning to produce a backlash within its own rank and file. Nor were the dissidents without organized spokesmen, since the Communist Party began to openly challenge AWU policy, tarnishing it with the sobriquet of being "the bosses' union."[98] The British Preference League's demand for 100-percent-Britisher employment ran counter to the AWU's longstanding position that a cutter must be unionist, whether Britisher or alien, but which then extended union protection to its foreign-born members.

The specter of non-renewal of the sugar embargo due to alien involvement in the industry, raised by the British Preference League, clearly caused concern. Government officials sought to reassure growers that the sugar embargo was not in serious jeopardy, while emphasizing to critics that the Britishers far outnumbered foreigners in the ranks of both the cutters and the growers.[99] The necessity for damage control, however, was underscored when a member of the British Parliament's House of Commons gave a speech in that body denouncing the privileged position in the Commonwealth market of Queensland sugar with respect to its counterpart from the British West Indies, a questionable state of affairs given alien control of the Australian industry. Queensland's agent general in London was quick to reply, noting that the Italian presence in North Queensland had been greatly exaggerated by its opponents.[100]

In the face of these developments, the aliens, and the Italians in particular, began to stiffen their backs. During the previous assaults on their status, the Italians exhibited extreme caution, preferring to let their consuls and sympathizers, such as Father Kelly of Ingham and Brisbane's Archbishop Duhig, state their case. No doubt there had been a belief in the Italian community that their position was precarious at best, and self-serving statements or actions could possibly exacerbate the situation. Whether it was a sense of desperation spawned by Great Depression conditions, collective frustration at being scapegoated yet again, or simply a question of the influence of certain charismatic individuals within the Italian community is uncertain. What is clear, however, is that, for the first time, there was a widespread mobilization among North Queensland Italians in defense of their rights.

This new propensity was spearheaded by the Danesi brothers of Innisfail, presaged in April of 1930 when they convened a meeting of their fellow countrymen to denounce the latest attack in *Smith's Weekly*.[101] The sensationalist newspaper had published another of its tasteless articles trumpeting, "Innisfail, Nightmare City of North Queensland, Town of Dreadful Dagoes Looks Calm but Foreign Scum Oozes from Its Highways...."[102]

L. Danesi, secretary of the Italian Progressive Club, denounced the newspaper. A petition was signed by several hundred angry Italians of the district and given to local Vice-Consul Luciano, who then telegraphed it to Consul-General Grossardi. It demanded that a formal protest be lodged with Commonwealth authorities, accusing the newspaper of defamation.[103]

Similarly, when the British Preference League first raised its head, Innisfail Italians were quick to respond. A protest meeting was called at the shire hall in early June that was attended by six hundred persons, some drawn from considerable distances. Chairman Carlo Danesi read four motions:

1. To enquire of the competent authorities of Queensland and of the Commonwealth if those Southern Europeans and more particularly the Italians who have been allowed to enter Australia shall have the same privileges of cutting cane as the British born, when farmers are willing to give them the contract?
2. [To determine] if those Southern Europeans and more particularly Italians who have gained the duties of Australian subjects by Naturalisation have thereby gained the same rights?
3. To ask the AWU if those Southern Europeans and more particularly the Italians who have joined this Union shall have the same right to work as British born members?
4. The Assembly decides to invite all Southern Europeans and more especially Italians to boycott all members of these nations who will not fall in with these requests.[104]

The question of the status of naturalized residents was a particularly thorny one. It seems clear that some Italians believed that, by undergoing naturalization, they would qualify as British, whereas the proponents of British Preference insisted that birthplace defined ethnicity. In the two-year period 1929–1930, 263 Italians in the Herbert district alone applied for naturalization. However, when the Gentlemen's Agreement failed to recognize their status for purposes of the British quota, many were disillusioned and threatened to return their citizenship certificates to the British governor general.[105]

Formation of the British Preference League evoked a prompt acerbic response from Italians outside of North Queensland as well. Italian Consul-General Grossardi was quick to denounce its purpose.[106] In Italy, Arnaldo Mussolini, Benito's brother, penned two articles in the newspaper *Il Popolo d'Italia* denouncing anti-Italian actions in the Queensland canefields and holding the League responsible. A concerned British embassy in Rome reported this development to Australian authorities.[107]

North Queensland Italians continued to organize as the cutting season progressed. At the Tully sign-on in late June of 1930, six or seven Italian farmers, following Grossardi's instructions, insisted upon hiring Italian cutters, prompting fears of trouble in the district.[108] In October, there was an appeal to all Italians to contribute to a fund to defend the sugar industry against attacks in southern Australia opposing renewal of the sugar embargo.[109]

By year's end, there was an incident at Tully that again exacerbated tensions between Italians and Britishers. About thirty Anglos attacked a house where some Italians were meeting, and a brawl ensued. There was a gunshot and sticks, bottles and razors were brandished. Two Anglos and two Italians were hospitalized.[110]

Debate over the sugar embargo increased tensions resulting from the Gentlemen's Agreement, and formation of the British Preference League together caused the Australian Parliament to commission one of its periodic inquiries into the state of the sugar industry. In places like Cairns and Innisfail, representatives of the League testified before the Commission. Mr. J. B. McCarthy of the Cairns branch stated his organization's view of Italians succinctly,

Italian newspapers are printed in the country; they have their own priests and minister of religion wherever possible and an attempt was made to start an Italian school but failed. Some Italians have been here for four years and have not been able to speak a word of English. The foreigner rarely mixes with the Britisher. When trouble starts they rush to their own Consul whether naturalized or not. This should show clearly that they recognize their own country only.[111]

During October and November of 1930, the Commission continued its hearings in several districts of North Queensland. At Cairns, Innisfail, and Ayr representatives of the British Preference League, which claimed a membership of one thousand,[112] gave lengthy testimony depicting the Italians as clannish and given to such unfair business practices as exploiting their fellow countrymen by paying them less than award rates, while offering exorbitant prices to gain control of farms. Unfortunately for the League, a number of influential Anglo-Australians refuted such accusations. This was especially surprising, since, by then, the country was deeply ensconced in the Great Depression.[113]

The strongest defense of the Italians was provided by Mario Melano, the acting Italian consul in Townsville. He noted that he was not an official spokesman for most North Queensland Italians, since, as naturalized citizens, they were British subjects. His government was currently actively engaged in discouraging emigration to Australia from Italy. Given that most Italians currently arriving to effect family reunions were women and children, and their numbers were now exceeded by departures of Italians from the region, "…the foreign problem in the sugar industry…has lost its importance; it will not be a question of trying to prevent new foreigners from coming in, but of trying to persuade them from walking out."[114]

Melano added that it was untrue that Italians had their own priests (there was only one of Italian descent in North Queensland), that he was unaware of any attempt to start an Italian school in the area, and that because of the many naturalizations of Italians, the workload in his office had declined to the point that steps were being taken to downgrade the consulate in Townsville to a vice-consulate.[115]

In light of the evidence, the Sugar Inquiry Committee concluded in its official report,

> ...the committee finds it difficult to accord the inclusion of so-called aliens into the sugar industry the significance sought to be placed upon it by some witnesses. Even so, it would appear impossible to recommend any procedure to delimit such penetration which under all the circumstances, would be ethical in conception, and equitable and practicable in enforcement. Indeed, the ultimate view in respect of the "alien" element engaged as sugar-canegrowers may well be that their acquirement of a real interest in land enhances rather than detracts from the value of such naturalized citizens as the component units of strategic outposts in the north....
>
> With regard to the number employed as field hands, it would seem that a proportion of the number of persons of foreign birth so employed would be directly attributable to the existence of a high percentage of compatriot farmers who would not unnaturally be willing to employ them, and the same remark applies to cane-cutters....; if they can secure work...from their farming compatriots, and from some Australian farmers, it is difficult to see how they can be denied.[116]

There were even those who raised their voices against the exploitation of Italian farm purchasers. The Cairns member of the Queensland Parliament, Mr. O'Keefe, called for government intervention. He denounced those farmers in his and nearby districts who were selling out to desperate Italians at ridiculous prices. In his words,

> I do not mind these farmers making a profit, but I think the Govt should protect individuals, whether they be foreigners or otherwise, who do not receive value for the consideration agreed on.... If it is not robbery, it is next door to it. At the beginning of the year a sugar farm at Binda was sold for £35,000, the purchaser being a foreigner. I notice the Premier laughing. Probably when he was in Cairns trying to win the Cairns seat he heard the story about the terms of sale. The agent responsible for selling the farm borrowed £2000 at 6% from the farmer. The agent in turn lent

that money to the Italian purchaser at 12% interest. The Italian, in turn, paid that £2000 to its original owner as a deposit on the farm. What chance has that Italian of making "a go" of that sugar farm? It is up to the govt to legislate against such transactions. It is a shame to permit these foreigners to be taken down.[117]

In January of 1931, the British Preference League branch in Innisfail demanded that 90 percent of the cutters in the coming season be Britisher.[118] The League also threatened to oppose the sugar embargo unless the 90 percent quota be adopted throughout North Queensland, with 100 percent Britisher employment the goal within three years.[119] Aliens clearly had good cause for worry regarding their prospects within the sugar industry, and, in February, Herbert district Italians formed *L'Associazione dei Produttori Italiani nell'Industria dello Zucchero* (The Association of Italian Producers in the Sugar Industry).

By June, the organization had a total of 1,045 members distributed throughout North Queensland, but concentrated primarily in Ingham, Innisfail, Babinda, and Tully.[120] *L'Associazone* was conceived as a mutual-aid society, and planned to defend the interests of both Italian farmers and workers while seeking an amiable accommodation with the British in the interest of Australian national harmony and prosperity.[121]

The 1931 season was entirely devoid of labor friction.[122] This was so despite the fact that British penetration was apparent in districts such as the Herbert, albeit not as great as that espoused by the British Preference League. It transpired despite the government's decision to increase the workweek to 48 hours for field hands and millworkers, and 44 hours for canecutters, thereby reducing the number of employees in the industry.[123] In "normal" times such a measure would have been debated exhaustively by the AWU, but Great Depression conditions clearly continued to make all parties cautious.

In 1932, the British Preference dispute flared up mainly in the Burdekin, focused in particular upon Kalamia Mill. It was there that the millworkers voted not to process cane until the goal of employing 86 percent Anglo canecutters was met. Several growers, including many foreigners, boycotted the sign-on, declaring that they were cutting their own cane. While it is true that many cut themselves, clearly, foreigner canecutters were also engaged surreptitiously. The dispute carried over into the 1933 season. That year, the sign-ons at Pioneer and Inkerman Mills went smoothly, whereas the standoff continued at Kalamia Mill. The whole matter was being adjudicated in the courts, prompting some farmers to argue that the idling of Kalamia Mill was costing the district thousands of pounds, while urging that the Mill crush cane while awaiting the court's decision regarding the "Gentleman's Agreement."[124]

In 1933, the focus of industrial relations shifted temporarily from British Preference *per se* to cane-cutter demands over pay and procedures in light of a deadly threat to the health of the men posed by Weil's disease. The first occurrences were in Ingham during the latter part of the 1933 season. The symptoms included high fever, jaundice, the disintegration of internal organs, and sometimes death. By October of 1934, there had been 134 cases recorded in Ingham resulting in at least seven fatalities. Ninety percent of the victims were canecutters, with the remainder being farmers closely associated with work in the paddocks. Given the ethnic makeup of Ingham's sugar industry, it was essentially an "Italian disease."

It was determined that the rat population was the carrier of the malady, transmitted to the soil through urination where the moist conditions then favored the growth of the bacteria. The disease entered its victim through skin abrasions that were the common lot of the canecutters. Medical authorities urged the men to replace their customary open sand shoes, shorts, and short-sleeved shirts with more protective footwear and clothing. At the same time, it was felt that burning the cane prior to harvesting might be a means of sterilizing the soil.[125]

By late August of 1934, strike meetings of canecutters were held in Ingham and Halifax. The Ingham gathering (attended by two hundred men) was unsanctioned by the AWU but was attended by Communist organizers. It was resolved to strike immediately over the demand that all cane be burned before cutting, and that the men be paid the green-cane rate for harvesting it (traditionally, if a paddock was accidentally burned by the cutters, as happened, they received a discounted rate in recognition that a scorched field was easier to clear).

The wildcat strike in Ingham was resolved rather quickly when the farmers agreed to pay the green-cane rate,[126] and, in return, were partially compensated for the difference by the Canegrowers' Association. The problem quickly transcended the Ingham area, however, since, by late September, cases of Weil's disease were reported from as far north as Innisfail.[127] A month later, Queensland's director of health and medical services declared the whole of the North Queensland coast to be affected.[128] The premier announced that Weil's disease would henceforth be included on the industrial diseases schedule, thereby making its victims eligible for workman's compensation.[129]

The spread of Weil's disease to Innisfail and other northern districts exacerbated the standoff between the union and its dissidents, providing the latter with a *cause célèbre*. In October of 1934, there were wildcat strikes at Innisfail and Goondi during which a "no-confidence" motion in the AWU was proposed. The Goondi meeting, attended by six hundred cutters who were addressed in both English and Italian, passed the censure of the AWU along with a call to form an independent Sugar Workers' Union.[130] Meanwhile, the proponents of British Preference were gleeful, since, quite coincidentally, the occurrence of Weil's disease had been restricted to the two districts that were the bastions of the Italian cutter (the Herbert and the South Johnstone). While the confrontation leading to industrial strife in the two districts was largely between Italian cutters and Italian farmers, the British Preference movement saw it as an opportunity to replace the Italian cutters with Britishers during the 1935 season.[131]

In 1935, a major confrontation erupted in the Italian stronghold of Innisfail between the AWU and the so-called Rank-and-File Movement. The latter took a strong stand against displacing any man with previous experience, alien or Britisher, in the pending sign-on.[132] Serious industrial strife spread throughout several districts further to the north. When cutters in the Mourilyan area demanded that the cane be burned, the Queensland Canegrowers' Council and the AWU objected. The Arbitration Court found that there was insufficient evidence of Weil's disease in the district and refused to issue a burn order.[133] There were then wildcat strikes at Innisfail, Goondi, Mourilyan, Tully, and Hambledon—opposed by the AWU.[134] Conversely, workers at Babinda, South Johnstone, and the Burdekin refused to join in.[135]

North Queensland seemed poised on the brink of economic catastrophe or even unbridled violence. The confrontation clearly transcended the ostensible health issue. Rather, on the one hand, it reflected a fundamental power struggle between the AWU moderate unionists and the Communists for control of the workers' movement, while, on the other, it shook to its very foundation the longstanding relationship between labor and management. Once it was no longer clear that the AWU could control its membership, the farmers and their associations adopted a siege mentality, calling for police reinforcements and forming a strike-compensation fund.[136]

The strikes persisted for several weeks, but, by mid-September, the Rank-and-File rebellion was over. The farmers had demonstrated a willingness to let the cane go unharvested (it would continue to grow for the following season), content to draw some compensation from the Queensland Sugar Growers' Council's strike-damage fund. Short-term economic hardship was deemed preferable to setting a precedent by acceding to the demands of non-sanctioned (by the AWU) strikers.

Eventually, the issue of Weil's disease was largely eclipsed by improved health measures, development of an effective serum, a rat-control program, drier weather, and the institution of cane-burning as a regular practice throughout North Queensland. For present purposes, however, the events of 1934–1935 are of interest, since they represent the high watermark in Italian organizational activity and labor activism. It is also interesting that neither Basques nor non-Basque Spaniards were involved in any kind of leadership role, despite the fact that they were also "Southern Europeans." The strikes were not exclusively ethnic in character, but, given the makeup of the canecutter labor force in the most affected districts, Italians provided the backbone of the Rank and File Movement. Henceforth, the alien worker could no longer be taken for granted by either the AWU[137] or management—Italian or otherwise. The strikes over Weil's disease, then, provided a context for Southern European labor to express discontent with the status quo, while testing its ability to change it.

So, in retrospect, it is clear that, by the mid-1930s, the British Preference movement had achieved a qualified victory. In the five years from the 1930 through the 1934 sign-ons the number of British cutters in the industry had increased by 47 percent, while the alien cutters grew by only four percent. 747 new cutter jobs had been added over the period, of which 632 went to Britishers. Nevertheless, while British Preference had eventually co-opted most of the new positions, it had not actually eroded the absolute number of alien cutters.[138] Aliens continued to predominate in certain districts. At the 1933 sign-on in the Herbert, of the 864 men hired (plus one Finnish gang of unspecified numbers), 737 were Italian, 47 were Finns, 23 were Spaniards (including Basques by this time), and 14 were Yugoslavs. A scant 43, or 5 percent of the total, were Britishers.[139]

New Zealand journalist F. E. Baume visited North Queensland at this time to research his novel *Burnt Sugar*.[140] It is the bildungsroman of an Italo-Italian, Mario Zobella, son of a canefarmer in the fictional town of Eulaville (likely Innisfail). It had an International Hotel, which, like its rival Cosmoplitan Hotel, catered to the areas of many non-Anglo ethnic groups.

The novel begins with an Anglo cutter from Mackay, Blue Martin, entering the Zobella farm after being refused work by Domenico Maggion for being a "drunken loafer." Martin had been turned away at four other farms as well:

> Down past George Walker's; on the winding road by Pietro Garrini's gate and Giuseppe Prenza's mail-box he walked, and a black hate surged over him. At Primo Zobella's tidy trellis-work gate, announcing the path through the cane to the homestead Wallarobba, Martin saw young Mario Zobella, aged nine, Primo's son.
>
> In his stride the cane-cutter reached the child. Mario looked up and smiled.
>
> "What's your name?" asked Martin.
>
> "Mario Zobella, mister."
>
> Something cracked behind Martin's ear. He yelled:
>
> "You dirty little dago! Won't give a decent Australian a job, eh?"....
>
> "I'll teach you dagoes!" he shouted.
>
> He kicked Mario in the ribs. The little boy's eyes opened wide with amazement. Then, with the searing pain of two broken ribs rushing him into unconsciousness, they closed.[141]

Until then, the Zobellas had employed a mixed gang that included one veteran Anglo cutter. Mario's mother, Marta, dismissed the man and vowed to only use Italians henceforth. Primo, an alcoholic, died soon thereafter in an accident. Mario's now widowed mother fell under the spell of a local Italian physician, Dr. Marchesini, who was a Fascist that lauded Mussolini and everything Italian while denigrating Australia.

Marta vowed to raise her only child to be a proper Italian and forbade him to use English with her. Mario gradually rebelled, finding the restrictions to be suffocating. He aspired to becoming an Australian. His best friend was Charlie Yip Wong, son of a Chinese importer married to a white Australian woman. He even fancied himself in love with Cora, Charlie's sister. Mario's hero was his schoolteacher, Albert Green, who was a Marxist humanist—the Communist anathema to Dr. Marchesini.

Mario snuck out of his house to attend Charlie's twenty-first birthday dance, after having been forbidden to do so by his mother. Charlie's Chinese family had contracted an Italian band for the event. But then Marta appeared at the ball, horsewhip in hand, and beat Mario publicly. She then marched out of the hall and committed suicide by wading into the nearby crocodile-infested river.

The now orphaned Mario was more anti-Italian than ever. He was not quite of age, so a local pharmacist, Andrew Talbot, became the trustee of his cane farm. Twenty-year-old Mario worked it and he decided to hire good cutters irrespective of their nationality (rather than just Italian ones).

Meanwhile, the waterside workers of the nearby port went on strike and refused to load sugar on the three vessels that awaited it. The strike was legal and the farmers had no legitimate gripe, given that the mill had already paid them for their sugar. However, Dr. Marchesini and Ragnelli, the president of the local Fascist club, announced that they were going to lead their primarily Italian canefarmer membership to the docks to load the sugar themselves. This was an illegal act, opposed even by the Italian consul in the Far North. Both the consul and Mario joined the citizens who were deputized by the local police constabulary to confront the strikebreakers. The authorities prevailed, but the main union organizer was killed. The confrontation triggered days of violence in which Britishers vandalized Italian property and vice versa. Mario's home was burned to the ground and his sugar set afire (hence the novel's title).

Mario had a head for figures, and on Talbot's advice, he completed a correspondence course in accounting. The young man aspired to getting out of sugar-growing and dreamed of becoming a proper Australian businessman, eventually residing in Sydney. It was now that Charlie's father, Wong Yip, wrote to his friend, the Jewish shopkeeper Harris Mendes in the fictional interior Queensland town of Harbutt (likely inspired by Hughenden), recommending Mario for employment. The offer was forthcoming, and on his way to the thoroughly Anglo place, Mario changed his identity to Mark Zobel. He spent five years in Harbutt, amassing capital and leading a proper Anglo life. After Mendes died, Mark moved to Sydney where he repeated his success, carved a niche within Sydney high society, married an Aussie bride, and fathered an Aussie son.

When his boy was three, Mark took a business trip to Brisbane. He was exhausted and fighting influenza. He decided that he needed a break—his first real vacation since moving to Sydney. It was at this point, much to his own confusion and chagrin, that he was drawn to Eulaville and his roots. The Far North was awash in a killer cyclone with the rivers on the rise, but the feverish young man was bent on heading north. He managed to catch the last train before rail service was interdicted and made it "home." Mario Zobella was back and driven to visit the site of his homestead, even though his house no longer existed. He traveled alone into the teeth of the storm and was drowned by the rising waters of the river that bordered the property.

At one point in the novel, Andrew Talbot is contemplating the passersby on the main street of Eulaville and notes that:

> Two Dutchmen went past, talking gutterally. Italian children played in the gutter. A Chinese taxi-driver swung past in an elaborate crimson-painted car; a Jugoslavian woman walked stolidly to the Street of the Little Houses [red-light district]. A khaki-clad [Anglo] policeman ambled past; two Maltese women talked their explosive Levantine. A mountainously fat Greek waddled, wet-faced, towards an hotel. Over the Consulate the Italian flag fluttered and the coat of arms stood in front of the doorway. "Festivita Importanti." There were always important festivals on which to fly the flag. A pock-marked Russian sat in the gutter and held his reeling head in his hands. Rain came out of a clear sky and drenched everyone. And in the quiet after the patter of the

drops half a dozen languages raised their tones to the Australian sky while a Chinese and Scotsman regarded them.[142]

Interestingly, for our purposes, an author as sensitive as was Baume to the ethnic makeup of the Far North in the early 1930s makes no mention anywhere in his book of the obviously low-profile Spaniards—let alone the Catalans and Basques.

We have noted that, by World War I, there was discernible concern in some North Queensland circles that aliens, and particularly Southern Europeans, were displacing Anglo-Australians on the sugar properties. However, the situation was considerably more complicated than a simple substitution of alien farmers for British ones. Rather, between 1918 and 1926, the sugar acreage of Queensland had increased from 160,534 to 266,519 acres. Improved cultivation techniques had increased the tonnage from 1,674,829 in 1918 to 3,548,421 in 1927, and its sugar content was generally higher.[143] Thus, the growth profile of the industry was in part accommodating the increased percentage of alien growers without necessarily reducing Anglo participation in absolute terms. For example, in Hinchinbrook Shire the numbers of Italian canefarmers more than tripled from 122 in 1921 to over 400 by 1930.[144] During the same period, however, the number of non-Italian farmers also increased, albeit more modestly, from 199 to 275.[145] L. D. Henderson notes that much of the Italian increase involved the parceling of existing larger farms into smaller units.[146] At the same time, Italian land speculation pioneered felling of the bush in the Long Pocket area and 12,000 acres along the Stone River.[147]

By May of 1931, pro-British elements in North Queensland were protesting against amendments effected by the Central Cane Prices Board in allocating cane assignments. It was alleged that many aliens had received them, and that the industry had become "foreignized" further. Some Anglo farmers in the Tully area telegraphed Queensland's premier, demanding that no more assignments be made to aliens until their cases were reviewed. They contended that some Anglos continued to hold the cane assignments in their own names while leasing their land to foreigners. Both the Returned Soldiers' and British Preference Leagues denounced the practice as disguised penetration of the industry. The

Queensland authorities in Brisbane, however, refused to regard the practice as illegal.[148]

While the issue of alien ownership of freeholds and leases occasionally surfaced in the press, it was actually the object of a behind-the-scene struggle that, left unchecked, threatened to disrupt Great Britain's and Australia's relations with Italy. In September of 1929, the premier of Queensland informed the British governor general of Queensland (Great Britain's highest official in the state) that the royal Italian consul had presented a formal protest regarding certain legal constraints on Italians in Queensland with respect to landholding. At risk was the 1883 Treaty of Commerce and Navigation between Great Britain and Italy.[149] Among the terms of the agreement was the guarantee that,

> The subjects of each of the contracting parties in the dominions and possessions of the other shall be at full liberty to exercise civil rights, and therefore to acquire, possess, and dispose of every description of property, movable and immovable. They may acquire and transmit the same to others, whether by purchase, sale, donation, exchange, marriage, testament, succession *ab intestato*, and in any other manner, under the same conditions as national subjects.[150]

At specific issue was a Queensland law stipulating that the leases to aliens could not be of more than twenty-one-years' duration.[151]

Premier Moore took no immediate action. However, the following year he was forced to respond to a request by the British Preference League that there be an inquiry into the sale and leasing of cane lands to Italians. The premier did not mince words when stating,

> The Government has no power to interfere as between vendor and purchaser or lessor and lessee in the case of sale or lease of sugar farms, where any such sale or lease does not contravene a State or Federal law. Further, neither the State nor the Federal Government has the power to pass any law that would discriminate against Italians in regard to such matters, as there is an existing treaty, between the British and Italian Governments that would not permit of any such action being taken.[152]

There were no further developments regarding the land-tenure matter until 1933, when Premier Moore's successor, Premier Forgan Smith, was again confronted with it. In informing the British governor in Queensland of correspondence between himself and the Italian royal consul-general in Sydney, he noted that any attempt to provide immunity to Italians from the provisions of The Leases of Aliens Restrictions Act of 1912 would provoke much hostility in North Queensland. The premier argued that, at present, the Italians who became naturalized did so in order to qualify for freeholds. If, by open-ended leasing, they could achieve the same goal of control of land, the incentive to become citizens (and, by inference, assimilated) would be removed.[153]

In 1934, the Italian ambassador to Great Britain contacted the British Foreign Office, urging that the British government convince Brisbane to amend its lease law to exempt Italian nationals from restrictions on aliens in accordance with the provisions of the 1883 treaty (acceded to officially by Queensland in 1884).[154] Premier Forgan Smith replied that Queensland's laws regarding freeholds and land leases actually antedated the 1883 treaty. He observed that, until quite recently, no one had ever questioned their validity. He further made the somewhat forced argument that non-naturalized Italians has been permitted to become *de facto* owners of freeholds by finding a British subject willing to act as trustee (but subject to the orders of the Italian freeholder). In this roundabout fashion, Italians were able to secure for themselves the rights guaranteed under the treaty.

Changing tack, Forgan Smith concluded by stating that any attempt to visibly alter Queensland freehold and land-lease law to accommodate Italians would be inflammatory and worsen Italian-British relations in the North. He also warned,

> In the Herbert and Johnstone River Districts of North Queensland, Italian Nationals are in the majority, and naturally give preference of employment to their compatriots. If, therefore, such people are permitted to take up land on equal terms with British subjects, there is no doubt that within a short period of time—probably within the next twenty years—North Queensland will be in danger of becoming in fact an Italian Colony secured by means of peaceful penetration.[155]

In June of 1935, the British Foreign Office informed its embassy in Rome that, under the trustee system, Italian nationals had access to freeholds and that Italian leaseholders enjoyed full (if unspecified) protection in actual practice, so there was no need for amended legislation on Queensland's part.[156] In late 1935, Senator Pearce, Australian minister of external affairs, declared that the Queensland Aliens Act of 1861, promulgated prior to the 1883 treaty between Great Britain and Italy, precluded Queensland giving full force to the reciprocal rights with regard to the land-tenure provisions of the latter. However, the trustee system made the impact of the Aliens Act upon Queensland Italians negligible.[157]

Archbishop Duhig quickly denounced the statement, noting that it was common knowledge that Italians were not being accorded their just quota of cane-cutting jobs and full property rights as guaranteed by the treaty.[158] The prelate's contention evoked a retort regarding the employment issue from Messrs. Hives (of the Sugar Producers' Association) and Doherty (of the Queensland Canegrowers' Council). They argued that the Gentlemen's Agreement had resolved a thorny issue for the Queensland and Commonwealth governments, brought order to the industry, and was supported by Italian and British growers alike.[159]

At this juncture, the debate simply ran out of steam. Possibly the effects of the Great Depression made some of the issues academic, as both Italian and Anglo property owners suffered financial reversals. Henderson, for example, documents the decline in Italian farm ownership in the Herbert in the early 1930s.[160] Between 1932 and 1938, there were twenty-four bankruptcies filed by Italians in the Hinchinbrook Shire, most of them farmers.[161]

In the decade of the 1930s, there was another discernible trend in the relationship between Italians and the land. By the late 1920s, the sugar-peak system was fully instituted, thereby placing an absolute limit on the amount of acreage that could be planted to the crop. This, combined with depressed prices and the fear that the British Preference movement might limit opportunities in sugar growing for aliens, prompted at least some Italians to look for alternatives. Some experimented with vegetable farming.[162] Italians were among the first to attempt tobacco growing in Hinchinbrook Shire, and many relocated to Mareeba in the Atherton Tablelands to grow that crop.[163] Similarly, by the 1930s, some Italians from North Queensland had resettled in the Griffith area of New South Wales where they engaged in fruit horticulture.[164]

In these regards, Spaniards would follow the Italian lead. They, too, grew orchards and vegetables in the South, and tobacco in the Atherton Tablelands. There is also evidence that they were attracted by the new copper veins discovered in Queensland's former gold districts. There was a growing Spanish presence in Mount Morgan and Mount Cuthbert by 1941, and Mason notes that, "significant numbers of Basques worked as 'copper gougers' in Malbon."[165]

The Black Shirt and the Black Hand—The combination of a dramatic increase of North Queensland's Southern European population in the 1920s, the anti-immigration debates in the aftermath of the Ferry Commission report, the emergence of the British Preference movement, and the effects of the Great Depression was a potent mix easily capable by itself of fueling and fanning anti-alien sentiments. There were, however, two additional factors that created genuine fear and loathing of Italians among their detractors and ambivalence among their defenders. Reference is to the growing confrontation between Italian Fascists and their compatriot foes, on the one hand, and the emergence of an alleged Italian ethnic crime wave, on the other.

During the 1920s, Italian Fascism was a legitimized political movement. Mussolini's successes antedated those of Hitler and did not initially evoke the specter of global conflict. Rather, *Il Duce* had many admirers both within and outside Italy as he strutted on the world stage. According to his supporters, he brought a degree of discipline to a notoriously undisciplined people and garnered at least some of the crumbs from the banquet at which Europe's powers divided among themselves jurisdiction over most of the non-Western world. He had negotiated the historic Concordat with the Vatican whereby the Italian state and the Catholic Church ended the feud that had raged between them since 1870. In short, Mussolini had restored to Italy a measure of national pride and international respect, while exorcizing her of deep-seated civil-religious strife.

The question of greatest relevance to the current study is how Italian Fascism was viewed in the emigrant diaspora. There is no simple answer as the issues were complex. Mussolini's rise to power in Italy was ultimately at the expense of the political left (despite his early personal history as a Socialist). The brutal tactics of the Fascists caused many leftists to go into exile. The established diasporas of Italians in North America, southern South America, and Oceania provided a ready avenue of escape. Therefore, many of Mussolini's bitterest opponents ended up abroad in the preexisting overseas Italian collectivities.

At the same time, a large segment of the established immigrants in such host societies were either apolitical or politically conservative (particularly if they owned land, a business, or were professionals). Then, too, Mussolini's drive for national glory translated into a potential source of ethnic pride for Italians of the emigrant diasporas—a penumbra effect, as it were. Accustomed to the barbs of their racist detractors, who denounced Italians at every turn, it would have been surprising had not most Italians everywhere cheered on *Il Duce*—at least initially. In the 1920s and early 1930s, few Italians anywhere saw the impending tragic future that lay ahead as Fascism played out its internal logic. While the foregoing statements are applicable in a general sense to all of the Italian diasporas, it is equally true that the particulars differed from one to another. It is to such refinement for the Australian case that we now turn.

It is impossible to understand fully the Australian response to Italian Fascism without considering, as well, the attitudes toward its chief foil—Bolshevism. By the early teens, there were at least some Italian Bolshevists in Australia.[166] In 1918, when confronted by industrial strife, a Colonial Sugar Refining official informed his headquarters that strike leader O'Malley had twenty "cunning agitators," mainly Russians and Spaniards with IWW (International Workers of the World) tendencies. They were vandalizing tramways and bridges and were said to possess dynamite.[167] By 1925, the *Melbourne Age* editorialized that Australia should be on guard since "Mussolini and his Fascists have made things uncomfortable for the Communists who blighted the land, and it is not improbable that some of them have carried their criminal instincts over the seas."[168]

It seems that, as early as 1925, both Pro- and Anti-Fascist Italians were settling in Queensland.[169] The presence of the former was descried and denounced by *The Worker*.[170]

In late 1926, there was an "Italian celebration," in Melbourne,

With great enthusiasm the members of the Italian Fascismo and the Italian community in Melbourne celebrated the anniversary of the armistice berween Italy and Austria on Nov 3, 1918 and the birth of the Fascismo movement on Oct 28, 1922, as the guests of the Italian Consul General (Commendatore Grossardi).

Fifty black Fascists figured in the picturesque ceremony at Hawthorn, where the Fascismo flag, after consecration, was handed over as the gift of Donna Grossardi to the Fascists.

A remarkable scene was that in which Count di San Marzano, recently appointed Consul for Italy in Brisbane, and who, like the Consul General wore the black shirt of the order, called upon the Fascists present to kneel during one minute's silence in commemoration of the Italian dead in the Great War and of the 3000 Fascists who perished after the war in conflicts against Bolshevism and Communism. Count Marzano, who left Rome only six weeks ago, brought a personal message of greeting from Mussolini.[171]

In 1927, the *Italian Bulletin in Australia* instituted a regular section called "*I Fasci in Australia*" that carried news of the different Fascist cells throughout Oceania. *Fasci* were functioning in Melbourne, Sydney, Adelaide, Geraldton, and Wellington (New Zealand).

In 1928, *The Worker* noted that the Italian consuls in Australia were under orders from Rome to ensure that the loyalties of Italian emigrants remained directed toward Italy.[172] Labour had considerable grounds for concern, given that the *Italo-Australian* had recently published an article regarding Australia entitled "A Land of Strikes," in which it was noted that the Fascist government in Italy had resolved that problem by making such industrial actions illegal.[173] In 1929, the Australian Workers' Union supported formation of the League of Australian Friends of Italian Freedom. Its object was to encourage political freedom in Italy, while countering Fascist propaganda in Australia.[174]

In 1929, Mr. Bruce was asked pointedly in the Commonwealth Parliament if the Italian Fascists were not requiring members in Australia to wear party badges, send their children to Italian schools, and register with a *fascio*? The prime minister replied that no one would qualify for naturalization without first renouncing former allegiances, and that non-English-language schooling was actively discouraged in

Australia.[175] Meanwhile, *Smith's Weekly* stated that Italy's Fascists had declared that persons of Italian descent remained Italian citizens for up to seven generations no matter where they were residing. Given Italian penetration of North Queensland, the sugar bounty could be regarded potentially an Australian subsidy of the Mussolini government.[176] Also of concern was the fact that Italian vice-consuls in Australia were said to be requiring those Italians petitioning to bring out their spouses and children to join the Overseas Fascist Party as a precondition for processing the necessary paperwork.[177]

Fascism was not simply an ethnic issue, and despite occasional statements of concern by politicians and the press, there were Fascist sympathizers in the wider Australian public. In Europe, the movement had started with disgruntled war veterans and many Australian ex-servicemen were attracted to some of its tenets. Particularly appealing was the Fascist emphasis upon discipline and patriotism for the youth.[178] In 1931, a group called The New Guard, which advocated formation in Australia of a corporate state modelled along Fascist lines, emerged in New South Wales. The movement was worrisome to its opponents (particularly Labourites).[179]

A potent force favoring Fascist Italy was the Catholic Church. Gurdon opines that its Australian hierarchy was more strident in its support of Mussolini than the Vatican itself.[180] The most prominent spokesman in Queensland for the Fascist cause was Brisbane's Archbishop Duhig. Educated in Italy, the prelate was a lifelong indomitable Italophile,[181] a love that carried over to *Il Duce*. In 1927, Duhig described Mussolini as a "great Christian knight."[182] That same year he traveled to Italy where he discussed the problem of Italian immigration in Australia with the dictator himself. Duhig was particularly euphoric over the Concordat of 1929.[183]

The archbishop's enthusiasm notwithstanding, Fascism met with considerable resistance among Queensland's Italians. The struggle between Fascists and their foes in North Queensland was far from peaceful or benign. As early as 1922, the Italian Club in Babinda had founded a relief fund to help workers and their families that had suffered under Fascism.[184] By 1925, there is a specific reference to Fascist activity amongst the Italians of North Queensland, but the proponents were clearly outnumbered by their adversaries. Thus, when a large number of Italians converged on Ingham and Halifax on a Saturday night there was political trouble,

> Late in the afternoon a political argument occurred in Ingham and it is said one man was having Facisti [sic] tendencies, was chased down the street and only escaped a severe handling by bolting through a boardinghouse. Another brawl occurred immediately afterwards, and the police were obliged to arrest four of the principals who were taking a leading part. At Halifax the same night a similar disturbance occurred, when an Italian, supposed to be a member of the Facisti [sic], was ordered to drink a bottle of castor oil, for the misdeeds, it is stated, of his party. On refusing, he received many punches, and was being severely handled when a policeman took matters in hand, and, by a little tact, eventually succeeded in quietening the mob.[185]

It seems clear that the Fascists were drawn mainly from the farmers' ranks, though few appreciated the full implications and future consequences of their adherence to the movement.[186] Prominent members of the Italian and non-Italian community were prone to welcome the Italian vice-consuls into their midst. In October of 1928, Count di San Marzano was feted in Ingham at the Italian-owned Noorla Hotel, welcomed formally by Dr. Piscitelli, and toasted by the shire chairman and police magistrate. The latter praised Mussolini in his speech. Count di San Marzano thanked the assemblage and singled out Father Kelly for creating understanding between local Italians and Britishers.[187]

The following April, there was a mass held at St. Patrick's in Ingham to commemorate signing of the Concordat between Italy and the Vatican. Count di San Marzano attended, and, amid considerable lauding of *Il Duce*, announced formation of a group of Italian *Ex-Combattenti* (War Veterans) in Ingham. Such organizations were the backbone of the Fascist movement in Italy.[188]

In 1929, a *fascio* was established in Innisfail. At the inauguration ceremony, the Italian Vice-Consul Luciano noted, "Italians in this district were Facists [sic], or at least sympathisers with Facist [sic] rule."[189] This provoked a response from the British segment of the population, which placed placards throughout the town declaring, "The Italian Consul is in Innisfail to organize Fascism. We don't want Fascism here, Italian workers—so says the British worker."[190]

In the Herbert, the *Comitato Anti-Fascista dell'Herbert River* (The Anti-Fascist Committee of the Herbert River) had been founded.[191] In late 1929, four Fascists were beaten in Ingham, and, in early 1930, Count di San Marzano was assaulted in the town and his badge stripped from his uniform. According to Cresciani, "This same Consul was repeatedly beaten and spat upon during his visits at Ingham, Banda and Cairns, and was eventually and humiliatingly driven to accept police protection when he went to Innisfail."[192]

The key figure among the Anti-Fascist group in the Herbert was an anarchist named Frank Carmagnola. He had escaped from Italy in 1922 and settled as a canecutter in North Queensland. He later moved to Sydney and Melbourne, where he founded an Anti-Fascist newspaper, *La Riscossa*. Another important Anti-Fascist was Mario Cazzulino, a Socialist. Cazzulino and Carmagnola had traveled to Australia on the same vessel along with two or three other Anti-Fascists, all escaping Italy in fear for their lives.[193]

By 1930, the Anti-Fascist movement in Melbourne experienced a schism. Frank Carmagnola resettled in the Ingham area where he continued to publish *La Riscossa* in reduced format.[194] When Anti-Fascists of the Herbert district organized a ball in December of 1931 in the Halifax Masonic Hall, followed by another Anti-Fascist meeting in the *Club Italiano* of Ingham attended by hundreds, *La Riscossa* noted triumphantly, "…in this district with pride we can affirm that no Italian has the courage to declare himself openly a fascist."[195]

Meanwhile, the newspaper regularly published warnings to Queensland Italians to boycott Fascist sympathizers and business establishments—which it named.[196]

In late 1931, there was an incident that epitomized the confrontation between the opposing camps in North Queensland. On December 26, Italian Vice-Consul Mario Melano of Townsville traveled to Ingham on a visit. Twice before, his attempt to organize a local *fascio* failed, and he left town after being insulted and spat upon. While Melano now claimed to be on a personal visit, and with no intention of engaging in politics, he did wear his black shirt and party badge. Anti-Fascists confronted him outside the Noorla Hotel, led by Carmagnola and Tom Saviane. The group became quite agitated in denouncing Mussolini and accused the vice-consul of spying on them in order to send back information on Anti-Fascists abroad so that Italian authorities could retaliate against their family members still in Italy. Melano received a blow that required him to seek medical attention. Later that evening, he reappeared with some supporters and they were put to flight by about fifty Anti-Fascists. The police arrested Carmagnola and another man. The situation was tense, as it was rumored that the Anti-Fascists planned to storm the jail to release the prisoners.[197]

The Anti-Fascists immediately organized a defense committee to raise funds for the legal expenses of the two defendants.[198] Their trial was held in Townsville in February and they were acquitted. The proceedings provided Carmagnola with a platform for his virulent Anti-Fascism and received extensive coverage in the wider press.[199] A letter from Anti-Fascists, signed "The Outpost," was sent to the *Herbert River Express* warning Melano and Piero Lalli of Ingham to cease their Fascist activities.[200]

About this time, however, the Anti-Fascists in Australia suffered severe reversals. In part this was signaled by the Commonwealth authorities' suppression of *La Riscossa*.[201] Carmagnola himself came under close police scrutiny and was branded in one report, "…a cause of trouble and agitation wherever he goes."[202] There was an unsuccessful attempt to strip him of his Australian citizenship and deport him to Italy, a plan supported by the Fascists as well as some employers' groups in Australia.

If the Anti-Fascists were no longer the same force to be reckoned with, they still possessed a capacity to harass their opponents. In 1934, when the Italian warship *Armando Diaz* visited Cairns, the Anti-Fascists printed leaflets encouraging the crew to jump ship. One man did so and was hidden by the Anti-Fascist underground.[203] Also, during the 1934 Weil's disease strike in the Herbert, Carmagnola and his followers were very active, cruising about the district overturning trucks transporting cane to the mills.[204] Again, that same year, when Italian Consul-General Ferrante planned to visit Ingham, leaflets denouncing him were circulated in the Herbert, and the visitor had to be afforded police protection.[205]

Meanwhile, *Smith's Weekly* warned that Mussolini had dispatched two secret agents to North Queensland to work against the British Preference League. According to the newspaper, *Il Duce* planned to press the British government to lobby Canberra for special treatment of Italians in the canefields. Failing concessions, Italy planned to embargo importation of Australian wool.[206]

About this same time, a *fascio* was formed at Babinda, the only one to function successfully in North Queensland. The members had their banner and occasionally held parades, such as the black-shirted rally of 1937.[207] It also intimidated its foes, subjecting several of the most outspoken Anti-Fascists to beatings.

The Italian invasion of Abyssinia in 1935, and subsequent intervention in the Spanish Civil War, sobered many of Mussolini's Australian supporters—Italian and non-Italian alike. The Abyssinian campaign, in particular, discredited Fascism as an international political movement, relegating it instead to the status of parochial Italian nationalism with imperialistic pretensions. In 1935, the new Italian consul in Melbourne issued as his first act a denunciation of Italians who were seeking naturalization in droves rather than standing with their Italian compatriots in the homeland in common pursuit of "Italy's greatness."[208]

Nevertheless, when Great Britain supported the League of Nations' sanctions against Italy in an attempt to force Mussolini to abandon Abyssinia, there was considerable ambivalence in Australian political circles. At stake was Australia's favorable trade balance with Italy, as well as critical geopolitical considerations. Australian officials feared that embroiling the British fleet in a Mediterranean dispute could well weaken the British navy's capacity to defend Oceania against an increasingly bellicose Japan. Consequently, the Australian government urged London to seek an accommodation with Mussolini over the Abyssinian issue.[209] At the same time, it sought to assure its citizenry that British sanctions were having minimal effect upon Italo-Australian relations.[210] Since 1933, 3,000 Queensland Italians had been naturalized.

The issue was tailor-made for a sectarian dispute between Australia's Protestants and Catholics. The Australian Catholic press, recognizing the obvious need for the Church to maintain good relations with Mussolini, and possibly sensing an opportunity to extend Catholic influence on the African continent, defended Italy's Abyssinian campaign. If Catholics were in the minority within the Australian nation, they were a majority in the Irish-dominated union movement, prompting Labour Party officials to join with the Catholic Church in justifying the invasion (citing Britain's own colonialist past as precedent).[211]

Protestant opposition to the Abyssinian campaign was widespread and outspoken. For example, in late 1935, a pastoral letter condemning it was read in the churches throughout Victoria. The missive was signed by the heads of the Church of Christ, the Methodists, Anglicans, Presbyterians, Baptists, Congregationalists, and the Salvation Army.[212]

Meanwhile, Archbishop Duhig went on the offensive in Queensland. Despite the pope's calling for prayers for peace, Duhig argued that Italy had a civilizing and evangelical mission in Abyssinia tantamount to that of Great Britain's historical role in Australia. The Abyssinians would ultimately benefit from European conquest, as had the Australian Aborigines.[213] Protestant churchmen in Queensland were quick to denounce the archbishop as a defender of Italy's grab for economic resources and the Catholic Church's quest for more temporal power.[214] In 1936, the Italian Consul General decorated Archbishop Duhig in Brisbane with the title of "Knighthood of Commendatore," in honor of the prelate's services to Italy and Queensland's Italians.[215]

Italy's involvement in Abyssinia and, subsequently, Spain had profound repercussions within Australia's Italian colony. Convinced Fascists were, of course, supportive. For example, in Ingham they formed a committee to raise funds for the Abyssinian campaign, with some women donating their gold wedding bands to the cause.[216]

Conversely, other Herbert Italians issued their "Manifesto Against War,"[217] and, in October of 1935, Italian canecutters met in Mourilyan to pass a resolution stating,

> That this meeting of Italian cutters forwarded a protest to the Italian consul in Sydney, demanding that the invasion of Abyssinia cease, and that this be forwarded to the Italian Government, as we consider that all the teachings of civilization have been outraged by the unprovoked attack on the rights of Abyssinians to develop independence and peace.[218]

When the Spanish Civil War broke out in 1936, Duhig was quick to support the rebels. He denounced the lack of religious freedom in Spain, praised Franco, and referred to the rebellion as "...a great awakening...." Duhig declared, "I ask for your prayers for the Catholics of Spain against this diabolic un-Christian force of communism."[219] He subsequently denounced the Australian press for its support of the Spanish Republic.[220] In his view, the Spanish conflict was but the present manifestation of godless Communism's assault on Christianity (and Catholicism in particular), "...yesterday it was Russia and Mexico, today it is Spain, tomorrow it may be Britain and the day after Australia."[221] Fernández-Shaw notes:

> Regarding the Spanish Civil War, the Catholic hierarchy adopted an "official" posture: Archbishop Kelly of Sydney, and his Coadjutor Archbishop Gilroy, Archbishop Mannix of Melbourne, Archbishop Duhig of Brisbane and Bishop Foley of Ballarat, among others, supported Franco without doubt and congratulated themselves upon his victory.[222]

According to Gurdon, such stands by Roman Catholic prelates produced a virulent backlash and sectarianism of the worst kind. The Catholic Church was denounced by some of its critics as a Fascist organization. He also attributed formation of the United Protestants' Association and the Protestant Labour Party directly to the climate created by the debate over Abyssinia and Spain.[223] Both organizations were opposed to the immigration of European Catholics, Italian in particular.

Consequently, the conflict proved divisive for the labor movement. Its right-wing branch, predominantly Irish-Catholic, espoused the unions' traditional isolationism—a silence that gave tacit approval to Franco's "crusade" against atheistic and anticlerical Spanish Republicans; whereas the pro-Soviet leftist unionists empathized with the Republic and viewed the Civil War as but one manifestation in the ongoing struggle to the death between Fascism and Socialism.[224]

For most Australians of the day, Spain was a distant and exotic country, and its Civil War of little direct relevance to them. Then, too, Australians were part of the Commonwealth, and Great Britain was one of the architects of the "Non-Intervention Policy" whereby most of the world denied military assistance to either side of the conflict (ignored by Franco's allies, Germany and Italy, as well as the Republic's Soviet-Union supporter).[225]

With the exception of the *Queensland Guardian* newspaper, most of the Australian press provided limited coverage to the Spanish conflict and generally sided with Franco.[226]

The Spanish Civil War also occasioned splintering in the ranks of Australia's Southern Europeans. Anti-Fascist Italians rallied to the Spanish Republican cause. They were prominent in the formation of North Queensland chapters of the Spanish Relief Committee, and several volunteered to fight in the International Brigade.[227] Some North Queensland Spanish nationals returned to Europe to fight against the rebels (I have found no evidence of any joining with Franco). According to Mason: "It is noteworthy that no Basques returned to fight, the relatively rapid collapse of the Basque front reinforced Basque apathy towards broader Republican policies."[228]

Catalunya and Euskadi[229] (albeit not Navarra) were the two strongest bastions of resistance against the rebels. Given Catalans and Basque predominance within the ranks of Queensland's Spanish nationals, the potential of their conflicting with North Queensland's Fascist Italians was considerable. Consequently, it is not surprising that four Basques were arrested in Home Hill for a barroom brawl. One defendant reportedly said, "…We come over from Ayr clean Italians up; Mussolini, Franco no good…." While another declared, "…Dirty Dagoes—we clean 'em up…."[230]

There were no fewer than sixteen branches of the pro-Republican Spanish Relief Committee (SRC) in the Far North. Interestingly, there is no evidence of a chapter in Ingham—the epicenter of North Queensland's Basque settlement. Mason speculates that, initially, Basques sent relief directly to kinsmen until they were cutoff from Euskadi when the Basque front collapsed in August of 1937. Most of the SRC activity dates from later that year, or after the Basque cause was lost.[231] Ayr and Innisfail alone provided 20 percent of the funds raised for it the first year throughout all of Australia. Innisfail's Catalan Gabriel Sorli was a known Anarchist and Anti-Fascist, and the Communist Party targeted both the Goicoechea family and the Spaniard Durán in the Burdekin. The latter joined and became the leader of the local chapter.²³² Innisfail Anti-Fascists founded the Australian branch of *Solidaridad Internacional Antifascista* (the International Anti-Fascist Solidarity), an anarchist organization²³³ that declared itself to be democratic and open to all. Its leader was a Navarran and former Patagonia settler, Francisco Martínez. While centered among Innisfail political radicals, it included three Ingham Basques (Izaguirre, Bilbao, and Astorquia). Regarding the latter, Mason opines that they were likely more Anti-Franquists than convinced political leftists.²³⁴ In 1939, the sugar workers in Innisfail as a whole approved a voluntary levy on their wages for Spanish Relief.²³⁵

It is clear that the act of collecting funds for the Republican Cause in the Spanish Civil War was enough to have you investigated by Australian authorities during World War II, concerned, as they were, with the possibility of Anarchist fifth columnists. There is the letter dated January 4, 1941, from the Cairns inspector of police regarding Victor Moizes Erviti. The man was born in Pamplona, entered Australia on January 20, 1930 (at Brisbane), and he then went to Mourilyan where he became a canecutter. He remained an unnaturalized bachelor. He was hardworking, Anti-Fascist, and probably a Communist. "I am informed that during the recent Spanish Civil War this man assisted in this District in the collection of funds in aid of the Spanish Government Forces."²³⁶

In November of 1937, the Italian Progressive Club of Mourilyan celebrated its twelfth anniversary. In his address, C. Danesi, one of the founders, noted,

> The club was founded to keep the Italians in social contact. Its objects are to raise the moral and material status of the Italian people not only in Mourilyan but in all North Queensland. The club has fulfilled its purpose in the past as to material assistance by financial contributions to the Innisfail Hospital and Ambulance and other necessitous causes. It also defended the interests of the Italians at the time when attacks were made by the British Preference League. Thanks to the existence of our club much of the tendency to racial discord has been overcome, and amicable and cordial relationships exist between the Australian and Italian populations....

There was no Italian Fascist press as there is now published in Sydney which could villify the Italians who have liberty and democratic institutions and who hate tyranny, by branding them "renegrades" [sic] and idiots. There are some people who say that this club is Fascist; others who say it is Communistic; and yet others again who claim that it is not sufficiently Italian. The club concerns itself only with the interests of the Italians in Australia—only with local and Australian social matters and has to date never propogated Communistic, or, for that matter, Fascist views or doctrines…

The majority of the Italians deplore the Fascist aggressor in Spain; they are stricken with horror when confronted with the facts of the aerial bombardment of defenceless women and children, as at Barcelona and elsewhere.… We have only to think of the horrors of the civil war in Spain and the bloody aggression in China, to realise what such carnage in this country of our adoption would mean, and look to our wives and children, thinking of the women and children of Spain and the bloody aggression in China, not forgetting, too, the Abyssinian victims of aerial bombs.[237]

The longstanding and bitter conflict in Australia between the black shirts and their Anti-Fascist foes ended with the outbreak of World War II, when, ironically, the leaders of both groups were interned together as part of the general treatment of all Italians in Australia as enemy aliens.[238]

The issue of ethnic crime is considerably murkier and fraught with hyperbole. In describing certain events in North Queensland during the 1930s, Harvey states:

Search the crime records of any country; analyse the set-up, or probe the cause of any saga of violence, study the chain of vicious deadly wrecking; of blazing guns and shattering bombs; of homeless despair, death maiming, misery—and nowhere, surely, could you find a more macabre era of horror than the Reign of Terror which held sway in North Queensland during the murder-studded decade which extended from 1931 to 1941.[239]

The author then presents an undocumented argument in which several bombings, threats, letters of extortion, and eleven murders are stitched together with innuendo and assertions in order to portray a picture of pervasive Italian criminal activity. While the Harvey book (published in 1943) fails to present evidence, its rhetoric reflects accurately the livid reportage regarding the activities of an alleged Black Hand Gang operating within the Italian community. It also established a defamatory tradition that persists to this day, as the same story is revisited over and over again by journalists and filmmakers.[240]

It seems that, prior to the 1930s, neither Italo-Australians nor their Anglo detractors believed there was organized ethnic crime activity in Queensland. There were a number of homicides among Italians in the teens and 1920s, all of which were treated by the police and the popular press as crimes of passion, stemming from love triangles, disputes between employers and employees, or between business partners. During the testimony regarding an Innisfail bombing in 1925, there was no suggestion that it might have been the work of a secret society, though the circumstances might well have led to such a conclusion. It was about the same time that *Smith's Weekly* and *Truth* began to vilify the Italians of North Queensland in every imaginable fashion. Had there been the slightest rumor of Black Hand, *camorra*, or Mafia activity, they would have been the first to seize upon it, yet that is one accusation the two newspapers failed to make.

Of equal interest was a confidential addendum to the Ferry Report's evidence elicited from a North Italian in Innisfail to the effect that,

> ...like all Northern Italians he had no time for the Southerners (Sicilian, Calabrese) and that the Northerners' pet hope is that something will be done by the Government to block them altogether. All Northerners cherished the same brotherly sentiments towards their swarthy compatriots privately and will express them privately, but that, valuing their lives and property they do not wish to compromise themselves by voicing them public.[241]

This statement reflects a perception that South Italians were capable of vendettas and violence. It fails, however, to make specific reference to criminal secret societies, which, had they existed, would have reinforced the argument that Sicilians and Calabrians should be excluded from Australia.

Evidence from Ingham suggests that the proportion of southerners, Sicilians in particular, in North Queensland's Italian population was on the rise. When an Italian Catholic priest visited the town in 1923, he contacted 288 Italian families with a total of 1,902 individuals. Of these, 1,469 were from northern Italy, 11 from Sardinia, 21 from central Italy, 31 from mainland southern Italy, and 365 from Sicily.[242] The aggregated figure of 396 southerners (mainland and insular) totals 20.8 percent of the Ingham sample; a figure that is quite consonant with Italian Consul-General Grossardi's claim that southerners represented one-fifth of Italian immigration in Australia as a whole.[243]

Henderson finds that, after 1926, there is a pronounced shift in the Old World origins of Herbert River Italians, despite the stated policy of both the Australian and Italian authorities to use the nomination system to bring immigrants along established lines, facilitated and guaranteed by bona fide sponsors. Normally, this would have meant that the sponsor was a kinsmen and/or fellow villager of the intending immigrant. Henderson analyzes the birthplace and year of arrival in Australia of 749 Herbert River Italians seeking naturalization between 1928 and 1938 and finds that some communities that previously sent emigrants to North Queensland ceased to do so while others became involved in Australian immigration for the first time.[244] Overall, there is a noticeable shift in the proportion of southerners. Of her sample, 241, or 32 percent, were from South Italy (228 being Sicilian).[245] In his study, J. A. Hempel determined that between 1920 and 1938, of the total Italian immigration in Queensland as a whole, 6.8 percent were from the mainland South, while 31 percent were from Sicily.[246] In Borrie's sample of 641 male Queensland Italians entering prior to 1941, Sicilians (311 individuals) constitute nearly half.[247] Clearly, such results vary significantly according to whom was contacted and thereby became "sampled."

Henderson compares her results with those of Borrie and concludes they suggest that Sicilian immigration into the Herbert River was likely male-biased.[248] Coupled with her other finding that much of the post-1926 immigration of Sicilians involved persons drawn from communities previously lacking Australian emigration, a picture emerges of a

South Italian immigration in North Queensland that was growing in magnitude and which included a large contingent of males who lacked (or had limited) kinship and friendship networks among established Italo-Australians. The arrival of so many South-Italian "strangers" must have enhanced the existing fears and prejudices within the North Italian community. Additionally, there was another small contingent within this Sicilian-dominated influx of southerners, namely the Calabrians. Few in numbers, they were to play a disproportionate role in North Queensland's "ethnic crime wave" of the 1930s.

By 1930, there was clear recognition of possible Italian criminal society activity in Australia. In December of that year, the *Herbert River Express* quoted an article in the Southern press that maintained two Italian secret societies were operative in Australia with branches in Sydney, Melbourne, Adelaide, Brisbane, and North Queensland.[249] In January of 1931, the newspaper featured a homicide in Sydney in which an intruder was shot dead by an Italian storekeeper from whom he was attempting to extort money. The Italian community of Sydney was reluctant to discuss the matter, but it was felt the extortionist represented the *camorra*.[250] About the same time, *Smith's Weekly*, in one of its periodic attacks on Italians, vilified Sicilians and equated North Queensland to Chicago because of its "countrymen of Al Capone."[251]

By 1932, notably in the Herbert and the Johnstone River districts, there were several extortion attempts reported to the authorities in which Italian canefarmers and businessmen were threatened with violence if they failed to pay protection. It is likely that there were others as well that the fearful victims declined to disclose. Several of the extortionists were accused, arrested, tried, and convicted. The *modus operandi* scarcely qualified as the strategy of an experienced criminal organization with international connections, as was contended by some journalists.

On the other hand, the frequency of the attempts and their references to a sinister Black Hand Gang clearly made both the Italian community and the Australian police nervous and watchful. In 1933, these fears were exacerbated when an Italian canefarmer in Mourilyan received a gunshot wound after ignoring a demand letter. For the next five years, culminating with the bombing death of the Calabrian Vicenzo

D'Agostino in Ingham, the ostensible head of organized crime in North Queensland, several murders within the Italian community were attributed to the Black Hand Gang.[252]

From the outset, the alleged Black Hand incidents caused grave concern that the sugar embargo might be jeopardized should the Australian public become convinced it was underwriting "foreign terrorism." Proponents of British Preference perceived an opportunity, arguing that if 100 percent Britishers were employed in the sugar industry the undesirable alien element would be forced to migrate elsewhere.[253]

For his part, the chief of the Commonwealth Investigation Branch assured the public that all aliens suspected of belonging to secret societies were under surveillance. He noted that the present trouble seemed more a matter of inter-family feuds than the work of "terrorists."[254] The Italian consul-general in Australia declared the Black Hand did not even exist in Italy, and that every nationality had its bad elements, the suppression of which was a police matter.[255]

There were appeals for moderation. In 1934, the Brisbane *Courier-Mail* noted that, while there was a Black Hand Gang, it surely numbered no more than six to possibly a score of members. The group was intimidating the Italian community, and one Italian canefarmer in Ingham was said to have sold out through fear of it. However, one extortionist had been deported to Italy, and this was having the effect of scattering the delinquents.[256] *The Telegraph* published an article that declared the Black Hand Gang was a mere fiction and fabrication of "febrile imaginations." Rather, there was a delinquent element that preyed upon weaker members of the Italian community. Indeed, the Italians themselves were organizing to counter these malefactors, most of whom were mere tyros in crime. While the criminals were mainly southerners, the Sicilian element was not without its good qualities. Given time, the Sicilians and Calabrians became good Australian citizens, just like their northern Italian counterparts.[257]

By 1937, the *North Queensland Register* responded to rumors that undesirable aliens were to be rounded up and deported by stating that, while there might have been some sort of Black Hand threat earlier, Commonwealth authorities had dealt with it effectively. In 1934, the immigration laws were changed to permit deportation of undesirable aliens indicted for a crime for up to five years after their arrival in Australia. Several suspects in North Queensland had been deported and were treated harshly by the Mussolini government on their return to Italy. The newspaper opposed any further measures targeting Sicilians in North Queensland for deportation, since most had resided there for more than five years. Many had become naturalized citizens and were therefore immune to anything short of draconian efforts to deport them.[258] Commonwealth Minister for the Interior Paterson declared his ignorance of any cooperative scheme between Commonwealth and Queensland authorities to deport Sicilians from North Queensland.[259]

Such assurances notwithstanding, irresponsible journalism fanned public concern. In the summer of 1937, Paterson denounced an article appearing in the *Manchester Empire News* as a gross misrepresentation of the situation. The article contended that, "Men and women are being tortured and killed, bombs are being thrown, and in some cases blood feuds are being carried out with such intensity that whole villages are forced to live behind barricades."[260]

The Telegraph sent a reporter to North Queensland who debunked the Black Hand threat. The article noted,

> Police officers in the North smile when the name "Black Hand Gang" is mentioned. They deny that there was ever such an organization in North Queensland. Responsible Italians are equally emphatic on the point. The reason given for the occasional use of the name of the dreaded Mano Nera is that the mythical gang has been so widely publicized in certain southern newspapers that a few hoodlums have recognized a possible method of extorting money by exploiting its name.[261]

Harvey contends that the surveillance and internment of Italians during the war effectively destroyed the Black Hand Gang. In point of fact, by 1939 the phenomenon had run out of steam, since, by that time, the Italian community refused to be intimidated by would-be extortionists. However, in a sense, all North Queensland Italians had paid a price, given that the sensationalism surrounding the Black Hand crimes fed into the stereotype of the dangerous Italians as Australia and Italy moved toward war.

Alien Internment—In the fateful year of 1939, as the world was once again poised on the brink of catastrophe, the situation of Italians in Australia grew increasingly tenuous. Germany and Italy, battlefield allies in Spain, forged their "Pact of Steel." However, when Hitler invaded Poland without consulting Mussolini, and then attacked France, the Italians refrained from entering the war. Great Britain engaged in a futile diplomatic effort to win Mussolini over to the Allied cause, or at least convince him to remain neutral.

Meanwhile, a nervous Australia began to gear up for the impending conflict. By May of 1939, the Aliens' Registration Bill was under debate in Canberra. Martens, parliamentarian from the Herbert, argued against some of its measures, noting that the children of naturalized aliens were becoming fluent English-speaking Australians.[262] However, the legislation was passed.

In September, the minister of defence ordered all aliens in Australia to report to their local police. They were required to supply four photographs of themselves and to sign a loyalty oath. Hotelkeepers were to maintain a list of their alien clients. Enemy aliens (Germans) had to receive official permission in order to change residence. Failure to register made any alien subject to internment.[263]

By early October, there was a rush to comply. In Ingham one thousand aliens had already been registered. A fourteen-day grace period was announced, after which tardy registrants would be assessed a £50 fine. The *Herbert River Express* asked its readership to inform any alien friends of the situation. Both the local photographers and police were swamped by the workload.[264] For their part, the Commonwealth authorities were also buried in an avalanche of naturalization applications from German and Italian nationals.

For the next several months, there was tension within Australia's Italian community regarding its homeland's possible involvement in the war. The speculation ended in June of 1940, when Mussolini declared war on France and Great Britain. That same month, Australia initiated a program of alien internment aimed primarily at German and Italian nationals. The position of Spanish ones remained nebulous. Mussolini and Hitler had aided Franco in the Spanish Civil War, but Spain had yet to enter the global fray on the side of the Axis.

In July, two Basques and one Catalan resident in North Queensland applied for naturalization. Australian officials were in a quandary over the requests. They opted to delay, for a few months, the applications of Spanish nationals with less than ten years' residence in order to better determine Spain's posture within the global conflict (it remained neutral). At the same time, they decided to proceed immediately with the naturalization of any applicant who had been in Australia for more than ten years.[265]

According to the *Herbert River Express*, news of Italy's entry into the war was greeted with grim silence in the local Italian population. Many felt that Mussolini had committed a grave error. In mid-June, eight constables arrived from Townsville to begin rounding up "tabbed" Italians in the Herbert district. The lists of potential detainees had already been prepared prior to Italy's invasion of France.[266] Warnings were issued against demonstrations, and the initial detentions elicited no violence or protest. The particular targets of the exercise were the influential and "clever" members of the Italian community.[267] In Ingham, several prominent farmers and businessmen were detained.

Whatever respect and acceptance Italians had earned through half a century of hard work in North Queensland was dissipated in the hysteria of the moment. Even in Ingham, unquestionably the most tolerant community of the Far North, there was a notable anti-Italian backlash. Italians were dismissed from their employment at the mills and were prohibited from working for the shire. Giuseppe Cantamessa resigned his post as Hinchinbrook Shire counselor.[268]

Initially, the roundup focused exclusively upon males who were identified by local internment committees as potential subversives. While the policy stated that the internees were to be treated reasonably well unless they attempted to escape, in fact implementation reflected the whims of local officials.[269]

By government decree, un-naturalized Italians lost most of their civil rights. They could no longer sue for debts or be plaintiffs in litigation. Anglo-Australians, however, could proceed against them in any court. All monetary remittances to Italy were prohibited. Businesses of internees were to be operated by court-appointed controllers, with profits going into a trust fund from which their families would receive a living stipend after the costs of operating the trust were met. The controllers were responsible for ensuring that no property under their aegis was transferred into the hands of other enemy aliens.[270]

Theoretically, there was an appeal process, but it offered little prospect of success. The internee had to solicit permission to make an appeal from the committee that had interned him in the first place.[271] Although the internments were carried out selectively, there was mounting pressure from patriotic groups, such as: the War Emergency Organization;[272] the Returned Services League;[273] The Sailors', Soldiers' and Airmens' Fathers' Association;[274] and the Country Women's Association;[275] to effect detention of all enemy aliens in Australia. Beginning in April 1941, Australia began to receive the first of what would ultimately number 18,500 Italian POWs captured in the fighting of the Middle East.[276]

With the memory of World War I still relatively fresh, from the outset of the new conflict there was fear in the sugar industry of an impending labor shortage. In the best of times, cane cutting was arduous, seasonal, and, hence, highly compensated. Many men lacked the necessary stamina and drive to be cutters. Under war conditions, the ranks of the existing Britisher canecutters were depleted by enlistments, removing the most able-bodied. Other industries offered good wages, the opportunity for overtime, steady employment, and better living conditions than those obtaining in the sugar industry. Of particular concern in at least some sugar districts was the fact that, unlike in the earlier war, the Italian canecutter was an enemy alien and thereby subject to restrictions.

The Queensland Canegrowers' Council faced its own predicament. It had, of course, many Italian members, but was dominated by Anglos who were fearful that, as Australian farmers themselves enlisted in the armed forces, aliens remaining in North Queensland would be in a position to buy up their properties (as happened during World War I). The Council therefore passed a secret resolution urging the government to prohibit any sales to enemy aliens until after the conflict. It also asked that all "enemy born subjects," naturalized or not, be disenfranchised. While seemingly harsh recommendations, the Council also went out of its way to state that many alien Queensland growers were doing their part in the national war effort by contributing to patriotic funds.[277]

That year's annual conference of the Returned Soldiers passed a motion that prohibited the sale or lease of land to enemy aliens for the duration of the war and three years after. It was aimed specifically at the Italians. They also approved motions calling for the internment of every enemy alien and prohibiting their release, while re-interning any who had been released to date. Furthermore, enemy aliens were to be prohibited from sailing anywhere off the Australian coast, including for fishing purposes. The only motion that failed to carry was, "that it be an offense to speak any language but English in streets and public places."[278]

In early 1942, there was another round of internments throughout Queensland. In the Far North it was touted as the largest campaign to date. Ingham authorities used boats to ford flooded rivers in order to detain enemy aliens residing on remote properties.[279] By early March, more than ninety persons had been apprehended in the Herbert alone.[280] According to Diane Menghetti, "By late March nearly every Italian household in the district had suitcases prepared; no-one knew whose door would be knocked on next."[281]

Enemy aliens not subject to internment were given the option of volunteering for military service or being conscripted into the Civilian Alien Corps. The CAC was to be assigned to civil work projects,[282] much like the home-guard Civilian Construction Corps. Meanwhile, no enemy alien or naturalized internee was eligible for protection of his property under the national war-damage insurance scheme.[283] Canberra, however, resisted pressures for more draconian measures, arguing that the selective internment program had guaranteed national security.[284]

The year 1942 represented the high watermark of Australian vulnerability to a Japanese invasion and fear of possible fifth-column activity from within. In January, given the gravity of the war situation, schools in North Queensland were closed. In March, brownouts were mandated in the coastal districts. In July, the Japanese bombed Townsville. Some North Queenslanders sent their families south, and many farms and businesses were operated with skeleton staffs.

In February 1942, a curfew was imposed on all aliens, requiring them to remain in their homes between 8 p.m. and 5 a.m. Violators were subject to heavy fines, jail sentences, or internment.[285] About this same time, a campaign was launched in North Queensland to break up an Italian spy ring said to be radioing information to Japan.[286] Representatives of most of the local authorities north of Townsville met at Atherton and demanded that English be the required vernacular throughout the area, and that all foreign-language publications be outlawed.[287] The Returned Soldiers' League (RSL) initiated a campaign to have all interned enemy aliens declared subversives, subject to deportation after the war. Their property was to be seized and redistributed to returning ex-servicemen. The RSL further urged that, henceforth, aliens should not be allowed to own more than 10 percent of the property in any district.[288]

Meanwhile, rumors proliferated that many Nazis and Fascists were still at liberty in the Far North, and that the measures to confiscate firearms from aliens had failed.[289] The Italian Marshall Caviglia was purported to have said that for years Italian emigration to Australia had been carefully selected in order to pave the way for a Japanese takeover.[290] The Country Womens' Association raised the specter of a slaughter of the Britishers in North Queensland, accompanied by mass rapes.[291]

The leader of the opposition in Australia, Mr. Fadden, called upon Commonwealth Prime Minister Curtin for internment of all enemy aliens in the country, including females, and asked that all certificates of naturalization issued during the preceding five years be reviewed. Curtin refused, declaring the measures taken to date to be sufficient. Nevertheless, it is clear that the internment program impacted North Queensland considerably more than any other part of Australia. According to Lamidey, fully 43 percent of the state's resident male alien population was interned, compared with only three percent in Victoria.[292]

In late September of 1942, Mr. Jesson, in a speech to the Queensland Legislative Assembly, surveyed the damage done to his district (the Kennedy, which includes the Herbert River area) by the war measures. He noted that North Queensland had been more adversely affected than any other part of the nation. Thousands had fled the Far North out of fear of the fifth columnists, driven by irresponsible journalism, such as the scare article by Mr. Connolly that had appeared recently in the *Sunday Mail*. In Hinchinbrook Shire, the economy was in a shambles. The prewar population of 12,500 had been reduced by 3,700, which included 1,000 enlistments, 1,000 evacuations, 900 departures of persons going south to work in the CCC and other defense projects, and 800 internments and conscriptions of aliens into the CAC. The Army had requisitioned 110 tractors, depriving the district of sufficient machinery to cultivate its crops. Numerous farm and business failures were imminent.²⁹³ Strategic parts of the district, such as the section along the road linking Ingham with its port of Lucinda, the town of Halifax, and the area around Macknade and Victoria Mills (deemed vulnerable to sabotage), had been totally purged of their Italian residents.²⁹⁴

In late 1942, there was a Royal Commission conducted in part to determine the impact of the internment of Italians upon farm management and labor relations in the sugar districts of North Queensland. The evidence is somewhat incomplete but is sufficiently comprehensive to illustrate that internment had removed more than one thousand alien growers, cutters, and field hands. Certain areas were impacted more than others. Thus, in the Herbert, the combined totals for Macknade and Victoria Mills alone constituted about one-third of the interned growers and nearly half of the cutters and field hands reported to the Commission. Conversely, the mills near Cairns (Mossman, Babinda, Mulgrave, and Hambledon) were affected more moderately, and those near Mackay scarcely at all. An adverse side effect of this outcome was to set districts and growers against one another as they competed for scarce manpower. Districts like the Herbert, which were crushing at 60–70 percent of capacity, advocated even-handed government allocation of available cutters throughout North Queensland, while districts that were producing at 90 percent of capacity or better were fearful their cutting force might be pirated by desperate farmers in grossly undermanned areas, employers who might be willing to pay a premium to get workers.²⁹⁵ This, then, was the climate when Jesson made his war-conditions' speech in September of 1942.

By late 1942, the growing American military presence in North Queensland, and the major naval defeat of the Japanese in the Battle of the Solomons, diminished fears of an enemy invasion. The anti-alien measures in Australia had peaked, and no new significant ones were being implemented. Consequently, a few politicians were emboldened to call for reevaluation of the internment program. Not surprisingly, the elected representatives from the Herbert were in the forefront of the initiative.

In early October, Mr. Martens, federal member, called for the assignment of internees to farmwork. He denied that they were potentially dangerous and declared them to be victims of systematic political discrimination, since most of the naturalized ones were members of the Australian Labour Party. He noted that overly zealous officials had recently attempted to intimidate alien women with the threat of internment. He denounced conditions in the holding area where internees were temporarily confined while awaiting assignment to a camp. At the camps themselves they were in the clutches of prejudiced Australian officials. Martens declared to be ridiculous the call by the Returned Soldiers' League to confiscate internees' farms for redistribution to ex-servicemen. In requesting the provisional release of internees, Martens noted that many were avowed Anti-Fascists who fled Italy in fear of Mussolini. Despite being interned in Australia, many continued to raise money for Australia's war effort.[296]

Jesson was even more outspoken in his defense of enemy-alien internees. He noted that many were the victims of malicious denunciations by vengeful neighbors: "God-fearing citizens are being put behind bars to suit the ends of somebody else." One Italian who had been in Australia for forty-seven years, married to a Scottish lady, and with four sons in the Australian Armed Forces, was interned! Such abuses led Jesson to conclude, "When this war is finished, if the story is ever published, it will astound decent, honest Australian people."[297] Despite such sentiments, the release of the internees was a slow and cautious process. It was not until late 1944 that the last Italian internee was freed, despite Italy's surrender to the Allies in September of 1943.

From the first fears, in 1921, of an "Italian invasion" to the outbreak of World War II, the Italian community had served as the lightning rod of controversy over the entry of Southern Europeans into North Queensland. However, the war measures themselves had removed the main bones of contention. For the duration of the conflict, Italian immigration was interdicted, assuaging fears of an alien takeover. War-induced labor shortages made British-preference a moot point as a desperate sugar industry scrambled to survive. The labor shortage in the immediate aftermath of the conflict made ludicrous the shrill calls by hardliners to reimpose the labor-quota system. Fears of Italian Fascism and ethnic crime were also ameliorated by the war, when potentially dangerous individuals were incarcerated easily, even if at times by means of unsubstantiated (possibly anonymous) allegation. The internments had the further effect of shattering Italian settlements. With their ranks decimated, a fearful and resentful North Queensland Italian community retreated behind its closed doors. By striking the lowest possible ethnic profile, Italians lessened any public concern over the formation of Little Italys or a viable Italian fifth-column.

Notes

1. William S. Bernard, ed., *American Immigration Policy: A Reappraisal* (Port Washington, New York and London: Kennikat Press, 1969), 25.
2. Gillies to Bruce, June 9, 1925, Queensland State Archive, PRE/A849, 1.
3. Ibid, 4.
4. Ibid, 3.
5. Commonwealth of Australia, *Commonwealth Parliamentary Debates, 1925* (Canberra: Government Printer, 1925), 458.
6. Ibid, 459–61.
7. Ibid, 932.
8. *Townsville Daily Bulletin*, July 15, 1924, 6.
9. Ibid, August 12, 1924, 4.
10. *North Queensland Register*, August 24, 1925, 30.
11. Ibid, July 20, 1925, 63.
12. Ibid, July 27, 1925, 59.
13. Ibid.
14. Ibid, December 29, 1924, 32.
15. Ibid, January 26, 1925, 18.
16. Ibid, April 20, 1925, 44.
17. Ibid, May 4, 1925, 36.
18. Ibid, May 11, 1925, 36.
19. *Corriere della Sera*, July 10, 1925, quoted in Fleetwood Chidell, *Australia—White or Yellow?* (London: Heinemann, 1926), 77.
20. Ibid, 85–86.
21. April 21, 1927, passim. Australian Archives (ACT): CRS A445, item 211/1/2, Part 1, Department of Immigration Correspondence Files 'Policy Series.' 'Immigration of Italians to Australia' 1927–1929. [April 21, 1927].
22. A census of the Italian population in the Herbert River taken in 1923 showed that, of the 1,902 individuals, 633, or approximately one-third, were from the province of Alessandria alone. See Father Mambrini, "Report of a Month's Visit to the Italian Settlement on the Herbert River, North Queensland," *The Record* 3 (10), May 11, 1924, 55–57; 3 (11), June 1, 1924, 33–34. ["Visit"].
23. April 21, 1927, 15.
24. Ibid, October 25, 1926, 35.
25. Ibid, November 1, 1926, 13.
26. Ibid, October 25, 1926, 57.

27. June 21, 1927, Australian Archives (ACT): CRS A445, item 211/1/2, Part 1, Department of Immigration Correspondence Files 'Policy Series' 'Immigration of Italians to Australia' 1927–1929.
28. Commonwealth of Australia, *Commonwealth Parliamentary Debates*, vol. 116 (Canberra: Government Printer, 1927), 109.
29. Ibid, 111.
30. Ibid, 117; 125.
31. Ibid, 400.
32. Ibid, 408.
33. Ibid, 412.
34. *Italo-Australian*, December 31, 1927, 1.
35. Cordasco, *Italian Mass Emigration*, 285.
36. Commonwealth of Australia, *Commonwealth Parliamentary Debates*, vol. 120 (Canberra: Government Printer, 1929), 43.
37. *Courier-Mail*, March 30, 1928, 6.
38. Mason, "Agitators," 90.
39. *Herbert River Express*, January 1, 1930, 2.
40. Ibid, April 7, 1931, 6.
41. Michael A. Gurdon, "Australian Attitudes to Italy and Italians, 1922–1936: With Special Reference to Queensland." B.A. thesis, University of Queensland, 1970, 105. ["Australian Attitudes"].
42. Commonwealth of Australia, *Census of the Commonwealth of Australia, 30th June, 1933*, vol. 1 (Canberra: Commonwealth Government Printer, 1933), 294; 298.
43. Ibid, 294; 298; 844.
44. Ibid, 292; 294; 296; 298.
45. Ibid, 844.
46. *The Worker*, July 17, 1924, 10.
47. *North Queensland Register*, April 6, 1925, 13.
48. Ibid, April 21, 1925, 25.
49. Ibid.
50. Ibid, May 4, 1925, 8.
51. Ibid.
52. Ibid, July 27, 1925, 48; Ibid, November 2, 1925, 11.
53. Ibid, May 11, 1925, 16.
54. Ibid, 17.
55. Ibid, 20.
56. AWU Northern District Secretary Letter, July 27, 1925, Queensland State Archives, PRE/A849.
57. Quoted in Mason, "Agitators," 11
58. *North Queensland Register*, May 11, 1925, 17.
59. Ibid, June 29, 1925, 13.
60. Ibid, June 1, 1925, 5.
61. Ibid, 63.
62. Ibid, June 22, 1925, 44.

63. Ibid, 85.
64. Ibid, July 6, 1925, 6.
65. Ibid, June 29, 1925, 12.
66. *Smith's Weekly*, October 9, 1926, 1.
67. *North Queensland Register*, December 13, 1915, 90.
68. *The Worker*, May 7, 1925, 14.
69. *North Queensland Register*, September 7, 1925, 13.
70. Ibid.
71. Ibid, August 2, 1926, 18.
72. Ibid, August 9, 1926, 1.
73. Ibid, 21.
74. Ibid.
75. Ibid, 21.
76. Ibid, 31.
77. Ibid, August 23, 42.
78. Ibid, May 18, 1925, 15.
79. *The Worker*, June 29, 1927, 6; 11; Ibid, July 6, 1927, 11.
80. *Courier-Mail*, June 18, 1927, 17.
81. *The Worker*, July 13, 1927, 7.
82. Ibid, May 23, 1928, 10.
83. *Herbert River Express*, June 6, 1928, 4.
84. Ibid, June 26, 1929, 4.
85. Ibid, August 7, 1929, 6.
86. Ibid, May 19, 1930, 4.
87. Ibid, May 28, 1930, 5.
88. Ibid, April 14, 1930, 2.
89. Ibid, April 25, 1930, 5.
90. *Home Hill Observer*, May 1, 1930, 3.
91. Ibid, May 22, 1930, 5.
92. Ibid, June 19, 1930, 2.
93. *Herbert River Express*, June 19, 1930.
94. Ibid.
95. Ibid, June 23, 1930, 2.
96. Ibid, June 20, 1930, 5.
97. Ibid.
98. *The Worker*, June 11, 1930, 6.
99. *The Australian Sugar Journal* 22, no. 2 (1930), 253.
100. Ibid, 22, no. 7 (1930), 40–2.
101. *Smith's Weekly*, March 29, 1930, 1.
102. Ibid.
103. *Herbert River Express*, April 14, 1930, 3.
104. June 9, 1930, Queensland State Archives, Correspondence A/12225 [June 9. 1930].
105. Henderson, "Italians," 291–92.
106. *Herbert River Express*, June 9, 1930, 2.

107. Ibid, June 27, 1930, 2.
108. Ibid, June 25, 1930, 2. Italian growers in Tully in fact had a history of resisting British Preference guidelines. In 1927, they formed the Italian Producers' Club and issued a statement to the effect that,

> Considering that the Italian cane planters, after so many hardships and expenditure, had to endure great losses last year owing to work not being properly done by some canecutters employed at the Tully mill, we ask the Government for the liberty to grant cane cutting contracts to all those exhibiting [union] tickets without making any distinction of nationality, as long as the work is done properly, and according to the rules, so that in this democratic land of Queensland, ruled by a democratic legislation, all the workers may enjoy the rights of this legislation (*North Queensland Register*, March 7, 1927, 35).

109. *Herbert River Express*, October 2, 1930, 2.
110. Ibid, December 4, 1930, 3; 6.
111. Commonwealth of Australia Committee of Inquiry into the Sugar Industry, 1930, *Reports of the Sugar Inquiry Committee* (Canberra: Government Printer, 1931), 184.
112. Ibid, 180.
113. By 1932, Australia would have greater unemployment and workers' unrest than any other nation.
114. Ibid, 398.
115. Ibid, 402.
116. Ibid, 13.
117. *Home Hill Observer*, August 21, 1930, 6.
118. *Herbert River Express*, January 24, 1931, 2.
119. Ibid, January 27, 1923, 1, 2.
120. Giuseppe Luciano, *La guida annuale per gli Italiani del Queensland* (Brisbane: N.p., 1931), 41.
121. Ibid, 42; 44.
122. *Herbert River Express*, December 17, 1931, 5.
123. Ibid, October 1, 1931, 6.
124. *Home Hill Observer*, June 22, 1933, 2.
125. G.C. Morrissey, "The Occurrence of Leptospirosis (Weil's Disease) in Australia," *The Medical Journal of Australasia* 2, no. 1 (1934), 496-97.
126. *The Australian Sugar Journal*, September 4, 1934, 326.
127. *North Queensland Register*, September 22, 1935, 10.
128. Ibid, October 20, 1934, 7.
129. Ibid, October, 13, 1934, 71.
130. Ibid, October 27, 1934, 45.
131. Ibid, October 20, 1934, 15.
132. Ibid, May 27, 1935, 16.
133. *Herbert River Express*, August 3, 1935, 2.
134. Ibid, August 10, 1935; Ibid, August 13, 1935; Ibid, August 25, 1935; *North Queensland*

Register, August 31, 1935, 7; Ibid, August 17, 1935, 71; Ibid, August 24, 1935, 8; Ibid, September 7, 1935, 76–77.
135. *Herbert River Express*, August 22, 1935; Ibid, August 27, 1935; *North Queensland Register*, August 31, 1935, 7; Ibid, September 14, 1935, 8; Ibid, September 21, 1935, 8; 71.
136. The novel *Sugar Heaven* (Sydney: Modern Publishers, 1936) by Jean Devanny captures the flavor of the events of 1935 from the strikers' point of view. See *North Queensland Register*, September 28, 1935, 18, for the AWU viewpoint. Also see Diane Menghetti, *The Red North*, Studies in North Queensland History, No. 3 (Townsville: History Department, James Cook University, 1981), passim. [*The Red North*].
137. Cris D'all Osto recounts abuses as late as the 1950s. He monitored the sign-ons for farmers and is certain that the AWU enrolled all new immigrants in order to collect dues, but that their union card lacked its ballot portion. It had been torn off by AWU officials who would then vote with it as they saw fit (Douglass field notes).
138. *The Australian Sugar Journal* 26, no. 5 (1935), 235. In the interest of accuracy, it should be noted that W. D. Borrie, in his seminal work *Italians and Germans in Australia* (Melbourne: F. W. Cheshire, 1954), 113–14 [*f*], makes several errors with respect to the British Preference system. He contends that it (1) was instituted in 1933, (2) affected only Cairns and Innisfail, (3) called for a 25 percent Britisher/75 percent alien ratio in the canecutter workforce, and (4) accommodated naturalized aliens from the Britisher quota. These discrepancies were first underscored in Henderson, "Italians," 243–44.
139. *Herbert River Express*, May 24, 1933; Ibid, June 5, 1933.
140. Baume, *Burnt Sugar*, passim.
141. Ibid, 14.
142. Ibid, 152–53.
143. *Herbert River Express*, March 23, 1928, 4.
144. Henderson, "Italians," 156.
145. Ibid, 123.
146. Ibid, 156.
147. Ibid, 167.
148. *Herbert River Express*, January 13, 1931, 5.
149. September 23, 1929, Queensland State Archives, Correspondence, A/12225. [September 23, 1929].
150. Treaty of Commerce and Navigation between Great Britain and Australia, 1883, Article 15, Queensland State Archive, Correspondence, A/12225.
151. September 23, 1929.
152. *The Australian Sugar Journal* 22, no. 4 (1933), 252.
153. September 18, 1933, Queensland State Archives, Correspondence, A/12225.
154. August 14, 1934, Queensland State Archives, Correspondence, A/12225.
155. November 22, 1934, Queensland State Archives, Correspondence, A/12225.
156. June 12, 1935, Queensland State Archives, Correspondence, A/12225.
157. *North Queensland Register*, November 16, 1935, 43.
158. Ibid, 61.
159. *The Australian Sugar Journal* 27, no, 9 (1935), 480–82.

160. Henderson, "Italians," 162.
161. Ibid, 163.
162. Ibid, 118.
163. Ibid, 118; 120.
164. Price, *Southern Europeans*, 129–30; Rina Huber, *From Pasta to Pavlova: A Comparative Study of Italian Settlers in Sydney and Griffith* (St. Lucia: University of Queensland Press, 1977), 57–58.
165. Mason, "Agitators," 40.
166. *North Queensland Register*, December 5, 1921, 76.
167. CSR Collection, BEA, Australian National University, Letter File II, Victoria Out, August 22, 1918.
168. *Melbourne Age*, March 23, 1925.
169. *The Daily Standard*, April 17, 1925, 10.
170. *The Worker*, January 8, 1925, 13.
171. *North Queensland Register*, November 8, 1926, 24.
172. *The Worker*, November 7, 1928, 9.
173. *Italo-Australian*, October 20, 1928, 1.
174. Gurdon, "Australian Attitudes," 100–1.
175. Commonwealth of Australia, *Commonwealth Parliamentary Debates*, vol. 120 (Canberra: Government Printer, 1929), 63.
176. *Smith's Weekly*, April 13, 1929, 3.
177. Price, *Southern Europeans*, 214.
178. Gurdon, "Australian Attitudes," 100–1.
179. Ibid, 32–34.
180. Ibid, 120–29.
181. Don Dignan, "Archbishop James Duhig and Italians and Italy," in *Altro Polo: Studies in Contemporary Italy*, ed. Ian Grosart and Silvio Trambaiolo (Sydney: Frederick May Foundation, University of Sydney, 1988), 163–70.
182. *The Worker*, February 2, 1927, 15.
183. Gurdon, "Australian Attitudes," 123.
184. *The Worker*, December 14, 1922, 15.
185. *North Queensland Register*, March 2, 1925, 16.
186. Interview conducted by the author with Mario Cazzulino in Ingham, 1980.
187. *Herbert River Express*, October 31, 1928, 5.
188. Ibid, April 17, 1929, 5.
189. *Johnstone River Advocate*, September 10, 1929, 1.
190. Ibid.
191. Gianfranco Cresciani, "The Proletarian Migrants: Fascism and Italian Anarchists in Australia," *The Australian Quarterly* 51, no. 1 (March 1979), 6. ["The Proletarian Migrants"].
192. Ibid, 9; 17.
193. Mario Cazzulino interview.
194. Gianfranco Cresciani, "Italian Anti-Fascism in Australia (1922–1945)," in *Affari Sociali Internazionali*, numero unico (Milan: Franco Angeli Editore, 1978), 150. ["Italian Anti-Fascism"].

195. *La Riscossa*, December 5, 1931, 4.
196. Cresciani, "Italian Anti-Fascism," 18.
197. *Herbert River Express*, December 31, 1931, 2.
198. *La Riscossa*, January 15, 1932, 1.
199. *Herbert River Express*, February 13, 1932, 2; 6.
200. Ibid, 2.
201. Cresciani, "Italian Anti-Fascism," 150.
202. Cresciani, "The Proletarian Migrants," 14.
203. Ibid.
204. Ibid.
205. Cresciani, "Italian Anti-Fascism," 152.
206. *Smith's Weekly*, August 4, 1934, 3.
207. J. M. Bertei, "Innisfail," B.A. thesis, University of Queensland, 1959, 74.
208. *North Queensland Register*, September 7, 1935, 36.
209. Gurdon, "Australian Attitudes," 46–47.
210. *North Queensland Register*, October 19, 1935, 8.
211. Gurdon, "Australian Attitudes," 126–27. It should be noted, however, that within the ranks of Australian Catholics there was a liberal branch as well. While the mainstream (the hierarchy and Catholic media) were the heirs and proponents of the conservative views of Pope Pius IX, as stated in his *Syllabus of Errors* (1864) and reiterated by English Catholic theologian Ronald Knox in his *The Beliefs of Catholics* (1927), Australia's liberal Catholics had much in common with their North American counterparts who differed with the Vatican on a number of doctrinal issues. Some of the younger Australian clergy found much to admire in the liberal propositions of their civil society; particular those that exalted the rights of the individual and tolerance for others. Campion, *Rockchoppers*, 25–28.
212. *North Queensland Register*, October 19, 1935, 8.
213. *Courier-Mail*, October 7, 1935, 10; Ibid, October 9, 1935, 12.
214. Ibid, October 9, 1935, 13; Ibid, October 14, 1935, 11.
215. *North Queensland Register*, July 4, 1936, 12.
216. Mario Cazzulino interview; Henderson, "Italians," 288.
217. Gianfranco Cresciani, *Fascism, Anti-Fascism and Italians in Australia* (Canberra: Australian National University Press, 1980), 123.
218. *North Queensland Register*, October 26, 1935, 44.
219. Ibid, July 27, 1936, 14.
220. Ibid, October 19, 1936, 14.
221. *Sydney Morning Herald*, August 3, 1936, 6.
222. Fernández-Shaw, *España*, 325. In 1943, Gilroy tried to have a radio commentator, Emery Barcs, reproved by the Australian Broadcasting Commission: "for suggesting that Guernica had been bombed by Fascists during the Spanish Civil War." Campion, *Rockchoppers*, 40–41.
223. Gurdon, "Australian Attitudes," 133–35.
224. Judith Keene, "A Symbolic Crusade: Australians and the Spanish Civil War," in *La Mistica Spagnola: Spagna America Latina*, ed. Gaetano Massa (Rome: Centro di Studi Americanistici, 1989), 145–46. ["A Symbolic Crusade"].

225. Ibid, 141–42; 144.
226. Mason, "Agitators," 147–48.
227. Menghetti, *The Red North*, 68–69. Alberto Urberuaga of Ingham told me that there was a French Basque called "Laburdi" (for the name of his territory of origin) who collected money for the Republican cause. He also worked the migrant committee for a successful candidate from Ingham to the Australian or Queensland Parliament. He was the only French Basque in Australia that Alberto had ever heard of (Douglass field notes).
228. Mason, "Agitators," 152.
229. The information flow from Euskadi to Queensland's Basque Australians was interdicted with the collapse of Basque resistance to Franco in 1937. In Innisfail, local Spaniards pooled resources to purchase a radio that was capable of receiving broadcasts from Europe so they could monitor events. (Ibid, 147).
230. *Home Hill Observer*, April 9, 1938, 3.
231. Mason, "Agitators," 168.
232. Ibid, 156.
233. There was a falling out when the Sydney leadership of the SRC objected to Innisfail's SIA dividing its relief funds between the SRC and the anarchist SIA in France. Even after dissolution of the Innisfail SIA, eighteen Spanish nationals in Innisfail (including two Basques from Ingham) continued to receive the American Anarchist publication, *Cultura Proletaria* (Ibid, 162; 165). Australian authorities had them under surveillance and the police believed that Torrente was the publication's local Queensland agent, when in fact it was the much more circumspect Basque, Pedro Careaga (from Aulesti) (Ibid, 208).
234. Ibid, 210. Australian authorities were suspicious of the initiative and interned one of its members, Miguel Torrente, during World War II (Ibid, 161).
235. Keene, "A Symbolic Crusade," 146.
236. Australian National Archives, Brisbane, Anarchism in Australia File, BP 242/1, Q 25027.
237. *North Queensland Register*, November 6, 1937, 11.
238. Gianfranco Cresciani, "The Bogey of the Italian Fifth Column: Internment and the Making of Italo-Australia," in *War, Internment and Mass Migration: The Italo-Australian Experience 1940–1990*, ed. Richard Bosworth and Romano Ugolini (Roma: Gruppo Editoriale Internazionale, 1992), 11–32; Donald Dignan, "The Internment of Italians in Queensand," in *War, Internment and Mass Migration: The Italo-Australian Experience 1940–1990*, ed. Richard Bosworth and Romno Ugolini (Roma: Gruppo Editoriale Internazionale, 1992), 61–73; Douglass, *From Italy*, 236–54.
239. John R. Harvey, *Black Hand Vengeance* (Sydney: Invincible Press, 1943), 5. Whew!?
240. A prime example is the article in *Parade* magazine (author unspecified), "'Al Capone' of the Canefields," no. 348, November 1979, 23–25. It details the life of the supposed head of the Black Hand Gang, Vincenzo Dagostino [sic], and his violent demise.
241. Confidential Addendum to Evidence Book of the Ferry Report.
242. Father Mambrini, "Visit," 56.
243. April 21, 1927.

244. Henderson, "Italians," 66.
245. Ibid, 56.
246. J.A. Hempel, *Italians in Queensland: Some Aspects of Post-war Settlement of Italian Migrants* (Canberra: Australian National University, Department of Demography, 1959), 33.
247. Borrie, *Italians*, 81.
248. Henderson, "Italians," 64–65.
249. *Herbert River Express*, December 27, 1930, 5.
250. Ibid, January 27, 1931, 2.
251. *Smith's Weekly*, August 29, 1931, 14.
252. Douglass, *From Italy*, chap. 8, passim.
253. *North Queensland Register*, January 13, 1934, 16.
254. Ibid, January 6, 1934, 13.
255. Ibid, January 20, 1934, 69.
256. *Courier-Mail*, February 3, 1934, 12.
257. *The Telegraph*, June 30, 1934, 9.
258. *North Queensland Register*, January 9, 1937, 18.
259. Ibid, 32.
260. Quoted in Ibid, August 14, 1937, 57; also see Ibid, August 7, 1937, 10.
261. "The Italians in North Queensland." Reprint of an article from *The Telegraph*, Copy in CSR Archive (Sydney), Box N.1.0., Folder 3.
262. *Herbert River Express*, May 16, 1939, 3.
263. Ibid, September 12, 1939, 2.
264. Ibid, October 3, 1939, 2.
265. July 11, 1940, Australian Archives: CRS A659, item 40/1/7984, Department of Interior, Correspondence Files Class 1, 1939–1950, "Treatment of Spaniards in Times of War" (1940).
266. Diane Menghetti, "The Internment of Italians in North Queensland," in *Australia, the Australians and the Italian Migration*, ed. Gianfranco Cresciani (Milano: Franco Angeli Editore, 1983), 89. ["The Internment"].
267. Ibid.
268. Ibid, 90.
269. Ibid, 90–91.
270. *Herbert River Express*, June 15, 1940, 5.
271. Ibid, June 20, 1940, 5.
272. Ibid, November 7, 1940, 5.
273. Ibid, April 8, 1941, 3.
274. Ibid, February 10, 1942, 2.
275. Ibid, March 19, 1942, 2.
276. Alan Fitzgerald, *The Italian Farming Soldiers: Prisoners of War in Australia, 1941–1947* (Melbourne: Melbourne University Press, 1981), 1; 5.
277. February 27, 1941, Australian Archives (ACT): CRS A461, item J 325/7/1, Part 2. CA 12. Prime Minister's Dept. Correspondence Files, Multy-Number Series, Third System, 1934–1950, "Sugar Industry Employment of Foreigners" (1942–1943).
278. *Home Hill Observer*, March 13, 1942, 2–3.

279. *Herbert River Express*, February 24, 1942, 2.
280. Ibid, March 3, 1942, 2.
281. Menghetti, "The Internment," 93.
282. *Herbert River Express*, February 14, 1942, 2.
283. Ibid, April 25, 1942, 2.
284. Ibid, May 7, 1942, 2.
285. Ibid, February 14, 1942, 2.
286. Ibid.
287. Ibid, February 17, 1942, 2.
288. Ibid, February 26, 1942, 6.
289. Ibid, March 5, 1942, 2.
290. Ibid, March 12, 1942, 3.
291. Ibid, March 19, 1942, 2.
292. N. W. Lamidey, *Aliens Control in Australia, 1939–46* (Sydney: N. W. Lamidey, 1988), 52–53.
293. *Herbert River Express*, October 1, 1942, 4.
294. Menghetti, "The Internment," 101.
295. *Report of the Royal Commission Appointed to Investigate Certain Aspects of the Sugar Industry* (Brisbane: Government Printer, 1943), 29; 101; 156; 264; 332; 401; 483; 586; 602; 607; 641; 787; 798; 830; 871; 921; 1003.
296. *Herbert River Express*, October 8, 1942, 4.
297. Ibid, October 13, 1942, 3.

CHAPTER 6

Rehabilitation and Renewal

Configuring a New Era—In retrospect, it is fair to say that World War II could have been a more devastating experience for Italo-Australians (and, by extension, Southern Europeans) than was the case. When we consider the anti-Italian sentiment in some quarters that followed World War I, despite Italy's role as an ally in that conflict, one might have expected worse once the Italian homeland became Australia's enemy in the second global conflict. Nevertheless, after that later one most Anglo-Australians became more concerned about their future than the past. Had not the nation just missed being invaded by Japan? Did it not remain next to a teeming Asia well aware of the discriminatory White Australia Policy? If not Japan, what about China or Indonesia?

In 1945, a Department of Immigration was created in Australia with Arthur Calwell as its first minister (1945–1949). He was a strong advocate of renewed European immigration, particularly of that continent's war refugees. In his view, best exemplified by his slogan "populate or perish," Australia needed renewed European immigration both to bolster its national defense and to provide workers for its depleted labor force. He was particularly in favor of accepting Europe's refugees from the recent world war.[1] His latter stance was telling, since he had been a labor organizer and entered Parliament in 1940 as a member from his native Melbourne.[2] Son of an Irish-American father, he was a staunch Roman Catholic and Celtic loyalist (he even spoke Gaelic). Consequently, while he remained a staunch defender of the White Australia Policy and ardent opponent of Asian immigration, he was not against Southern Europeans, and particularly Italians.

As Australians debated the issues, the only naysayers were the Returned Soldiers' League and a few ultrapatriotic groups. In early 1944, the RSL annual conference urged that Italian nationals be declared ineligible for naturalization.[3] A representative of the Queensland Country Party demanded in the Queensland Legislative Assembly that a loyalty test for Italians be devised after the war.[4] In April of 1945, the RSL renewed its contention that the property of subversives ought to be seized for redistribution to ex-servicemen, and its present owners deported. The League insisted that all POWs in Australia be returned to their country of origin, and that there be no new naturalizations of enemy aliens for five years after the war.[5] Shortly thereafter, Mr. Jesson of the Herbert was lampooned in print as a political comedian who was pandering to the Italian vote.[6]

This was being played out against the backdrop of an international initiative to resettle persons displaced by World War II. In 1944, the United States had taken the lead in convening forty-three other nations into a United Nations Relief and Rehabilitation Administration (UNRRA). It should be noted that the actual United Nations itself was not founded until October 24, 1945. One of its first priorities was to deal with the repatriation of displaced persons and resettlement of those who were unable or unwilling (one and a half million persons) to return to their homeland. So, on February 12, 1946, the General Assembly of the nascent UN established the International Refugee Organization (IRO) as its first international agency.[7] Its mandate was to expire on December 31, 1951, since it was believed that the problem should be resolved by then. In the event, its work would continue until March 1, 1952, when the agency was dismantled.[8] The IRO was assisted in its work by an extraordinary number of private entities—ranging the gamut from Catholic, Protestant, and Muslim church organizations to the Boy and Girl Scouts.[9]

Australia was one of the original members of the IRO, committed in principle to accepting displaced persons (DPs) on humanitarian grounds. By 1947, the inflow of "kith and kin" Britishers was evident, scarcely surprising given the devastation of the European economy, including that of the British Isles. That same year, Australia committed to accepting on humanitarian grounds 4,000 DPs. The intention was to raise the number to 12,000, and, ultimately, 20,000 annually thereafter. The eligible were single men up to forty five years of age, single women forty and under, and married couples with children as long as the parents were under fifty years of age (these parameters were eventually liberalized). In keeping with Australia's longstanding preference for northern European immigrants, the program was initially limited to "Balts" (Lithuanians). The intending newcomers were to be vetted carefully by the Commonwealth government to ensure that they were medically fit and capable of making a positive contribution to the Australian economy.

The immigrants were given excellent treatment. While they had to agree to remain in their initial employment for a year before enjoying freedom of mobility and occupational choice,

> From the time of arrival at the reception centre in Australia until employment was found for them, the migrants were paid a special social service benefit at a rate equivalent to the normal unemployment allowance; meals and accommodation were furnished at a nominal charge, essential clothing was provided free of charge, and the immigrants were given instruction in the English language and in the Australian way of life.[10]

When the United States agreed to take in 200,000 displaced persons, Australia committed to matching that goal. Then, in October of 1948, Australia informed the IRO that it would accept 100,000 DPs over the next two years. In the event, 75,000 entered the country in 1949 and another 60,000 in 1950. Australia broadened the program to non-European refugees as well. New reception facilities were constructed in the country. By 1951, concerns over a housing shortage and a tightening labor market prompted Australia to reduce its monthly intake of all categories of immigrants to an average of fewer than 1,000 per month. Nevertheless, Australia received 182,159 refugees in all, making it the second largest recipient of IRO DPs after the United States.[11] Of the 70,535 Italian-national DPs resettled by the IRO, 14,079 entered Australia. It might be noted that Spanish Republican refugees were eligible under the program, but, of the 9,988 Spanish nationals resettled by the IRO, Australia received only 84.[12]

As Australia entered the postwar period, there was a serious attempt to accommodate returning servicemen by resettling them on the land.

The Queensland branch of the RSL continued to advocate that the sugar holdings of enemy aliens be confiscated for this purpose. In early 1946, a Royal Commission was appointed to look into the matter. One area that came under particular scrutiny was the Abergowrie district in the Herbert. The president of the Herbert branch of the RSL argued for creation of a new sugar-producing district there, with its own sugar mill and allotments restricted to ex-servicemen. When queried about his organization's advocacy of expropriation of alien holdings, he dissented.[13]

By mid-1946, the Returned Soldiers' League was isolated in its call for such expropriations. In June, the RSL's Queensland president claimed to have received much abuse and several threats—all demanding that he lay off the Italians. He complained that the northern-district delegates of the organization feared victimization should they continue their anti-Italian rhetoric (particularly in places like Ingham and Innisfail). He declared that the League's resolutions were being ignored or held in contempt by government officials. Nevertheless, he urged his delegates to redouble their efforts lest the Far North be lost forever.[14]

The political impotency of the RSL over the Italian issue was underscored further when its plan to expropriate farms was ignored. Indeed, its alternate plan to create major new sugar districts for servicemen also stalled. After the deliberations of the Royal Commission, it was resolved not to construct any new mills, but rather to simply increase, by a mere 3 percent, the sugar peaks in the existing ones in order to accommodate at least some returning ex-servicemen.[15]

At a conference of the RSL in April of 1947, the Ingham delegate broke ranks with the majority over the issue of the deportation of internees. He declared that, in Ingham, Italians and Anglos got on well. Such sentiments notwithstanding, the conference passed resolutions calling for closure of all foreign schools and a prohibition of speaking foreign languages in public places. Violators of the last provision were to be given twelve months to learn English or be subject to deportation should they fail.[16]

The RSL's advocacy of increasingly stringent, anti-alien measures was more a sign of its own political isolation than a viable threat to Australia's Italians. The political reality of North Queensland was reflected more in the estimate that, of 8,000 registered voters between Townsville and Lucinda Point, some 4,000 were Australian-born or naturalized

Italians. While Jesson (with strong Italian support) held the Kennedy District for Labour, he barely defeated the Queensland People's Party candidate, who nevertheless traveled among the electorate with an Italian interpreter.[17] In short, running an anti-Italian campaign was not a viable political option.

It was one thing to rehabilitate the established Italo-Australian population in the postwar period; however, the renewal of Italian immigration was a political challenge of a different order. Possibly the first public pronouncement on the issue came as early as 1944, when emotions still ran high and some Italians remained in internment camps. It was in October of that year that Mr. Theodore, not surprisingly also from the Herbert, stated that immigration from Italy should be renewed after the war. Equally predictable, the proposal was roundly denounced by the Queensland Country Party.[18] By May of 1945, the indomitable Archbishop Duhig assailed the anti-alien stance of the Returned Soldiers' League and exhorted his countrymen to accept Italian immigration once again. He declared the purported assistance of Italians to Japan during the war to be sheer fantasy. The nation needed population and could not depend upon war-ravaged England for it.[19]

At about the same time, the North Queensland chapter of the *Italia Libera* movement, an Anti-Fascist organization, held a meeting in Ingham to celebrate the defeat of the Axis. The delegates called for the renewed immigration of democratic Italians as part of Australia's future defense policy.[20] Jesson also entered the fray, noting that the nation must become a model of interracial cooperation, like the United States [sic],[21] if it wished to be a great power in the Pacific.

By mid-1946, there was concern in Queensland regarding a continuing shortage of canecutters. The anticipated improvement in the labor situation on completion of the war failed to materialize. Rather, the Australian economy had entered a period of dramatic growth, making a labor scarcity pan-national. The difficult and seasonal work in the sugar harvest failed to compete with other occupations. Consequently, in August of 1946, R. Muir, secretary of the Queensland Canegrowers' Association, met in Townsville with Commonwealth authorities to urge renewed immigration.[22] Italo-Australian farmers wished to admit fellow countrymen; however, relations with Italy remained in limbo. In the aftermath of the recent conflict, Australia had resolved not to renew the

1883 Treaty of Commerce and Navigation. So some sort of new agreement remained to be worked out.[23] By year's end, the remaining Italian POWs were being returned to Italy, despite the fact that 40 percent of them wished to stay in Australia.[24]

In 1947, there was again a labor shortage in the sugar industry. J. Armstrong, Queensland minister of immigration, toured the Far North and stated that relatives of Italians already settled there should be allowed into the country.[25] Queensland Premier Hanlon countered immediately that state law barred the entry of more Italians should they be intending farmers.[26] At this time, the thousands of Spanish Republicans exiled from Franco's Spain were nevertheless excluded from most Displaced Persons' assistance, much to the chagrin of their Queensland relatives.[27]

Meanwhile, in late 1947, the sugar industry embarked upon an initiative with Commonwealth authorities in anticipation of a labor shortage during the 1948 season. In 1946, the number of Displaced Persons in refugee camps in Europe and the Middle East had stood at 1.25 million individuals.[28] In 1947, Australia agreed to accept 12,000 of them annually.[29] Consequently, the Queensland sugar growers requested 1,000 Balts out of this first contingent to be employed as canecutters. At the same time, there were some misgivings regarding the suitability of such northerners. It was felt they would have to be selected carefully to ensure that only healthy and young single men were obtained.[30]

The industry would clearly have preferred the familiar Italians, but it was noted that they were technically still enemy aliens as no peace treaty had been signed with Italy. There was also some concern over the possible danger of submarining the displaced-person alternative for the industry should it somehow become intertwined with political controversy over the nation's policy regarding Italian immigration. The Queensland Canegrowers' Council did, however, recommend that, in addition to 1,000 Balts, a quota of 400 Italians be nominated directly by Queensland farmers. Such nominees would have to pass security clearance by Australian officials before departing Europe, and would have to agree to work as cutters for a minimum of two years.[31]

One month after their initial proposal requesting 1,000 Balts, the Queensland Canegrowers' Council and the Australian Sugar Producers' Association sent a joint letter to Commonwealth authorities asking that the number be increased to 1,750 displaced persons. They assured Canberra that local AWU officials had been consulted and had no objections. Despite the fact that Australia and Italy signed a Treaty of Peace in September of 1947, the industry recognized the necessity of meeting with representatives of the Returned Soldiers' League prior to finalizing a plan to admit the nominated Italians.[32]

That "courtesy" proved a failure, since the war veterans passed a resolution approving the introduction of displaced Poles and Balts but opposing that of former enemy aliens. The Ingham sub-branch dissented, arguing that renewed Italian immigration would be beneficial. Nevertheless, the industry dropped its request for 400 Italians, but upped its estimated need for displaced persons to 2,200. It was further noted that the true demand would likely be on the order of 2,500–2,800 men, since some would be required as replacements for those who could not withstand the rigorous work.[33]

Possibly encouraged by Article 16 of the new Constitution of the Italian Republic that went into effect on January 1, 1948, and removed all the Fascist restrictions on Italian emigration, R. Muir made a public appeal for Italian immigration. He noted that the 1948 crop promised to be abundant, and that 300,000 tons could rot in the fields if immediate steps were not taken. North Italians could be nominated by persons already resident in Australia and enter the country under three-year cutting contracts. The AWU was in favor of the plan and opined that any suggestion that the new immigrants might become a "Fascist force" was absurd. While the cutters would surely contain some ex-soldiers, who fought against the Australians, it should be remembered that, "…the enemies of yesterday are the allies of tomorrow."[34]

The plan was supported by both a representative of the New South Wales Sugar Millowners and the secretary of the Herbert River Canegrowers' Association. The latter argued that, after the British, the Italians made the best cutters. Finns, Spaniards, Yugoslavs, and Maltese were also good men, but were few in numbers.[35] In 1939, or the last "normal" season, the ethnic composition of the canecutters within the Herbert River District's two mills had included 667 Italians, 232 Britishers, 24 Maltese, 20 Finns, and 11 Spaniards.[36] Consequently, it was to Italy that the industry must turn in the current labor crisis.

The Herbert River Canegrowers' Association noted that, in the 1947 season, the cutter force in that district had been approximately half its prewar level. An extensive advertising campaign throughout the nation attracted a number of men to the area for the 1947 sign-on. However, "Of 385 men introduced to the district as a result of the recruiting campaigns, 275 left…after varying periods of a few hours to a few weeks." Consequently, the industry's only hope was renewed immigration: "The backbone of what is left of our cutting strength today is comprised very largely of Italians, but it is well to remember that they are ageing and will not continue for many more years at this class of work. Of last year's cutters nearly 300 were of Italian origin."[37]

Italians demonstrated both skill and staying power when it came to "…one of the hardest and dirtiest jobs in Australia."[38]

Meanwhile, the effort to obtain displaced persons encountered difficulties. Premier Hanlon of Queensland sent the Commonwealth minister of immigration a letter expressing concern over the news that no more than four to five hundred displaced persons would likely be available for the 1948 season.[39] Canberra replied that an effort would be made to raise the figure to one thousand cutters for Queensland and New South Wales.[40] This fell far short of the industry's anticipated needs. Commonwealth authorities therefore also approved the entry of five hundred North Italians, to be nominated by Italians already resident in Queensland. Premier Hanlon praised the scheme, and then Muir, no doubt anticipating RSL opposition, noted it would benefit returning soldiers as well, since many had sugar properties and needed canecutters.[41]

The plan was approved by the AWU, which declared that 2,500 additional men were needed. Regarding Italians, AWU officials characterized them as "excellent workers [who] had proved good unionists and…first class citizens."[42] Predictably, the Returned Soldiers' League denounced the scheme as giving preference to ex-enemy aliens over Britishers, which could lead to "…setting up predominately Italian communities in the north [which] would merely perpetuate the 'Little Italy' which caused great concern during the last war."[43]

Such sentiments notwithstanding, there was reason to believe that Australia was actually facing an Italian immigration *problem* that might exacerbate the labor crisis in the sugar industry. Since the war, the shipping shortage had allowed maritime lines to charge exorbitant freight fares between Europe and Australia. The return trip, however, was half or less given the reduced demand for passage. This meant that Italians sojourning in Australia found it quite economical to return to Europe and to a post-Fascist Italy. After the recent discrimination and internments, some Italo-Australians were understandably fed up with Australia. The country was therefore experiencing a net loss in her Italian population.[44]

While Italians could again enter the Queensland sugar industry, it scarcely thrust them into the vortex of Australia's emerging new immigration policy. Each nominee had to have a nominator in Australia willing to assume full responsibility for his welfare. The nominator had to endure an investigation by local police as to his suitability as a sponsor. A landing permit for the nominee was then issued by the Australian immigration authorities. The intending immigrant then had to present it to British consular officials in Italy in order to apply for an Australian visa. The nominee had to furnish a medical certificate and evidence of a chest X-ray as well. All travel arrangements were to be made and paid for by the nominator or nominee.[45]

In short, it was all pretty onerous. The issue of transportation cost caused immediate concern, and in itself discouraged many potential immigrants.[46] When the first Italian nominee arrived in May, nominated by his father, it had taken twelve months to complete the process and his fare was an astronomical £322, a sum subscribed by several of his relatives.[47]

The Italian nomination scheme triggered a spate of letter writing in the Queensland press, most of which was pro-Italian. At the same time, the emphasis upon North Italians caused one influential Innisfail Italian to denounce Muir's implicit rejection of Sicilians. He argued that Sicilians had proven their worth in Queensland and should not be the objects of discrimination.[48]

By July 1948, eight hundred Balts were working in the sugar harvest; few had failed and more were on the way.[49] Indeed, by year's end, the Balts, and, subsequently, Polish displaced persons had resolved the manpower shortage for the 1948 harvest. However, it seemed equally clear that the long-range solution rested with the Italians. Consequently, when, in July, Commonwealth Minister of Immigration A.A. Calwell toured North Queensland, he addressed the issue. In Ingham, he announced that Italian authorities had set a national goal of 250,000 emigrants annually, and that Australia hoped to have an Italian immigration plan in place by Christmas. He urged racial tolerance toward continentals comparable to that exhibited in the United States [sic]. While British immigration was preferable, it was unrealistic to expect that it could provide the millions of persons who should eventually inhabit North Queensland.[50]

Calwell's Italian initiative continued to be opposed by certain groups in Queensland. During the spring, there had been an RSL protest march in Brisbane,[51] and the organization's Northern District Council passed a resolution against the plan to introduce five hundred Italian nominees. Significantly, there was internal dissent.[52] Shortly thereafter, Queensland's Country Party considered a motion to ban Italians, prompting Archbishop Duhig to make yet another pro-Italian public statement.[53] The motion was defeated.

Meanwhile, it seemed that wheels were turning in earnest to facilitate Italian emigration to Australia. The US government had made two vessels available to Italy under the Marshall Plan, and it was anticipated that 1,400 Italians might arrive on them in Australia in August.[54] The manager of the Italo-Australian Transport Company in Sydney left for Rome in July to speed up the Italian emigration process. He hoped to bring out 215 immigrants monthly.[55] Despite all such measures, however, there was still considerable residual fear in Queensland regarding Italian immigration. When, in November, three Italians disembarked in Brisbane, authorities assured the public that they would be carefully monitored for two years and deported if necessary.[56]

A further development was the founding in Sydney (1948) of the FCIC, or Federal Catholic Immigration Committee. According to Ignacio Garcia,

> Its objectives were to provide spiritual care for all catholic migrants, to assist in their integration into parochial and community life, and to act in liaison with the Government and other organizations in the interests of Catholic migration. Included in its activities were, apart from the recruitment of immigrants abroad, the distribution of religious publications and leaflets of instruction in various languages, the appointment of ships' chaplains, and the disposition and support of priests of required nationalities to work with their fellow nationals in camps, hostels and par-

ishes. In the field of operations, the FCIC granted travel loans, did counseling of migrants, carried out processing and documentation tasks, and assisted in the reunion of families and in the placement and integration of migrants.[57]

Fears regarding it notwithstanding, by 1949 Italian immigration was again being accepted as a fact of life. Indeed, one proponent was emboldened to suggest they be provided with the same governmental support extended to displaced persons. He also recommended that Australia send a free shipload of sugar to Italy in appreciation for past Italian contributions to the industry.[58] Meanwhile, an Italian minister visited Australia to explore immigration possibilities, and announced that the Italian consulate in Brisbane was to be reopened.[59] Part of the purpose of his trip was to explore the possibility of settling Italians on farms in Mareeba (tobacco) and Cooktown (peanuts).[60] Of considerable symbolic significance, at its annual conference the Queensland chapter of the RSL rejected, by a narrow margin of 25–24, the usual resolution to oppose enemy alien immigration. Not surprisingly, the opposition to the motion was organized by Mr. Pearson of Ingham.[61]

While renewal of Italian immigration received considerable lip service, it was also true that its postwar phase remained in its infancy. By late 1949, only seven hundred Italians had entered Queensland since the conflict,[62] all presumably through the vehicle of individual nominations. At the same time, the situation was being monitored closely by Commonwealth officials. According to one report, two thousand landing permits had been issued for Italians, but at least one thousand who had requested employment-related entry had yet to arrive.

The 1950 sign-on was a good one, primarily due to the number of Italians seeking employment.[63] By November, the situation had changed due to the early departures of Italians and Maltese cutters seeking other forms of employment in the robust Australian economy.[64] This prompted concern of a renewed labor shortage at the 1951 sign-on.

In January of 1951, Muir traveled to Europe as the sugar industry's representative to facilitate the immigration of British, Irish, and Dutch potential canecutters (the Dutch under the terms of a pending agreement between Australia and Holland). He believed that at least 750 to 1,000 additional men would be needed for the 1951 harvest.[65] By April, it seemed that the shortfall would be greater than anticipated. Many of the previous year's cutters had settled permanently elsewhere and did not plan to return to Queensland. It was feared that the farmers and their families might have to cut their own cane during the 1951 season.[66] Clearly, the problem was not simply how to attract labor from distressed European economies, but also how to hold it throughout even a single harvesting season—not to mention beyond.

It was at this juncture that steps were taken to formalize Italian immigration into Australia. Commonwealth Minister of Immigration Holt announced that Australia was negotiating a plan with Italy that would permit fifteen thousand Italians to enter annually.[67] By August, it could be stated that seven thousand Italians had come to Queensland since the war, and that three hundred were on their way as part of the recently concluded agreement.[68] According to its terms, Italians would be recruited and screened by Australian officials in Europe for a two-year labor contract in Australia. The intending immigrant would receive £25 from each of the two governments toward the £120 fare from Europe. The immigrant could also borrow an additional £60 from the Italian government, to be paid back within two years. Single men and women between eighteen and thirty-five years of age, childless married couples under thirty-five, and families in which the male head was under forty-five were eligible for such assistance. The immigrant was to receive all the benefits of an Australian worker in a comparable position, with the exception of credit toward a retirement pension.[69]

The only opposition to the plan came from the RSL, which belatedly expressed its preference for renewed German immigration instead. Its request that the five-year/75,000 Italians immigration program be renegotiated to accommodate 25,000 Dutch, 25,000 Germans, and 25,000 Italians was ignored.[70]

The newly institutionalized Italian immigration scheme represented a potential, albeit not automatic, solution to the endemic labor shortage in the sugar industry. Commonwealth authorities informed Muir that the program was not meant to be a substitute for the existing private initiatives that were already bringing Italian nominees into Queensland. In fact, in keeping with her defense needs, Australia placed the highest priority on immigrants who were skilled tradesmen. Consequently, specific nominees who would be assigned to their nominator were not eligible for assisted passages. However, Commonwealth officials did agree to accept lists of potential immigrants, at least some of whom might be released to the sugar industry.[71]

Meanwhile, by July the labor shortage within the industry was so acute that the growers petitioned Canberra to arrange for an airlift from Europe to Queensland of several hundred Italians. This was rejected as impractical from logistical and cost standpoints.[72] A frustrated industry spokesman reported to the Commonwealth authorities that the growers were losing confidence both in the government and in their own industry representatives. While it was clearly too late to salvage the 1951 season, it was suggested that Muir stop in Rome on his pending trip to Europe to confer with Italian and Australian consular officials.

It was of particular concern to the industry that the immigrants for the canefields should be introduced directly to the Far North, and that they be contracted as canecutters for a specified period of time during which they would be precluded from any other form of employment. The present system whereby they entered Australia through southern ports exposed them to the cajolery of persons seeking their service. It was also felt that recruitment at the Italian end needed improvement, since there was suspicion among the growers that Italian authorities were selecting their least desirable rural workers for emigration to Australia. It was therefore suggested that a farmer of Italian descent and a government official thoroughly conversant with the sugar industry be sent to Italy to advise in the recruitment process.[73]

Other critical issues were raised with immigration officials. The industry felt that the arrival of the immigrants in North Queensland should be timed carefully. There should be two stages in which one batch arrived just prior to the sign-on and the other a couple of months later to provide replacements for the inevitable erosion in the cutters' ranks. Were the immigrants to arrive too early and be given temporary employment, they might become established in occupations other than cane cutting. Another concern was that Manpower, the agency allocating immigrant employment, should be encouraged to return cutters to the industry after their first season. What to do with the men during the slack season was a major worry. It was argued that with the current depressed level of sugar prices the growers could not afford to carry men though the down time. While some might find private-sector temporary work elsewhere in Queensland, the government should be involved in the solution as well.[74]

In early September, upon his return from a tour of North Queensland, the Commonwealth immigration minister approved the plan to have Muir visit with both Italian and Australian officials in Rome. The suggestion to send an Italo-Australian farmer and an official of the Department of Labour and National Service to help effect recruitment in Italy was also approved in principle.[75]

Meanwhile, by late October industry representative Muir had visited Rome and met with the Australian Legation and Italian authorities. The Australian officials were favorably disposed to a plan to send over the two recruiters. They felt that it was a particularly effective way to energize the ninety-two regional labor officers in Italy, many of whom to date had been relatively indifferent to Australia's attempts to recruit immigrants. The main problem with the plan was that, after promising high wages in cane cutting, there could be dissatisfaction if all the recruits could not be placed within the industry and some were then diverted to lower-paying work. It seems that there was already a nucleus for recruitment, since none of the men listed by growers as potential candidates for the 1951 harvest had as yet been contacted.[76]

Muir was greatly encouraged by the visit. He thanked the immigration minister for his reception in Rome and noted that the recruitment plan seemed feasible. He did find that Italian officials were extremely touchy on the issue of limiting the program to single men, and also insisted the actual recruitment be done by them. It was therefore politically impractical for the two Australian recruiters to work directly with Italian regional labor offices.

It was at this juncture that the plan began to encounter headwinds within the Department of Immigration. The dispatch of two special recruiters seemed to impugn the competency of the existing Australian officials operating in Italy. The goal of recruiting one thousand cutters prior to knowing the precise needs of the sugar industry during the 1952 harvest was risky; should some fail to find employment it would be embarrassing for the government. The problem of slack-season unemployment of the men remained real and unresolved.[77] Furthermore, were the sugar interests given preferential treatment, other Australian industries might demand the same. In light of all of the foregoing, the Department was unwilling to send the recruiters to Italy. It did, however, promise to effect recruitment with the existing staff and offered a free berth on the migrant ship from Italy to Australia should the sugar growers wish to send their representatives to travel out with the immigrants to counsel and orient them during the voyage. All of the other expenses of its two employees would have to be borne by the industry.[78]

By this time, the scheme was clearly bogged down over procedural and cost issues. The Queensland Canegrowers' Council therefore decided not to dispatch a representative to Italy. Instead, it offered to send an Italo-Australian farmer to the Australian port of entry migrant center to assist in the selection of men for the industry. The Council also resolved to publish a pamphlet and produce a film, to be made available to the Australian Department of Immigration officials effecting recruitment in Italy.[79]

There was evidence of two new initiatives that would affect the future recruitment of immigrants for Australia. By 1951, the German, Italian, and American Catholic laity and clergy believed that the Church should become active in migration matters, particularly given the large percentage of Catholics among postwar Europe's refugees and displaced persons. So, in 1952, Pope Pius XII established the ICMC, or International Catholic Migration Commission, including a loan fund to assist destitute migrants with transportation costs. It exhorted Catholics around the world to welcome and assist foreigners fleeing their homelands.[80] The Vatican's main protagonist in the new initiative was Archbishop Giovanni Battista Montini (the future Pope Paul VI). He believed that the Church needed to become involved in the displaced persons' crisis, since many of them were Catholics. The ICMC held its first triennial International Congress in 1952 in Barcelona. During the 1950s, it would assist 150,000 migrants, of whom 2,623 were from Spain.[81]

The second development was secular; proposed in 1951, it was known initially as the PICMME, or Provisional InterGovernmental Committee for the Movement of Migrants from Europe. The following year, it was renamed the ICEM, or InterGovernmental Committee for European Migration. In late 1951, it assumed the mantle of the UN's sun-setting IRO. The ICEM would not be constituted formally until November

30, 1954, although some of its components were already working on its mission to promote the humane and orderly migration of refugees, displaced persons, and labor migrants.[82]

The Vatican also expressed its concern over the plight of refugees and migrant communities in general. In the summer of 1952, Pope Pius XII issued his *Exsul familia* apostolic constitution that integrated new directives on migrant care into Canon Law—including the provision of chaplains of their same nationality to migrant communities. The Australian hierarchy, and Archbishop Duhig in particular, were not pleased, given that they stood firmly against creation of "national" churches on the ground. However, they had little choice but to comply. Duhig consented to the arrival of migrant chaplains of eight different nationalities—including Spaniards. This facilitated the arrival in Brisbane of Father Portella, a Galician, and Father Tomás Ormazabal, a Gipuzkoan, in the Far North. The former had little impact upon Queensland's Basque Australians; the latter would become their own priest.[83]

By May of 1952, Australian officials in Italy had recruited 250 single males who were about to embark from Naples.[84] There is no evidence of additional formal recruitment of Italians for the 1952 harvest, which, in retrospect, turned out to be a blessing. In fact, by January of 1952, it could be stated that during the previous six months Australia had admitted 72,000 immigrants, of whom 9,200 were Italians.[85] By mid-year, however, the immigration euphoria had withered as there was an evident glut of jobseekers in the national labor market. Many new Australians of diverse nationalities sought employment in the sugar industry, making the 1952 sign-on one of the most successful of the postwar period.[86]

By July, there were indications of trouble. Unemployed Italians housed at Bonegilla Camp in Victoria State (converted from a facility for interning enemy aliens during the war into a processing center for the new immigration) were irate, because they had been held there for four months without work. Many had families to support in Italy and demanded jobs or repatriation. There were rumors of impending riots and threats to burn down the camp. By one estimate, 3,200 Italians were implicated.[87] While initial reports in the newspapers were exaggerated, clearly there was a genuine problem. Italian consular officials and Australian authorities cooperated to find a solution. Action was particularly imperative, since the Italian assisted-migrant scheme was in full swing, and there were many immigrants in the pipeline. Thus, if in September there were 1,100 Italians in migrant centers still awaiting their first employment, 450 were on vessels headed for Australia, and an additional 300 were about to embark from Italy.[88] The Italian consul made a personal appeal to North Queensland's Italo-Australian farmers to try and absorb 400 of the newcomers, arguing that the glut had taken everyone by surprise.[89]

In late October, there was a riot of 250 unemployed Italians in Sydney that had to be quelled by police, and with injuries. The Italian consul refused to receive the demonstrators. The incident caused a minor diplomatic flap between Australia and Italian authorities. There was concern of possible Communist agitation among the unemployed newcomers.[90] There was also indication that the men in the migrant centers were organizing. In November, the Trades and Labour Council of Queensland published, in both English and Italian, the demands for employment or repatriation by at least some of the men in the camps,[91] prompting fears that there could be an embarrassing (for the government) common front between the disgruntled immigrants and the Australian labor movement. By year's end, it was decided to suspend, temporarily, the Italian assisted-migrant scheme, limiting the entry of Italians to privately sponsored nominees until such time that the economic conditions warranted a renewal of the program.[92]

Just prior to the 1953 sign-on, there were far too many unemployed Italians in the cane districts. In Ingham all barracks were full, men were camping out, and more were on their way. Italian consular officials were urging southern-Italian newspapers to publish warnings to intending emigrants, noting that an unemployment crisis in the canecutter workforce seemed imminent.[93] By July, an Italian official touring North Queensland opined that future Italian immigration would be sparse, and should be limited to family units that might engage in tobacco growing and other forms of farming. However, even this could not begin until the current economic crisis was over.[94]

Nevertheless, by October there had been so many defections in the ranks of the cutters that some gangs were extorting bonuses from desperate farmers and Aborigines were being hired for the first time since the war.[95] At the same time, it was clear that much of the labor force would dissipate at the end of the season.

After the mixed experience of 1953, and with growing disillusionment with the Italian cutter, the growers proposed that certain new strategies be adopted. First, the amount of retention money should be increased to discourage mid-season defections. Second, it was believed that organized recruitment of cutters should be initiated in Spain as well as Italy. Third, it was resolved that every effort should be made to develop an efficient mechanical harvester.[96]

As the 1954 season approached, there was again concern over the availability of adequate labor for the industry, despite the anticipated arrival of Italian, Greek, and German immigrants.[97] Indeed, at the sign-on there was a shortfall, and about one-third of the men hired had no previous experience; once again some Aborigines were retained.[98] Efforts to effect recruitment in Italy foundered, and there was an attempt to fill the anticipated demand with last-minute campaigns in Trieste and Malta.[99] Some five hundred men were recruited in the former and two hundred in the latter. In June, the men were en route to Australia, but, in the belief that by then most of the canecutter jobs were taken, the government diverted the newcomers to other employment.[100] By September, many of the gangs were undermanned; more than four hundred men had left the Ingham area alone. The Germans and Greeks proved useless; the Italians and Spaniards were working out. On balance, however, replacements in the gangs had themselves been replaced and the situation bordered on the disastrous.[101] It was at this juncture that a desperate industry again began to look to the possibility of recruiting its own cutters in Europe.

By mid-1954, the Australian government was prepared to renew Italian immigration under the earlier bilateral agreement. However, rather than the original goal of fifteen thousand immigrants annually, the target was reduced to two thousand workers and two thousand dependents.[102] The decision was made amid signs of growing strain between representatives of the sugar industry and the officials of the Department of Immigration.

From the inception of the cane-gang system of sugar harvesting near the beginning of the century, there had been the endemic problems of having sufficient men for the sign-on, a backup pool of replacements for those unable or unwilling to complete the season, and the inevitable dissolution of the labor force at harvest's end. As the familiar pattern played itself out against the backdrop of assisted-immigration schemes, there was plenty of room for frustration on all sides.

The growers were quick to cite the poor quality of the recruits, contending that Australian immigration officials in Europe were ill-prepared to select suitable men for sugar harvesting. In September, the representatives of the sugar industry went on the offensive, arguing that something had to be done to ensure that immigrant men under contract fulfilled its terms. The main problem, however, was the recruitment itself. It seems that a Spaniard (Basque) from Ingham had personally secured forty men in Spain for the previous season, all of whom remained in the industry as successful cutters, whereas forty-seven of the fifty-seven immigrants sent to Hinchinbrook Shire by the Department of Immigration had already defected. Therefore, it was imperative that a "farmer-selection scheme" be implemented in Spain and Italy, as well as on the island of Korcula (Yugoslavia) that, according to one canefarmer, was reputed to have "particularly hard working people."[103] The notion that previous recruitment had been flawed, resulting in men unsuited for cane cutting, had been stated publicly by the president of the AWU as well.[104] Regarding Spain, the industry informed the minister of immigration,

> Since Spaniards who have come to the Ingham district in the last two or three years have done well as canecutters, and have apparently settled down well to this work, we earnestly hope that your Government will...arrange for a cane grower of Spanish origin to visit Spain to select men suitable for cane cutting. We believe that the Government would have to make special arrangements for this, since there is no assisted migration scheme in operation between Spain and Australia, but we do ask that every possibility be explored for attaining Spaniards of the right type for cane cutting, even if such migrants had to meet their own fare to this country. Could arrangements be made whereby transport could be arranged for selected Spaniards on condition that they repaid their fare over a period of two years?[105]

For their part, immigration officials felt the growers were unwilling to take positive steps to address the problem of slack-season unemployment. This meant a whole new contingent of immigrants was required each year, since few would return to cane cutting after finding alternative employment. Clearly, the work in sugar was undesirable, particularly for men with families. Consequently, whenever there were prospects of employment in other industries the cutters were quick to defect from the gangs. On the subject of nationalities best suited for the work, a frustrated immigration official noted, "On previous occasions the industry has expressed preference for Italians, Greeks, Spaniards and the latest suggestion has been Yugoslavs would be best suited for cane cutting. Next year, no doubt, they will be pressing for Eskimos."[106]

The same official noted there is little sugar cane to be cut in Europe, so it was impossible to select for suitable cutters beyond picking men of reasonable background (rural), physical strength, and stamina. Immigration officials ought to be as capable of making a selection as were sugar growers.[107]

Then, at a meeting with sugar-grower representatives held in the autumn of 1954, the Department of Immigration agreed to several industry proposals. Immigrant centers were to be established in North Queensland so that dependents of cutters would have a place to stay while the men were working in nearby areas. The first (near Townsville) was to be opened for the coming season, and a second (at Cairns) during the following one. One or two representatives of the industry were to be sent to Europe for the recruitment, with their fares and expenses (but no salary) paid by the government. It was also agreed that at least one immigrant vessel should come directly from Europe to a North Queensland port (or at least Brisbane), in order to avoid the accusation that southern-port disembarkations exposed intending cutters to alternative employment opportunities.

Rejected was a proposal by the industry that recruitment could be attempted in Spain, and that the Australian government would advance passages to Spanish nationals and then be reimbursed once they were employed. There were allusions to "confidential reasons" that had been communicated verbally, but not in writing. It therefore remains unclear whether reference was to the political sensitivity regarding Franco's Spain, in particular, or a general ambivalence toward advancing and then collecting the fares of immigrants of any nationality. In the event, there was a fear that the whole immigration program could be compromised by the proposed scheme for Spaniards.[108] There was also doubt that, in the absence of a bilateral agreement, Spain could be counted upon to contribute part of the cost of such a program.[109]

Such sentiments notwithstanding, the wheels were in motion to further explore a Spanish alternative. In 1954, the Spanish Catholic hierarchy established a *Comisión Cátolica Española de Migración* (CCEM), or Spanish Catholic Migration Commission, as a branch of the ICMC—presided over by Basque-surnamed Cardinal Arrieta y Castro.[110] So there was now a "Catholic bridge" between Europe and Australia intent upon facilitating emigration from the former to the latter—its Old-World anchor being the ICMC/CCEM and the FCIC its New World one. Established migrants in Australia wishing to sponsor relatives from Spain could request assistance (through the Spanish Consulate in Australia) from the CCEM. It assisted with preparations of the documentation and travel plans.[111]

Given the lack of formal diplomatic ties between Australia and Spain, it was the ICEM liaison officer in Madrid, an Italian national named Edgar Storich, who initiated negotiations of possible Spanish emigration to Australia. In 1954, he approached Spanish officials regarding the possibility of Spain joining the ICEM.[112]

On July 17, 1955, the Spanish government passed a bill to create the *Instituto Español de Emigración* (IEE), or Spanish Institute of Emigration, under the Department of Labor and designed to not only regulate but facilitate migration. It would eventually be presided over by an intergovernmental committee chaired by the minister of labor. The Ministry of Foreign Affairs would play a key role also, particularly through involvement by a director general of emigration consular affairs, a post first held by the Basque Félix Iturriaga.[113] It was in 1955, as well, that Spain appointed Santiago Ruiz Tabanera consul general in Sydney, charged with exploring migration possibilities.

On October 29, 1955, Monsignor Crennan, head of the Australian FCIC, met in Madrid with the Spanish minister for foreign affairs, Martín Artajo. Crennan had just toured parts of Spain to ascertain the interest in Australia of potential Spanish emigrants. He was acting in a semi-official capacity for the Australian government. He told Artajo that Australia would pay part of the passage of Spanish migrants, but they should be industrial workers, given that his country was no longer a strictly agrarian one. He proposed that there be a bilateral agreement predicated on the one that Australia had signed with Italy. In light of the lack of formal diplomatic ties between their two countries, Crennan believed that the Australian representative in Paris, or some other European venue, should be accredited in Madrid. Crennan assured Madrid that the Spanish missionaries at New Norcia would work with the two governments to attend to the spiritual needs of these Catholic newcomers.[114]

Shortly thereafter, or on November 17, 1955, Tabanera met in Canberra with Tasman Hayes [sic],[115] head secretary of the Australian Department of Immigration, and they drafted a memorandum. Tabanera insisted that any such Spanish migration program would be contingent upon the two countries establishing formal diplomatic ties. For his part, Heyes opined that the first step would be for the Spanish government to complete a questionnaire to be provided to it by the Australian side. He also believed that the ICEM needed to be involved through its representative in Australia. Mr. Wendling, head of the Australian ICEM mission, had no problem committing his cooperation, particularly since Spain had just requested membership in his organization.[116] In the event, the Australians dillydallied for a month before sending Tabanera the promised questionnaire (that Madrid never would fill out). In short, despite the enthusiasm in the trenches, as it were, higher-ups within the administrative hierarchies of both countries ignored or impeded the initiatives rather than furthering them.

Meanwhile, shortly after Christmas of 1954, a three-man Italo-Australian delegation left for Italy to assist Australian consular officials there in the selection of canecutters for the upcoming season. They were F. M. "Nando" Pavetto and P. Lalli from Ingham and A. Lando from Ayr. Pavetto and Lando were growers, while Lalli was the Italian consular representative in the Herbert.[117]

The delegation arrived in Rome the second week of January and quickly became bogged down in negotiations with several agencies.[118] First, there were three weeks of discussions with officials of the ICEM, the key organization for funneling displaced persons to host countries. The ICEM had strict guidelines and wanted guaranteed year-round employment for the migrants for a minimum of two years. The delegation was authorized by the sugar industry to promise only the usual seasonal work. The Australian government was asked to guarantee slack-season placement for the men. Both the ICEM and British officials wanted the recruitment to begin in troubled Trieste, an international sore point due to its many displaced persons, but the delegation resisted because of the sugar industry's limited and mixed experience with immigrants from there. The Italian government urged recruitment in those parts of Italy suffering the greatest unemployment. In addition, single men only were wanted, whereas the Italian government wished that married men be included. Ultimately, there would be a compromise to include three hundred married men in a contingent dominated by bachelors.[119]

For their part, the delegates preferred to recruit in those areas of North Italy and Sicily that had provided Queensland's earlier cohorts of successful canecutters. Sicilian canefarmers were insisting that the delegation secure Sicilians. However, that agenda caused ambivalence among Australian consular officials. They still believed that northern Italians were more desirable (and less controversial) than their southern counterparts.[120] Muir had earlier argued for the inclusion of, indeed a special preference for, Sicilians, reasoning that North Italians and Sicilians disliked each other. There were a large number of Sicilian canefarmers in North Queensland and they preferred their compatriots. The Sicilian worker had proven to be durable and reliable.[121]

The complicated negotiations in Rome dragged out, placing the delegation under considerable pressure if the immigrants were to be obtained, processed, and transported to Queensland in time for the 1955 sign-on. It was not until early February that actual recruitment began.

In addition to the three Italo-Australians, the selection team consisted of an Australian Legation officer, a representative of the ICEM, two or three secretaries, security officers, and medical doctors. The security personnel did the initial screening of the applicants in order to weed out Communists and their sympathizers. Nando Pavetto conducted the first interview with the candidates who passed the security screen. He examined their hands to make sure they were calloused from manual labor and approved only those with robust physiques (many of the slightly built were referred to other channels and ultimately emigrated to Australia for other lines of work). Pavetto queried the men regarding their backgrounds and asked to see their ID cards listing occupation. As it turned out, some of the applicants had as many as three cards that they produced depending upon the circumstances. Lando and Lalli then explained the nature of cane cutting to the men, and what they might expect to earn and save. Each candidate was then required to demonstrate his literacy by reading from a third-grade primer[122] and was given a preliminary medical screening. Those who passed all of the foregoing tests were sent to Milan or Treviso for a thorough medical exam and chest X-ray.

It was the goal of the delegation to recruit 1,500 men. However, it quickly became apparent that a significantly greater number would have to be interviewed in that many were failing the selection process. Also, there was considerable erosion among those who passed. Some had second thoughts and others were pressured by their families to relent.

When the delegation arrived in Sicily, it first went to Messina, since the Sicilian veterans in Queensland were in the main from either there or Catania. The chief Italian labor official in Sicily, however, wanted recruitment to be focused upon other parts of the island where unemployment was greater. After considerable negotiation and further delay, the delegation prevailed and began to travel to the hometowns of Queensland Sicilians (it had an extensive list of names of possible candidates). The delegates met with local officials and received promises of many applications. Once the processing began in Messina, it was anticipated that 90–100 men could be interviewed daily, whereas an average of 120 applied. The effort was not without its critics. While the Mafia was silent, several landowners opposed the loss of field labor and one Communist schoolteacher campaigned actively against the scheme.

After three weeks of successful recruiting in Messina, the delegation went to Enna, largely to please Italian officials, since it was *terra incognita* for the recruiters. Pavetto was favorably impressed with the men there, but a new impediment appeared. The Australian liaison officer objected to the applicants' negroid appearance, examined the cuticles of their fingernails, and pronounced them to be unacceptable. Despite the objections of a medical doctor, the ruling remained in effect. The Sicilian recruitment ended in Siracusa. Most of the applicants there were mariners and showed little promise for cane cutting.[123]

The delegation then returned to Rome, where it met with the chief officer of the Italian emigration service. He was from Sardinia and clearly wanted some recruitment there. After another two-week negotiation, the delegation agreed to accept four hundred Sardinians in return for permission to begin recruitment in Udine (near Venice). The Sardinian initiative was a success. Then, a few men were obtained from the Brescia, Milan, Bergamo, and Piedmont areas, the places of origin of many of Queensland's earliest Italian settlers. However, relative prosperity throughout these areas diminished the appeal of the opportunity to cut sugar cane.

When the delegation again returned to Rome, it found that the rate of rejection had been considerable, so an additional four hundred men were required. Again, at the urging of Italian officials, the recruiters traveled to the Abruzzo, a region of high unemployment. This proved fortuitous, since the local authorities cooperated fully and a contingent of experienced rural workers was selected.

The main contingent of the recruits was to be sent to Australia in two ships. The vessel *Flaminia* would carry 800 men for distribution throughout the sugar districts north of Mackay. It departed Italy on April 24 with 799 workers (one defected at the last minute) and 150 of their dependents.[124] Most of the men were between twenty-one and twenty-five years of age. Lalli accompanied the group, lecturing them several times on conditions in Australia and showing them a motion picture of cane-cutting techniques.

The arrival of the *Flaminia* was awaited with great anticipation in North Queensland. About half of the recruits were to disembark in Cairns and the remainder in Townsville. The Brisbane office of the Commonwealth Department of Immigration issued elaborate instructions to its staff and dispatched several officers to Thursday Island to board the vessel in order to begin the processing of the migrants prior to the arrival in Cairns on May 24. It was hoped that the men could be made available to the industry within two days after disembarking.[125]

The *Flaminia* reached Cairns on May 27, and, by month's end, the men were on their way to the individual sugar districts. 410 converged on Ingham alone and were quickly placed. The *Herbert River Express* noted there was general satisfaction with their appearance and urged that every effort be made to accommodate them, given that they were the likely future of the industry. It cautioned that the method of selection could not be repeated indefinitely, so these were the laborers to be counted upon. They must be enticed to remain in cane cutting after their two-year ICEM contracts expired.[126] For its part, the Cairns branch of the New Settlers League urged the government to recruit a shipload of Italian women who would work as domestics and hotel staff. It was felt they would marry the "newby" single males and thereby stabilize this most recent wave of the Italian presence in North Queensland.[127]

While the *Flaminia* was en route, Pavetto remained in Italy to finalize arrangements for sending out the remainder of the recruits. Approximately one hundred "rural workers" deemed suitable by the recruiters for agricultural work, but not the most physically demanding work of cane cutting, departed Italy on May 12 on the *Aurelia*. Meanwhile, preparations were underway to send seven hundred men on the *Toscanelli*. Pavetto was encountering last-minute difficulties in that there were some defections, late additions, etc. When it was rumored that only six hundred men would embark, he noted that tardy recruitment might cover the shortfall. In a pinch, some of the men on the *Aurelia* might be turned into canecutters. Pavetto informed Muir that the difficulty stemmed in part from the failure of the anticipated numbers of applicants from Perugia and Aquila (Abruzzo) to materialize.[128] Pavetto and Lando traveled to Australia aboard the *Toscanelli*. Writing in late June to Muir, Pavetto observed that, after enduring severe weather, the vessel was about to make port in Fremantle. Muir had asked that the men not be formed into cutter gangs before arrival, but it had proven impossible to prevent them from doing so on their own. Pavetto believed this to be advantageous, particularly since the recruits were from six distinct regions in Italy and had a strong desire to remain with their like kind.[129]

The *Toscanelli* contingent disembarked in Sydney in early July. After processing, most were sent to the New South Wales sugar districts; however, 269 of the men were directed to Queensland.[130] This was indeed fortunate for the Queensland growers, since there were already signs of erosion in the cutters' ranks. By September, in Ingham it could be said that, of the contract Italian cutters brought to the district for the season, more than 100 had drifted away. Only a small percentage had permission to leave and the authorities were attempting to track down the remainder.[131] Still and all, near the season's end, the *Herbert River Express* declared the recruitment a success, noting that it was unrealistic to expect every man to work out.[132]

Neither industry officials nor Commonwealth authorities seemed displeased. Initial reticence evaporated in the afterglow over a job well done. New lines of cooperation had been established. For instance, by late 1955, nominations to sponsor individual immigrants from Italy were pouring into the Department of Immigration from all over Australia, creating a bureaucratic logjam that translated into as much as a twelve-month delay. Commonwealth authorities expedited the entry of those earmarked for the Queensland canefields.[133] After the harvest, exit interviews conducted with a cohort of cutters recruited for the 1955 season suggested that most were happy with the work. More of those who came on the *Flaminia* directly to North Queensland expressed their intention to return for the next season than did cutters who landed in southern Australian ports. A number of the men planned to spend the slack season working in tobacco near Mareeba or on the railroad in western Queensland.[134]

Despite a desire to build upon the previous year's success, the sugar industry was unable to field a team of recruiters for the 1956 season, and therefore relegated selection to the Commonwealth Legation in Rome. Unfortunately, the official there most conversant with the growers' needs had been transferred to Copenhagen.[135] There was also a desire in some governmental circles to insist that sugar growers, like other Australian industries, make provisions for their own labor supply in the future. It was argued that, while it was too late not to go forward with a 1956-season recruitment, such Italian immigration should not be allowed to become a "hardy annual."[136]

Initially, the industry and government disagreed over the target number of European recruits for the coming year. The former wanted one thousand, while the latter believed eight hundred would suffice. There was the perennial problem of estimating in January the industry's labor needs the following June without knowing how many experienced cutters would show up for the new sign-on. The industry opted for a liberal projection to ensure a proper labor supply, while officials were more cautious—fearing a surplus and cognizant that ultimately the government was responsible for the immigrants during the slack season.[137] Government opinion prevailed, and, in February, Australian officials in Rome were ordered to recruit five hundred men (and up to two hundred dependents) for North Queensland, as well as an additional three hundred single men for the sugar districts of New South Wales.[138] In Ingham, the newspaper editorialized that conditions were improving in Italy to the point that potential migrants would think twice before leaving. Meanwhile, Spain remained impoverished.[139] The success of the Spanish cutters introduced by one particular private nominator [likely the Mendioleas] was extolled against the backdrop of fear that the Italian pool might dry up.[140] It was also stated that future recruited canecutters should be drawn from more than one nationality, with specific mention of Spaniards [Basques] and Austrians [Yugoslavs].[141] That autumn, the newspaper reiterated its stand that Spaniards should be recruited as an alternative to Italians; noting that the possibility had been vetted two years earlier but foundered due to the lack of diplomatic and consular relations between Australia and Spain.[142]

Regarding the private nominators, there is a certain *pro forma* pattern to the applications of both the Mendioleas and Badiola. While they were sprinkled over a number of years, the applications tended to state the same net-worth and annual income of the nominator—the Mendioleas £9,000 net-worth and £600 annual income; Badiola £10,000 net-worth and £1,500 annual income. The nominee was likely listed as a "cousin" or "nephew" with a rural manual occupation. In the case of the Mendioleas, the name of the nominator might range from Teresa (certainly in the majority) to Johnny to Rufino to Aniceto. In short, the applications sought to demonstrate the financial wherewithal of the nominator (i.e., capability of ensuring that the immigrant would not become a ward of the state, without providing the government with too much detail), while invoking at some level a kinship (in some cases, a friendship) bond between the sponsor and aspiring newcomer and, in the case of the Mendioleas, obviation of the possible perception that one person had assumed too many "burdens." This specificity may be considered against the reported propensity of the Mendioleas and Badiola to sponsor "strangers," i.e., the kinsmen, friends, and fellow villagers of recently arrived immigrants, including non-Basque Spanish nationals. In an interview, John Mendiolea told me that he could not recall anyone failing to repay his family's cash advancements toward application and passage costs.

It should also be noted that there emerged in each of the key centers of Basque settlement unofficial hosts. In the Burdekin, the Achurra household was the likely first stop and first bed for the newcomer from the Basque Country.[143] In Ingham, there were at least three—the Mendioleas, the Balanzateguis, and the Badiolas. I was also told in the Sydney *Gure Txoko* about Mario Gavazzi, husband of María Balanzategui (sister of Sabin, Bingen, and Gotzone in Ingham). Mario was North Italian and the couple met in Ingham. He or she would meet the ship of many a Basque newcomer, take them to their house for the night, and put them on the train for the Far North the next morning.[144]

Notes

1. Marie Kabala, "Immigration as Public Policy," in *The Politics of Australian Immigration*, ed. James Jupp and Marie Kabala (Canberra: Australian Government Publishing Service, 1993), 16. ["Immigration"].
2. Between 1960 and 1967 he was the Labour Party's leader during a period in which it was the opposition.
3. *Herbert River Express*, February 22, 1944, 2.
4. Ibid, October 5, 1944, 2.
5. Ibid, April 21, 1945, 4. The fear was that the prisoners-of-war would attempt to stay on rather than be repatriated to their war-ravaged homelands.
6. Ibid, May 17, 1945, 4.
7. Louise W. Holborn, *The International Refugee Organization: A Specialized Agency of the United Nations. Its History and Work 1946–1952* (London, New York, Toronto: Oxford University Press, 1956), 1. [*International Refugee Organization*].
8. Ibid, 67.
9. Ibid, 146–49.
10. Ibid, 394.
11. Ibid, 394–95.
12. Ibid, 439. Between them, Argentina (2,923) and Venezuela (2,623) accepted no less than 70 percent of the Spanish nationals. Both were longstanding (several centuries) destinations of Basque emigration.
13. *Herbert River Express*, April 11, 1946, 2.
14. Ibid, June 8, 1946, 2.
15. Ibid, September 14, 1946, 3.
16. Ibid, April 8, 1947, 2.
17. Ibid, April 3, 1947, 3.
18. Ibid, October 5, 1944, 2.
19. Ibid, May 17, 1945, 4.
20. Ibid, May 19, 1945, 1.
21. Ibid, May 26, 1945, 4. The United States was still racially segregated at the time. Indeed, whites and African Americans were strictly segregated in the American military forces sent to the Pacific during the recent conflict.
22. Ibid, August 17, 1946, 3.
23. Ibid, August 22, 1946, 2.
24. Ibid, December 24, 1946, 2.
25. Ibid, July 27, 1947, 2.

26. Ibid, July 29, 1947, 2.
27. Mason, "Agitators," 176.
28. *Herbert River Express*, August 31, 1946, 2.
29. For a discussion of the process from the perspective of a DP see V. L. Borin, *The Uprooted Survive: A Tale of Two Continents* (London: Allen and Unwin, 1959).
30. October 15, 1947, Australian Archives (ACT): CRS A445, item 199/1/3, Department of Immigration, Correspondence File S 'Class 16,' 1951–52, "Qld. Sugar Industry Employment of Migrants."
31. Ibid.
32. November 21, 1947, Australian Archives (ACT): CRS A445, item 179/1/3/, Department of Immigration, Correspondence File S 'Class 16,' 1951–52, "Qld. Sugar Industry Employment of Migrants."
33. January 28–29, 1948. Australian Archives (ACT): CRS A445, item 179/1/3, Department of Immigration Correspondence File S 'Class 16,' 1951–52, "Qld. Sugar Industry Employment of Migrants." [January 28–29, 1948].
34. *Herbert River Express*, January 31, 1948, 2.
35. January 28–29, 1948.
36. January 22, 1948, Australian Archives (ACT), Department of Immigration, Correspondence File S 'Class 16,' 1951–52, "Qld. Sugar Industry Employment of Migrants." Interestingly, Spaniards were somewhat more prominent in the ranks of the canegrowers. While Finns and Maltese owned five farms respectively in the district, fifteen farms were under Spanish ownership in 1948 (versus 302 Italian farms and 134 British ones).
37. Ibid.
38. Ibid.
39. January 28, 1948, Australian Archives (ACT): Correspondence File S, item 179/1/3, Department of Immigration, Correspondence File S 'Class 16,' 1951–52, "Qld. Sugar Industry Employment of Migrants."
40. February 4, 1948, Australian Archives (ACT): CRS A445, item 79/1/3, Department of Immigration, Correspondence File S 'Class 16,' 1951–52, "Qld. Sugar Industry Employment of Migrants."
41. *Herbert River Express*, February 5, 1948, 2.
42. February 23, 1948, Australian Archives (ACT): CRS A445, item 179/1/3, Department of Immigration Correspondence File S 'Class 16,' 1951–52, "Qld. Sugar Industry Employment of Migrants."
43. February 26, 1948, Australian Archives (ACT): A445, item 179/1/3, Department of Immigration, Correspondence File S 'Class 16,' 1951–52, "Qld. Sugar Industry Employment of Migrants."
44. February 3, 1948, Australian Archives (ACT): CRS 445, item 211/1/6, Department of Immigration, Correspondence File S 'Class 16,' 1951–52, "Immigration of Italians to Australia."
45. *Herbert River Express*, March 2, 1948, 3.
46. Ibid, May 1, 1948, 2.
47. Ibid, May 13, 1948, 4.
48. Ibid, July 8, 1948, 2.

49. Ibid.
50. Ibid, July 24, 1948, 4.
51. Ibid, March 1, 1948, 2.
52. Ibid, April 1, 1948, 2.
53. Ibid, July 27, 1948, 2.
54. Ibid, June 5, 1948, 2.
55. Ibid, July 29, 1948, 2.
56. Ibid, November 2, 1948, 2.
57. Ignacio García, *Operación Canguro: The Spanish Migration Scheme, 1958-1963* (Sydney: Spanish Heritage Foundation, 2002), 19. [*Operación*].
58. *Herbert River Express*, March 26, 1948, 4.
59. Ibid, March 1, 1948, 2.
60. N.d. (circa 1949), Australian Archives (ACT): Department of Immigration, Accession BT 541, item 60/6993, Aliens Inspecting Officer to Commonwealth Migration Officer, Brisbane, Correspondence File, "Italian Migration to Queensland," 1949-1952.
61. *Herbert River Express*, June 7, 1949, 3.
62. Ibid, October 4, 1949, 2.
63. Ibid, May 13, 1950, 2; Ibid, May 27, 1950, 3.
64. Ibid, November 23, 1950, 2.
65. Ibid, February 1, 1951, 2.
66. Ibid, April 12, 4; Ibid, April 14, 1951, 4.
67. Ibid.
68. Ibid, August 9, 1951, 4.
69. Ibid, August 21, 1951, 4.
70. Ibid, December, 18, 1951, 1.
71. July 11, 1951, Australian Archives (ACT): BT 61/1, item 49/12796, Department of Immigration, Correspondence File, "Italian Migration to Queensland," 1949-1952.
72. July 18, 1951, Australian Archives (ACT): CRS A445, item 179/1/4, Department of Immigration, Correspondence File S 'Class 16,' 1951-52, "Qld. Sugar Industry Employment of Migrants."
73. August 9, 1951, Australian Archives (ACT): CRS A445, item 179/1/4, Department of Immigration, Correspondence File S 'Class 16,' 1951-52, "Qld. Sugar Industry Employment of Migrants."
74. August 27, 1951, Australian Archives (ACT): CRS A445, item 179/14, Department of Immigration, Correspondence File S 'Class 16,' 1951-52, "Qld. Sugar Industry Employment of Migrants."
75. September 13, 1951, Australian Archives (ACT): CRS A445, item 179/1/4, Department of Immigration, Correspondence File S 'Class 16,' 1951-52, "Qld. Sugar Industry Employment of Migrants."
76. October 26, 1951, Australian Archives (ACT): CRS A445, item 179/1/4/, Department of Immigration, Correspondence File S 'Class 16,' 1951-52, "Qld. Sugar Industry Employment of Migrants."
77. October 30, 1951, Australian Archives (ACT): item 179/1/4, Department of Immigration File S 'Class 16,' 1951-52, "Qld. Sugar Industry Employment of Migrants."

78. November 15, 1951, Australian Archives (ACT): CRS A445, item 179/1/4, Department of Immigration, Correspondence File S 'Class 16,' 1951–52, "Qld. Sugar Industry Employment of Migrants."
79. "Immigration" n.d. Australian Archives (ACT): CRS A445, item 179/1/4, Department of Immigration, Correspondence File S 'Class 16,' 1951–52, "Qld. Sugar Industry Employment of Migrants."
80. The ICMC continues to function at present and maintains staff and programs in more than forty countries. It has a stellar record of having assisted the world's refugees throughout its existence irrespective of their religious affiliation.
81. García, *Operación*, 17.
82. During its first decade of existence, the ICEM facilitated the emigration of over one million people, mainly Europeans. Somewhere between 30 and 40 percent were war refugees, the remainder were persons seeking a better future and/or desirous of effecting family reunions with relatives abroad. In the cases of the truly needy, the ICEM provided loans for transportation costs. By 1959, Italy had provided 241,000 of the ICEM's total migrants, the highest figure for any sending country. Australia, a founding member of the ICEM, had received 230,000 of its migrants, making it the leader among recipient nations. 170,000 of these were DPs, a total second only to that of the United States. Jean I. Martin, *Refugee Settlers: A Study of Displaced Persons in Australia* (Canberra: Australian National University Press, 1978), 1.
83. Mason, "Agitators," 243–45.
84. May 9, 1952, Australian Archives (ACT): CRS A445, item 179/1/4, Department of Immigration, Correspondence File S 'Class 16,' 1951–52, "Qld Sugar Industry Employment of Migrants."
85. *Herbert River Express*, January 8, 1952, 3.
86. Ibid, May 31, 1952, 3.
87. Ibid, July 19, 1952, 1; Ibid, July 31, 1952, 1.
88. Ibid, September 30, 1952, 2.
89. Ibid, October 4, 1952, 1.
90. Ibid, November 1, 1952, 1; Ibid, November 14, 1952, 1.
91. The Trade and Labour Council of Queensland, n. d. Australian Archives (ACT): BT 140/1, item 52/12009, Department of Immigration, Correspondence File, Accommodation of Agreement Migrants released at emergency employment in migrant hostels, 1952–1955.
92. *Herbert River Express*, November 6, 1952, 1.
93. Ibid.
94. Ibid, July 23, 1952, 1. The official was a representative of the Institute for Credit to Italian Workers Abroad. The Institute had already helped Italian families to settle in Argentina, Brazil, and Chile. It was announced in the fall that a plan might be framed for fifty families in Queensland whose passages from Italy would be 80 percent paid by a two-year loan from the Institute (Ibid, October 27, 1953, 1). Establishing any such Italian "colonies"' was opposed by the RSL. This opposition prompted the Queensland government to announce that there was as yet no formal agreement (Ibid, November 10, 1953, 1).

95. Ibid, October 24, 1953, 1.
96. Ibid, March 16, 1954, 2.
97. Ibid, April 27, 1954, 2.
98. Ibid, May 29, 1954, 1.
99. April 15, 1954, Australian Archives (ACT): CRS A445, item 179/1/4, Department of Immigration, Correspondence Files Multiple Number Series (Policy Matters), 1951–1955, "Qld. Sugar Industry Employment of Migrants," 1954.
100. June 1, 1954, Australian Archives (ACT): Accession BT 170/1, item 54/6619, Department of Immigration, Correspondence File: "1. Employment, 2. Sugar Industry, 3. Migrants ex 'Flaminia' May 55—Precedents and procedures," 1954–1955.
101. *Herbert River Express*, September 23, 1954, 1.
102. August 3, 1954, Australian Archives (ACT): CRS A445, item 211/1/25, Department of Immigration, Correspondence Files Multiple Number Series (Policy Matters), 1951–1955, "Requisitions for recruitment of Commonwealth nominees in Italy for financial year 1954," 1954–1955.
103. September 29, 1954, Australian Archives (ACT): CRS A445, item 179/1/25, Department of Immigration, Correspondence Files Multiple Number Series (Policy Matters), 1951–1955, "Employment of New Australians in Queensland sugar industry."
104. Ibid.
105. October 18, 1954, Australian Archives (ACT): CRS A445, item 179/1/25, Department of Immigration, Correspondence Files Multiple Number Series (Policy Matters), 1951–1955, "Employment of New Australians in Queensland sugar industry," 1954–1955. [October 18, 1954].
106. October 1, 1954, Australian Archives (ACT): CRS A445, item 179/1/19, Department of Immigration, Correspondence Files Multiple Number Series (Policy Matters), 1951–1955, "Qld. sugar industry employment of migrants," 1954.
107. Ibid.
108. Ibid.
109. October 18, 1954.
110. Over the next few years, it would establish seventy-seven field offices, sixty-four diocesan delegations, three diocesan sub-delegations, and eight assistance offices in places of embarkation. It coordinated the activities of other Catholic entities such as *Caritas* and *Acción Católica* (Catholic Action) and *Juventud Obrera Católica* (Catholic Worker Youth) regarding emigration matters. It dispatched chaplains to migrant communities and published both a monthly newsletter and magazine called *Emigrantes Trasplante de Catolicismo* (Catholicism's Transplanted Emigrants) with 25,000 subscribers (García, *Operación*, 17–18). García creates considerable confusion regarding the magnitude of emigration from Spain to Australia between 1925 and 1959 facilitated by the ICMC (and CCEM). He states that, of the 3,985 persons entering Australia under the program, 2,623 were Spanish nationals. He cites as his source the book *Immigration in Latin America* (p. 253) authored by one "F. Bastos de Roa" (Ibid, 17). That book was actually written by Fernando Bastos de Ávila and it states on its page 253 that Australia admitted 2,716 migrants with ICMC travel loans. The 2,623 figure is the exact number of Spanish nationals entering Venezuela

under the IRO's program, as cited in Holborn, *International Refugee Organizations*, 439. The coincidence is too obvious. As if the error in itself were not bad enough, Totoricagüena perpetuates it by citing García's figures in her own book on Basques in Australia (Totoricagüena, *Australia*, 127.)
111. Ibid.
112. Between 1957 and 1961 (inclusive) the ICEM, through its Spanish branch with the acronym CIME (*Comité Intergubernamental para las Migraciones Europeas* or Intergovernmental Committee for European Migrations), would facilitate the emigration of nearly 60,000 Spanish nationals, largely to Latin American countries. 2,548 of these migrants went to Australia, peaking with 1,818 in 1961–1962 (García, *Operación*, 14–15).
113. Ibid, 10–11.
114. Ibid, 20–21.
115. García misidentifies him since his surname is actually Heyes. I will employ the correct one in what follows, even when citing García as my source. Again, Totoricagüena compounds García's error.
116. Ibid, 22.
117. Unless otherwise specified, the following description of the 1955 recruitment is based upon a personal interview with F. M. Pavetto in Ingham in 1981.
118. Founded in Geneva in 1952, the ICEM was charged by the United Nations High Commission for Refugees with aiding displaced persons of the recent world war (mainly the European venue, but including some refugees from the Pacific as well). Australia was a founding member of the High Commission and Spain would join it after entering the United Nations in 1955.
119. Australian Department of Immigration correspondence suggests the growers were reluctant to include married men since the cane barracks were unsuited for families. Actually, New South Wales growers opposed recruiting married cutters, whereas Queensland ones were more favorably disposed toward them on the grounds that families might settle in their area permanently and thereby stabilize the workforce. In their view, too many of the more mobile single men drifted away to other locations and occupations. The Australian government wanted permanent settlers at this time and favored married men. The Townsville and Cairns Migrant Centers were destined for families only. So the 300-married-men quota was a compromise forged within Australian circles and is mentioned in documents prior to the arrival of the delegation in Italy. For example, see December 23, 1954, Australian Archives (ACT): Accession BT 170/1, item 54/6619, Department of Immigration, Correspondence File: "1. Employment, 2. Sugar industry, 3. Migrants ex 'Flaminia' May 55—Precedents and procedures," 1954–1955.
120. The Australian chief migration officer in Rome was informed by the Department of Immigration as follows: "No approval was given for the recruitment of any specific number of Sicilians but it was agreed in principle to accept a number of them, although their selection was not particularly favored. However, once the proposal seems reasonable and it is agreed that the Canegrowers may do their first selection in Sicily, the maximum number selected from that area [is] to be limited to 300. See

February 14, 1955, Australian Archives (ACT): Accession BT 170/1, item 54/6619, Department of Immigration, Correspondence File: "1. Employment, 2. Sugar Industry, 3. Migrants ex 'Flaminia' May 55—Precedents and procedures," 1954–1955. [February 14, 1955].
121. December 31, 1954, Australian Archives (ACT): Accession BT 170/1, item 54/6619, Department of Immigration, Correspondence File: "1. Employment, 2. Sugar industry, 3. Migrants ex 'Flaminia' May 55—Precedents and procedures,"1954–1955.
122. It would seem that this was perfunctory since the Department of Immigration noted in its instructions to the chief migration officer of the Australian Legation in Rome, "Literate applicants would be preferred but the literacy test should not be enforced in respect to otherwise intelligent persons considered suitable for cane cutting. This exception applies only to cane cutters, of course." See February 14, 1955.
123. Three gangs were recruited in Siracusa and all subsequently failed to work out.
124. Breakdown of Italian Migrants on SS Flaminia, n.d. Australian Archives (ACT): Accession BT 170/1, item 54/6619, Department of Immigration, Correspondence File: "1. Employment, 2. Sugar industry, 3. Migrants ex 'Flaminia', May 55—Precedent and procedures," 1954–1955.
125. Introduction of Migrant Labour for Cane cutting in North Queensland. Procedural Instructions for Relating to the Arrival of 950 Italian Assisted Migrants on the *M.V. Flaminia*, n.d. Australian Archives (ACT): Accession BT 170/1, item 54/6619, Department of Immigration, Correspondence File: "1. Employment, 2. Sugar industry, 3. Migrants ex 'Flaminia', May 55—Precedents and procedures," 1954–1955.
126. *Herbert River Express*, June 2, 1955, 2.
127. Ibid, June 30, 1955, 2.
128. May 15, 1955, Australian Archives (ACT): Accession BT 170/1, item 54/6619, Department of Immigration, Correspondence File: "1. Employment, 2. Sugar industry, 3. Migrants ex 'Flaminia' May 55—Precedents and procedures," 1954–1955.
129. June 29, 1955, Australian Archives (ACT): Accession BT 420/1, item 55/8241, Department of Immigration, Correspondence File: "'Aurelia' Nominal roll," 1955.
130. July 15, 1955, Australian Archives (ACT): Accession BT 420/1, item 556831, Department of Immigration, Correspondence File: "'Toscanelli' Ex Italy with canecutters 3-5-55 due Sydney 7-7-55," 1955.
131. *Herbert River Express*, September 8, 1955, 1.
132. Ibid, November 26, 1955, 2.
133. September 5, 1955, Australian Archives (ACT): Accession BT 420/1, item 55/14526, Department of Immigration, Correspondence File: "1. Employment, 2. Sugar industry, 3. Qld. Canegrowers Council requests position regarding outstanding form 40 cases," 1955–1956.
134. November 18, 1955, Australian Archives (ACR): Accession BT 541, item 60/6993, Department of Immigration, Correspondence File: "1. Employment, 2. Sugar industry, 3. Policy and procedure re recruitment for canefields," 1954–1965.
135. November 24, 1955, Australian Archives (ACT): Accession BT 541, item 60/6993, Department of Immigration, Correspondence File: "1. Employment, 2. Sugar industry, 3. Policy and procedure re recruitment of labour for canefields," 1954–1965.

136. December 12, 1955, Australian Archives (ACT): Accession BT 541, item 60/6993, Department of Immigration, Correspondence File: "1. Employment, 2. Sugar industry, 3. Policy and procedure re recruitment of labour for canefields," 1954–1965.
137. January 10, 1956, Australian Archives (ACT): Accession BT 541, item 60/6993, Department of Immigration, Correspondence File: "1. Employment, 2. Sugar industry, 3. Policy and procedure re recruitment of labour for canefields," 1954–1965.
138. February 15, 1956, Australian Archives (ACT): Accession BT 541, item 60/6993, Department of Immigration, Correspondence File: "1. Employment, 2. Sugar industry, 3. Policy and procedure re recruitment of labour for canefields," 1954–1965.
139. *Herbert River Express*, July 7, 1956, 2.
140. Ibid, July 5, 1956, 1.
141. Ibid, July 3, 1956, 1.
142. Ibid, October 27, 1956, 1.
143. In her oral history interview with Carlos Orue, Elisabeth Achurra recalled that her father, José Francisco ("Patxi") Achurra, assisted dozens of Basques to come by arranging their papers and lending them their fare. Their household was the first stop of most newcomers and also served as a reunion place for the Basque population of the Burdekin virtually every Sunday. She was referring to the period prior to the formation in the Burdekin of the ethnic ("Spanish") voluntary associations of the 1960s and 1970s. Her uncle, Benito, was the first to immigrate in 1924. She states that her father immigrated in 1920 and came with his brother José María. That is incorrect as Patxi came in 1930 (sponsored by Benito) and alone. Benito married an Australian woman and they were childless, eventually moving to Townsville and investing in several real estate projects. José María was in Australia by the early 1930s, when he was killed in a car accident in the Burdekin. Patxi had intended to earn money and either go back to the Basque Country or send for his family (he left a wife and son there). In the event, his strategy languished and was then interdicted by the Spanish Civil War and World War II. It was not until 1947 that he was able to bring his family to the Burdekin via the USA. The family had been separated for no fewer than seventeen years! (Orue Urazandi interviews).
144. Douglass field notes.

CHAPTER 7

The Spanish Alternative

North Queensland's Spanish community escaped World War II largely unscathed. Non-naturalized individuals were required to register as aliens. However, excepting the surveillance of a few by the Australian authorities, Spanish nationals were ignored. Despite his close identification during the Spanish Civil War with Hitler and Mussolini, Franco kept Spain out of the global conflict. Also, North Queensland's Spanish population was in the majority Catalan and Basque, Franco's most implacable battlefield foes. This defused any possible concern regarding their loyalties in the minds of at least informed North Queenslanders.

At the same time, events in Europe did interdict Spanish immigration for a while. For nearly a decade after World War II, Spain was a pariah nation as the victorious powers sought to remove the continent's last Fascist dictatorship peacefully by means of an economic and political boycott. It was not until 1952, when the United States, as a part of its Cold War strategy, signed an agreement with Franco for military bases, that Spain began to reenter the world community.

On December 14, 1955, Spain was admitted to the United Nations, sponsored by the United States. A few months later, or on March 23, 1956, it joined the ICEM. Obviously, the prospects for concluding a migration program between Spain and Australia were improving. In April, there were three new initiatives, all involving the Australian Catholic Church. First, a Spanish missionary at New Norcia, Father Eugenio Pérez (backed by the Catholic bishop of Ballarat) proposed establishing an agricultural colony of Spanish (or Italian) nationals. In the event, this plan proved abortive when the Spanish government felt that it was untimely.

Second, on April 18, 1956, Monsignor Crennan visited the Spanish consulate in Sydney. His meeting with Tabanera was pretty much a rehash of his previous one with Artajo, albeit that Crennan was now suggesting that Spanish immigrants should be willing to accept agricultural employment if offered. It would seem that he was now coordinating his efforts with the Queensland sugar industry. Despite the Spanish consul's strong recommendation that Madrid pursue an "interchange of diplomatic missions," the proposal languished as Madrid processed Father Perez's plan.[1]

Then there was the third initiative, the one that would eventuate in a bilateral agreement. At a conference in early April, sugar-industry official Muir noted that Italians and Basques were the best canecutters.[2] John Ignatius Armstrong,[3] an Australian Labour Party senator in the Australian Parliament, facilitated an agreement that the Australian government should send two representatives to Spain to negotiate the possibility of recruiting two hundred Spanish nationals for the 1957 sugar harvest (it was obviously too late to do so for the 1956 one). The Australian representatives were to be Muir and R. E. Armstrong, the Australian high commissioner and head of the Australian Migration Office in London.[4] Shortly thereafter, Muir argued that an attempt should be made to recruit five to six hundred Basques for the 1957 season.[5] Just as Australian officials emphasized white European appearance when recruiting North Italians (as opposed to Sicilians), the Department of Immigration would equate northern Spaniards to northern Europeans.[6]

As the sign-on approached, the *Aurelia* left Italy destined for Cairns. Muir was arguing that the projections had proven low and that 1,500 immigrants were needed. His request for them was denied, though it was noted that the 300 men destined for New South Wales might be diverted to Queensland should conditions warrant.[7] On May 17, the *Aurelia* arrived in Cairns and landed 658 migrants including dependents.[8]

Meanwhile, there was nervousness in the industry, as too few of the 1955 Italian cutters returned for the 1956 sign-on.[9] Voices were raised to the effect that other possible areas of Europe should be targeted for migrant recruitment, possibly Austria and the Basque provinces of Spain. The Basques were proving particularly reliable workers. It was clear that conditions in Italy were improving to the point that cane cutting in Queensland held less attraction there, while rural Spain continued to be impoverished.¹⁰ Government officials were open to the suggestion, fearing that the continued focus upon Italians could produce a backlash reminiscent of past reactions during periods of intensive Italian immigration.¹¹

In August, the Ingham newspaper renewed its appeal for Spanish immigration. It claimed that local Spaniards had brought out hundreds of men over the years¹² and that about 100 of them currently resided in the Herbert. Most were in the sugar industry; some forming their own gangs. One was a baker and another was in construction. Most of the men were Basques and several had come to Australia with their wives. In one instance, an Ingham sponsor (the Basque Mendiolea family) bought out seventeen nominees. The newspaper touted this as the most comprehensive private immigration scheme operating in North Queensland. It also noted that the effects were cumulative, since each new arrival was a potential future sponsor.¹³

The nomination of a Spaniard by Ingham Basque Pascual Badiola was rejected that same month by a Commonwealth migration official,

> Because of the very considerable increase in the applications for admission to Australia of nominated southern European migrants paying their own fares, and of the need to ensure that the total number of migrants each year does not exceed the figure determined by the Government, it has become necessary for the time being to accept applications only for the entry of close relatives who are dependent on their sponsors and will rely on them for sustenance when in Australia.¹⁴

Upon further inquiry, Badiola's agent was informed that it was impossible to say when, or if, policy would change regarding eligibility.¹⁵ Nevertheless, about this same time the *Australian Sugar Journal* reported,

> In all over the past two or three years, the comparatively small number of Ingham's Spanish origin families have assisted several hundred young men to come out. At present it is estimated, that there would be close to a hundred Spaniards either working in the harvesting or on farms.... Quite a large percentage of the young men are from the Basque country in north west [sic] Spain.

Established families of Spanish origin not only assist the migrants to pay the passage here. They make special efforts to ensure that the newcomers are absorbed in the community as a whole. People in the Ingham district believe that the nominations and assistance by the families will have a "snowball" effect. New settlers will, in time, assist other members of their families to migrate.[16]

Mason interviewed José Larrazabal (married to a Mendiolea daughter) who reported that one of the Mendiolea brothers would meet new Basque migrants at the Ingham train station, interview them as to their backgrounds, and: "Those from rural villages and market towns were sent to the best farms, whilst those from coastal villages were sent to farmers with less cane to cut." The former were deemed to be the likely best cutters and the point was to sustain the Basques' excellent reputation in this regard.[17] In October, the *Herbert River Express* reported that the district's Canegrowers' Council was working through local Spaniards to determine emigration interest in Spain.

In December, Muir, after attending an international sugar conference in Geneva, and accompanied by R. E. Armstrong, visited Madrid to explore the possibilities of a migration program. The main problem continued to be the lack of diplomatic ties between Spain and Australia.[18] Consequently, the ICEM facilitated the discussions. The Spanish nationals who had entered the Herbert district during the past year had proven outstanding, and all had repaid their fare advances. The newspaper argued that Spaniards might become a complement (rather than an alternative) to the Italian canecutter.[19]

By year's end, there were attempts to recruit Spanish nationals for the Burdekin as well. Three Spanish growers (all Basques) in the district nominated ten Basques, claiming to have introduced previously a total of ten Spanish nationals between them, all succeeding as canecutters.[20] The activities of the three nominators were supported by the Ayr District Canegrowers' Executive and the Kalamia Mill Suppliers' Committee.[21]

Meanwhile, possibly in concert with the Ayr requests, Badiola appealed to the Queensland Canegrowers' Council to intervene on his behalf with the Commonwealth immigration officer. Appended to Badiola's petition was a list of thirteen Spanish nationals (Basques) introduced during the previous two years, all of whom were still cutting cane.[22]

Within a few days, Muir had forwarded Badiola's request to Canberra, along with those from Ayr, while noting,

> I would strongly urge that all applicants supported by Mr. Badiola or the Mendioleas from Ingham, in regard to Spanish migrants, should receive urgent and sympathetic consideration.... Quite a number of Basques have come out here following on the selection of another Mr. Badiola who is living in Spain, but who was at one time living in Ingham. He is the brother of Mr. Badiola referred to in this correspondence.[23]

Muir was informed that, since there was no agreement between Spain and Australia, the sponsors were proposing to bring in the canecutters as full-fare immigrants (that is, non-assisted). Such entry, however, exempted them from the assisted-migrant's scheme's two-year obligation to work at cane cutting. The previous year's full-fare immigrants had inflated the number of Italian arrivals to the extent that it became difficult to manage efficiently the assisted-migrant program for the sugar industry. However, it was decided that the pending nominations should be approved in light of Muir's recommendation.[24] At the same time, there was concern since "...it was not proposed to introduce a procedure which would lead to all nominations being channeled through these people [Badiola and the Mendioleas]."[25] The Brisbane office was ordered to approve some nominations to be screened by the British consul in Spain, and on condition that the nominators provided evidence that the immigrants would be guaranteed employment in the sugar industry.[26]

In early February, industry representatives, government immigration and labor officials, and a spokesman for the AWU met in Brisbane to set the recruiting goal. The union called for a review of European recruitment, arguing that the national labor market was softening and the jobs might be needed for persons already in Australia. There was skepticism that the Britisher cutter would suddenly reemerge, and planning proceeded to bring in 200 Spanish nationals, 300 Italians, and 300 "Austrians" (who were actually Yugoslavs still in Austrian refugee camps). A disappointed Muir argued that the industry would require a minimum of 1,300 new immigrants.[27] The AWU opposed the more modest plan to introduce the total of 800 European immigrants.[28] Immigration officials, concerned by renewed (albeit mild) AWU opposition to immigration, agreed with the 800-men target, while noting that, if required, the additional 500 men might be obtained in Australia among the ranks of the other immigrants arriving from Europe, yet undesignated for a specific industry.[29]

By this time, Australian Department of Immigration authorities were negotiating with the Spanish Government to introduce two hundred canecutters and up to fifty of their dependents. They were optimistic and felt that the men could arrive in Cairns by May first.[30] Muir reported that, during his visit to Spain the previous year, the Spanish authorities expressed serious concern that the rights of Spanish nationals be protected by some strong organization. They cited the poor experiences of Spaniards in other countries. Muir had informed Madrid that the AWU was the appropriate guardian of the right of all of its members.[31]

The Australian embassy in Rome sent a negotiating team to Spain where it encountered difficulties. The Spanish officials demanded to know the cost of living in North Queensland. They presented the Australians with a list of the high prices of specific items (kilo of beef, pair of trousers, bottle of beer). The Australians felt that the declared costs were those occurring in urban areas rather than the rural districts of the Far North; but were impressed by the Spaniards' thoroughness. One official noted, "…these chaps are quite spry and want the information as exact as possible."[32]

By May, the Ingham Rotary Club had sent two Basques, Alberto Urberuaga and Juan Azpiri, to Gatton College in Brisbane (the Agricultural College of the University of Queensland) for a short course designed to help them convince new immigrants to stay on the land. The two men were scheduled to address the Club upon their return.[33]

The wheels were also in motion to recruit 300 Spanish nationals for the 1958 harvest, introducing them in three 100-men contingents. The first would be scheduled to arrive in mid-July, as it was then that the need for replacements would begin to be apparent.[34] When, over the protestation of Muir, the target figure was reduced from 300 to 150 Spanish nationals, the AWU withdrew any opposition to the now modest 1958 recruitment goal.[35]

A pleased Commonwealth official noted that it should be possible to absorb the Spaniards, "…without attracting too much notice or criticism."[36] There seemed to have been nervousness regarding reaction to a quantum jump in Spanish cutters, since, despite all the favorable press given to the Spaniards during the 1957 season, there were only 45 Spanish nationals among the 4,545 cutters working north of Townsville.[37] At the same time, it was necessary to absorb them smoothly and quickly within the sugar industry, given that, from Madrid's viewpoint, it was an experiment that would be monitored closely.[38] Italians and Yugoslavs were simply left out of account as all efforts now focused upon Spain.

Nevertheless, by mid-March the Spanish government had broken off negotiations regarding recruitment for the 1957 season, arguing that there was too little time to complete them satisfactorily.[39] The recruiting effort was once again focused upon Italy. Then, on April 15, 1957, R. E. Armstrong sent the Duke Primo de Rivera, Spanish ambassador in London, a communication stating that the European recruitment for the 1957 harvesting season was already concluded, but that Australia would be interested in exploring a migrant-assistance program for the sugar industry for the fiscal year 1958–1959.[40]

In late May of 1957, the *Toscana* reached Cairns with nearly five hundred intending cutters from Italy. At the Ingham, Tully, and South Johnstone sign-ons there had already been a surplus of labor on offer. The AWU declared that it would not issue union cards to the new migrants until all existing members were employed. Five of the intending cutters decided to remain on board the *Toscana* for its voyage to Sydney, while about four hundred disembarked in Cairns to face uncertain prospects. The recruitment in Europe of an additional three hundred men (along with two hundred of their dependents) was put on hold.[41]

The usual attrition in the ranks of the cutters once the work began resolved the problem. After spending a few weeks in the Cairns' migrant center, the *Toscana* contingent was absorbed into cane cutting. However, the experience was unnerving for all concerned. Immigration officials generated statistics that showed that, of the 4,546 Queensland cutters in the previous season, 2,938 were European immigrants who had entered Australia prior to 1957. Factoring in the likely return to the paddocks in 1958 of much of the 1957 *Toscana* contingent, some Australian officials believed the industry needed no further assistance.[42]

A critical meeting was held on June 4, 1957, in the Madrid office of the IEE. The Australians were represented by Tasman Heyes and R. E. Armstrong. The director and assistant director of the CIME attended, as did a representative from the Spanish Ministry of Foreign Affairs and the director of the IEE, General Rodríguez de Valcárcel. They hammered out an agreement that was based largely upon the 1951 one between Australia and Italy. Regarding costs of passage, the Australian government would provide 85 US dollars, Spain was to give 50, and the migrant (with possible assistance from ICEM) had to contribute 35 dollars. The recruits would depart Barcelona for Australia on April 15, 1958, with Cairns as their destination. According to García,

> Spanish migrants eligible for assisted migration under this document were: single men from 18 to 35 years of age; childless married couples up to 35 years; and family units, provided the breadwinner was not over 45. Owing to the shortage of accommodation, married men were to proceed to Australia in advance of their wives and children. The assisted migrants would be Spanish workers that had been recruited by the Spanish authorities on the basis of numerical request lodged by the Government of Australia, and had been finally approved by the appointed Australian representative. The migrants undertook to remain two years in the employment to which the Australian Government allocated them, or to refund the cost of the assistance received towards their passage fare prior to departure, should they not remain in Australia for the agreed period. After this two years period, provided they have no [sic] proved unsuitable for settlement, migrants could remain indefinitely in Australia, and choose any employment and place of residence they desired. The memorandum guaranteed to all migrants the same wages, accommodation and general conditions of employment prevailing for Australian workers in the same occupation. Similarly, they would also be entitled to workers' compensation and other social service benefits.[43]

There remained but one sticking point between the two sides. The Queensland canefarmers wanted Basques—period. For the Spanish government this was anathema. The Basque Country in some ways continued to be treated as a conquered enemy by Madrid, and its *de facto* cultural genocide policy there remained in effect. The IEE produced a "Report on the Areas of Recruitment of Canecutters to Migrate to Australia" that stated the climate of Andalusia and the Canary Islands was akin to that of Queensland—certainly more similar than that of the Basque area. Furthermore, in Malaga, Almería, and Granada there were 4,930 hectares of sugar cane employing 3,300 men. Canary Islanders were familiar with machete-work and thousands had emigrated from there to the sugar properties in Latin America. The document also noted that Andalusians were already migrating to industrial employment in the Basque provinces, a highly industrialized part of Spain, so it made no sense to recruit rural laborers there.

Tabanera communicated these points to the Australians. Madrid also informed Armstrong in London that all Spaniards had an equal right to migrate. By concentrating the recruitment on Basques alone, the rights of other citizens would be violated. Should the Australians not relent on this demand, the negotiations were over. Nevertheless, on June 26, Armstrong reiterated that the recruits must be Basques. The decision in Madrid, given Armstrong's "stubbornness," was to freeze everything until formal diplomatic ties could be established between the two countries.[44]

In the event, the impasse was resolved almost immediately in early July. Harold Holt, director of the Australian Department of Labour, was just concluding a two-month tour of several European nations (Great Britain, Denmark, Germany, Holland, Switzerland, and Italy). García underscores that the newspaper coverage in Australia of the trip was extensive, but that Holt's final stop, Madrid, was initially left out of the account. It seemed that Australian officials themselves held a bias in favor of northerners versus southerners, whether dealing with Spaniards or Italians, as well as with Europeans as a whole. Then, too, there was still the anti-Southern Europeaner (or "Latin") bias within certain sectors of Australian society. Opposition to Italian recruitment had not abated entirely, and there was the possibility of exacerbating matters by announcing a new recruitment program for Spanish nationals. This was particularly true given that news of Spain in the Australian press focused primarily upon the internal resistance (including guerrilla violence) to the Franco government and labor strife. In effect, the Australian government would be seen to be negotiating with a Fascist dictatorship.[45]

Holt met with officials from the Spanish government and the ICEM, and it was resolved to modify Basque "exclusiveness" to a "preference" for Basques. In practice, this would mean that the recruiters would concentrate primarily in the Basque Country. At this point, the potential Spanish recruitment became public knowledge in Australia. Shortly thereafter, there was the annual meeting called the Australian Citizenship Convention, essentially dominated by conservative Protestant nativists, at which Prime Minister Menzies defended the Spanish program against its critics.

On September 11, Tabanera met with Harold Holt and Athol Townley, head of the Australian Department of Immigration, and was informed that Australia remained interested, but that there was still the ticklish matter of convincing the Australian public of the merits, particularly given the recent downturn in the Australian economy.[46]

In October, Townley wrote to Valcárcel informing him that Australia only wanted three hundred men and possibly some dependents in the first recruitment. Heyes and Armstrong would assist with it on the ground in Spain. Valcárcel then suggested to Heyes that the Australian selection team should operate in Bilbao between February 1 and 11, 1958, and in Madrid from the 11th to the 15th. The emphasis would be to screen out applicants who were not of Basque origin. Tabanera was delighted, and informed Madrid that he expected to open his new legation in Canberra in December of 1957, which would be the prelude to a successful negotiation of formal diplomatic ties between the two countries.[47]

The optimism proved premature, as Australia sent word in November that the plans were on hold due to concerns over the economy. Valcárcel met with officials of the Ministry of External Affairs and the ICEM and informed both Tabanera and Holt of their frustration. Preselection of the three hundred men had already commenced with the involvement of the Organization Sindical. The Spanish side also put the pointed inquiry to Holt as to whether the Australians were placing their recruitment of Italian nationals on hold as well?[48]

On December 3, 1957, Heyes wrote Madrid. Holt had advised him that the final number of recruits had been reduced to 150 single men. Their departure should be in mid-July (i.e., they would be midstream "replacements" during the 1958 harvesting season). They would disembark in Brisbane for immediate transport to Ingham. Henceforth, C. I. Waterman, chief migration officer in Rome, would be the contact instead of Armstrong in Rome. Given the reduced number, the selection should be confined to Bilbao. The Australian government would now provide 100 dollars of the passage costs of each recruit instead of 85. The IEE agreed.[49]

On January 16, 1958, Waterman and the Australian recruiters met with Valcárcel and ICEM officials in Madrid. By March, two Australian immigration experts had left Madrid for Spain's northern provinces to recruit 150 men for the sugar industry.[50] They were anticipating approval of the plan, although negotiations with Spanish authorities were still "up in the air," and could, in the view of one Commonwealth official, still fail.[51] By March 23, 400 Spanish nationals from the provinces of Bizkaia, Gipuzkoa, Araba, and Navarra, as well as some from Santander, Huesca, and Teruel,[52] had applied, and 249 of them had been preselected. A liberal Catholic cleric, Edmund Campion, recalled the extreme Protestant attitude as reflected in the publication *Rockchoppers*, regarding the arrival of the Spanish nationals in 1958. He stated that, for Protestants, "It is inconceivable that the Catholics could profess sincere loyalty to the British Crown. To be a non-Protestant supposed potential disloyalty."[53] Consequently,

> The arrival in Brisbane at the beginning of this month of a contingent of Spanish immigrants is something that should disturb every true Australian. The specious plea that we need these migrants for labour in the sugar fields is so much poppycock. The natural increase of the Italians will provide more than enough labour for the industry. It is particularly disturbing when one realises that they are all Basques. That particular group has been described by many impartial authorities as the most fanatical R.C.s [Roman Catholics] to be found anywhere. Another characteristic is that they commonly have families of up to 20 children.[54]

By May, the 166 who had received final approval for what had been named *Operación Canguro* (Operation Kangaroo) were informed that they were to proceed by train to Trieste for embarkation June 26 on the *Toscana*. 159 men (all single males or unaccompanied married men) did so. Also aboard was Father Tomás Ormazabal, a Basque Catholic priest destined by the CCEM to minister to the religious needs of North Queensland's Spanish Catholic community.[55]

Ormazabal expected to stay in Queensland for two years, although it turned out to be for the rest of his life. He was ultimately based in Tully where he organized gatherings of Spaniards in the local Irish Club. He was quoted as saying, "On Sundays I hold Mass twice in Dimbulah, and a third one in a suburb called Mutchilba. I preach a sermon in English, and another much the same in Italian, because it so happens that all these Spaniards already speak Italian and the Italians constitute by far the greatest part of the audience."[56] He traveled extensively throughout the Far North, and depended upon the generosity of his flock to cover his travel expenses. He learned to leave his car unlocked and parked strategically so that it could be filled by the faithful with provisions while he was ministering to the congregation. He became a critical node in an employment information network that operated among Spanish nationals throughout North Queensland.[57] According to Mason,

> Spanish-speakers' contact with the migrant chaplain remained predominantly pragmatic and social, rather than religious. Basques were satisfied to have the opportunity for religious services performed by a Basque clergyman, and Ormazabal occasionally married Basque couples. Yet, many established Basques preferred that Australian priests performed such sacraments, recognising the social capital accrued by the decision. Rather, Ormazabal's reception can be seen in the social context of Basque religiosity and collective identity, and he was most influential when re-enacting central features of Basque cultural and social memories.[58]

Ormazabal found himself at the center of tensions within the ethnically and politically diverse Spanish communities. Basques felt that local Castilians' and Andalusians' perceived aloofness towards the chaplain derived directly from his birthplace. Projecting a sense of historical injustice, Basques felt his situation reflected local Castilians' attempts to sustain a privileged position in Spain's ethnic hierarchy. Faced with navigating this microcosm of post-bellum Spain, Ormazabal offered local Spanish-speakers assistance to find family members who had been displaced during the Civil War. Whilst this was superficially apolitical, it distanced him significantly from Franco's regime and its traumatic policy of "disappearing" its former adversaries. Ormazabal's actions aligned with those of the many local community members who sent funds to the Basque Government-in-Exile and refugee support groups. Although Ormazabal was careful that such activities did not compromise his position as a Government-sponsored chaplain, his actions gave some moral recognition to Basques' sense of injustice and assimilated their experiences within historical narratives of resistance to imperialism.[59]

In the event, Tabanera had some sort of difficulty in getting his legation certified in Canberra. Shortly after the *Toscana* arrived in Brisbane on August 9, Tabanera was reassigned by Madrid to Manila.[60] Meanwhile, in June, Senator Armstrong passed through Madrid on a trip to Lourdes and Dublin. He met with General Franco himself and subsequently praised the dictator. He told Valcárcel that R. E. Armstrong had been relieved from his London posting due to his "stubbornness" in dealing with Spain. He also argued that there should be another Spanish recruitment the following year of five hundred persons, preferably childless couples.

The Herbert River Canegrowers' Executive opined that all of the Operation Kangaroo recruits should be assigned to the district, because the idea had originated there.[61] The men arrived in early August. By that time, the Herbert River Executive had reduced its request to ninety of them.[62] By August 14, fifty-six of the "Spaniards" had been allocated to the Herbert's Victoria and Macknade Mills.[63] At about the same time, the Department of Immigration denied the private nomination of a Spanish national that had been submitted through Muir, presumably preferring to channel future Spanish immigration for the sugar industry through the assisted-passage scheme.[64]

By season's end, the 1958 Spanish recruits were being touted as outstanding cutters. The *Herbert River Express*, in an article headed "Spanish Basque Migrants Regarded as Outstanding," urged that more Basques be recruited for the 1959 season, with their arrival timed to coincide with the sign-on.[65] In early January, it could be stated in the Herbert that 56 percent of the previous season's Spanish cutters remained in the district, billeted in the barracks and assisted by the established Spanish-nationals' growers. It seems that seasonal employment opportunities in the South had proven scarce, and those few men who pursued them were expected back in the district shortly.[66] By February, the newspaper reported the largest contingent in years of cutters remaining in the Herbert during the slack season. Some Basques had headed south as "work scouts," and others were expected to follow, but it was believed that all intended to return for the 1959 sugar harvest. There were many unemployed Italians in evidence as well.[67]

It might be noted that, by about this time, canefarmers were complaining about the labor competition from the tobacco industry in the Atherton Tablelands. By then, there were many established Italian and Spanish growers there, most with ties to the cane gangs of the Far North. While fruit-harvesting season in the South readily complemented cane cutting, and the men moved from one short term (a couple of weeks) engagement to another, the tobacco season began in November (or a few weeks before the end of the cane harvest around Christmas). It seems that the tobacco growers were offering cutters a higher wage and thereby attracting individuals and whole gangs away from the sugar harvest at precisely that point in the season in which they were most difficult to replace.[68]

As the sign-on approached, there was again apprehension regarding a possible labor shortage. It was anticipated that 350 Spaniards were on their way to Australia, but it was rumored that they might be inferior to the previous year's batch.[69] Fears were allayed somewhat at the sign-on when all of the *Toscana* Spaniards returned and were forming their own gangs (as opposed to the 1958 season when they were dispersed in lots of two or three to existing "mixed-nationality" ones).[70] Meanwhile, the new contingent of 169 Spanish adult males recruited for the so-called *Operación Eucalipto* (Operation Eucalyptus) departed Bilbao on the *Montserrat* on May 5. In July, the *Herbert River Express* noted that sixty of the men had been allocated to the district and were due to arrive shortly.[71]

It was by this juncture that the transition from Italians to other nationalities, and particularly Spaniards, was becoming evident. The last three immigrant ships from Italy carried a total of but 273 "rural workers," of whom only eight had come to the Herbert River to cut cane.[72]

On June 12, 1959, the newly appointed Spanish Consul General (Basque-surnamed) José M. Garay arrived in Australia to assume his post and welcome the second contingent of Spanish immigrants. Garay complained that diplomatic ties between the two countries were as yet not normalized. Spain should have a legation (an ambassador) rather than just a consulate in Australia. There should be an Australian immigration agent in Spain—as it was, Commonwealth officers in Rome and Paris were still selecting the Spanish applicants for emigration to Australia. When the Spanish Consulate was transferred from Canberra to Sydney, a disappointed Garay absented himself regularly for significant periods of time. Basque-surnamed Vice-Consul Fernández de Viana became the de facto administrator of the operation. He had been heavily involved in Spanish immigration issues for years.

There were also several signs that the new Spanish presence in North Queensland was becoming well established, and within a remarkably short period of time. In September, Alberto Urberuaga, son-in-law of Ingham's Pascual Badiola, was named Australia's representative to the Second World Congress (concerned with the Spanish emigrant diaspora) to be held in La Coruña. He had also agreed to assist in the recruitment (labeled *Operación Emu* or "Operation Emu" by the IEE) of a third contingent of Spanish nationals for North Queensland.[73]

Meanwhile, the recruitment in Spain had produced a sizeable contingent of emigrants. Urberuaga had been assigned to recruit family units. Consequently, when the *Monte Udala* departed Bilbao on December 19, it carried 55 married couples, 77 children, and 214 single males or unaccompanied married men.[74] Upon their arrival in Australia on January 21, 1960, or well before the sign-on, the immigrants were first housed in the Bonegilla Migrant Centre. The Australian government helped place the men. Some went to pick grapes in rural Victoria, while others were sent to Wollongong for industrial employment.

The timing of the arrival of the *Monte Udala* caused some consternation in the sugar industry. Would the men still be available by the sign-on in late May? In February, a carpenter from the contingent arrived in Ingham and found work in his trade. A nervous *Herbert River Express* speculated that the men might not have been selected for cane cutting.[75] Rural workers were wanted, not tradesmen. The newspaper noted that the most successful recruitment to date was when three Italian selectors from North Queensland went to Italy, a model that should be pursued in Spain.[76] Meanwhile, Urberuaga, who had returned with the *Monte Udala* contingent, informed the Ingham Rotary Club that Spain was disposed to send many emigrants to Australia.[77]

The following month, an advertisement appeared in the *Herbert River Express* stating that those willing to employ Spanish domestics should contact Mr. Balanzategui. It seems that a group of Spanish women had just arrived in Australia, and twenty to thirty remained unemployed in the Migrant Centre in Victoria. They were part of a plan by the Australian government to balance the sexes (at least somewhat) and thereby stabilize the new Spanish presence in Australia.[78] As early as the mid-1950s, there was awareness that many assisted-migrant single males from Europe were unhappy without women of their own background. However, it could work both ways. Mason notes that, although many such marriages lasted, some failed and were "set aside."[79] The Australian Department of Immigration was encouraging male migrants to nominate for immigration their younger sisters of marriageable age. There was also a willingness to facilitate the entry of the fiancée of a single male migrant. The purpose of both policies was to help alleviate the sexual imbalance in the migrant population.[80] There was the example of Jenaro Urionabarrenchea who had agreed to bring out a "Miss Egana" and marry her. According to the testimony at an inquest by two of his Basque fellow workers, Jenaro was so remorseful that he shot himself.[81]

The women in the Melbourne facility were the first Spanish nationals of what was labeled in Spain the *Plan Marta* (Martha Plan) after the biblical figure (Luke 10). There were many Greek women in the group as well. While the real intent was to introduce potential brides, the program was configured to recruit domestic help for Australian families. The women would stay initially in a migrant center, and potential Australia employers would recruit them from there. About a hundred Spaniard males (some who had traveled great distances) met the first plane. The Spanish press reported that the Australian minister for immigration was present. On descending, two of the women danced a Spanish dance accompanied by all of the men clapping in the background.[82]

There were several subsequent flights of *Marta* women, but there would be a series of disconnects. The idea was to send women to North Queensland to stabilize the single-male "Spanish" immigrant work force that was predominately Basque. Yet only slightly more than a third of the women were themselves ethnically Basques, having been recruited from throughout Iberia. In the event, this had the effect of producing some "mixed" marriages between Basques and non-Basque Spanish national spouses. There was also a certain unwillingness of the women to proceed to Queensland after entering in the South. In 1962, out of a contingent of sixty-seven *Marta* women, only ten proceeded to Queensland and then it was to Brisbane, where there were few Spanish nationals, and not to the Far North.[83]

As the 1960 harvest approached, preparations for recruitment in Europe, and particularly Italy, were lagging. It was not until March 3 that it was resolved to recruit 900 men in Europe, with 500 to arrive before the late May sign-ons and the remaining 400 later to serve as replacements.[84] Once again, the late start made it impossible to meet the schedule, which led to a buck-passing exchange between government and industry officials. Only 303 potential Italian cutters reached Australia by May. Consequently, there were fears of a possible shortage of 1,000 cutters north of Townsville.[85]

The actual sign-on did not bear out the dire predictions. Italian consular officials elsewhere in Australia funneled men to North Queensland. Most of the *Monte Udala* contingent came north for the sign-on as well. In fact, many of the men had already sorted themselves out into gangs.[86] In the Herbert, there was actually a surplus of willing cutters; concern there shifted from a possible shortage of cutters to the inexperience of the candidates. Fully 40 percent of the men had never cut cane before.[87]

The Italian presence in the ranks of the cutters was diminishing. There were twenty-four nationalities apparent among the 998 cutters working in the Herbert—including 220 Spaniards, 134 Yugoslavs, 50 Germans, 45 Hungarians, and 44 Finns. Italians with previous cutting experience continued to anchor the workforce. However, 131 of the Spanish nationals had cut previously, making them an increasingly important factor within the occupation.[88] Indeed, after the sign-on, there were 658 Spanish nationals in North Queensland (including 66 women) distributed primarily among Ayr, Home Hill, Tully, Innisfail, Ingham, Babinda, and Cairns.[89] Nearly half were concentrated in the Herbert River District.[90]

On July 23, the *Monte Udala*, having departed Santander, arrived in Melbourne with 370 Spaniards, of whom 155 were assigned as replacements for the remainder of the 1960 season.[91] The Department of Immigration officer who processed them commented on their fine appearance and good humor. He noted,

It must be added that all prior conceptions in relation to the arrival of dark complexioned Spanish migrant types have been completely upset...as in appearance they are very akin to the Northern European types and although smaller in stature could be taken for German, Swiss and Southern Dutch migrants.[92]

Furthermore, many of the men had made immediate inquiry as to the possibility of nominating fiancées and relatives. The official urged that their settlement in Australia be expedited.[93] Nor were the Spaniards left to their own devices. Félix Iturraga, representative of the Spanish government, arrived with the July *Monte Udala* contingent and traveled to Ingham with sixty of the men. He was to conduct a personal inspection of the living and working conditions of Spanish nationals in North Queensland.[94]

Meanwhile, there were signs of problems with Italian immigration. Apparently, Italian officials were discouraging the finer class of North Italian labor from emigrating (Italy, and particularly the North, was in the midst of pronounced economic growth that is sometimes referred to as the "Italian Miracle").[95] Of the 1,500 employment forms that Australian authorities intended to send to northern Italy, no fewer than 1,200 of them were redirected by the Italian government to the South.[96] Sugar industry officials were increasingly displeased with the quality of arriving Italian workers, and planned to meet with the Italian consul to register their protest.[97]

By the summer of 1960, the success of the recruitments in Spain was evident to all parties. Edgar Storich had accompanied the *Monte Udala* group that arrived in Melbourne on August 8, 1960, and he informed the IEE that the Australian officials were favorably impressed with the immigrants. Spanish officials Valcárcel and García Lahiguera visited Canberra. Before departing Spain, Valcárcel stated in a newspaper interview that not a single immigrant to date had been repatriated at government expense, thereby underscoring the thoroughness of the vetting process. His only complaint was that some Spanish newspapers had exaggerated the wages paid in Australia for manual labor. Lahiguera was on record as being very pleased with the Australian treatment of Spanish nationals. Indeed, Spanish officials were so content that they were prepared to provide at least 2,500 emigrants annually to Australia. For their part, the

Australian authorities were proceeding cautiously as they better assessed how the Spanish immigrants were assimilating into the country's way of life.[98]

Meanwhile, the Australian Catholic Church was also proactive. Monsignor Crennan continued to visit Spain, and, in May of 1960, Cardinal Gilroy led seven hundred Australian Catholics on a pilgrimage to Fatima. They then stopped in Madrid and were received by Franco himself. The encounter received much favorable coverage in the Spanish press, underscoring the high standard of living in Australia and the fact that there were two million Catholics in the country.[99]

Monsignor Crennan was also instrumental in the creation of the *Plan Marta*, and in alleviating any concerns among the Spanish Catholic hierarchy that the unchaperoned women would be exposed to moral danger. It was agreed that the women would be recruited from throughout Spain by the CCEM through its parish networks and Diocesan Migration Committees.[100] Before departing for Australia, the women (almost none of whom were domestic servants in Spain) were to attend a month-long training course in a Madrid convent. There, they would be taught the fundamentals of preparing Australian cuisine, the general skills for domestic service, and a little basic, employment-related English. The placement (and subsequent welfare) of the women was to be overseen by Father Tierney, the director of the Roman Catholic Immigration Office in Sydney.[101]

In theory, they were required to remain in domestic service for two years; in practice, many left their initial employer before the contract time was up and either married or went into a different line of work—none were prosecuted or deported for such transgression.[102] In the event, although some of the women were from the Basque Country, few of them left the urban worlds of southern Australia. So, the impact of *Plan Marta* on the Far North was rather minimal. Several, however, married ex-canecutters who had relocated permanently in the South.

In 1963, a priest named Father Nicanor accompanied a *Plan Marta* contingent to Brisbane where he was assigned to a parish, presumably to minister to the Spanish-nationals' spiritual needs. His impact, as well as that of his predecessors, Father Portella and Father Casado (a refugee from China), was minimal even in the Brisbane environs, let alone the Far North. Father Nicanor had been expelled from Cuba after the

Revolution.¹⁰³ Father Eutiquinano also fled Cuba, and, after a brief stint in Venezuela, arrived in Brisbane in 1964. Similarly, at least two nuns, including the Basque Sister Esperanza Ybarrolaburu, fled Communist China and ended up in Brisbane.¹⁰⁴

There would be two more recruitments of Spanish nationals in northern Spain called "Operation Karry" and "Operation Torres." The 372 migrants in the former left Santander on the *Monte Udala* in June of 1960 and disembarked in Melbourne on July 23. The 425 migrants in the latter embarked in Santander on the same vessel in December, and arrived in Melbourne as well on January 21, 1961.¹⁰⁵ The two contingents included a few Basques, but there is no evidence that these recruitments were as focused upon the Basque Country *per se* as were the earlier three. Both the timed arrivals (the first after the 1960 sign-on and the second well before the 1961 one) suggest that few, if any, of these immigrants were destined for the North Queensland sugar industry. While *Operación Canguro* migrants had their fare paid in full, those in Torres contributed 3,500 pesetas toward it and were required to have ten dollars for their initial expenses upon landing in Australia.¹⁰⁶

Appendix One details the Basque cohort present in all five of the "operations," a total of 384 individuals, by town of residence before departure (in most cases the same as birthplace). A comment is in order regarding them. Until now, when speaking of the origins of Basques in the Far North, Aulesti, Amoroto, Nabarniz, Markina, and Lekeitio (and their ancillary communities) predominated. In these new recruitments, there are but four immigrants from Amoroto, two each from Aulesti and Markina, and one from Nabarniz. It may be presumed that intending migrants to Australia immediately after World War II found sponsors among their established relatives and fellow villagers in the cane districts, and then entered Australia along such channels rather than through the formal recruitments. This will become more evident when we consider the many biographies of immigrants detailed in Chapter 11.

Of the 384 new recruits, no fewer than 25 came from Bermeo, 22 from Gernika, 21 from Bilbo/Bilbao, 12 from Mungia, and nine each from Mutriku and Donostia/San Sebastián. This reflects the recruitment effort in Bermeo, Mungia, and Mutriku. It also reflects the fact that the two largest cities of Bizkaia and Gipuzkoa were likely to have workers from other areas of Iberia that took advantage of the program, not to mention Basque urbanites more likely to read the media in which the programs were announced than were their rural counterparts. Finally, there is a major shift toward Navarra. No fewer than 144, or 37.6 percent, were Navarrans. There was active recruitment there (and word of mouth), particularly in central and southern reaches of the province.

Over the next two years (June of 1961 through April of 1964), there would be eight sea voyages of Spanish assisted migrants: one of which left from Cadiz, three from Vigo, and four from Barcelona—all destined for Melbourne (although several disembarked some of their passengers in Fremantle). There is little indication that Basques were included in those contingents or that any of these immigrants ended up in Queensland's Far North. After 1961, more and more immigrants began arriving by air. In 1963, 1,348 Spanish nationals did so, whereas only 661 came by boat.[107]

By 1960, there was another crucial development that was to affect the sugar industry's labor demand, and, hence, its need for immigrant workers. In that year, the Herbert River Canegrowers' Association established the Herbert River Mechanical Harvesting Committee that purchased two Massey Ferguson mechanical harvesters for trial use in the paddocks.[108]

By the time it was decided to field-test the mechanical harvesters in the Herbert, one phase of the harvesting process was already on the way to full mechanization. By far the most onerous part of the canecutter's task was the manual loading of cut cane for transport to the mill. Beginning in the mid-1950s, the industry began the transition to mechanical loaders. It was a time of dramatic expansion of the Australian sugar crop, due both to improved farming techniques and the increase of acreage included within the sugar peak. Mechanical loading made it possible to harvest the surplus without increasing substantially the number of cutters. For their part, the canecutters welcomed their liberation from hand loading. While they were paid less per unloaded ton, their increased cutting efficiency (relieved from the loading interruptions) more than compensated for the lower rate, actually providing them with a significant pay increase. By 1960, over 2,000 mechanical loaders were processing almost half of Australia's sugar crop.[109]

The prospect of mechanizing the cutting phase of the harvest was, of course, attractive to the mill owners and sugar growers. It promised liberation from the perennial difficulty of recruiting a suitable labor force and vulnerability to industrial strife from it. No longer would an edgy industry await each new sign-on with trepidation, concerned over the rate of return of the previous season's workforce scattered to the winds during the slack season. No longer would the defectors have to be replaced midstream during the harvest. It would not be necessary to engage in the complicated negotiations with Australian authorities and foreign governments to secure annual contingents of new-chum, immigrant canecutters. In short, the mechanical harvester represented the ultimate rationalization of the harvest.

From the canecutters' perspective, the prospects were altogether different. Their very survival as an occupation was at stake. Given this, they mounted surprisingly little resistance. This probably reflected the seasonal nature of their work and their lack of cohesiveness and continuity as a pressure group. To the extent they were represented at all, it was by the AWU. The immigrant cutters were ambivalent at best about that organization. It seemed more concerned with the status of Britishers within the sugar industry. Many resented paying for a union ticket that restricted in many respects their flexibility, rather than facilitating it. Notably, the AWU championed fixed hourly rates and opposed the preference of many foreign cutters to be paid by the ton. They were willing to work extra hard and longer hours to maximize their pay. The union also opposed using the spouse of one of the members as the cook for the gang—a common practice among the immigrants. Rather, the AWU wanted each gang to have a paid position for its cook. And so on.

Clearly, the mechanical harvesters (assuming they worked) could be phased in as some cutters defected and others failed to return for the next season's sign-on. Initially, it looked like the mills would advance the capital for the expensive technology and lease it out to the growers. That caused some ambivalence in the latter's ranks, as anything that gave the mills more leverage boded ill. After all, it was also a part of their annual negotiating (along with the sign-on) to hammer out a price from the mills for their cane. Since the harvesters were going to require a substantial outlay of capital, most growers preferred pooling with three or four others to buy a single machine that they then shared.

Over time, mechanical harvesting would become a profession in its own right. Indeed, many foreign cutters took the lead in pooling their savings to buy a machine (and loaders as well) and then contracting out their services to growers on a fixed per-acre or tonnage basis. However, that development lay in the future.

During the 1960 season, eleven mechanical harvesters cut 68,000 tons of cane throughout Queensland.[110] While this was insignificant in terms of the overall crop, the tests were deemed successful. The manager at Victoria Mill announced his plan to acquire additional harvesters;[111] and articles began to appear declaring that the mechanical harvester was the wave of the future that would formulate the last revolution in the sugar industry.[112]

By 1961, the days of the manual canecutter were indeed numbered, although a conservative sugar industry was not yet prepared to believe that his disappearance was a foregone conclusion. For the next few years, there was continued perennial anxiety over the sign-on. Thus, in February of 1961, the Queensland Canegrowers' Association complained about the practice of simply selecting "rural workers" in Italy for cane cutting. In its view, the Department of Immigration should have employed once again a selector with both Italo-Australian and sugar-growing backgrounds.[113] Government officials were unconvinced. Indeed, by the sign-on, an unexpectedly large number of *Monte Udala* Spaniards were returning of their own accord (about eighty in Ingham alone). The Queensland regional director of the Department of Labour and National Service was surprised that so many men left high-paying jobs in other parts of Australia. He noted,

> It was not possible to gain any real reason from them as to why they had done this but our general impression was that information had been circulated mainly through foreign publications that the crop was good and in particularly good cutting condition; even though the season would be short, the possibilities of making good money were great.[114]

The official opined that, while mechanization was still unsatisfactory, it had reduced the overall demand for cutters in North Queensland by five hundred men and promised to make further reductions in the future. The willingness of immigrant cutters already in Australia to return for the sugar harvest, combined with the shrinking demand for manual cutters, might mean that further recruitment in Europe was unnecessary.[115]

Consequently, formal recruitment of Spanish nationals ceased, although there continued to be an influx of privately nominated ones. The Mendiolea family in Ingham, having recently sponsored twenty-four Spanish nationals, continued to file new nominations. In approving a mid-1961 request, a Department of Immigration official noted that it was appropriate to accept applications from unrelated sponsors, since the Spaniards entering in this fashion were few in number—or about five per month during the previous year.[116]

Beginning in 1961, the emphasis in the assisted-migration program evolved beyond indentured single male workers and married men entering alone to other considerations. That same year, there was an attempt to stabilize the Spanish population of North Queensland by including female immigrants. In October, twenty-four Spanish women arrived in Brisbane and thirty-six more were due shortly, both under the auspices of a group called Catholic Immigration in Queensland.[117] 1961 witnessed creation of a new program, the Assisted Nominated Dependents' Scheme, whereby both the Australian and Spanish governments contributed money toward the passage to bring out close family of persons already in Australia. This was broadened to include affianced who could enter by paying their passage and a £200 deposit, the latter to be returned once the marriage had been consummated. Family units were also encouraged to immigrate, paying their own way, but possibly in part with credits arranged through the CCEM and the ICEM. There was also a premium upon skilled workers needed in Australia who were free to pursue their trade (or any other) once in the country. In short, on balance, the new policies were designed to establish immigrants as valuable and permanent members of Australian society. Their collective impact was noticeable almost immediately, since 4,326 Spanish nationals entered in the 1962–1963 fiscal year.[118]

The 1962 season proceeded without a hitch. In the Herbert, the number of Spaniards within the ranks of the canecutters rose to 284, or 29 percent of the total. For the first time, the Italians represented somewhat less than half the total (456 of 985 men).[119]

In 1963, the Herbert River Canegrowers' Council polled its membership to determine the interest in sending a recruiter to Italy or Spain at an estimated cost of £1,100. The proposal was rejected by an overwhelming majority of respondents.[120] The nervous secretary of the Herbert River district's Canegrowers' Executive wrote the Italian ambassador in Canberra requesting his assistance in securing Italian immigrants for the sugar industry.[121] The request was treated in cavalier fashion and simply referred to Rome.[122] There is no evidence that the Italian government acted on it. Of particular concern to the industry was the news that only Yugoslavs, rather than the better-suited Italians and Spaniards, would be introduced into North Queensland for the 1963 harvest.[123] The concern proved unwarranted, since, in the Herbert, that remained one of the last bastions of manual harvesting; at the 1963 sign-on there was no difficulty attracting the 852 cutters that were required for Victoria and Macknade Mills. Rather, there was an influx of jobseekers from Mackay and Innisfail due to mechanization in those districts.[124]

In 1963, the Spanish government terminated the agreement with Australia under which, during the previous six years, four thousand assisted immigrants from Spain entered Australia. By 1961, the Australian economy declined and the labor supply exceeded the demand. This meant that newcomers in the reception camps were languishing as the government struggled to place them. In late June of 1961, one thousand Germans in Bonegilla demonstrated in the streets, demanding work or repatriation to Europe. On July 17, two hundred Italians, joined by many Yugoslavs, held their own demonstration, protesting among other things that the Germans were now being favored in employment allocations. Then, about one thousand persons of many nationalities smashed the employment office and threw rocks at the police, one of whom ended up in the hospital. When the Italian vice consul from Melbourne visited the camp, he retreated after being booed by his fellow nationals. They complained about having been deceived by Australian authorities and the Italian government's migration officials alike during the recruitment process. Some Spanish immigrants had just arrived at Bonegilla, and they now threatened to create a disturbance if they were not provided timely employment. Spanish vice consul José Luis Díaz was asked by Australian authorities to intervene, and he urged his countrymen to be patient.

Relations between Italy and Australia were strained by the Bonegilla disturbances and were monitored by the Spanish consulate. The Spaniards had their own grievances with Australia at this juncture. Both Commonwealth and State government authorities had been working with Spain on a scheme that would introduce one thousand Spanish nationals into Western Australia for a railway-construction project. By November 10, 1962, three planeloads of Spanish nationals had arrived and were in the Holden Migrant Accommodation Centre at Northam. Five days later, the *Aurelia* landed many more in Fremantle. Soon, there were over a hundred men and dependents (more than four hundred Spaniards in all) in the facility, and they eventually marched on the nearby town in protest over the lack of work.

Mason documents the history of the Basque Isildro Goñi Basarte, who entered the country in January of 1962 with his wife and three sons:

> He remained unemployed and exasperated at Bonegilla migrant hostel for four months, before he left to find work on his own. Although he worked for Queensland Railways, Pilar and the children were obliged to stay in a succession of hostels for over six months, and accrued substantial debts. Unable to find steady work in Queensland that suited a family, they eventually left to settle in urbanized Geelong, Victoria.[125]

Finally, there was the issue that Australia now wanted certified skilled workers, but there was a severe disconnect between the Spanish and Australian systems of certification. A particularly stark example was Spain's desire to send some of its surplus of medical doctors, and the near impossibility of their qualifying to practice in Australia given the differing academic systems and English language barrier.[126] There was also a problem of Spanish "white collar" workers falsifying their credentials and sometimes securing a recommendation for a fee (read bribe) from a high-placed Spanish official in order to be selected, with the expectation that once in Australia they would be able to secure manual laboring employment at high wages. They found that the wages did not meet their expectations nor were they physically suited for such work. In short, the recent difficulties made it into the Spanish press (which, given the Franco regime's severe censorship of the media, sent a strong signal that the Spanish government was unhappy). The press campaign against the agreement then became the regime's excuse for cancelling it.[127]

There was the added factor that Spanish Consul General José Luis Díaz was biased against the introduction of Catholic Spanish nationals into a Protestant-dominated Australia. He sent a series of hyperbolic reports to Madrid, stating that the claims of Australia's higher standard of living and wage scale vis-à-vis Spain were exaggerated. The circumstances of the average Spanish national in Australia were a "disaster," a conclusion that he supported with anecdotal evidence from a few cases. He simply ignored the fact that thousands of Spanish nationals had immigrated willingly, adapted well, and were happy with their decision.[128] He also told Madrid that several other European countries had interdicted assisted emigration of their citizens to Australia—an unfounded assertion.[129]

By this time, Spanish emigration to several Latin American destinations was robust and the movement of guest workers to a recovering Europe was gaining strength. So, Australia no longer ranked high in Spanish-emigration priorities.[130] If, between August of 1958 and March of 1963, 7,814 Spanish nationals came to Australia,[131] during the first nine months of fiscal year 1963–1964 only 316 Spaniards entered the country. The Spanish authorities did agree to allow close relatives of persons already in Australia to emigrate in order to effect family reunions. However, Spain's participation in the assisted-migrants program was essentially interdicted after having operated for but a brief six years.[132]

In 1964, the demand for cutters in the Herbert declined dramatically from the previous year (560 versus 852 men). The number of Spaniards surpassed that of Italians (253 versus 203).[133] By 1965, there were 822 mechanical harvesters cutting 5.3 million tons of cane, or 37 percent of the total Queensland crop.[134] That year, only 300 cutters were contracted in the Herbert (129 Spaniards and 107 Italians), barely 25 percent of the numbers required a scant five years earlier.[135] Eighty percent of Victoria Mill's cane and 90 percent of Macknade's was harvested mechanically.[136] The era of the canecutter was over, closing a major chapter in the history of Southern Europeaner immigration in Australia.

Soon after cessation of the assisted-migrant program, Ramón de la Riva replaced Díaz as Spanish consul general in Australia. In April of

1963, he produced a report for the Spanish Ministry of Foreign Affairs. Consul de la Riva believed that the image of Australia in the Spanish press was critical to the success of any future migration scheme. In his view, between 1957 and 1961, or when assisted-migration prospered, Australia was depicted as "paradise," whereas in 1962–1963 it was "hell."[137] In his report, he stressed that any future migration should be clearly publicized as long-term and not for two years (as many Spaniards thought). He noted further that manual laborers do well in Australia; office workers do not. Third, he observed that, as individuals, most of the migrants were positive about their experiences, but when asked collectively in meetings they tried to outdo one another in stressing the problems encountered. He acknowledged that the migrant ran a greater risk in the entrepreneurial Australian labor market than in the Spanish one that protected his job. Furthermore, the Australian migration officials have exaggerated the virtues of their migration program.[138] In effect,

> Australia is neither paradise nor hell.... Emigration to this country suffers mainly from flawed selection. Migration can be resumed, provided the selection is properly made: white collar workers, no; labourers, yes; skilled workers, only with guarantees.... The Spaniards are well thought of here, and the authorities try to increase their quota.... There is no guarantee of employment in a country of absolute free employment.[139]

Meanwhile, the Australian government upgraded its presence in Spain by establishing a consulate in Madrid in the summer of 1963. It also actively negotiated continuation of the family reunification program. At the initiative of the Australians, the following October they met with Spanish officials of the Ministry for Foreign Affairs in New York where discussions were held regarding the terms under which a renewal of the migration flow might transpire. Attention was given to such issues as guaranteeing employment in Australia in their specialty to immigrants, restricting immigration in periods of high unemployment in Australia, and reducing the length of migrant stays in the receiving centers. The Australian government also withheld information, waiting more than a year before announcing cessation of the Spanish Assisted Migrant Program and then stating that Spain had ended it because of the scarcity of skilled workers for its own burgeoning economy.[140]

Consul De la Riva traveled to the Far North after the collapse of the migration plan and was received cordially by Ingham Basques despite his representation of the despised Franquist government. Queensland Basques also petitioned the Sydney consulate for financial support in establishing a social club, but to no avail.[141]

Despite the ongoing interest of both sides, the flow of Spanish assisted-migrants would not resume until 1968 when, on July 25, 168 of them landed at the Sydney airport.

Notes

1. García, *Operación*, 24–26.
2. April 5, 1956, Australian Archives (ACT): Accession BT 541, item 60/6993, Department of Immigration, Correspondence File: "1. Employment, 2. Sugar industry, 3. Policy and procedure re recruitment of labour for canefields," 1954–1965.
3. Armstrong was a fervent Catholic and was described by the Spanish consul general in Sydney as "the best friend Spain has in Australia" (García, *Operación*, 26).
4. Ibid.
5. May 4, 1956, Australian Archives (ACT): Accession BT 541, item 60/6993, Department of Immigration, Correspondence File: "1. Employment, 2. Sugar industry, 3. Policy and procedure re recruitment of labour for canefields," 1954–1965.
6. As late as 1963, a Brisbane officer noted of Luis Perez that he seemed "to be a decent type…and very clean. He is completely Caucasian in appearance." Quoted in Mason, "Agitators," 230.
7. Mason, "Agitators," 230.
8. Introduction of Migrant Labour for Cane cutting in North Queensland per M. V. "Aurelia" ex Genoa 17th April, 1956, n.d., Australian Archives (ACT): Accession BT 512/1, item 56/4159, Department of Immigration, Correspondence File: "1. Employment, 2. Sugar industry, 3. Arrangements for introduction and reception of Italian migrants ex 'Aurelia' at Cairns, May 1956," 1956.
9. *Herbert River Express*, June 21, 1956, 2.
10. Ibid, July 5, 1956, 1; Ibid, July 7, 1956, 2.
11. June 6, 1956, Australian Archives (ACT): Accession BT 541, item 60/6993, Department of Immigration, Correspondence File: "1. Employment, 2. Sugar industry, 3. Policy and procedure re recruitment of labour for canefields," 1954–1965.
12. I am the indirect source of an error regarding the magnitude of this process. García states, "In one remarkable case of chain migration, Teresa Mendiolea, from the Ingham district, helped 700 Basques migrate to Australia, in many cases advancing their travel costs" (García, *Operación*, 28). He cites Grassby. Grassby (*The Spanish*, 52) cites me as his source. Indeed, I did correspond with him while we were both working on our books and shared with him my preliminary observations regarding Basques in North Queensland. I told him that over the years the Mendioleas assisted "several hundred" Basques (and other Spanish nationals) to

immigrate. I believe that my "several" was transitioned into "seven" in his work. I have no recollection of ever recording such a precise number of such recruits from my informants (Teresa's descendants). Grassby's figure then gets repeated, e.g., Fernández-Shaw, *España*, 336; Mason, "Agitators," 217.

13. *Herbert River Express*, August 16, 1956, 1.
14. August 2, 1956, Australian Archives (ACT): Accession BT 583/1, item 61/8196, Department of Immigration, Correspondence File: "1. Employment, 2. Sugar industry, 3. Individual cases," 1956–1962.
15. September 16, 1956, Australian Archives (ACT): Accession BT 583/1, item 61/8196, Department of Immigration, Correspondence File: "1. Employment, 2. Sugar industry, 3. Individual cases," 1956–1962.
16. *Australian Sugar Journal*, September 15, 1956, 492. Mason cites numerous examples of nominations of friends and relatives in the Basque Country by established Queensland Basques (Mason, "Agitators," 188–89).
17. Mason, "Agitators," 218.
18. The two countries would not exchange ambassadors until 1968.
19. *Herbert River Express*, October 27, 1956, 1.
20. December 18, 1956, Australian Archives (ACT): Accession BT583/1, item 61/8196, Department of Immigration, Correspondence File: "1. Employment, 2. Sugar industry, 3. Individual cases," 1956–1962.
21. January 2, 1957, Australian Archives (ACT): Accession BT 583/1, Department of Immigration, Correspondence File: "1. Employment, 2. Sugar industry, 3. Individual cases," 1956–1962.
22. January 3, 1957, Australian Archives (ACT): Accession BT 583/1, item 61,8196, Department of Immigration, Correspondence File: "1. Employment, 2. Sugar industry, 3. Individual cases," 1956–1962.
23. January 8, 1957, Australian Archives (ACT): Accession BT 583/1, Item 61/8196, Department of Immigration, Correspondence File: "1. Employment, 2. Sugar industry, 3. Individual cases," 1956–1962.
24. February 5, 1957, Australian Archives (ACT): Accession BT 583/1, item 61/8196, Department of Immigration, Correspondence File: "1. Employment, 2. Sugar industry, 3. Individual cases," 1956–1962.
25. February 15, 1957, Australian Archives (ACT): Accession BT 541, item 60/6993, Department of Immigration, Correspondence File: "1. Employment, 2. Sugar industry, 3. Policy and procedure re recruitment of labour for canefields," 1954–1965. [February 15, 1957].
26. February 21, 1957, Australian Archives (ACT): Accession BT 583/1, item 61/8196, Department of Immigration, Correspondence File: "1. Employment, 2. Sugar industry, 3. Individual cases," 1956–1962.
27. February 7, 1957, Australian Archives (ACT): Accession BT 541, item 60/6993, Department of Immigration, Correspondence File: "1. Employment, 2. Sugar industry, 3. Policy and procedure re recruitment of labour for canefields," 1954–1965. [February 7, 1957].
28. *The Worker*, February 12, 1957.

29. February 8, 1957, Australian Archives (ACT): Accession BT 541, item 60/6993, Department of Immigration, Correspondence File: "1. Employment, 2. Sugar industry, 3. Policy and procedure re recruitment of labour for canefields," 1954–1965.
30. February 15, 1957.
31. February 7, 1957. The concern of Spanish authorities likely reflects the circumstances of Spanish Basque contract sheepherders in the American West. During the 1950s, there were difficult negotiations regarding their status between the sheepmen's associations and the Spanish and US governments (Douglass and Bilbao, *Amerikanuak*, 310–15).
32. February 12, 1957, Australian Archives (ACT): Accession BT 541, item 60/6993, Department of Immigration, Correspondence File: "1. Employment, 2. Sugar industry, 3. Policy and procedure re recruitment of labour for canefields," 1954–1956.
33. *Herbert River Express*, May 4, 1957, 1.
34. November 21, 1957, Australian Archives (ACT): Accession BT 541, item 60/6993, Department of Immigration, Correspondence File: "1. Employment, 2. Sugar industry, 3. Policy and procedure re recruitment of labour for canefields," 1954–1965.
35. February 6, 1958, Australian Archives (ACT): Accession BT 541, item 60/6993, Department of Immigration, Correspondence File: "1. Employment, 2. Sugar industry, 3. Policy and procedure re recruitment of labour for canefields," 1954–1965.
36. Ibid.
37. Canecutters Engaged at Sign-ons for the 1957 Season, Australian Archives (ACT): Accession BT 541, item 60/6993, Department of Immigration, Correspondence File: "1. Employment, 2. Sugar industry, 3. Policy and procedure re recruitment of labour for canefields," 1954–1965.
38. Labour for the 1958 Harvest, Australian Archives (ACT): Accession BT 541, item 60/6993, Department of Immigration, Correspondence File: "1. Employment, 2. Sugar industry, 3. Policy and procedure re recruitment of labour for canefields," 1954–1965.
39. March 19, 1957, Australian Archives (ACT): Accession BT 541, item 60/6993, Department of Immigration, Correspondence File: "1. Employment, 2. Sugar industry, 3. Policy and procedure re recruitment of labour for canefields," 1954–1965.
40. Ibid.
41. *Courier-Mail*, May 25, 1957, 5.
42. November 21, 1957, Australian Archives (ACT): Accession BT 541, item 60/6993, Department of Immigration, Correspondence File: "1. Employment, 2. Sugar industry, 3. Policy and procedure re recruitment of labour for canefields," 1954–1965.
43. García, *Operación*, 38.
44. Ibid, 40.
45. Ibid, 40–41.
46. Ibid, 41.
47. Ibid, 43–44.
48. Ibid, 44.
49. Ibid, 44–45.
50. *The Telegraph*, March 4, 1958.

51. March 11, 1958, Australian Archives (ACT): Accession BT 541, item 60/6993, Department of Immigration, Correspondence File: "1. Employment, 2. Sugar industry, 3. Policy and procedure re recruitment of labour for canefields," 1954–1965.
52. The Spanish government insisted that 26 men from Santander be included to blunt domestic criticism of an exclusive Basque preference (Ibid, 56). Those from Huesca and Teruel were probably working in the Basque Country at the time of their recruitment (or had a relative there who informed them of the opportunity) (Ibid, 175, fn. 87).
53. Campion, *Rockchoppers*, 100.
54. Ibid.
55. From an interview with Alberto Urberuaga, Ingham, 1980.
56. García, *Operación*, 154–55.
57. Mason, "Agitators," 247–50; Robert Mason, "Repositioning Resistance: Basque Separatism, Religion and Cultural Security in Regional Queensland, 1945–70," *Queensland Review* 20, no. 1 (2013), 42–43.
58. Ibid.
59. Ibid, 10.
60. García, *Operación*, 46.
61. *Herbert River Express*, May 6, 1958, 1.
62. Ibid, August 9, 1958, 1.
63. Ibid, August 14, 1958, 1.
64. August 18, 1958, Australian Archives (ACT): Accession BT 583/1, item 618196, Department of Immigration, Correspondence File: "1. Employment, 2. Sugar industry, 3. Individual cases," 1956–1962.
65. *Herbert River Express*, November 29, 1958, 1.
66. Ibid, January 3, 1959, 1.
67. Ibid, February 12, 1959, 1.
68. García, *Operación*, 101–2.
69. *Herbert River Express*, April 30, 1959, 1.
70. Ibid, June 11, 1959, 1.
71. Ibid, July 16, 1959, 1.
72. Ibid, July 14, 1959, 1.
73. Ibid, September 22, 1959, 1.
74. Nominal Role of Approved Migrants Embarked on SS 'Monte Udala' on December 19th, 1959 from Bilbao to Melbourne, Australian Archives (ACT): Accession BT541/1, item 60/307, Department of Immigration, Correspondence File: "'Monte Udala' Assisted Passage Scheme," 1959–1963.
75. *Herbert River Express*, February 1, 1960, 1.
76. Ibid, February 13, 1960, 2; Ibid, March 22, 1960, 1.
77. Ibid, February 25, 1960, 1.
78. Ibid, March 12, 1910, 4. By mid-March, one intending bride was in Ingham awaiting the return of her affianced who was in Western Australia engaged in seasonal work before returning to the Herbert for the sign-on (Ibid, March 17, 1960, 1).
79. Mason, "Agitators," 233.

80. García, *Operación*, 104–5.
81. Inquest of Jenaro Urionabarrenechea, 5th of April, 1957, Queensland State Archives, JUS-N 1293, 246–57.
82. Ibid, 106–7.
83. Mason, "Agitators," 235.
84. March 3, 1960, Australian Archives (ACT): Accession BT 541, item 60/6993, Department of Immigration, Correspondence File: "1. Employment, 2. Sugar industry, 3. Policy and procedure re recruitment of labour for canefields," 1954–1965.
85. *Herbert River Express*, May 10, 1960, 1.
86. Ibid, June 2, 1960, 1.
87. Ibid, June 9, 1960, 1.
88. Ibid, June 11, 1960, 1.
89. Canefarmers who have nominated Spanish Migrants, Australian Archives (ACT): Accession BT 583/1, item 61/8196, Department of Immigration, Correspondence File: "1. Employment, 2. Sugar industry, 3. Individual cases," 1956–1962.
90. *Herbert River Express*, August 11, 1960, 1.
91. October 19, 1960, Australian Archives (ACT): Accession BT 541, item 60/6993, Department of Immigration, Correspondence File: "1. Employment, 2. Sugar industry, 3. Policy and procedure re recruitment of labour for canefields," 1954–1965.
92. July 28, 1960, Australian Archives (ACT): Accession BT 541/1, item 60/7021, Department of Immigration, Correspondence File: "'Monte Udala' at Melbourne 22/7/60," 1960–1962.
93. Ibid.
94. *Herbert River Express*, August 16, 1960, 1.
95. Jon S. Cohen, "Economic Growth," in *Modern Italy: A Topical History since 1861*, ed. Edward R. Tannenbaum and Emiliana P. Noether (New York: New York University Press, 1974), 171–96.
96. *Herbert River Express*, June 30, 1960, 2.
97. Ibid, August 16, 1960, 1.
98. García, *Operación*, 48–49.
99. Ibid, 50.
100. Ibid, 106.
101. Ibid, 108–9.
102. Ibid, 110–12. García notes that the program settled into a goal to send sixty women four times annually. By the time that Spain interdicted the assisted migrant program in 1963, at least 747 single women from Spain had entered Australia (Ibid, 93; 107).
103. Mason, "Agitators," 249.
104. Ibid, 251–54.
105. García, *Operación*, 94.
106. Ibid.
107. Ibid, 114; 116. García notes that the air passengers failed to bond as "mates," as did the boat passengers during their lengthy voyage—ties that often carried over once in Australia.
108. *Herbert River Express*, January 10, 1960, 1.

109. Geoff Burrows and Clive Morton, *The Canecutters* (Melbourne: Melbourne University Press, 1986), 59. [*The Canecutters*].
110. *Herbert River Express*, January 10, 1961, 1.
111. Ibid, October 18, 1960, 1.
112. Ibid, October 27, 1960, 1.
113. *Herbert River Express*, October 27, 1960, 1.
114. February 15, 1961, Australian Archives (ACT): Accession BT 541, item 60/6993, Department of Immigration, Correspondence File: "1. Employment, 2. Sugar industry, 3. Policy and procedure re recruitment of labour for canefields," 1954–1965.
115. Ibid.
116. July 7, 1961. Australian Archives (ACT): Accession BT 583/1, item 61,8196, Department of Immigration, Correspondence File: "1. Employment, 2. Sugar industry, 3. Individual cases," 1956–1962.
117. *Herbert River Express*, October 10, 1961, 4.
118. García, *Operación*, 52–53.
119. *Herbert River Express*, June 16, 1962, 1.
120. Ibid, February 5, 1963, 1.
121. March 22, 1963, Australian Archives (ACT): Accession BT 541, item 60/6993, Department of Immigration, Correspondence File: "1. Employment, 2. Sugar industry, 3. Policy and procedure re recruitment of labour for canefields," 1954–1965.
122. April 2, 1963, Australian Archives (ACT): Accession BT 541, item 60/6993, Department of Immigration, Correspondence File: "1. Employment, 2. Sugar industry, 3. Policy and procedure re recruitment of labour for canefields," 1954–1965.
123. May 1, 1963, Australian Archives (ACT): Accessions BT 541, item 60/6993, Department of Immigration, Correspondence File: "1. Employment, 2. Sugar industry, 3. Policy and procedure re recruitment of labour for canefields," 1954–1965.
124. *Herbert River Express*, May 25, 1963, 1.
125. Mason, "Agitators," 269.
126. García, *Operación*, 55.
127. Ibid, 61–69.
128. Ibid, 74–78.
129. Ibid, 75.
130. Ibid, 72.
131. Ibid, 91.
132. *The Sydney Morning Herald*, June 25, 1964, 11.
133. *Herbert River Express*, May 23, 1964, 1.
134. Burrows and Morton, *The Canecutters*, 171.
135. *Herbert River Express*, June 19, 1965, 1.
136. Burrows and Morton, *The Canecutters*, 187.
137. García, *Operación*, 88.
138. Ibid, 82–83.
139. Cited in Ibid, 83.
140. Ibid, 81–82.
141. Mason, "Agitators," 278.

CHAPTER 8

Basques in the Antipodes

Colonizing the Far North—We have considered the settlement of Spanish nationals (including a few Basques) in nineteenth-century Australia and found that it was concentrated mainly in the urban South and dominated by Catalans. We also analyzed the recruitment by Hughes in 1907 of a contingent of the latter for the Queensland sugar industry. We might note that eight migrants in the Hughes expedition went ashore in Melbourne, where they were convinced by countrymen not to proceed to Queensland because of its primitive conditions.[1] Thenceforth, Spanish nationals arriving in the South tended to remain there.[2]

We have the narrative of Josee (Josephine) Canals, daughter of Catalan immigrants in Melbourne. Her father, from Montgat, arrived in 1910. Her mother, from Barcelona, came with her family at fourteen years of age (she already had two brothers in Victoria). Her future father-in-law reached Melbourne in 1912. All three families settled in the city permanently.

Josee's father had a fruit shop in Albert Park, but then decided to specialize in fish-and-chips—there were already eight or nine Spanish families in that line of work. They met regularly in the Melbourne market and helped one another when needed. The families would also picnic together on occasion—"we all knew each other and were like a big family." By the turn of the twentieth century there was a Barcelona Club in Melbourne. Her husband was of Catalan descent as well, and his family was in the fish business. So, the young couple eventually took over his family's enterprise and ran it until his death.[3]

She speaks proudly of the Catalan Stephen Morell. Born in Melbourne in 1869 to a restaurant owner, Esteban, from Vila-seca, the boy was taken to Spain by his family where he received his early education.

The Morells returned to Australia in 1883 and Esteban developed many business holdings. He owned the Princes Bridge Hotel in Melbourne and had pastoral properties in Queensland. He served on the boards of Carlton and United Breweries, Equity Trustees, Melbourne Cooperative Brewery, Victoria Insurance Co., Windsor Pictures Co., and the Melbourne Tramways Trust.

Son Stephen attended Scotch College and was a champion rower on the Yarra River for his school in 1896 and 1897, and today there is a bridge over it named for him. He became president of the Mercantile Rowing Club and Victorian Rowing Association and also served as vice president of the Melbourne Cricket Club. He was knighted in the 1930s, and also served as Lord Mayor of Melbourne.[4]

Josee's grandmother lived with her parents and spoke nothing but Catalan. So Josee maintained that language, learning no English until she went to school. She has visited Catalunya six times (as of 2000) and her granddaughter studied Catalan at Barcelona University. Josee was a founding member in 1986 of the *Casal Catalá* (Catalan House) of Melbourne.[5] She is aware of Catalans elsewhere in Australia, but not the Far North. She notes:

> I know that there are Catalans in other parts of Australia who have probably left their mark for their hard work and enterprise. For instance, I know people, some of them my husband's family, who settled in Kalgoorlie and Coolgardi in Western Australia because of the gold rush. A branch of the Parer family went to Brisbane.[6]

Lola Waring (nee Sans) reports that in 2000 there were 817 Parers on her Australian family tree. There are also at least seven streets in Melbourne named after Parers and four after Barcelona. She recalls Damien Parer who was a famous war correspondent and photographer in World War II. He was killed in action in 1944. Then there was Ray Parer, who was in the British Airforce in 1919. He participated in the first England-to-Australia air race. He later went to New Guinea and flew single engine planes there. Finally, she reports that a branch of the Parer family moved to Brisbane, and that the present (2000) federal minister for resources and Queensland senator, Warwick Parer, is a descendant of it.[7]

We might also contemplate the episodic arrival in Cairns, in 1917, of a contingent of disillusioned Spanish nationals, mainly Catalans, who re-emigrated from Patagonia enticed by the rumors of Spanish land ownership in Australia. For the latter half of the nineteenth century, Argentina had pursued an active immigration policy that included attracting northern Europeans. There had been a Welsh colonization scheme whereby people from that region of Great Britain were proffered incentives and short-term land leases. By 1914, there were some 4,000 living in southern Chubut Province where they were engaged in competition with Spanish immigrant groups. Over time, the Welsh found themselves in danger of losing their identity as their youth assimilated into Argentinian society.

By century's end, the British were highly influential in Argentina (having financed much of its railway infrastructure and refrigerated meat industry). In the first two decades of the twentieth century, Australia was interested in populating its North, particularly the vast Northern Territory (whose white population was only 4,000). Through its Commonwealth ties, it offered the Chubut Welsh incentives (a loan to pay for the voyage, infrastructural assistance, and free land), as well as the prospect of establishing their own semi-autonomous settlement where they could govern themselves and maintain their customs—including language. There was precedent, as Australia had received three previous contingents of Welsh colonists, and there was now considerable favorable publicity about the new plan in the Australian press regarding "our" British kith and kin.[8]

There were, however, two major problems. The recruitment of Welshmen in Chubut for the venture did not succeed as planned. So, its backers signed up Spaniards, in the main Catalans, who had entered Patagonia both as intending settlers and as recruits to construct a railway from Buenos Aires to Chubut. Many of the latter were drawn from the ranks of Catalunya's disaffected Anarcho-syndicalists and they brought their political views with them. After completion of the railroad, several settled in Chubut, where they became tenants on large agricultural estates. In 1912, they were an integral part of a sharecroppers' rebellion against the local landlords. Some of the recruits for the Australian venture were drawn from these ranks. To make matters worse, there were tensions between the Welsh and Spanish immigrants in Chubut itself over access to land. The former viewed the latter as unruly political radicals. The Spaniards regarded the Welsh as privileged by the landowners and the government.[9]

The second obstacle was the timing. The initiative was launched in 1913 (when the planet was poised on the brink of catastrophe) and then realized in 1915. World War I exploded before the recruits' departure, and the conflict's immediate consequences gave the Australian public pause for thought. As their economy nosedived, the concern over the country's capacity to absorb the new immigrants became palpable. Nevertheless, the vessel, the *Kwantu Maru*, left Port Maldyn, Argentina, for Australia in May of 1915.[10]

There were 220 Patagonians in the expedition, but, in the event, only 28 Welshmen sailed compared to 113 intending settlers of Spanish origin. There were also 45 Russians and 30 Italians on board.[11] There were tensions between the several groups in the port of departure and then aboard their ship. The Spaniards claimed that the vessel's officials and accompanying Australian representatives favored the Welsh. The Spaniards elected leaders to voice their complaints, and the main one, Antonio Vendrell, was incarcerated twice during the voyage to Australia. The leaders were articulate spokesmen; steeped in their Marxist view of world history. The Spanish women, imbued with Anarchist gender egalitarianism, were actually the most unruly. In Aukland, they refused to remain on board when ordered to do so. They confiscated arms and a launch to go into the city in search of fresh vegetables and tobacco. They knocked unconscious some of the ship's crew who tried to manhandle them on their return. In Melbourne, the Spaniards met with a Catalan resident, Antonio Martínez, who served as their interpreter. It was agreed that the vessel would carry two additional police officers to maintain order during the remainder of the journey to Darwin.[12]

When the expedition arrived in the Northern Territory on August 4, 1915, it encountered hostile protesters who heard that the newcomers would depress wages and take absented servicemens' jobs. The Spaniards felt particularly threatened, and armed themselves with rifles, revolvers, and knives before disembarking. They exacerbated tensions by refusing to contribute to the AWU's Patriotic War Fund, and they ended up in a camp living in tents for months during the quagmire created by the rainy season.

As a requirement of their passage-assistance, several of the Spanish families had signed an agreement that required them to work on railway construction for a year or forfeit £8. They were settled in Pine Creek, where they were to build the railway from there to Darwin. Single men were separated from them and sent up the projected line into the bush. The wages were less than promised, and the families at Pine Creek demanded they be increased. This was denied and the supervisor of the project had their credit with the butchers and grocers cut off to force an end to the Spaniards' work stoppage. The Spanish women in Pine Creek summoned the single men for help. They commandeered a locomotive and arrived in the town fully armed. They vandalized the telegraph wires to Darwin and threatened the local constable, vowing to hang the supervisor if he did not restore the Spaniards' credit with the merchants. The supervisor backed down.[13]

The strife continued when the single men returned to work, only to find that they were expected to purchase their own picks and shovels. They went on a "go-slow," and then burned their tools in protest. Forty-one of the protesters were still unemployed a month later. The Spaniards also refused to recognize the authority of the ganger assigned to them and elected their own. At this point, some of the Spaniards absconded while others went to work for the Vestey plant in Darwin, a newly opened facility with an Argentine connection.[14]

When it closed, in 1920, the Northern Territory's acting administrator arranged for a boat to take 216 unemployed persons, including many Spaniards, to Cairns to cut sugar cane.[15] One of the Chubut recruits, Antonio Villalba, had preceded them there, and he arranged for their reception in collaboration with the established Catalans from the 1907 Hughes recruitment. Some of the newcomers to the Far North stayed for but a few months before migrating south to Melbourne. There, they appointed a woman, Trini García, as their spokesperson, and requested that the Australian government repatriate them to Argentina. She was unsuccessful, and so many of the recalcitrant returned to North Queensland.[16] One of their numbers, Lorenzo Durán, later described the work in the Far North as disgusting—the kind done only by blacks in Cuba. It was his intention to go back to Argentina where he could "live like white people."[17]

Nevertheless, many remained in the Far North. It could be stated subsequently that, "A small Patagonian community of mixed Welsh, Spanish and Italian descent still remains in the Cairns-Gordonvale area today" (descendants of Villalbas, Duráns, Saenz, Camerero, García, Vacca, and John Richard Davies) and that there was a similar cluster of Spanish Patagonians in Innisfail (the Villalbas, the Duráns, and more than one Martínez family).[18] It should be noted that most of these Spanish nationals were Andalusian and Catalans; not Basques.

Another interesting case is that of the Catalan Bruno Tapiolas. I interviewed his widow in Ayr in 1981. She refused to speak Spanish with me because her husband always insisted on English in the household. None of their children learned Spanish; her forty-year-old son is taking a University course to try and learn it now. Bruno came in 1912 to Innisfail as a bachelor. He cleared scrub for farmland. A Spaniard there convinced him to go to Sydney to open a restaurant together. They did, but it failed. Bruno headed back north on a steamer. He had a Basque stowaway under his bunk who was discovered by the crew. Bruno had to pay the man's fare. When they arrived in Townsville, he gave the stowaway a gold crown and never saw the man again.

He went back to Spain and married in 1922. By then, he had a cane farm in Ayr. She noted that Basques worked for them. She showed me a photo taken before 1922 of an all-Basque five-man gang. One was Balanzategui, who later moved to Ingham to farm. She noted that Basques are physically stronger, but Catalans are better at business. The Basques would go to Sydney and blow their money; Bruno never did that, he stayed in the Far North and studied English in his spare time.

As we have seen, only a handful of Basques entered Australia during the nineteenth century, in the main solitary males mostly imbued with an adventuresome spirit. They certainly were not chain migrants moving along established networks of kith and kin. Even though the latter half of the nineteenth century was a prolific period for immigration schemes targeting both individuals and potential "colonies" for the world's settler societies, fueled both by the policies of host countries to increase their populations while developing their economies and by entrepreneurial agents and shipping lines that sought profit in the human traffick, there were no significant attempts to recruit Basques for Australia.

Nevertheless, the pace of Basque immigration in the southern continent picked up noticeably during the first quarter of the twentieth century. Despite the failure of the CSR's agent Thomas Hughes to recruit canecutters in Bilbao in 1907, Basques were about to become involved in the Queensland sugar industry. Indeed, that particular avenue would evolve into the Basques' main entrance into Australia. However, there were some interesting side doors as well.

The following analysis will once again rely upon Charles Price's data gleaned from Commonwealth Naturalization Records between the years 1903 and 1946. As noted earlier, this is not a random sample of any particular subset of immigrants—some were more motivated to seek citizenship than others—and it is certainly not a comprehensive summation of the total number of the subset's Australian immigrants. However, one of the huge advantages of these records is that, in many cases, the application details the applicant's former residences. So, first let us consider the personal histories of some of the more interesting Basque immigrants who did not go to Queensland's Far North:

1. In 1905, the twenty-two-year-old Joseph Betos of Bilbao applied for citizenship having entered Australia in 1903. He was a bachelor seaman and gave his residence as Pyrmont, N.S.W. He came to Australia from Victoria, British Columbia.

2. In 1918, forty-seven-year-old Antonio Pena of Bilbao applied after a six-and-three-quarter-year residency in Port Pirie, South Australia, where he worked as a smelterhand. He was married to an Australian woman and had two infant daughters. He traveled to Port Pirie from Cardiff, Wales.

3. In 1930, forty-five-year-old Doroteo Wroite (no doubt Uriarte) of Bilbao applied after having entered Australia in 1912. He was married to a "South American" and had no children. He came to Fremantle from England. His residencies included seven years in South America, two years in Mexico, two years in England, six years in Kalgoorlie, seven years in Fremantle, and five years in his current residence of Brusselton, all in Western Australia. He listed his occupations as fisherman and labourer.

4. John Julian Tellechea of Santesteban (Doneztebe), Navarra, applied for citizenship in 1937. When he arrived in Australia in 1899, he was twenty-seven and married to an Englishwoman. In 1901, they had a daughter, their only child. They had come to Australia from England via New Zealand. He had lived in the British Isles a total of eight years after a year-long round-the-world tour when he was nineteen. The couple resided in Sydney and its suburbs for thirty-three years before moving to the Brisbane area. They lived in the suburb of Darra near the city, and he listed his occupation as poultry farmer.
5. Forty-two-year-old Francisco Zuazo of Gasteiz, a man married to a "Spanish" wife and with five children, listed his occupation as labourer. He had been in Argentina for ten years and a total of twelve in Darwin before applying for citizenship. He had likely been a Vestey Group employee.

Then there are the interesting cases of a number of Navarran clergymen who settled in Western Australia. Stephen Moreno (born in 1888), Henry Moreno (born in 1891), and Urbano Giménez (born in 1891) were all Catholic priests residing in New Norcia when applying for citizenship. They were all from Corella, Navarra, and entered Australia in 1908 (probably coming out together). Their tender ages on entering suggest that they came as intending seminarians at the New Norcia mission and then remained there after ordination. There was now a clearly established tie between New Norcia and Corella. In 1913, twenty-one-year-old Roman Rios came from the Navarrese town to New Norcia, as did eighteen-year-old Thomas Gil in 1916, nineteen-year-old Isidore Ruiz in 1921, and twenty-one-year-old Plácido Sesma that same year. Three other individuals give us some insight into the process. In 1927, Ramiro Ausejo, Ildefonso Garcia, and Theodore Hernández, all from Corella, applied for citizenship, having entered the country in 1921. García and Hernández were both twenty-two years old when applying and Ausejo was twenty-four—all listed their occupation as "clerical student." In 1925, another Navarran, Jose Yarbayo, came to New Norcia at nineteen years of age and was a priest there in 1942 when applying for citizenship. He was from Estella (Lizarra). Then there was Anselmo Catalan, from Corella, who was thirty-eight when he entered Australia in 1916. Four years later he applied for citizenship, listing his occupation as "abbot."

All of the above were residing at New Norcia at the time of their application—so there was a strong, maybe even predominant, Corella contingent within the ranks of the mission's Benedictine monks—at least during the teens and twenties.

There were also at least three Navarran priests in Western Australia who were not at New Norcia at the time of their naturalization, albeit they were New Norcia spinoffs. William Jiménez (from Corella) entered in 1908 at eighteen years of age. He lived at New Norcia for nine years (obviously as a seminarian) and for the last two was the parish priest at Moora, Western Australia. Emiliano Ross (did he Anglicize his surname?) was seventeen upon entering in 1925 and was a parish priest in Pithara, Western Australia, when applying in 1940. He had resided at New Norcia for seven years, Fremantle for one, Perth for two and a half, and now Pithara for four and a half years. Serafín Sanz, from Villatuerta, Navarra, entered in 1931 at eighteen years of age and was a missionary at Drysdale Mission, Western Australia, when applying for citizenship in 1943. He had lived in France for two years before traveling from there to Fremantle. He spent seven years at New Norcia (that seems to have been about the time it took for a seminarian to become an ordained priest). He then spent a year in Sydney before moving to Drysdale, where he had resided for the past four years.

Mention might be made of the Navarran Gregorio Navarro. He was from Corella and eighteen when he entered in 1908. Might he have come with the three intending Corella seminarians—the two Morenos (brothers) and Giménez who entered that same year? Anyway, when he applied in 1926, he listed his marital status as single, his residence as Fremantle, and his occupation as cook. One could have speculated that he was a seminary dropout were it not for the list of previous residences on his application. He had lived for two years in Perth, one and a half in Bunbury, three months in Palgarup, and now seven years in Fremantle—with no evidence of a stay at New Norcia.

If we then turn to the Queenslander Basques who entered Australia between the turn of the century and the beginning of the Great Depression in 1929, a very different picture emerges. Queensland Basques have never heard of Lehimas de Arrieta, or of any of the nineteenth-century Basque settlers that we have identified in other parts of Australia. Rather, their perception is that Basque settlement in the southern continent began in Queensland. There is a kind of founder's myth that refers to some merchant mariners from the Bizkaian town of Lekeitio who jumped ship in Sydney and then somehow ended up in North Queensland, where they entered the ranks of the Southern European canecutters.

Appendix 2 lists sixty-five Basque immigrants who settled in Queensland during the first three decades of the twentieth century—all males. The earliest to do so was eighteen-year-old Aniceto Menchaca who entered Australia in 1907 (or the year of the Hughes recruitment but certainly not enlisted by him). When he applied for naturalization two years and nine months later, he was residing in Stone River in the Herbert. While a major sugar district, he gave his occupation as "carpenter" and his birthplace as "Bilbao." This seems to have been a clear case of an immigrant communicating his birthplace to a bureaucrat as some better known city rather than his actual obscure town or village. Queensland's prominent sugar-growing Menchacas were from Mungia. Aniceto stated that he had come directly from Bilbao to Sydney. He resided in Sydney for four months before ending up in Ingham (Stone River) for two and a half years.[19] He then returned to the Basque Country to reside in Lekeitio, known there as "Mungia," where he became an ardent recruiter for workers for the Australian sugar industry.

In 1911, Johan Menchaca came to Queensland and three years later applied for citizenship—listing his Australian residence as Beeva (also in the Herbert) and his occupation as "labourer" (this was a common self-identification of canecutters). Johan was three years younger than Aniceto and also claimed to have been born in Bilbao. He stated that he had come directly from Spain to the North Queensland port of Townsville, and that he had lived in Beeva for the past three years. While I cannot be certain, it seems likely that the recently naturalized Aniceto assisted his younger brother to join him in Queensland. It may have been that, by then, Aniceto had a cane farm on which he employed his brother. If indeed the case, this would be the earliest example of Basque chain migration in the state. That, in turn, would lend substance to a Menchaca (and Lekeitio) founders' story.

Then there is the case of the Ugartes. In 1909, Juan (John) Ugarte Ynchaurraga, from the Bizkaian village of Ereño, came from Buenos Aires to Fremantle (which again smacks of a merchant mariner). After two weeks, he made his way to Cloncurry, Queensland—at that time a booming mining district (had John heard of it while on port leave in Fremantle?). In 1910, Tomás Ugarte Ynchaurraga traveled directly from Spain to Brisbane and then resided in Innisfail for four years before applying for citizenship. In 1911, nineteen-year-old Eloy (Elvig) Ugarte Ynchaurraga came directly from Spain to Cairns. He then spent a year and a half in Cloncurry (with his brother John?) before moving to Innisfail where he was a canefarmer when applying for citizenship in 1923. Is it possible that Tomás attracted Eloy to his side in 1913? In 1914, both applied for citizenship, both were residing in Innisfail, and both were cutting cane. Meanwhile, when John applied for citizenship in 1923, he stated that he had lived in Cloncurry until 1917 before relocating to Innisfail (where he was a canefarmer in South Johnstone when filing). Was he attracted to Innisfail by Elvig and Tomás?[20] It was common practice for relatives and/or fellow villagers to work together in the same cane gang.

On April 6, 1912, sixteen Bizkaians arrived in Fremantle having embarked in Marseille on the French vessel *Caledonien* (Table 2).

This may have been the first "group" exodus of Basques toward Australia. Koldo San Sebastián states that the Sesmas, as did Ypiñazar, stayed first in Sydney before continuing on to Queensland. In 1913, Gabriel Sesma was on board the *Bombala* from Brisbane to Sydney, accompanied by a Basque, G. Azcarraga. In 1914, Sesma made another voyage from Melbourne to Sydney on the *Canberra*. The following year, he again arrived in Sydney from Brisbane on the *Wyreema*, this time accompanied by the Basque Pio Iturriaga. Was he Sydney-based at this time and employed in coastal navigation? When he filed for Australian citizenship in 1926, he was a canefarmer in Ayr and stated that he had resided for two years in Innisfail, two in Melbourne, and ten in Ayr. He had been issued an alien registration card on March 9, 1917, while residing in Innisfail.

Meanwhile, Gabriel's brother-in-law, Valentín Ypiñazar, was working as a boilermaker for the New South Wales government in Balmain (near Sydney), home of many shipyards, when his spouse, Brígida Sesma, arrived on May 21, 1914, aboard the *Otway* with their two children. On April 27, 1916, Aquilino Sesma arrived in Brisbane from Sydney on board the *Wyreema*. Was this his permanent move to Queensland?

TABLE 2. Basque Arrivals aboard *Caledonien* in 1912

Name	Birthplace	Occupation
1. Ángel Alberdi	Aulesti	Vine Dresser [?]
2. Pedro Arangüena	Aulesti (?)	Farmer
3. G. Azcarraga	?	Gardener
4. Pedro Careaga	Aulesti	Carpenter
5. Ángel Cincunegui	Aulesti	Engineer
6. ? Galdos	Aulesti	Electrician
7. Ignacio Goicoechea	?	Carpenter
8. Pedro Hilaro	?	Butcher
9. José Inchausti	Aulesti (?)	Mariner
10. Domingo Plaza	Aulesti	Mariner
11. José Renteria	Aulesti	Engineer
12. Aquilino Sesma	Lekeitio	Engineer
13. José Gabriel Sesma	Lekeitio	Engineer
14. Anastasio Ugarte	Ereño	Carpenter
15. José María Urizar	Aulesti	Farmer
16. Valentín Ypiñazar	Zeanuri	Engineer

In 1921, Valentín and Brígida filed their intention to change their abode to Ayr. By then, the two Sesma brothers were established in the Far North. The Ypiñazar family (including four children and two infants) arrived via Townsville in the Burdekin on October 1, 1921. In 1923, Valentín filed for naturalization and his documents state that he had worked in Innisfail for two years at some point during his stay in Australia. He might have engaged in cane cutting or work in his profession as boilermaker at one of the mills, likely prior to his move to Ayr and possibly corresponding to his brother-in-law Gabriel's stint in Innisfail. The two men were close, because when Gabriel Sesma filed for citizenship, he noted that he was a canefarmer as a partner for the last three years in the Ypiñazar Co.[21]

In 1928, Juanita Ypiñazar Sesma, daughter of Valentín and Brígida, married Norberto Balanzategui of Ingham.[22] A few months later she died, likely in childbirth. It is a Sesma family tradition that Gabriel was very sympathetic to the Australian Communist Party, even possibly a member. Brígida was quite anticlerical. Their leftist politics were likely evident in Spain as well, possibly evoking persecution by the authorities and contributing to their decision to emigrate to Australia.[23]

There is also evidence that the Kwantu Maru connection from Argentina to Darwin was the avenue of at least a few Basque settlers in North Queensland. José Abreu of Begoña, Bizkaia, was a twenty-seven-year-old bachelor upon entering Australia. He, too, came directly from South America to Darwin, having resided in Argentina for twenty-two years (obviously having been taken there when five by immigrant Basque parents). When applying for citizenship in 1933, he was a waterside worker in Innisfail, Queensland (while a sugar town, he appears not to have been involved in that industry). Serially, his Australian residences had been Darwin for two years, then Innisfail for three and a half, Brisbane for three months, and Nanango (in southern Queensland) for two months, before returning to Innisfail—his home at the time of his application.

Faustino Martínez of Los Arcos, Navarra, stated that he had lived for ten years in Argentina and three in Darwin. From there, he went to Mourilyan. In 1924, he and his wife returned to their natal village in Navarra, ceding control of their sugar farm to their two eldest sons, Daniel and Lorenzo. In 1929, the two boys repatriated their parents to North Queensland. Nevertheless, in 1934, the parents again returned to Navarra along with their three daughters. Two of them returned to Queensland after just seven months, and the third remained to care for her aging parents and became entrapped in Spain by the Spanish Civil War. When Faustino died in 1948, Daniel sponsored the return to Queensland of his sister and seventy-year-old mother.[24]

Unlike the highly disparate and idiosyncratic personal histories of the Basque immigrants in other Australian states, there is clear patterning to the Queensland Basques' history—one that permits considering them a "colony" even if not the result of purposeful targeted recruitment like, for example, the inhabitants of New Italy. Particularly notable is the fact that fifty of the sixty-five Queensland Basques in the sample had never resided in another Australian state. *All* were residing in one of three major North Queensland sugar districts—the Burdekin (Ayr, Home Hill, Jarvisfield), the Herbert (Ingham, Stone River, Beeva, Victoria, Macknade, Lannercost), or Innisfail–South Johnstone (including

Mourilyan and Tully). The applicants averaged 22.5 years-of-age at entry and slightly over eleven years in Queensland before seeking citizenship. Thirty-five, or more than half of the applicants, were still farm labourers or canecutters. Conversely, twenty-seven, or 41 percent of the total, had acquired a farm.

Sixty of the sixty-five applicants were Bizkaian (there was one from Araba, one from Navarra, and three from Gipuzkoa—none from Iparralde). Of the Bizkaians, eight (or over 13 percent) were from the thousand-person village of Aulesti/Murélaga; counting the two Menchacas, another six were from Lekeitio. So, there is clear evidence of an emerging chain migration.

Forty-eight of the men were single, even after eleven years on average in the country. The spouses of the remainder (not counting three whose marital status was unspecified) included two Australians, one Italian, and eleven from "Spain." It seems clear that the Queensland Basque colony was constituted in the main by bachelors, but that some men were going back or sending back to the Basque Country for wives. There is no evidence at all of a single-adult-woman Basque presence—all of the applicants were male.

Twenty-six, or fully 40 percent of the sixty-five men under analysis, entered in a three-year span (1924–1926) of the decade of the twenties. While this was a period in which the cane districts were expanding sugar acreage into the surrounding bush, given the lag time in bringing such land on line, it seems unlikely that such development would create a stampede of Southern European immigration. It might be noted, however, that its Immigration Act of 1924 reduced the annual quota of Spanish nationals allowed to enter the United States to 131 individuals.[25]

I now conduct a similar analysis of San Sebastián's database (n = 377: 329 males and 28 females).[26] We have the birthplace (or residence upon emigrating) of 175 individuals. Of that total, 154 (88 percent) were from Bizkaia, thirteen from Gipuzkoa, four from Navarra, three from Araba, and one from Melbourne. The Bizkaian sample was overwhelmingly rural, with no fewer than 23 (15 percent) from the one-thousand-inhabitants village of Aulesti/Murélaga alone.

Only twenty-eight of his immigrants, or but 7.42 percent, were females. He found naturalization records for only twenty-eight persons;

however, he learned of the presence in Australia of nearly twice as many (sixty-four) through the electoral rolls. Presumably, they could not have voted without being Australian citizens. One served in the Australian Armed Forces during World War I and eleven did so during the subsequent planet-wide conflict. While the earliest in his corpus to be naturalized did so in 1897, and there was a sprinkling of seven others until 1933, the real clustering was during World War II and shortly thereafter (twenty in all between 1939 and 1950). We might posit that the rise of Fascism, including Franco's dictatorship in their natal country, prompted some Basques in Australia to relinquish their Spanish citizenship.

Then there is the question of Australian residence. Of the 305 for whom it is possible to impute[27] residence, 276, or 90.5 percent, were in Queensland, of whom four resided in Brisbane and three were in Mount Isa. Of the Queensland residents, 131, or nearly half, resided in the Burdekin district (Ayr-Home Hill), another 93, or a third, lived in the Herbert, and 31 (11.2 percent) lived in Cairns/Innisfail. So, these three districts alone accounted for 91.4 percent of his sample of Queensland Basques. As for the other Australian states, eleven lived in New South Wales, as was the case with Victoria, and there was one in South Australia.

Occupationally, as well, there was considerable clustering. Of the 116 individuals for whom we have information, 64, or 55.2 percent, were cane growers and thirteen were canecutters or haulers. Another thirteen were in the sugar districts and listed as "labourers" or "transporters"—possible alternative identifications of cane workers. There were seven miners, five mariners, and four waterside (dock) workers.

At the same time, a few entries give additional tantalizing information unique to particular individuals. There is the intriguing question of sponsorship of intending immigrants by established persons in Australia. We can cite several early examples from both Ayr and Ingham. Regarding the former, as early as 1924 G. Sesma sponsored an immigrant and J. Plaza supported two the following year. In 1930, Ayr's Benito Achurra nominated four newcomers and Landa two. In 1930, in Ingham we have Elortegui sponsoring four immigrants and V. Balanzategui two. In short, between the two towns we can identify no fewer than ten sponsorships in March and April of 1930 (there may have been more). One might surmise that there was a desire to emigrate a few months after Europe entered the Great Depression, and some established Basques in North Queensland facilitated such departures before Australia closed its doors.

By the decade of the 1920s, there is clear evidence, then, of active sponsorship of aspiring newcomers by established persons in Australia. It is equally clear that this often entailed the nominator's relatives and/or fellow villagers in the Old World. It is also evident that immigrants were coming in small groups. San Sebastián identifies forty immigrants who entered between 1923 and 1925 inclusive. On October 18, 1923, four[28] persons arrived in Brisbane from Toulon on board the *Orsova*. Two were women, suggesting that Basque emigration to Australia was beginning to "mature." In February 1924, five[29] men arrived in Sydney on the *Cephee*, probably having embarked in Marseille (that vessel's French home base). On April 4, 1925, the *Ville de Metz* made port in Fremantle having departed Le Havre. On board were six Basques.[30] On May 28, 1928, the *Ville de Strasbourg* reached Fremantle from Marseille with four[31] Basques on board. Similarly, of the eighteen Basque arrivals in 1930 recorded by San Sebastián, six[32] arrived on March 18 in Fremantle on board the *Orontes* having embarked in Gibraltar. On April 20, the *Orsova* docked in Fremantle, having come from Marseilles with five[33] Basques.

A couple of caveats are in order. First, just because there were more than one Basque on board a particular ship does not mean that they were, in fact, traveling together as a group. The scheduled sailings were weeks apart and may have been booked by individuals who were then surprised to find other Basques on board. In the case of the 1912 sailing of the *Caledonie*, with sixteen Basques, there could have been two "groups"—those from Aulesti and the Sesma clan from Ereño. Second, it is not necessarily clear that the arrival of an individual represents his/her year of first entry into Australia. Return visits to Europe were the aspiration of most Basque Australians and their descendants (although more plausible over time due to improvements in transportation systems).

There are a few interesting cases of persons who had previous immigration experience in multiple countries. The mariner Juan Estanislao Chacartegui left Australia in 1920 destined to join his brothers in Idaho (the epicenter of Bizkaian sheepherders and ranchers in the United States). His last Australian residence was Innisfail—so it seems likely that he moved there from either Sydney or Melbourne to check out the sugar scene before deciding to leave for North America. Alejandro Lecube entered Australia in 1927 and was residing in Buenos Aires in 1939. In 1915, Antonio Onaindia Laca from Amoroto entered Australia and became a canecutter after having herded sheep in Idaho and Nevada for twenty years. His nickname was "Tony Bronco." Immigrant José Maguregui was, at some point (unclear as to whether before or after his Australian sojourn), a *jai alai* player in the United States.

It should be noted that all such data bases are more akin to still photographs than they are to videos. By this I mean they generally give us a snapshot, a frozen image, rather than a dynamic sequence. If we consider "residence" and "occupation" as examples, the documentary source may well list only the single answer that pertained to the question at the time it was posed. In this fashion, the likely fact that the respondent may have had several residences and different occupations during his stay in Australia is simply left out of account. It should also be underscored that San Sebastián's entries are uneven in that many sources provide only partial information. We have discussed the disparity between the naturalization records and the electoral rolls. Some of the men are identified as having served in Australia's Armed Forces, but we cannot be sure that none of the others did so.

Another question is that of political radicalization. It would seem that at least some of the Basques that ended up in Australia were exposed to the leftist politics that characterized the industrial urban areas of Bizkaia in the late nineteenth and early twentieth centuries. Mason dwells at length on the role of radical leftist politics in the community, albeit as expressed through the activism of a few, largely Catalan, individuals.[34]

Mason states that the postwar Spanish nationals immigrating into Queensland were "both overwhelmingly radical anticapitalists and Catalan."[35] Few Basques were involved in radical politics in their adopted country. An exception was Frank Bilbao, who was detained by Australian authorities for seditious activities—he was a Communist. Other Basques with tarnished reputations were Francisco Churruca, Nicolás Arrieta,

"Pikua," from the farmstead of the same name, and Cecilio Basurco, who arrived together in Australia from Austria in 1927, having been described as "deserters" in Spanish records. Basurco ultimately composed verses entitled "Mutriku'tik Australia'ra" (From Mutriku to Australia).[36]

Mason details the Iberian origins of Queensland Spanish nationals by decades, between 1910 and 1940, and finds that Catalans dominated between 1910 and 1919 (with fifty), while Bizkaians (with thirty) were in second place. In Europe, Catalan emigration began to decline after 1921, and, for the decade of the 1920s, Mason found that another thirty Bizkaians entered Queensland while only seventeen Catalans did so. During the 1930s, forty-nine Bizkaians managed to reach the area as opposed to just eight Catalans.[37] In short, the Catalan community was aging and becoming far less of a factor in Queensland's mix of Spanish nationals, whereas the Basque presence was robust and on the increase.

We might consider one last snapshot of Basques in the Far North at mid-twentieth century. Between September 12 and 19, 1948, there was a major Congress in Biarritz organized by the International Society of Basque Studies (*Sociedad Internacional de Estudios Vascos*). Its theme was the Basque presence in many countries throughout the world. Manuel de Inchausti (a returned Basque from the Philippines) prepared a "Preliminary Note" on Basque residents (and toponyms) in several countries, including Australia. The details for that continent were sketchy at best. The report regards Basques resident only in the Herbert, the Burdekin, and Innisfail/Cairns in Queensland's Far North. There is no mention of Basques in Mount Isa or other Queensland venues like the Atherton Tablelands, although we know for certain that there were some by then. Interestingly, Melbourne and New South Wales are also missing entirely. Again, we know that there were at least a few Basques there, but they were off this radar. The report therefore provides (plausible) negative evidence that, in 1948, Australia's Basque presence was overwhelmingly in three districts of Queensland's Far North.

And for each of these, the data are interesting. It would seem that De Inchausti had one main informant who was residing in the Herbert. The report detailed all Basques living there. His coverage for the Burdekin is a bit sketchier, and even more so for Innisfail/Cairns. For the Herbert, De Inchausti counts twenty-seven adult males and eighteen women (plus two Catalans married to Basque men). There were eighteen children. Four women were listed as dressmakers and two as stenographers. Six adult men had no listed occupation and were presumably cancutters or at least farmworkers. There were twenty-one canefarmers in all, including one widow (Romualda Menchaca de Iraegui). In the Burdekin, there were seventy-one Basque men, twenty-two Basque women (plus a Catalan married to a Basque), and twenty-one children. There were thirty-seven canefarmers (including a widow) and twenty-one men had no listed occupation and were therefore likely canecutters or farm laborers. There were two dressmakers. Among the men, eight were listed as "transporters" and two as *corredores*. One suspects that they were engaged in cane haul-out rather than carrying freight over long distances. In Innisfail/Cairns there were twenty-six Basque men, three children, and but two women (clearly undercounted, since I know of the presence of some wives). The two women were Basques, whereas there were Basque/Catalan and Basque/Spanish unions in the area as well. Of the listed men, ten were canefarmers and a like number had no stated occupation. Two were entered as "proprietors" of businesses, one man was a building contractor, and another a miner. In all, the three areas had a reported Basque population in 1948 of 211 individuals. There is likely some undercounting, but I suspect the demographic snapshot was only slightly blurred.[38]

Finally, the European birthplace of 126 persons is given. All but fourteen, or 89 percent, were Bizkaians; there were eleven Gipuzkoans (eight of whom were from Mutriku), and three Navarrese.

Of the Bizkaians, twenty were from Aulesti-Gizaburuaga, fifteen from Amoroto, eleven from Lekeitio, eleven from Nabarniz, and ten from Markina-Xemein. In short, the data confirm the Old World origins of the Basque population of the Far North as stated to this point in our argument.

Mason states:

> The primacy of economic conditions explains the sharp decline in Catalan emigration from its peak in the early 1920s. Whilst Basques were well established in Queensland and migrated on the basis of developed local networks, Catalan migration was not

similarly embedded. Key Catalan sponsors, such as Bruno Tapiola [*sic*], were successful businessmen able to offer employment, but few non-Basques could provide such scope and consistency of opportunity...Catalan settlers in Queensland had not been as commercially successful as the Basques. They migrated decades earlier, but were hampered from the start by their indentured status, and a lack of community networks to pool their resources. They had waited several years before they could afford their own farms. Although financially secure by the Cold War, they lacked similar networks of contact with Spain, and sufficient economic incentives to entice family and friends to Queensland.[39]

I differ with Mason's explanation. We have already considered the chain migration of Catalans to Melbourne along dense village and kinship networks. One can tickle out similar behavior among Catalans in the Far North. Once the 1907 recruits became established, they served as magnets for subsequent Catalan immigration. They certainly maintained a sense of ethnic distinctiveness (like the Basques) within the larger collectivity of Spanish nationals that persisted for decades. The Catalans of the Burdekin were the prime movers of the Spanish Society of North Queensland, founded in the late 1960s. Nor, in my experience, are Catalans in the Far North less successful economically than Basques. Indeed, in Ingham there is little distinction, whereas in the Burdekin there are some prominent Catalan fortunes (including that of Bruno Tapiolas). Nor can we ignore the stunning success in Mena Creek of José Paronella. Furthermore, the recruitment of Basques on cane-cutting contracts in the late 1950s was quite equivalent to the 1907 recruitment of indentured Catalans. Basque immigrants aspiring to farm ownership in Queensland, like their Catalan (and Italian) counterparts, worked as manual laborers for years before succeeding—often by pooling resources with fellow ethnic cutters. In short, I find nothing distinctively Basque (or Catalan), either in technique or outcome, in what I consider to be a Southern European (notably Italian) pattern of socioeconomic mobility within the sugar industry.

I do agree with Mason's conclusion that, of all of Queensland's Spanish nationals, anti-Franquism was most prominent among the Basques. Their support for Basque nationalism increased, as did the importance of their language (despite the fact that use of it was declining among the immigrants and their descendants) and culture as symbols of ongoing resistance to the Spanish dictator.[40]

Southern Europeans in Pre- and Postwar Queensland—There remains the question of the extent to which World War II and Australia's anti-alien measures impacted the numbers and the circumstances of Italians and Spaniards in Queensland. It is possible to infer at least part of the answer by comparing the relevant data in the 1933 and 1947 national censuses (which bracket much of the Great Depression and all of World War II), on the one hand, and the available information regarding land tenure, on the other.

Of immediate interest, as reflected in Table 3, is that, despite the anti-immigration climate during the period in question, Queensland's population of Italy-born persons was actually slightly higher in 1947 than in 1933 (8,541 versus 8,343)! That the period was one of maturation of the Italian community is reflected in the sex ratio of immigrants. We have noted the surge of Italian immigration between the 1921 and 1933 censuses. Constituted in the main by single males or solitary married men entering Australia to gain an initial foothold before sending for fiancées or spouses, the sex ratio in 1933 stood at 2.6 males for each Italy-born female. Conversely, by 1947 the ratio was down to 1.7 to 1, suggesting that there was a female bias in the Italian immigration of the intervening period as women effected family formation or reunion. Then, in the next seven years, it surpasses 2 to 1—suggesting that the most recent immigration was largely male.

During the brief intercensal period from 1947 until 1954, Queensland's Italian population nearly doubled to 16,795 individuals. Despite all of the opposition to their renewed entry into Australia, the established foothold clearly served effectively to sponsor kinsmen and others. This doubling antedates the formal recruitments of the mid-1950s.

A second discernible trend is the broadening of the Italian settlement pattern within Queensland. In 1933, almost a third of the state's Italy-born population lived in the Hinchinbrook Shire (Ingham). An additional third lived in Johnstone (Innisfail) and Mulgrave (Cairns) Shires. By 1947, the combined total for the three shires represented less than half (46 percent) of Queensland's Italy-born population. Greater

TABLE 3. Italy-Born Persons Resident in Queensland as Registered in the 1933, 1947, and 1954 National Censuses

1933 Census				1947 Census				1954 Census			
M	F	Total	%	M	F	Total	%	M	F	Total	%
I. Greater Brisbane											
166	66	232	2.8	517	262	779	9.1	1731	495	2226	13.2
II. Atherton Mareeba[1]											
335	86	421	5.0	303	164	467	5.5	631	357	988	5.8
III. Ayr (Burdekin)											
386	134	520	6.2	437	276	713	8.3	882	475	1357	8.0
IV. Cardwell											
226	90	316	3.8	205	130	335	3.9	450	178	628	3.7
V. Douglas											
168	78	246	2.9	139	101	240	2.8	226	100	326	1.9
VI. Hinchinbrook											
1815	771	2586	31.0	1190	748	1938	22.7	2010	942	2952	17.5
VII. Johnstone											
1112	464	1576	18.9	748	473	1221	14.3	1565	676	2241	13.3
VIII. Cairns[2]											
701	273	974	11.7	487	281	768	9.0	1062	417	1479	8.8
IX. (Mackay area) Pioneer-Mirani											
234	89	323	3.9	213	111	324	3.8	417	168	585	3.5
X. Stanthorpe											
59	38	97	0.1	235	149	384	4.5	pages missing for 1954 census			
X1. All Queensland											
6005	2338	8343	100	5386	3155	8541	100	11248	5547	16795	100

[1] Listed as Tinaroo and Woothakata in the 1933 Census
[2] Listed as Mulgrave in the 1947 and 1954 Censuses

Sources: Census of the Commonwealth of Australia, 30th June 1933, pp. 292, 294, 296, 298; Census of the Commonwealth of Australia, 30th June 1947, pp. 236, 238, 240, 242; Census of the Commonwealth of Australia, 30th June 1954, pp. 51, 52, 54, 58.

Brisbane was emerging as an urban alternative (9.1 percent), while the Darling Downs (Stanthorpe) and the Atherton Tablelands together accounted for 10 percent and represented a growing agricultural alternative to the sugar industry for Queensland Italians. This tendency is also apparent in the 1954 statistics. While the traditional venues held their own, indeed increasing their numbers dramatically in absolute terms, it was greater Brisbane that experienced the highest percentage increase in its Italian population (from 9.1 percent to 13.2 percent of the state's total). The city's Italians had nearly tripled in absolute numbers (779 to 2,226).

Since Spaniards were not enumerated by shire in the 1947 census, it is impossible to replicate the foregoing exercise for them. However, macro-statistics for the entire nation would suggest that between the censuses there was considerable stasis in Australia's Spain-born population (1,141 in 1933 versus 992 in 1947).[41] It is plausible to infer processes of maturation and settlement dispersion similar to those noted for the Italian collectivity. It is during this period that several Spanish families became established as farmers (notably in the Burdekin, the Herbert, and the Johnstone Districts, as well as the Atherton Tablelands). Spanish geographical mobility within the sugar industry was also becoming more pronounced. In 1948, a representative of the New South Wales mill owners expressed admiration for Spanish canecutters and settlers, while adding that they were scarce.[42]

Mason provides an analysis of the Old World origins of 158 Spanish nationals recorded as residing in Queensland sometime between 1945 and 1956 and finds that 57 percent were from the three Basque provinces and 7 percent were Navarrans, as opposed to only 8 percent from Catalunya.[43] In short, by mid-century, Basques were the predominant "Spanish" element within Queensland society.

Another barometer of the relative position of Southern Europeans within North Queensland society during the pre- and postwar periods is land tenure. We have noted the trend throughout the first three decades of the twentieth century for some Southern Europeaner canecutters to employ their savings in the purchase of cane farms. Table 4 profiles landownership according to ethnic origin as reflected in the rate books for Hinchinbrook and Ayr Shires. It demonstrates that in Hinchinbrook Shire, between 1929 and 1957, there was steady accrual of landholdings by both Italians and Spaniards. Of particular interest is the fact that,

TABLE 4. Land Tenure by Ethnic Origin: Hinchinbrook (1929, 1939, 1957) and Ayr (1937–38, 1953–54) Shires Compared.

	Hinchinbrook							Ayr Shire			
	Year							Year			
	1921		1939		1957			1937–38		1953–54	
Ethnic Origin	Acres	% of total	Acres	% of total	Acres	% of total		Acres	% of total	Acres	% of total
Anglo–Australian	166,475	76.4	194,125	76.4	318,576	80.1		602,940	94.7	545,579	94.1
Italian	45,825	21.0	55,773	21.9	75,369	18.9		29,043	4.5	30,254	5.2
Spanish	1,681	0.8	1,860	0.7	4,055	1.0		2,890	0.5	3,966	0.7
* Others	4,007	1.8	2,336	1.0	—	—		1,651	0.3	—	—
Totals	217,988	100	254,094	100	398,000	100		636,524	100	579,799	100

* For 1957 in Hinchinbrook Shire and 1953–54 in Ayr Shire this category is aggregated with the "Anglo–Australian" one.
Sources: Shire of Hinchinbrook Valuation and Rate Book, 1929; 1939; Hinchinbrook Shire Council, Assessment Rolls, 1957; Ayr Shire Council, Valuation Register and Rate Book, 1937–8; Ayr Shire Council, Valuation Register and Rate Book, 1953–4.

between 1939 and 1957, the acreage controlled by Italians increased considerably, but that of Spaniards more than doubled. In Ayr Shire, in the periods 1937–1938 and 1953–1954, the figure for Italian-owned property remained practically constant, while that for Spaniards increased by about 25 percent. In short, despite the internment of Italians and all of the negative rhetoric surrounding the issue of Southern European "penetration" of North Queensland, Italians and Spaniards actually increased their holdings between the pre- and postwar periods. The rate books failed to distinguish the use (sugar or otherwise) of the assessed acreage, and also do not reflect leaseholds as such. We know from oral histories that Southern Europeans often leased acreage, but we have no means of quantifying the amount in the district as a whole.

Consequently, Table 5 provides a better idea than does Table 4 of the extent to which Southern Europeans were engaged in sugar production in the two districts in the year 1950. The statistics presented herein incorporate cane from leased farms as well as owned ones, while detailing the ethnicity of the producer rather than just the landlord. In the Herbert, fully 63 percent of the growers were Italians, producing 67 percent of the crop. In the Burdekin, by contrast, Italians accounted for only 27 percent of the growers and 30 percent of the tonnage. The percentage of Spanish growers (4 percent) and tonnage (also 4 percent) was nearly identical in the two districts. In short, in some districts of North Queensland, notably but not exclusively the Herbert, rather than suffering reversals during the Great Depression and the war years, Southern Europeans, and particularly Italians, actually expanded and consolidated their position within the sugar industry in both demographic and economic respects. The gains, while less striking, were discernible in other districts as well—such as the Burdekin.[44]

A tiny anecdote captures the extent to which Basques were integrated into the region's Italian-dominated Southern European culture. Cris Dall'Osto, Ingham's titular Italian sub-consul, was called upon from time to time to interpret in court cases involving Italian nationals. He was doing so in a manner that involved technical terminology concerning geology and blueprints. At one point neither Cris nor the Italian spectators could think of the right Italian word for a particular term. As they all struggled, suddenly the Australian-born Basque, Iñaki Badiola, shouted it from the back of the room, much to the amusement of all present.[45]

TABLE 5. Number of Growers and Peak Tonnage by Ethnic Origin: Herbert and Burdekin Districts (1950)

Mill Area	Anglo-Australian and Others			Italians			Spanish		
	# of growers	% of total	Tons grown	% of total	# of growers	% of total	Tons grown	% of total	# of growers	% of total	Tons grown	% of total

Mill Area	# of growers	% of total	Tons grown	% of total	# of growers	% of total	Tons grown	% of total	# of growers	% of total	Tons grown	% of total
Macknade Mill	57	26	83,546	27	151	70	217,206	69	9	4	12,876	4
Victoria Mill	110	38	97,647	29	169	58	219,740	65	12	4	19,729	6
Combined Totals Herbert Mills	167	33	181,193	28	320	63	436,946	67	21	4	32,605	5
Inkerman Mill	141	65	129,125	63	72	33	68,771	34	5	2	6,306	3
Kalamia Mill	121	70	20,553	66	42	24	8,209	27	11	6	2,172	7
Pioneer Mill	121	74	113,863	70	34	21	41,127	25	8	5	7,749	5
Combined Totals Burdekin Mills	383	69	263,541	66	148	27	118,107	30	24	4	16,227	4

Source: *Queensland Government Gazette*, May 17, 1950, no. 158, pp. 2111–2112, 2039–2041, 2054–2055, 2057–2059, 2158–2160.

Notes

1. Douglass, *Azúcar amargo*, 81.
2. Mason, "Agitators," 41.
3. Josephine Canals, "The Catalans and Their Place in Melbourne's History," in *The Spanish Experience in Australia*, ed. Carmen Castelo (Jamison Centre, ACT: The Spanish Heritage Foundation, 2000), 9. ["The Catalans"].
4. Ibid, 9. Also see Catalan Footprint.
5. It has a physical locale that is supported by the *Comunitats Catalanes D'Exterior de la Generalitat de Catalunya* (Catalan Communities Abroad of the Generalitat of Catalunya). It teaches Catalan and sponsors an annual celebration on Catalan National Day. It had 150 members as of 2016.
6. Ibid, 11.
7. Waring, "Lola's Memories," 74–75.
8. Ibid, 69–70.
9. Ibid, 74–75.
10. Ibid, 70–71.
11. Michele Langfield and Peta Roberts, *Welsh Patagonians: The Australian Connection* (Darlinghurst, NSW: Crossing Press, 2005), 215. [*Welsh Patagonians*].
12. Ibid, 224–26; Mason, "Agitators," 75–77.
13. Ibid, 78–80.
14. William Vestey was born into a prominent merchant family in Liverpool. In 1876, he went to Chicago where he worked in a meatpacking facility owned by his father. In 1897, he founded the Vestey Group, along with his brother. They invested in cattle ranches in South America and built meatpacking plants in Uruguay and Argentina, specializing in exporting refrigerated products to England. In 1914, the Vestey Group built a meatpacking facility in Darwin. William Vestey was admitted to British peerage in recognition of his role in provisioning Great Britain from South America during the First World War.

    In 1920, the Vestey plant in Darwin was bankrupt and closed, putting many migrants out of work. The destitute men requested Government assistance that was not forthcoming. They marched on Government House, the Spaniards among them singing the "Internationale." The territorial administrator refused to meet with them and they burned his effigy. The Spaniards then charged some nearby fortified positions and threw their machine guns into the sea. An alarmed administrator requested that a Royal Australian naval vessel be brought into Darwin harbor to restore his authority (Ibid, 81).
15. Langfield and Roberts, *Welsh Patagonians*, 229.
16. Mason, "Agitators," 81. She would later serve as the main organizer of the SRC branch in Innisfail. Her husband, Jack, was a Communist and he returned to Spain to fight on the Republican side during the Spanish Civil War (Ibid, 151; 153).
17. Langfield and Roberts, *Welsh Patagonians*, 230.
18. Ibid, 229; 231.
19. Price Collection, passim.
20. Ibid.

21. Ibid.
22. Ibid. He had entered Australia in 1921, likely sponsored by his brother Vicente who was established in canefarming in Ingham.
23. Ibid.
24. Mason, "Agitators," 186.
25. Douglass and Bilbao, *Amerikanuak*, 304–5.
26. San Sebastián, "Basques," passim.
27. In some instances, the immigrant's destination is specified. I have sometimes been able to identify a locale from such evidence as place of residence when applying for naturalization or place where pursuing an occupation. Obviously, the exercise is not flawless, but at least suggestive.
28. María Garramiola, José Goicoechea (from Jatabe), Romualda Menchaca, and Saturnino Onaindia. We will meet the latter two below as pioneer canefarmers in Ingham and Innisfail, respectively.
29. Benito Achurra Calzacorta (Berriatua), Claudio Anchia Bastarrechea (Mallabia), Martín Buruaga, José Epelde, and José Telleria.
30. Félix Ayo, José Goicoechea, Valentín Madariaga (Xemein), Félix Plaza, José Totoricagüena, and Santiago Ynchausti.
31. Enrique Elorduy, Alberto Fernández de Viana, Justo Goicoechea, and Sebastián Goitiandia.
32. Saturnino Achurra, Angela Araquistain (Ondarroa), León Badiola (Amoroto), B. Elortegui, Joaquín Elortegui (Jatabe), and A. Erezuma. All had been recommended by Pedro Elortegui Azcorra, a canefarmer in Ingham. Pedro had immigrated in January of 1928, arriving in Fremantle as the only Basque on board the *Orvieto* from Toulon.
33. T. M. Achurra, Antonio Aguirre (Abadiño), A. Ansotegui, Antonio Azpiazu (Mutriku), and A. Urquidi. All had been recommended by a canefarmer in Ayr named Benito Achurra.
34. Of particular note was the anarchist and atheist Salvador Torrents of Mataró, an industrial city in Catalunya, who arrived in Essendon, in 1915, with fellow Mataroan and political radical, Juan Jordana. They quickly resettled in Innisfail, Queensland, where they hoped to acquire a farm. They purchased sixty acres of scrubland at Mena Creek with borrowed money, and then engaged in the backbreaking labor of clearing it for a sugar paddock (Mason, "Agitators," 43–47).
35. Ibid, 85.
36. In Antonio Zavala, *Ameriketako bertsoak* (Tolosa: Auspoa, 1984), 103–8. See Appendix 3.
37. Mason, "Agitators," 91; 93.
38. Manuel de Inchausti, "Los Vascos en el Mundo," *Anuario de Eusko-Folklore* 29 (1980), 91–94.
39. Mason, "Agitators," 190–91.
40. Ibid, 212.
41. Commonwealth of Australia, *Census of the Commonwealth of Australia, 30th June, 1947*, vol. 1 (Canberra: Commonwealth Government Printer, 1947), 644.

42. January 29, 1948, Australian Archives (ACT): CRS A445, item 211/1/6, Department of Immigration, Correspondence File S 'Class 16,' 1951–52, "Qld. Sugar Industry Employment of Migrants."
43. Mason, "Agitators," 194. Derived from records in the National Archives of Australia (Brisbane).
44. Ibid, 128.
45. Douglass field notes.

CHAPTER 9

Coming Together

Much work, reasonable pay, and little play in the company of one's mates were the fate of the immigrant generation. Home was a barrack, a barn, a tent, or the backseat of a vehicle. Most returned to the Basque Country, but a few married and planned an Australian future. Eventually, wherever there was the smallest of critical masses, maybe forty or fifty families and bachelors, there emerged the idea of forming a *txoko*, or Basque Club.

A definitional feature of any immigrant diaspora is the tendency of its members to create ethnic networks within the host society. Lacking such interaction with fellow ethnics (immigrants from the homeland like oneself, as well as the "New World" descendants of former fellow immigrants), the individual remains a generic citizen who happened to be born elsewhere while speaking the local language with an accent. Within virtually every immigrant collectivity there is the potential of creating, over time, a critical mass of a sufficient number of ethnic-aware persons maintaining a web of intra-ethnic-group ties to beget formal voluntary associations. These "clubs" assume a variety of forms and functions. They may acquire a "clubhouse," possibly leased, purchased, or constructed after years of scrimping together the funds. Alternatively, the "meetings" might be in the homes of individuals or the hall of a service club or parish church, mosque, or synagogue. The activities may be entirely recreational and limited to a picnic or festival, likely held on the day or days of particular significance in the ethnic homeland. It is quite common for the group to foster its folk music, dances, and costumes. Not uncommon is the attempt to teach the ethnic language, particularly to the children in an attempt to preserve it (an exercise usually fraught with difficulty and frustration). The clubhouse may contain a restaurant, a commercial enterprise designed to purvey the ethnic cuisine both to satiate its members and to raise funds for the club's expenses. Members are usually dues-payers and, in some cases, there are public funds (usually modest) from agencies in the homeland or a host society committed to preserving the culture abroad.

We shall now consider how virtually all of the foregoing has characterized the Spanish and Basque collectivities of Australia. Before examining the particulars, however, several caveats are in order. In writing a book about "Basques in the Antipodes" I make the underlying assumption that there are persons in Australia that choose to identify as Basques, even though they do not carry a passport with such designation. I further assume that this fact informs at least a part of their persona and behavior. At the same time, I would underscore that there are many immigrants in Australia with Basque ethnic credentials (genealogy, birthplace, etc.) who are indifferent to them. They may be like me with respect to my Irish and Scottish roots. I am aware of them, but without that fact affecting my daily life in virtually any fashion (if we except my "Irish guilt"—having been raised in an Irish Catholic household before becoming my present agnostic and agonistic self). In short, I have no way of documenting such individuals and, therefore, of stating their proportion within the universe of this study.

When it comes to membership in voluntary associations, we are truly dealing with committed individuals—but here again they vary among themselves in magnitude of commitment. Notoriously, the real work (decorating the hall, cooking the meal, cleaning up the mess) in voluntary ethnic associations devolves upon a few persons, the truly dedicated. The very survival of the organization sometimes turns on their continued willingness to serve; their imperviousness to "burn out."[1]

Finally, I would note that in no event is the immigrant actor (let alone her descendants) a full-time (or even significantly part-time) ethnic. This can vary according to whether all members of the household are of the same ethnic background and employ the language as the vernacular within the intimacy of home life. However, even "pure" actors, during the course of their day, maintain their prime interaction with non-ethnic school or workmates, neighbors, tradesmen, and the extant media (most of its programming in the national language), etc. Therefore, even the most "ethnic" of immigrant actors is likely to go days on end without an ethnic moment or encounter outside the home. "Being Basque" in a host society is therefore largely episodic and recreational.

We have early evidence of the existence of a "Barcelona Club" among the Catalans of Melbourne at the turn of the twentieth century.[2] There was also a Spanish Club in Queensland during the mid-1920s, presumably based in Brisbane where the violinist Luis Amadeo Pares resided. He tells us: "As president of the newly formed Spanish Club of Queensland, a novel experience awaited me in the sugar towns of Babinda, Innisfail, Ingham and Tully, where Spaniards and Italians were residing." When he toured the Far North giving recitals, he was greeted every morning by "Catalans, Basques and Andalusians," and, each day by nine in the morning, "the charivari was in full swing."[3]

Mason reports a dense ethnic network of Spanish nationals evident in the Innisfail area by the 1920s. Indeed, the Catalan barber and canefarmer, Gabriel Sorli, took bankruptcy in 1916.[4] Mason cites Torrents, who reported that there were two or three restaurants in the town that served Spanish food and as a meeting place for Spanish nationals. There is the case of the Basque Saturnino Fernández (likely a Navarran), who arrived in Fremantle in 1916 and went to work in that city's Madrid Restaurant. He then moved to Sydney where he continued in the hospitality industry before moving to Innisfail and becoming a chef in a local restaurant. Catalan Joe (José María Donatiu) owned the movie theater in Innisfail for many years and he also had a cane farm nearby.[5] Navarran Peter Goñi was running a tavern in the town.[6] Miguel Martínez ran a boardinghouse in Innisfail's Chinatown and the Catalan, Gabriel Sorli, presumably financially solvent, did so on Ernest Street. Mason notes that they both brought together single men (in the majority among the immigrants) and served them as a node in an ethnic employment network.[7] The boardinghouse run by Teresa Mendiolea did the same for Spanish nationals in the Ingham area.

I would regard these to be rather informal precursors of the later more elaborate clubs considered below. These earliest, informal infrastructures focused on the celebration of picnics and/or organizing other outings for a small number of insiders. Between the world wars, they are somewhat implicated with the confrontation between Fascism and

Bolshevism in the European homelands of both Spaniards and Italians. Indeed, we have considered the development among Italo-Australians of both pro- and anti-Fascist associations and newspapers. Many Catalans were also leftist political radicals. Basques were less engaged with Anti-Fascist radical politics. While most were anti-Franquist and pro-PNV, and therefore favored European Basque independence (to varying degrees), Basque nationalism was fundamentally conservative, pro-capital, and Catholic. The active anticlericalism of Southern European anti-Fascists in Australia was off-putting for most of the Basque-Australian immigrant community.

"Anticlericalism," then, was a complicated set of issues producing stances that were not always mutually consistent. Mason notes that, to the extent that anticlericalism existed among Basque Australians, it was due to "a lack of empathy with the Irish emphasis of the local Church."[8] At the same time, he recognizes that there was also a tendency for many a local community to esteem its local pastor if he seemed sympathetic to their needs—including the Maltese priest Father Alfred Lanzon and then Father Clancy in Ingham.[9] He also notes that during the Spanish Civil War images of atrocities perpetrated by Republicans against Catholic targets (church burnings, executions of priests and nuns) were accepted at face value and even condoned by some Spanish nationals, but not the Basque Australians.[10]

I would qualify the foregoing as a partial explanation. It might be further noted that, prior to and during the initial stages of the Spanish Civil War, Basque authorities had appealed unsuccessfully for Vatican recognition that they were loyal Catholics and should not be confused with "Red" Republicans. When Church fathers, including the Spanish and Basque bishops, sided with Franco and labeled his rebellion a holy "crusade" against godless Communism, Basque nationalists felt betrayed. Some Basque parish priests opposed their bishops and served as chaplains in the Basque army; a number of them were subsequently executed, incarcerated, or exiled for this.

I would further note that Basque religiosity is clearly gendered. When asked, Basques of both sexes acknowledge their Catholicism and almost all would insist upon a Church wedding, baptism, and confirmation for their children, not to mention a Catholic funeral upon bidding farewell to this life. However, attendance at mass in the "Old Country" is as much a function of peer pressure and unwillingness to incur the ire of the influential parish priest. Among Basque emigrants throughout the world, "church-going" tends to be a female activity. The same was true among Basque Australians.

It might also be noted that the acceptance by local Basques of local priests in the Queensland context was also qualified. Mason notes that there were five Spanish priests stationed in North Queensland before 1945. Three of them were Augustinians and the other two were likely so. Three arrived in Cairns in the late 1920s, and all were relatively young. They came as the result of an agreement between Queensland's Augustinian order and that of Manila.[11] The priests' clear objective was to learn English. One of these Cairns' clergymen served as assistant parish priest in Innisfail during part of 1928 and 1929. All three of the Cairns' priests were Castilian, and Mason concludes that they had little impact upon the local Spanish community. That is scarcely surprising given the antagonism toward Madrid of many Catalans and Basques, the two most prominent subgroups among North Queensland Spanish nationals.[12] In my experience these five priests were not even a part of the collective memory of North Queensland's Basques. No one ever mentioned them to me, their baseline for ethnic religious ministry being the arrival in 1959 of the Reverend Tomás Ormazabal, a Basque.

We might conclude this section by describing one fairly spectacular, if bizarre, example of a "Spanish" ethnic initiative in North Queensland. The Catalan José Paronella worked first in Italy, Switzerland, and France before emigrating to Queensland in 1912. He cut cane and worked in the mines before acquiring a block of bushland near that of Torrents in Mena Creek. He was not a political radical but certainly qualified as a maverick. While he courted priests and politicians to further his business interests, in 1924 he paid a fine of £1,000 for having refused to pay income tax.[13] Mason tells us that, by the 1930s, Paronella was directing his energies to creating a fantasy public recreational destination:

> Together with his wife, he built the pleasure park in a self-consciously Spanish style with a crenellated castle, grand staircase, and house that overlooked Mena Creek falls. The park contained a theatre, cinema, tennis courts, café and pool, and was frequented by a cross-section of the local community. From its

inception though, the park was a particularly important venue for local Spaniards. It not only hosted occasional Spanish dances, but its technological achievement and beauty were a source of pride to Spaniards, and provided a visual statement of their culture and presence.[14]

The *Centros Españoles* of Victoria and Sydney—There is a sense in which the true associative presence of Basques in Australia begins with the founding, in 1960, of the *Centro Español* in Melbourne and, in 1962, the Sydney Spanish Club. Several Basques resident in the two cities were among the founders and earliest officers of the respective organizations.

According to García, in November of 1960, a group of Melbourne-resident Spanish nationals leased premises for get-togethers on Spring Street, moving their venue the following year to Swanston Street, across from city hall. Then, in 1963, they moved again to Elizabeth Street, and, in 1964, formalized the *Centro Español* and named a famed professional boxer, Ricardo Marcos ("Bolita"), their first president. By then, there were 527 members. The membership included many Basques, as was certainly the case with the Sydney *Centro Español*. Notwithstanding that the membership was growing (706 by the following July), the *Centro* had financial difficulties and struggled to pay its £173 annual rent. So, it moved again, now to La Strobe Street. The *Centro* opened daily, but really only prospered on weekends (its members were mainly working class). A special function, such as a festivity or dance, might attract two hundred participants. Its social life was centered upon bar culture and Victoria only permitted liquor sales once monthly—a day of considerable celebration in the *Centro*.[15]

Beginning in 1962, with the arrival in Melbourne of a Catholic priest, Father Sánchez, the *Centro Español* (which de facto was in the main anti-Franco) experienced competition. The new arrival, quite pro-Franquist, had, during an earlier sojourn, gathered about himself a group of Spanish sympathizers who became known as *el club del cura* ("the priest's club").[16] Upon returning to Melbourne, he obtained funding from the IEE to establish a physical *Hogar Español,* or "Spanish Home." The Spanish Consulate viewed him as an unwelcome competitor for funding and influence.[17] Then, too, the Melbourne *Centro Español* experienced an internal schism led by two pro-Franquists. They formed a competing

Club Hispano-Australiano that syphoned off tens of members of the Spanish Club, thereby debilitating it. The members of the *Hogar Español* and the *Club Hispano-Australiano* referred to themselves as "those of the flag," and called the *Centro Español* "the Communists' club."[18]

Meanwhile, in 1963, seventy Spanish migrants in Geelong, Victoria, founded their own club. It was the idea of Samuel Nieto, a man who entered Australia in the mid-1950s. He was elected president by the first General Assembly. The membership grew to 130, or more than a third of the Spanish nationals residing in Geelong. The organization functioned only on weekends, and its prime challenge was to obtain an elusive liquor license. The Club organized Spanish-language and religion classes for its children, attended by fifty. Interviewed in 1965, its president noted that committee meetings were held weekly in the home of one of its members and there was a monthly party held at the Viscount Slim Hall, attended by most of the Spaniards resident in Whyalla. Couples paid 30 shillings and singles 20 shillings to enter, and that included all the beer and refreshments one desired.[19]

In Canberra, by 1964, classes for Spanish children were organized. Christmas of 1965, a member of the colony was killed in an auto accident and the idea of founding a club was vetted at his funeral. On October 16, 1966, the Spanish-Australian Club of Canberra was inaugurated. There was immediate internal controversy, particularly surrounding the establishment of the Spanish Embassy in Canberra in 1967. In 1971, a building site was purchased, and a migrant owner of a construction company helped erect a building. The new club was opened to the public in August of 1973.[20]

That same year of 1973, a *Casa de España* began functioning in Whyalla, South Australia. It was never able to afford its own premises, particularly as the number of Spanish nationals in the area actually declined.

García notes that the idea of forming a Spanish Club in New South Wales germinated in discussions among Spaniards frequenting Sydney's Catholic Club. He distinguishes two groups that converged in the common project. First, there was the cohort of largely single men in their twenties from the organized recent recruitments in Spain, who frequented the Kings Cross Hotel, largely on weekends. Forty-five or fifty of them were in attendance. They were annoyed by the NSW drinking laws at the time that forced closure of public drinking establishments at 6 p.m. Totoricagüena states that,

> This group often continued on down the street to the cafeteria Brazil, where the Hungarian Jewish owner was willing to serve alcohol even though he had no liquor license to do so. The secret password was to ask for "cold tea," and one would be served a glass of wine, but if the police happened to enter, all had to pretend that it was a private party in order to evade fines.[21]

There was another group of Basque friends that gathered regularly in the Five Ways Hotel in Paddington.[22]

The single women from the *Marta* flights were the second contingent. They met regularly and attended mass together in St. Mary's Cathedral on Albion Street. They began renting the premises of the League of Catholic Women for dances. Several had Spanish-national boyfriends who accompanied them. García mentions that the Basque Valentín Ugarte, brother of one of the Marta women, used to bring his friends—including additional fellow Basques, such as José Luis Goñi, and Navarrans "Santiñan" and Mariano Escribano.[23] Goñi reached Australia in 1959 and cut cane in North Queensland for a single season before moving to Sydney.[24]

Enter Fernando Largo and Roberto López de Lasala. The former arrived in Australia in 1952 and settled in Sydney. The latter was a Basque-surnamed descendant of a grandfather that was a Carlist general who took refuge in the 1870s after his defeat in the final Carlist War. Roberto's father was a sea captain who married a Portuguese woman in Macao and then settled in Manila. Roberto was orphaned at fourteen and went to Hong Kong, where he was apprenticed to the John Manners & Co. concern. By age twenty-seven, Lasala was the assistant manager in Canton, and, in 1949, became the managing director and chairman of the board. He had a passion for racing and owned eight horses, winning, in 1966, one of Australia's major races. By then, Manners owned a fleet of twenty ships, as well as real estate and businesses in Alaska, Brazil, Argentina, Indonesia, Timor, and England. Fernando Largo was Lasala's personal driver and property manager of several Manners' buildings in Sydney.[25]

Largo brought the new Spanish migrants and Lasala together for a meeting in July of 1961. Manners had its offices on the seventh floor of a building at 88 Liverpool Street. There was a cafeteria on the ground level and an Indian restaurant above it, both managed by Lasala's son-in-law. Lasala agreed to allow the Spaniards to use the ground floor free of charge on Sundays, and the restaurant as well on occasion. By September, the Spaniards had a foundation to run things with membership dues of £6 for married men, three for single women, and one for wives. It was one of the first migrant clubs in Sydney to admit women and accord them the right to vote. The leadership immediately passed a motion prohibiting the discussion of religion or politics on the premises.

So, the Spaniards began to organize Sunday dinners and the odd dances, both staged with volunteer labor. They then evolved into sponsoring excursions—the first being an outing to Katoomba during which a Spanish couple were married. The foundation needed 220 members in order to qualify for a liquor license, and it was not easy to recruit them. Some Sydney Spanish nationals were leery of the Club, and others thought its membership fee excessive. Many lived at considerable distances from the location and could not imagine frequenting it. Conversely, some Spaniards living elsewhere in Australia, or just passing through Sydney, joined. A few underaged people were enrolled, and some of the women, were listed as "Misters," thinking the subterfuge would enhance the likelihood of approval of the license application.

In the event, by March of 1962, there were 220 members and the first General Assembly was held that approved a constitution and named Lasala the first president. In April, the Club was registered with the authorities and by June it had a liquor license. Then, when the Indian restaurant closed soon thereafter, Lasala leased to the Club the first two floors of the building for five years—at £3,260 annually for the first year and £4,000 thereafter. The premises were remodeled and Lasala sold the fixtures to the Club on favorable terms. Poker (slot) machines were introduced on the first floor as one source of income to meet expenses.[26] There was a formal inauguration of the Sydney Spanish Club on October 6, 1962. In the membership register of 1962, there are 43 Basque surnames.[27]

The enterprise immediately entered into a series of economic and political crises. When the first annual general meeting was convened on February 17, 1963, the Spanish Club was in financial difficulties. While some members were critical of Lasala, and even accused him of embezzlement or mismanagement, he survived as head of the governing committee. In August, he appointed José Luis Goñi as assistant manager after the embattled general manager resigned. The public facilities, and particularly the restaurant and bar, were leased out to an operator. In October, Lasala himself resigned after being criticized as an exploiter of immigrants for personal gain. In fairness, he had saved the enterprise to date by providing his personal guarantee to its bank. Several non-Spanish Australians were admitted as members, notably the Club's chief banker, Sydney Stott.

Stott and several other Anglo-Australians had been founding members when they inaugurated the Sydney Hispanic Society on October 27, 1960—a friends of Hispanics organization. It could not have been more eclectic, having been proposed by the Basque-surnamed ambassador of the Philippines to Australia, a Mr. Ezpeleta, and first presided over by Carlos Zalapa, a Mexican businessman who also served as Brazilian Consul in Sydney. He all but monopolized imports in Australia from Spain (mainly olive oil). It was about this same time that a Spanish Chamber of Commerce began functioning in Sydney to facilitate trade and investment between Spain and Australia. Similar societies were founded in Melbourne and Canberra. According to García, "They preceded the clubs, and then ran a parallel existence with them." They were "made up of middle-class people who held their meetings in English; migrants who approached them soon found out that, with some exceptions, they did not fit it. These were in fact Australian societies."[28]

The next few years were a stormy period for the Sydney Spanish Club in which committee meetings became sounding boards for disgruntled members to gripe. There were disputes over whether children could be in the bar (against Australian law, but common in Spain), and disputes sometimes broke out between employees trying to observe the (somewhat liberalized) closing hour and drunken patrons refusing to leave even then—sometimes requiring police intervention. In 1965, members of the losing faction challenged results of the annual election of officers. They alleged irregularities, and, on April 30, the president and four committee members resigned. It then became so difficult to find anyone willing to exert leadership that it became necessary to appoint an Australian, Lancelot Hickey, as president. He was replaced the following year when the General Assembly made Ángel López president of a committee of reluctant officeholders. Even the excitement created by the victory in a Davis Cup match of Spanish tennis star Manuel Santana over Australian legend Roy Emerson failed to assuage tensions within Sydney's Spanish community.[29]

By the following year, the leadership faced the decision of continuing to rent the premises or purchase them, against the backdrop that Lasala was considering selling the building. It was decided (by 35 votes versus 19) by a Special General Assembly convened in September of 1966 to purchase the building with quarterly payments and to borrow A$50,000 for necessary renovations. The upstairs premises were to be leased out to existing tenants, and the Spanish Chamber of Commerce took over the former Manners' headquarters on the seventh floor. Lasala died shortly thereafter, or in May of 1967, touted (hyperbolically) in one of his obituaries as the richest man in Australia.[30]

If governance and policy of the Spanish Club were stormy matters, the organization enjoyed considerable growth and proliferation of activities. Between November of 1963 and June of 1966, membership nearly doubled from 882 to 1,570. Weekends, the restaurant and dance floor were crowded with people coming from as far afield as Wollongong and Canberra. Free Spanish lessons were offered to non-Spanish members and English instruction was provided to monolingual Spanish nationals. There were movie and cabaret nights (including flamenco dance shows). And, in 1964, 175 books in Spanish were ordered as the foundation of a cultural library. A café famed for its coffee (it had Sydney's first expresso machine) became popular and a source of income. The first *mus* tournament was held in 1964 and became an annual event. That same year, the Spanish Club held its first soccer match between a team of single men and marrieds (the latter captained by the Basque Julián Oriñuela). In 1966, the Club fielded a team to compete in matches sanctioned by the Soccer Federation of NSW.[31]

To this point, we are considering the associative expression of a shared Spanish nationality—as expressed in one's passport. As we have considered, however, this masked the ethnic plurality of Iberian peoples. Virtually all of the Spanish Clubs experienced internal dissidence—some of it class-based—not to mention religious and political divisiveness. The very fact that there was a tendency to prohibit discussion of religion and politics itself underscored the hovering, ever-present seriousness of these issues. A subset of political contentions, certainly for at least some Basques, Catalans, and Galicians, were their desire for self-determination vis-à-vis Madrid.

Both the Melbourne *Centro Español* and the Sydney Spanish Club experienced schisms in their memberships. Galicians in the former founded their *Club Gallego* in 1965 with premises next to the Central Market in North Melbourne. It aspired to having a good library, a choral society, and a Galician dance group. Its first president underscored the "pride of putting another link on the chain of Galician centres throughout the world."[32] Similarly, the Asturians in the Sydney Spanish Club founded their *Centro Asturiano de Sydney*. It held its first general meeting in June of 1965. It soon had more than 100 members and rented premises at Rushcutters Bay. The Asturian Club had little staying power and was dissolved in April of 1967.[33]

Melbourne *Gure Txoko* — It was in 1964 that Juan Antonio Ugalde, along with his brothers, Tomás and Juan, as well as Javier Iriondo, decided to start a Melbourne *Gure Txoko*.[34] The *Txoko* admitted some non-Basque Spanish members. There was underlying tension, however, such as when during *Aberri Eguna* celebrations they were prohibited from singing their songs in Spanish. It was the original intention of the founders to purchase a building (or building site) for a clubhouse, but the total membership never exceeded seventy families, so the costs of such a project were prohibitive.[35] It was decided instead to lease a locale on Stable Street.[36] By then, many Melbourne Basques were involved in *pelota* at several *frontones*, appended to Roman Catholic churches in the city. It seems that Irish Catholics were also fond of playing the game, as were non-Basque Spaniards. There was some talk as well about starting a team of Basque oarsmen.[37] It failed to materialize but would have been in keeping with a centuries-old *trainera*, or rowing, tradition of coastal Bizkaia and Gipuzkoa.

From her interviews with Melbourne Basques, then, Totoricagüena describes a fairly rich Basque cultural life in the city just prior to the founding of *Gure Txoko*. In addition to the *pelota*, the household of the three Ugalde bachelor brothers, known as "Anbeko," the name of their family farm in Gernika, was a meeting place for several Basque bachelors. The home of the Ugaldes' married sister, Lucía, her husband

Celedonio Moreno Tejada, and their four children, was an informal boardinghouse, known to practically every Bizkaian arriving in the city. The Ugaldes worked to secure employment for the newcomers and organized dinners, picnics, celebration of *Aberri Eguna* on Easter Sunday, and the Day of Saint Ignatius on the last day of July. The *San Ignacio* celebrations included athletic competition such as woodchopping and tugs-of-war. The mass was sung by an impromptu Basque choir, led by Joseba Urquidi and accompanied by the *txistu* music of Javier Amorebieta. Many of these events were held in a *frontón* rented from a church. The Molina Restaurant was another popular gathering point for Melbourne Basques.[38]

The first major event in the new clubhouse was the wedding of Ramón Arrien. It filled the facility to its 100-person capacity. Funerals were common and attended well, the membership serving as the surrogate family of the deceased.[39] Totoricagüena notes,

> "…The rent in 1964 was $12 per week, which soon went to $16 and then to $18 per week…. The members raised the money to buy our own tables and chairs, kitchen utensils, all the cutlery, plates and glasses," said Antonio Torrijos. Luis Mezo painted a map of *Euskal Herria* on one wall, the Basque flag, *Ikurriña*, and the coat of arms of the Basque territories on another wall. They displayed large cloth Basque and Australian flags and a banner which read "Euzkadi Gatik Alkartuta," translated as "gathering together for the Basque Country."[40]

The *Gure Txoko* began organizing day excursions to places like Donnybrooke and Hillside, the bus departing from the clubhouse. Members had their own key and could use the premises as they desired. On Friday and Saturday evenings, the *Gure Txoko* was usually filled with single men drinking and playing cards. Sundays were families' day. Accordingly,

> Gure Txoko members volunteered as cooks and organized themselves by way of families choosing specific Sunday dates and a calendar sign-up was established with designated families cooking for the entire membership. A printed menu in Euskara wrote "Jateko Lerrokada", the list of food. Jesús Egiguren had a butcher

shop and the meats were purchased from him, and Antonio Torrijos ordered the groceries from an Italian grocer, "San Remo," and also from "El Catalan," who delivered wine and groceries for the Sunday meals. Torrijos worked at "Maxims" and was able to learn the business of restaurant and bar supplying and had help cooking from Julián Alcántara and Ramón Arrien. It was very difficult to get a liquor license in Melbourne and the Gure Txoko was not permitted to sell any alcohol, so members brought their own wine and beer. "The police raided us three times, and once when we were preparing for Minister Arthur Calwell's visit. So when we told them Calwell was coming they left us alone after that," said José [sic] Antonio Ugalde.[41]

There was the occasional formal dance with hired live music. There were special events for members only and others that were open to non-Basque, nonmembers as well. From 1965 through 1972, Juan Antonio Ugalde taught Basque to about three or four students. By the late 1960s and early 1970s, *Gure Txoko* fielded a soccer team that played against those of other ethnic clubs in Melbourne. There was particular friendly rivalry in this regard with the *Club Gallego*.[42]

In an interview with Javier Iriondo and his wife, they noted the tendency of bachelor Basques to belong to both the *Club Español* and the *Txoko*. They had a better chance of meeting single women at the larger former one. So, several *Txoko* members married non-Basque Spanish wives and, under their influence, drifted away from the Basque Club.[43]

J. A. Ugalde was always a prime mover. We have already met him at the beginning of this book as a leftist and Basque nationalist. During the late 1960s and early 1970s, he penned several treatises such as "In the Name of Truth and Justice" (an exposé of Franquism) and "The Importance of the Basque Language." He distributed them among people in Melbourne's Spanish Club, the parishioners of several Catholic churches, and even among the membership of the Italian Club (to which he belonged as the spouse of an Italian national). He also sent information regarding the activities of Melbourne Basques to the Basque-government-in-exile and the publication *Eusko Deya*, and corresponded with other diasporic Basques, such as those of Mexico.[44]

The activities of *Gure Txoko* were almost exclusively recreational and cultural. However, when, in 1970, charges were brought against several ETA members and sympathizers for assassinating a suspected torturer of the Franco regime, and a military court in Burgos handed out several death sentences, there was outrage and appeals for clemency throughout the world. A number of Melbourne Basques met at the *Gure Txoko* and took the tram to city hall to demonstrate against Franco. Ugalde organized the Melbourne demonstrators for a bus trip to Canberra to protest the Burgos trial before the Spanish embassy in the Australian capital. An educated Mildura Basque, Pablo Orive [*sic*-Oribe], was interviewed several times on Australian radio during which he described the authoritarianism and lack of civil rights in Spain. He and other Melbourne Basques met with the Parliamentary representatives, including Arthur Calwell, to educate them on the sad realities of Franco's dictatorship. The Basques of Sydney and North Queensland also wrote the Australian ambassador in Madrid demanding that he denounce the trial.[45]

In 1966 and 1967, there was an initiative by some members to raise the funds to purchase the clubhouse, but it failed. The Club chugged along for several years afterwards, but, in 1975, the steam ran out. After about a decade of existence, the *Gure Txoko* closed its doors and the property became an Argentinean club.[46]

Sydney *Gure Txoko* — The decision of some Basque members of the *Centro Español* to establish the Sydney *Gure Txoko* several city-blocks away at 344 Liverpool Street was, in part, a reaction to the agenda and ambiance of the Spanish Club. Regarding both the Asturian Club and *Gure Txoko*, García states,

> They were not meant to compete with, but rather to complement the main Spanish Club, and their members were often members of it. However, sometimes there were tensions. These clubs were created because their members felt that their identity was not totally preserved and represented in the main club; the latter regretted their appearance as it was seen as creating divisions and draining the effectiveness for the whole community. A similar situation occurred in Melbourne and Whyalla.[47]

It is fair to say that a number of Navarrans would continue to prefer the *Centro Español* instead of *Gure Txoko*, but it is equally true that several Basques from all four divisions of *Hegoalde* joined and frequented both organizations.

Totoricagüena notes that *Gure Txoko*, founded in 1966 and still in operation since its inception, is the longest standing Basque association in Australia. We have already remarked upon the involvement of many Basques in the Sydney Spanish Club, including the appointment of José Luis Goñi as assistant manager in 1963 and the role of Julián Oriñuela in the organization, in 1964, of its bachelors' soccer team. It seems that Oriñuela's home tended to be a meeting place for a coterie of Sydney Basques—according to one, "his house was like its own *txoko*."[48] Both men were Basque nationalists after their families fled Franco's Spain.[49]

The group of Basques considering forming *Gure Txoko* relied upon the advice of Ramón Peñagaricano, a Basque Argentinean married to an Australian he met in Germany before migrating to her homeland. He was employed as a high school teacher, totally fluent in English, and conversant with the laws governing associations in Australia. His father had been one of the founders of a Basque association in Argentina. Ramón was proposed as the first president of the Sydney *Gure Txoko*. He sent a letter to Eusebio Illarmendi informing him that he had been nominated to be the new club's first vice president. The Sydney Basques were well aware of the *Gure Txoko* in Melbourne and were visited and advised by two of its prime movers, Iker Ercoreca and Alberto Ansoleaga. Ansoleaga had a brother, Abel, living in Sydney who would join the first directorate of the Sydney *Gure Txoko*.[50]

Organizational meetings were held in the Oriñuela home and he recruited several potential members in the Spanish Club. On July 31, 1966, twenty or thirty people in attendance met and launched the "Basque Society Gure Txoko." They elected officers—Peñagaricano became president, Illarmendi vice president, Julián Quintana secretary, José Luis Olabarriaga vice secretary, Julián Oriñuela treasurer, and Abel Ansoleaga vice treasurer.[51]

The first order of business was to find a locale where the club could meet and also construct a *frontón*. Peñagaricano contacted a real estate agent, but the search ended differently. According to Totoricagüena,

Fortunately, at the same time, Mariasun Salazar noticed that across the street from her own small businesss on Liverpool Street, a building was for sale. Salazar and her husband, Benito Bañuelos, investigated and found that the nephews of the recently deceased owner, Mr. Tuohy, wanted to sell the building. Salazar contacted the newly formed board of directors of the Gure Txoko, and assisted with the contacts and negotiations to first rent and then later to purchase the property for a good buying price of $15,736.00 Australian dollars.

In order to raise this money immediately, Julián Quintana, Julián Oriñuela and Ramón Peñagaricano went to the Bank of New South Wales to request a loan and volunteered themselves as the personal guarantors. Additional loan guarantors included Eusebio Illarmendi, Francisco Montero, and José Arregui.[52]

They then employed a combination of their personal ties among Sydney's Basques, combined with a scanning of the telephone directory for Basque surnames, to compile a mailing list with which to convene a meeting at the site. About fifty to sixty people attended. They were asked to join the new club and provide A$200 as an entry fee in order to secure the building. Some declined on the grounds that they viewed the initiative as divisive, given the existence of a Spanish Club a short distance away on the same Liverpool Street. Others simply could not afford it. Twenty-six in all committed.[53]

In 1967, it was decided to construct a *frontón* in the backyard of the property and there was a campaign to raise funds for the materials. The work was to be done on a voluntary basis—made particularly effective given the employment of many members in the construction industry. A cement worker even traveled regularly from Canberra to participate. By the following year, the *frontón* was ready for play. That year, the Club celebrated its first *pelota* tournament and initiated a *mus* championship among the membership as well.[54] Beginning in the 1970s, several times annually the *frontón* was converted into an outdoor movie theater for the screening of both adult and children's films.[55]

The Club celebrated three feast days in particular—*Aberri Eguna*, or Fatherland Day (a Basque Nationalist Party event in Europe), held Easter Sunday, the Feast of Saint Ignatius (patron saint of Bizkaia and Gipuzkoa) on July 31st, and the festival of Saint Fermín (the patron of Navarra and the object of the famed festival in Pamplona held throughout the second week of July). Clearly, there was the intention of including Navarrans along with the other Basques of the remainder of Hegoalde, as well as accommodation of Basque nationalism (tempered by a policy from the outset to avoid "politics" on the premises).

As with the Melbourne *Gure Txoko*, an exception regarding political action was made during the Burgos trials of 1970. The president of the Sydney *Gure Txoko* at that time, Julián Oriñuela, organized a protest demonstration in front of the city's Spanish consulate. It seems that some members quit the Club over this action.[56] He was irritated generally by the pro-Franco slant to coverage of Spain in the media and continued over the years to send letters to the editors of several newspapers. Totoricagüena cites the one to the *Sydney Morning Herald*, dated July 1, 1975:

> Dear Sir,
> Your newspaper has been publishing news about the sufferings of the Basque people under the Franco dictatorship.
>
> Sometimes our fighters are being made to appear as terrorists and enemies of the society. For this reason we would like to make it clear that the real enemies of our society are no others than the uniformed authors of legalized violence thru force against our people since they were invaded in June of 1937, putting an end to Euzkadi (Basque Country) autonomy as part of the Spanish Republic.
>
> The Basque people is claiming, demanding and fighting for a change in the present structure of government which is subjugating and slaving our country.
>
> We are openly fighting for the recognition of the Basque people's rights to restore in our country a democratic rule as well as economic, social and cultural strongly binded together to repulse any movement or ideology intended to destroy any of them. We are for the integration of Euzkadi within a united Europe constituted not according to convenient frontiers as present but by the natural communities composing them. We mean a united Europe in which all nations are integrated with equal rights and obligations.

It's not dignify for a nation which is suffering slavery patiently, and more is the people with chains around their bodies but free with a string spirit. Unfortunately they are victims, but not rebel slaves. This is what our Sabino Arana said. It's our ideal as Basque people. For this the Basque people is being persecuted without mercy by Franco's dictatorship.

We fully support our countrymen unconditionally from here! For the Basque,
Julián Oriñuela[57]

Meals became the prime activity of *Gure Txoko* with special ones prepared on feast days and weekly ones as a matter of course. For years, Wednesday nights were the occasion of a *pelota* match followed by a meal and then *mus*. This was primarily a male event, particularly among Sydney's Basque bachelors. For a time, a couple of recent Basque immigrants offered Basque language lessons followed by a dinner on Monday nights. Women volunteers did most of the cleaning and were likely to help with the preparation of regular Sunday noontime meals.

There was also a tradition of conceding an upstairs living quarters to a Basque couple whose presence provided round-the-clock custodianship of the property, deemed essential given that the facility was located in a somewhat crime-infested neighborhood and would otherwise be vacant for much of the week.[58]

In sum, there was a spirit of intimacy and camaraderie in *Gure Txoko*. Members each had their own key and could use the building for family events. A core of members with dual membership in the Spanish Club became increasingly postured more around the Basque one. Totoricagüena cites the statement of one female member as characterizing the relations that developed among its women as "sisterly."[59] Nevertheless, for nearly the first two decades of its existence, women had no formal vote in the administration of *Gure Txoko*. Indeed, if one was married to a non-Basque who participated along with his spouse, he, but not she, could vote. That was changed in the 1980s.[60]

Gure Txoko, like all of the other associations we have considered to this point, had its problems with the country's strict liquor laws. It had no license and sought to finesse the problem by selling coupons that could be redeemed for alcohol rather than through direct cash transactions at the bar, a palliative that was not always enforced.

In 1971, an undercover policeman entered and purchased a beer. A short time later, the Club was raided, and 3,000 bottles of beer confiscated. *Gure Txoko* was cited for selling liquor (and tobacco) illegally. A fourteen-month court case ensued, and, when the Club actually prevailed, the police were ordered to return the beer. However, there had been adverse consequences. The Club had struggled to meet its bank payments, given the loss of revenue. Some members became afraid to frequent *Gure Txoko* after the raid. In response, the leadership organized a picnic held in nearby Centennial Park. This set the stage for its own tradition that has lasted down to the present, namely, that of holding picnics in several of Sydney's parks. That allows for athletic competitions, such as foot races, cricket, and soccer competition among the young that would be impossible on *Gure Txoko*'s premises.[61]

Soccer gained considerable support in the Club, and it formed its own informal adult team to play against those of other ethnic communities. On one occasion, the Spanish ambassador invited the team to play against Spanish clubs from Sydney, Melbourne, and Wollongong—*Gure Txoko* purchased uniforms with the red, white, and green colors of the Basque *ikurriña* for the occasion. As in Spain, soccer became a surrogate of the struggle over political sovereignty of the Basque Country.

In 1985, Antonio Esparza of the Sydney *Txoko* was visiting the Basque Country and participated in the international *mus* tournament. When he returned to Sydney, he urged the Club to become involved by sending its annual champion to the international event. Several members of the *Txoko* told Totoricagüena that they regard this to be the first outreach to other Basque diasporas around the world, as well as a means of placing the Sydney collectivity on their radar. Since 1986, the Sydney *Txoko* has sent its team to the world championships (held in a different annual venue in Europe and North and South America).[62]

1989 proved to be a watershed year in terms of the relations between Basque Australians and the Basque homeland. In the spring of that year, the new *Txoko* president, Antonio Esparza, was in the Basque Country and called upon the Basque government. Since 1986, Josu Legarreta, of the Department of Culture of the Basque government, had been charged with overseeing relations between Eusko Jaurlaritza and the Basque diasporas throughout the world—particularly their cultural associations and clubs. Esparza provided Legarreta with an overview of the Basque collectivities in Australia and made specific requests on behalf of the Sydney *Txoko*. He needed educational materials—books, journals, and videos—so that the Sydney community, particularly the young, could learn more about their heritage. He also wanted assistance in holding a Basque cultural week in his city to showcase its Basques to the wider public. He envisioned it encompassing the *Txoko*'s Saint Ignatius Day festival.

Esparza was profiled in the next issue of the Basque government's journal *Euskal Etxeak*. Curiously, this initial statement of the Basque government regarding its Australian diaspora underscored their fame as restaurant workers and owners (the latter, at the time, Esparza's profession). There was no mention of the Far North and its predominant Basque involvement in its sugar industry (at all levels from canecutter to farm owner), despite the fact that Esparza himself had once been a canecutter and harvester-owner there.[63] If Australia had yet to discover its' Basques, the Basque Country was in the process of discovering the Basque Australians!

Legarreta moved quickly in support of the Sydney event. He traveled to Australia for it, accompanied by the *txistulari* Gotzon Tueros (Bizkaian), the weightlifter Iñaki Gil (Araban), and the woodchopper Mikel Mindegia (Navarran). The festivities were held between July 8 and August 2 in the Festival Market Place, Darling Harbour. It received considerable media coverage and literally hundreds of Basques from throughout Australia were in attendance. One drove the 3,900 kilometers from Perth to be present. Mikel put on an exhibition with two Australian woodchoppers, George Quigg and world champion David Frost. The two Australians acknowledged to the crowd that the Basques were the planet's best when it came to their style of woodchopping. At the closing lunch, a recently formed Sydney choir performed, under the direction of Mr. Laca from Bermeo, followed by emotional singing of classic Basque songs by the audience.[64] *Gure Txoko* had no dance group of its own, and therefore requested that the Spanish Club dancers learn and perform some Basque dances, which they did.[65]

That same summer, the Department of Culture and Tourism of the Basque government sponsored the trips of forty-two diaspora youths to the Basque Country, including that of Damian Blake, son of an Irish father and a mother from Bilbao. It also paid the return visit of thirty-four diasporic *aitonak* ("grandparents") who had emigrated decades earlier and did not have the wherewithal to make a return visit to their beloved homeland. Among their number was at least one Australian Basque.[66]

In the autumn of 1989 (November 6–12), the *Primer Congreso Mundial de Centros Vascos* (First World Congress of Basque Centers) was held in Bahía Blanca, Argentina. The Basque government was resolved to document the profiles of the multitude of Basque associations (and their needs) as part of a broader project of understanding the magnitude and nature of its multiple diasporas. Antonio Esparza and Rosa María de Amezaga of the Sydney *Gure Txoko* represented Australia at the Congress.

The first Basque cultural week in Sydney was such a success that it was resolved to repeat it annually forever. That proved illusory, but the following spring the Txoko's *Aberri Eguna* celebration was modified to accommodate the commitment. In the words of Totoricagüena,

> *Aberria Eguna*, celebrated on Easter Sunday, was an annual event at the *Gure Txoko* building, but in 1990, several circumstances coincided to aggrandize it and Mariasun Salazar suggested moving it to Centennial Park as a mass, picnic and barbecue event. That year it was even extended to an entire "Basque Week." The year before, Julian Oriñuela had been elected President, and with his officers, Carlos Orúe, Mariasun Salazar, Eusebio Illarmendi, Miguel Urdangarín and José Antonio Urbieta, he wrote a letter to the Basque Government's Department of Culture, where Josu Legarreta was responsible for relations with the Basque communities abroad. They asked for the Basque Government's financial assistance in sending to Sydney a *txistulari*, and after several difficulties in finding a person that was willing to travel so far, they found the perfect combination of a Basque musician and scientist; a txistulari and oceanographer who had always wanted to travel to Australia, Dr. Javier Urrutia. Urrutia was the

Director of the Institute of Oceanography in Donostia-San Sebastián and during his stay in Sydney he combined *txistu* and drum music performances with presentations about nature and science. The *Aberri Eguna* of 1990 stretched to a week including a Sunday open-air mass with Basque music at a small forest in Centennial Park and a barbecue picnic with people dressed in traditional folk costumes, even with *abarkak*, or traditional leather shoes that had been sent by the Department of Culture and had been given free to members who wore the Basque clothing. There were games for children, several groups of *mus* players enjoying a hand, and singing from family tables. Members of the Basque community organized an excursion to Huskisson-Hyams Beach, and enjoyed stretches of the world's whitest sands. They challenged each other to a tournament of golf (with an ikurriña at the holes instead of the traditional white flag). Each day's bus ride included music and song, and all were awed by Dr. Urrutia's explanations of nature and especially by his conference given at the *Gure Txoko* regarding the contamination of the planet and the deterioration of the ozone layer.[67]

In 1991, the Basque trio *Txori Alai* (Happy Bird), featuring an accordion, *txistu*, and tambourine, toured Australia. It was sponsored by the Basque government and performed in Sydney as a part of the 25th-anniversary celebration of the *Txoko*. The band was already famed for its performances in the Basque Country and tours of Argentina, Uruguay, and the United States.[68]

In 1995, the Basque government formalized the World Congress event.[69] That year, the delegates from Australia were the three from the Sydney *Txoko*. Beginning in 1999, participation was extended to Melbourne and North Queensland as well.[70]

That same year, Josu Legarreta visited Australia for a second time. He was in the Sydney *Gure Txoko* and attended the Saint Ignatius Day festivities in Melbourne at Gumbuya Park. He also traveled to Townsville where he met with personnel in the Spanish Society of North Queensland and also with city officials. There was discussion of the Basque government funding a *frontón* in the city, but it never happened because the city's officials failed to donate the proposed public site to the project.⁷¹

None of Legarreta's successors have visited Australia, although the current one (2019), Gorka Álvarez, intends to when the time is right. During the Sixth Congress of Basque Collectivities organized in Vitoria/Gasteiz in 2015, Sydney was represented by Manu Martín and North Queensland by Begoña Bengoa and Stephen Mendiolea. Melbourne had no representative. In recent years, Australia has sent no young people to Gaztemundu and last year the Sydney *Gure Txoko* was the only Australian entity to solicit a Basque government subsidy.

In 2017, the Basque government reorganized itself internally in terms of its regional outreach to the various Basque diasporas. Australia was included in Europe and Asia (Shanghai and Tokyo). Manu Meaurio is the representative overseeing Basque governmental affairs with it, and a preliminary meeting was convened in Paris in 2017. In 2018, regional meetings were held for South America in Buenos Aires and for North America in San Francisco. The various threads will be brought together during the Seventh Congress of Basque Collectivities in the Basque Country in October 2019.

In 1980, I visited the Sydney *Txoko* and presented a slide show regarding Basques in the American West that I had prepared for the Basque Studies Program of the University of Nevada, Reno. There were about fifty people present and it was greeted with great interest and many questions. It seems that the social calendar of the *Gure Txoko* was dominated by farewell parties for people moving back to the Basque Country, ostensibly permanently. That night was no exception, as a Mrs. Blasco was about to return to Bilbao. She had come twenty years earlier as a correspondence bride. But her husband was an alcoholic and she hated it there. She was leaving with her daughter, but her two sons planned to remain with the father. She was disturbed by that, as the two teenagers were, in her view, practically bikers at this point.

Former *Txoko* president, Rafael Alegría, told me that there were by then several cases of Basques coming to Australia from South America as part of the country's latest influx of Latin Americans. He noted that his wife was babysitting for a Chilean woman whose father was from Bera (Vera de Bidasoa), Navarra. He also noted the clustering of Basque bachelors in this city by recounting the case of Matias Mendiolea. He, a bachelor, purchased a large house and then rented out rooms to four different Basque bachelors. So, five *mutil zaharrak* were living under the same roof.

On another occasion that same week at the *Txoko*, I met a man from Donostia who had been in Australia since 1950 and he recounted his life's story. He had been a *gudari* during the Civil War and ended up in Germany at the end of World War II. He worked for the next five years there as a factotum for the American occupying forces. He then married a German and emigrated to Australia with A$40,000 in his pocket. He had no Basque or Spanish connections there. One day he was strolling in the park and heard someone speaking Spanish. He approached the man and it was Alberdi, an ex-*pelotari* who had played in Shanghai before fleeing when Mao took over. Alberdi's wife, a Russian Jew, had relatives there so they relocated to Sydney. The two married couples met regularly for the next year or so to socialize and go to the movies. Neither knew any other Spaniards here. Alberdi subsequently moved to Manila, put in a restaurant there, retired, and then died. The narrator had subsequently become a gambler, lost all of his money, and his wife. He now works as a dishwasher.

I also interviewed together Benito Bañuelos and his friend, Luis García. We met in the home of the former. Both men were construction workers in Sydney. Benito was from Bilbo and Luis from Viana, Navarra. They were clearly reluctant at first to do the interview, but Mrs. Bañuelos insisted. She, too, was from Bilbo and very proud of her cousin there, a renowned *txistulari*. She had sent the children back to Bilbo on two occasions; Benito has never returned. Both men came in the recruitments—Benito on the *Montserrat* and Luis on the *Toscana*. Both had cut cane in the Far North and had interesting nomadic histories. Both had worked construction in Mount Isa. Both had visited Darwin looking for work. Both worked briefly in Outback towns near Darwin. Benito had worked for fourteen months constructing a rail line from an iron mine to a coastal port in Western Australia. Luis had worked for six months in Indonesia (New Guinea) for an American gold-mining concern. He had also done other work in New Guinea.

Luis was married to an Aragonese woman. She and two of her sisters were present. My wife, Jan, conversed with them while I did the interview. They were very critical of *Gure Txoko*. The women there, like the men, were divided into factions along political lines. Also, the men were masochistic and scarcely paid attention to females. Benito weighed in by stating that most Basques in Sydney did not go to the *Txoko*; they preferred the *Club Español*. He cited the case of a Gipuzkoan who hardly knew Spanish who went to the *Txoko* and tried to converse in Basque. He found that most of the members were speaking in Spanish and was disgusted. For that, he could go to the *Club Español*. He now did so regularly, and he never frequented the *Txoko*.

North Queensland Spanish Society—The Spanish community of the Far North, while more impressive in absolute numbers, was not nearly as concentrated as were the Spanish nationals of greater Sydney and Melbourne. However, early on there were premonitions and precursors of formal association in the Far North, whether in Innisfail in the 1920s or the St. Ignatius festival in Ingham in the late 1950s and early 1960s. The latter lasted for possibly no longer than four years, during which the Basques of the Hinchinbrook organized a Saint Ignatius Day celebration in Ingham's Library Hall. The event attracted visitors from as far away as the Burdekin. That attendance reflected the male bias in the canecutter workforce, given one event's 237 men, 71 women, and 33 children.[72] There was also a Spanish festival in the Tully area,[73] and a formal Spanish Society in the Atherton Tablelands, regarding which Mason states,

> Clubs were rarely the scenes of explicit ethnic tensions, and members instead focused on the services they provided. It was these services that acted as the platform for sublimated hostility. Where families of Basques formed an overwhelming majority, individuals were rarely sensitized to regional difference and hesitated to create a formal club. Where no single ethnic majority dominated, as was the case in the tobacco farms surrounding Mareeba, regional difference became much more significant. Fixed meeting places accentuated regional differences, since they required administrative frameworks and institutionalized rules. The relative priority placed on dances such as the *flamenco* became symbolic

points of contention in broader historical and personal disputes. Catalans and Basques resented the prioritization of non-Catalan and Basque music.[74]

Mason further observes that there were similar problems within the membership of a Brisbane Spanish Club founded in 1972 by Father Portela. His emphasis upon conservative Catholicism and the apolitical did not play well with Basque and Catalan members. In practice, "apolitical" implied castigating "anti-Spaniards," meaning regionalists advocating the division of Spain that had led to the fratricidal Civil War. The echoing by the Club of Franco's celebration of Hispanic unity (*Día de la Hispanidad*), on October 12, likewise did not sit well with most Brisbane Basques and Catalans.[75]

The history of the North Queensland Spanish Society is of particular interest. By the late 1960s, the Catalans of Ayr were celebrating the Day of the Sardana, an initiative that eventually incorporated the Basques and their Feast Day of Saint Ignatius. In 1970, on the initiative of Agustín Adarraga of Townsville, a Spanish Society of North Queensland was founded.[76] Appendix IV provides a list of the membership by residence. Adarraga served as its second president (Joe Goicoechea was briefly its first). In 1971, Adarraga organized North Queensland's "First Basque Festival." Held on Saint Ignatius Day at the Trebonne Hotel in the Hinchinbrook, and initiated with a mass by Father Ormazabal, its attractions included, "…stone lifting, *txingas*, *pelota*, *mus*, Basque dancing and a painting competition for children which was said to have attracted 350 entries from all over Queensland."[77]

The Spanish Society of North Queensland still persisted in 2000, with annual celebrations of Saint Ignatius Day (Basques), the Day of the Sardana (Catalans), and the feast day of Our Lady of Pilar (Spaniards), with a mass followed by lunch in the Ayr Returned Soldiers' League hall. Rather than athletic events, the ageing population was more likely to engage in the (Italian) card game *brisca*.[78]

There were other, less formal, initiatives. For example, in 1980, I visited a gathering of the *Club Ibérica* held in the home of Floren Laucirica in Ingham. Its primary purpose was for each member to contribute one dollar to a soccer pool. The older men were playing *mus* and the younger were engrossed in billiards on Floren's table. In addition to Basques, there were two brothers from Santander and a Galician present.

Ingham and Ayr both had an International Club, built and dominated by Italians. The Ingham one had a "Spanish table" in its food area, which is where its Spanish and Basque members sat during meals.[79]

The Basque Club of North Queensland—In 2002, largely through the initiative of Joe Goicoechea and with the collaboration of Mary Arrate and Pedro Mendiolea, a Basque Club of North Queensland was founded in Townsville. It has its own clubhouse and continues to function to this day. The details of its history are provided in my interviews with Joe Goicoechea, Amaya Arrate, Mary Arrate, and Stephen Goicoechea in the Coda of this book.

Nostalgia—Many Basques returned to Euskadi after a stint of varying lengths in Australia. Just as they could never leave their homeland legacy behind upon emigrating, they reentered Euskadi with an Australian one. They and their descendants were formed, in part, by Australian memories and stories. Beginning about 1980, Bizkaian and Gipuzkoan returnees began holding an annual luncheon get-together in Gernika. It was attended by some Navarrans as well. There was a major exhibition of Basque life in Australia one year in Gernika as well.

Totoricagüena notes that one hundred Navarrans, in 1994, decided to form an *Asociación Navarra Boomerang* (Navarran Boomerang Association). In 1996, there was an exhibition in Pamplona city hall of photographs and Australian memorabilia (cane knives, kangaroo skins, etc.). It was sponsored by the municipality, the foral government of Navarra and the major Navarran savings bank *Caja Rural de Navarra*, as well as two corporate donors—*Gráficas Ipar* and *Eroski*.[80]

Totoricagüena notes, "What had been established decades ago in Melbourne and Sydney with the Basque *Gure Txoko* associations, and with the *Club Español* organizations in both cities, was in a way now being duplicated in reverse."[81]

On January 14, 1995, about ninety members of the new association held their first meeting in Villafranca (Alesbes), Navarra. They approved statures and elected officers.

Totoricagüena visited many returnees in their homes in southern Navarra and recorded their impressions of Australia.[82] She notes that most displayed Australian imagery in living rooms. It was reminiscent of Basques in Australia adorning their walls and surfaces with photos and bric-a-brac from the Basque Country. One Navarran, Plácido Iñigo, declared to the newspaper *Noticias de Navarra* that Australia "is the best country in the world."[83]

Sport—It seems fair to say that one of the robust fields of social scientific inquiry over recent years has been the study of sport. Within my discipline there is a distinguishable subfield denominated "the anthropology of sport." In the Basque case, there is a growing library of analysis of soccer—particularly Bilbo's Athletic team. We have already noted the emergence of soccer in the Sydney Spanish Club and *Txoko*, as well as the rivalry and competition between them. Similarly, the demonstration of Basque sports—such as tugs-of-war, weight lifting and weight-carrying, and woodchopping—is an intrinsic part of Basque festivals, whether in the homeland or throughout the emigrant diasporas. Australia was no exception. After soccer, probably the Basque sport to garner the greatest attention is the handball/*jai alai* complex that runs the gamut from amateur matches to professional world championships and is played against village church walls or in sports' palaces capable of seating more than a thousand spectators in exotic places like Djakarta, Havana, Lima, Caracas, Miami, Manila, and Mexico City.

We have already considered the importance of *pelota* to Melbourne's Basque community, played in various *frontones* owned by the city's Catholic parishes, and the construction of a *frontón* at the rear of the Sydney *Txoko*. These developments in southern-Australian urban centers postdate the construction of a standalone *frontón* in the rural hamlet of Trebonne near Ingham in the Far North. Inaugurated on November 28, 1959, it was a business venture funded by an Italian, Joe Sartoresi, owner of the Trebonne Hotel. Sartoresi was encouraged to build it by Félix Jayo and Alberto Urberuaga as an amenity that might augment his already substantial trade from his Spanish and Basque clientele. Since he had never seen the game played, the two Basques took him to the Mendiolea farm, where, on Sundays, there was a semipublic barbecue that attracted a number of local Basque families and bachelor canecutters. The day's socializing included makeshift handball games played with tennis balls against a high backwall of the farmhouse. Sartoresi was impressed, particularly by the amount of beer being consumed.[84]

He resolved to build a proper facility and set about applying for the necessary local permissions and contracting with a designer and builder.[85] Alberto Urberuaga and Agustín Adarraga of Townsville obtained plans from the Basque Country for professional courts, but they were far too large for the Trebonne site and had to be modified. The structure was built over a six-week period. Father Ormazabal blessed it at the inauguration. The first match pitted the Jayo brothers (Félix and José María) against Juan Cruz Arriaga and Tomás Monasterio. All were dressed in traditional handball-player costume (white shirt and trousers, red sash, and espadrille [*alpargatas*] footgear). The Jayos were victorious.[86]

When Alberto Urberuaga went to Spain, in 1959, to attend the Second World Migration Congress and then to recruit canecutters in the Basque Country, he returned with six *pelota* balls and six *palas* and four *paletas* (bats). In the event, the bats were used infrequently, given the diminutive size of the Trebonne court.[87]

On June 24, 1960, a Spanish Handball Club was created with Pascual Badiola as president and Joe Satoresi patron. Vicente Goitiandia and Juan Mendiolea were vice presidents, Alberto Urberuaga was the treasurer, and Bingen Balanzategui was the secretary. Membership was 10 shillings annually. As its purpose, "The Club was responsible for holding barbecues to raise money for the upkeep of the *Fronton*, to purchase seating and to maintain a kitty of goat skin *pelotas* which were purchased from the Basque country."[88] Over the years, it was variously referred to as the Handball Club, the Trebonne Handball Club, and the Spanish Club.[89]

Both Spaniards and Basques played in the *frontón*, but only the latter held formal competitions. These annual elimination matches terminated in a trophy presentation for the winners held in the Drill Hall of the Ingham Showgrounds (the majority of the competitions were won by Felix Jayo). The trophies were donated by the Spanish Club, Lee's Hotel, Gino and Maria Manini (publican partners in the Trebonne Hotel), and Joe Sartoresi. The formal competition lasted only until about 1967, and for most of that decade,

...the *fronton* attracted both single men and families of a Friday night and also Saturdays and Sundays. The men would go into town of a Saturday morning to have a few beers. Challenges would go out. After lunch they would gather at the *fronton*. Saturday afternoon games could be guaranteed to attract a good crowd. Up to 200 people could gather, particularly on nights when there was a dancing and a barbecue organized by the Spanish Club.[90]

The *frontón* served as a civic focal point for other organizations engaged in evening get-togethers and/or fund-raising events. These included the Trebonne State School, Forrest Home State School, Helen's Hill State School, Herbert River Small Bore Rifle Club, Ingham Golf Club, Tennis Association, Roma Soccer Club, C.M.F., St. Pius X Parish, and the Canossian Home Appeal.[91]

Other Basque sporting performances and events held in the Hinchinbrook included weight lifting (*harrijasozaile*), weight-carrying (*txingas*), and tugs-of-war (*sokatirak*). Indeed, in the 1950s, or before the construction of the Trebonne Hotel's *frontón*, prior owner Agostino Rotondo sponsored Sunday tugs-of-war that pitted Spanish, Basque, Italian, and Yugoslav teams against one another.[92]

In 1964, the Basques put on a weight-lifting exhibition as a part of the Hinchinbrook's annual Maraka festival. In 1965, it included a cane-loading competition and the trophy (designated the Mendiolea Memorial Cup in honor of the late Rufino Mendiolea). That year, the weightlifting competition came down to two competitors from Ayr, attracting a large number of spectators from the Burdekin.[93] Such competitions also became standard fare at the Trebonne barbecues. One, in late 1964, included a weight-throwing context in which a ball and chain were employed. The *txingak* competitions became so popular that they evolved into a fixture of Ingham's annual Italian festival (employing the weights imported by Ayr's Agustín Arrate family).[94]

By the late 1960s, the *frontón* fell into disuse. By this time, the era of the manual canecutter was over. In 1971, Ramón Pla leased the Trebonne Hotel. During the following decade, there is evidence of the occasional weight-lifting competition held there, but no mention of *pelota*. Father Ormazabal died in 1973 as well.[95] The Handball Club lingered for a few years until Alberto Urberuaga handed over the accounts to John Mendiolea, and he donated the residual monies to the Blue Nursing Service.[96]

While the Trebonne *frontón* passed into history, its presence and structure remain in the collective mentality. Bianka Vidonja Balantzategui and Barbara Debono recommended in 2001 that the *frontón* be restored and displayed with historical plaques as a tourist attraction. Their proposal was rejected.[97] However, that year Vidonja Balantzategui did manage to have the structure entered in the Queensland State Heritage Register.

Boxing was always popular among the migrants. In 1932, there was a "Great International Boxing Contest" in Ingham between the Italian Caesare Pane and the Basque F. Arrilliaga, both over six feet tall. The former won when the Basque was disqualified for a foul.[98] Not just Basques, but rather all Spaniards followed with intense interest the careers of the two Basque heavyweight contenders on the international scene—Paolino Uzcudun and "Urtain" (José Manuel Ibar Azpiazu).

Australia, like the Basque Country, is famed for its woodchopping competitions. Argentina, New Zealand, Canada, and the United States have their woodchoppers as well. For all of these nationalities, save the Basques, the major annual competition was that held in Sydney at its Royal Easter Show. In Australia and the rest of the world, it is customary to chop softwoods that are deployed vertically. The chopper stands on a plank that is driven into the side of the trunk while topping it. He moves the plank lower as he completes successive toppings. In the Basque Country, hardwood trunks are arranged horizontally and the chopper stands on them while stroking between his spread feet. Aside from the differing arrangements, techniques, and consistency of the wood, there is the issue of the quality of the axes. As it turned out, the Australian ones were superior to the Basque ones (harder and therefore capable of holding a sharp edge longer).

The inevitable transpired, when, in the 1970s, a team of Basque woodchoppers came to Sydney to challenge Australians. They, and their supporters, were certain that they would win. They did not, in part due to the superior quality of the Australians' axes. In 1977, the Basque champion, Arriya II, entered the Sydney Easter Show competition. A newspaper account described his challenge against Victorian champion Martin O'Toole, son of Jack O'Toole, Australia's greatest axeman of all time, as "the coming of age of wood chopping in Australia." Two thousand spectators witnessed the competition won handily by the Basque farmer. Arriya II was planning to take twenty Australian axes home with him, some given to him by his Australian competitors (now companions) at the Easter Show.[99]

In November of 1982, the third international championship of *aizkolariak* (woodchoppers) was held in Donostia. The city had inaugurated the first one in 1976. A trio of Basques had competed the previous April in Sydney, during which there were three hundred participants in all. Now, a Basque trio, which had triumphed in two elimination competitions held in the Basque Country in September, was taking on a "world team" including the Australian champion O'Toole brothers. There were compromises on format—it being agreed ultimately that half of the trunks would be of softwood and half of hard; similarly, half would be arranged vertically and half horizontally. Sixteen thousand spectators witnessed the Basques' victory. It was the largest crowd to date to ever witness a woodchopping event.[100]

Celebrities—While Australia is devoid of notable Basque figures in state and national politics (Ramón Jayo, mayor of Ingham, being the most prominent to date), there are some celebrities in the entertainment business that deserve mention. Frank Bennier (Benier) was a famous cartoonist. Born in South Australia in 1919, he was of fourth-generation Basque descent. Yet, despite such genealogical distance from the Basque Country, he always wore a *boina* to display his Basque heritage. His father was a bushman turned copper miner. When his son demonstrated artistic talent and interest, he was sent by his genitor to Mount Gambier to split fence posts and do physical work on farms in order to become a proper man. It did not work. Frank became a regular cartoonist in the *Adelaide News* and then moved to Sydney where he worked in animation. He illustrated the book *Now Listen, Mates!* by essayist John O'Grady (Worthing, England: Littlehampton Book Services, 1982). Frank died in 1998.

There are three singers who merit attention. Stewart D'Arrietta (his spelling) is a direct descendant of Jean Baptiste de Arrieta. He is a prominent singer with a six-person band. In addition to his own compositions, he performs works by Leonard Cohen, Tom Waits, Randy Newman, and John Lennon. He was a big success at the 2016 Edinburgh Fringe Festival and has a popular recording called *My Leonard Cohen*. Stewart is a member of the Sydney *Gure Txoko*, although he is there infrequently. He has never been to the Basque Country, or to Camden Park for that matter.

Then there are the Trápaga siblings. Monica Maria is a jazz singer/songwriter and actress. She was the presenter in a children's series called *Play School* on Australian television from 1990 to 1998. She has been part of several musical groups: Pardon Me Boys, Monica and the Moochers, and Monica Trapaga and the Bachelor Pad. She was born in Wahroonga, New South Wales, and is the youngest child of a Basque-Chinese father and Catalan-American mother. They were living in the Philippines and relocated to Sydney in 1963. In 2016, she was the head juror on the Australian jury for the Eurovision Song Contest. She has also authored two cookbooks.

Monica's older brother, Juan Ignacio Trápaga, has the stage name of Ignatius Jones. He was born in the Philippines. He is an events' director, journalist, actor, and the front-man for the shock-rock band Jimmy and the Boys. At one point, he was in the same band, Pardon Me Boys, as his sister Monica. He has acted in two Australian TV series and has had minor roles in several motion pictures. He worked on the 2000 Sydney Olympics opening and closing ceremonies, the opening ceremony of the Shanghai 2010 World Expo, and the Vancouver 2010 Winter Olympics. In 2017, he received the Lifetime Achievement Award at the Australian Events Awards.[101]

Heralds—There has never been a "Basque press" *per se* in any language in Australia,[102] no doubt reflecting the lack of sufficient critical mass to constitute a viable readership. The closest thing to an Australian Basque press was coverage of Basque topics in the nation's Spanish-language newspaper, *El Español en Australia*. It began as a mildly pro-Franco and highly pro-Church publication with a strong emphasis upon Spanish and Australian governmental policy, particularly as they configured immigration. There was a section on world news with a bit of an emphasis upon Latin America. The newspaper was clearly anti-Communist and somewhat anti-Labour Party (and unions) in its coverage of Australian affairs. Its treatment of the United States, Vietnam, and Australia's decision to ally with the Americans against the Vietcong were also mildly supportive, despite the reticence of many male immigrants to be conscripted to fight in it.

From the outset, there was considerable emphasis upon news of the Sydney *Centro Español* that did not obfuscate its internal divisions. In 1966, the initiative of some of its Asturian members to create their own club (while remaining members of the Spanish one) triggered a debate that received treatment in both editorials and letters received by the editor. Its critics viewed it as both unnecessary and unnecessarily divisive.[103] The Basques founded their *Gure Txoko* that same year, and, curiously, it was not even mentioned in the journal. Indeed, prior to the Burgos trial, there was scant mention of Basques and Basque matters at all. Even ETA went unremarked upon in its early years, and the few references to Basque nationalism regarded the Basque posture during the Spanish Civil War. Of greater interest to *El Español en Australia* were the budding careers of several Basque boxers, including the rise of Urtain as the heir apparent of Paolino Uzcudun.[104]

By the Burgos trial (1970),[105] the newspaper was shifting leftward. Its former blanket defense of the Catholic Church became silence; its support of center to right politics in Australia become openly pro-Labour, particularly with the ascent of Al Grassby as minister for immigration (1972–1975) under Gough Whitlam and the architect of Australian multiculturalism.

All through the first half of the 1970s, *El Español*'s treatment of Francisco Franco became increasingly critical. There was coverage of ETA violence, as well as the rise of Basque nationalist politics. There was a tendency to conflate the two and then reject their particularist view. Both contradicted the historical evidence that the Basques were the oldest Iberians and hence foundational Spaniards. Far from representing interests of truly noble Basques, nationalism was the political pretense of cynical opportunists pursuing their own personal interests.[106] Some of the coverage of Basques was historical and benign, including feature stories on the origin and significance of the Tree of Gernika[107] and the recovery of the language through the *ikastola* school movement.[108] Neither did the increasing number throughout Spain of protests, strikes, the dismissal of government ministers, incarcerations, and even torture escape notice.[109] The return of Basque Bishop Añoveras to his bishopric of Bilbo/Bilbao, after having been detained and threatened with deportation for criticizing the Franco government, was touted as a victory for the Spanish Catholic Church.[110] The rise of the monarchy and Franco's agonistic decline (including the loss of successor when ETA assassinated Admiral Luis Carrero Blanco in 1973) were reported regularly.

In short, by Franco's death, the newspaper conceded that it was about time—reproducing, while not without quite endorsing, the more radical sentiments of some of its readership. Then, too, after the dictator's demise, *El Español* published a few letters from persons who lamented the passing and predicted chaos to come.[111]

By this time, *El Español en Australia* was becoming more of a Latin American publication than Iberian one. As part of its multiculturalism, Australia accepted many refugees from the several civil conflicts throughout Latin America. Most were fleeing right-wing dictatorships, and news of the activities of Chileans, Colombians, Peruvians, Brazilians, and Bolivians, including of their clubs, began to crowd out the former emphases, including in the advertisements. Coverage of Latin American affairs became openly pro-democratic. Dictators were upbraided and their demise celebrated in the pages of the Australian paper (Castro's Cuba was given somewhat of a pass).[112] Indeed, from about 1980 on, after the Spanish transition to democracy was consolidated, news of Iberia had a two- or three-page section in the middle of the publication and just before "Women's Affairs" and "Sports." The twin subjects of ETA's ongoing campaign and the affairs of the newly established Basque autonomous government received fairly extensive treatment within this reduced space.[113]

The Australian press covered Basques in extremely perfunctory, generally negative fashion. There was the indictment of the "Italian" Vincente Ugartiburu, accused by a Townsville magistrate of having had carnal knowledge with a minor under twelve years of age.[114] We might cite the petty crime of Domingo Arregui and Domingo Murelaga, accused in 1934 in Innisfail of having stolen fishing nets from the Russell River. In their defense, they argued that people had been stealing fish from their traps. In the course of the investigation, Arregui was found to be in possession of a stolen battery that he used in his boat. He admitted stealing it from a car three months earlier, along with another man who took a generator. He was fined £5 or a month in jail in lieu of payment.[115] That same year, two "Spaniards," Y. Bilbao and M. Aboitiz, were killed in Queensland when their lorry overturned.[116]

If Anglo-Australian press coverage of the Spanish Civil War, influenced as it was by the Catholic Church, was essentially pro-Franco, there was change over time. Certainly, the world's ostracism of the Spanish dictatorship demanded critical assessment of it. When, in 1960, several hundred Basque priests defied their own hierarchy and petitioned the Vatican to stop supporting the regime, it was reported in the Queensland *Catholic Leader* and the secular press. Mason notes that Queensland's Catholics viewed the protest as a matter of individual liberty, whereas Queensland's Basques "framed the action as the traditional defence of their community whose unique identity and cultural difference had been divinely ordained since time immemorial."[117] In 1937, José Guerricadbetia [Guerricabeitia] and Gregoria [Gregorio] Totorico [Totorica] were injured in a mine explosion at Charters Towers. As they were entering the shaft a benzene gas tank exploded and threw Guerricabeitia to the surface. He went to town to give the alarm and his seriously burned mate was extracted from the tunnel and taken to the hospital. According to a newspaper account, "Misfortune continues to dog a party working the mine at Ravenswood," since they arrived in the town a few months earlier and their leader, José Renteria, had fallen from a hotel balcony and was killed.[118]

Eusebio Illarmendi told me that one of his fellow townsmen from Zarautz made national news here. It seems that he was working in a machine shop in Gove, Northern Territory, when his boss told him to clean up the place as Prime Minister Gordon was coming there for a visit the next day. The Basque had refused, claiming that it was not part of his award (job description).[119]

Mention should also be made of a 1967 article, "The Basques—Strongmen of the Canefields," written by Larry Foley as a feature piece for Australia's *People Magazine*.[120] Foley is a consummate scrivener who weaves a compelling tale. His piece reads like a detective story in which he pursues the rumored presence of Spaniards in Ingham to the largely

Basque initiative of the *fronton* in Trebonne.¹²¹ His key informants are Alberto Urberuaga and Johnny Mendiolea. We are taken on a marvelous intellectual journey from the prehistoric origins of the Basques, the uniqueness of their language, and their emigration throughout the centuries and around the globe to a description of *pelota* and weight-lifting spectacles that he witnessed in Trebonne. Foley's visit documents a propitious moment, since the festivity that he witnessed transpired on the eve of the mechanization of the sugar harvest, the transformation for Basque immigration in Australia that it supposed, and the waning days of the Trebonne *fronton*'s active life. He was particularly impressed with the weight-lifting competition,

> The drama is enacted on the back of a flatbed truck which, flood-lighted, makes an ideal stage, like a boxing-ring without ropes, and gives the close-packed audience a good view.
>
> Two men take the centre of the stage: the contestant and his second. The contestant takes the end of an immensely long, black woolen sash, paid out by his second, and turns around and around slowly, so that the sash winds itself around his waist, forming a wide, thick bandage.
>
> The donning of the sash has an air of ritual. The hubbub dies. Tension mounts. Three men are seated importantly on sandbags against the truck cabin: timekeeper, judge, and keeper of the official count. The crowd presses right up against the side of the truck. They are already loud with exhortation and advice....
>
> The big truck shudders. The judge signals a clean lift. Everybody counts out loud: One!....
>
> Up she goes again...Right this time! Thirteen! The count goes on. The din is terrific. In their passionate involvement the spectators seem to be trying by the sheer power of their vocal cords to help raise that cruel deadweight over those last agonizing inches on to the now-bleeding shoulder. By comparison, the conventional weight-lifting contest is like a prayer meeting.¹²²

Summing up his experience, Foley concluded, "And it all reminded me of two things I'd once read about the Basques; first whatever the Government, they're agin it; second, it is beneath his dignity for a Basque to admit he may be wrong."¹²³

It is fun to accompany Foley as his fellow traveler, but it might be noted that his are but a few lines about Basques scribbled on the Australian vastness. If anything, they underscore the paucity of Australian awareness of this "little weird mob"[124] in their midst.

Australians had another exotic glimpse into the Basques' emigratory legacy when the noted journalist and author, Robert Langdon, produced two books on the possible genetic legacy of Basques in the South Pacific.[125]

Australian Basques are sometimes mentioned in the press in various newspapers in the Basque Country and publications of the Basque government. Prior to creation of the present Basque government, in the late 1970s, there were a few stories published in the Basque homeland by feature writers who visited Australia and published their impressions. A freelance journalist, Joseba Etxarri, was a frequent visitor to the Basque concentrations throughout Latin America and the American West. He made a single two-month trip to Australia as well, accompanied by his parents. His father had once intended to emigrate there but did not. He remained curious about the place. Joseba was particularly prone to attend celebrations and other events in the Basque diasporas. He then published vignettes regarding them in his electronic newsletter Euskalkultura.com (subtitled "Basque Heritage Worldwide" and published in English, Basque, and Spanish). It is still maintained by the Basque government and contains information from the Basque diasporas throughout the world.

Euskal Telebista (Basque Television) and *Radio Euskadi* (Basque Radio), as well as public media outlets of Basque government, have all touched upon the topic of the Basque Australians. There is the activity of Julian Iantzi, born of Basque parentage in the United States, but resident for many years in Euskadi. He is a television personality, writing and appearing in many shows on both Basque and Spanish national television. He is the creator of the currently popular reality show on *Euskal Telebista* called *El conquistador del fin del mundo*.

Julian and his two siblings were born in California. Their father, from Lesaka, lived in California for twenty-three years, thirteen years in sheepherding and sheep-ranching and then ten in cattle. He was living in Dixon when his children reached school age, and he decided to return to the Basque Country to educate them and effect a family reunion. A few years ago, it was his idea to organize a festival of ex-herders from Navarra and Iparralde, and the response was tremendous. A lunch, attended by more than five hundred persons, was held in the *frontón* of Lesaka. Unfortunately, the elder Iantzi died the week before. His daughter, Laura, then founded an association called *Euskal Artzainak Ameriketan* (Basque Sheepherders in America). Julian was considering doing the same for Bizkaian herders. He accompanied his sister when she organized a contingent of ex-herders to attend the last Boise *Jaialdi* (2015) and filmed a documentary of Basques of the American West that appeared on *Euskal Telebista*.

Next, he traveled to Australia for filming. In Sydney, someone took him to the *Gure Txoko*. He had known nothing of its existence. When he returned to the Basque Country, he was struck by the lack of awareness there of the Basque compatriots in Australia. He began posting on social media information that he had learned about their history. He was struck by the parallels between it and the one he had always imbibed about sheepherders in the American West—the hard life, the language difficulties, the struggle for acceptance, the ultimate triumph through persistence. He began receiving feedback from his audience—particularly descendants of ex-canecutters—with anecdotes and offers of family photos. It was then that he decided to explore forming an association predicated on the one that his sister created for ex-sheepherders. In cooperation with three daughters of ex-canecutters, Amaia Urberuaga, Tere Gabiola, and Leire Goirigolzarri, a luncheon was convened in Gernika on November 25, 2018, which was attended by about 250 persons.[126]

It was then that *Euskal Australiar Alkartea* (Basque Australians Together) was launched. It now has a board consisting of a president (Amaia Urberuaga Badiola),[127] two vice presidents (Teresa Gabiola Bereciartua and Loren Arkotxa Meabebastarretxea), a secretary (Leire Goirigolzarri Etxeandia), a treasurer (Jugatx Azkue Azkue), and four regular board members (Esther Korta Gabiola, Julian Iantzi Mitxelena, Karlos Aguirre Fernández, and Antonio Onaindia Laka). In late March of 2019, a similar meeting was held at the Hotel Hola of Tafalla, attended by more than 100 Navarrans. They are in the process of forming their own association—*Navarra Boomerang Australia Alkartea* (Navarran Boomerang Australians Together). There is an eighteen-day excursion scheduled for the second half of July of 2019 to Australia that is already fully subscribed (fifty participants, a Basque Television crew, and, possibly, Basque government officials). Led by Amaia Urberuaga, it will begin in Cairns, then travel to Ingham, Townsville, Home Hill, Brisbane, and, finally, Sydney.

So, the Basque public now finds its canecutter, like its sheepherder of the American West, to be a fascinating and even iconic figure.

There have been several novelistic treatments of Basques in various Latin American venues and the United States. Those of the American West have their literary spokesman in Robert Laxalt.[128] Basque Australians have yet to fictionalize their experience or record it in book-length format. Amaia Arrate wrote a charming account of her childhood memories ("Footprints in the Pig-Pen: A Basque Memoir"), but only self-published a few copies for her siblings and cousins. Jenny Goicoechea has produced three tomes, with a fourth in progress, on Joe's life, replete with many newspaper articles and magnificent photographs. However, it, too, exists in only a handful of copies circulated among family members.

We do have the poem sent from Australia by Cecilio Basurko, a Basque immigrant (see Appendix III). He entered the country in 1927 along with three other Basques, all army deserters. It is not clear when the verses were composed or sent, but it seems probable that it was within a few years after their arrival. The verses are entitled "Mutriku'tik Australia'ra" (From Mutriku to Australia). They were sung by a woman in the *baserri* Matzuri (presumably, albeit not certainly, situated in Mutriku). One of the verses stated the intention that they be printed and sold to make money for their author (a form of publications known as *bertso papera* that was often marketed at rural festivals). Again, it seems likely, although uncertain, that the *bertsolari* in question was Cecilio.[129]

The only extensive treatments of Basque Australians are my comparative study of Basque and Italian immigrants and Gloria Totoricagüena's subsequent work.[130] If the Basque presence in Australia has been heralded mainly in newspaper articles in both Australia and the European homeland, I might also mention the travelogue by a Bizkaian author, Manuel Leguineche. His book, *La Tierra de Oz* (The land of Oz), details a several-week tour of Australia that he made at the turn of the twenty-first century. It is replete with incisive observations of the country and its people, informed by the author's reading of key Australian authors like Patrick White and Robert Hughes, as well as my book. He uses *Azúcar amargo* to discuss the Basque presence in Queensland, including anecdotes from it about places—Ingham and Ayr—and people like Teresa Mendiolea, Pascual Badiola, and Alberto Urberuaga.[131]

There is, of course, a pronounced shift to the Internet. When Josu Legarreta first visited the Sydney *Txoko* in 1989, he agreed to send it the Basque press. This began with the Sunday edition of the newspaper *Deia* and the Monday one of *Diario Vasco*. Writing in 2008, Totoricagüena stated that, "Today the Gure Txoko no longer receives any paper copies of any Basque homeland newspapers. Members search for information via the Internet or via cable television, or SBS Spanish daily news broadcasts on Australian television."[132]

Notes

1. I did a similar analysis of Basque Americans and was able to conclude from census data on Basque Americans and the memberships of the more than thirty Basque voluntary associations in the United States that only about one in eleven persons who self-identified as wholly or partly Basque in the census pertained to a Basque club. William A. Douglass, "Basque Immigration in the United States," *Boga: Basque Studies Consortium Journal* 1, no. 1 (2013), 13.
2. Canals, "The Catalans," 9.
3. Pares, *I Fiddled*, 88.
4. *North Queensland Register*, May 22, 1916, 5.
5. Santina Lizzio, *Basilisk: Township of South Johnstone* (Cairns: Bolton Print, 2006), 63; 78.
6. Mason, "Agitators," 123. There is evidence of mixed career strategies that might involve cane cutting or farming during that season as well. For example, in 1934, Goñi was among the first to contract Weil's disease, so he must have been cutting cane at the time. He had been sponsored by Daniel Martínez and then married Marina Villalba, a woman born on the *Kwantu Maru* during its voyage from Argentina to Australia (Ibid, 119).
7. Ibid, 126.
8. Ibid, 137. We have already noted Queensland Bishop Duhig's support of Italian Fascism, a sentiment echoed by Father Kelly of Ingham (Ibid, 142).
9. Ibid, 140.
10. Ibid, 139.
11. Two Spanish Agustinian priests were sent from Manila to Thursday Island, probably to minister to the substantial Philippine population at Keriri (Ibid, 142).
12. Ibid, 141.
13. Ibid, 127.
14. Ibid, 128.
15. García, *Operación*, 144–46.
16. Ibid, 154.
17. Ibid, 157–58.

18. Ibid, 158.
19. Ibid, 146–47.
20. Ibid, 146–49.
21. Totoricagüena, *Australia*, 214–15. Totoricagüena seems to be conflating and confounding García's account (García, *Operación*, 129–130) of the formation of the Sydney *Centro Español* with the subsequent creation a few years later of *Gure Txoko*.
22. Totoricagüena, *Australia*, 215.
23. García, *Operación*, 129–30.
24. Totoricagüena, *Australia*, 212.
25. García, *Operación*, 131–32.
26. Ibid, 133–34.
27. Totoricagüena, *Australia*, 213.
28. García, *Operación*, 142–43.
29. Ibid, 136–39.
30. Ibid, 131; 139.
31. Ibid, 139–43.
32. Quoted in Ibid, 146.
33. Ibid, 143.
34. Javier Iriondo stated that the move was resented by the members of the Spanish Club. They regarded it as schismatic and unnecessary dilution of Melbourne's already small Spanish population (Douglass field notes).
35. Totoricagüena, *Australia*, 201.
36. García, *Operación*, 146. Totoricagüena states that the location was 16 Stawell Street and was leased from a Maltese owner (Totoricagüena, *Australia*, 201).
37. Ibid, 195–96. She notes that, in 1925, one Jules Minvielle, a recent immigrant from Cairo, was denied a permit to build a "pelote Basque Stadium" in Melbourne. Totoricagüena speculates that this might mean that there was a sufficient critical mass of Basques in the city by that time to make such an enterprise viable. Maybe, yet unlikely—given that it is unsupported by any other evidence. In fact, by this time, *jai alai* was a popular international sport because of the wagering. Basque *fontones* were operating in places like Buenos Aires, Montevideo, Santiago de Chile, and Manila—all cities with significant Basque populations. But they were also present in Jakarta and Shanghai. In fact, even in the Basque Country today few *frontones* would be viable without non-Basque "tourist" spectators and bettors.
38. Ibid, 196–99.
39. Ibid, 203.
40. Ibid, 201.
41. Ibid, 203–4. Totoricagüena calls him "José" here and subsequently after correctly giving his name as "Juan" (correctly) at the beginning of her exposition of the history of the Melbourne *Gure Txoko*.
42. Ibid, 201; 203.
43. Douglass field notes.
44. Totoricagüena, *Australia*, 207.

45. Ibid, 204–6.
46. Ibid, 206–7.
47. García, *Operación*, 143.
48. Totoricagüena, *Australia*, 211.
49. See the individual sketches of the lives of both Goñi and Oriñuela in Chapter 11 of the present work, [INSERT PAGE RANGE IN PDF VERSION].
50. Ibid, 215; García, *Operación*, 144.
51. Totoricagüena, *Australia*, 215.
52. Ibid, 216.
53. Ibid, 216–17. Totoricagüena provides thumbnail sketches of each of the founders. Among them only one was a woman, Teodora Torrontegui, and there was a single non-Basque, Alfonso de Miguel from Madrid, who had many Basque friends (Ibid, 218–19).
54. Ibid, 220–21.
55. Ibid, 232.
56. Ibid, 231.
57. Reproduced in Ibid, 230–31.
58. Ibid, 221–24. Totoricagüena reproduces as the first two appendices of her book the original statutes of the Melbourne and Sydney *Gure Txoko*s (Ibid, 323–46). Her Appendix III is the revision of the latter effected in 1984 (Ibid, 349–67).
59. Ibid, 224.
60. Ibid, 223–24.
61. Ibid, 226.
62. Ibid, 235–36.
63. *Euskal Etxeak*, nos. 2–3 (June–July 1989), 27.
64. Ibid, nos. 4–5 (August–September 1989), 22–23.
65. Totoricagüena, *Australia*, 239.
66. *Euskal Etxeak*, nos. 4–5 (August–September 1989), 18–19; 27.
67. Ibid, 233–34.
68. Ibid, 240.
69. It has sponsored one every four years since (and counting).
70. Totoricagüena, *Australia*, 236–37.
71. Most of the foregoing regarding Josu Legarreta's activities was provided to me by him in a personal communication on February 18, 2019.
72. Bianka Vidonja Balanzategui and Barbara Debono, "The Fronton: A Basque legacy in tropical Queensland," *Journal of the Society of Basque Studies in America* 21 (2001), 26. ["The Fronton"].
73. Mason speaks of the Spanish woman in Tully who was inspired by the festival organized by local Sicilians to convene (date unspecified) six other Spaniards of the town to stage their own celebration with "regional Spanish dance and food" (Mason, "Agitators," 242).
74. Ibid, 273.
75. Ibid, 275–76.
76. See Appendix IV for its original membership list by families and residence.

77. Vidonja Balanzategui and Debono, "The Fronton," 26.
78. Ibid, 26–27.
79. I attended a dinner there with José Larrazabal and Dolores Mendiolea (his wife), Johnny and Conchi Mendiolea, and Tomás and María Ibañez and sat at the Spanish table. There was one Australian of Sicilian descent seated with us—a friend of all. Conchi told me that Mari Ibañez had planned to come after dinner was served in order to save the A$9.00 for her plate. Conchi underscored it as an example of how immigrants lived deprived lives here in order to invest back in the homeland (Mari has a couple of apartments there). At one point, José and Félix Jayo's wife danced a *jota*, to the great delight of the entire crowd (Douglass field notes).
80. Totoricagüena, *Australia*, 273.
81. Ibid, 275.
82. Ibid, 279–85.
83. Ibid, 275.
84. Vidonja Balanzategui and Debono, "The Fronton," 19.
85. Ibid, 19–21.
86. Ibid, 22.
87. Ibid.
88. Ibid.
89. Ibid, 23.
90. Ibid, 22–23.
91. Ibid, 23.
92. Ibid, 25.
93. Ibid, 24–25.
94. Ibid, 25.
95. J. Cunningham, "The Toughest Game of All," *Courier-Mail*, "Leisure," November 27, 1980, 4.
96. Vidonja Balanzategui and Debono, "The Fronton," 27.
97. Ibid, 28–29.
98. *Herbert River Express*, May 10, 1980, 5.
99. *Sydney Morning Herald*, April 9, 1977, 2.
100. *El País*, November 7, 1982.
101. According to Manu Martin, neither of the Trápaga siblings are members of *Gure Txoko*, but there is a Juan Trápaga in the Club who is likely a relation.
102. This was unlike the situation in several Latin American nations and the United States. In the latter, by the late nineteenth century, there were two Basque-language publications in California—*Escualdun Gazeta* (1885) and *California-ko Eskual Herria* (1893–1898). The former is actually the first Basque-language newspaper ever founded on the planet (including the Basque homeland).
103. An Asturian defender wrote,

> With such a quantity of distinct characteristics, it is natural that an organism like the actual existing one in Sydney, has not been able to totally satisfy all Spaniards, despite all the efforts and good will that the Directive

has always displayed, given that to satisfy some would be to fail others. If there would be a competition of Aragonese *jotas* (Spain's most beautiful), the Galicians would want one focused upon *muñeiras*, the Andalusians *flamenco* and we Asturians would say the *xiringelu*, even though we know that dance is only known among Asturians, but to us it is more enjoyable than *flamenco*, even though that may be famous throughout the world… (*El Español en Australia*, June 23, 1965, 1).

104. Ibid, January 15, 1969, 7.
105. The newspaper reported the statement of the defendants (Ibid, December 16, 1970, 1) and Franco's reluctant (faced with international condemnation) commutation of their death sentences (Ibid, January 6, 1971, 1).
106. Ibid, April 14, 1971, 2; Ibid, December 8, 1971, 3; Ibid, December 15, 1971, 3; Ibid, February 6, 1974, 9.
107. Ibid, September 19, 1973, 4.
108. Ibid, May 30, 1973, 4.
109. Ibid, June 30, 1973, 1.
110. Ibid, March 20, 1974, 1.
111. Ibid, March 13, 1976, 4.
112. Ibid, May 15, 1979, 10.
113. For example: Ibid, March 28, 1978, 1; Ibid, October 24, 1978, 1; Ibid, October 31, 1978, 1; Ibid, April 24, 1979, 19; Ibid, July 31, 1979, 1; Ibid, September 19, 1979, 20; Ibid, October 30, 1979, 1; Ibid, January 8, 1980, 14; Ibid, February 3, 1998, 1.
114. *North Queenland Register*, March 8, 1915, 80.
115. *Cairns Post*, March 10, 1934, 5.
116. *The West Australian*, July 18, 1934, 18.
117. Totoricagüena, *Australia*, 239.
118. *Warwick Daily News*, February 27, 1937, 1.
119. Douglass field notes.
120. Larry Foley, "The Basques—Strongmen of the Canefields," *People Magazine* (October 18, 1967), 12–17.
121. "It was an item on the printed program for the annual festival at Ingham, North Queensland, that led me to the discovery of a little weird mob of migrant settlers who are in many ways more Australian than the Australians. The program said, 'Spanish Weightlifting Contest.'" (Ibid, 12).
122. Ibid, 12; 13.
123. Ibid, 17.
124. Ibid, 12.
125. Robert Langdon, *The Lost Caravel* (Sydney: Pacific Publications, 1975); Robert Langdon, *The Lost Caravel Re-explored* (Canberra: Brolga Press, 1988). For a synopsis and discussion of the Langdon thesis that Basque seamen from the Spanish caravel, the *San Lesmes*, which disappeared in 1526 after traversing the Strait of Magellan and later shipwrecked in the South Pacific, sowed their genes there, see Douglass, *Basque Explorers*, 203–5.

126. Euskalkultura.com (http://www.euskalkultura.com/english/), November 15, 2018; Ibid, Novembr 16, 2018.
127. Amaia still returns to Australia from time to time. Between 2006 and 2011, she rambled around the country in her camper van and logged almost 100,000 miles. Last year she spent a month in Melbourne. Her only brother, Javier, moved to Spain in 1980 and lives in Madrid. She has no family in Australia, so would not consider moving back there permanently.
128. David Río Raigadas, *Robert Laxalt: The Voice of the Basques in American Literature*, Occasional Papers Series, no. 13 (Reno: Center for Basque Studies, University of Nevada, Reno, 2007).
129. In Antonio Zabala, *Ameriketako bertsoak* (Tolosa: Auspoa, 1984), 103–8. [*Ameriketako*].
130. Douglass, *Azúcar Amargo*; Totoricagüena, *Australia*.
131. Manuel Leguineche, *La Tierra de Oz: Australia vista desde Darwin a Sydney* (Madrid: Aguilar, 2000).
132. Totoricagüena, *Australia*, 239.

CHAPTER 10

Basques in the New Australia

To Sojourn or Settle—We have noted that there are as many migrant histories as there are migrants. While this book deals primarily with discernible collective patterns, from the viewpoint of the individual actor the migration process was idiosyncratic. The decision to leave familiar kith and kin, friends, fellow villagers, and parishioners was never taken lightly. Even if one anticipated moving along an established network of facilitators, the act of traveling thousands of miles to a new land was daunting. It certainly entailed crossing more than international borders; there were the cultural and linguistic ones as well. The latter were more pronounced for those Basque immigrants who opted for the Anglo worlds of the United States or Australia, as opposed to the less-alien Latin American alternatives.

I would argue that few Basques emigrated to the Anglo world with the intention of settling permanently. That is to say, they left Euskadi as sojourners. But, then, along the way some had a change of mind (and heart) and opted to settle permanently in the host society. Others could never quite make up their minds (as we shall see when we detail individual life histories in successive chapters). They might sojourn, save up money for the return to birthplace, do so, attempt to become reestablished there, fail, and reemigrate to the former (or even possibly a new) overseas' destination. If the rhetoric regarding such moves tends to be the search for "security," the outcome resembles more what the Basque writer Pío Baroja entitled *inquietudes* or "restlessnesses" of his globe-trotting mariner protagonist Shanti Andia (*Las Inquietudes de Shanti Andia*, 1911). It calls to mind the emigrant's lament of becoming trapped somewhere between two cultures without really pertaining to either.

Mason recounts his Mareeba informants' (2004) contention that the only Spanish nationals to stay in Australia and gradually assimilate were those who failed to save up enough for an eventual return to Spain.[1] Well, yes and no. Certainly, there were a few such cases, but even they were relative. How much one needed to accumulate before returning to the homeland was always an idiosyncratic calculation. It was influenced by what the return might entail (paying off the mortgage on a family farm, setting up a small business, buying a truck to enter Spain's commercial transportation network, purchasing an apartment as a place to live while engaging in salaried employment, etc.). Certainly, those who opted to buy a farm or a mechanical harvester in Australia had sufficient capital to contemplate a return to Euskadi instead. Others settled in Australia after becoming enamored with the country and its many personal freedoms compared to Franco's Spain. Then there were those who married an Australian citizen (possibly an Anglo Australian or, initially, more likely the descendant of former Southern European immigrants) unwilling to abandon kith and kin to emigrate herself to Europe. And so forth.

Mason furthermore detects a disconnection between the older generations of established migrants in the Far North and the subsequent newcomers. It is worth quoting his findings:

> Many of the pioneer migrants resented the relatively high level of Governmental support now offered, and felt it symbolized the new arrivals' lack of commitment to their adoptive society. Basques' family networks mitigated some of this tension, and Basque leaders "made a very real effort towards the assimilation and welcoming of the newcomers". Established settlers did offer occasional support, but many felt the new arrivals' cultural values were at odds with remembered Spanish traditions. Although some migrants recalled that contact between the groups was amicable, prominent families did not recall any contact with the new settlers. Non-Basques sensed their cultural differences from older settlers, and realized that Spain's postwar social norms had altered radically. Newer migrants felt that "the old people don't look good to the young fellows who come from Spain". Without

sustained family contacts and shared experiences in Spain, the two groups lacked a consensual framework of what might constitute shared *Hispanidad*.[2]

Inquietudes (not to mention *idiosincrasia*), indeed!

Those Basques who did settle more or less permanently in Australia became the parents of a generation of "true" Australians, and potentially the grandparents of even "truer" ones. There is, then, the question of the extent to which such descendants were influenced by, and continued to maintain (or not), their ethnic heritage. An obvious intent of all of the Basque (and Spanish) voluntary associations that we considered earlier in Chapter 9 was the preservation of a Basque heritage among future generations. Their success would be somewhat qualified.

Mason notes that, in general, the Australia-born were likely to favor "Anglo-Celtic groups such as the Rural Youth or Junior Farmers" as best addressing their cultural and financial realities. Acquisition of higher education, valued by their immigrant parents as well, became the vehicle for social and economic mobility. The four children of John and Conchita Mendiolea and the three of Agustín and Mary Arrate are classic examples: Johnny Mendiolea and Michael both became schoolteachers. Tommy, after teaching as well, moved to Sydney and worked as a steward for Qantas Airways on its Sydney to London route. Stephen Mendiolea has his own businesses and lives in Townsville. None remains in farming. Amaya Arrate is also a schoolteacher and her sister, Idoya, is a nurse. Of this cohort, only John Arrate remains in agriculture as a part-time sugar farmer. Even he commutes (by air) to a job as a mechanic at a zinc, lead, and silver mine in the Queensland outback.

We could also cite the case of Joe Goicoechea, who, while born in the Basque Country, came to Australia as a young child. Joe would become a major force in the construction business of the Far North, and he ran for mayor of Townsville on three occasions. Today's mayor of Ingham, Ramón Jayo, is the son of the baker Felix Jayo and his wife, Pilar Astorquia, of Trebonne.

Then there is the subject of marriage. While the immigrant generation tended to practice ethnic-group endogamy (whether marrying an Hegoalde-born spouse or an Australian Basque), or, to a lesser degree, a spouse of other Southern European extraction, all of the Mendioleas, all of the Arrate children, and Joe Goicoechea and Ramón Jayo as well, married Anglo-Australians.

A Demographic Mosaic—The two world wars were watershed events in Australian history. If the Commonwealth of Australia was created formally in 1901, arguably, the new nation faced the same challenge underscored by that champion of Italian unification, Massimo d'Azeglio, when, in 1861, he stated, "We have made Italy; now we must make Italians." More than one observer of Australia has attributed their common involvement in World War I as the experience that "made Australians" out of the inhabitants of the continent's several colonies. The new nation lost 61,527 of its men in combat and suffered more than 200,000 casualties in a population of roughly five million. There is scarcely a town in Australia without its prominent monument to the fallen—usually with the names of the local ones etched upon it. The War Museum in Canberra is Australia's national shrine.

We have considered in depth one of the guiding principles from creation of the Commonwealth through World War II—The White Australia Policy—and the challenge that immigration from Southern Europe posed to it.[3] World War II underscored Australia's vulnerability and need to rethink its future. Today's Australia, with its 24,496,800 inhabitants,[4] is an entirely different country than that of the 3,788,123 inhabitants in 1901 or the 7,465,157 Australians in the year 1946. The huge increase reflects a postwar willingness to admit massive numbers of immigrants. Not only has Australia opened its doors to people from every continent, she has been the refuge for the victims of many human calamities. For example, the population of Nepal-born persons increased from 4,567 in 2006 to 24,635 in 2011. During that five-year period the Himalayan kingdom endured much civil strife. Then, too, there are the Iraqis (74,955), Lebanese (76,451), and Egyptians (36,533), many of whom were fleeing Middle Eastern conflicts.[5] Between 1947 and 1971 alone, the percentage of Australians who were foreign-born doubled from around 10 to 20 percent of the national population.[6]

Australia's Southeast and Far East Asian population has exploded. In 2011, the (mainland) Chinese (318,969), Vietnamese (185,039), Filipinos (171, 233), Malays (116,196), South Koreans (74,538), Indonesians (63,159), Singaporeans (48,646), Thais (45,466), Japanese (35,377), Taiwanese (28,628), Cambodians (28,330), Burmese (21,760), and Laotians (9,932) totaled no fewer than 1,147,273 people. South Asia provides similarly dramatic figures: India (295,363), Sri Lanka (86,413), Pakistan (30,221), Afghanistan (28,598), Nepal, (24,635), and Bhutan (2,455), or a total of 467,685.[7]

There was also the British Commonwealth factor. The Canadian (38,871) and New Zealand (483,396) numbers certainly reflect this (albeit in the case of the latter there is a sort of "shared destiny of close neighbors" effect as well). Australia clearly served as a refuge for whites concerned with the blacks' accession to power in South Africa (145,683) and Zimbabwe (30,252). Migration from Hong Kong to Australia (74,451) relates to China's assumption of political control of that former British colony. One might also surmise that the high figures for nonwhites from Hong Kong, Singapore, and Malaysia were partly facilitated by the membership of those entities in the Commonwealth.[8]

This is not to say that there were no ups and downs along the way. In 1973, the Gough Whitlam Labour Government formally repudiated the White Australia Policy, culminating a process that began in the late 1940s.[9] It passed the *Australian Citizenship Act 1973* that removed all privileges enjoyed by British citizens in relation to their citizenship, voting rights, and visas. It also abolished the distinction between Europeans and non-Europeans regarding immigration possibilities in Australia.[10] In 1974, the Department of Immigration was effectively dismantled by shifting its key function to other ministries. The prime minister characterized the Department of Immigration as, "outmoded, outdated, and 'incurably' racist."[11] Australia was a signatory, since 1966, of the UN's Convention on the Elimination of All Forms of Racial Discrimination, but it had never been ratified by the Australian Parliament. The Whitlam government remedied that with its *Racial Discrimination Act 1975*,

> The legislation made it unlawful for a person to discriminate on the grounds of race, colour, descent, or national or ethnic origins. It guaranteed equality before the law without distinction as to race, nationality, or ethnicity. It established the grounds for the

appointment of a commissioner of community relations to administer the legislation, with the power to examine complaints of racial discrimination with the assistance of a Community Relations Council.[12]

Whitlam appointed Parliamentarian Al Grassby (himself of Spanish descent)[13] as minister for immigration, and, during his tenure, "ethnic politics" became a factor in national elections. Grassby was the architect of a formally diverse Australia. He was skeptical that immigrants could be assimilated completely into Australian life, and therefore advocated multiculturalism for the nation. It was predicated upon developments along those lines in Canada.[14] He visited the capitals of several Asian countries to present their leaders with Australia's new immigration policies regarding them and was welcomed. He created six immigrant taskforces to learn from the immigrants themselves how reforms should be formulated and implemented.[15]

Ironically, under Whitlam/Grassby the annual quota of immigrants was scaled back considerably, and the newcomer's potential for contributing to the Australian economy was emphasized. Australia was accepting 140,000 immigrants when Whitlam took office and, by 1975, was only admitting 50,000.[16] Whitlam himself was capable of discrimination for political reasons. When Saigon fell, he opposed admitting South Vietnamese refugees on the grounds that they were anti-leftists who would likely support the Liberals over Labour.[17]

Grassby was the object of death threats and would himself become the victim of a racist campaign. He lost his seat in the Australian Parliament in 1974 but was then appointed immediately by Whitlam to be the government's special consultant on community affairs.[18]

By 1984, the country was awash in what has been called "the Blainey debate."[19] Reference is to that noted historian's call for review of a national immigration policy that threatened to transform Australia's essentially European character into a multiracial and multicultural society riven by internal discord among contending ethnic groups. The discussions ranged widely over an array of economic, social, and human rights' issues, but without effecting genuine policy reform.[20] Tavan notes that this was just the beginning of a series of polarizing debates over immigration that continue down to the present; as often degenerating into invidious labeling of one's opponents rather genuine discourse in search of consensus and solutions.[21] That summation rings particularly true for both Europeans and North Americans at the present stage in our own debates over immigration.

And what of this book's Southern Europeans: Italians and Spaniards in particular?[22] In the 2011 census there are 185,401 persons reporting Italy as the birthplace of one or both of their parents, while 916,121 claimed Italian ancestry.[23] Of the latter, 116,263 lived in Queensland.[24] We might compare that figure with the 16,795 figure for Queensland Italians in 1954 (See Table 3, Chapter 8). In roughly half a century, the state's Italian population had increased nearly sevenfold!

Persons with Spain-born parents in Australia as a whole in 2011 numbered 13,057; while 92,952 persons claimed Spanish ancestry[25] (no comparable statistics were reported for Queensland). While there are some grounds for suspecting confusion of Latin Americans with Spaniards in the "Spanish" figures, beyond a doubt the postwar population of non-Basque and non-Catalan Spaniards in Australia increased exponentially.

If Spain had interdicted the assisted-migrants' agreement with Australia in March of 1963, neither government was inextricably opposed to renegotiating it. For their part, Spanish authorities wanted to keep the Australian door open in the event that it was needed at some time in the future. For his part, the head of the CIME argued that the flaws in the system had resulted from the insistence of both Australian migration officials and the IEE to become overly involved in the recruitment. Of the 3,500 Spanish emigrants recruited by his agency, not a single one had complained or been repatriated. Should the program be resumed, he recommended that the recruitments be conducted exclusively by the CIME.[26]

Then there are the Catalans and Basques, who had been the main components of Australia's Spanish nationals' immigration in the period prior to World War II. Persons reporting Basque ancestry for all of Australia totaled but 612 individuals in 2011, which, nevertheless, exceeded the Catalans (171).[27] While the number of Basques in Queensland is not specified, there were 48 persons in the state reporting that the Basque language was used in their home.[28]

In short, we can now make the following generalizations about Basque immigration in Australia.

There were four phases:
1. The nineteenth-century precursors who arrived individually and pursued idiosyncratic careers, albeit sometime related to Australia's mining boom and seafaring.
2. The pioneers in the Queensland sugar industry closely affiliated with established Catalans and influenced considerably by the dominant Italian element among Queensland's Southern Europeans.
3. The prominence of Basques among the formal recruits of the three official recruitments of Spanish nationals for Australia in 1958–1960.
4. The post-canecutter era in which former Basque cutters devised new strategies within the Australian economy, often moving out of the sugar districts to urban destinations in the South (Sydney and Melbourne in particular). Their numbers were complemented by Basques entering the country to study or work—often as professionals.

It should be further noted that each phase built somewhat upon its predecessor. Thus, the few established Basques among the precursors were a likely source of information about the Queensland sugar industry that convinced the early Basque pioneers of the Far North to settle there. They, in turn, instituted their own chain migration from the Basque Country and were a key factor in the three formal recruitments of 1958–1960. Mason opines that fully 70 percent of the Basques immigrating during and after this period went to either the Herbert or Burdekin, and another 15 percent chose Mount Isa. The dissemination throughout Australia of the Queensland collectivity established potential sponsors of the eclectic migrants of the post-canecutter era that lasts down to the present.

Notes

1. Mason, "Agitators," 265.
2. Ibid, 266.
3. For fuller treatment of the evolution of the policy throughout the twentieth century, see Gwenda Tavan, *The Long, Slow Death of White Australia* (Melbourne: Scribe Publications, 2005), passim. [*The Long, Slow Death*].
4. Estimated as of June 20, 2017; see entry "Population of Australia" in Wikipedia.
5. Commonwealth of Australia, Department of Immigration and Border Protection, *The People of Australia: Statistics from the 2011 Census* (Canberra: Australian Government Printing Service, 2014), 3–8. [*People of Australia*].

6. Peter Lloyd, "The Political Economy of Immigration," in *The Politics of Australian Immigration*, ed. James Jupp and Marie Kabala (Canberra: Australian Government Publishing Service, 1993), 64.
7. Commonwealth of Australia, *People of Australia*, 3–8.
8. Ibid. Australia and New Zealand tout a "Trans-Tasman" relationship whereby, with wrinkles over time, they waive border control, taxation, and work permit requirements for one another's citizens.
9. Stuart Harris, "Immigration and Australian Foreign Policy," in *The Politics of Australian Immigration*, ed. James Jupp and Marie Kabala (Canberra: Australian Government Publishing Service, 1993), 26; Jeremy Bruer and John Power, "The Changing Role of the Department of Immigration," in *The Politics of Australian Immigration*, ed. James Jupp and Marie Kabala (Canberra: Australian Government Publishing Service, 1993), 111; John Warhurst, "The Growth Lobby and Its Opponents: Business, Unions, Environmentalists and Other Interest Groups," in *The Politics of Australian Immigration*, ed. James Jupp and Marie Kabala (Canberra: Australian Government Publishing Service, 1993), 196–99.
10. Tavan, *The Long, Slow Death*, 199.
11. Ibid, 202.
12. Ibid, 200.
13. He was lionized by the Spanish community and became the object of many adulatory articles in the *El Español en Australia* newspaper. For example: Ibid, April 25, 1973, 1; Ibid, June 13, 1973, 1; Ibid, November 7, 1973, 4. By January of 1974, Grassby had issued a blanket amnesty for all illegal aliens in Australia (Ibid, January 30, 1974, 1. When the political opposition lambasted him for doing so, the newspaper equated Grassby to Raffaello Carboni, the hero of the Eureka Stockade rebellion (Ibid, February 6, 1974, 4). When, in June, Grassby declared that "You do not build a nation with fears," the newspaper gave his pronouncement headline treatment (Ibid, June 12, 1974, 1). In November, the Spanish organ canonized Grassby as "a humanist more than politician" in a major feature article (Ibid, November 6, 1974), 11.
14. Tavan, *The Long, Slow Death*, 201–2.
15. Ibid.
16. Ibid, 200.
17. Ibid, 205; Michelle Grattan, "Immigration and the Australian Labour Party," in *The Politics of Australian Immigration*, ed. James Jupp and Marie Kabala (Canberra: Australian Government Publishing Service, 1993), 130–31.
18. Tavan, *The Long, Slow Death*, 203.
19. Geoffrey Blainey, *All for Australia* (North Ryde, New South Wales: Methuen Haynes, 1984).
20. Kabala, "Immigration," 16–18.
21. Tavan, *The Long, Slow Death*, 218–33.
22. Price, "Ethnic Character," passim. According to Price, an analysis of the birthplaces of all 14,694,861 Australians in 1981, projected over past generations as well, reflects 10,553,997 persons of British origin. Italians, with 603,241 persons, occupy second

place followed closely by Germans with 578,898. The next largest category of Europeans is Greeks with 298,088.
23. Commonwealth of Australia, *People of Australia*, 5; 57.
24. Commonwealth of Australia, Department of Immigration and Border Protection, *The People of Queensland: Statistics from the 2011 Census* (Brisbane: The Queensland Government, 2014), 132. [*People of Queensland*].
25. Commonwealth of Australia, *People of Australia*, 7; 60.
26. García, *Operación*, 80.
27. Commonwealth of Australia, *People of Australia*, 55; 56. One might posit that this also reflects the greater tendency by then of Catalans to identify as "Spaniards" than was the case of Basques.
28. Commonwealth of Australia, Department of Immigration and Border Protection, *People of Queensland*, 93.

CHAPTER 11

Voices

To this point, our narrative has depended upon secondary sources and documentary evidence (newspapers and government records primarily). We may now shift the approach to personal stories.

In the course of my research, I interviewed more than one hundred individuals, many of whom I taped. I also applied lengthy questionnaires (a couple of hundred queries) to approximately twenty-five North Queensland Basques (and their spouses) and twenty-five to Basques residing elsewhere in Australia (mainly Sydney and Melbourne, but also in Griffith/Yenda and the logging districts of Victoria and South Australia). The questionnaires and field notes date from the year 1980. Shortly thereafter, my research assistant, Iban Bilbao, interviewed for me another twenty-five Basques in the Basque Country who had returned to their homeland after a sojourn in Australia. It is impractical to reproduce all of this testamentary evidence; not to mention that many of their accounts have much in common. In what follows, I present the life stories of particularly exemplary individuals, on the one hand, and a few extraordinary ones, on the other. In this chapter, I have divided them into clusters predicated by the respondent's residence at the time of the interview.[1] Chapter 1 presented my experiences and impressions gleaned from a return visit in 2002 and the Coda updates them in 2018. We also have several published accounts of the lives of individual Basque Australians. In this regard there has been an impressive initiative to tell the life stories of women. All are far more sensitive to the women's lot than was I in my earlier book (Douglass, *Azúcar Amargo*, page 430).[2]

Hinchinbrook

John Mendiolea*#& —We were four brothers, Rufino, Aniceto, Antonio, and me, and one sister, Dolores. My father, Tomás Mendiolea, had been in America for twelve years before he went back to Murélaga [Aulesti] and married my mother. They lived in a *baserri* in Zubero and everyone in the family began to die of tuberculosis. When my maternal aunt passed away there, the doctor told my mother that she wasn't going to last long if she stayed in the Basque Country. He told her to emigrate. She asked if he meant America, and the answer was that America was too wet and cold. He recommended Australia. So, when Rufino was four, Antonio was two, and she was carrying Aniceto, she left for Australia. They barely knew anyone. There was maybe one man from Aulesti already here. My father had savings from America and paid the passages of three men from Murélaga who came out with them to Australia.

They met on board the ship a Spaniard named Mariano Camarero who had been to Australia before. They all got off in Townsville and he told them there were a few Spaniards, Basques, in Ingham. Pascual Badiola and his brother had been here for about a year. Aniceto Menchaca, Mrs. Iraegui's brother, was here. The Balanzateguis were in Innisfail at the time.

This farm is 320 acres; that makes it a fairly big one. Our peak is 7,600 tons. That is how much cane we are authorized to send to the mill. We could produce more than that by using intensive methods, more fertilizer, for instance. But we don't because we can't be certain that our mill, Victoria, would take the additional cane. The worth of a farm is determined by its sugar peak more than by acreage.

My brother, Aniceto, and I are fifty-fifty partners now and we run it together. Most of the year we don't work too hard. The three weeks of planting is our busiest time and we put in full days. But the rest of the year we might have leisurely coffee at 6 a.m., go to the paddocks for three or four hours, come home for lunch and a siesta until mid-afternoon, and then a couple of more hours in the fields.

Our family leased this farm in 1946. Before that, my parents had a farm in Longpocket. They came to Australia in 1925 and my father cut cane for a while. They then put in a boardinghouse in town for a couple of years. About 1929, they leased the farm in Longpocket from a man named McQueen, it had about a 1,300-tons peak. I was born there. We had that place for three years. Its cane looked great at first, but as the season progressed it was attacked by a disease and we might cut only 800 tons.

So, my parents left that farm and they leased a very good property close to this one. They were there for thirteen years (1933–1946). The owner was named Nielsen and he had a brick-works in town—plenty to do without dealing with farming too. He had this farm and another, and his two boys didn't want to work them. So, he had had several tenants before we leased this one. Three or four Spaniards working together leased it for a while before us. One of them was a Basque-surnamed Urigüen. One bloke would work the farm while the rest worked cane. After the first man paid off his farm, they would lease another and repeat the process until they all had one.

We did very well on that Nielsen property. We had good years and made good money. Even during the war years, we did fine. There wasn't much cane grown then, and we had to cut our own.

During the war, my father and Aniceto joined a cane-cutting gang. Ceto was only seventeen at the time. When they got their first pay, my father went to the ganger and asked why his son was given wages rather than a full share like everyone else? The answer was, "he's just a boy." Father replied that Ceto cut cane as well as anyone else and that maybe he lagged behind when it came to loading it. But Father was a champion loader. He had been a competitive stone-lifter in Spain before he came here. So, he said, "Listen, I load way faster than anyone else here, so I more than make up for Ceto. He gets a full share or I'm going to cut off your dicks." Next day Ceto had his money.

By then, we were three brothers working together, since, in 1939, Rufino leased a farm near here with his partner, Santos Alberdi, a Basque from Markina. Alberdi was hard to get along with. He had to be the boss in everything, even though he couldn't drive a tractor. My brother was the only one who got along with him, because he never talked back.

My mother used to have a big garden and raised chickens. She sold that produce in town. She worked very hard and earned quite a bit. She barely had to ask my father for anything out of the sugar proceeds to pay household expenses. That was mostly on her.

My father died in 1950. In 1948, my parents went to Spain for a holiday with my eldest brother Rufino and my sister Dolores. Aniceto, Antonio, and I stayed here to run the farm. Father had been suffering for years; he had terrible pains in his stomach. When he got back from Europe, he went to an American chiropractor in Tully. He had a good reputation and he was recommended by a Spaniard [Basque] surnamed Muguira from Ayr. That doctor put my father on a strict diet for twenty-one days to clean out his system. Every day he was supposed to drink a glass of water and then vomit it up. My father couldn't do that part; he would choke. But after the treatment he felt much better. He was running up and down the Tully beach. But then Father died from a coronary occlusion. My mother felt he choked to death.

When we leased this farm, the former renter wasn't well. He was hurt in an accident when a piece of his machinery fell into the creek. He was on his own and couldn't keep up. It was right after the war, so he couldn't find any laborers. Rufino and his partner worked a couple of paddocks for the man, and my father and we three brothers farmed a couple of others. We were getting to a stage where all of us boys were old enough to farm. We were a growing family. So, we started to inquire into buying a farm in Macknade. The owner of this one, an Italian, Camillo Zavattaro,³ heard about it and asked why we hadn't talked to him first? We said that it was our understanding that he wouldn't sell and he denied that.

We entered into an agreement and drew up the papers to buy this farm. We were supposed to pay £18,000 down. My parents went to the notary office in town to complete the purchase. The officer was Miren Balanzategui and she told them to wait while she conferred with the seller. And then it turned out that his finances made it impossible to sell. He owed taxes on the previous year's crop and other things to the point that most of the down payment would go for income taxes. So, he came out and said that he would lease us the farm for the coming year and sell it to us in the next tax cycle—or about Christmas time. But then that came around and he still had a tax problem. He couldn't clean all of that up in one year. So, he offered to lease the property to us for seven years. We insisted on fifteen and Zavattaro and his wife finally agreed to that. Some people told us that they were being duplicitous, but they weren't. Many Italians were after them to sell, but they refused. "Where were you when we needed you? The Spaniards stepped up."

In 1949, the Zavattaros wanted to sell both this farm and the Hinchinbrook Hotel that they owned in town and move to Brisbane. They intended to buy a hotel there. That purchase was in escrow. My parents were still in Spain, so they came to me, Antonio, and Aniceto. But we couldn't put the money together, and, by the time my parents came back, the hotel in Brisbane was gone.

The Zavattaros came to us again in 1955; we still had a few years to go on the lease. The word around town was that they wanted about £80,000, and we just sat on our hands. Then their agent came to us and said that the price was £55,000. We thought that was fair and agreed. Every price that the Zavattaros ever proposed to us was fair. When we first leased the place there were twenty-three horses on it and two tractors. I have never done business with a finer person than Camillo. He was always true to his word. We four brothers bought the farm. By then, Rufino had dissolved his partnership with Alberdi.

In the early 1950s, there was a real shortage of canecutters. We sponsored several men to come out from Spain—maybe thirty or forty. We met their train when they got to town, and we would take them to Duffy's store to buy proper clothing for cane cutting. Then it was off to the Royal Hotel for a welcoming drink. They came home with us and stopped off for maybe a week or two until they had work. If a man arrived in January, he might have to stay in our barrack until May or June when the gangs were formed. A Mr. Livingston was chairman of the local Canegrowers' Board, and, one day at our kitchen table, he asked us, "Why don't they [the Australian government] bring out Basque immigrants?" He started to make inquiries through the Immigration Department and that's how it all started. We said that we could help by finding candidates.

Before and after the formal recruitments, we brought a lot of men out, or signed sponsorship papers. An immigrant might come to us and say that his brother wanted to join him, but they needed an Australian sponsor to get approval. You had to promise them employment. But we really only had to pick them up, usually in Townsville, and bring them back here. We signed a lot of those letters. We were involved in bringing out more than a hundred men.

My mother's system was to pay for a man's passage, send him some pocket money for the trip, and then arrange to have someone meet him on his arrival. We then took him to town to buy his clothing. We advanced him £20 to buy his gear and added £7 as a fee for the costs of processing his papers, the seals on them, etc. So, he might owe £375 in all. Every Saturday there would be a line of men coming to pay Mother back. Most managed to liquidate their debt in three or four months. Most showed up with their first paycheck and she would always say, "Send it to your mother so she will know that you are well and employed here. There's no hurry in paying me back."

I remember one time that seven men arrived at the very end of the season and had no work. Mother knew the cane inspector well and got him to arrange employment for them on the tramline that CSR was repairing in Abergowrie. They knew no English, so I spent a couple of weeks with them as interpreter.

There were also a few cases of men jumping ship and going to cut cane. In 1952, the vessel *Ardaiz* landed in Lucinda and a man from Pedernales [Sukarrieta] jumped ship here. Then, in Bowen, another four jumped off—all Basques. They ended up cutting cane around Ayr. Later, a second ship reached Cairns and another two Spaniards jumped off.

My mother knew that the two who settled in here were illegals and kept her distance from them. Everyone knew what they were. Then, someone denounced them to the police and they were rounded up in Stone River and put in jail in Ingham. We took them some food and wine. They had to go through the formalities of a legal hearing. Nothing much came of it. We signed a letter assuming responsibility for them and they were alright.

Last year a bloke came to me and asked if I could fix his papers. He was in trouble with the Franco government and decided to get out. He got a tourist visa and came here but didn't leave. I discussed his situation with Cris Dall'Osto, the local Italian consul who is kind of our ambassador, but there was nothing to be done. He just had to keep hiding until they changed the immigration law, or they caught up with him and deported him.

In about 1975, brother Rufino sold me his one-third interest in the farm for A$60,000 down and then A$10,000 a year for five years. He and his wife moved to the Basque Country and bought a place in her hometown of Lekeitio, planning to stay. But the cost of living there was going up sharply, so, in 1980, they returned to Ingham. It is unclear what they will do here, but they will have to decide on something, because life is getting more expensive here as well. My wife, Conchi, had an apartment in Lekeitio that she sold recently for A$48,000 in order to pay down our debt here.

The total farm peaks of a person's individual holdings are one amount, and then you have your mill peak that is assigned by the sugar board. It determines how much sugar you can send to the mill. It is based on the history of your production. When there is an expansion, the mill is given more peak that it divides among its suppliers—those who have a history of meeting their peak. We have always been part of Victoria Mill. We can only sell to it. We could not supply Macknade even if we wanted to.

The past couple of years [late 1970s] there has been a surplus on the world sugar market. We were only allowed to sell so much. So, we carried over some sugar hoping for a better year. But that doesn't work out well. The sugar content goes down in the mature cane and there can be rain damage. Cane falls down and rots if there is too much rain, and you start getting suckers taking over. It also disrupts your rotation system. So, you can carry cane over or plow it under. These past two years we have had thirty acres of cane that the mill would not accept. We just plowed under 21 acres and carried over nine. It was all part of our rotation. We normally replace our cane every four years. We are allowed to harvest 85 percent of our net-acreage. The other fifteen is fallowed. So, we knocked down the most mature cane, chopped it up with a grass thrasher, and plowed it under. That old cane is hard to get rid of. It doesn't rot easily.

I have maybe fifteen or sixteen paddocks. There are different sizes. We fallow about 65 acres every year. Once the cane is harvested you plow the stubble under. It all depends on the weather. Some farmers harvest their fallow field at the beginning and others at the end. I like to wait until toward the end to get the highest return off the taller cane, but if it starts raining early that is a mistake. It becomes very difficult to burn a wet field and harvest its cane properly. Once the fallow field is clear, you might plant beans as a legume crop to improve the soil. Sometimes we do and others we don't, depending on the rest of the workload at the time. If you planted beans, maybe in January you knock them about with a rotary hoe. You don't want them to flower. You hope there isn't too much rain, as you want the paddock pretty dry to be able to work it correctly. So, you use a disk harrow and then plow under either the grass or beans. You cross rip the ground with a disk harrow until the old vegetation is plowed under and the soil is fine.

So, then you plant your cane in late spring. You might go to the Government Experimental Station and ask for "sticks" of some new variety that you would like to test. Maybe two hundred, and they just give them to you. You can also buy sticks of the varieties that you prefer. It takes two to two and a half tons of cane per acre to replant cane. Sometimes we use our own cane that we cut for planting. You take that to the mill, and they boil it to kill off the diseases that occur around here. You use that clean cane to replant next year. The oldest cane they use is two years old—or three at the most. Any older than that, it becomes hard to treat for disease. Some diseases are spread by the harvester. So, they should sterilize the blades whenever they change paddocks, but oftentimes they don't. Some of the disease cuts down yield from maybe thirty tons to the acre to twenty.

[Johnny's wife, Conchi, commented on the sad history of Pedro Martín Urizar. He is a bachelor and an alcoholic. He left Spain because he had a drinking problem there after his fiancée dumped him for another man. He worked as a canecutter in Ingham and sent back money to his parents in Spain for safekeeping, and with it the father bought an apartment that he put in his name only. Conchi noted that Pedro is not the only immigrant to have that disappointing experience.

Pedro then worked all over Australia in construction, particularly in Western Australia. He had not been back here for years. Then Johnny heard that Pedro was staying in a local hotel and went there and brought him here to live. They gave him work around the farm.

One night, I attended a farewell party at the Mendioleas for Gino, the North Italian former owner of the Trebonne Hotel, and his wife. They were moving permanently to Lekeitio—her hometown.

Former Shire Chairman, Sicilian Sam Cavallaro, and his wife, Pearl, were in attendance. Pearl told me as an aside that Sam was working in an accouting firm and his boss decided to sell. Sam wanted to buy it but didn't have the money. Teresa Mendiolea lent it to him without asking for security. Cris Dall'Osto later told me that Sam, his partner, was the Mendioleas' accountant and that he arranged for the fare payments and money transfers of all of the immigrants sponsored by Teresa and her sons.]

José María Aguirre * # & —I was born in Morga and we moved to Muxika when I was eight. My father was a farmer. I helped him on the farm. When I was sixteen, I went to work in an arms factory in Gernika. I was just a kid and they paid me little—25 *pesetas* a week. Before I turned eighteen, I told Father that I wanted to go to Australia. I had a brother already there, and I believed that it would give me more opportunity than working in Gernika. My father was a little disappointed. I think he was counting on me to take over the farm one day. All he said was, "In Australia, too, the dogs go about barefooted." He meant that there had to be people struggling to make a living there, too. My brother sent me a ticket and Father gave me £25 for pocket money.

So, off I flew by myself in November of 1958. I arrived in Sydney not knowing anyone. I had a pocket dictionary to help with a few English expressions. My ticket was good to Townsville and I managed to get on a flight that arrived in the evening. I had sent a telegram to my brother and expected him to meet me. It went to the farm where he cut cane, and it was now slack season for him. Eight days earlier he had left. With my dictionary, I communicated with an Australian at the airport. He took me into Townsville and got me a room for the night. The next day I boarded a train to Ingham.

There was absolutely no one to meet me. By then, everyone knew that there were Spaniards turning up regularly, so someone in the station led me to the Victoria Hotel. He told me that there would be Spaniards there. In the hotel, I ran into a Basque who told me that my brother had left a few days earlier for Mareeba to pick tobacco. There was no work in Ingham, so, two days later, I took the train to Mareeba. I found employment with an Italian there. We talked a little in English, a little in Spanish, and a little in Italian. I had never left the farm before, so, I didn't know languages, but I had my dictionary and I picked up a few words of Italian as I went along. So, now I had a job picking tobacco.

I ran into a few Basques in town. A couple of them knew my brother. He had telegraphed my family asking why I hadn't shown up? He thought maybe I had run into some last-minute delays in obtaining my travel documents. Father's reply had gone to the sugar farm in Ingham and they didn't know how to reach him in the Atherton. So, it was still sitting there. I didn't see my brother for six weeks after I arrived in Mareeba. By then, of course, we were working on different farms.

He had been cutting cane in Australia for a year and was a ganger. They were now veterans and he told me that I should join a gang of newcomers. It would be too hard for me to cut with veterans; I would lag behind. "You won't have to kill yourself as much."

So, six of us newcomers formed our gang. My brother arrived in 1957 by ship and I came on my own by plane before the second boat of recruited immigrants arrived in 1959 in time for that season. I joined a gang with five of those newcomers—all from Muxika. My brother set it up. All of them returned home after cutting seven or eight years and are all in Gernika now [1980].

The first year, I cried every night. I wasn't even eighteen yet and was still growing. The others were older. I did fine with the loading up to eight or ten tons a day. To that point, no one was better than I. But, after that, I didn't have the strength to keep up and we needed to do at least twelve. By the end of the day, I was worn out. My hands were blistered and bleeding, and many evenings I was too sore to even shower or eat. The soap burned my hands. One night my brother visited me and soaked my hands with vinegar to toughen them up. Eventually, your hands become hard as cement. You could stick a needle in them and you wouldn't feel any pain. The first six or seven weeks were awful, but then I hit my stride. That first year I made £600.

After the second season, I went back to Mareeba to the tobacco. I picked in Mareeba for nine years in all. It was hard work, but compared to cutting cane, it was a holiday. Tobacco required its study. You needed to learn how to distinguish the different grades as you filled your sack. Maybe it would weigh fifty pounds by the time that you started a new one. That weight was nothing compared to cane loading. In tobacco, at that time, we earned £15 per week and most places gave you your keep. After my first year, I understood tobacco well enough to work on contract. To do that you had to know how to grade the leaves according to their texture and color. There are various categories, and you need to separate the leaves properly or the buyers might reject the bundle. We were paid on contract—one shilling per pound. The farmer had to have confidence in your grading ability. The first year on contract I might have picked only five or six pounds a day, but then I got better at it and so did the money.

After I picked tobacco the first year, I returned to Ingham and planted sugar cane for a few weeks before the cutting season began. They paid us £1 per chopped ton that we planted. It wasn't bad money, and then it went up to 25 shillings a ton. You could earn £5 or £6 a day. It was also a good way to get your body and hands hardened for the cutting season.

The second year, my brother asked me to cut with him. By then, he was twenty-seven and I was eighteen. He had me work with him so we could keep the same pace together. That year my brother and I cut with the Uriona brothers and Juan Uriarte. We were all from Muxika. Uriarte was from the *baserri* next to ours. We cut on three Italian farms along the road to Trebonne. We made good money. After that season we went together to Dimbulah to pick tobacco. It was then that I had an opportunity to plant my own crop. I had an Italian friend and we share-farmed a plot of land owned by another Italian. By the second year, the farm owner asked me to be his partner and we planted 26 acres. That year I did not go back to cane cutting.

My partner was very clever, as are many Italians. He had acquired the right to bring some bush under production, and he needed someone to clear it for him. I was due 26 percent of the profits outright, and we would then split the rest. You were supposed to sign a formal contract to that effect. I did so before a lawyer and my partner said he would the following day. I didn't look at the contract carefully when I got my copy. He hadn't signed it. Then I got a letter that I couldn't understand. The crop was now about three-quarters grown, and he didn't need me any longer. My partner was throwing me out.[4]

There was an Australian bank manager who was good to me and pointed out what my partner was trying to do. He explained that to me slowly in English. I understood him. I have always jumped right in when it comes to the language, whether I speak well or not. I am not shy. He sent me to a local agent who spoke some Spanish, even though she was Italian. She got me an attorney that forced my partner to sign the contract. He made it clear to the Italian that we could prove that I had my rights even if he hadn't signed the document.

My partner wasn't happy, but he had no choice other than to take me back. We harvested that crop together without ever exchanging a single word. We worked in total silence and it was very unpleasant. It turned out well enough, since, that year, I made £8,000 in the tobacco. Of course, it was very uncomfortable. I would go to see my brother and just sit and mope. He told me that I had to get out, because it was ruining my life. He wanted me to go back to cane cutting, but I thought of looking for another business. I was unsuccessful in that, so I joined my brother's gang. There were five of us, all Basques.

Before, the difference between a good cane gang and a poor one was the number of cutters needed. The mill might send the same number of bins per day to both, but the good gang would figure out how to work with one fewer cutter. If things were going well, it might send a member to pick tobacco earlier than the slower gang. So, if they were all friends, the tobacco salary would be added to the gang's sugar money, and then all was split in equal shares.

Our gang agreed before the start of the year that, if anyone was hurt and couldn't work, he would still get a full share. One year, a guy in our gang spent thirteen weeks in the hospital and we supported him. There were times when someone was laid up for, say, three weeks, and he did the domestic chores while the rest of us worked harder to make up for him in the cutting. We all got along well. Some of the Italian gangs just threw out the weakest cutter;[5] we Basques were better at working together. As we veterans improved, we would send someone to tobacco early this year and then the next we would try to find an additional contract with another farmer, and that way cut a little more cane. Our gang worked together better than any other here. We always got along. My brother was the ganger and we were all from Muxika. Our gang cut for two Italian farmers and two Anglo ones.

By law, you could only work between 6 a.m. and 6 p.m. Most of us actually put in more hours than that. The loading was the hardest part. You were expected to cut and load twenty tons a day. In good cane you could finish the week's quota in four or four and a half days. We bought our own food, and cooked and cleaned for ourselves. We ordered our supplies once a week, and they were delivered by the store to the barrack. The fourth year we hired a woman to cook and clean for us. Otherwise you had to send someone from the paddock a half hour before each meal to cook it. Life was a lot easier when you didn't have that bother, and there was someone to do the housecleaning and laundry. You never felt like doing those chores after cane cutting from dawn to dusk.

After a few years, we bought a mechanical cane loader for £1,800. We would cut in the morning and used our loader in the afternoon once the cane was dry. If you loaded in the morning, while the cane was still wet, you had to do it manually. But that loader helped a lot. It made us more efficient and the work was easier. When it started raining and the soil was soaked (about eight weeks out of the season), the farmers made us load by hand. Our machine would damage their field.

The second year we had the loader we got a contract just doing haul-out for other growers, and I would go there with the machine and do that while the rest of our gang cut for our farmers. So, we were expanding and earning more. The fourth year, we invested in a trailer to haul out cane instead of having to lay rails for the tram system. That was even more efficient, so we were progressing. We stayed together for nine years in all. During maybe seven slack seasons I picked tobacco in Mareeba.

Saturdays and Sundays, we went to town to the pubs. That was our only real expense. We didn't know the language and we pretty much stayed to ourselves—no girls. So, we saved our money. My first year, I ended up with £1,500. In three years, at that rate, I could have bought an apartment in Gernika.

I was interested in welding, and there was an experienced Aussie welder here who let me hang out with him in the slack. I became a good enough welder to look for slack-season work as a rigger. It was about 1966 that I worked in Gladstone for four months as a rigger in a nickel refinery with two Basques and three Spaniards. We lived in the Company's barracks. Another time, I went to Townsville and worked for the Honeybrook Electrical Company for five months, installing steel posts for powerlines.

Maybe in 1966, my brother and I made a trip to Spain. Then, in 1967, I went South in the slack with seven friends, all Basques. We took four cars, two in each. We didn't work much. We were tired and wanted to see more of Australia. One of them is married now and lives in Griffith. I was curious about life here in Australia other than in North Queensland. I wanted to see if I could buy a farm somewhere else.

First, we went to Sydney for four days. We were in the *Gure Txoko* and the *Club Español*, but I didn't like the atmosphere there. In the Spanish Club, they saw us as cash-flush cutters from Queensland and came to us every day asking for money for this or that. I asked questions about the cost and conditions of living in Sydney and wasn't impressed with the answers. I was happy to leave.

So, we went to Griffith and found work picking fruit. We did that for a little while and then went to Melbourne. We were in the Basque Club there. I didn't know anyone, but I liked Melbourne better than Sydney. Not the city itself, but the surroundings. If things had worked out differently, I might have bought a hundred acres there and grown vegetables.

We went on to Adelaide without knowing anyone. We didn't meet a single Spaniard and were there for three weeks. We picked grapes for a while outside the city. It was actually a little tough, since we hadn't worked for eight or nine weeks and were out of shape. The first four or five days were hard. That was the year that Australia changed from the pound sterling currency to the dollar, and we made about A$500 each picking grapes.

While I was in South Australia, I received a telegram from home saying that my father was gravely ill. One of my friends drove me to Sydney, and I had a plane ticket to fly to Spain the next day. I went to the Spanish Club and asked for help in getting my passport stamped and cleared for the trip, and they didn't assist me at all. They declared it to be impossible in such a short time. I went to an Australian agency; all I needed was a stamp in my passport. The agent declared it to be an emergency and I was on the plane the next day. I went to Spain and stayed for thirteen months—during which time Father died.

I returned to Queensland and I went into partners with Ciriaco Lejarcegui in a truck for hauling out cane. We did that for two years. It didn't pay as well as cane cutting. I didn't have the money to buy my own truck, and splitting the income was a dead end without a future. So, that slack season of 1970, I had an opportunity to buy a backhoe for A$12,000. I had a trial period of six weeks learning how to run it before finalizing the purchase. The owner just paid the gasoline and my keep while I worked on his jobs. I took it to Mount Fox and it might have been a good opportunity, but it began to rain the second day and the project was shut down. I went back to Ingham and gave the machine back to the owner. I didn't buy it. I went to Greenvale and worked in a nickel mine. There were several Basques working there at that time.

After two months, I went back to Ingham and bought a harvester along with José Luis Echeandia from Ereño. He lives in Ayr today. He had another harvester with his brother-in-law, Iñaki, who is now in Spain. I had a chance to buy a used machine; one not in very good condition but it came with the owner's cutting contract. The contract was good even if the machine wasn't. So, José Luis agreed to buy in with me. We paid A$23,000.

We were partners for five years. He got married and moved to Ayr. We never had a problem; but he left, so I bought him out. Almost all of our employees were Anglos. By that time, there was no new immigration and almost all of the Basques here had their own businesses. So, you had to hire Aussies. I stayed in business by myself with that machine. Then, two years ago, I bought a new one.

To make a good living with a harvester, you have to know something about mechanics. You can't afford to lose time with breakdowns and paying specialists to make your repairs. The harvesters are temperamental. I have a relationship with an Asturian who has a harvester. If one of us breaks down, the other tries to cover by cutting after hours, and helps with the repairs as well. If your motor goes out, you will be down for three or four days waiting for a new one to be delivered and then installing it. Some pay someone to cover for them in a pinch, but I have never had to do that.

Many people have gone broke with a harvester. I know three Australians who have done so recently. The competition is keen and there are always salaried guys willing to pool their money and buy a harvester, if they can get cutting contracts. They may try to underbid you with some or all of your farmers. Then, too, some farmers get their own harvester. Maybe two or three of them go together to do that. If there are sons to help it makes sense; if they have to contract for loaders, it is tougher. A group of six farmers lost A$5,000 each last year on a harvester because they had a falling out. A farmer with his own equipment gets a tax break when he purchases it.

To own a successful harvesting business, you have to be a mechanic. I have to service the machine daily, changing out all the cutting blades. The bushings have to be greased every other day as well. I spend all of every Saturday on maintenance, changing the belts, etc. You replace the six gallons of oil once a week and all of the air filters every four weeks. Chain lasts about 40,000 tons; but only half that in sandy soil because of the abrasion. It costs over A$8 per foot and the harvester has more than a hundred feet of chain. The hydraulic system has 48 gallons of oil that needs to be changed frequently. All of the gaskets have to be replaced every season. During the past year, I spent A$5,000 on spare parts alone; I can't afford to pay a mechanic on top of that and must do most of my own work. I only pay a specialist to service the hydraulics. At the end of the season, I spend a few weeks essentially rebuilding my equipment. You have to treat your harvester better than your mistress!

The costs of everything keep going up. I paid A$64,000 two years ago for my new harvester. Last year it would have cost A$74,000, and, today, it is worth A$103,000. It has become a so-so proposition to buy a harvester and everything else you need as a start-up harvesting business.

I have ten farmers that I cut for. I do everything—burn the cane, cut it, and do the haul-out. About two weeks before the season, we always have a tough negotiation. We had a harvesters' association for a very short time, a year or two. But none of the havesters want to work on salary. We all prefer contracts, and that potentially places us in competition with one another. The Sugar Cane Board, which is controlled by the farmers, determines the minimum price per ton to be paid each season for harvesting. You can then insist on more, and it is between you and your farmers to agree or not.

So, a couple of years ago our association set a higher price. The farmers refused to pay it and we delayed the start of harvesting. But then a couple of our members broke ranks and we all had to go back to work. That "strike" failed completely; the association was dead. So the farmers hold the power and are very tight, particularly the Italians. They will brag to you about how they saved A$20,000 in taxes by expensing something, and then fight to the end to keep from paying you five cents more a ton (that could also be expensed on their taxes).

I quoted this year a price of between A$3.75 and A$3.90 a ton to my farmers. For that I do everything. The contract might be for five years, but the specific rate is negotiated annually according to market conditions. I get along with my farmers pretty well; I have had the same ten for twelve years now. You have to be careful to treat them equally. You might cut 5 percent of one farmer's cane before moving on, and then no more of his until you have harvested 5 percent of everyone else's. The harvester travels at more than twenty miles an hour on the highway, so moving around isn't a problem.

Then there are the cane inspectors. Thank God for them. They come to the paddock every day. It is they who adjudicate if the harvester and farmer disagree over whether a premium should be paid for harvesting snarled cane or in wet conditions. The inspectors make sure that the cane being loaded is clean (few weeds and roughage). The farmer is paid by weight. If the cane is "dirty," the mill can reject it and fine the operation as well. In such a case, I am liable for 25 percent of the fine and the farmer pays the rest.

A harvester and the loaders for it cost about A$120,000. A harvester needs three or four men to operate it. I cut about 35,000 tons with a machine in 20 weeks. Before, a good gang of six to eight men harvested about 8,000 tons a season. So, the machine uses far less labor. I pay all the expenses. My employees put up "their two hands." I have a Basque, Frank Larragan, who has been with me for four years and an Aussie for the last two. They each drive a loader. Sometimes I have to add a third temporarily for the extra haul-out if the paddock is far from the tram. I usually drive the harvester. It is about a seven- or eight-hour day and, at the end, we burn cane for the next morning's go.

If all goes well, the money is good. I have made as much as a 50 percent profit, after expenses, in some seasons. I once grossed A$96,000. This year I paid my haul-out contractor A$19,500 for five and a half months' work. But, in a wet year you are lucky to make wages. The going is slow and very hard on your equipment.

The machines are all pretty dangerous. The harvester weighs seven-and-a-half tons and flips over easily, particularly in wet soil. Fortunately, it does so in slow-motion, so you usually have time to either jump or prepare yourself to go with it. There have been a few deaths and several injuries. The loaders turn over easily even on the highway. They are very top heavy, and you are going along at thirty miles an hour with 12 tons behind you. You are always rushing since you are on contract basis and want to make five round-trips an hour ideally.

Right now, the harvesters from Ingham are all in Ayr planting cane. They will be back here at the start of next season. We used to go somewhere down South in the slack, but not so much any more. That is over. The quality of immigrants has gone down. Most now are Spaniards. They demanded more than us. They knew their rights the first day in the country, but some never learned their obligtions.

Many Basques worked here to buy apartments in Spain. Before, in a year-and-a-half on cutters' wages you could buy a 200,000-*peseta* apartment in the Basque Country. I know a guy who bought four in Gernika and then returned there. He is still a bachelor. My brother went back to Europe with A$10,000 and he bought an apartment in Gernika that cost him about 500,000 *pesetas*. He and our cousin purchased a truck for a million-and-a-half *pesetas* for transporting freight. He didn't have enough money for all that, so I loaned him A$12,000. A year later he wrote and said everything was going great and he bought another truck. Together they now have six.

He wrote recently and said I should go back and be their partner. I replied that both he and our cousin are married, but I am a bachelor. We would be too many partners; maybe with different opinions. Not good. I could end up working in a factory there, and I am too used to my freedom now to adjust to that. In Australia, I am my own man.

Three years ago, I built my own house during the slack. I am still a bachelor and I have two stories. I live upstairs and my mate, Sancho Lamiquiz, lives downstairs. Sancho did all the interior finishing in his unit.

I wanted to learn how to be the manager of a hotel. The owner of the Belvedere in Ingham gave me my keep and a little bit of cash. I have been there for the last three slacks. I now qualify for my license, and they want me to sell the harvester and take over the hotel. But I am not convinced. I wouldn't mind having my own hotel one day, but to sell my business and work for someone else is not appealing. They pay me good money, A$300 a week. That work does bother me sometimes, for instance, when some drunk calls me a "Bloody Wog." Still, if I didn't have my own business, I would probably accept their job offer. But, if I work hard in my business, it is security. If I sell it and go to work for someone, and then lose that job for whatever reason, I will have nothing. I am back to square one. That is my fear. But one day I might own my own hotel; maybe two years from now when I turn forty.

In the slack season of 1977, I didn't feel well and took the whole time off for holidays. I went to the Gold Coast for three weeks. I then visited the tobacco district in Texas just to look around. There were opportunities there if one had money. I then went to the North Coast around Cairns. There were things you could do there, too, if you were married. But, a bachelor like me…? In a lot of businesses, you need a wife to help you. There is opportunity there; I had A$25,000 cash in hand and could have raised maybe fifteen more. You could do a lot with that. But marrying an Australian? Bringing a Spanish woman here? I don't know about that.

Anyway, that trip kind of opened my eyes. I decided to build this house and settle down here. I pretty much constructed it myself, helped by several friends. I used a borrowed backhoe to dig the foundation and a farmer let me use his truck to carry sand for cement. I paid for the gasoline and then cut cane for him for a week in return. So, with other friends helping as well, this house cost me very little. An Italian cabinetmaker did my kitchen. He didn't charge me anything. He has a sugar farm as well where I have cut cane for him for nearly ten years. He lets me park my harvester in his barn and doesn't charge me a thing. Then I put Sancho downstairs as my companion. He was helping me a lot and eating his meals with me, and I decided he might as well live here as well and share the expenses. He was about to turn fifty. Until then, I had always lived in cane barracks.

I hope to go back to Spain next Christmas for a visit, but, to tell the truth, I don't think I'll stay. I am better off here in this country. And if I return, I would like to move south here in Australia. I want to try something new. I want to spend six months in Brisbane working in a hotel. I want to learn how to do the books and to mix fancy drinks. Here it is all whiskey; nothing complicated. So, I am not a real bartender yet. I want to learn to be one and I have to go to Brisbane for that.

I have a girlfriend here who works with me in the hotel, and we are thinking of going south together. I think I should have about A$150,000 in hand before making that move. We wouldn't be partners; she would work for me. She is experienced and once had a chance to lease a hotel here from a large company. She wanted me as her partner, but I declined because I didn't know enough about the business at that time. I would have been too subordinated to her. Now I am no longer afraid, because I know something about all aspects of the hotel business. But the truth is that I can make a reasonable living if I just stay with my harvester.

Félix Jayo * # & —I was born in 1930 in Aulesti, Bizkaia, and attended school there for four or five years. My parents were from there and Father herded sheep for six years in the USA before returning to his *baserri*. Mother worked as a domestic servant in Bilbo for two years.

I immigrated here in 1949. I wanted to avoid military service and Teresa Mendiolea, my mother's first cousin, was on a visit and offered to help me. She arranged my papers and advanced me my passage. My parents were happy about my decision.

Four cousins and I set out from Aulesti to catch the boat to Australia. We were headed for Genoa, but we confused it for Geneva and ended up in Switzerland. We were turned back at the Swiss border. I sailed from Genoa to Sydney and spent forty-eight days at sea. I was traveling as well with my uncle, José Urigüen, my mother's brother. He first came to Australia in the 1920s, was a canefarmer in Ingham, and knew English. Johnny Mendiolea met our boat and put us on a train to Ingham. I was impressed by the size of the country. There were adjustments to make. I had my first meal without wine.

We arrived in February and I liked Ingham. I lived with the Mendioleas and my first job was planting cane for them. I then cut their cane that first season. Our gang included Jesús Gárate from Markina, Saturnino Achurra from Amoroto, Cornelio Careaga and Juan Unamuno (my first cousin) both from Aulesti, my brother José María, and Sol Morales, an Andalusian. Jesús was our ganger.

That first slack, I went to Ayr to work as a busboy in a café leased by Morales. I returned to Ingham to plant cane before the next harvest. I was the ganger and we cut for the Mendioleas and some other farmers. My men included Juan Unamuno, Ignacio Malaxechevarria from Aulesti, Juan Azpiri from Lekeitio, and an Italian and his wife (our cook). We were a very efficient gang and we were able to get extra work towards the end of the harvest on farms that were lagging.

That slack season, we went to Mount Fox to cut timber for railroad sleepers for Victoria Mill. I went there with Unamuno, Malaxechevarria, and Azpiri. I bought my first vehicle in 1952, a Leyland truck. My aunt, Teresa Mendiolea, found us work that slack, cutting sleepers for Victoria Mill in Mount Fox. We did that for the next two years and cut cane in Ingham during the harvest season. We went to Abergowrie. There was an Italian gang that was in trouble as it was way behind schedule. Tony

Mendiolea went to the union organizer and got us that contract as their replacement. We were six in all (including two of my old gang). I was the ganger. Ganger is like being a pimp for poor prostitutes. You fielded all the flak and got nothing extra for it.

That slack, my former partners at Mount Fox, and I went to Abergowrie to cut sleepers on a contract that we bought from Gino Paris. We stayed for two years. Then, Juan Unamuno and I sold our shares to the other two partners and I purchased the bakery in Trebonne from an Australian (at the time it was leased out to an Italian). I paid £7,000 and then had many expenses as the place needed major remodeling. I own two pine stands in Aulesti that I inherited from my father. It was 1956. I went to Trebonne with Juan Unamuno and my brother, José María, and am here still.

I married María Pilar Astorquia from Aulesti in 1964. I met her on my first trip back to the Basque Country. I was there for one year and we married. I brought her back to Australia with me. Her father was deceased, and she was caring for her mother. María Pilar began working as a domestic servant at eleven years of age and had spent eight years in that capacity in Orozko, Gernika, and Bilbo. Her father's brother, Juan Astorquia, lived in Innisfail and was a canefarmer.

I know some English but would still take an interpreter along if I had to meet with a lawyer or doctor. I never attended classes here and just picked it up in the hotels and dating Australian girls. I read the *Herbert River Express* and *El Español* (every week). My wife gets womens' magazines from Spain. I used to listen to ethnic radio, but no longer. I know some English, Spanish, Basque, and Italian. I was naturalized in 1955 in order to own a business. Also, to avoid problems with the military if I visited Spain. Two years ago, we joined the International Club here. We are Catholics and attend mass almost every Sunday. At home, we use Basque exclusively. Our children still understand it.

I have a cousin, Jesús Urigüen, who came to Australia in 1958 and lives in Weipa where he works in construction. In 1963, I arranged the papers for my brother, José Luis Jayo, to immigrate here. He paid his own passage. He was here until 1968 and now lives in Bilbo where he works for Firestone. In 1964, I arranged the paperwork and advanced his passage to my brother-in-law, Félix Astorquia. In 1965, I did the same for my wife's first cousin, Alberto Idoeta from Aulesti.

I have many Australian friends, several of whom buy my bread. I also serve as the interpreter between Spanish gangs and Anglo farmers. I like to drink every Monday in the Longpocket Hotel owned by my good Aussie friend Frank. He buys my bread. I think that we Basques were more esteemed by Australians before. We had a good reputation as the best canecutters. Since the harvest was mechanized, that esteem has diminished.

Some Australians are industrious, but most are not. Most spend what they earn. I have been insulted a few times in the hotels, but nothing important. I don't really see much difference between Basques and Spaniards. But if I enter a hotel bar filled with both, I inevitably gravitate to the Basques. I like Italians. They are good people. They are my major clientele. Well, there are some who aren't too reliable. We have an uncle in Innisfail, Astorquia, but we have little to do with them as they are cold. I think it is because his wife is Catalan.

María Pilar likes Australia—the political freedom. She was naturalized in 1967. We visited the Basque Country, France, Germany, Austria, Switzerland, and Italy in 1975. We were gone for about a year. We would like to go back to the Basque Country for a visit with the children when they finish school, but only for a visit. I would not object to anyone other than an Aborigine that my child chooses to marry. A Basque would be nice, since it would help me to converse with him or her. I would not really like to see my children move permanently to the Basque Country. We have sacrificed to educate them here for an Australian future. Hopefully, one that is better than mine. They have attended the Canossan and St. Mary's private schools here in the Hinchinbrook, and Ramón went to the Mount Campbell Catholic School in Charters Towers.

It was a mistake becoming a baker. You get up in the middle of the night to bake bread and then spend all day selling it. You never get a vacation. Farmers have time off. It is the easiest work in the world. You sit around for six months out of the year. I could have bought a cane farm in Abergowrie when I purchased this bakery. There were maybe fifty returned-soldiers' farms, and most were on the market at a low price. Today, there are maybe only four or five Anglos left there.

We plan to retire in Trebonne.

[I then took a ride with Félix in his bread truck while he made deliveries. We passed the farmhouse of a Basque farmer and he commented that the owner, born here of immigrant parents, is married to a woman who is half Aussie and half Aborigine. It seems that his parents were appalled when their son started dating her and sent him to the Basque Country for an extended stay in the hope that he would meet and marry someone there. It didn't work. When he returned, he married his present wife. Félix also pointed out two farms owned by Chinese, several by Finns, and one by a German. There was also a farm leased by a Hindu family from its owner. In short, the Hinchinbrook countryside was indeed multicultural.]

Juan Unamuno # —I was born in 1925 in Markina. I attended school for only one year. Father was from Barinaga and had cut sugar cane in Cuba for one year. Mother was from Aulesti and my parents lived on her *baserri*. I had a brother, José, who died in America where he was herding sheep. My brother Ignacio lives in Mungia and owns a taxicab after having herded sheep in the USA for eight or ten years. None of the other nine siblings (in all) emigrated.

I immigrated here in 1949 and before coming I was working on the *baserri* and felling pines in Aulesti. I had done 30 months of military service in Logroño and Elizondo, Navarra, and had been a baker for two years in Markina. My family was poor, so, I came to Australia to make some money. I was unsure for how long I might be here. My aunt, Teresa Mendiolea, was visiting Aulesti and suggested I come. She made the arrangements and advanced my fare. She even gave me £15 for pocket money. It took me two years to pay her back.

I was on the *Toscana* for forty-six days from Genoa to Sydney. Johnny Mendiolea met the boat. He was vacationing in Sydney and didn't know us. He walked along the wharf saying out loud, "*Euskaldunak batzuk emen badira?*" ("Are there some Basques here?"). My pocket money was spent by then, and he gave us more and put me on a train to Townsville. There, two Basques met me and sent me by train to Ingham where the Mendioleas were waiting in the station. It was right after the harvest, so for the next six months I stayed in the Mendiolea barrack with no work, but food provided.

I cut cane for them that first season and, after two weeks, everything hurt. My hands and shoulders were bleeding. I wanted to go home, but I liked the pay envelope full of pounds every fortnight. Our gang was cutting fifty or sixty tons a day and earning 13 shillings per ton. I was working with Jesús Gárate from Markina, Saturnino Achurra from Amoroto, my cousins Félix and José María Jayo, and a non-Basque Spaniard.

That first slack I worked with my three cousins on the CSR tram. Teresa Mendiolea talked to the cane inspector of Victoria Mill and found us that work at Mount Fox. I made £60 per week.

We returned together to cut cane the next two seasons and the two slacks went back to Mount Fox. Then, we had a chance to buy the sleeper contract from an Italian, Gino Paris, for £3,000. Teresa Mendiolea lent us that money and we purchased a lorry for £750 as well. We cut 50,000 sleepers that first year and made £36 per hundred. But we had to pay Gino Paris £13 per hundred for the use of his sawmill equipment.

We then went as a group to a sawmill 46 miles from Ingham and cut lumber on a per-board-foot contract. We did that for a year, but then the forest inspector declared our timber source to be off-limits, so we went to Abergowrie to cut cane. Johnny Mendiolea cooked for us there. We next cut sleepers in Abergowrie for six months on our original contract with CSR and then Azpiri and Malaxechevarria bought out Félix and me for £2,000. Then Félix, his brother José María, and I bought the bakery in Trebonne for £9,000—three each. I built a house in Trebonne that year and the two brothers lived together. We three worked the bakery and that first year was very tough. I was in that for the next seven years and then sold my share and my house for £4,000.

It was 1954, and I found work on a farm in Halifax for the Catalan, Bubé, as caretaker while he went to Spain. I worked at Macknade Mill as well. Bubé paid me £55 per week. I cut cane there along with Aranas from Gernika and Ignacio Aristi, a Gipuzkoan. I was there for one year. It was bad cane and we couldn't finish the harvest. I had to bring in a mechanical harvester to do so.

I then bought a house in Ingham for £2,350 and an Italian came looking for me. He wanted a full-time farmworker. So, I rented out my house in town and moved to the farm with my wife and family. I made A$150 weekly and did that for three years.

The farm was sold, and I moved back to my house in Ingham. But then another Italian farmer came to me with the same proposition and I sold my town house for A$14,000 and moved to his farm. It has a 10,000-ton sugar peak and I am paid well whether I work or not. I have sick pay and free rent and utilities. I have four weeks of paid annual leave, although I don't go anywhere. I clear about A$700 per month. I didn't buy my first car until 1964.

I married my wife, Carmen Badiola, in 1960. She is from Ondarroa and I knew her brother here. He put us in touch, and we exchanged photos and began corresponding. I sent for her, provided her fare, and we were married two months after she arrived. She was thirty and working in Ondarroa as a seamstress and helping on her parents' *baserri*. She was one of nine children. Her younger brother, Esteban, is a factory worker in Elgoibar today, but was a sheepherder in the USA for three years and a canecutter in Australia for six. Her next brother, José, is a stonemason in Ondarroa and was in Australia for thirteen years. Her sister, Edurne, is a housewife in Vancouver. She has been in Canada for twelve years after living here for five. Her brother, Loren, is a gym coach in Ondarroa after five years in Canada and eight in Australia. The youngest, Jesús, lives in Bilbo after having been in Australia for two years. He doesn't work since he literally won the lottery.

When Carmen came to Australia to marry me, the Mendioleas hosted the wedding at their house and two hundred people attended. We then stayed with the Mendioleas for two months. I can't even begin to say how wonderful they were to us and how grateful that I am.

Within six months of coming here I knew Italian, but it took me ten years for English. I have never attended classes here. I learned English by talking with my fellow-workers when they were Australians. I do not listen to shortwave radio, although I used to. I have never been anywhere other than here in Australia. I don't write home, my wife does. I read the *Herbert River Express*, and, once in a while, *El Español*. Teresa used to give me some issues of publications from Spain. I was naturalized in 1954. Aunt Teresa told me to become a citizen in order to enjoy full rights here—pension, health insurance. I do not belong to any social club. I have few friends. Johnny Mendiolea is the best. I go to a hotel only occasionally. I don't frequent any particular one. I am Catholic, but do not attend Mass often.

At home, we use Basque, and, at work, Italian. I use Basque exclusively with my children. I insist they speak it at the dinner table. I prefer to have Australian close neighbors, there is too much prying and envy among Basques, but I like to have them in the wider community. In the hotels, I usually drink with them. Basques are a good race. They are more tranquil than Spanish. Spaniards are volatile. When we invited them to the Saint Ignatius festival, they ruined it. There were fistfights. Italians are like Basques; some good, some bad. About 80 percent of the Australians accept us, particularly those in Ingham. Some have helped me along the way. I think, on the whole, Australians are well educated, but there are some donkeys, too. Aussies are big drinkers and like to fight. I was once at a dance with Matias Mendiolea and an Aussie girl brought us a drink. Some guy didn't like that, and we ended up in a fistfight.

I would like my children to marry Basques. Australians would be so-so. Aborigines or Sicilians would be bad. I would not like my children to return permanently to the Basque Country. They are Australians now.

I have never helped anyone to come here. My cousins wanted to and and I advised them against it. The work is very hard here. If you bring someone and it doesn't work out, it is your fault. I don't want that kind of responsibility. We have never been back to the Basque Country. Maybe we will go one day, but only for a visit to relatives. We plan to retire here. I would like to buy a house above the flood plain.

Juan Azpiri # —I was born in 1925 in Ispaster. My mother was from Amoroto and Father was from Ispaster. Neither had ever emigrated and they lived on a *baserri* in Lekeitio. Both are now deceased. We were seven children, six alive. Three have never emigrated and three of us came to Australia. I live here in Ingham and work in a sawmill. My brother, Antolín, is a stonemason (*albañil*) in Ayr. He came to Australia in 1954. Domingo lives in Vancouver where he is a laborer. He was in Australia from 1956 until 1970 when he left for Canada. I brought both of them here by advancing their passage money.

I immigrated here in 1952. I thought of saving money and returning to Spain after a few years. I first wanted to go to the USA but was unsuccessful in arranging the papers. Tony Mendiolea came to the Basque Country on a visit and told me about Australia. He arranged for my papers and the Mendioleas lent me my fare. I came to Sydney by boat along with six other Basques. The Mendioleas sent an Italian to meet our boat and put us on a train to Ingham. My first job was cutting cane for them. I liked it. No worries. I worked with Félix Jayo (the ganger), Juan Unamuno, Ignacio Malaxechevarria from Aulesti, Julian Eguia from Lekeitio, Rufino Zárate from Bilbo, and Fernando from Bilbo as well.

During the first slack, I went to Mount Fox to make sleepers along with Félix, Juan, and Ignacio. I did that from 1953 to 1955. We bought a contract from Gino Paris. I then sold my share to Ignacio's brother and left because I became very ill with asthma.

For the next two years, I could not work. I was in the hospital in Brisbane for two months one time and then one-and-a-half months another. In 1958, I went to Spain for twenty-two months.

I returned in 1960 and cut cane that season for the Mendioleas. That slack, I went to a sawmill in Mount Fox and became ill again. I got a job with the Goicoechea Construction Company in Mount Isa for five months driving a truck. But the dust was too much for me, and I was unable to work for the next year. The next year, I went back to the sawmill in Mount Fox and am there to this day. I commute from Ingham.

By 1971, I was married, and my wife and I had the Victory Café in Ingham. She ran it while I worked in the sawmill. We sold it because of the poor business. I make A$170 per week. My son, John, is a clerk in a hardware store and he makes A$100 weekly. We built our house thirteen years ago for A$8,000 and £750 for the land. In 1958, I bought an apartment in Lekeitio for 200,000 *pesetas*.

I have never gone to class here to study English. I am still uncomfortable in it. I always seem to hang out with Basques, Spaniards, or Italians. We get the *Woman's Weekly, TV Week, People, the Herbert River Express,* and the *Townsville Daily Bulletin*, mainly for the children. Sometimes, friends give me issues of *Hola* and *La Semana* from Spain, and *La Fiamma*, the Australian-Italian newspaper. I joined the Foxwood Club at work seven years ago and the International Club and Noorla Bowling Club here in Ingham last year. I also joined the Iberian Club when it was founded nine months ago.

I became a citizen in 1961, mainly for Australian medical care and pension. I am a Catholic but attend Mass only on Easter and Christmas. Our son and daughter both attended Catholic school in Sydney. He was at the Gilroy Convent School here and then Saint Patrick's in Sydney. Milagros is fifteen and attended Santa María's here and is now at Our

Lady of the Rosary in Sydney. We have made four two-week trips there to see our children.

At home, we use Basque and Spanish and eat Spanish cuisine. We insist that the children use Basque and Spanish with us. They will learn English on their own. I see other Basques frequently. I go to the Central Hotel as that is where they hang out. I go every Friday to the Iberian Club and Sundays to the International Club. At work, I use a little Italian and a little English.

I met my wife, Rosaria Arrillaga, in 1958 in Lekeitio on my trip back to Spain. We were married in 1959 and I brought her back with me. She and her parents are from Mendexa. Her brother, Pedro María, herded sheep in the USA for three years. Her father's brother, now deceased, lived in Trebonne when she came. Her cousin, Frank Arrillaga, lives in Mount Fox.

When I came, Basques were viewed very well here. With the later recruitments of Spaniards that changed somewhat. I have never had a real problem with discrimination. I think Basques and Spaniards are pretty much the same. I don't agree with the prejudice of some Basques against Spaniards. Italians, with a few exceptions, are fine.

It was a good idea for me to come here. I have not enjoyed the best of health, but the climate in Ingham is probably better for me than is Spain's. Life here is easy and some who left to go back now regret it. I hope to go to Spain next year to see the soccer championships, but for a visit only. I plan to retire here in Ingham.

Tomás Ibañez * # & —I was born in Bilbao in 1925 and went to school for only fifteen months. I know Spanish, Basque, Italian, and some English. I never knew my real father. I heard that he was once a sheepherder in Elko, Nevada. My mother married Juan Balanzategui of Yurreta [Iurreta]. She was from there as well. I have three step-siblings. Lucia is a housewife and seamstress in Ontario, Oregon. Juan works in Durango in a factory after cutting cane in Australia from 1952 to 1969. Jesús was here from 1955 until 1962, and is now a warehouseman in Durango.

Before immigrating here in 1950, I was a farm laborer in Bedarrona and Muxika. I wanted to emigrate to save up money and purchase a house in the Basque Country. I thought of going to the USA but could not find a sponsor. Then a Balanzategui aunt of my stepfather who lived in Stone River told me about Australia. Leandra Araquistain (married to Aniceto Menchaca) was also a distant cousin. She paid my passage and her brother, Julián Araquistain, gave me my first job. It took me forty-two days at sea to reach Brisbane. When we first made land in Fremantle and went ashore for a visit, it was so hot that the cars were covered with gunny sacks. We retreated to the boat for its air conditioning. I was worried, since I feared it might be hotter in Ingham. Afterall, it was in the tropics. A Spaniard met us in Brisbane and gave me a train ticket to Ingham and £10 from Pascual Badiola. There was another Basque immigrant with me, headed for the Mendioleas.

I lived with Julián and he became my best friend. We played cards, went to the Trebonne Hotel, fished, and watched movies together. I saved money and started paying off my passage and sending money home to my impoverished family. I cut cane for Julián for four years until he sold his farm and moved to Spain.

The first slack, I went by train to pick fruit in Victoria. I was with my stepbrother, Juan, and two other Basques. We got that job passing through Sydney. Basques there told us about Mildura and the Government Employment Office found us that work and gave us round-trip tickets ex-Sydney. I can't remember what we made, maybe A$4.00 per hundred buckets. There were six of us Basques picking together. Our expenses were considerable, and we only had ten or twelve weeks of work. So, we didn't save money.

In the 1953 slack, I went to Townsville to work for construction for three or four months with my stepbrother Juan and Domingo Ibarra. In 1954, I went to Mildura to pick fruit, and then Melbourne. In Melbourne we went to the headquarters of a railroad and got work replacing tram tracks. I made £24 weekly. We sometimes went to the Spanish Club for dinner. I was there for two months and then returned to Ingham to cut cane for the Balanzateguis in Stone River with my stepbrother. There were two other Basques and three Italians in the barracks.

My next move was to the Elortegui farm to be its caretaker while they went to Spain. At first, I was alone, but then my other stepbrother, Jesús came. I received a regular salary plus 20 pence a ton for the sugar produced. I did that for fifteen months until Elortegui returned. I then went to cut cane with my two stepbrothers on the Güazo (Italian) farm. Güazo was Elortegui's brother-in-law. We cut with another pair of Basque brothers.

The next slack I was again in Mildura picking fruit with Juan. A Basque living there found us that work. Four Basques lived and picked together. After ten weeks, the harvest was over, and we three brothers went to Sydney. A friend from Bilbo, Diez, found us work in a mower factory and we lived in the house of our relative, Miren Balanzategui. I made £26 per week. After two months, it was back to Güazo's cane. The next slack I remained in Ingham unemployed.

The following season, Espilla told us that Reinaudo had lost his former gang. We went to him and got his contract. All three of us brothers worked there with other Basques. That slack I went to Mildura with Juan and our cousin, Miguel Balanzategui. We went to the same farm as the year before.

It was then that Miguel and I decided to go to Spain for a year. I took a gift for someone from here to the town of Viana. That was when I met María Fernández, my wife. I knew her father's sister's son, Valentín Ruiz, in Australia. He now lives in Canberra. Anyway, we were married, and I brought her back to Australia in 1960. Her parents were unhappy. No one in the family had ever emigrated and Australia seemed so far away. We went to live in the Reinaudo barracks, and I cut with my stepbrothers and other Basques.

The next two slacks, we stayed in Ingham and during the harvest cut for Reinaudo. Then we went to Shepparton to the fruit. My stepbrother had been there the year before. I traveled with Milagros and two other couples—Fernando and Milagros Echebarri and Eusebio and Nieves Arrizubieta. We got A$3 a bin and could pick about five per day. We were there for sixteen weeks.

In the 1966 slack, we went to Shepparton to the farm from before. We picked fruit for one month and then moved to Yenda, NSW, for the grape harvest for another eight weeks.

I cut cane for Reinaudo until 1968. He and I were the only ones cutting. That slack, it was back to Yenda with a Navarran, a man from Santander, and my stepbrother Juan.

The next year, we went to Spain for a year and then to Mount Isa on our return. I went there with Juan, Pedro Monasterio, and Félix

Astorquia. We were working on installation of a new copper mine and lived in a barrack. I went on to Gunpowder, Queensland, by myself. There, I worked with two Basques and some other Spaniards. I made A$215 weekly.

It was then back to cut for Reinaudo. By then, I was doing cleanup behind the harvester. In 1973, I was back in Yenda at the earlier farm. Then it was back to Reinaudo for the harvest. After it, we went to Spain again for five months. Then, once Reinaudo's harvest was over, I went by myself to Yenda to pick fruit. I made A$30 daily, seven days a week.

In 1977, I went to Green Valley to work as a laborer opening up a new mining town. Then it was back to Reinaudo, which is where I work still.

I once went to an employment office in Brisbane along with other Basques. We wanted work on a tramline. We came from the fruit-picking and none of us spoke English. There were many other people applying for the work. Well, they looked at our hardened hands and hired us straightaway. At one point, Mari accompanied me South. She tried to pick fruit, which was prohibited. She fell off a ladder and broke her arm.

I earn A$184 per week for eight months and about A$225 weekly during the sugar harvest. We have a house rent-free. María works two days a week at the Canossans in Trebonne and earns A$74. Our son, John, works for Foxwood Timber and makes A$130 per week. We have a rental income of A$600 a month from an apartment in Spain. We bought an apartment in Galdakano [Galdakao] in 1969 for 700,000 *pesetas* and a plot of land that same year in Viana for 130,000. María has a house in La Bastida, Navarra, that she purchased for 2,500,000 *pesetas* in 1975.[6]

It took me five or six years to learn some English. I listened to the radio, went to the movies, and picked up some in the hotels. I read the *Herbert River Express*, the *Townsville Daily Bulletin*, the *Sydney Morning Herald*, and *National Geographic*. I used to read *El Español*, but no longer. I also read for a while *La Fiamma*, *Il Globo*, and *Corriere della Sera*. I get *La Semana* and *Deia* from Spain every week. I have a shortwave and listen every day to broadcasts from the USA and *Radio Nacional de España*. I get the BBC from London sometimes and programs from Chile and Rome occasionally. Last year, we joined the International Club and the Iberian Club here. We are Catholics but only attend church on Easter and Christmas. Our three children have all attended parochial school here.

I was naturalized in 1966 for no particular reason. María is not naturalized. She doesn't like it here. She hates the discrimination and has great difficulty with English. We went back to Euskadi in 1969 for a year and toured Spain as well. In 1976, we went for five months and went all over Spain. In 1977, María went with our daughter while I stayed here. At home we use Spanish with the children, not Basque. Spanish is more important. They will pick up English in school. At work, I use Italian. It is not important for me to be around other Basques and Spaniards, but it is for my wife. I see other Basques frequently. Last week there were many at Aniceto Mendiolea's funeral. I believe Basques are more sincere than Spaniards and would like my children to marry one, or at least a Spaniard. There are many different kinds of Italians. North Italians are more like us than the Sicilians.

I helped many to come to Australia, maybe twenty in all. I was not a citizen and had no property, so I couldn't sponsor them myself. But I went around to the farmers and found them sponsors. I also lent the passage money in most cases. I did that for both of my stepbrothers. In 1955, I helped my cousins from Bedarrona, Andrés and Jesús Arando. In 1957 and 1958, it was friends from Ispaster, Eugenio, Sabino, and Pedro Corta. Then there were two from Ea. The only time I got burned was by a distant cousin from Andalusia that I helped in 1965. He was here a few weeks, complained about everything, and just disappeared.

Life is easier here than in Spain, but more interesting there. We both want to retire in the Basque Country—Lekeitio or Ea—but it may be hard if our children remain here.

Some Australians accept us, and others don't. I always try to go through a Basque connection if approaching Australians for a job, since the Basque worker has a great reputation.

Félix Astorquia * # & —I was born in Aulesti in 1945 and attended school for nine years. My mother was from Gizaburuaga and Father was from Aulesti. He was a carpenter and butcher. They never emigrated. We are five siblings and only María Pilar and I have emigrated. She lives in Trebonne and has a bakery with her husband, Félix Jayo.

Before coming here in 1963 I was helping my parents on the *baserri* and going to sea as a merchant mariner for three weeks at a time. I wanted to make one million *pesetas* and return home to buy an apartment in Gernika (you could get one for 150,000 to 200,000 then), put the rest in the bank, and go to work. I considered the USA. I had relatives there, but my sister was here in Australia and this opportunity came up first. I learned of conditions here from Félix Jayo who came back to Aulesti on a visit and that's when he married my sister. My father's brother, Juan Astorquia, lived in Innisfail, but I had no contact with him. Félix lent me £400 for my passage. My parents were fine with the decision. Father said that, if it didn't work out, I could always come back to the *baserri*.

I came by sea headed for Sydney. In Melbourne, a few of us went ashore to look around. Well, we ended up drinking in a pub and then lost our way and missed the sailing. An Australian in Melbourne helped us to get a train ticket to Sydney, and we went from there to Townsville by plane where I was met by Félix.

My first employment was with the Mount Fox Timber Company. Juan Azpiri was working there and got me that job. I stayed with him and his wife and child. I only made £13 weekly. I hated the place. The language was a problem and we had no electricity. Primitive. There was nothing to do but work. I preferred working to having time off, at least when you were busy the hours went by faster. I wanted to go home. I actually cried the first few days. There were a few other Basques there as well. On weekends, I sometimes visited my brother-in-law in Trebonne. I was at Mount Fox for four months.

I then went with Azpiri and other Basques to the Mendiolea farm to plant cane. We found that work through Félix Jayo. I ended up cutting there with Alberto Idoeta (Aulesti), José Luis Jayo (Aulesti), Hilario Marqués (Lekeitio), and José María Iturriaga (Gernika). I made £1,000 for the season. In my spare time, I went fishing in the Herbert River, played a little *pelota* in Trebonne, played some cards, and watched TV in the Mendiolea house. That first season, I paid Félix back his loan and sent another £400 to my father.

The first slack, I went to Shepparton, Victoria, along with Hilario, Alberto, and Félix Jayo to pick fruit. We flew from Townsville to Benalla and then by train. We considered Mareeba and the tobacco, but when I missed the boat in Melbourne a Spaniard there told me about the opportunity picking fruit in Shepparton. We lived together in a barrack and worked ten or eleven hours six days a week. We earned £6 to £7 daily. We were all Basques there. Alberto Idoeta was my first cousin and we hung out together. We didn't really save anything as our trip expenses were high.

I returned to cane cutting with Alberto. By then, the Mendioleas were using a mechanical harvester. So, we went to Giru as we heard they weren't using harvesters there. I cut alone for a Basque farmer from Amoroto. I liked working by myself since no one ordered you around and you could go at your own pace. I cut twelve tons per day and made £12. There were twenty-two Basques in Giru at that time, and I was with them in the hotel on Sundays. I could have saved money, but I spent it too. I was young and went around with guys who had cars. After that harvest, I went to Trebonne to work in the bakery for Félix. I made A$45 weekly and stayed with the family. I was there for the next two years.

But I felt too tied down and decided to return to Shepparton to pick fruit. By then, I had my car (purchased 50-50 with my cousin in 1965) and I drove along with a guy from Santander. We had no work lined up, but I knew it would be easy to find. We picked for several farmers over the next four months. When the harvest was finished, I drove back to Ingham along with José Luis Jayo. I planted cane for the Mendioleas and then heard that Alberto Urberuaga needed two men. He was still cutting manually rather than with machines. We were four Basques in the gang, and I made A$25 a day.

That slack, I went with Alberto Idoeta to a vegetable farm in a suburb of Melbourne. He had been there before. We went in his car. We were three from Aulesti, one from Amoroto, and one from Navarniz [Nabarniz]. Two of us had been cutting in Ingham and three in Ayr. We had little free time—we picked six days a week for eleven or twelve hours. One of the guys hunted rabbits in his spare time, so we didn't have to buy meat. I made A$1 per hour. That year, I sent A$5,000 to an aunt in Spain so she could pay off the mortgage on her apartment.

After four months, it was back to Ingham to plant cane for several farmers. Then I went to work for Fabián Mendicute (from Lekeitio) on his harvester. I was working there with Alberto Idoeta. When Fabián's cousin left for Spain, he needed someone to do his haul-out. I lived with Félix Jayo while doing that. I didn't pay room and board because I helped out in the bakery.

The following slack, I went to Mount Isa with Pedro Monasterio and

Tomás Ibañez. We had no contact there. We stayed in a boarding house owned by an Italian. His brother was a contractor and he hired us to build a warehouse. I made A$2 per hour. I was only there for three weeks. I had a fiancée in Ingham and wanted to get back to her. I received a telegram from Félix Jayo saying that a contractor needed someone, and I got that job. I lived with Félix and worked with Antonio Azpiazu of Aulesti.

I worked construction from February to June and then went back to hauling-out, this time for Antonio Esparza. He had purchased Mendicute's harvester. I made A$18 per week. Esparza and I were the only two Basques; the other two men were an Italian and an Asturian.

After the harvest, I took two months off to get married and then took my wife to Aulesti for eight. When we returned, I went to work hauling-out for an Italian harvester. We lived with my father-in-law (Rotondo) on his cane farm. I made A$18 per day. That slack, I went to Lannercost to pick tobacco. I made A$13 per day between January and March. I then planted cane for a few weeks and went back to hauling-out with the harvester of the year before.

I then went to Trebonne to take over the bakery as a full partner while Félix went back to Spain for an extended visit. My father-in-law had a house in Trebonne, and we lived with him. I did that for fourteen months until Félix returned. I then went back to the same Italian harvester to do his hauling-out.

I believe that migration to the South during the slack is about over. The young bachelors today are looking for steadier work year-round. They go into construction or logging—jobs that are for all twelve months. They now realize that your expenses traveling around, and losing a day here and there due to weather or whatever, makes it impossible for you to save much money.

It was now 1975 and I bought a general store in Trebonne. Between 1975 and 1978, I continued to do haul-out for the Italian harvester as well on wages. In 1978, I bought a tractor (A$12,000) of my own and a double-bin trailer (A$6,000), and now I work for the same Italian on a contract basis. I make about A$24,000 annually. My wife has some land here that she inherited, and I own one-quarter of the *baserri* Gadaur in Aulesti, also inherited.

I met my wife, Janet Rotondo, at a dance in Longpocket in 1968 and we married in 1971. She was eighteen and an only child. Her parents would have preferred that she marry a Sicilian. She was born in Ingham and her folks were both from Messina. Her uncle owned the store that I later bought, and she had clerked for him for eleven years. We lived for a while with her parents and they came to like me. They wouldn't charge us rent, but they did split the beer bill!

I learned English in about two years. I had a Spanish-English grammar. I dated a lot of girls. I never listen to ethnic radio, just the standard Australian station for news. Since 1975, I read the *Herbert River Express* and the *Courier-Mail*. Infrequently, I buy in Ingham *El Español* and *La Semana* magazine. I was naturalized in 1970 since I planned to go to Spain and had not done my military service there. I also felt it was safer, politically. In politics here, I favor Labour. I belong to no social clubs. We are Catholics but go to church very infrequently. At first, I hated Australian cuisine but became more accustomed to it. My wife cooks Basque-style and some Italian dishes at home. We use English and Spanish (Janet learned it during our visit to Aulesti).

Our son and daughter are small. I try to teach the boy Spanish, but he prefers English. It is important to me to live around other Basques. I frequent the Central Hotel in Ingham because a lot of Basques hang out there. I do not belong to any social clubs.

It is up to my children to choose who they will marry. Australians would be so-so and Aborigines no. I haven't had a lot to do with Australians. I once had a fistfight with one and later he was in a hotel proclaiming, "all Spaniards are bastards." I see no difference between Spaniards and Basques. Both are hard-working. Italians are about the same. It all differs from person to person more than group to group. Generally, I have been treated well and plan to retire right here. If my children want to go back to Europe to live one day, it would be their choice. Who am I to say that they can't? I migrated. But now, I imagine I will retire here. My wife and children are all Australians. I no longer dream of the million *pesetas* and the return to live in the Basque Country.

Floren Laucirica*#& —I was born in 1926 in Gernika. I attended school for six years. Today, I speak Basque, Spanish, Italian, and English and read all four. My father was a farmer from Gernika, and mother was born in Ajangiz near there. Neither ever emigrated. We were seven children, and several have migration experience. My sister, Gregoria, lives in Mareeba and is a vegetable farmer. José is a farmer and factory worker in Gernika today, but was in Australia for eight or nine years. Jesús is a factory worker in Gernika, too, but after spending two years in France and three-and-a-half herding sheep in Idaho. Secundino[7] was a merchant mariner and now lives in Millicent, South Australia, working in a paper-pulp factory.

Before coming here in 1963, I was a stonemason (*albañil*) in Gernika and Natxitua (my wife's hometown). I tried to borrow 100,000 *pesetas* from my father to start a construction business and he refused. So, I asked one of my brothers here to arrange for me to come. I'm not sure why. I had a good life in Spain—a car and money in my pocket. I once thought of going to Uruguay. I even filled out the papers, but my lawyer in Bilbo was dodgy and I changed my mind. I also considered Fernando Po. I knew about Australia from my siblings here. They said you could make £1,000 in a year here and that was enough to build a house. At that time my two brothers lived in Ingham and Home Hill and my sister was here in Ingham. It was my brother José who arranged my papers and lent me my fare. My parents were against the plan. They were elderly and feared they would never see me again. But they didn't try to talk me out of it.

I flew from Europe (SAS) to Sydney and then Townsville where my brother picked me up at the airport in his car. He had found work for me as a stonemason with an Italian contractor. My boss knew some Spanish, so it was easy to communicate. I had a terrible first impression. It seems that a fifteen-foot carpet snake that lived in the Ingham library for rat control had escaped and was in the main street. I almost died when I saw it. I expected snakes in the cane paddocks and bush, but on main street?!!! Had I had a return ticket, I would have left that night.

I stayed in Ingham at a boardinghouse that had several Basque boarders. My friends were Juan Balanzategui and Tomás Ibañez from Durango. On weekends we pub-hopped with many Basques. I earned £26 per week and sent most of it to Europe. I was married and with two kids when I came here by myself. I brought the family out eighteen months later.

After three months on that job, I went to Texas, Queensland, to pick tobacco. I also worked on building a house and barn while there. My sister and brother-in-law, Pedro Acha from Araba, used to go there and told me about it. I went by myself. I was working for an Italian, Oreste Macussi, and lived on his farm. I made £1,000 in eleven months. My best friend was Jaime Aberasturi. We hunted rabbits together on weekends. He was from Rigoitia [Errigoiti].

I wanted to bring my family there, but Mancussi would not give us a house to live in. So, I had a chance to cut cane with my brother, José, and went back to Ingham. José was the ganger and we lived in the Salvatore-Spina farm's barrack. I earned £70 to £80 per week cutting on contract. We were all Basques, my two brothers, my brother-in-law, and Pedro Monasterio. I spent my leisure time hunting pigs, turkeys, and ducks in Abergowrie. I bought a car and some furniture in anticipation of my family's arrival. I cut cane for two seasons and then the purchaser of the Spina farm asked me to work for him permanently. My family was here, and we lived in a renovated barrack. I earned A$65 per week. I worked alone and did that for eight years.

We went to Macknade Mill and both my wife and I worked as cooks in our leased restaurant. They gave us living quarters. It was a bad proposition, because the Mill set the menu and its pricing. We did that for two-and-a-half years and saved no money. I went back to the farm for eighteen months. Now we lived in a rented house in Ingham and I was making about A$90 weekly.

I then began to have my own business as a stonemason and still have. We make about A$28,000 a year. That includes my son Joe who earns A$150 a week as a boilermaker, my daughter Mary who earns A$103 per week as a travel agent, and Begoña's A$60 weekly as a part-time cook in the Roma Café. We built a house here for A$70,000 two years ago. We have no other investments other than some CSR shares that have lost half what we paid for them.

My wife, Begoña Yribar, is from Natxitua, as was her father. Her now-widowed mother is from Nabarniz. Her father had herded sheep in Idaho and Nevada for many years. She is one of seven children. Her sister, Luz María, lives in Longueuil, Quebec. Another sister, Belen, is a housewife today in Gernika, but was here in Australia for seven years.

It took me about ten years to learn English. I never attended classes here. I just learned it through give and take. I read the *Herbert River Express* in English, *Deia* in Basque, and, for many years, *El Español* and *La*

Semana, *Hola* and *El Gol*. I used to listen to Spanish language broadcasts fom Tokyo, Spain, and France, but no longer. We are Catholics but go to church infrequently. We use Basque at home[8] and some English with the children.

I joined the Australian Accordion Society six or seven years ago, the Herbert River Angling Club four years ago, and the International Club two. I founded the Iberian Club here nine months ago and it meets Fridays in my home. I am its president. I drink infrequently in the Belvedere Hotel (Basques there), the Station Hotel (my fishing club meets there), and the Lucinda Hotel (because of two Basque friends nearby).

I have some Australian friends. Robert is married to a Spaniard. Kevin always hangs out with Spaniards and is the president of the fishing club. We fish together. Martin was once my neighbor and does my taxes.

It is tremendously important to me to have other Basques around. I see someone daily. Today it was Pedro Aranas when I went to his hardware store to buy materials. Yesterday, it was Domingo Murelaga, an old man who lives alone in Lucinda. I try to give him company a few hours almost daily, otherwise he has no one. I see many Basques at the International Club and I founded the Iberian Club to keep us together.

In 1966, I was naturalized. I thought it necessary to work more easily in my stonemason profession here. Begoña became an Australian citizen in 1970. We favor no particular political party.

Some Australians are prejudiced against us, but there are all kinds. It gets better all the time. I was helped here my first year by an Englishman. I find most Aussies to be lazy, the worst in the world. Five percent are industrious. They dislike seeing you work hard. They gamble a lot and can't save their money. Many will save only for their next holiday. None wants to work more than eight hours. I have never had real altercations. Whenever I see one coming in a pub, I just buy the man a drink and walk away. As far as Basques-versus-Spaniards goes, I really see little difference in the two groups. Both have good and bad. There is a rub over the language difference. I find Italians to be two-faced. The northerners are the best. About 80 percent of them are like Basques. Sicilians have extremes. Some work hard and are thrifty; others are gamblers and spendthrifts. [Their son, Joe, has a Sicilian fiancée and, at first, they were unhappy about it, but now find her delightful.]

We like it here but miss the Basque Country. We have never been back and miss family. Begoña's mother is nearly eighty and we want to see her. We would like to see our children move to Euskadi. They would love it. Life is easier here, but better there. We want to retire in Europe. But only if at least one of our children with our grandchildren settles there. If they all remain here, it would be very difficult.

[Floren and I traveled together to Dalbeg, along with Agustín Arrate, to visit Santiago Mugica. Santiago has four farms and is doing well. He has two A$50,000 Deere tractors and recently someone had put sugar in the gas tank of one. He said, "if it were an Englishman, he would have done the job right, whoever did this made a mistake." Whenever Floren and Agustín spoke negatively of Aussies, Santiago objected. He noted that many worked hard and were shrewd. The most recent farm purchases in Dalbeg were all by Aussies.

Floren then recounted that when his brother and a companion arrived in Ingham unannounced, Tony Mendiolea saw them wandering down the street and said, "you're Basques, no?" They were very excited as they knew no one here. They told Tony that they wanted to cut cane, but he was skeptical as they were of slight build and had bland hands. He found them a gang, and both Tony and Rufino visited them weekly to see how it was going. Their hands were all blistered and wrapped in handkerchiefs. So, Tony went to the cane inspector and asked him to send that gang fewer bins. He didn't tell them as they would have been irritated. By the end of the season, the newcomers were doing fine. They were even overloading the bins, cranking down the loads with chains to make extra money. The mills didn't like that as it could damage the bins. But the cane inspector liked the gang and looked the other way. Floren noted that some of the gangs cut cane by moonlight to get ahead.[9]]

José María Inunciaga # & —I was born in Gernika in 1941 and attended school for eight years. My father was born in Mendata and Mother was from Gernika. They were farmers there and neither ever emigrated. Mother remarried after my father died, so I have stepsiblings. Sabino Aranas is the eldest and is an iron-rigger in Newcastle, NSW. Before that he was a merchant mariner. My three stepsisters live in Gernika and all are hairdressers.

Before I came here in 1961, I was doing farmwork with my stepfather and working in an arms factory in Gernika. I couldn't earn enough to get ahead and wanted to come here for five or six years to buy a house in Spain and return there. I thought of going to the USA, but knew no one there. I learned about Australia from returnees from the first recruitments in 1958 and 1959. My cousins, José María and Benedicto Aguirre, were living here in Ingham. José María lent me the money for my passage.

He met me with Johnny Mendiolea at the Townsville airport. I was to cut for the Mendioleas in José María's gang. I had a poor first impression. The work was very hard and there were no diversions. This was a sad place. We were José María, his brother Benedicto, Félix, Juan and José María Uriona from Muxika, and another Basque from there. I earned £700–£800 and paid back my passage.

In the slack, we went to Mareeba to pick tobacco. José María was growing it in partners with an Italian and we went there. Then it was back to the cane in Ingham, once again to the Mendioleas.

The following slack it was back to Mareeba, but to a different farm. I went with Bendicto Aguirre and José María Uriona. I picked with the two Aguirre bothers, Félix Uriona, Jaime Mendizona, and a Yugoslav and two Italians. I made £23 per week.

Then it was back to Ingham for the cane. I was now a ganger. We had Lamiquiz from Muxika, Félix Ituarte from Aulesti, Antonio Longarte from there, and Manuel from Lekeitio. Then it was back to Mareeba, this time with my stepbrother, Sabino Aranas. I brought him here in 1964 by paying his passage. We picked with two Australians.

It was now 1965, and I partnered with José Antonio Longarte, Félix Ituarte, and Ciriaco Lejarcegui to buy two used harvesters (£10,000 each). We got a contract from a group of six farmers. Ciriaco had done haul-out for them and knew they had lost their harvesters. I lived in a barrack with Ciriaco, Juan Lamiquiz, Gregorio Ituarte (Félix's brother), Sabino Aranas, and Pedro Acha. I made A$7,000–A$8,000 a year.

I next went to Gladstone, Queensland, to work construction. I was by myself. José María Aguirre was there and sent for me. I lived with him in a barrack. I made A$1.50 an hour. There were lots of Spaniards there among the thousand workers in all—including Juan Lamiquiz. I worked for five months and then returned alone to Ingham to harvest cane.

Next slack it was to Griffith to pick fruit. I went with Antonio Longarte, Félix Ituarte, Juan Lamiquiz, and Ciriaco Lejarcegui. We found that work through an employment agency in Ingham. We made A$8 a ton in the grapes. We finished in April and I went alone to Texas to pick tobacco for a couple of months, and then back to Ingham for the harvest.

Then, it was off to Griffith and Tenterfield with Antonio Longarte as the year before.

After cutting cane in Ingham, I went the next slack to Mareeba with Tomás Gárate. We had an Italian farmer's name and called him from Ingham. We made A$62 a week on a grading contract. I used to stay in Tenterfield two months longer than anyone else to continue grading tobacco. I was good at it after Mareeba. They were not and didn't want to go through the hassle of learning how to grade.

I met my wife, Françoise Dodin, in 1971 when we were both picking tobacco in Texas. We married in 1972. She was born in Nantes, France. Her mother was from there and her father was a plumber by trade. Françoise is one of eleven siblings. When her brother, Christien, wanted to emigrate to New Caledonia, the parents decided that they and some of their younger children should as well (the older ones were established in France). They came first to New Caledonia, then to Adelaide, and eventually to Texas, Queensland. Françoise was nineteen when we married, and her parents were not pleased. They wanted her to marry a Frenchman. Her parents moved back to France after her father retired and live in Paris today. Her brother, Christien, lives in Brisbane and works on the railroad. She has another brother, Bernard, working in a shoe factory in Adelaide.

We partners in the harvester then bought our own 200-acre tobacco farm at Bambaroo in the Hinchinbrook for A$50,000. I lived there with my wife. The idea was that I would work it and the partners would help. So would Juan Lamiquiz. Then we would all pick in the slack. Meanwhile, I would receive some income from the cane harvesting in compensation for staying on the tobacco farm. It was all logical, but in practice, there were problems and rubs. You were in A$10,000 to A$12,000 each year before you realized any income. I stayed there for four years and then we sold the farm for A$55,000. That was a bad decision because it is worth A$200,000 today. It was 1975 and Ciriaco went out on his own. He sold out and the rest of us bought another harvester.

In 1976, I went to Texas, Queensland, to pick tobacco. Juan Lamiquiz came with me. We earned A$2.40 an hour. And then it was back to the cane. That year I cut with Félix and Gregorio Ituarte and Antonio Azpiazu. Then it was to Texas with Juan Lamiquiz and Félix Ituarte. That year Martín Ituarte joined us.

We repeated the pattern the next two years. Then my wife and I did the Texas routine in my car and we lived in a cottage during the next harvest. For the last two seasons, we have remained here in Ingham during the slack. I do some cane planting but am mainly unemployed.

When I first came here the language was a real problem. I did not date because of it and to save money. I never attended classes here. I learned English after marriage. Françoise doesn't know Spanish and I don't know French, so we use English at home. For the last four or five years, I read the *Herbert River Express*. Before that it was *El Pueblo Vasco* and *La Gaceta del Norte* by mail subscription (no longer), *El Español*, and *La Fiamma*. I buy *El Español* regularly in Ingham. I have a shortwave radio and listen to *Radio Nacional* in Spain for sports. In 1968, I joined the *Club Español* in Sydney and the Ugali Club in Griffith. I am a member of the Iberian Club here for the last nine months. I was naturalized in 1979 to possibly go to Spain. We are Catholics but attend church infrequently. Our kids go to Catholic school.

I have not been back to Europe yet. I correspond regularly with my mother—every few weeks. Our children are seven and five, and I tried to teach them Spanish but gave up. They prefer English. It is more important that they learn Spanish than Basque. It is more useful. I like living near other Basques. I probably see at least one five days out of seven. I search out Basques and Spaniards in the pubs.

We built our house three years ago for A$46,000. In 1964, I bought an apartment in Gernika for A$5,000 and my parents live there today. In 1977, we partners bought two harvesters for A$53,000 and, in 1979, a used one for A$25,000. The tractors and other equipment cost maybe A$30,000. I make about A$20,000 annually. I didn't buy a car at first. I always took the train South since a car seemed frivolous when I was saving to move back to Spain.

I would prefer that my children marry a Basque or Spaniard. Anyone else would be okay except for Chinese or Aborigine. Basques are the same as Spaniards. Italians can be a little over the top.

I hope to go to Spain soon to see my parents before they die and introduce them to my wife and children. I plan to retire here, maybe in Brisbane if not Ingham. I like it and go there on vacation to see my brother-in-law. It is too hot here and Brisbane has a better climate.

Ciriaco Lejarcegui # &—I was born in Arbatzegi-Gerrikaitz in 1939. I completed primary school and today speak Basque, Spanish, Italian, and some English. My father was born in Ibarruri and mother in Arbatzegi. They are both farmers in Muxika and neither ever emigrated. I am one of seven offspring. Two of my brothers are professional *pelotariak* and have lived in the USA. Juan Pedro competed in Djakarta as well.

I came to Australia in 1960. Before emigrating, I was a mechanic in Gernika while living with my parents on the *baserri*. I wanted to avoid military service and I didn't like my job in Spain. I thought about migrating as a mechanic to Valladolid. I had been too young for the two recruitments of emigrants for Australia, but I had friends who came that way and they wrote to me about this place. In particular, there were José María Aguirre and Juan Lamiquiz. José María arranged through the Mendioleas for me to come. I borrowed half of my fare from a cousin in the Basque Country. Father was upset and offered to buy me a car so I could commute to my job in Gernika from Muxika. I refused.

It was a difficult trip as it was my first. I was on a French airline and knew no French. When I got to Sydney, someone in the airport called the Spanish Club and said a man needed help. They put me on a train to Ingham.

My first job was cutting cane in Abergowrie. I got that through the Mendioleas. It was very boring, hard work. The barracks were miserable, and it was cold in the mornings. I cut with all Basques. My best friends were José María and José María Inunciaga from Gernika. We went to the pubs and movies on Saturday nights. The language was a difficulty, so, we didn't go to dances.

The first slack, I went to Mareeba to the tobacco with Sabino Uzin from Forua. The farmers came looking for us in the train station and hotels. We only stayed for three weeks as the work was hard and the food bad. We left to pick in Texas. We had no contact there, but had heard there was plenty of work. We picked for three months at 60 cents an hour.

Then, Sabino, another Basque, and I went back to Ingham to the cane. That season, I cut with José María Aguirre, his brother, the Uriona brothers, and one other Basque. We bought a loader together and contracted work on the side for 40 cents per ton and made extra money.

I left early, in September, to plant tobacco in Texas on the farm where I worked the year before. I was there with Sabino Uzin and one other Basque. In April, it was back to Ingham to the same gang and farm. I operated the hauler. Then it was back to Texas to pick tobacco. That year, I traveled with Jenaro Ibarruengoitia. We made 70 cents an hour.

The next cane season I was back in Ingham. I bought a haul-out outfit and worked on contract. I had three and went from farm to farm. I made 40 cents per ton.

The following slack, I went to Riverton, Queensland, to pick tobacco with Angel Duñabeitia, an Uriona brother, and a guy from Ondarroa. It was forty miles from Texas; I just decided to change farms.

After completing my three haul-out contracts in Ingham, I next headed to Mount Isa to work for the Goicoechea Construction Company. I worked with several Basques and *Santanderinos*. I put in a lot of overtime and worked sixteen hours a day, seven days a week, for an average of 90 cents an hour. I did that for four months before returning to the cane.

It was 1965 and I went to Spain for three months. When I returned to Ingham, I bought into a harvester partnership (two harvesters) with Félix Ituarte, José María Aguirre, Tony Longarte, and Ramón Pla (son of a Catalan immigrant). We paid £10,000 for each complete harvesting outfit. We had contracts with two groups of farmers. In all, we were three Asturians, two *Santanderinos*, and four Basques.

The next slack, I went with Félix Ituarte to Victoria to pick tomatoes and then to Griffith. We picked fruit and felled trees as well. We heard about it from Basques who had been there. Then Félix and I headed back to the cane where we harvested in the same places as the year before.

The following slack, I went south with a *Santanderino* to pick tobacco and then by myself to Griffith to the fruit. Afterwards, it was back to the cane in Ingham.

The following slack I had an operation on my ear and stayed in Ingham and went to work in the Bonanno machine shop. It was now 1968. I lived in a boardinghouse with nine Basques in all. It was operated by

Antonio Azpiazu and his wife. Félix Ituarte and José María Aguirre lived there as well. I earned A$1 an hour and stayed there for two-and-a-half months before cutting cane with the same gang. Then, we bought a tobacco farm together in Bambaroo and that slack I worked on it picking tobacco.

In 1969, I sold out of the harvesters and farm and got married. I went back to work for Bonanno and bought my house for A$12,800. The next season I cut with Juan Lamiquiz, José María Aguirre, and an Australian. We cut 17,000 tons and made A$2.70 per ton.

That slack I went to Griffith by myself where I had picked before and made A$980 in four months. Then it was back to the cane. In 1972, I bought the harvester that I still have today, and that slack was back working for Bonanno again.

I still cut with my harvester and in the slack usually worked for Bonanno. In the slacks of 1977 and 1978 I worked on the wharf in Lucinda as a laborer and made A$320 weekly.

When we went South, one of the advantages was that you were casual labor and didn't have to buy a union ticket. You got your money in cash and didn't declare taxes on it. You set up a bank account in a local bank with a false name and deposited your check into it. You drew that out without a problem when you left.

I met Rosa Norma La Spina, in 1968, here in Ingham, and we were married in 1969. Her parents were vegetable farmers. He was from Catania and she from Udine. Her mother was against her marrying a Spaniard, but her parents now like me. Rosa considers herself to be Italian in addition to Australian. She was a shop's assistant for my harvester partner, Ramón Pla, when I met her and is now a housewife. There were many adverse comments among my Basque friends when I told them about my intention of marrying her.

It took me about six years to learn English. I attended class for one month here in Ingham. I didn't date Australian women because of the language. I learned Italian much quicker and more easily. Rosa and I use English and some Italian at home. After marrying, I began reading the *Townsville Daily Bulletin* and the *Herbert River News*. I buy *El Español* every week here in town. I never listen to ethnic radio. I was naturalized in 1963 because I had evaded military service in Spain and to have more rights here in Australia. Three years ago, I joined the Noorla Bowling Club and last year the International Club. I joined the Harvester association in 1966. We are Catholics, but do not practice. Our seven-year-old daughter goes to Lourdes Catholic School.

We have two lots in Forrest Beach. I purchased one six years ago for A$4,500 and the other two years ago for A$5,000. Two years ago, I purchased a garage site here in Ingham for A$11,000. I have a harvester that I paid A$25,000 for in 1972, a tractor I bought in 1975 for A$3,000, and another purchased in 1976 for A$10,000. I have two trailers that cost A$7,000.

I have been to the Basque Country for three months in 1965, four months in 1967, and again for four months in 1977. That trip we went to Málaga and Italy as well.

It is important to me to be around other Basques; they are my closest friends here. I would like my children to marry Basques and wouldn't mind if they moved to the Basque Country one day. I see myself retiring here on an Australian beach. There is good opportunity and equality here. Middle-aged and elderly Australians treat you well, particularly in Ingham and, to a degree, in Griffith. The unions have too much power and strikes, and I find the climate in Ingham to be too hot. Australians are poor workers and never save. They should find a place off the coast and name it "Music Island" and put all the Australians there, keep them well fed and with "no worries," and repopulate this continent with immigrants.

Tomás Gárate # & —I was born in Garai, Bizkaia, in 1946. I know some English, but mainly Spanish, Basque, and Italian. I went to school for eight years. My father is from Gernika and Mother from Yurreta [Iurreta]. They live in Matiana-Abadiano [Matiena-Abadiño], Bizkaia, and he is a foreman in a factory. Neither have emigrated, although Father's father was in the USA, I imagine herding sheep. We are eight siblings and six have never emigrated. My brother, Ignacio, is a tobacco grower in Mareeba.

Before coming here in 1965, I was a turner and solderer in a factory in Matiana-Abadiano. I had an aunt, Ramona Gárate, and uncle, Lorenzo Duñabeitia, from Muxika here. They were here from 1957 until

1969 and now live in Canada, where he is a carpenter and she a cook. The Duñabeitias arranged our documents and advanced the passage for Ignacio and me. We were thirty-five days on a boat to Brisbane. There was another Basque named Arrizmendieta on it. He had been here before and helped us get on the right train.

My first job was cutting cane in Ingham with a mechanical harvester. It was harder work than I anticipated. I worked with José, Francisco, and Pedro Uriarte from Bakio, Francisco Javier Larragan from Arrieta, and my brother. We earned £25–£30 per week and that season I paid back my passage. I then went to Mareeba with José Uriarte and two other Basques to the tobacco. A farmer from there came to Ingham looking for workers. I made £28 weekly plus board. When I had time off, I played soccer and hung out with two Basques who played guitar. In April it was back to Ingham to plant cane.

That second season, I cut with a Navarran and my brother. My uncle and aunt found us the work. I made £10 daily. Then it was back to Mareeba. After another cane harvest in Ingham, when I cut with the brothers Ramón and Luis Goirigolzarri from Urduliz and a Navarran from La Ribera, I was off to Griffith. We were twelve or thirteen Basques in five cars. There were many looking for work, so, we had a hard time finding it. I harvested grapes for A$5 per ton with my cousin, Juan María Mugica from Gernika, and a Gipuzkoan from Zarautz. I spent a week in Sydney and then finished that slack in Texas picking tobacco for a couple of months.

I started cutting cane the next year (1968) with the same gang and on the same farm as the year before, but halfway through the season I switched to a farm in Abergowrie. Two of our gang left early for Mareeba that year and we were unable to finish that Ingham cut and lost our retention money. That next slack, I picked tobacco in Ingham on a farm owned by two Basques. We were three Basques picking and the wife of one was our cook. I made A$14 per day.

The next cane season I worked behind the harvester in Ingham for Ciriaco & Company. I stayed with other Basques, including Azpiazu— and his wife cooked for us. The next slack, I picked tobacco here in Ingham again, but on a farm owned by an Italian. He was a friend of my future father-in-law. I made A$120 weekly. In April, I graded tobacco for a Spanish farmer here. I then returned to Ciriaco for the cane harvest doing haul-out. I married and rented a flat. That slack, it was back to tobacco for the Italian farmer from the year before.

There was a split in Ciriaco & Company, and I went to work for Tony & Company doing its haul-out. We bought our house for A$11,500. I was working with Antonio Azpiazu and Félix Ituarte. I then spent another slack picking for the Italian tobacco farmer. In February of that year, I went to Greenvale to work construction for A$150 per week. We were three or four Basques who traveled there together. We went back the following slack as well.

In 1975, I bought my own tractors and trailers and did haul-out for Tony & Company on contract for 60 cents per ton. I have continued doing that every year until the present. That slack, I worked as a manual laborer for Victoria Mill here in Ingham.

In the 1976 slack, I went with Félix Ituarte to Mareeba to pick tobacco on contract for 12 cents a pound. In 1977, I planted cane in Ayr for A$10 per acre. I did that alone and stayed in my cousin's house. In the 1978 slack, I picked tobacco at first for the Ingham Italian grower and then went back to Ayr to plant green cane. In 1979, I worked on the wharf in Lucinda for A$200 weekly and then finished up in Ayr planting cane again. Last slack (1980), I worked for Gino Paris in his sawmill for a few weeks and then went to Ayr to plant cane.

I own equipment worth about A$9,000 and, in 1967, I purchased an apartment in Abadiano [Abadiño] for 275,000 *pesetas*.

I met my wife, Norma Perdella, in 1968 at dances here in Ingham. We married in 1970. She was twenty-three years old. She was born in Inglewood and her parents were from Mantova, Italy. She worked in a pharmacy here for eleven and a half years as head of the assistants. She now works two days a week in the delicatessen of Woolworths.

At home, we speak in English and Italian. We tried to teach our daughter Italian, but gave up. She prefers English. I have never attended classes here. I learned most of my English from my fiancée beginning in 1968. We get *TV Week*, the *Post*, *People*, the *Herbert River Express* (for the last ten years), and occasionally the *Townsville Daily Bulletin*. Sometimes, I buy *El Español* in the store. I only listen to ethnic radio when I am in Mareeba with my brother. He likes it.

In 1969, I joined the Rangers Soccer Club. I was on the Ingham squash team from 1969 until 1973. I am a member of the Noorla Bowling

Club since 1978 and the Iberian Club since last year. We are Catholics but seldom attend Mass. I am not naturalized but need to do so if I want to return to Spain. I could have trouble there over military service. I have never been back and would not consider moving there permanently unless its politics change. I want to go for a visit next year to see the World Cup play.

I have never sponsored or helped anyone to immigrate here. Nevertheless, I have many relatives here. My cousins in Australia from Gernika include José Mugica, who came in 1963 and is a carpenter today here in Ingham. His brother, Juan María, came in 1964 to cut cane and is now in Sydney. Their brother, Miguel, was here as a canecutter from 1961 until 1967 and now lives in Gernika. Then there was my uncle, Cosme Gárate, who came in 1960 and died that year in Mareeba. My cousin, Gregorio Gárate, came in 1962 and is a stonemason in Mareeba. Finally, my cousin, Agustín Castrejana, came in 1961 and lives in Ayr today.

I see other Basques frequently. Antonio Longarte and I are close friends and work together. We see each other almost every day. I think Basques work harder than Spaniards, but, in some ways, they are more educated than are we. Italians are pretentious. They are falser than Spaniards. Australians are prejudiced and call us Wogs. Actually, Basques are pretty well viewed. I have found employment just by saying I was Basque. Australians are poor workers and savers. I would not want my daughter to marry one, never an Aborigine. I prefer she marry a Basque. I wouldn't mind retiring one day in the Basque Country. Life is more interesting there than here. For now, I want to improve my house or maybe move to another above the flood plain. I intended to stay for five years and fifteen have gone by.

[His wife, Norma, was present during the interview and noted that Spaniards are more open and like Italians more than do the Basques. When Tomás announced his plan to marry her, there were many adverse comments among his Basque friends. Basques are clannish and aloof. She would never marry one again and would object if her daughter did so. She added that her sister had married a Basque and he committed adultery. They divorced and he had the gall of accusing her of being responsible for his adultery. She thinks Basques make little effort to assimilate here. She then excepted Tomás from her indictment of Basques in general.]

José Antonio Longarte # & —I was born in 1941 in Aulesti. I completed five years of school in Europe and speak Basque, Spanish, Italian, and some English. My mother was from Markina-Etxebarri and Father from Bolivar [Bolibar]. They farm in Aulesti. Neither has emigrated. I am one of three siblings and neither of the other two have emigrated.

Before I came here in 1962, I worked for two years in the marble quarry in Aulesti and then four years in a factory in Eibar. I couldn't save in Eibar and wanted to go somewhere to earn some money. I also wanted to avoid military service. I preferred going to the USA, but couldn't arrange for a sponsor. I learned about Australia when Tony and Johnny Mendiolea came to Aulesti on a visit. I knew others from Aulesti in Australia, but we had no correspondence. Anyway, Johnny Mendiolea fixed up my papers in Australia; Tony helped me with the paperwork from the European end and lent me my fare. I flew to Townsville with two Basques destined for Ingham and two others headed to Ayr. The Mendioleas met our plane.

It was the end of the 1962 harvest and so I worked for three weeks on the Mendiolea farm. It took me a few months to adapt to Australia, but I liked it. I then went to Mareeba to the tobacco. I traveled alone. An Italian farmer had come here and recruited me. I picked tobacco there with Imanol Osa from Ondarroa (he had been on the plane with me) and Javier from Gernika. We earned £20 per week after taxes and keep. I paid off my passage.

I returned to Ingham to plant cane for the Mendioleas and then went to a gang in Stone River. Tony Mendiolea found me that position. I cut with Imanol Osa, Eusebio Diaz from Arteaga, and Esteban from Gernika. We made £8 per day.

That slack, I went to Mount Isa with Félix Ituarte to work for the Goicoechea Construction Company. I worked with three other Basques and two Spaniards and earned £55 per week. We did that for four months, and then Félix and I went back for the cane harvest. Our gang included Juan Lamiquiz and Imanol Achabal. The next slack I went to Texas to pick tobacco with Félix Ituarte and Ciriaco Lejarcegui. We had nothing specific awaiting us, but had heard there was great demand for workers. We earned nine to ten shillings an hour.

It was now 1965, and I bought into two harvesters with Félix Ituarte, José María Inunciaga, Ciriaco Lejarcegui, and Ramón Pla (a descendant of Catalans). I cut that year with Félix and his brother, Gregorio, and Antonio Azpiazu. The original harvesters were flawed and the contracts small, but you still came out better than today.

That slack, I went with Félix to fell trees in Victoria for a paper-pulp plant near Melbourne. Félix wrote to a Basque friend he had there. We bought our own chainsaws and worked on contract. We made £15 to £20 daily and it was good work. We did that for three months and then returned to Ingham a little early to attend the wedding of Ramon Pla's daughter.

After the cane harvest, the next slack I went with José Inunciaga to Griffith to pick grapes. We did that on contract for six weeks. By working many hours, we did well. I did that for the next three slacks and then, in 1969, I went back to Mareeba with Félix Ituarte and Sancho Lamiquiz.

During the 1970 cane harvest, in our gang Gregorio Ituarte was replaced by Serafin Madariaga from Aulesti. That year, our partnership bought a tobacco farm here in Ingham and in the following slacks we picked there.

I married and, from 1974 until 1979, spent the slacks here in Ingham employed in a brickworks. The last two years I have just collected unemployment.

In 1972, our harvester partnership broke up and I now have two harvesters with Félix Ituarte and José María Inunciaga. We have Tony & Company. Last year, we all worked with Tomás Gárate and one Italian.

I met my wife, Maria Novelli, here in Ingham in 1968 and we married in 1970. She was born in Conzano, Alessandria, and was two in 1950 when her parents brought her here. So, she grew up in Ingham. Her father worked as a laborer at Macknade Mill for twenty years until his recent death. He cut cane for ten years. He was recruited by an agent in 1949, and then sent for his family the following year.

My English is still poor. I learned most of what I know by working my second year with Australians in Mount Isa. I have never attended classes here. We get the *Herbert River Express* and the *Townsville Daily Bulletin*, but only Maria reads them. I get no newspapers from Spain or buy any here. I used to listen to shortwave radio broadcasts from Spain, but no longer. They don't come in clearly. Tonight, I am calling back to Aulesti for the first time in eighteen years. Iñaki Badiola's wife and one of the Jayo wives set that up. I just joined the Noorla Bowling Club and, nine months ago, the Iberian Club.

I was naturalized in 1975. After marrying, I knew I would be staying here. I have never been back to Spain, but I would like to go for a visit, and I don't want problems regarding military service. We are Catholics but go to church about once a year. Our ten-year-old son, Robert, attends convent school. We bought our house in 1975 for A$19,000 and then remodeled it. I bought my first car in 1966. I own part of two harvesters worth maybe A$100,000. We have tractors and trailers as well. We are three partners.

I think Spaniards are just as good as Basques. We are both a bit clannish. I guess I prefer to be with Basques. I like Italians. They work very hard. I have worked well with and for them. Australians don't like us. They call us Wogs. I personally have never had any trouble with them. I really like it here and will likely retire in Ingham. In 1964, we had a very difficult year with bad weather. Félix Ituarte and I considered emigrating to the USA. But then, we bought the harvester and stayed.

[Maria Novelli was present and noted that the Basques are as clannish as Sicilians. At any function, Basques always sit together. They also prefer to marry their own kind. She feels like an outsider.]

Francisco Javier Larragan # & —I was born in Arrieta, Bizkaia, in 1947. My mother was from there and Father was from Fruniz [Fruiz]. I attended seven years of school. Today, I speak Spanish, Basque, Italian, and English. My weakest language is English.

We were living in Muxika when I emigrated. My eldest sister, María Teresa, lived here in Australia from 1962 until 1966 and is now a housewife in Gernika. My older brother, Jesús, was a ranch worker in the United States for six years and is now a laborer in Muxika. My two youngest sisters have never emigrated and live in the Basque Country.

Before coming here, I worked on a rented *baserri* in Rigoitia, Bizkaia, after first doing the same on a rented one in Arrieta. In 1964, I came here to my sister. I planned to stay for just three years. I considered going to the United States because I had an uncle there but preferred coming to my sister instead. She wrote me about life here. She sponsored me and sent me the passage money. My parents thought it was a good idea. I was on a boat for thirty-two days from Genoa to Brisbane. An Italian family and some Spaniards helped me catch the train to Ingham, and my sister met me at the Ingham station.

My sister and brother-in-law, Miguel Mugica from Gernika, were on the Reiteri farm and I worked with them. We stayed in its cane barrack. I made £22 per week. My brother-in-law was a ganger, and I cut with him the first year. There was Miguel, the brothers Francisco and Ángel Uriarte from Bakio, and me. I saved my money and paid off my passage and bought an apartment in Durango by the end of the second year.

In that first slack, my brother-in-law and sister went to Ayr and I stayed on in Ingham. I managed to get a day or two of work with Victoria Mill fixing its tramlines.

After the second season cutting cane here in Ingham, Miguel, Teresa, and I traveled together in their car to Texas, Queensland, to pick tobacco. We went from farm to farm and I ended up working on one by myself. I made £20 weekly. I saved up enough to buy my first car.

From there we went together to Ayr. I became the haul-out man for the gang and made A$150 a week. I worked with Miguel, a guy from Aulesti, and Johnny Muguira, a Basque Australian and son of a Burdekin canefarmer.

That slack I went to Mareeba with Miguel and Teresa. I stayed there with Ángel Uriarte and another guy, Jesús, from Bakio. That year, rather than returning to cane cutting, I went with Ángel Uriarte to Gladstone to work construction. Miguel and Teresa moved back to Spain, to Gernika, and have lived there ever since. We heard the money was better in Mount Isa and went there. I didn't like it and stayed for only a week before deciding to go back to cane cutting in Ingham. I had my car by then, and Ángel came with me. First, we planted cane for the Mendioleas and then cut for them along with José, Ángel's brother.

The next slack it was back to Mareeba along with Ángel. I did that for four months and then went to Griffith to pick fruit. José and Francisco Uriarte came with me. We made about A$200 per week.

I then returned to Ayr to do haul-out during the cane harvest. The Uriarte brothers came with me. We worked on the same farm that I knew from before when I hauled-out for Miguel. In addition to Johnny Mugira and José Uriarte, we had Juan María Mugica, who was my brother-in-law's brother.

Then it was back to Mareeba to the tobacco, this time with Juan María. After the harvest was over I drove to Griffith to the fruit. This time, José Uriarte and Ramón Goirigolzarri (from Urduliz, Bizkaia) were with me. From there, the three of us returned to Ingham to cut cane—still by hand. Ramón was a ganger and set up the contracts. I cut with him, his brother, José Luis, and the two Gárate brothers (Tomás and Iñaki from Garai, Bizkaia). I made A$400 weekly.

Then, it was once again to Mareeba along with José Luis Goirigolzarri. This time I went to a different farm and made A$150 and keep for a week. From there it was to Griffith to the fruit with Ramón and José Uriarte.

The next season in Ingham I worked at haul-out for wages. Tony Esparza was our ganger and we cut on the Mendiolea farm. The other two in our gang were Italians. Afterwards, it was back to Mareeba, with José Luis Uriarte, for the tobacco harvest and then on to Texas.

It was then that my life took a turn. I met my future wife, Carol Ann Morris. She was born near Brisbane. Her father is a laborer. That year, when I came back to Ingham, I worked as a hauler for José María Aguirre and lived in the Central Hotel. She was serving at the bar in a hotel. That slack, Carol and I went to Greenvale where I worked as a backhoe operator. I made A$250 weekly. I stayed there for two and a half years before moving back to Ingham to plant cane. That year of 1975, I went to Spain alone for three months to visit my family. I took out Australian citizenship before going as I was afraid of being conscripted otherwise into the Spanish Army.

When I came back, José Uriarte and I worked for an Italian doing haul-out, after which I went to work for Victoria Mill as a laborer. I just went there on my own and asked for a job. Carol and I lived in a flat in Ingham. I made A$160 per week that slack. The following year I bought my own haul-out outfit and worked for José María Aguirre. I have been working for him in that capacity ever since during the cane harvest.

That 1977 season, I went back to Griffith with José Uriarte to the fruit. Then, in both 1978 and 1979, I went to Texas along with Carol and our infant son. We had housing on the farm and I made A$200 per week. I now own a tractor and two trailers for haul-out and am my own businessman.

This year [1980], I intend to stay right here in Ingham during the slack season. My son is eleven and in school; you can't just take off. I want to take Carol and the children to the Basque Country next year so she can meet my parents and they can know their grandchildren. I like Australia. It was a good idea to come here. You can get ahead. You are free to express your opinions without fear of reprisals. One day, I would like to own a farm here or close to Brisbane. I would not mind retiring in Brisbane. Carol's parents live near there and it has a good climate.

I never had problems with Australians or dating Australian girls. I once had a fight over a girl, but it was about her and not my ethnicity. Most Australians view Spaniards and Basques well—Italians, not so much. Basques are more formal than Spaniards; better at keeping their word. The farmers always asked if you were a Basque or a Spaniard as they preferred hiring Basques. Italians are good people but a little bit false. If you say something bad about one to another, he is likely to pass it on.

I belonged to the AWU for cane cutting but dropped my membership in 1972 after I began working for myself in haul-out. I just joined the Noorla Bowling Club here and am in the Iberian Club as well. In Griffith, in one of my years there I joined the Ugali Club for about three months. It was social. I have been in the Sydney *Gure Txoko* once when passing through the city.

I read an issue of *El Español* every month or two that I buy here. Since knowing Carol, I read the *Herbert River Express*, the *Townsville Daily Bulletin*, and the *Brisbane Courier-Mail*. I don't listen to any radio broadcast from Europe. Carol is a Methodist, but doesn't practice. We are raising the children Catholics, even though I seldom go to church.

I try to teach my kids a few words in Basque and would like them to marry a Basque. After that a Spaniard, Italian (well, a Sicilian would be so-so), an Aussie, or whatever. I would not want them to marry an Aborigine or Chinese.

Carol's parents were very accepting of me.

Innisfail

Saturnino Onaindia*& —I'm Bizkaian and live here in Mena Creek (Innisfail). I am married to a Catalan and we have two sons. One is married to Elizabeth Balanzategui from Ingham, herself the daughter of a Basque-Catalan union.

I was born in 1906 in Torino (Italy); my father was working there. He was from Ibarruri and had been a *pelotari*. When I was two, the family moved to Alexandria (Egypt), where Father was a runner [wager-taker] in the *frontón*. He then went to Barcelona and, in 1914, to Cuba in the same profession. I was given to an uncle to be raised on his *baserri*. I herded his sheep as a child and received little education. At the time I didn't mind, but, after I came to Australia, I thought about it and found my childhood to have been unfair.

I came to Australia in 1923; Father paid for my passage. I had two cousins in Oregon and wanted to go there. I put in my application, but there was at least a two-year delay. The English Consul in Bilbao said that entry into Australia was easy, so I came here instead.

My cousin was married to a sister of Ángel Lazcano. He came to Australia in about 1916 or 1917 [actually, in 1912] and had a cane farm in Innisfail. He was an ex-cutter who received a perpetual lease on Crown land. I went to work for him as a farmworker until 1929. Then, I worked as a canecutter for fourteen or fifteen years. My first gang had Valencians, Andalusians, and two Italians. I was the only Basque. The second year, I cut with two Navarrans, two Valencians, two Italians, and a Catalan. In 1932, I married a Catalan; her parents immigrated here in about 1916 or 1917. Eventually, I got my own sugar property here.

I received letters in impeccable Spanish from my father, brother, and sister, and it embarrassed me not to be able to reply to them in proper grammatical language. I became determined that my English would be better. I made friends with a local schoolteacher, and he gave me some instruction and novels to read for practice. In my spare time, I would go alone to the bush and read them out loud. Some I read with a dictionary five or six times.

Many of the Anglos here didn't like migrants. They called us "Dagoes." I hated that word. I would tell them that they didn't even know what it meant—but they used it as if calling us dogs. When people laughed at my English I would ask: "So how many languages do you speak?" In their ignorance they thought of themselves as superior. I remember once being at a dance and the leader of the band told the girls to pick out a boy to dance with. An Australian girl asked me, and, while we were on the floor, I spoke up and she noted my accent. She didn't say anything, but I saw the look on her face. She regretted dancing with me and that hurt.

Eventually, I came to understand Australians better. They might dislike us, but they preferred hiring us to native Aussies because we were more dependable. During the hard times, the Depression, many native Aussies were out of work and "Waltzing Matilda" down the road, unable to feed their families. So, their complaint was legitimate—but should have been directed at the government and not against the immigrants.

There were never many Basques here, and sometimes I would travel in the evening to nearby towns to play *mus* in someone's home. I think of Australia-born Basques as "second-class" ones. I have lost much of my capacity to speak Basque through lack of practice here. I sometimes go to Ingham to see Basque friends, and once I was in Teresa Mendiolea's boardinghouse and she scolded me for talking in Spanish all the time.

I learned Italian as well. Wherever there are Italians, their language dominates. I have only known four Italians who bothered to learn Spanish. Sometimes Spaniards feel slighted when they are with Basques who keep talking in *Euskera*. Once, a Spanish vessel arrived in Lucinda and about half the crew was Basque and the rest Spaniards. The Ingham Basques organized a dinner for the Basque crewmen and didn't invite the others. The local non-Basque Spaniards considered organizing a dinner for the Spanish crewmen, while excluding the Basques. It didn't happen, and, generally, the Basques and Spaniards in North Queensland got along.

[During our interview, Saturnino showed me a book of Basque verse and a photo, one of the Basque coastline. He asked me to send him the etymology of his surname. Elizabeth Balanzategui was present, and she asked me to send her a copy of Robert Laxalt's *In a Hundred Graves*. She had heard of it. She also noted that her daughter once won a prize at an Ingham costume dance when she wore her Basque folk outfit. Elizabeth also remembered that there was a big dust-up in Ingham during the 1962 Saint Ignatius dance when someone went to the podium and shouted "Viva Franco."[10]

We continued on from Innisfail to Mission Beach to meet with Juan Azaguirre from Mallabia, Bizkaia. He had come to Australia fourteen years earlier to work on a cane property there owned by Saturnino Onaindia. Juan's uncle had a summerhouse nearby, and, through him, the young man was offered a cane-cutting job by Saturnino. However, he was laid off during the slack season every year and had to go to Mareeba to pick tobacco. He found this to be costly and disruptive, so he jumped at the chance when offered year-round employment near Mission Beach by an Italian farmer. He now lived here with his Galician wife.

When Juan noticed that I was contemplating the decorations in his house that consisted largely of Spanish imagery (bullfighting posters, etc.), he remarked: "That is not my country; this is my country," pointing at the Basque escutcheon on his living-room wall. Nevertheless, he was quite happy to be in Australia and away from the Basque politics that are "completely out of hand." He bemoaned the fact that he was losing his Basque language competence due to the lack of opportunities to use it here in Innisfail.]

Mareeba

Pedro Acha*#& —I was born in 1929 in Llodio [Laudio], Araba. I went to school for five years was all. Today, I speak Italian and Spanish, as well as broken English. My father was from Areta, Álava, and was a truck driver. Mother was from Llodio. My brother, Fernando, tends bar in Llodio and was in Australia for five years beginning in 1965.

Before coming here in 1961, I worked in an iron-smelter in Arrancudiaga [Arrankudiaga], Bizkaia. I would have gone anywhere as long as it got me out of Spain. I learned of Australia from my brother-in-law here in Ingham, Joseba Laucirica. He advanced my fare. By then, my parents were both deceased. I was married and had children.

My first impression of Ingham was poor. It was hot, the language was impossible, cane cutting was hard work, and there was a snake in the thatched roof and possums in our barrack's kitchen. I cut with seven other Basques on contract and made £7 to £10 per day. It varied. My best friend was José Luis Lezamiz from Arteaga, Bizkaia. We hunted and fished together, went to the pub, and bought a car fifty-fifty. I purchased my part of that car eight days after arriving in Australia. I was proud of that. Between the car and paying back my fare and sending money to my wife, I didn't save that first season.

The first slack I went to Mareeba by myself to pick tobacco. I went to the hotels and the farmers came looking for us. I picked with a Navarran. I can't remember his name. I earned £15 clear of food and taxes.

I went back to Ingham and got assigned to a gang by approaching the Cane Growers' Association. I cut with five other Spaniards, again on contract, and made the same as the year before. Pepe Llera from

Santander was my best friend there. We hunted, fished, and pub-crawled together.

I brought out the family and that slack we picked fruit in Griffith. We lived in a cottage there and I made £15 a day. When we finished, it was off to Tenterfield to pick tobacco.

I eventually ended up cutting cane in Ayr and picking tobacco in the slack season in either Dimbulah or Mareeba. That was the routine year after year.

Then, four years ago, I bought a sixteen-acre vegetable farm in Mareeba for A$25,000, and that is where I am today. My wife and I make about A$20,000 per year. But it varies. This year, I was paid A$19 per box in Cairns for tomatoes that cost me A$4.50 to produce on just two acres. One trip to Cairns, I grossed A$3,000, and, for the season, A$30,000. Yet, last year I received A$2 per box and sold them at a loss. Our son, Feliciano, teaches manual arts and makes A$200 per week. I have about A$6,000 in equipment between a used tractor and water pumps for irrigation. In 1959, we bought the house we live in for A$5,000.

I met my wife, Gregoria Laucirica, in 1952 at a festival that she was attending in my town. We were married in 1955. It took me two years to learn enough English to get by. I am still learning some every day. I sometimes read the *Cairns Post*. I might buy an issue in the store of *El Español, La Fiamma, Il Globo, La Semana, La Gazzetta Illustrata*, and *El Caso* from time to time. I try to listen to ethnic radio almost daily. I was naturalized in 1976 to have full rights here. I favor the Labour Party. In 1977, I joined the Mareeba International Club. I go to the Dunlop Hotel once a week as Spaniards hang out there. I am Roman Catholic, but do not go to church.

I have only assisted two people to come here. I fixed the papers and advanced the fares for the brothers José and Fernando Larrazabal from Arrieta in 1964.

We speak mainly Spanish at home. I prefer that the children learn it before English. Then come Basque and Italian. I see no difference between Basques and Spaniards. We might speak different languages, but we are all Spanish. There are good Italians and bad; generally, they are false. I would not object to my children marrying anyone except an Aborigine or maybe a Chinese. I have never had any real problems with Australians. Some are industrious and some are not.

I have never been back to Spain and want to go when I can afford it. Maybe in four or five years. It would only be for a visit. It might have been a mistake emigrating; my friends in Spain are pretty well-off now. When I lived in Spain I made twice as much as many others but it is never enough. If you put 5,000 *pesetas* in your bank account, you were unhappy because it wasn't 5,025. So, I emigrated and now, for the last four years, I have a farm and work seven days a week. My last day off was Christmas months ago.

I like it here but struggle still with the language and some of the customs. I love the hunting and the fishing on the Great Barrier Reef. I want to retire near the sea with a big fishing boat. I might even do a little commercial fishing.

[Gregoria, his wife, listened in to the interview, as did Camilo Madrid. They were all three scheduled to attend a dance at the International Club.] Camilo commented, "he who emigrates chooses an illness. His life will never be the same. If he earns A$200 in a week, he'll try to put A$210 in the bank! I returned to Spain in 1961 and bought a bar. But I was unhappy and sold it to return here. You will never belong fully to either place ever again."

Pedro suggested that Gregoria go along with Camilo and that he would join them. She refused, saying, "I know if I leave, he will go back to work on the motor he's repairing and will never show up at the dance."

Camilo discussed his latest initiative. "This year I started the Hispanic Center of Far North Queensland here. There are twenty-six member families so far and we have had three barbecues. I am president, Camilo Jr. is secretary, and Roberto Urquiza is treasurer. Most of the members are Castilians and Andalusians, and we have a few Basques. We are modelling ourselves after the club in Ayr and received a copy of its statutes from the Spanish embassy in Canberra. Two of our members are from Cairns. We expect to get more from there and Dimbulah."

Camilo noted that most tobacco farms were selling for between A$100,000 and A$300,000. Many (like sugar farms) have more acres than they need to grow their peak. Most have around a ten-ton tobacco peak and it is valued at A$4,000 to A$4,500 per ton. In this area, the smallest farms are around six-ton peak (there are only about ten that size) and forty-ton peak (only two). One can buy and sell tobacco peak independently of any particular plot of land.

There are many risks associated with tobacco growing. The present government, unlike Labour before it, tends to use the tobacco quota as a pawn in its international trade negotiations. Presently, Australia is importing 40 percent of its tobacco consumption and domestic growers are receiving a low average price of A$3.76 per kilo. You are also vulnerable to winds, hailstorms, etc. The unmechanized farms are facing a major manpower shortage, since the mechanization of the sugar harvest has wiped out the seasonal canecutter labor source. The farmers have had to hire Australian pickers, many of whom prove to be unsatisfactory.]

Roberto Urquiza*#&—I was born in 1950 in Erandio, Bizkaia. I attended five years of night school after primary. I know Spanish, Italian, and English. I know no Basque as it was illegal when I was growing up. My father was born in Bilbao and was an upholsterer before he died. Mother was from Deusto and now lives with me here in Mareeba. I have three siblings. Isidoro lives in the Basque Country and is a merchant mariner. María del Carmen came to Australia sixteen years ago and sews in a garment factory in Brisbane. Juan José came to Australia in 1975 and is a fitter-turner in Dysart, Queensland (Brisbane).

I was working as an upholsterer in Leioa before I immigrated here in 1969. I wanted to leave for political reasons and to avoid military service. My brother-in-law was in Australia and told me about it. He and María del Carmen lived in Dimbulah at that time. They helped with the papers and I borrowed my fare from a loan company in Spain. I flew from Sydney to Cairns and then went to Dimbulah by car.

My first job in Australia was with the Steelcon Company in Atherton. It was based out of Mount Isa. After upholstering, I found work with a sledgehammer to be very hard. But after a week, they taught me to be a dynamiter. That was easier. I lived in an apartment by myself and earned A$63 weekly. In my spare time, I read a lot and went to the movies. I paid off my fare the first year.

After three months, I went to Dimbulah to pick tobacco. The farmer offered the job to me when we met drinking in a hotel. I worked with two other guys, one a Basque—Patxi Larrazabal. I made A$68.50 weekly, including room and board. After the harvest, I went to Ingham with José Uriarte to cut cane. We lived and cut together in Trebonne that season with five others. We recreated together—met girls, went to dances, got drunk, played *mus*.

That slack, José Uriarte and I went back to Dimbulah. We worked for my brother-in-law and made A$80 per week. That cane season, I went back to Ingham with my brother-in-law to plant cane as his wife had gone to Spain for a visit. I then cut in Ingham alone that season. I averaged A$150 per week. But then I left after two months as the cane was poor, fallen to the ground, and tangled. So, my brother-in-law and I went to Mareeba. Someone came to our boardinghouse looking for workers. I made A$85 weekly.

After two-and-a-half months, I was doing judo training in a gym and was offered a job by another farmer. I stayed with him for the next two years. Then, I left for Texas with a Spaniard (Gustavo González) to pick tobacco. It was arranged from Mareeba. I made A$1.40 an hour.

After the harvest, Gustavo and I went to Brisbane and I found a job as an upholsterer for A$120 weekly. I was there for five months until my employer went broke. I found another job in Brisbane through a newspaper ad with a different upholstery firm at A$130 weekly. I was there for two years and was married in Brisbane. It was then that I decided to move to Mareeba to start the upholstery business that I own today. My wife is a self-employed hairdresser. Between us we make more than A$28,000 annually. We rent our house for A$140 monthly.

It took me a year to learn English, mainly by reading and talking. I dated a few Australian girls. I started reading the *Reader's Digest* in 1980. I don't subscribe to newspapers. I no longer listen to shortwave radio but used to. I would tune in Radio Moscow, Radio Peking, Radio Madrid, Radio Euskadi, and Radio Pirenaica. I was naturalized in 1975 in order to have full rights here. I wanted to be Australian. Australia is a better country than Spain. I joined the Italo-Australian Club in 1974 in Brisbane to socialize. I am a member of the Mareeba International Club since 1978. I favor Labour in politics and am an atheist. I go to the Masterton Hotel for a drink every day because that is where my friends are. We speak in English. It is not important to me to be around other Basques, but I prefer that my daughter marry one. We use some Spanish at home, and English as well. There is considerable difference between Spaniards and Basques in thinking, character, culture, and tastes (particularly music). I don't like Italians in the least.

I met my wife in 1974 at a soccer match in Brisbane. We were married in 1975. Her parents were very opposed, but they later accepted it. I see them infrequently (gratefully). In 1975, I helped my mother and brother to immigrate; she now lives with us in Mareeba.

I may go back to Spain in 1982, mainly for a visit and to watch the World Cup soccer competition. I plan to retire here. The good things about Australia are the business opportunity, the beer, and the freedom. The downsides are the job opportunities (mainly manual), the beer (alcohol abuse), and the Aborigines.

Townsville

Agustín Adarraga*& —I was born in Hernani, Gipuzkoa, into a large family of twelve children. My father, Luis Adarraga Gorrochategui, and one of his brothers were married to two sisters. Between the two couples, they had twenty children. Father had studied in Orthez, France, for three years and was fluent in French. At our dinner table you were allowed to speak Basque or French, but never *Castellano*. If you were caught speaking two words of Spanish, you lost your cider; three words cost you dessert. I only spoke to my father in Basque until the day he died.

My father and his brother manufactured chocolates. Father educated all of his children; almost all became engineers. I did my military service for about a year and became a second lieutenant in the Spanish Army. Then, since I was good in mathematics, Father sent me to the same college in Madrid that a couple of my brothers had attended—the Jesuits' ICAI or *Instituto Católico de Artes Industriales* (the Catholic Institute of Industrial Arts). I studied there for three years, but hated it. When I became old enough to defy him, I transferred to the University of Zaragoza to study veterinary medicine. In 1954, I even pursued my degree in it at the University of Glasgow. Back in Spain, I got my degree at the University of Zaragoza. That is where I met María. She is from Catalunya and was doing graduate work there as well in nursing.

Anyway, the economy in Spain was very bad and I was unable to find work as a veterinarian. My father asked me to join him in the chocolate business, and I agreed to do so for two years to see if there was a future in it for both of us. I began considering emigrating. We had friends and family in both Venezuela and Mexico. I also thought of Argentina, since I might be able to practice as a veterinarian there, but it didn't work out. Then, I saw a newspaper ad for Operation Emu and applied. They wanted workers for the sugar and they didn't like my appearance. I showed them a photo of me digging ditches as a laborer in Zaragoza, and they were unimpressed. I told them that I was physically fit and was not afraid of hard manual labor. I passed their tests and was told to report. I wanted to bring María with me, and they insisted that we be married. So, we wed two weeks before boarding the ship. It was assisted-passage and we only had to pay £30 each toward the fare.

We left in December of 1959. We stopped in the Canary Islands and many of the men went with prostitutes and caught venereal diseases. When we reached Capetown, I arranged for them to go ashore for treatment. Some of the mothers on the boat asked my advice when their children were ill. By the time we reached Melbourne, I had become the leader of the group.

We wanted to see the city, but they loaded us onto a train like prisoners and told us that we could not get off until we reached Bonegilla—a real concentration camp. I went to work in the hospital as a kind of nurse's aide, cleaning up the doctors' waste, and as an interpreter. I knew some English and could fumble around with a dictionary. About a month later, an Italian was going to Melbourne and took me along in his car. I went looking for work and interviewed at a hospital. I couldn't really understand them and kept saying "I beg your pardon..." But I didn't understand when they repeated themselves.

When I got back to Bonegilla, I told María to pack up as we were moving to Melbourne. "Did you get a job." "I think so." Anyway, when I went back, I got through their iron gates easily enough, but then they made me leave just as fast. I didn't have a job. I kept applying, and after a few days found work with CSL [Commonwealth Serum Laboratories] processing blood plasma collected in rural shires. We worked all day in a cold room; temperatures near zero. I made £6 per week doing that. I made friends with an Australian veterinarian and he helped me apply for work in my profession. But the offers I got were to "clean the stables." That was a nonstarter.

After six months in Melbourne, we moved to Brisbane. Alberto Urberuaga had told me that, if I ever needed work, he could give it to me in the sugar industry. So, I thought that, if Brisbane didn't work out, we could move to Trebonne. It was difficult at first. I applied for a manual laborer job, but they didn't want me. My appearance was too refined. I asked a Greek restaurant owner for work, and he asked if I knew anything about the business? I replied no, but that I had a lot of experience eating in restaurants! He gave me three-hours' work a night. I also got a job in a tavern; that lasted for six days.

I was, of course, applying for better positions, and, given my Melbourne experience, I was offered a job as a biotech assistant for the Red Cross. We were investigating hemophilia. The director of the Brisbane Red Cross facility also took note of me. He was a Russian and empathized with my situation as a migrant. I wanted to enroll in the University of Queensland and get a doctorate. The head of my lab said I didn't need it. He was moving to another lab and wanted me to go with him. But I felt that you have to have the credential to get ahead, no matter what else you can claim. The Red Cross director agreed to give me time off to attend classes if I would stay. So, now I was working and attending classes as well.

The idea was to get a Bachelor's of Science degree. They offered me six credits for my previous studies in Spain. The first year, I concentrated mainly on English. I made two Aussie friends at the University who helped me a lot. They were very generous with their time. It took three years in all, including night classes, to get my degree.

My credential and experience were in pathology and bioscience, and it was then that an opportunity became available. There were hospitals in both Cairns and Townsville with openings in their state-funded laboratories. Since I was beginning to lecture in my field, I chose Townsville General Hospital because of the city's James Cook University.

It was now 1967, and, after about six months on the job, María and I made our first trip back to Spain. We were open to the possibility of staying there. I tried to get work, but without much success. A former professor of mine and two of my classmates (one teaching in London) urged me to get my doctorate. They thought that, once I had the degree in hand, they could nominate and support me during the oppositions' competition for a regular academic position at some Spanish university. The problem was that I would need about another five years of graduate study to reach that point. It seemed too long, and we decided to return to Australia to make our lives here permanently.

María became a nurse in the pathology division of the Townsville

General Hospital and still works in it. There was a division of labor between my supervisor and me. He headed the Townsville Pathology Lab and I was the *de facto* head of the three or four others under him. In all, between doctors, nurses, and other staff, about fifty-five persons were reporting to me. It was a big responsibility, but very fulfilling. I learned that good administration meant anticipating matters before they became a problem. To do that, you needed to know your people well, including their family arrangements and life challenges. No two were the same. My boss didn't understand that, or was simply not interested.

And then he retired. So, for the next seven years, I was either the interim head of the whole operation or second in command under a new director who lasted for just a few months. In 1987, I traveled to France to visit the Pasteur Institute in Paris to become acquainted with what it was doing in AIDS research. That was a forbidden topic in this country. After that trip, we began taking blood samples here in Townsville; the only other lab in Queensland doing so was in Brisbane. We still analyze about fifty samples a week for AIDS here in the Townsville General Hospital.

At age 63, I decided to retire as well. It was then that I went into sport full-time.

I come from a family of sportsmen. My father was the cycling champion of the entire Basque Country, including the Pays Basque.[11] He received Spain's "Sportsman of the Year" award. My cousin, Manuel, was the founder of the Hernani Rugby Club, before performing on the Spanish champion *Atlético de Madrid* team in that sport.

My brother, José Luis, was a four-time national champion in Spain in *balonmano* (handball). Bernardino was a decathlon and pentathlon champion in the 1950s at the Spanish national level. Fernando held the national pole-vaulting record.[12] I was a serious *balonmano* and *pelota* player. I recall playing against Bishop Setien (diocese of San Sebastián). He was actually pretty good. I was on a Spanish national handball team three times. I also played on the Hernani rugby team. When I was in Zaragoza studying, some weekends I had to commute back to Hernani for a match. We were the Gipuzkoa champions.

Anyway, after moving to Townsville, one day my personal doctor, Joe León, said to me, "You are a Basque, so you know how to play *pelota*. You should try squash." I agreed and he arranged a game for me. I showed up wearing my white shirt and pants, and red cummerbund, like we dressed for a match in the Basque Country. Everyone was in shorts and they just laughed at me.

In *pelota* and *pala* you use your shoulder, but squash is all wrist. My shots kept hitting the ceiling, but it was an easy adjustment. I was playing the courts' pro and he ran me around a lot. Squash is ninety percent stamina, and I was a big drinker and smoker. But I am very determined, so I began training. I did that for a month, abstaining and running. I went back, and no one in the club could give me competition, except the pro. He taught me a few squash tricks and I won every title in North Queensland. I then competed in the state and nationals. I was the Queensland champion in my age bracket several times. I represented Australia in competitions with New Zealand, and then went to the world championships in Toronto. I became world champion in my age bracket (50–54). I was fifty-four at the time. The next year, I went to Hernani to promote the game, but no one was interested. That same year, Geoff Hunt and Heather Mackay[13] came here to Townsville to play competitive matches with me.

My son, Austin, started playing squash as a child. When he was eleven, he was in Spain visiting relatives in Madrid perfecting his Spanish. That year, Spain had its first youth squash championship and he entered. He was the runner-up to a seventeen-year-old champion. Austin was the highest-ranked player in Spain for five consecutive years. He played on the professional tour during the 1990s. He was once the eleventh-ranked men's professional player in the world. Jansher Khan, the eventual champion, eliminated him in the semifinals of the 1992 world championships held in Johannesburg. Austin was later the pro at squash facilities in Madrid and in Brisbane.

Anyway, after retiring I devoted my time to promoting squash. The country's Squash Federation certified coaches at what was called "level one." Then it created a special "level two" category with international standing, and there were only four of us—including Geoff Hunt, Heather Mackay, and myself. I became the first Junior League squash coach in Australia. I started a squash association here called the JLA. The initials stood for *Jai Alai*, though few understood that. We had ninety members, 60 percent of whom were youths.

In 2000, I was awarded the Queen's Australia Sports Medal for that year. It was given to me at a ceremony by British Governor General William Dean, and is signed by John Howard, Australia's prime minister.

In life, I wear three hats. My first is my Basque heritage. I understand the love of Aborigines for this land, since I have the same feeling for my Basque Country. When I was little, Mother took us every year on a pilgrimage to the Monastery of Aranzazu. I study Basque for at least an hour every day. I just love it. My Basque is before *Euskera Batua*. Father Villasante invented that. In my time, we didn't read or write Basque, we just spoke it. Now they have a Basque word for everything. For cemetery we used to say *kanposantua*, an obvious borrowing from the Spanish *camposanto*. Now they say *ilerria*. I estimate that at least 20 percent of my Basque came from Spanish. I study my Basque grammar and my Basque-Spanish dictionary.

I read the Hernani newspaper every day on the internet. I travel to the town almost every year. The first thing I do is climb our mountain, Adarra. My brother, Juan Bautista, died three or four years ago and we scattered his ashes in a dolmen there. It was his wish. He was a great *espatadantzari* [sword dancer]. I then drive my beloved coast from Donostia to Elantxobe. I drink cider and eat *membrillo* and Idiazabal sheep's cheese. I often go at fiesta time and record the music so I can listen to it back here. I have many, many articles about Hernani and other Basque topics. Here is an image of the main altar at Aranzazu before it was remodeled. My house here in Townsville I call Arkaitza.

My second hat is Spain. I took a loyalty vow to it when I became an officer in the Army. I studied in Madrid and Zaragoza and married María from Barcelona. I have friends and family all over Spain—Cordoba, Seville, Madrid, Barcelona, Galicia. Two of my sons live in Madrid and are married to *Madrileñas*.

My third hat is Australia—my adopted country. I am very proud to be a part of it. I have given my all for Hernani, Gipuzkoa, Spain, and Australia.

Hernani is a main supporter of Batasuna and ETA. It is included in what is called the "ETA Triangle," along with Andoain and Urnieta. You could add Lasarte and Rentería [Errenteria] as well. During fiestas in Hernani, there are portraits of ETA prisoners strung from balcony to balcony. I disagree with *kale borroka* and political graffiti everywhere—all over my beautiful Hernani. I have many friends in Bastasuna, some of whom have served up to fifteen years in prison for belonging to ETA. We have drinks together, but we can hardly discuss politics. I tell them that I disagree first of all with the killing, and, secondly, for their lack of respect for the political opinions of others—including mine. That is not democracy.

I like [president] Ibarretxe, but I can't stand Arzalluz.[14] He is an opportunist who wants to separate the Basque Country from Spain. He is like the characters in *Gargantua and Pantagruel* who piss and shit on everything. I had a copy of that book. It was on the Catholic banned list, but I found a copy here in Australia. Father Ormazabal borrowed it on his last visit here. He was traveling south and, a few days later, he died in Mackay. So, I lost that book.

When I first arrived in Townsville, I wanted to start a Basque club here. But then I realized that most of the canecutters had left and we Basques were spread out and mixed among Spaniards. Also, we Basques are hard to manage; each is his own priest. So, I called some people together at my house to begin the Spanish Society of North Queensland. It must have been about 1970. I invited the two most prominent Spanish businessmen—Joe Goicoechea and Bruno Tapiolas. Father Ormazabal, a good friend, also attended, as did Johnny Mendiolea. Joe was made the first president and I was the secretary (and later the second president). I wrote the constitution. I put in a clause that limited terms in office to three years. I wanted to avoid the presidency being monopolized for years by any one individual [shades of Arzalluz].

We had some meetings in a Townsville hotel in which Joe was a partner. We decided to celebrate Spain's regional festivals. July 31, Saint Ignatius Day, was a big one. We held it in Trebonne sometimes with dancing, *txingas*, *pelota*, stonelifting for two days. Then there was the Day of the *Sardana* and, on October 4, the *Pilarica* (Aragón's Virgen of Pilar Day).

I wrote a newsletter for the Society for a number of years. Last year, Maialen Lujanbio, a female *bertsolari*, toured Australia. In my time only men were bertsolaris, but that is changing. I think she will be the next world champion. She was a great success here. We promoted her and about 350 spectators turned out. The Society is still going, although there is now talk of starting a Basque Club here. We shall see.

BURDEKIN

Agustín Arrate*#&^ 15—My name is Agustín Arrate. I was raised in the town of Markina, Bizkaia. My grandfather, also Agustín Arrate, was born on the *baserri* Txorixe. He had been in Chicago and that was his nickname in Markina. His kids were called "Chicagotarrak" or "the Chicagoans." My grandmother was from Burgos and I was raised in part by her. So, I spoke good Spanish. When I first went to school I was outraged by the teacher. He fined anyone for speaking Basque. The kids from the distant *baserriak* knew no Spanish when they started. I felt very sorry for them, having to go home to ask their impoverished parents for that money. My father, Jenaro, was a blacksmith, in partners with his brother, Patxi, and brother-in-law, Celes. They shod cows so they could pull plows, but then that disappeared. So, they opened a garage and automobile agency. I was working on my degree in mechanics, and so I went to work for them.

I was becoming of the age to do military service, nineteen, and I didn't want to. I was fed up with politics in Spain. I was a member of a dance troupe that toured villages and performed during their festivals. If you wanted to perform you needed permission from a Franquist mayor. You had to get down on your knees. One time, our mayor denied us permission because of our pro-Basque performances. I used to do clandestine things, like hang at night the prohibited Basque *ikurriña* from electric lines. I was in a mountaineering club and they were regarded with suspicion by the authorities. I had three friends in prison serving a year or two for pro-ETA activity—not violence, maybe just for distributing anti-Franco literature. Anyway, I was stained, as it were, not to mention fed up, and Father thought it better that I leave for eighteen months or so.

I had a friend in Venezuela, and he kept urging me to come there. He assured me that, with my mechanic's degree and experience, there was plenty of work for me there.

I came to Australia in 1962, to Ingham, to work as a mechanic in Bresciani Motors. I planned to stay two years and now [2002] it has been forty! Alberdi said that his uncle in Venezuela would advance me my fare. It was going to cost £250 that I didn't have. I spent a year trying to make the arrangements. I could never seem to get my exit permit. I think I had pulled a number and was standing in a long line. I hired an agent with pro-Franco credentials and even he became frustrated. He wasn't sure, but he thought that my being from a pro-Basque-Nationalist family was a factor. He suggested that, if I could go to France it might be easier to arrange my departure from there. Well, we were used to that—just get your hiking staff and slip through the mountains rather than a frontier post. I was within three days of doing that when the Australian opportunity came up. I flew out with a young man, Iñaki Arrate (no relative) from Olaeta/Lekeitio, who had an aunt in Ingham. He was destined to work in Félix Jayo's bakery in Trebonne. We traveled by plane with two guys from Aulesti headed to Ayr.

José Bubé, a Catalan with a Basque wife, Juanita Alberdi from Markina, sponsored me and got me that job. She was his second wife after his first wife, Juanita's sister, Josefina, died. Their brother, Santos, was here at the time and he was courting Segunda Bereciartua, my eventual mother-in-law. She was widowed but didn't marry him, so he went back to Spain and married there. They had another brother, Antonio, who had a cane farm in Ingham.

The Bubés met me at the airport in Townsville. The English national rugby team was touring Australia and was playing that day in Townsville. They took me from the airport to the match. It was the most boring thing I had ever seen. I knew nothing about that sport, of course. They then said we had a short drive to Ingham. A hundred plus miles later we arrived there after dark! That was my introduction to the vast scale of this place.

It was Saturday and I went to work on Monday morning at Bresciani Motors. They sold tractors and various brands of cars. They had recently acquired the Fiat Tractor dealership and had sold about sixty by then. A few weeks into my employment, they gave me an International truck with a crane and tools. It was my job to tour the district and provide maintenance and repairs to the tractors. Well, that was pretty easy since most were brand-new and with few problems. A few were two or three years old but well built and therefore didn't need a lot of attention. The farmers came to trust me. They would ask me to find them reliable cane-cutters among the Basques. I placed several of them.

I did that mechanical work for two years, but I knew that I couldn't pay back my passage with those wages and everyone talked about the big money to be made in cane cutting. So, I cut in Ingham for a year and then heard that conditions were better in the Burdekin. With the irrigation, the cane was always erect and evenly spaced, and you bent over less. I went there.

My first contract with a friend was on an Italian farm. It was undesirable, as he had too much cane for one cutter and not enough for two. It gave us a chance to break in, which was hard in the Burdekin as it was a bastion of British preference. But once you had a union ticket, you were guaranteed your own preference at the next sign-on.

Sometimes, farmers might hire a cutter without a ticket and tell them to tell the cane inspector or union organizer that he was just a farmhand should they come around. There was an Italian farmer in Home Hill who hired four Basques cutters. The union organizer refused to give them tickets and watched the property to make sure they didn't cut. The farmer put them up in his barracks and gave them spending money. The organizer kept telling the Italian to hire an approved gang. But the farmer was wealthy and stubborn and just replied, "I have my own gang here already." The standoff lasted for about a month until the organizer gave in. The pressure was too much for him; he probably feared it would become a cause *celébre*.

On the Italian's farm, I worked with a Navarran (his wife was our cook) and guy from Gernika. Iñaki Arrate was cutting as well and he asked me to change to his gang and I did. After the harvest, a man, Féliz from Olaeta, Imanol from Lekeitio, and I went to Atherton to pick tobacco. One of them had a car. We had no contacts, but getting a job there was easy. An Italian came looking for workers when we were drinking in a hotel and we signed on. We were there for four months.

I did not like picking tobacco. The climate was much cooler. You slept under a blanket and drank wine more than beer. You got up very early and there was dew on the crop. You picked ripe leaves and left the green ones and put them in a sack on your back. By the time it was over, it hurt your shoulders and back more than a bundle of cane. There were lots of snakes; really bad ones. They were all over the ground and even up in the tobacco at times. Unlike the sugar, they never burn tobacco fields and the bush comes right up to their edge, so the snakes proliferate. We picked from early December until the end of January and then fired up wood-burning ovens to dry the leaves. That was dirty as well and you could hardly breathe for the smoke. We finished in April.

By then, I was friends with the two Echeandia brothers from Gabika and we went to Ingham to plant cane before the harvest. While there, we heard of a cane-planting opportunity in Home Hill. One of the brothers went ahead and sent for us.

I would note that we always enjoyed ourselves. Yes, we made money and saved some, but we enjoyed life as well. The immigrants who hate it here are those who come with the idea of saving A$10,000 as quickly as possible. They never go to a barbecue or dance, and seldom to a pub. They stay isolated in the barracks. I liked dancing and was not afraid to jump right into English, with all my mistakes. I wasn't timid. Later, when we were going from the Burdekin to the Dimbulah to pick tobacco we stopped in Ingham for three days to a week to visit friends and just relax a little. One played the accordion and we went around partying with him.

We planted cane in Home Hill until the season started. There was a preference system here and, if you were a foreigner, you had to have a union ticket that showed you had cut the year before. We did not and the farmer who wanted to hire me went along to the sign-up. When we were told that there were seven of eight men who had preference and were still unemployed so we could not cut, my farmer objected. It seems that many of the Anglos (I call them *Sajones* or Saxons) would cut the easiest and best cane until September, since that's when it got hot and the remaining cane was more difficult, and then leave the farmer in the lurch. So, our farmer wanted me. Period. When the union official objected that I could not get the job done alone, I said I would find a partner. We prevailed.

I cut alone for two months, maybe 100 tons per week. Then I found an old, semiretired cutter named Lachiondo from Ea or Natxitua. He couldn't work all day but was great for about three-quarters of it. We finished that harvest together.

About October, the man who was doing our haul-out said that he was purchasing a farm and wanted to sell his outfit, his nearly new tractor and gear, for £2,500. It was a good price, but I didn't have that money. He kept insisting that I was young and had the necessary mechanical skills to be successful. He had contracts with eight farmers and so his business was solid. Maybe a week later, I was drinking in a hotel with a man from Lekeitio who was retired after cutting cane and picking tobacco in Transfield for many years. I told him about the proposition, and he offered to lend me the money at the same low interest he was getting for his savings in the bank.

So, I went ahead with the deal. The seller talked to all of his clients and they agreed to stay with me. I now had an outfit and 24,000 tons to haul-out. I did that work for the next four or five years and made good money. During the slacks, I would head for the tobacco. The third year, I was drinking in a hotel in Ingham on the way to the Tablelands when I ran into my old boss at the tractor agency. He said, "I need you here, you can't leave. I have many more farmers now and am desperate." "No, no we go to the same place in Dimbulah and they are expecting me." "Well, you can't go." I was conflicted as I felt I owed him something, but also to the farmer. Anyway, I ended up staying in Ingham on the condition that it would be for the slack only since I had my haul-out business in Home Hill. I did that Ingham stint for the next couple of years. I hung out with two young stonemasons (*albañiles*)—Badiola and Pete Aranas—and a couple of Basque carpenters. Of course, the young Ingham canecutters would be gone somewhere else for the slack, but these tradesmen stayed in Ingham year-round.

I met my future wife, Mary Bengoa, in 1964. It was the slack and some of us went from Ingham to Ayr for a festival. We met her father and he invited us home to dinner. Anyway, about that time, there was some new technology for loading and hauling that my farmers were urging me to buy. I wasn't convinced as it was unproven and very complicated to maintain. But my clients were nagging me.

In 1966, Mary and I were married. José Bubé and his wife stood in for my parents at the wedding here. Several of us married Basque girls born here. That was my case with Mary. We were seeing each other, and I told her that I had to make up my mind, since my family had a car dealership in Spain, and they wanted me to come back. By Basque custom that should have been mine, I am the eldest son. But my two brothers ended up with it.

In 1967, I moved to Ayr to my father-in-law's farm. The Bengoas had a nephew from Amoroto doing their haul-out and he wanted to go back to Spain. Peter was planning to leave for the Basque Country as well for an extended stay. He suggested that I take his place while he was gone. So, the Bengoas offered me a job to do their haul-out, and I took it.

That same year my father was killed in a freak accident. Standing in the portal of his house, he was hit by an out-of-control motorcyclist. I was twenty-six and the eldest in the family. I went to Euskadi in February of 1968 with Mary and our infant son, Johnny, to arrange Father's estate's affairs. I was able to get a twelve-month permit but was advised by Spanish authorities that it would be prudent for me to leave a day before it was up, because, otherwise, they would be coming for me. Our daughter, Amaya, was born while we were there. In September, I went to work in the Markina garage and then left for Australia and the Bengoa farm the following February.

Peter was home and he had married María Angela Malaxechevarria from Lekeitio and brought her back to Ayr. So, I continued to work with the two brothers-in law on salary. They paid me the going rate of A$5 per hour. I doubted that I had much of a future on the Bengoa place, since it would likely go to Mary's brothers. Also, I was still contemplating whether to stay in Australia or return home permanently to my family's business in Markina.

In 1971, I told my in-laws that I was leaving the farm to go back to cane cutting. I gave the excuse that I wanted to save more money to replace my old car. Cutting for a season, it would be possible for me to save A$3,000. They immediately raised my salary to A$7.50 an hour! Then the father came to me and said that Mary had an undivided interest in his farms, but that he was thinking that he would buy a different one for us, one instead in return for her shares in the others. He tied up a farm in Millaroo, even made an offer, and then took me to see it. It had good soil but seemed very far away from everything. Access to it was over a decrepit wooden bridge and John Bengoa was of the opinion that it would be washed away in the next flood. Somehow, we got out of that contract—probably by declaring we couldn't raise the money. It wasn't true, but it worked.

Anyway, a couple of weeks later I was chatting at the Lion's Club with my lawyer and he asked if I was still looking for a farm? He then said that he had the power-of attorney to sell a small one near Clare for its owner. It had eighty acres and a 1,000-ton sugar peak. It had been a soldier-settlement property. I liked the place and we bought it in 1971. With the mill expansions, today it has a sugar peak of 3,000 tons. But, those first few years, we grew vegetables as well. We had as many as nine women at the same time picking our green beans. We shifted its house to a block of land in the town of Clare, and I commuted daily to the farm to work it. I have three sows, many piglets, a few goats, and lots of chickens.

In 2000, Mary and I moved to Ayr to the place that she had inherited. Our son, Johnny, took over that house in Clare and improved it. Sometimes, when Basque farmers decide to move back to the Basque Country, they lease their farm to a canecutter rather than sell it. That way, they can always change their mind and come back without having to start over again. Some who want to retire, but don't have kids or whose kids have left farming, do the same thing to stop working and have a fixed income. I received A$67,000 last year from the mill. That was gross, before my expenses. Anyway, I could probably lease my farm for A$15,000 annually and retire to the Basque Country with no worries.

There are more Basques in the Burdekin than in Ingham. About thirty years ago they had more, but not any longer. When I came here in the early sixties, in Spain all we ever heard was "Ingham, Ingham." I once saw a magazine article that said there were 2,000 Basques in Ingham, but I don't think there were ever that many. In the Far North, Ayr is "Basque Country." A few years ago, there would be a couple of hundred Basques in the Burdekin Hotel on weekends. The Queen Hotel sponsored a Basque tug-of-war team (six men) and they competed throughout the region as far away as Bowen. They used any prize money to throw a big party. There was a rival Basque team in Giru and the competition between the two was furious. Giru also had a good Italian team. We started a soccer team lately. Some wanted it to be all Basques, but we included two Australian players. To have excluded them would have made us as bad as those Australians who used to exclude us from their teams.

It rains a lot more in Ingham than here. That is good for the farmers, but not for the cutters. The weather is better here for cane-growing. With irrigation, the crop is better; the cane is not on the ground or tangled up. In my time, if you made £15 in a day there, here you might make 25. I worked in Ingham and we cut 6,000 tons among four men, an average of 1,500 tons each. The last year I cut here, we five harvested 13,000 tons. It was a big difference. So, Basques came here and got married. We all came from Ingham. It was our landing-area in Australia. There was an Aboitiz who went from here to Ingham to cut cane. He was the only one to do so, and it was like a joke. Nobody did that.

It is easier to buy a farm in Ingham. The land is cheaper. In Ingham, the price is one hundred to one—one hundred dollars per ton of peak. Here you can get two hundred to one and a few years ago it was as much as three hundred to one. We are in the best sugar-raising place in the world, and the Burdekin has the highest sugar content in its cane. We have bigger expenses, too—the irrigation. We have been in a drought just when the sugar prices are down. Thank God for the irrigation. Many of the boys that once cut cane bought a farm here.

For me, the worst thing about cane cutting was changing the rails in the hot sun. You had to cover your hands with grass to do that to keep from getting burned by the hot metal. Many men were hurt by dropping a rail, and many tendons were cut by crossbars.

There was a main leader of the Basques in Ingham—Pascual Badiola. He brought out many people from Spain. Some moderate Spaniards and even Basques here didn't like his ideas; he was very Basque. But I give it to him. Whenever I went to Ingham for a *chiquiteo*, there was Pascual in the hotel wearing his *txapela* surrounded by about twenty people. He was an old man by then, in his sixties, and they were in their forties. But they just wanted to be with him. They asked him advice about everything, even lawyers and legal matters. After I came to the Burdekin, I didn't see him much, but whenever I went to his house, I was very welcome.

I learned from my father-in-law that a couple of Basques from here went back to Spain during the Civil War to fight on the Republican side. I think they raised a little money here for the Republicans, but that was before my time. I have always been very Basque. I came here because I needed to get out of Spain for a while. I was in a little political trouble.

I learned drawing in school, and one time I got a Spanish publication with a map of Euskadi. I drew a map of the Basque Country for Pascual from it, and, the next time I visited his house, it was framed and up on his wall. He was the strongest of Basque nationalists. You had better not talk to him in Spanish or he would call you out for it.

Teresa Mendiolea was a bit like Pascual. She did a lot for the Basques. She didn't like the Basque guys dating Australian girls. She would take them aside and tell them not to. She would say, "I know a good girl for you." She might be an Andalusian from one of those Andalusian families in Ingham. "She's not Basque, but she comes from a good family," Teresa would say. When Mary and I were still dating, we went to a wedding in Ingham. Her mother asked, "And where are you sleeping?" I said at the Mendioleas, and that was fine with her. That night Teresa put me in the bedroom with Aniceto; he was still a bachelor, and she said to Mary, "You sleep in my room with me; there are two beds." That was what I was expecting. With her you couldn't get any funny ideas.

We have many friends in Ingham should anything happen to us here in Ayr. Basques would be three-quarters of the people from Spain in the Burdekin. Then maybe twenty percent are Catalonians and five from the rest of Spain. The Catalonians can be real fanatics. The original idea of a festival came from them, maybe in the late 1960s,[16] and they excluded everyone else. They never invited us, even though we were in the majority.

[In the course of our interview, Agustín produced a clipping from the *Townsville Catholic News* from 1969. The headline was "the Day of the Dance," and I now quote the content,

> The most interesting day of devotion, feasting an dancing was held in Ayr on April 27. Approximately fifty members of the Catalan (Spanish) community of Ayr, Home Hill and Brandon celebrated the feast of Our Lady of Montserrat in their traditional way. The replica of the blackened Madonna, leant by Mr. Benito Droguet, was enshrined in St. Mary's Church Parkside and during the special Mass in Spanish candles were offered to Our Lady as they are in Montserrat.
>
> The celebrant was Father Tomás Ormazabal, E.L., and the epistle was read by Father Antonio Maldonado who has lately come to the diocese from Tokyo. Though Father Maldonado is a Spaniard, this was the first time that he had read the lesson in his native tongue.
>
> Congregational singing in Spanish and "Ave Maria" most feelingly rendered by Mrs. B. Tapiolas were features of the Mass. Later, at the Masonic Hall, M.H., the entire Spanish community sat down to a sumptuous feast prepared for the occasion.
>
> The Ladies present were given a corsage and the men a small replica of the Catalan Flag—four red stripes on a yellow background.

Especially iced cake, surrounded by a statue of the Black Madonna with two miniature children offering red roses, held pride of place on the table. Father P. J. Carroll, Abn (Parkside) presided and cut the cake.

The afternoon was given over to dancing in the Catalonian style designed for religious occasions. These dances are somewhat like a Folk Dance with everyone holding hands in one big family circle, before the image of our Lady. Quite a few of the dancers had donned their regional costumes for the occasion. This is the way in which the Catalonians honor their patroness all over the world.

The whole spectacle made one realize how dancing which to most Australians is merely a form of recreation and at times a morally questionable one at that can be turned to the glory of God, and that, while we have used drama, poetry, recitation and singing as means of worship, we have neglected to use the dance.

This is not so with the Catalan people.

Mr. George Sallais, a brilliant exponent of the Catalan dance has, in his repertoire many religious themes, including the Stations of the Cross and the Resurrection and we hope to see more of this religious form of dancing at a later period.

For the benefit of the curious the Region of Catalonia is situated in the North-east of Spain just below the border with France. Barcelona is the principal city.

It was here that Our Lady is said to have appeared during the Moorish occupation and rallied the Christians to drive the strangers from the land.

A Carmelite Monastery on the Serrated Mountains is a symbol of the faith and devotion of the people to the Blessed Virgin.

The little statue of the seated Madonna and Child, which is enshrined in Montserrat and duplicated in most Catalan homes, is blackened by carbon from many torches and candles placed before it over the centuries.

We hope that this third annual celebration of the feast of Our Lady of Montserrat in Australia will not be the last.]

But as the Catalonians got older and were fewer, eventually they came to us and asked to come together. So, in 1970, we formed an Ayr Spanish Club. Most of the members are Basques; the majority of Catalonians live further north. Both Mary and I have been its president. I remember when Franco became ill, an old Catalonian member wanted us to send him a telegram with our best wishes for his recovery. I announced that I wanted a formal vote so it would appear in the minutes that I had voted against it. I was beaten by Franco's *guardias civiles* when I was seventeen. The telegram was never sent. Whenever any Spaniard from here to Innisfail dies, we send a wreath to the funeral.

In 1975, we Basques in the Burdekin decided to have a Basque festival. So, we put up ten dollars each at a get-together, a barbecue that Mary and I hosted. People from Ingham came as well. There was friendly competition between us. We had *txingas* [weight-carrying] and weight lifting. A black fellow [Aborigine] attended as well. He liked to enter the *txingas* and was good at it. He once won second place.

We wanted to get two weights, proper ones with handles [as the sport had evolved in Spain] rather than the older ones from Ingham. About two months later, I went to Spain on a visit, and I agreed to commission those weights from Alberdi on the *baserri* Aritxinaga in Markina (he was famed for making them) and bring them back with me on the ship. I packed the handles in my luggage. I was careful to get receipts and proper accounting for everything. We had a bit of money left in the bank, maybe A$150. We donated it to the library for books. That was in the newspaper.

Since about 1970, we have a Spanish Society of North Queensland. It has around fifty families. Joe Goicoechea was the first president and my wife Mary was the second one. The Club has a circular [newsletter]. Before any festivals or anything, maybe thirty years ago, we used to have a lot of festivals—weight lifting, *txingas* [weight-carrying], tugs-of-war, and things like that.

We celebrate several holidays during the year: New Year's Eve, Saint Joseph's Day, and Sardana Day [the Virgin of Montserrat's feast day], the *Día de la Hispanidad* or Day of the Race (October 12) as the Spaniards call it.[17] Then we might have a couple of barbecues in between. We cover everyone. We don't get into trouble! Everybody is happy.

The Spanish Society just nominated Johnny Mendiolea for a Queensland government award given for helping migrants. Last year we nominated Mrs. Pla, a Catalana, from here and she won. We wanted to nominate the whole Mendiolea family, but the award is for individuals.

The non-Basque Spaniards in Townsville tried to form their own club. They struggled along for a while, but it did not survive. Some are now part of the Spanish Society for North Queensland, based here. We have considered trying to have a clubhouse, but we are too few to afford something like that. Also, we are fewer and fewer all the time. Maybe in the last ten years, twenty-five old people died. Some went back to Spain. Every year the Society tries to make a donation for civic causes—drug-use prevention among young people or the blue nurses who visit the elderly in their homes. Last year we gave three hundred dollars to the blue nurses and got our name in the paper—and a lot of blah, blah.

We hold our Saint Ignatius Day festival at the new International Club here. This year we did weight lifting, carrying, and stone dragging. I proposed that the club build a small *frontón* that would cost A$6,000. They have a good place for that. We could apply to Parks and Recreation for a one-third subsidy. I knew we could raise the rest of that money. My sister is the president of the International Club. At first, everyone wanted it, but then some people opposed the idea. So, I dropped the matter.

We never had much to do with Tully and Innisfail. There were just a few Basque families there; a lot of Catalans. In the Tablelands, Mareeba, there is a pretty active Spanish Club. It was started by a fellow named Acha. It is maybe a little bigger than our club. But it is for Spaniards way more than Basques. The last time I was there, they had maybe fifty-percent Basques out of sixty members. Here, we have thirty-five Basque families out of fifty members. We have five Valencians and then there are the Tapiolas and Comas Catalan families, as well as Droguet and Sallais from Townsville.

We used to perform Basque dances. Our mother taught dancing in Spain, and she was pretty good at it here—but it didn't work out. My two daughters haven't danced for four years. They live in Townsville and you can't get them to come. Many of the young people their age moved away.

Mary and I always speak Spanish between us [she is Australian-born]. I talk in Basque to the children. Amaya knows quite a bit of

Basque, but hardly any Spanish. I wanted the children to be able to talk to their grandparents back in Spain. When they went, people in Markina remarked that my children speak better Basque than theirs despite being raised so far away. I am proud of that. Mary's parents here in Australia appreciate it as well. Our mother [Segunda Bereciartua] now manages a store, but her English is not that good. So, she can use Basque with her grandchildren.

Many of the cutters went back to Spain, and it's sad for us here. Things are much better there than before, so I understand. My sister is a schoolteacher and she earns pretty good money. She is thinking of visiting us here, you can do that now. Some of them went down South, to Sydney and places like that. Hardly half a dozen new men have come in the last ten years.[18] Before, you would go to the hotel once a week on the weekend and there were always new faces. At one time, it was almost all Basques, but then the newcomers were from all over Spain. There might have been 300 to 400 Basque farmers and that many cutters in North Queensland; now there may be just 200 to 300 Basques between here and Mareeba. Most of the young people can't speak the language any longer.

I don't know what is going to happen with farming; or rather Basques in it. Johnny Mendiolea's children are now third generation and none of them is a farmer. Two are teachers, one is a mechanic, and one lives in Sydney. My two daughters are the same way. One is a schoolteacher in Townsville and the other is a legal secretary there. They don't want to come here anymore. City girls; they don't want to go to the bush. It is natural really. You want the best for your kids. You don't want them to have to do the dirty jobs you did. There is a successful canefarmer here, Jenaro Lequerica, from Nabarniz. When he was growing up, they were four brothers on the farm. His father would say three of you are going to school and one has to go to the mountains to care for the sheep. And Jenaro always put up his hand for that. Now he has two sons—one is an accountant and the other is a civil engineer. I don't know what will happen to that farm.

In our case it was a little different. When Mary's brother Johnny was twenty, the family bought a farm in Jarvisfield that he now runs. Peter was trained as a mechanic and worked at that in town for a while, but then he came back to run the home farm. The two brothers help each other. And, of course, Mary and I got our own farm here. So, all three of Pedro's children have farms today.[19]

[In the interviews for her book, Segunda expressed concern for the next generation:

> There will be nobody, nobody. Juan has three girls, none of them will carry on with the farm. They will not marry a farmer, because to get marry with a farmer one has to marry an Italian or a Sicilian, because Spaniards also do not keep farming. They all go to study. They earn good money. Rose Mary is working and earn a good salary, she went two or three times to Spain. Now, she went to America with her high salary. She does not think of getting marry. The others from Peter, they are still little. The boy is ten years old and the girl thirteen. Well I would be surprised if those stay on the farm. The Bengoa name in farming is over. Those of Mary's neither I don't believe. The boy is not interested. The girls, one is a teacher and the other a nurse, neither, no. There is finish the farms.[20]

I have always liked politics, both in the Basque Country and here. I was once a candidate here for councilman. In those days, there were four electoral districts and Clare was in the one most distant from Ayr. We felt abandoned. We were represented by two old-timer cattlemen. One had been in office for about twenty-five years and the other maybe twenty. They antedated much of the sugar expansion and many of us farmers felt left out. So, there was a meeting of about fifty or sixty voters, and it was decided to field a candidate in the upcoming election. We nominated Joe Bonanno, but he declined because he was too busy with his farm. We next proposed a sugar official who said he would have a conflict of interest. So, someone nominated me. I protested that my English was insufficient and that I was a foreigner. But they insisted and I accepted with the condition that they would help and that the campaign would be about our proposed agenda rather than critical of our incumbents *per se*. They paid my filing fees and ran some ads in the newspaper. We thought that the veteran incumbent was untouchable, but not the other cattleman. In the event, I lost to him by forty votes out of nearly five thousand cast.

They wanted me to run again in the next election. Some thought that we should have been more critical and wanted the next campaign to be more so. I did not run. However, I believe that I accomplished something. After my race, Clare received a lot of attention from City Hall. We got improvements to the connecting road, new streets, and gutters.

I have served on many committees here. I represented Clare, Millaroo, and Dalbeg in the oversight of the Old Peoples' Home. I was on the committee for the Farmers' Association and the one for Invicta Mill—our sugar mill. I have been president of the Spanish Club and the Clare Club as well. I was president of the Soccer Club. I have been a soccer referee, trainer, and on the directive of more than one soccer team.

[I attended a meeting of the Ayr Lion's Club with Agustín and was asked to give a talk about my project—a comparative study of Basque and Abruzzesi immigration in Australia. There were about five Italians in the club out of fifty-six members in all. Afterwards, we were having a drink with some of the Aussies and they started making "Bloody-Wog" jokes. One was a newspaperman who was in his cups, and he declared that Italians ended up with all the money because they grow marijuana. One asked, only half in jest, if I carried a weapon in the boot of my car for protection if I was going to hang out around the Mafia? That elicited from an Italian the response that Italians are wealthier because they work harder than convicts. He then told me to be sure to put in my book that if it weren't for the immigrants the Burdekin would be bush instead of farmland. The president of the Club noted that, three years earlier, someone gave a talk praising the contributions of the immigrant canecutter to the Burdekin's economy and was booed. However, all were interested in my project and asked to be notified when the book came out. The Aussies present were particularly down on Al Grassby. The president and two Aussie members took me aside and said that race relations in Australia were much better before Grassby and his multiculturalism. Back then, immigrants did their best to assimilate and become good Australians instead of sticking to themselves like now.]

José María Zabala # & —I was born in 1941 in Amoroto. Father was from there and Mother was from Mendexa. They were farmers in Olaeta when he died. Father had herded sheep in the USA for eight years. I was the youngest of seven siblings. My brother, Alberto, is a fisherman and he has been to Labrador in that capacity. Antonio is a canefarmer in Giru in the Burdekin. None of the others has ever emigrated.

Before I came here in 1961, I had worked in a sawmill in Lekeitio for two years and then on an animal-feed delivery truck in Olaeta for another two. I emigrated in order to avoid military service and to find a better future. I thought I would save some money and then go back to Spain. I thought about the USA but wasn't old enough at that time. I learned of Australia from my brother Antonio and my mother's cousin, Vicente Goitiandia, in Ingham. Antonio arranged my documents and advanced my fare as a loan. Mother was opposed; Father thought it was a good idea. I sailed from Italy to Brisbane along with another Basque. Antonio met the boat.

My first job was in Yetman, NSW, picking tobacco. My brother had friends there. I picked with several Italians, no Basques. I went to Ingham for the cane harvest and lived on the Vicente Goitiandia farm and cut for a nearby Italian farmer. My brother arranged that. I earned £70 per fortnight. I cut with José and Laureano Arrate and two other Basques from Mendata. When we finished, I went to Dalbeg to pick tobacco for an Italian grower. I worked with a man from Ereño and two Italians. After the harvest, I planted cane in Ayr and then, for the next four years, cut cane for Santiago Muguira there. I worked with my brother Antonio and the Muguiras.

The first slack, I went to Stanthorpe, Queensland, picking fruit. The second slack, I went to New Zealand on a working holiday and found a job in a sawmill for two months. I went with John Muguira. The third slack, I went to Mareeba to pick tobacco. By the fourth, I was married, and we went to Shepparton, Victoria, to pick fruit. I bought my first car in 1964.

I then cut cane in the Burdekin for Claudio Bilbao, earning A$4,000 that season. That first slack (1970), I bought a vegetable farm in Gumbu in the Burdekin for A$17,500 and grew some capsicums. I did so the second slack as well and, since 1971, I am a vegetable farmer. People said I was crazy to buy that farm. Most of those there were failed sugar properties owned by returned soldiers. They would set a goal of, say, A$6,000 and, when they reached it, they just plowed under the rest of the crop. They didn't like hard work. So, in bad years they had no contingency savings. The first year, I almost went broke. I sold 12,000 boxes of vegetables for only A$10,000. I barely made expenses and considered selling out. But last year, I grossed A$100,000 and netted about half. It is a hard life, sixteen hours a day, seven days a week, for six months, and then four fixing equipment. I now have two employees to harvest, but they are half-assed workers.

Soon after I bought my vegetable farm, Tororica bought one up the road. Today, we immigrants own all but two farms in the district. I am also in partners with my brother, Antonio, in his cane farm. In 1979, I paid A$150,000 for my half of the 3,200-ton-sugar-peak place. I would like to buy another sugar farm. Last year, I made A$50,000.

I met my wife, Cynthia Darwin, in 1965 and we married in 1966. We were introduced by mutual friends. Her parents raise sugar in Brandon. We have three children and they are members of the Church of England. I am Catholic, but do not attend church.

I have never attended classes here. For the first three years my English was too poor to date Australian girls. Then, I got engaged in my fifth year and my English took off. We use English exclusively at home with the children and between ourselves. I am thinking of enrolling them next year in Spanish language classes in Ayr. Since 1965, I read the *Ayr Advocate*, the *Home Hill Observer*, the *Bowen Independent*, the *Townsville Daily Bulletin*, and the *Sunday Sun*. I get no publications from Europe and do not listen to ethnic or shortwave radio. I see no point in it. Some Basques here are very closed. They remain more oriented to Europe than to here. I find that to be stupid. If you live here, you need to become involved here.

We joined the Ayr International Club in 1978. I was naturalized in 1965 in case I wanted to buy a business here. I favor the Country Party in politics. I go to the Burdekin Hotel once a week to have a few drinks with my Spanish friends there. I see Basques almost every day. I have never assisted anyone to immigrate here. In 1962, my cousin, Luis Eguia, came here and today he is a miner in Blackwater, Queensland.

I have never been discriminated against, but there is always an undercurrent. I have no preference regarding my children's choice of spouse as long as it isn't an Aborigine. Basques are more independent than Spaniards. Italians are very proud but have little substance. There is tension between North Italians and Sicilians like that between Basques and Spaniards. I have never been back to the Basque Country; I intend to visit but not stay. I plan to retire here in the Burdekin.

José Luis Echeandia # & —I was born in 1943 in Ereño. I completed primary school and know Spanish, Basque, Italian, and English. Father, who is now deceased, and Mother were from Ereño and farmed there. Mother now lives in Gernika. Father was in the USA herding sheep for ten years and then working on the railroad for four. We are four; the eldest, my sister María Angeles, was in Australia from 1960 until 1974 and is now a housewife in Gernika. I am second and live in Ayr as a canefarmer. The third, José Martín, is a factory worker in Gernika after having been in Australia from 1964 until 1976. My youngest brother, Domingo, is a merchant mariner and lives in Gernika.

I immigrated here in 1962. Before coming I worked in a sawmill in Gabika for a year and on a *baserri* in Ereño. I planned to stay for five years, earn some money, and go back. I learned of Australia from my sister who was here at the time and living in Halifax. She and my brother-in-law got Johnny Mendiolea to sponsor me. My brother-in-law lent me my passage. I flew from Madrid to Townsville and was met by him. It was like a homecoming.

My first job was in picking tobacco. My brother-in-law found it for me. My companions were a *Santanderino*, an Andalusian, and a Navarran. I was there for three months and then went to Ingham to plant cane and later cut for Paco Cao. I made £7 daily. Our gang was Fernando Jayo (Ereño), José Apraiz (Muxika), Ignacio Navarán (Arteaga), and Joseba Legarra (Ereño). There were too many of us, so I left early and went alone to pick tobacco in Dimbulah to the farm of the year before. After three months, I went into Ayr to plant cane with a Basque and a Portuguese. I stayed in an Italian boardinghouse in Home Hill. Then it was to Ingham to cut cane for Cao.

That slack, I went to Mareeba to the tobacco. Then it was to Ayr to plant cane and I stayed on during the harvest. I planted with the Portuguese for an Italian farmer and then we both stayed there to cut.

It was then off to Texas to pick tobacco. I went with my brother, José Apraiz, and Jesús Bengoechea. Jesús was with me on the flight to Australia. He had been to Texas before and had the contacts. We made 16 shillings an hour. In 1963, I bought half-interest in a car with a friend from Lekeitio.

In 1964, I cut for a different farmer in Ayr. There were two of us and we didn't have preference. The farmer told us to just show up for the sign-on. The union organizer refused to approve us and told the farmer to hire two preference cutters. He declined and the next week the organizer decided to look the other way. The harvesters were beginning to replace manual cutters and the organizer probably thought it wasn't worth getting into a formal dispute over us.

I next bought a harvester (1965) with my brother and brother-in-law to cut cane in Ingham. We had five contracts—three Italian brothers, one other Italian, and one Sicilian. We paid £11,000 for the machine and grossed that much the first year. We owners did the work and had an employee who was an Aborigine.

I cut cane for the next eleven years; six with the original partners. Then I bought half-interest in another harvester with José María Aguirre and worked with him for five years. During all of this time, in the slack I went twice to Griffith to pick fruit (1968 and 1973). The remaining years I went to Mareeba with the exception of 1973–1974 when I went to Spain. I also worked construction in Mount Isa for two months in 1973.

I did that harvesting work until 1977 and then decided that it was time to get out. We were breaking even or losing money and there was more competition. You are vulnerable to the farmers. A harvester without a contract is nearly worthless. I sold out and went to Ayr where I found a job at Kalamia Mill irrigating and then cultivating experimental cane. That is my job today. I work with six other Basques there.

I made A$14,000 before taxes last year. In 1976, we bought our home for A$24,000 and spent A$6,000 remodeling it. In 1970, I bought an apartment in Gernika and my mother lives in it now.

When I first came, the language was very difficult for me. It prevented me from dating Australian girls. It took me about four years to learn English. I went to night classes for a month in Home Hill in 1964. I had a Basque friend who knew English and he helped me with it. I made some Australian friends as well. I began reading newspapers a little bit when in Ingham, and, since 1977, read the *Ayr Advocate*. I would also read the odd issue of *El Español* and *La Fiamma* when given to me by a friend. My sister sends me a newspaper from Spain about once a year.

I listen to shortwave broadcasts from there occasionally. I have never belonged to a social club here. We are Catholics and go to Mass every other Sunday. I was naturalized in 1968 when I decided to stay. I wanted all of the rights. In politics, I favor the Liberal Party. I go to the Burdekin Hotel once a week because my friends are there.

I met my wife, Inmaculada Aguirre, in Europe. I was working for her father in Gabika in the sawmill when she was still a child. Her family migrated to Australia in 1966. The grandmother, Ventura Aguirre, and three aunts lived here in Ayr at that time.

Inmaculada and I married in 1976 when she was twenty-two. I continue to correspond regularly with my niece who is also my godchild. We don't mind Australian food but cook Basque-style at home. At home we speak Basque. We have an infant son and plan to teach him Basque. I would like him to marry a Basque, but anyone except an Aborigine would be alright. I think Basques are viewed more positively by Australians than are Spaniards. We are humbler and work harder. Some Italians are fine, but not all. In general, Australians are not good workers, but the exceptions work harder than we do.

I have only been back to Europe once (six months in 1974). I plan to return to the Basque Country but am not sure when. I have my feet here but my head in Euskadi. There is more economic opportunity here, but life is more interesting there. This place is boring. I would like to retire in Europe. My wife is willing to stay here or go back. Australia has more tranquil politics than does Spain and more freedom, too. No one controls you here. But taxes are too high in Australia and there is favoritism for the business class over the workers.

Juan Tomás Telleria # & —I was born in Amoroto in 1950. I completed primary school and today speak Spanish, Basque, Italian, and some English. My father was born in Gizaburuaga and worked in a sawmill in Lekeitio. He was in Australia for fifteen years as a canecutter. Mother is from Amoroto and never emigrated. My only brother, José Ignacio, is a merchant mariner in Lekeitio and never emigrated.

Before emigrating in 1968, I was a house painter in Lekeitio. Father was here in Ayr and I thought I would try it out. I wanted to avoid military service. I planned to possibly stay for good. I knew about Australia from Father's letters. His brother lived in Ayr as well, as did my mother's brother (Joe Gabiola). Joe arranged my papers and advanced me my fare. I came by plane to Townsville and my relatives all met me at the airport.

I went to work on the Nielson farm in Ayr and liked it. I found that employment through the Bengoas. In the slack, I went to Killara, Victoria, with four other Basques to harvest tomatoes. They had been there before. I earned A$1 per hour. I was there seven months and then returned to Ayr to work on Nielson's farm with Peter Bengoa. We finished his cane in three months and moved to the Bengoa farm to continue harvesting. Then it was back to Victoria to the tomatoes.

After six months, I was back in Ayr in the same cane. I cut with Peter again and we had Eusebio Asturi, Agustín Arrate, Antolin Azpiri, and Agustín Castrejana working with us.

I then went to Dimbulah to pick tobacco with Castrejana. He had done that there before. We made A$160 weekly after taxes. Five months later, I went to Ingham to plant cane and then returned to Ayr for the harvest. I cut with Peter Bengoa, Castrejana, two Basques, and a guy from Santander.

That slack, I went to pick tobacco in Dalbeg with José Aguirre, my future brother-in-law. After that, I returned to Ayr to plant cane and then did haul-out that season for an Italian farmer that came looking for me. I lived with my uncle and made A$120 weekly. I cut with Antonio Azpiri and the Italian boss. Then it was back to Dalbeg to pick tobacco with a Navarran, Santiago Mugica.

I then went to the Basque Country and Italy for four months in 1973. When I returned, I went to Greenvale and asked for a job with the John Holland Construction Company. I worked there for fourteen months. When that project was over, they sent me to Blackwater on another for nine months, and then for a month to Gladstone to build a coal-conveyor belt.

When I left John Holland, I went to Dimbulah to pick tobacco. I had been there and now picked with Italians for five months. I then went back to Ayr to the Italian farmer I had worked for before. I have been here ever since. In the slack, I work construction with my brother-in-law, and we plant some green cane.

My wife, Carmen Aguirre, was born in Gatika, Bizkaia, but came here with her family as a toddler. She grew up in Ayr. She was twenty-one when we married in 1977. I met her when she was a teenager picking tobacco in Dalbeg. We were engaged in 1976, but I knew her when she was thirteen. She works in Ayr as an office clerk. I make A$12,000 annually and she makes A$600 monthly. I bought our house in 1976 for A$32,000. I purchased my first car in 1969. We vacationed in 1977 on Hayman Island for five days, and I was also in Mount Isa once for five days looking for work.

It took me about four years to learn my English. I dated Australian girls for that purpose. In 1972, I went to night school for four months. We get *Woman's Weekly* and the *Ayr Advocate*. I used to buy *El Español* and *La Fiamma*, but no longer. I do not listen to ethnic or shortwave radio. In 1977, I joined the Returned Soldiers' League and, in 1978, the International Club. Both are social. I go to the Burdekin Hotel regularly because that is where the Spanish hang out. I am not a naturalized citizen. I correspond every few weeks with my mother and siblings. I call as well.

We have a six-month-old daughter. I would like her to marry a Basque or Spaniard. It will be up to her. But not an Aborigine and a Chinese would be so-so. Basques are very closed, more than Spaniards. There are all kinds in both groups. If you have to work for an Italian, they are hard taskmasters; if they work for you, they shirk.

Carmen became an Australian citizen in 1972. But we would both like to retire one day in the Basque Country. Life is easier here, but fuller there.

Enrique Lejarraga # & —I was born in Luno [Lumo], Bizkaia, in 1944. I attended primary school. Father was from there and a turner by trade. Mother was from Kortezubi. I am one of three siblings and am the only one in the family to have emigrated.

I came here in 1964. I had an uncle, Celestino Lejarraga, in Ayr and we corresponded. He told me about Australia, and I decided to come. He arranged the papers and lent me my fare. My parents had mixed feelings about it. I came by plane Madrid–Townsville. My uncle met me at the airport.

I found this to be a bit sad and boring. After two days of cutting cane for Muguira in Brandon with a Sicilian, we had a fight and I left. Through my uncle, I found work as a carpenter with a contractor in Ayr. I made £29 per week. There were four or five Basques working there, as well as some Valencians.

I did that for seven years and then went to Spain, thinking of staying. But I had not done military service, so I left again and came back to Ayr to work for the same boss. I spent another seven years until I set up my own business with Antonio Aguirre. We were together for one year, when Antonio decided to go back to planting cane. I returned to my old construction job and I work there today. I make A$485 a fortnight after taxes. I bought my first car in 1966 and my house, for A$7,500, in 1973.

I met my wife, Serafina Totoricagüena, in 1964 in an English class, and we were married in 1973. She was twenty-three by then. She was born in Navarniz [Nabarniz]. Her father came here first and then sent for the family in 1964. He cut cane for eight years, was a farmworker in Ayr for another ten, and then, five year ago, leased a canefarm in Clare.

I attended night school classes here in Ayr for four or five years. After my third year in Australia, I began reading the *Ayr Advocate* and the *Townsville Daily Bulletin*. I used to read *El Español*, but no longer. Sometimes I get publications from Spain from Agustín Arrate when he is through with them. I never listen to ethnic or shortwave radio. I joined the Returned Soldiers' League in 1976 and the International Club in 1978. I also belonged to the Soccer Club at one time; when I was a player. I go to the Burdekin Hotel weekends, because my Basque friends are there. We are Catholics, but only go to church a couple of times a year.

At home, we use Basque and English, about fifty-fifty. We have three small children and try to teach them Basque, but it is hard. I don't see a lot of difference between Basques and Spaniards. Basques are more extroverted. Italians are closed.

I was naturalized in 1970, mainly to avoid problems regarding military service when I visited Spain and was there for almost a year (I was considering staying). I went back again for four months in 1974. I correspond regularly with my parents and I want to move there permanently. I am not sure when. There is no comparison. Life in Europe is far more interesting. I like the hunting and fishing in Australia, but do not feel welcome. Australians view us the way Basques view Extremaduran migrants to Euskadi—outsiders. I have no real Australian friends.

Santiago Urzaa # & —I was born in 1940 in Navarniz [Nabarniz] and attended school for five years. I know Basque, Spanish, Italian, and English. My parents are from Navarniz. Father spent ten years in Idaho on the Simplot cattle ranch. I am one of six offspring. The eldest and youngest, both sisters, have never emigrated. My second eldest sister, María Jesusa, went to the United States in 1966 and is now in Los Angeles, where she is a meat processor for Farmer John's. I am next in order and the brother after me, Esteban, is a taxi driver in Ondarroa today, but was here in Australia from 1962–1969 and spent two years of that time in New Zealand. Finally, Juan lives in Portland, Oregon, where he works as an electrician. He spent some time in Colombia.

Before I came here in 1958, I worked on the *baserri* in Navarniz. I thought of staying for five years and then going back. I considered no other destination. My grandfather, Félix Plaza, and two uncles were here in Ayr and Home Hill. Félix arrived in the 1920s. My uncle, Juan Plaza, entered in 1949 and farms cane in Home Hill. Victor Plaza is deceased now. He came to Australia in 1943 and was growing cane in Clare when he died in 1967. My aunt, Venancia Plaza, was my mother's sister and married to Victor. She died in 1975. My first cousin, Jesús Plaza, is a construction foreman in Melbourne.

My uncle, Juan Plaza, helped me with documents and a loan. I flew alone from Madrid to Townsville and my uncle's friend met me and took me to his home. My uncle came for me the next day.

My first impression was shock at how quiet and dead it was here. My first job was planting cane for an Italian farmer. I stayed at my uncle's house and planted with Frank Artiach, Luis Ormaechea, Juan Urtubi, and George Muguira. I did that for two months and then cut cane in Home Hill on the Plaza farm. I made £75 per week. I worked with Juan Urtubi. I would cut there for the next six seasons. In 1958 and 1959, I stayed there during the slack and received unemployment. Then, in 1960, I went to Shepparton, Victoria. I flew to Melbourne by myself and then to the fruit. In Shepparton, I picked with Jesús Balanzategui and two Navarrans. After two months, we moved to Mildura for four months in the grapes. I returned to Shepparton and Mildura the following slack as well. I bought my first car in 1960.

During the 1962 slack, I went to Cooma to work contruction on a tunnel project. I made £75 weekly and was working with my brother, Esteban. I spent the next two slacks there; Esteban remained behind and worked in Cooma year-round.

In 1975, I went back to Spain for thirteen months. Then, in 1966, I cut cane for Tapiolas. I lived at Agustín Arrate's place and worked with my cousin, Jesús Plaza. That slack, I bought a truck to contract for haul-out. In the interim, I took it to Charters Towers and worked on a highway project for five months. I went alone.

For the next four seasons, I contracted for hauling-out work doing the harvest and in the slack did odd jobs around the Burdekin with my equipment. I did roadwork for the Shire Council and the Water Board. In the 1968 slack, I went to Mount Isa with my truck and contracted with the Goicoechea Construction Company for three months.

In 1970, I got married and began buying cane farms. The first cost A$61,000. The second, in 1972, was A$150,000, and the third, in 1977, cost A$220,000. They are 340 acres in all. I have had several employees over the last decade, none of them Basques. I once owned flats on Magnetic Island but sold them. Last year I earned A$62,000. I can't stand to have money sitting idle in a bank.

I met my wife, Santina Sgoi, in Home Hill in 1968 and we married in 1970. She was twenty-two at that time. She was born in Home Hill and her parents were from Sicily. They are retired canefarmers.

It took me four or five years to learn English. I never attended classes, I mainly learned at work. At home, we use English exclusively. I think it is important for my children to learn it. I make no effort to teach them anything else. It used to be important to me to live near other Basques, but no longer. Sometimes I go to the Burdekin Hotel and I see some there. Since about 1963–1964, I read the *Townsville Daily Bulletin*, the *Home Hill Observer*, the *Ayr Advocate*, and *Country Life*. I used to read *La Fiamma*, but no longer. I do not listen to ethnic radio. I belong to the International Club since 1977. I was naturalized in 1960 on the advice of my uncles. I used to support the Labour Party, but no longer care about politics. We are Catholics, but do not go to church often. I have two young sons and would like them to marry a local girl. She should not be an Aborigine and a Chinese would be so-so. Otherwise, the choice is theirs.

We were just in Europe on a three-month trip. We visited the Basque Country, Spain, and Italy, as well as the United States and Canada. I hope to go to Europe again next year. I don't see a lot of difference between Basques and Spaniards. Maybe Basques are a little more trustworthy than Italians.

I like Australia. It has good beer, a good climate, and a quiet life. I want to buy another farm. I would like it if they made the Aborigines work more and if the politicians would keep their promises. I plan to retire here.

Elias Alcibar # & —I was born in Lekeitio in 1934 and completed nine years of schooling. I know Basque, Spanish, Italian, French, and English. My father was born in Deba, Gipuzkoa, and my mother in Lekeitio. Father was a baker and farmer there but is now deceased. Neither of my parents ever emigrated. We are two brothers and we both came to Australia. Francisco is a railroad employee in Townsville today.

Before emigrating in 1951, I drove a truck in Lekeitio for a year and a half. I came to avoid military service, make some money, and go back. I thought of the USA, but that was too complicated then. My uncle, Pascual Badiola, was visiting Lekeitio and suggested I emigrate. My mother's brothers, Francisco and Floren Ituraspe, lived in Ingham, as did Pascual (Mother's mother's brother). Pascual sponsored me and advanced my fare. I came by boat with two brothers from Ereño. We sailed from Genoa to Sydney. There, we were met by some Ingham farmers who happened to be in the city, and we rode the train with them back to Ingham. I was only seventeen and overwhelmed by everything. I first thought I would just pay back my fare and return to Europe.

My first job was with Julián Araquistain. Pascual set that up. Some said that I was too young to cut cane, but Pascual insisted that I was physically strong enough to do it. I subsequently lost a year because I had to have disc surgery due to that first year. I cut cane with Tomás Ibañez and four Sicilians. One Sicilian rode me from the outset as I couldn't keep up. After a few weeks, I was cutting more than he could, and was riding him in return. The man's brother was the ganger and told me to shut up, but I refused. One night, it all blew up in the barrack. The Sicilian I had been tormenting chased me with a broom handle. I took it away from him and whacked him over the head with it. Tomás Ibañez ran into the dark and was gone all night. My friends told me not to return to the barrack as the Sicilians would kill me. I ignored the advice and went back. I told them, "If you try to kill me do it right, because if you don't you are dead." They left me alone and I finished the season with the gang.

After the harvest, a Basque friend and I came to the Achurra farm in Home Hill to clear bush for farmland. I did that with Hilario Achurra. I made £11 per week.

It was then back to Ingham where I cut cane for Vicente Goitiandia. Uncle Frank Ituraspe arranged that. I made £33 weekly and cut with Uncle Frank, Uncle Floren, Victor and José Urberuaga from Pedernales [Sukarrieta], and Cornelio Careaga from Aulesti. That slack, I went to Ayr to irrigate and apply sulphate to the cane. I worked at that for the Muguiras, Bereicuas, and one Australian. I bought a motorbike in 1952 and my first car in 1956.

That year, I remained in Ayr and cut cane for a Navarran, Santiago Muguira. We were Ramón Aguirre, me, and one Italian. The next two harvests I cut cane for the Bereicuas and in the slack applied sulphate on their paddocks.

In 1954, I bought a haul-out outfit and, in 1956, a truck. I contracted with several gangs to do their haul-out in Ayr until 1960. In the slack, I sometimes worked for the Burdekin Shire.

In 1961, I was unable to work for a year because of an operation and, in 1962, I went back to Spain. I bought a truck there with a partner and worked with him for nineteen months. I thought I might stay, but changed my mind. So, in 1964, I came back to Australia and bought another haul-out outfit. I did that work for three years and, then, in 1967, I bought a harvester and two years later another.

In 1969, I sold out here and went back to Spain to stay. I bought a taxi and drove it for three-and-a half years in Lekeitio.

In 1973, I returned to Australia and bought the harvester that I continue to operate today. In the 1974 and 1975 slacks, I worked for the mill repairing the tramline.

I met my wife, Julia Bereicua, in Ayr in 1952. I was working for her parents and first saw her when she was a teenager at family events. She was born here. We were married in 1958—she was twenty. Her father was from Amoroto and her mother from Navarniz. They were canefarmers in Giru and Ayr, but are now deceased. She is self-employed as a storekeeper. She sells children's clothing and makes about A$14,000 annually.

It took me three to four years to learn enough English. I attended six months of night classes in Airdale in 1954. I also mixed a fair bit with Australians. I have more Australian friends here than Basque ones in Spain. It was easy enough to date Australian girls. Julia taught English in the Basque Country at one time. At home, we use Basque, with the children in particular. We insist on it. We get the *Courier Mail*, the *Townsville Daily Bulletin*, and the *Ayr Advocate*. I receive *La Región* from Spain and used to get the *Boletín del Banco de Vizcaya*. My mother sends me *Deia* infrequently. I sometimes listen to shortwave broadcasts from Europe on my radio.

We are Catholics, but do not attend church. I was naturalized in 1958 in case I wanted to buy property one day. In politics, I favor Labour. I joined the Burdekin Squash Club in 1968. I have a good Australian friend, Joe, who was my neighbor and tennis and squash opponent.

Australians think highly of Basques, but don't like Spaniards and Italians. I had some fistfights over insults from less-educated ones. Basques are harder working and more serious than Spaniards. North Italians are fine, but Sicilians are not. They are like Spaniards. They have the same coloring and are half-castes.

I want my three daughters to marry Basques. The eldest did so last year. She married a young man she met in Lekeitio. I brought him here and he now does haul-out for me.

I resent the discrimination here. My son-in-law was playing soccer last week and happened to shout something in Basque to a recently arrived player on his team who didn't speak English. The referee blew his whistle, penalized him, and said, "Any more of that Wog talk and you are out of the game." He later apologized, but the damage was done.

I feel Basque nationalist but am not very political. I resent Spanish occupation of Euskadi. We are like the Jews. In our own homeland, we are told to speak "Christian" [Spanish], and here we are told to speak English. No one lets us speak Basque.

I made A$95,000 last year. We bought half of our house in 1974 for A$13,000. Julia inherited half and then we bought out her sister's other half. I inherited five or six lots in Lekeitio and, in 1979, bought an apartment there for five-and-a-half-million *pesetas*. My harvester and haul-out outfit are worth about A$200,000. I have made as much as A$1,200 in one day with them, but it is a lot of money to tie up in equipment that you only use for five months out of the year. We used to have a rental unit here, but our daughter now lives in it.

I went to Spain last year for three months to buy a house to prepare for our return. We plan to go there in the next few months to live. Life there is much more interesting than here. You can live well in Australia if you work hard. But it is a very quiet life. The bad things here are the climate (too hot), my occupation (mechanical harvesting is dirty work—lots of dust in the air), and this is too far from the Basque Country.

Iñaki Iturbe # & —I was born in Mendexa in 1935 and didn't finish primary school. I know Basque, Spanish, Italian, and English. Father and Mother were both from Mendexa as well and are farmers. Neither ever emigrated. I am one of four offspring. I am the second and am a welder in Ayr today. The youngest, Pedro, is a cement worker in Millicent, South Australia. In 1954, I arranged his papers and advanced his fare.

Before I came to Australia, in 1952, I had worked in Lekeitio in a fish factory for a year and was living on my parents' *baserri*. I emigrated planning to remain here. My grandfather's niece was in the USA and promised to help me go there. But when I wrote her about it, she didn't reply. I learned of Australia from a neighbor who had been there. Pascual Badiola of Ingham helped me with documents and my fare. My parents thought it was a good idea. They told me that, if it didn't work out, I could always return to the farm.

I traveled by boat from Genoa to Brisbane with about fifteen other Spaniards and Basques. I then went by train to Ingham and Badiola met me in the station. I wasn't all that impressed with Ingham, but I was always with other immigrants so language wasn't an issue. I arrived three weeks before the end of the harvest. Badiola gave me work on his farm. We were many Basques plus Camilo Madrid.

That first slack, I stayed on Badiola's farm as a laborer. The next harvest, I cut cane for the Mendioleas. I earned £1,000 for the season. I cut with Rufino Zarate (Bilbo), Marcos Marqués (Lekeitio), Ramón Azcarate (Lekeitio), Andrés Urberuaga (Pedernales [Sukarrieta]), Mateo Landaburu (Aulesti), Julián Egaña (Lekeitio), and Camilo Madrid (Valencia).

We all then went together to the Burdekin to cut cane in Home Hill. I got a job on the Odorica farm there. He and I cut together without anyone else. I stayed there for eight years, cutting cane during the harvest and doing farmwork in the slack. I bought my first car in 1956. During the 1957 slack, I went to Tasmania with an Australian friend and then to Mildura to pick fruit. In the 1958 slack, I picked tobacco in Clare and Millaroo.

I had met my future wife, María Pilar Eizaguirre, in 1951, at a dance in Amoroto—her hometown. I corresponded with her from Australia and, in 1958, we married by proxy and she came to be with me in Australia. She was twenty. She was one of four siblings and all have emigrated. Jaime was a sheepherder in the USA for three years and León worked in Germany for two years before also herding sheep in the USA for three. Her eldest brother, Juan, lives today in Millicent, South Australia, where he works as a pine-feller.

I now decided to go to South Australia on the advice of my wife's brother. He said the money was good and the work was year-round. So, my wife and baby daughter traveled to Mount Burr, South Australia, and lived in government housing while I worked at pine harvesting. I earned £70 a fortnight after taxes. I worked with Juan and two other Basques.

I spent three years in Mount Burr and then two more in Millicent. On weekends, I was learning to weld and so I switched employment to become a welder for an Italian contractor. I did that in Millicent for the next five years. During that time, in the summers I went commercial crayfishing. As a welder I earned fourteen shillings an hour and crayfishing I made A$132 per week. The first year of crayfishing, I worked for an Italian in South End, South Australia, and the next two for an Australian. We built a boat but lost it in a shipwreck.

In 1971, we went back to the Basque Country to live. I spent six months there working as a welder in Ondarroa. But, after nine months in all, we then changed our minds and came back to Australia. I planted some cane in Ayr at first and then found a job here as a welder. I still do that today. I make A$600 a fortnight before taxes. María Pilar works as a domestic and makes A$325 a fortnight. In 1975, we bought our house for A$35,000. I had a house in Mendexa, but sold it.

It took me two years to learn English. Odorica's children used it exclusively. I never attended classes. Since 1959, I have read the *Ayr Advocate*, the *Sunday Mail*, the *Home Hill Observer*, and car magazines. I received no publications from Spain. I used to listen to broadcasts from there on my shortwave radio. But not so much anymore. I was naturalized in 1958 as I wanted full rights here. María Pilar became a citizen in 1970.

We stay in touch with our relatives in Europe. We exchange letters every few months and call them at Christmas. When I lived in Millicent, I belonged to the Community Club there. Last year, we joined the International Club here. I go to the Burdekin Hotel every weekend to drink with my Basque friends. We like Australian cuisine; we are used to it now. But we like to cook Spanish-style. We are Catholics and go to church about six times a year. I would like my son to marry a Basque. My daughter is twenty and married here, in Home Hill, to a person of Sicilian descent. I would object if either married an Aborigine or Chinese, any other choice is up to them. I think Spaniards think too highly of themselves and put Basques down. I find Italians to be even more pretentious than Spaniards. Australians say nasty things about us, but most don't mean them. I have had a few insults, but nothing important.

We want to go back to Spain, but only for a visit. I would like to build a house here one day on an axis so I could turn it to enjoy whatever sun and wind I desired. I hope to retire here one day; anywhere in Australia on a beach.

[María Pilar chimed in that she dislikes the discrimination here. Her kids have told her that their schoolmates refer to the International Club as the "Wog Club." One daughter added that the teachers often pick on immigrant kids in class. She said, "We have to be a little bit better in everything than the Australians in order to be accepted as equals by them." Iñaki pooh-poohed her, "Australians are insincere, so that when they call you 'Wog' they don't mean it any more than when they call you 'Darling'." He added that he feels less discrimination from Australians than from the Australia-born offspring of immigrants.]

Valentín Astorquia # & ^ —I was born in 1933 in Mendaro, Gipuzkoa. I completed three years of school and speak Spanish, Basque, and Italian. My father was from Bolibar, Bizkaia, and Mother was from Aulesti. They were farming in Mendaro when he died. She lives there still. Neither ever emigrated. We are seven siblings and I am the eldest. The third, Joaquín, lives and farms in Mendaro but was in Australia. None of the others ever emigrated.

I was farming in Mendaro before I came here in 1951. I wanted to avoid military service and find more opportunity. I came with an open mind; to try it out. I looked into going to the USA but couldn't arrange for that. I had two uncles in Jarvisfield, José and Andrés Ybarlucea. José arranged for my passage and documents. Mother was very opposed; I was underaged and had to trick her into signing the parental permission papers. I flew from Madrid to Townsville with my cousin. My uncles met us at the airport.

I was young and very excited. I didn't mind anything. My first job was farmwork with my cousin for Uncle José. I earned £17 a fortnight. I did that for two years, but then wanted to earn more money. My uncle wouldn't let me cut cane for him, so I did so on a different farm. I still lived with Uncle José. I made £160 per fortnight. A Sicilian and I cut together, and I finished the harvest alone.

I then did farmwork for Luis Arroiti in the slack and cut for him the following season. I lived in his barrack and cut with three Australians. I can't stand unions. I always refused to join when a canecutter. My farmers paid my ticket. One time, an organizer told me that he would see to it that I never got another job in Queensland.

It was 1954, and I bought a truck and outfit to haul out cane on contract. I did that work on Rita Island for the next thirteen harvests. In 1968, I purchased a harvester in partners with an Australian. After three years, I bought him out. Today, I have that harvester and another leased one. During the slack seasons, I worked for the Shire Council, picked tobacco in Dalbeg, and fixed fencing for cattle ranchers. In the 1959 slack, I drove a truck in Brisbane. Two different slacks, I made cement pipes in Brandon and for another two was a bricklayer in Ayr. I took off one slack to build my own house there. Then, for three slacks I worked as a welder in Home Hill. In 1974, I leased a canefarm on Rita Island and live there today. I still run my harvesting business.

It took me about three months to begin learning English. My uncle was married to an Australian, so they used English at home. I was living there, and their kids only spoke English. I went to English classes in Jarvisfield for three years. Since 1951, I read the *Ayr Advocate* and the *Townsville Daily Bulletin*. I also read the *National Farmer*, the *Australian Sugar Journal*, and the *Australian Canegrower*. I have received no publications from Europe. I took out citizenship in 1952 in order to be able to own property here. I support the National Political Party.

I met my Australian wife in 1959 when I was best man at her cousin's wedding. We were married the following year. She was born in Eidsvold, Queensland. Her parents liked me a lot. She is Church of England. I am Catholic, but do not go to Mass. Our children are Catholics. I have no preference regarding who my children marry, although an Aborigine would be so-so. At home we speak English and I make no effort to teach the children Spanish. It is not important to me to live around other Basques. I have never helped anyone to immigrate. Some Australians discriminate against us, but I have never felt that. You can't trust Spaniards as much as Basques. Italians are not too bad, but Sicilians are less trustworthy.

Last year, I made A$30,000. I cut 30,000 tons and grossed A$300,000, but you have many expenses. In 1974, we moved on to this cane farm. I own the crop and equipment and pay 17 percent of the gross as rent. I bought my first car in 1953. I have a harvester and lease another. I own three haul-out outfits. In all, I would estimate that I own about A$600,000 in equipment.

I like farming and would not live in town. Here, you don't have to deal with as many people. I need to buy my own land, but the values keep going up. I have never returned to Europe and have no plans to do so. I would like my son to stay in farming, but only if we get our own land. The last letter I received was five years ago from my sister. I wrote my mother fifteen years ago. I like the climate, lifestyle, and freedom in Australia. Its downside is that there is too much industrial strife.

I hope to retire here on a beach someday.

Lorenzo Aguirresarobe # & —I was born in 1933 in Aya [Aia], Gipuzkoa. After primary school, I attended a college in Donostia for eighteen months. I know Spanish, Basque, Italian, and English. Father and Mother were from Aya. They farmed in Tolosa and he is now deceased; she lives in Orio, Gipuzkoa. We were nine children. I am the third from last and my two younger brothers came to Australia as well. Jesús is now back in Aya after being here and the youngest, León, lives in Dalbeg and owns a harvester. None of my other siblings emigrated, with the exception of one sister who lived in France for six months.

Before I came here in 1958, I worked as a cabinetmaker in Orio for ten years. I thought of going to Germany but couldn't get the documents. I really wanted to leave Spain for three or four years. A friend read about the recruitment for Australia and we applied. At first, my parents were very upset. We sailed on the *Toscana* from Trieste to Brisbane.

We spent two weeks in the migrant camp near Brisbane and were then sent by the government to Cairns. We immigrants were provided with an interpreter by the Immigration Service. He was an attorney who was Australia-born of Catalan parentage. Cane cutting was very hard work and wiped me out physically, but we were treated well. I cut for an Irish and an Italian farmer. Our gang included Pedro Zabaleta (Hernani), Pascual Garmendia (Hernani), Dionisio Iriondo (Legorreta), a guy named Altuna from Donostia, and a *Santanderino*. I made £500 for the season.

The first slack, I went with four Basques to pick tobacco in Dimbulah. I worked alone there for three months. I next went to Innisfail to cut cane. I did so with Pedro Zabaleta and the *Santanderino* from the year before.

My next move was to Sydney where I found work as a carpenter. I went by car with Altuna and one other Basque. I knew some English by then and had little trouble finding that work. In fact, I found jobs for the other two as well. I stayed there six months and made £26 per week. The three of us worked together. That year my brother, Jesús, was here and cut with us. In 1960, I arranged for Jesús to immigrate.

Then it was back to the tobacco, all four of us from the cane gang together. I did two more seasons in Innisfail and picked fruit in the slacks in Griffith.

It was 1964 and I decided to return to Spain to live. However, after five months there, I changed my mind and came back to Ayr. I found a cutting contract here through a friend I met at a dance. I cut with an Italian and lived in the house of some others and took my meals in a café. That slack, I went back to Griffith to harvest fruit. I cut cane in Ayr and harvested fruit in Griffith for two years, and then worked on a tunnel in Cooma for two months. 1968 was the last year I cut cane. That year, I purchased a cane farm in Dalbeg in partners with my brother, León. In 1971, I bought out his half. He farms nearby, but we don't get along very well. I am still here today and farm sugar, rice, and corn.

It took me about two years to learn English. I bought a grammar and talked with people here. I dated Australian girls from the start, it was easy. A few Australians discriminate, the majority do not. I was treated particularly well by them in Cairns. I was once insulted in a bar by a drunk and the barman threw him out. I used to get the *Ayr Advocate*, but no longer. I do subscribe to the *National Farmer*, but seldom read it. I get the *Australian Sugar Review* and the *Rice Journal*. I receive no publications from Europe. I used to listen to broadcasts on shortwave, but no longer. I belong to no social organization. I was naturalized in 1964 because I was thinking of buying land. I am Liberal Party in my politics.

I met my wife, María Dolores Olazabal, in 1965, when I returned to Europe. She is from Zarautz and I had actually worked in her house years earlier. I went back to Europe again in 1975 for a nine-month visit. After that, we began corresponding, and, in 1979, I brought her to Australia. Her parents were both deceased by then. She worked for twenty years as a secretary in Zarautz before coming to Australia. She is one of nine siblings. Only one other ever emigrated. Her sister, María Pilar, lives in Buenos Aires for the past twenty-five years. We are Catholics, but do not go to church often—funerals only.

We have no children. At home, we use Spanish. [She interjected her complaint, "He will only speak Spanish with me; I only get to speak Basque to the cat."] In the pub, I use English, Spanish, and Basque depending on the company. I have some good Spanish friends, but I like Basques. Still, it is not too important to me to live around other Basques. There are good and bad in both groups. I like North Italians, but not Sicilians. If I had children, I would prefer that they marry Basques. I would also emphasize a good education for them; it is the most important thing in life.

Last year, I made A$50,000. We bought this farm in 1968 for A$34,000. It has 138 acres. I also bought a lot in Townsville for A$10,500 on which to build apartments one day. My machinery is worth about A$150,000. We are too far from Ayr, I would like to have a farm closer to it.

María Dolores is not too crazy about life here. She is not naturalized and does not intend staying permanently. I prefer to retire in Australia. I tried moving back to Spain and didn't last. There, you are very controlled. The police treat you like a dog.

José María Urberuaga*&—My wife works in the Burdekin Hotel and my sister-in-law is married to the owner. I go there daily. Even though it is the hang-out for Basques here, I do not feel very accepted by them because I married an Australian woman. When I came, I tried to mix with Australians in order to learn English, so I avoided unnecessary contact with other Basques. Some Basque farmers have been here for forty years and still can't read English. I used to be a roustabout. I spent all of my money in bars and on Australian girlfriends. I was living with my wife before we married, and she was a barmaid then in the Queen's Hotel.

My brother, Andrés, jumped ship in Lucinda and the Mendioleas hid him out for two years. Another brother, Victor, immigrated, but didn't cut cane. He is lazy. He did some farmwork around here and then went to Mount Isa to work on Joe Goicoechea's Julia Creek-to-Darwin highway project. He drove a grader. Later, he stayed on in Cloncurry, married, and is still there. We hadn't seen each other for years until I recently passed through Cloncurry when driving a truck to Mount Isa for a friend.

Andrés brought me out, and the first two years I cut cane in Ingham the farmers there were almost broke. They paid you to harvest, but then expected you to cut green cane for seeding just as a favor for letting you live in the barrack during the slack. I got fed up with that and moved to Townsville. I couldn't speak English because Ingham was a "Little Italy." I couldn't find work, so I continued on to the Burdekin where I found a job cutting green cane through two Basques that I met in the Queen's Hotel.

The next year, I had a chance to get a cane contract on two farms. I needed help and sent for my brother in Ingham. He came with another set of brothers. We were going to cut on two different farms, and we split up the two sets of brothers. Brothers never really get along, and their arguments are always more serious than those between friends.

I once had a £200 bet arranged by Vicente Goitiandia of Ingham. Ingham Basques believed that Tomás Ibañez and Juan Unamuno could outcut anyone in the Burdekin. We would cut here and they there. I had cut cane in both places and knew that it was no contest. The cane in the Burdekin was bigger, and the cutting and loading much easier. I didn't want to accept the bet, but Goitiandia insisted. Florén Iturraspe and I finished by 2:30 in the afternoon and had cut twenty tons more than the Hinchinbrook guys. We blew that money standing rounds of drinks for everyone in several pubs that night.

I bought a harvester in partners with two Italians. It was old and kept breaking down. After six months, I walked away and lost my down payment and wages. One of the Italians went broke, but the other continues in mechanical harvesting to this day.

I became a locomotive driver for Pioneer Mill. I did that for eight-and-a-half years. During that time, I had four accidents. In the last one, I hit a semi-truck crossing the highway and sheered off its front end. It banged me up and scared me. I lost my nerve for loco driving and bought a haul-out outfit for A$15,000. The first year, I grossed A$14,000. But back injuries made it hard for me to drive it. So, the next year I hired a driver and only made A$4,000. I sold my equipment for A$20,000 and went back to Pioneer Mill and got the job that I still have today.

Félix Arangüena—[Committed suicide on July 2, 1957, by throwing himself out a train window near Gympie, Queensland. The following account is constructed from testimony at the inquest.] José Achurra of Ayr testified that he had been contacted in 1955 by the deceased with the request that he nominate him for entry into Australia. Achurra did not know the man [we have no evidence of Arangüena's town of birth and residence, or how he managed to contact Achurra], but agreed to serve as his sponsor and advance his passage money. The deceased arrived in March of 1956 and stayed with Achurra until July. He worked planting cane around the district and seemed happy. He then found employment on a highway project near Bowen. He would visit Achurra periodically. The last time he showed up looking frail and said that he had spent time in a Bowen hospital with an ear disorder. And it was then that Aranagüena "started to go queer." Sometimes he seemed normal; others he was obsessed that people were "talking about him."

Achurra suggested that he see a doctor about his mental condition, but Arangüena refused. He decided to go back to Spain instead, and asked Achurra to make the arrangements—which he did. The deceased left for Brisbane by train to catch a ship that was due to sail July 1, 1957. Achurra was mystified as to why Arangüena was on board a train headed back to Townsville on July 2.

[The other account is that of an Aussie passenger on the same train.] Arangüena came into his compartment and said that he was bound for Townsville to conclude some business before heading off to Spain to see his wife and family. He was untidy, unshaven for the last two or three days, and seemed despondent.

About 11:30 in the evening, Arangüena became very agitated and said he was going to the toilet. When he didn't return within fifteen minutes, the Aussie went to check on him. He banged on the locked toilet door and there was no reply. He got on his knees to look through a grate near the floor and saw legs standing on the toilet seat. Arangüena then stepped down and started banging the seat up and down, making a terrible racket. So, the Aussie went looking for a security guard.

When they returned, Arangüena was quiet, but would not open the door. And then they heard the window being smashed and it was clear that he intended to jump. The conductor forced open the door and they saw a broken toilet seat and glass from the window lying on the floor. The window frame was covered with blood and Arangüena was gone. The body was found next day along the tracks at Nambour, near Gympie.[21]

[I was told by Elias Alcibar of the suicide of another Burdekin Basque from Olaeta who never seemed to be able to save money to send to his family in Europe. One day, in a fit of depression, he plunged a butcher's knife into his chest after first cutting off his testicles with it.[22]]

Brisbane

José María Mugica ^[23] —I was born in Gernika and came to Australia in 1961. I didn't want to do my military service. I wanted to go anywhere, it didn't matter—North America, South America. My father suggested that I look into Australia because I had uncles and a brother here. I was just a kid, eighteen years old. Father suffered a lot in the Spanish Civil War. He was imprisoned in Bilbo and had many bad experiences there. Neither of us wanted me to serve in Franco's army.

My uncles were prepared to help me. I traveled by myself to Genoa to take the *Roma* to Brisbane. In Genoa, I boarded with other Basque passengers and two families from Valencia. My uncles had arranged for someone in Brisbane to meet me. I was in their house for three or four days, and then they put me on the train to Ingham. My relatives met me at the station.

It was March, and my first job was planting cane. I then cut for Pascual

Badiola and later for the Balanzateguis. The truth is that I would have gone back to the Basque Country after the first six months had I had the money to do so. I found everything very different here. The language was a major problem.

In the slack, we canecutters went south to harvest fruit, or north to the tobacco. Some went into construction, but that was more difficult. You needed to know some English for that. It was simpler to harvest with your fellow immigrants.

One year, I went to Robertson, NSW, with José Badiola from Bermeo. We traveled by plane and then bus. He had been there before working on the railroad in that town. It was after the cane harvest and just before Christmas. We were told that the offices were closed for a three-week holiday break. So, we went to the Shepparton area, a farm near Cobram, to harvest fruit for three weeks, and then returned to Robertson. Well, they hired José because he was a former employee, but not me.

I had to return to Cobram, and José helped me buy a train ticket and explained that in Albury I needed to change trains or get a bus. When I got to there I just panicked. The normal thing would have been to go to a hotel, sleep, and then, after breakfast, proceed. But that seemed daunting, because I couldn't ask for directions. An Australian asked me what I needed and I just said Cobram and showed him my £10. He got me a taxi and it cost me that to get to Shepparton. But the farm was another seven kilometers from town, so I put my gear on my back and started walking. After about two kilometers, the farmer that I had worked for before pulled up alongside me and said, "What are you doing here?" All that I knew to say was "work," "work." We went to his place. There were two Basque brothers from Bakio and some other guys doing the harvest. Those non-Basques were supposed to leave in a week. There was no place for us in the barrack, so the farmer let us stay in his stable sleeping on straw with the animals for a week. He wanted us to remain as he was very happy with our work. We wanted to stay, too, because he hired us on contract, and it paid well.

I have never felt discrimination here. Because of our language issue, Australians sometime make fun of you. You pretend you understand them, but they know immediately. You are silent when when you are supposed to laugh and maybe laugh when they say something sad.

But I have never felt discrimination for being a Basque or a foreigner *per se*.

I am a timid person by nature. It was therefore hard for me to leave my shell; particularly given my difficulty with English. What gave me confidence was sport. I am pretty athletic and was good at the Australian game of bowls. I began competing in Ingham and won some local competitions. I was named to the team representing North Queensland in the national championships and we won it all one year. So, I could compete with anyone in bowls which made me feel as good as everyone.

I also remember a gratifying day—very emotional—in Ingham. They had the Maraka festival and Dolores Mendiolea arranged for some of us to perform the *Espata Dantza*, complete with costumes, at Lee's Hotel. We had to do it over again by popular demand. Word got out, and we were asked to perform that evening at the Golf Club. They had set up a whole staging area and we received a wonderful ovation. Things like that stick in your memory. In those days there were maybe 900 Basques in Ingham during the cane harvest. Of course, half or more left during the slack. They used to celebrate Saint Ignatius Day by alternating it between Ingham and Ayr each year. As many as 300 Basques from the region attended it.

After several years of cutting cane and traveling during the slack, I started working for some Italians in Ingham as a cabinetmaker. I did that for fifteen years. I also married an Australian of Italian descent. I moved to Brisbane and do that same cabinetry work. My son is also a cabinetmaker here and my daughter is a bank clerk.

I maintained contact with my family from the outset, mainly through correspondence with my mother. But, in the early days we were very careful. Given Father's history as a separatist, we feared that our letters were being opened and monitored. We were careful not to say anything that might be compromising—so, it was hard for me to get real information about conditions there.

I have been back twice. I still have that in my heart—"Home is Euskadi." I know it would be hard to leave Australia since my grown children are established here and my wife is Australian. The ideal dream to me would be to spend six months here and six months there every year (laughter).

Griffith-Yenda

Ramón Goirigolzarri # & —I was born in 1945 in Urduliz and attended school for three years. I know Spanish, Italian, English, and some Basque. My mother was from Urduliz and Father from Gatika. He farms in Urduliz and worked in a factory as well. Neither have emigrated. I am one of seven offspring. Five never emigrated, although José Ignacio went to sea as a commercial fisherman for four years. My brother, José Luis, and I both came to Australia. I brought him here in 1957. He is now back in Urduliz working as a stonemason.

Before I immigrated, I worked in Urduliz in farming, was a cooking apprentice in Bilbao for three years, and then an electrician in Urduliz for two-and-a-half. I came to Australia in 1965. I took a brother's place as he had made all the arrangements and then changed his mind. I planned to be here for three years to save some money. I heard about this from cousins here who wanted to help their relatives to join them. Juan Manuel Goirigolzarri was living in Ingham and José Ignacio, his brother, in Tenterfield, Queensland. José Ignacio helped me with documents and my fare. My parents were opposed. They wanted the family to stay together in Europe. By then, none of us had left.

I flew to Townsville and was met by José Manuel. It was March and I was out of work for three months. I liked the place in general, but the language problem was tough. I was staying with my cousin in a farm barrack and then got work fixing a tramline. Each farmer was required to do so and mine sent me in his stead. That work only lasted a few days, and then I went to Ayr to plant cane. I went with the Azkue brothers who were also from Urduliz. They had been there before. I made £8 for the one week that I planted. It was then back to Ingham with the Azkues to the harvest. I got work through my cousin cutting cane on two different Italian farms. There were we two and two other Basques in the gang.

That slack, I went to Dimbulah to pick tobacco with the two Basques in the cane gang. The farmer came looking for workers in the hotel. I worked there for four months and then returned to Ingham. That year, I ended up cutting alone when the two others (Basques) in my gang left early. It was then back to Dimbulah with my brother. By then, I had helped him to come to Australia. We finished in a month and then went to Griffith to pick fruit for four months.

We returned to Ingham and I was now a ganger. I had my brother, José Luis, Frank Larragan, Tomás and Iñaki Gárate, and a Navarran. That slack, it was again to Mareeba for a month and then to Griffith for four to the same farms as before in both places. In the tobacco that year I made A$75 weekly. The next year was the same routine, although in the slack I traveled with José Uriarte.

After five months of picking fruit that year I found employment in a winery for nine months instead of returning to the cane. I then picked grapes in the next harvest with Juan Muguira in Yenda, and then worked for the next year on that farm there. I married and found work in the rice mill where I am still employed today.

I met my wife, Ann Bagatella, at a dance in 1967, and we were married in 1970 when she was twenty-one. Her parents are from Belluno, Italy, and her father is a farmer and butcher. She was born in Griffith. She works as a store clerk. I met her my first year in Griffith and we began corresponding. She even came to Ingham for an extended visit to be with me.

It took me about four years to learn English. It was hard to date girls here because of the language. I mainly picked it up in the hotels. Since 1972, I get the *Sydney Telegraph* and the Griffith newspaper. I used to read *El Español* but stopped two years ago. I get no news from Spain. I do not listen to ethnic radio. In 1968, I joined the Yenda Diggers Club. It is social. In 1975, I became a member of the Ugali Catholic Club and, in 1976, the Yenda Rugby League. I am one of its sport officials. I played on the Yenda team for four years. I was naturalized in 1976 in order to go to Spain with fewer problems. I don't care that much about politics here but lean a little towards Labour. I go to the Yenda Hotel once a week as my friends are there. I am Catholic but go to church about once a year. At home, we use mainly English and a bit of Italian. In 1977, we went to the Basque Country, Madrid, and Belluno, Italy, for three months.

I bought my first car in 1967 and our house in 1970 for A$9,500. I once thought of buying an apartment in the Basque Country, and even started some paperwork, but gave it up.

I have many Australian friends through rugby and at work. Some Australians view us favorably and others badly. Generally, Australians are not industrious, but the exceptions work harder than us. Some are thrifty and others not. I have not suffered discrimination, but others have. Basques are more introverted than Spaniards and harder working, Italians work hard, but are a bit false.

I like it here, particularly the sports. But life is generally more boring than in Europe. I would consider retiring in the Basque Country, but my wife is from here.

Juan Manuel Goirigolzarri # —I was born in 1937 in Lauquíniz/Laukiz, Bizkaia and completed primary school. My father was born there and Mother in Gernika. They live on a *baserri* in Lauquíniz and neither ever emigrated. I am the eldest and now have a bar in Urduliz after returning from Australia. Neither my sister nor my youngest brother emigrated. José Ignacio also went to Australia and now has a wine shop here in Urduliz. Before I went to Australia, in 1961, I worked in a quarry in Lauquíniz. I planned to earn some money and return to the Basque Country, which is what I did. I heard of Australia when the formal recruitments began. I had a cousin, Tomás Armaolea, in Ingham and he helped me to immigrate. My parents were very upset. I came by boat and was out of work for the first three months. I was very sad. I got my first job through Tomás cutting cane in Ingham.

In the slack, I went to Melbourne to meet my fiancée. She is from La Rioja and came out to marry me. I went to work in Melbourne in construction. I was there two months and then we returned to the sugar harvest. We lived in the barracks with four other Basques and I earned £8 daily. That slack, we stayed in Ingham and I did odd jobs. I cut cane in Ingham for the next two years and stayed and did odd jobs there in the slacks. The following slack we went to Griffith to the fruit. We went with a friend from Valladolid and earned £7 per day. We were there three months before returning to Ingham for the sugar harvest. That slack, we went with my brother to Dimbulah to pick tobacco for £7 daily. The following year I had my own contract to cut cane in Ingham and then it was back to Dimbulah. I then cut cane for a year in Giru and picked tobacco in Dimbulah.

I learned my little bit of English by just mixing with Australians. I really don't know it. I never read the English newspapers there. I bought *El Español* and *Blanco y Negro* from Spain once a month in the store. I used to listen to shortwave radio from Spain every day at six in the morning. I would not like my children to marry an Australian or Italian.

Basques are doers; Spaniards are talkers. North Italians are like us; southerners are bad. I prefer they marry a Basque. In my work in Australia I used mainly Spanish and a little Basque.

It was now 1967, and I decided to return to live in the Basque Country. I had purchased an apartment here in the Basque Country for 160,000 *pesetas* in 1963. We had never naturalized, and my wife disliked Australia, particularly that nomadic life there. I tried unsuccessfully to become a codfisherman and ended up in a factory job that paid 8,000 *pesetas* per month. I didn't like it, and decided to return to Australia.

My wife stayed in Europe. I first worked construction in Ayr until the cane harvest started and then cut cane and earned about £12 to £13 daily. In the slack, I went to Dimbulah by myself to the tobacco. By then, I knew that scene well. I earned £7 daily and was there for six months. I then cut cane in Giru with a guy from Urduliz. He had a contract. Between us we were doing the work of five men. I earned £18 daily. Then it was back to Dimbulah with him to the tobacco. I then decided to return to my family in the Basque Country in 1970. I really considered staying in Australia permanently, but life began improving in Spain about then. I bought my bar in Urduliz in 1971. I still ask myself whether it was a mistake to leave Australia? I would like to go back for a vacation, but it is an expensive journey.

Fernando Echevarria # — I was born in Miravalles [Ugao-Miraballes], Bizkaia, in 1924. I attended school for five or six years and speak Spanish, Italian, some Basque, and some English. My father was born in Bizkaia [Fernando couldn't remember the town] and is a blacksmith in Zeberio, Bizkaia.

My parents are divorced, and she lives in Arrigorriaga. My eldest sister, Consuelo, lives in Sopelana [Sopela] and is a cook. She was here in Australia for a while. My eldest brother, Juan, was killed in the Spanish Civil War. Daniel died when he was eighteen. Then there is me; I am a farmworker here in Yenda. My stepbrother José Manuel Isasi is a turner and lives in Donostia. He has never emigrated.

When I came here, in 1951, I planned to stay. I wanted a better life. I wanted to go to sea as a merchant mariner but was denied the necessary permit to do so by the city authorities; my family was Basque nationalist. I had been working in the same *"Misericordia"* (Care Home) near Bilbo with Félix Jayo and he suggested I come to Australia. He came first and a year-and-a-half later sent for me. He helped with the papers and got Teresa Mendiolea to advance my fare. My mother was unhappy. Before coming, I had been running the cow farm for the *"Misericordia"* for seven years, and, before that, worked for a year in a paper-pulp factory in Arrigorriaga and on a farm for another year in Derio.

I flew to Townsville and Félix and Teresa came to meet me. There were two other guys from Aulesti on the plane destined for Ayr. My first job was cutting cane with Félix for the Mendioleas. I didn't like it that first year, but later became accustomed to the place. I cut with Félix, his cousin, some other Basques, and an Italian. I stayed the first slack in Ingham, as there was no work anywhere. I then cut again in the town. That was my routine for the first five years. I never left Ingham.

After the fifth cane harvest, I went to Rockhampton to work on the railway. I found the job through the state Employment Office. I only stayed two months, as my fellow workers were all drunks. I continued by myself to Sydney. I had written to the Spanish consul, and he got me a job on the farm of the French consul. Again, I left after two months when I had an argument with a fellow employee.

I then went to Cooma to work on the railroad. I went there with some Basque friends from Sydney. They knew about that. I worked for six months and was then injured. I spent six months in Sydney recovering. I returned to Queensland and cut cane in Ingham the next season. This time it was in Bemerside on a different farm. It was now 1959, and I went to Spain for six months and was married there.

I next cut cane for the Balanzateguis in Stone River. I did that for two seasons without leaving Ingham during the slack. After the next harvest, I went to Mildura to harvest fruit and then to New South Wales to gather asparagus. From there, we went to Shepparton where I worked as a manual laborer and on a pipeline project. I was there for three years.

It was then that I returned to Ingham and found employment in the mill, briefly, and then cut cane for the next two years for an Anglo farmer. In the slack, we went to Dimbulah to pick tobacco.

It was in 1968 that we went to Griffith to harvest fruit and vegetables. I did that for two years and then bought the farm that we have today.

When I first arrived here, it was impossible to date Australian girls because of the language. It took me two years to learn some English;

I never attended classes. Rufino Mendiolea tutored me. Today, I read farm news and the local Griffith newspaper. I get *El Español* every week and sometimes the *Spanish Herald*. My wife likes *Women's Weekly*. Once in a while, I get *La Semana* and *España Hola* from Spain. We joined the Hamble Catholic Club in 1970 and the Yenda Diggers Club in 1972. I don't listen to radio broadcasts; I have bad hearing.

I met my wife, Milagros Ruiz de Gordejuela, in 1960, and we were married that same year. She was twenty-six and born in Luyando [Luiaondo], Araba. Her parents were deceased. Her father had worked in Bilbo in a shipbuilding firm. I was on a six-month visit to Euskadi and Madrid. My cousin introduced us. I brought her back with me to Australia. Before coming, she had worked for fifteen years as a domestic servant in Bilbo, Luyando, and Vitoria/Gasteiz.

I have never had problems with discrimination, although some Australians view us badly. Dennis was my Australian employer and we have a very close relationship. I don't want my children to marry Australians. A Spanish spouse would be alright, but an Italian so-so. I want them to marry Basques. Basques are maybe a little more noble that Spaniards, but pretty much the same. Most Italians are good people.

We speak Spanish at home. I stay in touch with my family, mainly by telephone, particularly at Christmastime, seldom by letter. We are Catholics and attend church regularly. In 1954, I assisted my sister, Consuelo, to come to Australia. She lived here for a while and went back to Spain. Her son lives here today, and I spend time with him and a Navarran family as well. I like socializing with Basques. I see someone every few days.

I make A$170 per week before tax, and my wife works in a winery in Yenda as a bottler. My eldest son (nineteen) is a fitter and makes A$110 weekly. The second son works at the Ex-Servicemen's Club and earns A$82 per week. My daughter (fifteen) works at Woolworths part-time and makes A$20 weekly. They all live at home. [He preferred not to state how much he paid for his farm.]

We are not naturalized. We like it here, but want to retire in Euskadi.

Eusebio Arrizubieta # & —I was born in 1931 in Ispaster. I went to school for four years. I speak Spanish, Basque, Italian, and some English. My parents were from Ispaster and farmers. Father, now deceased, was a sheepherder in the USA for ten years. Mother lives on the *baserri* in

Ispaster. We are eleven siblings. I live here in Griffith and Florén, who now lives in Gernika and works in a factory, herded sheep in the USA for three years. None of the others has ever emigrated.

Before coming here, in 1958, I lived and worked on the family *baserri*. I just wanted to save some money and then go back. I thought of going to the USA; Father was alive and liked that idea. But then a friend, Tomás Ibañez, told me about Australia and offered to advance me the money for passage. My parents were against the idea, but I decided to come anyway. I came to Brisbane by boat along with ten other Basques. Tomás met us and arranged for our train tickets north. He found me my first job in Ingham, planting cane. I didn't like the heat, but everything else was fine. I made friends quickly.

That season I cut cane with Tomás, his two stepbrothers, Juan and Jesús Balanzategui, and two other Basques. That slack, I went with Tomás's stepbrothers and two or three other Basques to Texas to pick tobacco. It was easy to find work there without knowing anyone. After the harvest, we went back to Ingham, where the same gang cut cane on the same farm.

That slack, I went to Tasmania to pick fruit along with the two Balanzateguis. We first went to Mildura and found no work, and then to Melbourne. It was there that we were told of the opportunity in Tasmania. We harvested there for three months and then it was back to Ingham to the same gang and farm.

The next slack, it was off to Shepparton to pick fruit. I went with the cane gang. Work there was on offer without connections. We harvested for three months, and then returned to Ingham to the same farm and gang. It was then that I decided to change and went to work on the railway. I traveled with my future father-in-law and a Navarran. We learned of that opportunity through friends. We only stayed three months as it was too hot and buggy. After cutting another season in Igham, I got married (1962). We moved to Shepparton for two months and then to Griffith.

After the harvest, I was offered a job as a farm laborer and did that for the next two years. I then cut cane one more time in Ingham and after that season returned to Griffith, where I live today.

I could not date Australian girls due to the language. I never attended school here. It took me five or six years to know English. I picked it up at work and in the street. For the last six or seven years, I read the *Sydney Morning Herald* at times and the Griffith paper regularly. At first, I read *El Español, Il Globo*, and *La Fiamma*. I used to receive *La Semana* from Spain, but no longer. I listen to broadcasts on my shortwave radio. We belong to the Hanwick Social Club since 1968.

I met my wife, María Victoria de los Angeles Ribero, in 1960. Her father is from Burgos and her stepmother from Bilbo. She was born in that city. When we met, her father was here working as a canecutter in Ingham and was a friend of Tomás Ibañez. They now live in Sopelana. The family came to Australia sponsored by Fernando Echarri of Yenda. He is the brother of her stepmother. We married in 1960 when she was eighteen.

We have a seven-year-old daughter. We speak Spanish at home and at work I use Italian. It is very important that Belinda learn Spanish. We plan to move to the Basque Country. My wife was naturalized in 1960 when she was sixteen. It was automatic when her parents took out citizenship. I was naturalized in 1973 to enjoy more rights here. I favor Labour in politics.

We prefer Spanish cuisine; we don't like Australian food. We are Catholics, but do not practice.

I prefer that my daughter marry a Basque. I would object to an Aussie and definitely an Aborigine or Chinese. I would not object to a Spaniard or North Italian. Spaniards and Basques have some friction, at times over language. I find Italians to be like Basques and Spaniards; maybe a little falser than Spaniards. I would note that it is better to work for an Australian than a European. The latter makes impossible demands on you.

It is very important to me to be around other Basques and I seek them out. We socialize with Uncle Fernando Echevarria and the Navarran Delgado brothers. They are from Corella and one is married to a woman from Madrid and the other to a Navarran. Almost every week, we get together in one another's house. On the other hand, Fabián Bereicua (whose wife is a Jehovah's Witness) and Ramón Goirigolzarri (whose wife is Australian-Italian) don't mix in much.

I make A$370 a fortnight as a farmworker, and my wife works for a few hours a week in a fish-and-chips shop. We own a house that we purchased in 1970 for A$5,500. I bought my first car in 1960. We went to Spain in 1977 for three months for a visit. I almost bought a fish-and-chips store but didn't because my wife has bad health here and wants to move back to Spain in a year or two. All of our family is there. We are saving our money for that.

Fabián Bereicua # & —I was born in 1924 in Amoroto. I went to school for six years and know Spanish, Basque, Italian, and some English. I read Spanish and Basque. Both of my parents were from Amoroto and neither ever emigrated. They were tenants on a *baserri* in Berriatua. We were eight children. Six never emigrated. My brother, Juan, came here in 1931 and lived in Ayr as a canefarmer until his death. I live here in Beelbangera, NSW, and am a farm laborer.

Before I came, in 1952, I was a farm laborer in Berriatua. I planned to stay here. I found out about it through my brother. He arranged my papers and paid my passage. My parents were deceased by then and we were orphans. Four of us Basques traveled together from Venice to Sydney. The brother of one of my shipmates met our boat and put us on the train to Ayr. At first, I was scared of people here and very timid because of my lack of English. Also, there were bugs everywhere. But I got used to it.

My first job was cutting cane in Ayr for my brother on a farm he leased. I cut about one-and-a-half tons a day and earned seven shillings per ton. In the slack, I cleared bush in Ayr, some for my brother. For the next two years, I cut for him during the sugar harvest and cleared land in the Burdekin in the slack. Then my brother's lease ran out and I worked on building a tramline from Giru to Clare. I did that for eighteen months until the line was finished. I then cut cane in Ayr. I did that for two years and in the two slacks went to Griffith to pick fruit.

My next job was in Pioneer Mill in the Burdekin. Six months later, I went back to Griffth to work on an Italian's farm in nearby Beelbangera. It was now 1970 and he offered me a permanent job. I am here to this day.

I learned English at work and by attending night school in Ayr for three months. At home, we use Basque and English—Basque with our son and English with our daughter. I would like them to learn our maternal language, but I won't force it on them. I read no English-language newspapers. I get *El Español* infrequently. I do not receive any publications from Europe. In 1971, I joined the Returned Servicemens' Club, and, in 1980, another social one. I was naturalized in 1957 because I was thinking of buying a house in Ayr and had to put it in my citizen brother's name. I vote but am indifferent in politics. Lucia is a practicing Jehovah's Witness.

My wife, Lucia Zabala, and I grew up together in Berriatua. We were married in 1955 in Ayr when she was twenty-three. She had worked for seven years as a domestic in Lekeitio, Berriatua, and Ermua before coming here. Her parents were not happy about it, because it meant she would be leaving for distant Australia. Our son is twenty-two and an electrician here, and our daughter is only seven. I have no objections to anyone they might marry as it is up to them. We have never returned to Europe. We would like to (I am not sure when), but for a visit only.

We have a good life here. I make A$147 weekly after taxes and Lucia earns A$30 as a domestic. I have steady work and would not like to own my own business. I am not very good with people. We bought our house in 1977 for A$17,000. I purchased my first car in 1953.

I have no Australian friends. Before, they didn't like us, but that is improving. Some Australians are hardworking, and others are not. Most don't save their money. I have never felt discriminated against. I see Spaniards as about the same as Basques. It has been nine months since I was with other Basques, I chatted with some at the Easter Show. We go to Sydney for a week once a year. I have many good Italian friends here.

I don't care where I retire as long as it is near my children. I would like to own three or four acres on which to raise animals.

[Lucia then commented that her parents were opposed to her coming here to Ayr. The tongues were wagging so she sent back a wedding photo to still them. She has never been back to the Basque Country and has little desire to go. She barely communicates with her family. She used to be critical of anything Australian, often without even having sampled it. She then discovered that there are many good things here, from porridge to religion.]

Traralgon/Millicent

Juan Eizaguirre # & —I was born in 1930 in Amoroto. I only attended school for three years. I know Spanish, Basque, Italian, and English. My parents were born in Amoroto and were farmers. Since Father died, Mother lives in Lekeitio. Neither ever emigrated. All four of us children did so. I am the eldest and am here in Millicent working as a pine-feller.

Jaime lives in Lekeitio after having herded sheep in the USA for three-and-a-half years. León works in a sawmill in Lekeitio after two years in Germany and then two stints as a contract sheepherder in the USA. The youngest, María Pilar, is in Ayr where she cares for the elderly.

Before I came here, in 1958, I worked in Amoroto and Andoain as a pine-feller and farmer. I didn't plan to stay in Australia but changed my mind. I considered going to Venezuela and even filled out the papers and made a deposit toward the costs. I was also on the waiting list for the USA, but then Australia came up. I read about the recruitment in the newspaper. I was in the first one with government-assisted passage. I knew no one in Australia. My parents were tenant farmers and approved but insisted that I return. I sailed on the *Toscana* from Trieste to Brisbane.

I was in the migrant camp near Brisbane for three or four days and was then sent to Ingham. I made bilingual friends there, so didn't have too much trouble for lack of English. I liked it here. I cut cane that first year with three from Amoroto and one from Ondarroa. The slack, I stayed on in Ingham doing farmwork for three months and then left for Kalangadoo, South Australia, to fell pines (my job in Europe). I left Queensland because it was too hot. I learned of that opportunity through an Italian in Ingham. I worked on contract with a Navarran and we earned good money. I did that for four months and then returned by myself to cane cutting in Ayr. By then, my sister was living in Home Hill. I cut with a guy from Gernika and a Sicilian. In the slack, it was back to Kalangadoo.

I returned again to the Burdekin during the next cane harvest and cut in Home Hill. I worked there with Hilario Achurra. That slack, I went to Mampoo, South Australia (near Millicent), to fell pines and am here to this day. I once spent a month in Darwin looking for work.

It took me about five years to learn some English. I never attended classes; I picked it up in the hotels and then with my fiancée. I read no newspapers, only sporting magazines. I receive no publications from Europe. I telephone my mother every month. In 1962, I joined the Millicent Gun Club, and, in 1970, the Port McDonald Football Club. I have also been in two or three other football ones.[24] I sometimes listen to *Radio Nacional* from Spain on my shortwave radio. I go regularly to the Grand Hotel because other Basques do. But it is not particularly important to me to live around other Basques.

I met my wife, Mary Pratt, in 1962. Her father was working in the timber like me and he introduced us. She was twenty-three when we married in 1963. I became naturalized that year in order to get married. We are both Catholics, but don't go to church every Sunday. We have two small children and they do. We speak English at home and with the children. I didn't like Australian cuisine at first, but now I do. We cook Spanish-style more often. I would not object if my children married an Australian, but I prefer a Basque. I have never had problems with Australians. Most appreciate us as we work hard. In Euskadi I never liked to be with Spaniards. They are two-faced. Italians are almost like Spaniards in that regard.

I make A$650 weekly and Mary makes A$192 in a paper-pulp factory. I bought my first car in 1960 and I paid A$6,000 for a house in 1972. I plan to go to Europe within the next two years for a visit. If Mother gets sick, I'll go sooner. If I didn't have my family here, I might return for good. Life is more interesting there than here. I will probably retire in Millicent. I like the football.

Cornelio Uriarte # —I was born in Sukarrieta (Pedernales) in 1929 and attended school for four years. I know Spanish, Basque, Italian, and some English. My father was from Rigoitia [Errigoitia] and Mother from Sukarrieta. She is deceased and they lived there when she died. They were farmers and neither ever emigrated. I am one of four. My eldest brother, Antonio, is a merchant mariner and he herded sheep in the USA for three years. The second, Pedro, is a farmer in Sukarrieta and never emigrated, nor did the youngest, Miren, who is married on a *baserri* in Murueta, Bizkaia. I am a timber contractor here in Traralgon.

I was on the *baserri* in Sukarrieta before emigrating in 1958. I planned to earn some money and return. Through neighbors, I tried to go to the USA, but was not successful. Then I saw on a bulletin board in the town hall the chance to go to Australia. My parents were not opposed, but Mother cried when I left. I was government-assisted and sailed on the *Toscana* from Trieste to Brisbane. I was in a nearby migrant camp. I found the food hard to take.

I was sent by the government to Innisfail to cut cane for an Italian farmer. I learned Italian quickly and so didn't need much English. I cut with some brothers from Bermeo. I stayed in Innisfail during the slack and worked on the wharf. I then cut cane the second year there for a different farmer.

That slack, I went to Canberra along with Valentín Astuy and some other Basques to work construction. They had a friend there who wrote them about the opportunity. I was there for five months and then returned to Innisfail to cut cane.

The next slack, I went with several Basques to Shepparton and Mildura to harvest fruit, and then back to Innisfail.

The following slack, I was in Melbourne and met a Basque who was looking for workers to fell trees for a paper-pulp mill. I went there in 1963 and remain in Traralgon to this day as a timber contractor. This year I made A$24,000 and my wife cleans schools and makes A$60 weekly. I bought my first car in 1965 and this house in 1973 for A$16,500. We also bought five acres here eighteen months ago for A$33,000. I would like to build a new house there one day.

I met my wife, Ester Fernández, in 1964 here in Melbourne in the Spanish Club. She is from Baracaldo [Barakaldo], Bizkaia. She came in the third expedition in 1960. She was working as a domestic in Bilbao for six years and then a factory for four years in Baracaldo before emigrating. She lost that job and decided to emigrate. In Melbourne she worked in Mercy Hospital for four years.

It took me five years to understand English. I never attended classes here. I used to listen to *Radio Independiente Pirenaica*, but no longer. We are Catholic, but do not attend church. I don't read newspapers often, but Ester does. We get the two local ones, *Woman's Weekly*, the *Sun*, and the *Weekly Times*. We receive by mail *Deia*, the *Correo Español*, and *Interviu* from Spain sometimes. We joined the Melbourne *Gure Txoko* in 1964. I used to go frequently to the Crown Hotel because that is where my Basque friends hang out. I see Spaniards as less serious and dependable than Basques. Italians are tricky; not too trustworthy. We have two teenaged sons. We always speak Spanish at home, but they resist. It makes them mad. I would like to see them move to Euskadi one day.

I became a citizen in 1967 to have more rights. Ester was naturalized in 1968 and likes it here. She would like to stay. I like it here. The only problem is too much industrial strife. I hated the work in Queensland, and it was too hot. I went back to Spain in 1967 for a visit for three months, and, then, I tried to move there in 1973, but I missed this and returned here. When I retire, I want to have a livestock farm in Victoria somewhere, unless, of course, I move back to Euskadi.

Lorenzo Garmendia # & —I was born in Atallo [Atallu], Navarra, in 1933. I know Spanish well and then some Italian, Basque, and English—maybe fifty percent. My father was from Oreja [Orexa], Gipuzkoa, and Mother was from Atallo. They farmed in Uztegui [Uztegi], Navarra, and are now both deceased. Neither ever emigrated. I am one of four siblings and the only to emigrate.

Before coming here, in 1959, I was a logger in Uztegui. I came intending to earn some money and return to Europe after a short time. I was considering the USA, but this came up first. I saw the newspaper announcement of the recruitment. I had a friend, Manuel Artaro, a Gipuzkoan, living in Queensland. He wrote me about Australia, and I decided to apply. My parents were unhappy about it. Australia was too far. I came government-assisted in the *Montserrat*. I was then in Bonegilla for two weeks before being sent to Gordonvale by the government.

I cut cane. The work was too hard and it was too hot. I earned £50 weekly. I then went to Mareeba to pick tobacco, along with a Bizkaian. It was then to Inglewood to finish the tobacco season and afterward to Ingham to cut cane. I had met a gang in the tobacco and came along with them to cut in Halifax. They were all Basques.

My next move was to Ferntree Gully, Victoria, to fell timber along with a Navarran and a Gipuzkoan. There was a priest here who had a connection there and we had jobs waiting. I made £50 weekly. I have been here since 1961, although I have changed contractor from time to time. I have always been treated pretty well by Australians and find the forest workers to be industrious and thrifty. They are now mechanizing timber-harvesting, so the day of the independent feller (by chainsaw) is about over. There are far fewer Basque here now than before because of that.

It took me ten years to understand English. I learned it working with Australians only. I never attended classes. I have read the *Sun* since 1972. I get no publications from Europe. I never listen to radio broadcasts and belong to no social club. I am a Jehovah's Witness, as are my wife and children.

I met my wife, Heather Blucher, at a Jehovah's Witnesses' meeting in

1977 and we married in 1978. She has two children by a previous marriage that live with us. We now have an infant daughter, Amaya. Heather was born in Mafra, near Traralgon. Her father drives a truck. Her parents are very accepting of our marriage. We use English exclusively at home. I would like to teach Amaya Spanish and Basque. I like being around other Basques, but it is not too important.

I earn A$600 per week. We purchased a house in 1978 for A$27,500. I bought my first car in 1963. I own two apartments that I bought in Donostia in 1965 and 1969.

I have been back to the Basque Country in 1965 for three months, 1969 for three months, and 1974 for six weeks. I will go again some day, but only for a visit. I like Australia and intend to retire here in Traralgon.

Miguel Jauregui # —I was born in 1941 in Amoroto. I attended school for ten years and know Basque, Spanish, Italian, and English. I am one of eight siblings. The eldest, Dionisio, lives in Shoshone, Idaho, and is a ranch foreman after twenty-four years in the USA. The third, Javier, lives in Portland, Oregon where he owns a restaurant. He has been in the USA for thirty years. The fourth, Luis, lives in Adelaide and is a landscaper. He has been here for nine years after twenty in the USA. My brother, Felipe, lives here in South End, South Australia, and is a commercial fisherman with me.

Before immigrating in 1962, I was a farmer in Amoroto. I came to avoid military service. I hoped to go back after a few years. I considered the USA, but one of my brothers wrote advising me against it. I met Johnny Bengoa from Ayr when he was visiting the Basque Country and went around with him. Johnny talked me into coming and arranged the papers, although my father paid my passage. He lent me the fare. I was due to go to the Army within a month after having passed my physical. I was able to get a passport when I told the authorities that I wanted to spend a few days in France before military service. I obtained my Australian visa in France and came here as a deserter.

I sailed from Genoa to Sydney. I was then on a train to North Queensland with four other Basques. I found Australia to be very different from Spain—boring.

I first worked on the Bengoa farm for three months and then cut cane by myself for an Anglo farmer. Bengoa had set that up. That slack,

I went with four or five Basques to the tomato harvest in Killara near Melbourne. We picked for a Valencian farmer. After five months, it was back to Ayr. That year I cut for an Anglo farmer along with Domingo Bereicua from Amoroto.

The following slack, I traveled with Domingo and three other Basques to pick fruit in Shepparton. Again, it was back to Ayr after five months. I shifted to an Italian farmer and was cane cutting by myself. That slack, I stayed in the Burdekin and worked on repairing Pioneer Mill's tramline. Then it was back to cane cutting for the same farmer as the year before.

The following slack, I went with five or six Basques to Shepparton. We were three months there and then the last two in Griffith. Then it was back to the Italian farmer in Ayr for the cane harvest.

The next slack, I went with my brother and three other Basques to Mount Gambier, South Australia, to fell pines. I wrote to my cousin, Juan Eizaguirre, and he found us that employment. After five months, I returned to Ayr by myself. It was now 1967, and I finished that cut and then returned to Mount Gambier. I worked in the timber for a full year and then had the chance to engage in commercial fishing for lobsters in South End for some Italians. For seven-months' work, we made A$17,000 in wages alone, and also received 25 percent of the catch. We were paid in cash, so we didn't declare it as income for tax purpose. I found that work through a Yugoslavian friend in the timber who knew those boat owners. I was now married and stayed in South End from 1968 until 1972.

I then went to Adelaide with my brother, Luis, to have a fish shop together. He arranged that. We worked together from 1972 until 1978. But my hands couldn't stand the preparation of the product, so, I went back to commercial fishing in South End. I did that with my other brother, Felipe. I still fish today.

I have never attended classes here. It took me about two years to learn some English by going out with Australian girls and at work. About six years after I arrived here, I began reading the *Adelaide Advertiser* and the Millicent newspaper. I received no publications from Spain. I sometimes listen to news from there on my shortwave radio.

I met my wife, Maureen Fosterson, at a dance in Mount Gambier. We were married in 1966: she was eighteen. Her parents were in favor of the marriage. She is a Protestant and active in her church, but our five children are baptized Catholic. That is my religion, but I don't attend Mass. I am a naturalized citizen since 1969. I intended going to Spain then, but was considered a deserter there. I needed the protection. Actually, I didn't make the trip and have never been back. I don't correspond with family in Europe; my brother does instead and gives me the news. I haven't written in eight years. I arranged for my brother, Félix, to come here in 1966 with his papers and passage. I helped Luis with his documents only in 1972.

I would object to my children marrying an Aborigine or Chinese, anyone else would be their choice. I think most Australians think badly of us and that it hurt my chances here. They will not insult you to your face but are backstabbers. I don't drink much, so I seldom go to pubs. That is where there is likely to be trouble. Basques are more introverted than Spaniards; Spaniards are showoffs. North Italians are like Basques; southerners are not noble.

I earn A$16,000 to A$17,000 annually. My wife and I are now divorced. I collect unemployment in the off-season. I bought a house in Adelaide, in 1977, for A$55,000. I purchased my first car in 1963.

I would like to go back to Spain in a few years, but only for a visit. I would like to retire one day in the Basque Country. I have been to Perth for two weeks on vacation and this year went on holiday for six weeks to North Queensland. I have been in Sydney many times, for a week at a time passing through. This is a better place to work and has more freedom, but Spain has more atmosphere. I like the climate here. There are downsides in Australia, such as the lousy politicians. Women here have too much freedom and the young people are libertine bums. I favor the Liberal Party.

Jesús Elordieta # & —I was born in Ereño in 1930 and finished primary school. I speak and read Basque, Spanish, Italian, and English. My parents were from Ereño and farmed there. Neither emigrated. We are four siblings. I am the eldest and live here in Sale, Victoria, and work as a rigger. My brother, Isaias, is in Canberra where he is an electrician. I helped bring him here in 1959—papers and fare. I visit him for a week every year.

Before emigrating in 1955, I worked on the farm in Ereño. I had a fiancée and wanted to come here for four or five years to save money and go back to marry. I considered no other destinations. I learned of this from Julián Araquistain, a canefarmer in Ingham, who was back in the Basque Country on a visit. He helped with the documents and lent me my fare. I repaid that plus he demanded 5,000 *pesetas* for his trouble. My father was opposed as he had two *baserriak* under his care and needed my help. I came by boat from Genoa to Brisbane, along with three other Basques destined for Ingham. We knew no English, and couldn't even order a meal. We pointed to some bananas and that's all we had to eat during the two-day train ride to Ingham. We got sick.

I liked the climate passing through Melbourne. Brisbane wasn't too bad, but Ingham was so hot. Plus, the season was just ending and there was little work. Sabino Balanzategui found us a few weeks on the Mendiolea farm. After the first week, a plane passed overhead and one guy threw down his machete and pointed up while saying, "If I could just grab onto the tail, I'd fly home this very minute."

Christmas Day we were about forty or fifty Basques at the Mendioleas'. That slack, I went to Griffith to pick tomatoes. Tony Mendiolea found me the work, as he knew an Italian farmer there. By doing that, he hoped I would come back to their farm the next cane harvest. I worked alone and made 70 cents an hour.

On the way back north, I met two guys from Aulesti who convinced me to go with them to Ayr instead of Ingham. The harvesting was easier in the Burdekin. I cut cane on the Alberdi farm. I made £35–£40 weekly. Then it was back to Griffith to the same Italian farmer. I liked it there and preferred working for wages rather than on contract, as you always knew where you stood.

I cut cane for Alberdi the next three harvests and picked in Griffith for the same Italian in the two slacks. The following slack, I tried tobacco-picking in Clare for a couple of days and hated it. I left immediately for Griffith again.

After that slack (1960), I went to Spain for eighteen months with a man from Ispaster and worked on the family *baserriak*. I planned to stay but changed my mind. I married while in the Basque Country.

I returned to Australia in late 1961 with my wife. My brother was in the South and told me that Moe, Victoria, was a good place. I went there and worked for six weeks in a sawmill—and hated it. Through a Basque there, I found a position with a cement works in Mundara, building a dam. It paid £33 per week. In five months, the project was finished, and I went to a power station laying cables near Morwell. Some Basques working on the dam told me about it. I was there for the next eight years.

In 1971, I was offered a job by the company in Tasmania and went alone, as my wife took the children back to Spain on a visit. She even thought of staying but changed her mind.

That Tasmanian work lasted for nine months, and then I was transferred to Yalloun, Victoria, to work on a power station. I was there for four years, but there were too many strikes and an Australian friend helped me get a job in a gas plant in Longford. I have been here ever since.

It was after my wife returned in 1971 from Spain that we decided to start "living" here rather than saving all the time. We bought our first car that year, and we purchased our house in 1977 for A$42,000. I make A$6.64 per hour and my wife makes A$68 weekly as a janitress.

In 1961, I attended night school for two months to gain some English. But I learned it mainly at work with many Australians. At home, I use Basque with my wife and mainly English with the children. At work, it is all English. I listen to shortwave radio from Europe every day.

Since 1963, I read the *Sun* and since 1974 the *Gippsland Times*. I used to read *Il Globo* for its sports and, since 1970, *El Español*. Infrequently, when we receive a package from Spain, we have a few issues of *El Correo Español*, *La Gaceta del Norte*, and *Deia*. In 1956, I joined the Ugali Club in Griffith. It is social. When we lived in Morwell, I went frequently to a pub that had much Italian clientele. Here, I see Cornelio Uriarte, Javier Iriondo, and Mateo Malaxechevarria a couple of days a week. We play cards.

I met my wife, Milagros Aboitiz, in 1953. She was from Ispaster and an apprentice seamstress with my aunt. She was adopted into a family with nine children. Eight of her step-siblings have emigrated. Rufino was in the USA for eight years, as were José (seven years), Benito (three years), and Eugenio (four years). Prudencio was in America as a ranch hand for twenty-five years before he died in Nevada. Miguel was five years in Australia before spending the last ten in the USA. Pedro was here in Australia for four years, and now lives in Gernika and works as a merchant mariner.

Australians discriminate a little, particularly against Italians. I am not sure whether being Basque helped or hurt me here. I never had any real problems, but others have. Australians are not hardworking, educated, and only one in a hundred is thrifty. Basques are humbler than Spaniards; they have a superiority complex. I like Italians and find them to be trustworthy.

This is a good place. Life is tranquil and you earn well. I owe no money and the kids are coming along fine. I plan to go to the Basque Country next week, but just for a six-week visit to see my bedridden father, but not to stay. Milagros would like to retire there after the kids are grown. I wouldn't mind either.

My eighteen-year-old son is very pro-ETA and is pleased with each bombing. I am not. I think he is pro-Communist as well. If I took him to the Basque Country, he would end up in jail for sure. His grandfather was always, "Euskadi this and Euskadi that." My son is now pro-Euskadi in everything. I guess it is in his blood!

Sydney

Julián Oriñuela * # & —I was born in Bilbo in 1934. After primary school I completed some industrial studies (*perito industrial*). I know Spanish, Italian, English, and a little Basque. Father was a coppersmith from Ordizia (Villafranca de Oria), Mother was from Erandio. They both lived in Bilbo when they died. Neither had ever emigrated, nor have any of my three siblings.

Before coming here in 1959, I lived in Leioa and was an electrician for seven years, including two at sea. My family was Basque nationalist and had a partly worker-owned factory in Pasajes [Pasaia]. We lost it during the Civil War. When we returned from abroad after the conflict, it was to Bilbo. When I went to the university, I refused to take the SEU loyalty oath and was expelled. I went to work in a factory as an electrician and was a union organizer. I was outspoken politically and got into lots of trouble. I was also on the organizing committee of a local festival that was busted when we played prohibited Basque music. So, I was fed up and wanted out for a while. I considered going back to sea and had a job offer in Belgium. But then I read of the recruitment for Australia and a friend of mine, Raimundo Aresti from Leioa, who had herded sheep in the USA, talked me into applying. He, too, was fed up with Spain and wanted to leave it again. I planned to stay in Australia for two years.

We were government-assisted and sailed on the *Montserrat*. My parents were alive and opposed the plan—particularly Mother. From Bonegilla, I was in a group of eight sent to Ingham by the government to cut cane. There, I worked with Raimundo, Sabino Ugalde, Eduardo Quintana, Máximo Inchausti, and two other Basque guys (one from Mungia and the other from Gernika). Sabino was from Leioa and was my best friend at this time. He had been in the USA and knew some English. I was able to earn £500 that season and then spent much of it looking for another job.

I traveled to Sydney with Sabino, Eduardo Quintana, and Máximo Inchausti. After two weeks, Máximo and I found work with the Water Board at £16 weekly. We stayed together in a Greek-owned boardinghouse. I lasted for two months, and, then, through the newspaper, I found better employment in construction. I rented an apartment in Paddington and lived there by myself. A Basque, Arraras, and his wife were in another flat in the same building. Now I was making £23–£24 weekly. My best friend at work was a New Zealander. I was there for six months.

I was between construction jobs and decided to go to Griffith to pick fruit. We lasted for only two days. It was the hardest work that I have ever done.

We went back to Sydney, and I accepted employment in the Chevron Hotel. Again, I found that through a newspaper ad. We made £40–45 weekly because there was lots of overtime. Two guys from Gernika were working there as well. I remained for two years and then went to work in construction on the Sydney Opera House. Again, I found that job through a newspaper ad. I continued living alone in Paddington. At first, I earned £30, but later became a foreman and made more. Eventually, there were several Basques there—Arregui, Arraras, Pascual Garmendia, a Navarran.

I did that work for twelve years, until the building was finished. I had a Spanish friend at the *Gure Txoko* who worked at a parcel-delivery firm and he found me work there as a driver. I was later promoted to supervisor in the depot. I changed firms but am still doing that same work today.

It took me one year to learn English. The first year I was here in Sydney, I attended night school. I began reading the press and learned a lot from my New Zealander friend. I never tried to date Australian girls because I had a fiancée in Spain, and she came out the second year I was here. From the first day I arrived, I tried to read English newspapers—the *Sydney Morning Herald* and the *Daily Mirror*. Ten years ago, I began receiving *Reader's Digest*, and, beginning last year, the *Golf Digest*. When I first came, I read *El Español*, but no longer. I also got publications from Spain, but not for a long while. I never listen to ethnic or shortwave radio.

In 1961, I became a member of the *Club Español* and served on its board. I was a founder of *Gure Txoko*, as well as a board member and its president. I joined the Eastern Suburb's League in 1975, the Randwick Golf Club in 1977, and the Mascot Social Golf Club in 1979.

When I first came to Sydney, we Basques and Spaniards were few and with little collective ambiance. The food was particularly distasteful to us. If you tried to cook at home, you had to buy your olive oil in a pharmacy. So, when the *Costa Brava* restaurant opened with delicious Spanish cuisine, there was a line at the front door from the beginning, including many Australians. When I first joined the *Club Español*, the waiters set up three tables that were reserved religiously for Basques only. That is how we Basques in Sydney really began to come together.

I met my wife, Matilde Marqués, in 1956 in Bilbo, before immigrating here. We were married in 1960 when she was twenty-four. She is from Burgos. She is one of nine siblings and her parents are farmers. None of them have ever emigrated. They were not too happy when she came here to marry me. I have never met her parents. I have never been back to Spain. Matilde made a trip in 1973 to visit family, but she likes it here and is fine with staying. She was naturalized in 1972. I do not write to Europe, but Matilde does.

I became an Australian in 1968. My parents died about then and, so, I knew I was going to stay here. I favor Labour in politics. I am a member of the Transport Workers Union since 1976. We are Catholic, but do not attend church.

I make A$18,000 and Matilde earns A$7,000 doing family daycare. We purchased our first car in 1967 and our house for A$27,000 in 1968. We own no other property. We spend two weeks on a beach every year during our holidays.

We have two young sons. At home we speak Spanish. We use a little English with the kids. It is important that they retain their maternal language. It is also important for me to be around other Basques. I prefer that my sons marry Basques. I do not want them to marry an Australian, an Aborigine, or a Sicilian. A Chinese would be so-so. We Basques are better viewed here than are Italians and Greeks. Being Basque has helped me to find work. Australians are not industrious, educated, or thrifty. I was once told in a Paddington pub to stop singing Basque songs by an Aussie. He was expelled and my friend and I were allowed to stay. I was once insulted by a woman on a train. Basques are more egalitarian than Spaniards. They are hierarchical and have an inflated opinion of themselves. North Italians are like Basques; southerners are similar to Spaniards.

I want my sons to visit Europe, but not to stay. I love the freedom and opportunity in this country. Also, it has many golf courses. I don't like some of its antiquated laws. Business here is monopolized by the wealthy. I also don't like Queensland's Bjelke-Petersen. I plan to retire in Australia. I want to live on a farm, possibly in North Queensland.

José Luis Goñi * # & — I was born in 1930 in Goizueta, Navarra. My father was a medical doctor from San Sebastián, and he was practicing there. My mother was born in Zarautz; so, we were Gipuzkoans, really. My father never emigrated, and mother's family fled to France during the Civil War and lived there from 1937 to 1939. We were also refugees in Belgium. I am the second in the family and my eldest brother, Ramiro, and my sister, Iciar, both emigrated to Caracas and are there now [1980]. María Loli lives in Paris. Only my youngest brother, Juan María, has never emigrated. He lives in Zarautz.

I came to Australia in 1959 as part of *Operación Eucalipto*. I just answered a government recruitment ad. I was fed up with politics in Spain and wanted to get out from under my parents' control. My father was a famous physician and cast a long shadow. They were very much against my coming here, and even tried to buy me off. I thought I would give it a try. I had no relatives in Australia. I could have gone to Venezuela, my brother was there and would have helped me, but I was looking for independence.

I was almost thirty when I emigrated. I had attended school for fourteen years and had a degree in technical (mechanical) studies. I worked for five years in a toy factory in Zarautz before leaving Spain. Today, I speak Spanish, Basque (very little), English, some Italian, and French.

I came on the *Montserrat* and there were three men, including Raimundo Aresti, who had herded sheep in the American West. They talked about getting work in that industry. They were certain that, with their experience and the millions of sheep in Australia, it would be easy. They were disillusioned, and, I believe, they only stayed in Australia for a relatively short time.

I was in Bonegilla for two weeks and was then sent, along with José Arregui, who was from Eibar, to Mossman to cut sugar cane. I liked this immense country immediately, but I didn't like cane cutting at all. Arregui and I cut together and were poor at it. After expenses, I probably netted about £3 a fortnight. It was a huge disappointment.

I hated Mossman; it was boring. Maybe it would have been different had I lived in Ingham or Innisfail where there were more Basques. I met a Hungarian in a hotel, and he convinced me to leave Queensland and go to Sydney. I had a friend there, Eusebio Illarmendi, and I knew I could stay for a while with him. So, Arregui, a guy from Cuenca (who worked in Eibar before emigrating), and I traveled to Sydney together. Many years later, Arregui was the godfather of my two eldest children.

All three of us newcomers to Sydney moved into a boardinghouse owned by a Portuguese. I worked there as a janitor for four months. I would hang out at the hotel in Kings Cross frequented by Basques, and some of them told me about the opportunity to work at BMC (British Motors Company). I was employed there and worked for a year before being laid off. I worked along with a Basque named Victorino Zarauz. I was unemployed for about eight months, and then became a kitchenman and dishwasher in the King's Cross Hotel. It was a favorite hangout for us Basques. There might be fifty of us there and only one or two Australians. All this time, I lived in the Portuguese boardinghouse.

After a short layoff, I was called back by BMC and worked there for another year-and-a-half before accepting the position as the assistant manager of the *Club Español*. But I couldn't get along with the man who had the restaurant concession, so, after six months, I went to the Menzies Hotel for kitchen work.

I liked Sydney and became involved with the Spanish community here. I was a founder of the *Club Español*, in 1962, and served as an officer. I was a founding member, in 1966, of the *Gure Txoko* as well, and, for a time, was its president. In 1977, I became a member of the Mount

Druitt *Club Español* and served as an officer and its president. I have also joined soccer clubs here and coached three teams. In Spain, I had been the trainer of the Zarautz soccer team and was even the first coach of the famous *portero* Iribar.

I eventually got a factory job in Smithfield and moved here to avoid the long commute. I have worked in a glass and steel factory and as an aluminum cutter. Between two factories, I have been here for ten years now.

I married my wife, Ana Moyano, in 1964. She came to Australia in 1961 as part of *Operación Marta*. She was from Málaga and had a sister residing here in Sydney. They lived together. I met her at one of the dances that were organized by the Spanish community before we had the Spanish Club.

We were both naturalized in 1967. It was more my idea than hers. I wanted to give up my Spanish citizenship, but she didn't. She has never been comfortable here and wants to move back to Spain. She has two sisters living here now and one in France, but most of her family is in Spain. Ana has problems with English. I studied it in school in Europe and on the boat. Right after I arrived here in Sydney, I began going to night school to improve my English. I read the *Telegraph* and *Mirror* newspapers regularly. I use English all the time at work. I also joined the Metalworkers Union in 1968 and favor the Labour Party. Still, I would say that my closest friendships are with Basques. I like to get together with them. I go to the *Gure Txoko* nearly every week. I like Spaniards, but Basques are more open. I used to read the *El Español* newspaper here, but no longer. Sometimes, my mother sends me Spanish publications from Europe.

We use Spanish at home with the children. They learn plenty of English in school and with their friends. They know a few words of Basque, but not much. We went back to Spain in 1975 for a three-month visit. I wouldn't mind if any of my children decided to move permanently to Spain, but I am happy here.

Ana thinks Aussies consider us, and our children, to be "Bloody Wogs." I believe that only some do, and I have never really experienced much discrimination. I have some good Australian friends and workmates. I think that Australians don't like Italians and Greeks but appreciate Spaniards more. Ana would like us to retire in Spain; she considers it to be her country. We'll see. [José Luis Goñi was both a gourmet chef who prepared many meals at *Gure Txoko* and an artist who designed posters for its *pelota* and *mus* tournaments. He died in Australia in 1993.[25]]

Eusebio Illarmendi*& —I was born in Zarautz in 1927. My father died when I was nine, so my mother was a housecleaner and raised my sister and me. Times were very tough for her. I became a mechanic, a turner-fitter. I completed my military service and was working in a factory in Zarautz that made electrical trams. Economic opportunity was very limited in Franco's Spain and a friend of mine (Imanol Arluciaga) and I decided to emigrate.

Well, Imanol had a sister working in the Canadian embassy in Paris and she suggested we go there. She arranged the papers, but we were rejected by the Canadians as citizens of a Fascist country! She suggested we go to Australia instead, and helped us with the papers in the Paris Australian embassy. We had to pass a medical exam in Bilbo by a doctor there approved by the British consulate. It handled Australia's affairs in Bilbo at that time. We crossed the French frontier and spent four days in Dax before embarking in Marseille. Neither of us had family outside of Europe. We paid our own fare—I borrowed the money from my mother, sister, and uncles.

There were six Spaniards on the ship; we were the only Basques. We went from France to Algiers, then Guadaloupe, Curaçao, the Panama Canal, Tahiti (where we stayed five days), and then New Caledonia. One of the Spaniards had a brother in Australia, and he wrote that conditions there were very bad. So, we two Basques and a shipmate from Alicante decided to stay in New Caledonia. Some French we met on board said that it was easy to get work there. There was a nickel-processing plant that needed skilled workers. It had electrical Siemens ovens sent there from Germany after the war that were used to process the ore. It was labor intensive as their elements had to be replaced regularly.

But to work we needed a permit. We went to the Police Commissariat for it and were told that we would have to post 15,000 francs as a good-conduct bond. We didn't have that money, so they agreed to let us make a 3,000 per month payment for five months.

The language of the place was French. I knew a little bit and Imanol more. He had a French brother-in-law. But it is a Latin language anyway, so we picked it up pretty fast. We lived in company housing and the pay was good. But it was always our intention to go to Australia. So, when our companion from Alicante heard from a friend of his in Sydney that conditions had improved there, we bought boat tickets. The police returned our deposit with interest! They had deposited the money in a bank, and we were given its interest as well. We had been working in New Caledonia for nine months.

In Sydney, we were met by three Spaniards and taken to Kings Cross. We found lodgings there used mainly by other immigrants. Two days later we were taken to the Holden car factory and employed immediately. There were many immigrants working there, a lot of Italian peasants, and most had no skills or experience. They were learning on the job. As soon as a man became a decent welder, he quit and took a better job. Holden was like a training ground, and its product was pretty shoddy. Anyway, we were the only two Basques. At that time, there were very few Basques in Sydney; quite a few Spaniards but not many Basques.

After three months at Holden, I was asked by a fitter from Bilbao to go to work for him. I did so, and our first job was in construction of a factory for the major English firm ICI (Imperial Chemicals Industries). It lasted for about three months, and then we went to Cooma to the Snowy Mountains Scheme to work on an electrical plant for it. There were many immigrants there. The salary was good and there was nothing to do, so you saved your money. It was too cold to drink much beer, so you didn't have that big expense of Queensland canecutters. Weekends we went hunting for rabbits for recreation and to cook up. But, the work was very dangerous. We worked for a while in the tunnels as dynamiters. One day I saw a Spanish guy almost killed by a falling rock and decided to quit. I went back to Sydney.

It was now 1956, and I had a fiancée in the Basque Country. We had worked together in the factory in Zarautz. So, I was now established and sent for her. We were married by proxy, as were the fiancées of two of my non-Basque Spanish friends in Sydney. The three women traveled out to Australia together from Rome on an Italian boat.

When they arrived, we all had a party. In those days the liquor laws were very strict—downright archaic—I remember eating a lobster that night washed down by tea. We bought a house in a poor neighborhood together with José Bilbao from Bilbao and his spouse. We shared it for a couple of years. One day, in 1959, we went to the beach together and on the way came across a subdivision development. My wife and I, as well as three other Spaniards, decided on the spot to buy lots there. Two later sold out, but the other friend and we built houses. We were in about A$9,000 in all, after paying £1,100 for the lot.

At first, I was a fitter here and then became a toolmaker. Toolmaking paid better. I worked at that profession in several different plants until my eventual retirement. My wife went to work in various factory jobs over the years, and together we worked hard to pay off the house.

In 1960, we went back to Spain for a visit, and, in 1971, made another nine-month trip to the Basque Country. That time, while we were gone, we rented out our Sydney home. We had no intention of staying in Europe, since Franco was still in power.

Most of the Basques in Sydney either stayed here after immigrating or after working a single season in cane cutting. The canecutters might come to Sydney in the slack season and go to work for the Water Board. Some stayed on and were employed there for many years. Even though the money was better, not everyone wanted to cut sugar cane.

If a man was married, he was more likely to remain in Australia with his family. But many were bachelors and most went back to Spain. There were always problems adapting here—particularly with language. It was not like South America where everyone speaks Spanish. I can't remember anyone here who was first in Latin America, except for a few professional *pelotaris* (maybe six or seven). Some came here from the Philippines after things became bad there. One of our *Txoko* members lived in the Philippines for several years.

About 1962, it was decided in Sydney to form a Spanish Club—*El Centro Español*. I was on the first directorate, but I only served for about one year. I was the only Basque on that board, although there were many others as club members. By then, there were many Spaniards here. We wanted to start up a *futbol* team. Quite a few Spaniards had come to Australia by then. Most stayed in either Sydney or Melbourne. I have pretty much pulled out of the Spanish Club since the Basques started the *Txoko*.

In 1966, two Basques came to see me. One was a young man from Tolosa; he was the main promoter of *Gure Txoko*. The idea had been floating around for a few years. We Basques sometimes got together in a certain hotel in Paddington. Other times we met in the Paddington private home of Ramón Peñagaricano. So, we formed a provisional directorate and compiled a list of all the Sydney Basques we each knew.

We contacted a real estate agent and he showed us a property at 344 Liverpool Street.

We then invited everyone on the list to come and view it. We had the key to the locale and about forty or fifty people attended. We suggested that each person put up A$250 so we could make the down payment. Not everyone liked that proposal or was able. So, we asked all who wanted in to move to one side of the room and those who didn't to the other. We then opened the door and told the dissenters to leave; we didn't want to waste any more of their time. Some of them eventually did join. There were about twenty-five founding members.

It was very difficult the first couple of years. We had to service the mortgage and needed to make repairs—paint, a new roof. We paid £2 per month as a quota. Not all of the members were Basques. Some were non-Basque Spanish sympathizers. Some Basques stayed away because they thought the club was political, anti-Franco. It was really not. It was like a gastronomical society, recreational. We are nothing more than a tavern with eating, drinking, and *mus*. In fact, there are few genuine cultural activities.

I see little future for the *Txoko* if we do not get new Basque immigration. Four members have died and many have gone back to Spain. The children of Basques who are born here have other interests. They are Australians at heart. They may have little more than a Basque surname. I don't think the youth are interested. The kids might come once in a while, but they prefer their friends and other activities. Then, too, many families live too far from the *Txoko* to come very often. It is too much of a project on your day off. So, they only show up for a big fiesta. We have always been very few in numbers. It is not like Argentina where you have thousands and thousands of Basques. There are maybe 150 Basques in Sydney. Without new immigration the *Txoko* will likely die out little by little.

We had a football team, but the players all turned forty together. We added some Portuguese and Spanish players just to keep it going; and that caused its own disputes. "Why should a Basque Club have non-Basques on its soccer team?" The same happened with the *pelotaris*. They all became older together and stopped playing. Many of our members are bachelors, so they aren't leaving descendants. The club is really male. There isn't a lot for women to do in it. Some member got mad for one reason or another, left, and never came back. If the *Txoko* dies the building goes to charity. No one will make money out of it.

We ran everything with volunteer labor. For ten years I worked Sundays on the *frontón*, beginning at 6 a.m., and then played on it. I remember fondly the Christmas, Easter, and *Aberri Eguna* celebrations and parties. The first *Aberri-Eguna* celebration, I brought the silverware and record player from my home.

This club was not in vain. All of what I am telling you is only my opinion; others might see it differently.

I am still a member of the Spanish Club, but I only go once a year, in December, to pay my dues. I might attend one other event during the year. I no longer have friends there: most of my friends are in the Basque Club. Some of us are members of both. The *Txoko* played against the Spanish and the Portuguese in soccer. They were informal matches, maybe around a picnic. We might bet half a cow and then cook it up for a barbecue. We had an internal *pelota* championship, but no longer.

I wrote the International *Mus* Federation to see if we could be included in the world competition, Franco Aguirre of the San Sebastián Department of Tourism came here two years ago, with some Basque woodchoppers who entered the Australian national competition. Aguirre was kind of an observer for the *Mus* Federation. But last year he was in Melbourne and Javier Iriondo[26] of the Melbourne *Txoko* wanted it to be named the Australian representative. I don't know him, and I'm not sure if there are more Basques in Sydney or in Melbourne. I had only two Basque friends in Melbourne, and they have both gone back to Spain. I think we'll get in. Our champion *mus* player is in Spain right now and offering to participate in this year's world competition there.

Rafael Alegría*& —Is from Hondarriba (Fuenterrabía) Gipuzkoa. His father was born in Hualde, Navarra, and his mother in Azpeitia. His parents settled in Irun where his father worked for a bus company and then a railroad transporting passengers to and from the French frontier and Donostia. Rafael spent three years of his childhood on the maternal family farm in Azpeitia owned by his uncle and aunt. There were several children in the Alegría family (three boys and three girls), and they alternated with one another in Azpeitia.

Rafael attended school until sixteen years of age. In his teens, he was at the Lasalle College in Irun. He then began working full-time and continued his studies in after-hours' evening classes. He worked full-time Saturdays and Sundays, so it was a very demanding life. He did not complete his education as he joined the Army to avoid serving in North Africa. By enlisting as a volunteer, Rafael was able to do his service in Irun. He was actually able to work one day at his civilian job and then go to the local military base the next. This went on for sixteen months.

Between 1963 and 1969, Rafael was employed in the Irun factory of La Palmera. It manufactured silverware and kitchen gadgets. So he gained considerable technical skill and experience. He met his future wife in 1967 when he was twenty-six. She came to Hondarribia for summer vacations. Her relatives lived in Madrid and owned a travel agency. She had been an airline stewardess and actually lived for a while in New York. Her father was a professional soccer player. Ana had an uncle and aunt in Sydney. It was because of them that the young couple decided to give Australia a try after marrying. They planned to wed and then honeymoon on board the ship that brought them here. At that time, Australia was looking for technicians and they both seemed to have appropriate experience. They thought they might try it out for a couple of years and then decide about the future.

Rafael had considered emigrating to Canada or England before his marriage in 1969. But then the Australia opportunity came up. When I interviewed him as president of Sydney's *Gure Txoko* (in 1980), I asked how the idea of emigrating occurred to him? He noted that living in Irun, right on the French border, gave you an international outlook. He and his siblings crossed into France regularly, sometimes to take classes in French. One of his sisters raised a son there until he was ten. Then, too, you saw fishermen departing regularly from the town for as far away as Terranova and Africa. They also knew about the emigrants to Latin America and the sheepherders in the American West. In sum, the possibility of going abroad was inherent in the Irun worldview.

Rafael then commented on the history of *Gure Toxko*: The Asturians in Sydney organized a Club about the same time that we did. It only lasted a short time because they tried to do things "*en grande*" [or "on a pretentious scale"], whereas we remained small and family-oriented. We held barbecues and picnics in parks. Under Australian law, an association had to have a minimum of 250 members. We weren't close, so we formed, instead, a corporation (*sociedad anónima*). All of the work here was voluntary. We celebrate *Aberri Eguna*, which is very well attended. The crowd scarcely fits in the building; if the weather allows, we spill into the *frontón*. We also do something around Christmastime (*Noche Buena*), given that many of our members are bachelors and lonely during the holidays. We organize *mus* and *la rana* (another card game particularly popular with women) tournaments and a *pelotari* championship. We hold a nice awards' dinner and give out prizes to the first- and second-place winners.

Every trimester, the directive meets to go over the books and report the Club's finances to the membership. They also assign volunteers for the upcoming quarter's weekly (weekends) duties.

During the year, there are several events, mainly picnics, in nearby Centennial Park. Our soccer team played there against that of the *Club Español*.[27] There are other competitions, like *sokatira* between both adult and juvenile teams. We baptized a tree in the Park as the "Tree of Gernika," and we had a racing competition in which the contestants ran to touch it and then back. There was always *mus* as well. We organized many excursions. In 1974, we went to Canberra to watch our soccer team compete in the Ambassador Cup championship. But our players included some Portuguee and Spanish players and that caused dissent, and ultimately a schism, in the *Txoko*.

Today, we have fewer picnics as the youth are growing up and have their own interests. Maybe the husband comes to the *Txoko* on Sunday while his wife and kids go to the beach. So, rather than unifying families, the Club now divides some.

It is prohibited to talk politics in the Club; but, of course, sometimes you can't help it. We painted the *frontón* red, green, and white—the colors of the *ikurriña*. Some, like Pascual Garmendia, believe that it was a political statement that should not have happened. It alienated some members.

The building is almost paid for now and it is my dream to have a second country house where retired members could live out their days, given that about half are old bachelors. Their lives are lonely and tragic. We may receive some money from the telephone company in compensation for the damage they did to our building when it built its new one next door. We'll see. If there is no agreement, there will be a lawsuit.

The *Club Español* has gone down. I don't belong any longer. One popular meeting point is the *Costa Brava* restaurant owned by a very sympathetic man named Álvarez. We have a guy here who won this year's *mus* championship in the *Gure Txoko* who is a professional card-player. He doesn't work; he makes his living playing cards against the Basques and Spaniards in Sydney. He plans to move back to Spain soon.

We also do beneficent works. Francisco Javier Montero, one of the founding members but then living in Bilbo, was injured and spending time in the hospital after having a finger amputated. He needed money and the *Txoko* set up a donor's fund and sent it to him. When some members from the *Txoko*, who happened to be in the Basque Country, visited him in the hospital, he was so moved that he started crying.

When José Arregui had a fatal heart attack while preparing his son's First-Communion party, the *Txoko* held a ceremony in the crematorium. As was his wish, the casket was adorned with an *ikurriña*. The family needed help. The Club donated A$500 from the treasury and individual members added to it—the total amount was A$1,900. Pascual Garmendia and I visited her house to hand it over.

The founders each put up A$200; but it was actually a loan rather than a donation. It earned one-and-a-half percent per annum. If you wanted to leave, maybe to go back to Spain, you were owed your original contribution plus interest. No one wanted the interest, and some just left their contribution as a donation to the *Txoko*.

Carlos Orue * & —My father had been an emigrant at one time. In 1960, he went to Spanish Guinea in Africa for a while in search of employment. My cousin and her husband came to Australia, in either 1959 or 1960, in one of the recruitments. They were from Villafranca, Navarra, and I still have family in that area. They returned to the Basque Country about 1974 and convinced my sister to join them, along with her husband and three children. My cousin's husband was a fitter and turner. He went to work in the steelworks of Wollongong in his trade. He later set up his own construction company; building and then selling houses. She learned Italian rather than English and went to work in Italian restaurants. Ex-prime minister Whitlam was actually one of her customers.

I was still in Spain when Franco died. Times were tough both economically and politically. The Franquists tried to blame the economic problems on the oil embargo. That might have been part of it, but the awful economic policies of the regime were at fault as well.

About then, I borrowed over a million *pesetas* from a bank to buy a truck to go into the transport business. I didn't have colaterral, but the banker agreed to work with me. Miren, my wife, went back to her old job in a fish-processing plant in Bermeo to help out a little. We had one son, Carlos, and, because of the times, postponed having more children. I lost that truck to the bank and then went to work for a short while in Amorebieta and then as a driver in Eibar for a cement manufacturer transporting material from a quarry. But things went from bad to worse. There were weeks in 1979–1980 when I went more than a week without a trip. Then my employer had to cut our wages.

So, in 1980, I acceded to the imploring of my sister and cousin and applied for an immigration permit in Australia. My sister was in debt, buying her house, and didn't have the resources to sponsor me. So, my cousin agreed to be our sponsor. I got my approval and, under its terms, had a year to decide. If I failed to, it could be renewed for another year if we simply passed the medical test.

I was playing cards in a bar one day with my friends and first news of the *coup d'etat* of the military in the Madrid Parliament was broadcast on the television. No one knew that I had my Australia-approval and I thought to myself, "Carlos, this is the last straw. Why stay here any longer." By two in the morning, the coup was over. The king had pronounced himself against it. I told Miren, "He took eight hours. He wanted to see how the reactions were. Had they been favorable for the rebels, I believe the king would have declared his support as well."

So, we renewed our application for Australia. While I was awaiting approval, I saw an article in the newspaper that said that Australia was looking for mechanics, fitters, turners, and other tradesmen. I didn't have those skills but knew a man who employed turners (*torneros*) in his pipe factory. I asked if I could come in for maybe three months in the afternoons after my driving job to learn how to talk the talk and then maybe pass the test when asked to take it by the Australians. He agreed and even offered to pay me for my work. I made several pipes. So, I reapplied as a turner. I was approved in September of 1981. Maybe three months later, I went to a meeting in Irun. There were twenty or thirty of us, all intending to emigrate as tradesmen. That's what the Australian government was looking for. Their representative didn't know Spanish, so he spoke to us in Italian, like it was close enough! He then told us several "bloody lies" about wages in the country and its pension system. So, they lied to me and I lied to them about my credentials. I had a falsified certificate saying that I was a turner. It was all a little ridiculous, because, after passing your test in Spain, when you got to Australia, they wouldn't recognize your credentials anyway. Maybe it was a labor-union thing, but they required you to get recertified in a technical college. That was a killer for many immigrants because of their lack of English.

I still hadn't received my final approval several months later and traveled to Madrid to ask the Australian authorities why? They were a bit dodgy and said it was in the line and would be acted on soon. They asked me how much money I had, clearly concerned that I could become a ward of the state. I had none, so, when I went back to Eibar, I asked my boss to terminate me from my job. He agreed to do so, and that qualified me for severance pay, maybe 200,000 *pesetas*. I informed the Australians and in early September had my permit, but with the news that they would no longer pay our fare. It seems that, as of April of 1981, they no longer did so. The fortunate thing was that I was never asked to take my turner test in Madrid; every other technician from Spain that I have met in Australia had to do that. Strange world, isn't it?

Anyway, I contacted the Comisión Católica in Bilbao and they were great. They found us cheap tickets and lent us the money to pay for them. We had an interest-free loan for two years and made no payment for the first three months after arriving in Australia. On December 4, 1982, we flew to Madrid with our son, Carlos. We were stuck there for twenty-four hours arranging some details and then flew to Paris. We had to sleep in the airport on benches that night. Next day, we began the twenty-four-hour trip, counting layovers, to Sydney. When we got there, I said to Miren, "We are never going back to Euskadi again, if only to avoid that damn trip."

We were met by my sister and we spent the next month living in her home. She told us that we should just relax as no one would hire us over Christmas holiday anyway. It was a great vacation. Then, in January, I applied for a job in the Wollongong steelworks, but the Australian economy was retracting, and they were laying men off rather than hiring. My cousin found Miren work making sandwiches and coffee in a café in the Red Cross Blood Bank about eighty kilometers from Sydney. By February, I had work as a part-time janitor in a nearby office building. My cousin found us a flat to rent and it was the worst place I have ever lived. In the winter, there was thick mold on all of the walls. But it was close to Carlos's school and he could walk there while we were both at work.

I kept applying for other jobs and was a little ashamed of my employment. I put that I was employed currently by an "industrial cleaning firm," another lie. Meanwhile, I studied English from 9 a.m. until 4 p.m. for ten weeks in a government-sponsored course for immigrants. I then ended up working as a janitor in a hotel complex. I was supposed to be temporary, replacing people on vacation. But they liked me and asked me to stay. There was a guy from Durango working in a restaurant there and he got me a job cleaning it from 6 a.m. until it opened at noon. By then, I was in the Sydney *Gure Txoko* and Múgica, a member from Gernika, asked if I would be interested in working for the Sydney County Council. It was the municipal electricity company that later changed its name to Sydney Electricity. I filled out my application and three months later was hired. I have been there for the past seventeen years.

Miren worked in that café for five years. She struggled with English and worked mainly in the kitchen. She was fortunate that a coworker was a Greek woman born in Egypt who knew many languages. She helped Miren with her English. Still, when she finally had to waitress, she memorized the menu by heart and could scarcely communicate with customers who asked for anything that was not on it.

We bought an apartment two years after arriving here. Then, four years later, we were given the opportunity to house-sit and maintain a fancy residence. We moved there and rented out the apartment. So, we had that additional income with which to pay off the mortgage on the rental quickly. We then sold it and bought our current residence.

I joined *Gure Txoko* in 1983,[28] shortly after arriving in Australia. I went on the Directive Board but was not very active. The next year, I got a call one evening to congratulate me. The Directive had just elected me vice president. I was new and didn't feel very qualified to contribute much. Actually, Mari Asun got me more involved. She brought me along. In those, days we had a Wednesday night dinner and a Sunday lunch (3 p.m.). There is some talk of covering the *frontón* to increase the dining space. It is almost never used for competition. The former players are too old. The court always had the defect that there is no room for spectators. It is so narrow that maybe only ten people could stand pressed against a wall to watch a match.

Gure Txoko now (1995) has 98 members. In terms of names, membership list has grown since 1980. But that is partly a function that women can now join on their own. In terms of families, there are fewer than before, and the number is dwindling slowly as people retire and move back to the Basque Country. Four or five members have died in just the last three years. Members pay A$20 annually as dues. We actually are considering raising it to maybe A$50 or even A$80 per year. The Board believes that the expenses of events should be covered by those attending them, but maintenance of the building should correspond to everyone. The current dues fail to cover that. [Carlos opined that the discussion would be controversial, and they would probably settle on dues in the range of A$40 to A$50.]

Most of the members of *Gure Txoko* belong to the *Club Español* or pay their dues there anyway. Some of the Spanish Club members resent or envy the *Txoko* and start false rumors about it. They are in a minority, however, and the two organizations cooperate on some things. There are non-Basque members of the Spanish Club who come to *Txoko* events—particularly the barbecues in Centennial Park. In recent years, the *Aberri Eguna* event is held there beneath the "Tree of Gernika." That tree is not an oak but has acorn-like nuts. The children dress in Basque costume. There is also a Christmas event held there around December 17. We barbecue meat and *chorizos*. It is very popular. The Centennial Park events draw more than those held at the *Txoko*—between 100 and 200 participants.

About four years ago we cancelled the Wednesday dinners. There were too few old bachelors left and it was a work night for everyone. The dwindling attendance did not warrant it. We still do the Sunday lunch. It is well attended.

During the past year's Easter Show, a group of Basque sportsmen came to Australia on their own—*aizkolariak* and weightlifters. There is a famed saw maker here who produces special ones for hand-sawing competitions here and in North America. The Basques were interested in learning about that. The woodchoppers and Ibarra and Mendizabal came, and they offered to put on an exhibition here in Sydney. They asked for our financial help and I approached several donors. One gave A$5,000 and he was able to raise an additional A$1,500. They got a lot of local television coverage.

Last year, *Euskal Telebista* sent a filming crew to do a documentary on Basques in Australia. The segment on Queensland Basques just appeared and the Sydney one is scheduled for next month. The documentaries are well done, and they include interviews with many people here. Australia, and particularly Sydney, are now in fashion as world-class destinations. So, the *Txoko* gets frequent visits from Basque tourists, professionals, and also backpacking students out to see the world.

The *Txoko* does not have language classes. We constantly receive letters from qualified people in the Basque Country offering to come here to teach Basque, but they require a salary. Apparently, there is a scarcity of such opportunity in the Basque Country at present. There seems to be the impression that Australia is a rich country and could afford easily to pay an instructor. That is not the case. The Board of the *Txoko* has enough on its hands just keeping the doors open. We do not have Basque dance classes either. We are all too old and our children are not really interested. We have even convened some young people to tell us what we could do to make the club more attractive to them, but they didn't really have any idea. They are all proud to be Basques, but don't see a need for the *Txoko* in order to feel that way.

I asked about their relations with Queensland Basques and Carlos replied that, "of the twenty-five founding members of the *Txoko*, twenty-all were ex-canecutters!" Nevertheless, there are few ties today. The Basques in North Queensland do not have their own Club, so it is difficult to interact with them. Nevertheless, any Basque Queenslander passing through Sydney is likely to visit *Gure Txoko*. Joe Goicoechea recently became a member. We would like to engage him more, because he has the resources to help us. But he lives too far away.

There is no Basque Church here in Sydney. Members attend the one closest to their home. There is a Father José Perea (from Bilbao), and he says Mass at *Txoko* events such as the Saint-Ignatius-Day festival.

Carlos and Mari Asun could not think of any recent Basque-with-Basque marriages. She spoke of her son's wedding. "He was the first boy in Australia to be named Aitor." When he married, she arranged to have a choral recording and the organist play the hymn of the Virgen of Begoña as the bride entered the church. Many of the elderly Basques in attendance became teary eyed.

Carlos noted[29] that, after he became president, the *Txoko* struggled mightily to pay its bills. But then the Basque government became involved. The first year of its subsidy program it gave *Gure Txoko* A$5,000. The next year, they failed to get their paperwork in on time and missed out. On the thirtieth anniversary of the Club's founding, *Eusko Jaurlaritza* gave it A$20,000. Since then, they have received a minimum of A$10,000 annually. That is about their annual cost for insurance, power, and water, so the subsidy makes a big difference. You cannot raise that kind of money just by holding a dinner among a few supporters. Without the subsidy, they might have closed by now. It is ironic that, if we have a building and a cultural center with a library on Basque culture, it is due to the drunken binges (*borracheras*) of people like Pascual Garmendia who had no interest whatsoever in books. It was their weakness that kept this place going.

I have a twenty-seven-year-old married to a Greek-Australian. I also have a daughter who lives forty miles from here. They both belong to the *Txoko* but do not come very often. There is little here for young people. They know English, period. So, they are bored as they sit around while their elders converse in Spanish. That generation speaks some English, but always lapses into Spanish without even realizing it. They are more comfortable in it. Many of us know no Basque. My wife, Miren, used Basque at home in Zarauz with her mother who knew little Spanish. But her father was from Galicia. Now, Miren understands some Basque, but after so many years away she can't speak it.

I go to Mass for someone's christening, marriage, or funeral, but for them not me. I believe that Jesus understands me. There can't be a single pope in heaven if it is true what the bible says about the greater difficulty for a rich man to enter the Kingdom of God than for a camel to pass through a needle's eye. The Catholic Church has very little to do with the teachings of Christ. As long as Franco is buried in the *Valle de los Caídos*, a church built with the sweat and blood of war prioners and blessed by the Church, I will not attend Mass.

Jesús Azcona*&^ —I was born in 1924 in Los Arcos, Navarra. My mother died in 1933 and Father was taking care of us four children. He was a telegrapher. Franco's beasts pulled him out of the house in the middle of the night and executed him. I have subsequently learned that he was a cultured and apolitical man. He had confronted the parish priest over the poor wages paid to field workers. It is also possible that a Fascist wanted his job. Anyway, it was some kind of envy and he was killed over it. I was twelve years old.

Our uncle and aunt in Estella [Lizarra] took us in, and, for a year, I earned one *peseta* a day as a baker's assistant. When I was thirteen, I went to San Sebastián on my own. I was so poor I couldn't afford shoes. I wore *alpargatas* that were frequently wet. I lived in a pension and paid one *peseta* for my bed. I took my lunch and dinner in a tavern for two *pesetas* a day. My sister was a domestic in a wealthy household, and sometimes slipped me pastries from its kitchen for my breakfast. I did odd jobs and survived as best I could.

In 1943, I moved to Mondragón [Arrasate] and got a job in an iron foundry. It had nearly one thousand workers. I worked there for a year and a half, and the owner only registered me for benefits for 200 days. They would hire full-time employees and list them as part-timers so they wouldn't have to pay retirement and health benefits. If an inspector came, you were expected to disappear or lie. That was capitalism under Franco.

I then did 33 months of military service in Morocco. It was horrible. We experienced hunger and maltreatment. The ignorance was astounding. Our sergeant, who had served in Spain's Blue Division that fought with Hitler's army on the eastern front, insisted that the Strait of Gibraltar was constructed by the Romans with picks and shovels! He believed it.

After the military, I went back to San Sebastián for six months and applied for permission to leave for France in search of better employment. I was denied a passport, probably because of my father, so I tried twice to sneak across the border near Irun. I was detained both times. After the second, I was serving a three-month prison term. An official offered to help me obtain legal papers if I would just fill out an application. I was afraid to have anything to do with the Regime, particularly after he told me that, should I be detained a third time making an illegal crossing, I would be sent to prison for two years of hard labor. So I ended up with a job in Barcelona as the ticket-taker in a zoo for six months.

I then began my career as a professional stowaway. I first managed to slip onto a ship that headed for the Canary Islands. Santa Cruz de Tenerife became my home base, and, over the next few years, I traveled the world. I was in many European ports, and Buenos Aires and Havana as well. At one point, a companion from Bilbao and I were found out in Rio de Janeiro and arrested. We were in jail until they could put us on a ship to Italy. During the voyage we were under close surveillance and one of the guards, a sympathetic man who had served with the Mussolini forces during the Spanish Civil War, told us that we should apply to the IRO as displaced persons. He wrote a letter of recommendation. I received an international passport, maybe because my father had been executed. My companion was turned down.

I was now able to work in Italy, but it was in terrible shape having been levelled during the recent war. We couldn't find employment, and someone suggested that we go to the IRO office and sign up for the displaced-persons emigration program.

I was living in Bagnoli on a former naval base built by Mussolini. I went to the Spanish consul and said that I wanted to go to sea. He said he could get me on a boat to Barcelona, but I refused to go back to Spain. I went to the IRO and took a series of medical tests and passed. I was offered Peru, Brazil, or Australia.

While awaiting news of a boat, I went to Rome with several Spaniards. We found work as extras in a couple of movies. We then went to see Father Echeverria, a Basque, who was in charge of the Vatican's program for refugee assistance. He gave us knickknacks, notepaper, and stamps and dressed us from head to toe in secondhand clothing. We left and went to a nearby flea market and sold everything. We went back to Father Echeverria on other occasions, and he would give you maybe 500 *lire*. We also went to the Communist Togliatti's office and got some assistance. It was all hand to mouth. We were three months in Rome.

Then I got my call to Naples from the IRO. I was to ship out on the *General Sturgis* to Australia. It was 1950. I was the only Spanish national among the 1,700–1,800 passengers. We had to sign an agreement to do whatever they told us for two years. After that, we would be free to live anywhere and choose our work. They put us in a holding camp and assigned me to work for the city hall of Sydney. I didn't like it there. I had many arguments. There were Aussies working just Saturday and Sunday, part-timers, who earned more than I. When I asked for that assignment, I was turned down. We immigrants were always viewed as second-class citizens, a little less than human, and fit only for manual labor. We were "Dagoes," which I think is a deprecative term for Greeks [sic]. Well. I can tell you that it was we foreigners who made Australia.

So, I was sent to the New South Wales Railway. There, I was an Aussie stonemason's assistant. We two lived together in a made-over boxcar. It had a kitchen. I learned English from him and had a dictionary as well. I would take hours to figure out an article in the newspaper. I did that work for the required two years.

During that time, I tried to emigrate to Argentina. My grandfather's sister had gone there, so I had relatives in the country. Anyway, for reasons never communicated to me, my application was rejected. Then, one day I was hanging out in the California Café, a favorite place for Spaniards in those days, and a couple of Spanish engineers talked to me about emigrating to Brazil. There was much work there. I went to Canberra on the train and asked a taxi driver to take me to the Brazilian embassy. Somehow, we ended up at the Soviet Union's one. They invited me in, but I went right back to the station instead and returned to Sydney.

I had wanted to emigrate because Sydney was such a sad place. It had one cement building. The food was terrible and there was almost no wine. The taverns had stringent closing hours. I have never seen such binge drinking anywhere as in Sydney just before closing—both men and women. It was disgusting. The ignorance about the world was astounding. I was once asked to write out my name by a shopkeeper who couldn't understand it verbally. I did so and he asked its nationality. When I said Spanish, he was surprised. "I thought Spaniards were black." We were refugees; not citizens.

My wife is Andalusian. I met her in Algeciras through mutual friends and brought her out to marry me. I will visit the Basque Country again, but will never move back. My married son and spinster daughter are established here. I have one granddaughter. They won't go to Spain to live.

My first job on my own was as a cook in a hotel. I did that for four or five years. I then went to work in a shoe-importation establishment. There were about a thousand employees; I was the only Spaniard. I have been doing that work ever since.

In the mid-1960s both the *Centro Español* and Gure *Txoko* wanted me to become a founding member and I refused both. I didn't want my name at the head of anything. I later joined the *Txoko* and have been a volunteer cook there for thirty years.

I have been back to Europe a couple of times. I returned to that fucking town of Los Arcos in 1978 and again in 1992, but only for a few hours to see one family with which I am still in contact.

Sylvino Bañuelos^—I was born in Bilbao and came here in 1963. I was one of maybe ten Basques on the *Aurelia* leaving Barcelona. There were at least fifty or sixty *Madrileños* on board. I came after the formal recruitments were over. I was helped by CIME, the Catholic Church's group. My brother, Benito, had come here in 1959, and he tried to help me, but couldn't. I was working in the Echeverria steel mill near Bilbao, making laminations. The wages were pretty good, but you could never save. I was a bachelor. I met my future wife in Bilbao. Her name is Fernández and she worked in a restaurant.

After arriving here, I worked for five months for the Water Board and then the railroad. I went to Queensland to undergo training to become a miner. I became impatient and went to Prosperpine on the Gold Coast to work for its Water Board for two or three months, and then it was back to Sydney to its Water Board. Proserpine is a very beautiful town. I then had a job opportunity with the American firm Utah Construction Company. They had a big project drilling a water tunnel in New Zealand. That was always my specialty—tunnels. In Sydney, you made £65 a fortnight and in New Zealand it was £100 plus room and board. There was a lot of urgency to complete that project, and they paid a lot of overtime. We were a thousand men and lived on board a ship, as there were no accomodations on shore. It was in the extreme south and it snowed all the time. But, of course, when you were in the tunnel that didn't matter.

Then, I was buried alive in a collapse. It made national television while they tried to extract me one stone at a time. I was almost given up for dead. I was seriously injured and spent six months in hospital. When I got out, I went to Spain for three months, but then returned to New Zealand to ask for my job back. I was there until we completed the project in 1969. I then went to Cooma to work on a tunnel project in the Victorian Alps. We were almost all Europeans working there.

In Sydney, I was on the board of the Spanish Club early on. When they were planning to start *Gure Txoko*, I was asked by Arregui to be a founder. But then I left for New Zealand while the plans were still in the works. I later learned from a man who came from Sydney to New Zealand after me that the *Txoko* had become a reality.

I have been to Spain many times. I was there in 1968 and then again in 1971–1972. That is when I met my wife—she was from Bilbao and worked in a restaurant there. We were married in 1973. I went back in 1985, 1989 (on a trip paid by the Basque government), 1991, and to a wedding in 1993. One of my trips was underwritten by the Spanish government's program to assist pensioners of the Sydney *Club Español* to return to the homeland.

I will go back again, but only for a visit. My wife wants to stay here. We took our son once, and he didn't like it. He doesn't want to go again.

Antonio Esparza*#& —I was born in Lorca, Navarra, in 1932. I completed eight years of school and then took a correspondence course. I speak Spanish, English, and Italian. My father was from Villatuerta, Navarra, and he was a farmer in Lorca. Mother was from there and is deceased. I am living here in Sydney and work as a chauffeur. I am one of five children and the only to emigrate. The youngest, Margarita, lives in France where she is a nun today.

Before emigrating, in 1958, I worked as a polisher in a factory in Eibar for three years. I tried to get to the USA, and also to the Dominican Republic. But then I saw the announcement in the newspaper for recruitment for Australia and I applied. Prior to leaving Spain, we immigrants were addressed by Menchaca and another canefarmer who told us about conditions and wages here—what we might expect to accomplish. It was all bullshit.

I came on the *Toscana* with government-assisted passage. It took forty-two days from Trieste to Brisbane. I was in a nearby migrant camp for two to four weeks and was then sent by the government to Tully to cut cane. It was September, so it was very hot. We were divided among farmers applying for us—A Scotsman, an Italian, and a Yugoslav. I cut with two other Navarrans, two Basques, and a Riojan. We made £7–£8 per day. My best friend was a man descended from Catalunya who helped all the Spaniards who came to Tully. At the end of the season, I told the priest, Ormazabal, to interpret for me with an Australian official to say that I refused to cut cane again. Don Tomás was reluctant to do so, as he believed the contract to be obligatory. The official confirmed that, but noted that, after two years, I was free to do anything I liked.

That first slack I went with Florencio Muñoz and Ciriaco Saenz by train to Newcastle. We heard that it was an industrial town, and we had all worked in factories. We failed to read the signs properly and ended up in Sydney. We couldn't find anyone that spoke Spanish. We were crossing the Harbour Bridge, and one of the guys lost his papers when his wallet fell into the sea. We went to King's Cross to sing in Spanish in the bars in hopes that someone would understand us and give us advice. We ended up in the Spanish Consulate and were directed to Cooma. We worked construction there for six months, and then I headed alone north to the cane—this time to Ingham. There I cut with another Navarran, three Basques, and a Yugoslav.

Then it was back to Cooma for my old job with Utah Construction Company. After another six months, it was off to the cane again. I was in the same gang, but we now cut for a Catalan farmer, Miguel. The following slack it was Cooma, and then back to Ingham to the same place.

I then changed my routine by going to Griffith in the slack to pick fruit. It was 1961. I asked around and found that work. By then, my wife was with me and we worked together. The next four slack seasons we did that.

In 1965, I bought a harvester with Ángel Sesma and Muñoz. That slack, I worked in Sydney at several jobs, including janitor and manual laborer. Then it was off to Griffith to pick fruit.

In 1966, I bought another harvester with several partners, and the following slack was back in Griffith. From 1968 on, I spent the slack in Ingham before moving South permanently.

Between 1969 and 1972, I was in partnership in three harvesters with Henry Miguel. We put one in Tully. In 1970, I bought the Victory Café in Ingham in partners with the Basque "Serenga."

By 1972, we were harvesting for the Mendioleas. After that season, I bought Miguel's share and, from 1972–1975, cut by myself for the Mendioleas and the Spinas.

In 1975, I sold my harvesting business and moved to Spain, expecting to stay permanently. I thought of buying a café or bar. Well, it had changed. Taxes were high and there was a lot of competition. We decided to move back to Australia in October of 1976. My wife and son really wanted to come back here.

We settled in Sydney and I contemplated putting in a restaurant with Spanish cuisine. I went to work as a solderer. We also went to Melbourne for four months.

I worked for one year at soldering and then found a job with the government in the motor division. At first, I was a mechanic, but soon they made me a chauffeur. I like my job. It is very easy. Some days you get no assignment; others you drive some dignitary to the airport and then sit around the rest of the day.

I met my wife, Paula Andueza from San Sebastián, in 1958, when we were both working in Eibar (she was a news agent). We were married in 1960 here, after I sent for her. She had been adopted as an orphan and had seven step-siblings. None have emigrated except her stepbrother, Fidel Lizarrazu, who works in a factory in Melbourne today. I arranged for his papers and advanced him his fare in 1965.

I knew English by my second year. I attended night school for two months in Ingham to learn it. Since 1959, I have been reading the *Telegraph*, the *Sun*, and Queensland local newspapers. I also used to read *La Fiamma*. I never listen to ethnic radio. We are not naturalized; maybe someday. I joined the *Club Español* and *Gure Txoko* in 1976. I have been president of the latter. I belong to the Saint George Club since 1978.

We made a six-month trip to Navarra in 1976 intending to stay but changed our minds. We bought a house in Sydney in 1976 for A$41,500. I make A$350 weekly and Paula makes A$250 per week as a domestic. I have security and little hassle. I owned businesses and they expose you to a lot of stress and risk. When we returned, I did not want to go back into the harvester business. You depend on contracts and your competition tries to undercut you. The farmers can cut you off—and then what?

We are Catholic but do not attend Mass. I would not like my son to marry an Australian or an Aborigine. I might retire here or in Europe. It depends on what our son decides.

Fidel Aldamiz # & —I was born in Ereño in 1932 and completed primary school. I know Spanish, Basque, Italian, and some English. My parents are both from Ereño and had a *baserri* there. Mother is deceased. Father herded sheep in the USA for twenty years. We are three siblings and I am the youngest. The second, Ángel, herded sheep in the USA for three years and now works as a carpenter in Ereño. I live in Sydney.

Before immigrating here, in 1959, I worked for four years in a quarry in Ereño and another six as a mechanic in the town. A friend talked me into coming. I planned to stay for two years and then go back. I didn't consider emigrating to any other destination. Our passage was government-assisted, and we sailed on the *Montserrat*. We were in Bonegilla for two weeks and were then sent to Innisfail. It was very hard at first. I didn't like the migrant camp, and then it was too damp in Innisfail. I was cutting with José María Azpiazu and Benito Bañuelos from Ereño, and two or three other Basques. I then went to Ayr with a friend to plant cane. We found work drinking in a hotel, when we met a Basque there. That season I cut cane in Ayr with Pedro Meabe (Ereño). We then went to Texas together to pick tobacco.

After the harvest, I went to Brisbane and found work with the Grace Brothers Construction Company. I just asked around among Spaniards and Italians. I made £17 weekly and worked with several Spaniards. I was there for two months and then returned to Ayr for the cane harvest. I cut with a *Santanderino*. Afterwards, I headed to Sydney on my own, looking for construction work. I found a job and lived in Paddington. There were no Basques but several Italians at my work. The building was finished, and I got married. I then found work in a foundry and did that for fourteen years. But then, I got laid off and secured employment as a maintenance man for the government of New South Wales. I do that work today.

It took me about two years to learn English. I picked it up just talking to people. I have never attended classes. Since 1959, I read the *Australian* and *Daily Telegraph* newspapers. I sometimes read *El Español*, but it is now too Latin-American. I used to read *La Fiamma*, but no longer. I get no publications from Spain. I listened to shortwave broadcasts at one time but stopped. I am one of the founders, in 1962, of the *Club Español*. I was in *Gure Txoko* from 1965 until 1978. In 1976, I joined the Returned Soldiers' League Club in Marrickville. I was naturalized in 1965 in order to enjoy full rights. We are Catholics and attend church twice monthly. My son went to the Lasalle Brother School and my daughter is in Saint Bridget's.

I met my wife, Lidia López, at a fiesta in the Basque Country in 1956. We married in 1962 when she was twenty-seven. She was born in Mundaka; her father was from Plentzia and her mother Kortezubi. Her mother died and her father remarried, so, Lidia was living with an uncle and aunt. Her youngest stepsister, Angelines, is a housewife in Sydney. None of her other four step-siblings, nor her brother, have ever emigrated. She came to Australia in 1961 to marry me. She was naturalized in 1974.

I have never been back to Spain. Lidia went with the children in 1973 for ten weeks to see her uncle and aunt. I correspond regularly with my mother. At home, we speak Spanish, Basque, and some English. It is important to teach our children Spanish and Basque. They will learn English on their own I think. It is nice to have Basques around, but it is not critical to me.

I earn A$220 monthly and Lidia makes A$135 as a domestic. My son is a panel beater and makes A$73 weekly. We bought our house in 1978 for A$50,000. We own four apartments that produce A$8,000 annually.

I think Spaniards are just like Basques. Italians are the same. Some Australians don't like us—call us "Wogs." I see a lot of differences among Australians. Most are not industrious, but those who are work very hard. Some save; others don't. I have never felt much discrimination. I like the climate here, the freedom, the working conditions. I believe that the unions are too strong. I also think Australia exports its raw materials and imports manufactured goods when we should be making them. I prefer that my children marry Basques. I would like to retire to the Basque Country, but it will be a problem if the children remain here.

Sabino Astuy # &—I was born in Bermeo in 1927. I attended four years of technical-arts studies after primary and secondary school. I am a fitter-turner. I speak Spanish, Basque, Italian, Portuguese, and English. Mother was from Arrieta and Father from Bermeo. They farmed in Bermeo, but both are deceased. Neither ever emigrated. We were ten children in all.

Seven never emigrated. María, the second eldest, was a domestic servant for many years in France. My younger brother, Valentín, is a manual laborer in Sydney.

Before I came here in 1959, I had worked in a factory in Bermeo, and then was a merchant mariner for three years. During that time, I jumped ship in New York and lived there for five months. When I emigrated to Australia, I planned to stay for only two years. I thought of going to Canada and initiated paperwork, but it was too difficult to arrange from Spain. My brother was in Australia and I wrote him. At the time, Valentín was cutting cane in Innisfail. My parents were not too happy.

I came out with government-assisted passage on the *Montserrat*. I remember a man named Aresti and two others who, like him, had herded sheep in the USA. They talked about getting herder jobs in Australia. They reckoned that with so many sheep here, and with their experience, they would find that employment easily. Of course, they were disillusioned; I believe they left Australia soon after our arrival. I was in Bonegilla for ten days, and they then sent me to Gordonvale to cut cane. I was a novice and the cane in poor condition. I only earned £20 a fortnight. After a month, I wrote my brother and he came for me and took me to Innisfail. I cut with him and a man from Busturia named Cornelio.

The first slack, I went to Tasmania to pick fruit. Our farmer in Innisfail had relatives there and he arranged employment for us. I was there one month and then went to Mildura. After the harvest was over, I went to Canberra to work construction for three months before returning to the cane in Innisfail. I joined a new gang. Even though I was a veteran, I was a weak cutter and wanted to work in a weaker gang. I cut with three Navarrans.

That slack, I went with the gang to Griffith to pick grapes. They had been there before. We did that for two and a half months and then I went to Sydney to meet my fiancée. I got work there in construction. I found that through a friend in the city. My wife and I stayed in an Italian boardinghouse at first. I have been in Sydney for eighteen years, always in construction. I have changed companies several times.

I never tried dating Australian girls, because I had a fiancée in Spain. It took me about six years to learn English. I never attended classes, but I had a recorded method and a grammar. I then used the language in the street. By 1959, I was reading the *Sydney Morning Herald*, the *Sun*, and the *Mirror*. I also read the Spanish-language *Extra* and *El Español*, and *La Fiamma* as well. At first, I also received *El Mundo Deportivo* and *ABC*, but not for the last eighteen years. I joined the *Club Español* in 1968 and have applied to the Eastern Suburb Rugby League Club. I was naturalized in 1976, because I wanted to vote after Fraser turned out Whitlam. I favor the Labour Party.

I met my wife, Margarita De Román, in 1958 at a festival in Donostia. She was from Burgos where her father was a sculptor. We were married when she was twenty-nine.

She had worked for six years in a factory in Burgos. We married in 1961, and her parents weren't very happy about it.

I earn A$400 per week and Margarita makes A$180 as a domestic. We bought our house in 1968 for A$14,500. I owned a car when I was cutting cane, but then did not until 1976. I own an apartment in the Basque Country that I purchased before coming here.

We are Catholics and go to Mass every Sunday. My three children attend parochial schools. At home, we use Spanish, mainly, and some English. It is important that the children learn Spanish; but never Basque. Besides, Margarita doesn't know it. We like Australian cuisine but eat Spanish-style at home. The last time I ate out was four months ago in the *Costa Brava* restaurant, and the time before that eight months ago in the *Club Español*. Both have Spanish cuisine. I used to see my Basque friends at the hotel, the Canberra Hotel in Paddington, but no longer. I have high blood pressure and cannot drink as before. It is not important to me to live around Basques, anyway. My brother, Valentín, is very active in the *Gure Txoko*, but I don't belong. In fact, I don't see Valentín often. Before, Basques were noble, but no longer. Now they are worse than Andalusians. No Basque has ever helped me here. Italians are like Spaniards—some good and some bad. They work as hard as Spaniards do.

I have never been back to Europe. Margarita has been three times. I continue to correspond every few months with my family there. I would like to go next year, but only for a visit. I might even move there after I retire. Margarita naturalized in 1976, and prefers to live here permanently. Actually, I like the character of the Australian people in general. The country has good government, an excellent standard of living, and a beautiful countryside. Before, I didn't like the atmosphere here, very boring, but now it is better as Australia has become more Europeanized.

Isaac Astoreca # & —I was born in 1933 in Gernika. I finished primary school. I know Basque, Spanish, Italian, and English. My parents are deceased and were from Gernika where they farmed. We are eight siblings. The eldest, María, lives in England and has been there for many years. The third, Pilar, lives in Sydney and came to Australia in 1966 after living for seven or eight years in England. I am second to last and live here in Sydney and work as a pile driver in construction.

Before coming here, in 1959, I worked for nine or ten years in an arms factory in Gernika. I first thought of the USA but knew no one there. I was looking for an adventure and thought of staying somewhere for a couple of years, was all. Then, I was talking in a bar in Gernika to a farmer, Urigüen, from Ingham, who was trying to recruit someone, and he convinced me. I applied to the recruitment program and came with government-assisted passage on the *Montserrat*. I was in Bonegilla for two weeks, and then they sent me to Innisfail to cut cane. I loved Australia from the first moment. It was clean, pretty, and well-turned-out. Perth was very nice. We were six in the gang—three Basques and three Spaniards. When I was cutting cane in Innisfail, I was told that the first Basques in the Far North came about 1923 from Argentina [echoes of the *Kwantu Maru* expedition].

The first slack, I went to Griffith with the three Basques. Tony Mendiolea found us that work. After the harvest, we came to Ingham to cut cane. Félix Jayo, the baker, got us that contract. We were five in all—four Basques and one *Santanderino*.

In the slack, it was back to Griffith to the same place as the year before. I was married by then and my wife came along. Then it was back to Ingham to the cane. By then, I was the ganger. I earned £80–£100 a fortnight. We five cutters were all Basques.

It was now 1962, and we went to Sydney. I found a job with an English construction firm as a pile driver. A brother of a friend in Ingham was working here in Sydney, he arranged that employment for me. I have been doing that work ever since.

I studied English on the boat and then used it at work. I never attended formal classes here. I dated some Australian girls. I was conversant within a year. Since 1964, I read the *Daily Telegraph* and the *Mirror* newspapers. I used to receive publications from Europe, but no longer. I do not listen to ethnic radio. I joined the *Gure Txoko* in 1969, and once served as its president. In 1974, I became a member of the Eastern Suburbs League Club, and, in 1977, the Paddington Returned Servicemen's League Club. Both are social. I became a naturalized citizen, in 1970, in order to get a security clearance to work on a construction project on a submarine base. I have been a member of the Building Labourers' Union since 1962.

I met my wife, Manuela Lizarralde, in Ingham in 1960. She came out then to the Herbert on an adventure to see the world. She only planned to stay for two years. She was born in Hernani, Gipuzkoa, as were her parents. She had been working for eight years in a factory in Hernani before emigrating. She is the only one in the family to emigrate across the ocean; three of her siblings worked in France and two still live there. She had a friend from Hernani, Tere Arraras, in Ingham, who came out on the first government-sponsored flight. Milagros was on the second. I met her at her welcoming party in Ingham. We were married that year. She likes Australia, and was naturalized in 1970, but wants to return to Europe to live one day.

Our daughter, Izascun, is eighteen and lives at home. She attends Holy Cross College. I prefer that she marry a Basque. We speak Spanish at home, and it is important that she learn it. It is critical to me to live near other Basques. We speak different dialects of Basque, so Milagros and I do not communicate in it. We are Catholic and attend Mass only occasionally. In 1966, I helped my sister, Pilar, to immigrate here. I arranged her papers.

My company once wanted to send me to Noumea for two years. I considered it but did not go. We visited Euskadi and France in 1975 for four months. Actually, we were glad to leave since our thirteen-year-old daughter was very pro-ETA and we feared that she would get in trouble.

I make A$6.27 per hour, plus extra pay for danger and travel. Milagros does not work. I have never owned a car. We bought our house, in 1972, for A$18,500, and it has tripled in value.

Lower-class Australians are jealous of us immigrants, but the middle class appreciates us a lot. Australian farmers are hardworking, but the city folk are not. I have never felt discriminated against. I think Basques are better workers than Spaniards and have a different way of thinking. I don't like Italians at all; maybe just a few. They are false and very stuck up.

I like it here; but I want to retire in Euskadi one day.

My wife and I are very disappointed with *Gure Txoko*. I was its president and we both worked hard to make it a success. I was cooking and she cleaned the whole place. But then politics got in the way. I felt that any Spaniard who entered had to respect Basque traditions, and I threw a few out for not doing so. Then, when *Gure Txoko* defeated the *Club Español* in soccer, the latter refused to turn over the circulating trophy. I threatened to personally burn the Spanish Club down and the trophy changed hands immediately.

Then, in 1974, the *Txoko* was invited to the soccer competition in Canberra. I felt that we could not field an all-Basque team and therefore should not compete. I called a general meeting of the membership and the vote was to abstain. However, other board members would not accept the decision. They met secretly, and then invited me to a meeting to reopen the matter. I blew up, resigned, and handed over my key. We have never been back.

[Their home is a virtual gallery of Basque symbols. The walls are adorned with Picasso's Gernika painting, a photo of the tree of Gernika and a framed oak leaf from it, both family escutcheons, a crest of Eskualherria, and a photo of Gernika—his hometown.]

Eduardo Quintana # &—I was born in Mundaka, Bizkaia, in 1928. I completed three years of primary school; my education was interrupted by the Spanish Civil War. We lived for two years in France as political refugees. I know Spanish, Basque, and some Italian and English. My father and mother were born in Ochandiano [Otxandio] and lived in Lamiako, Bizkaia, where he worked as a tax collector. After Mother died, he emigrated to Venezuela, where he is now retired. I am one of six siblings. Julián, the eldest, is now a boilermaker in Sydney. Begoña is a housewife in Bilbo. I am the third. The fourth, Elias, lives in Bilbo, but spent time in Australia. Miguel is a shopkeeper in Santurtzi and has never emigrated. The youngest, Ester, is a housewife in Venezuela.

Before I immigrated here in 1959, I worked in a factory in Lamiako for seven years and then as a solderer for eight. I left Spain looking for new horizons and opportunity. I was prepared to stay permanently in the right place. I would have preferred going to Canada, and looked into it, but it was closed. A friend of mine, Sabino Ugalde from Portugalete, had been in the USA and knew about Australia. When we saw the recruitment announcement we decided to come here together.

Our passage was government-assisted. We came on the *Montserrat* to Fremantle. I liked Perth. I did not like Bonegilla; it was a concentration camp. We were there for three days and then went to a different camp near Brisbane. It was better.

We were sent to Ingham to cut cane. We were eight in all; five had been in the USA. Our nickname became "the Americans' gang." We were all Basques. When the season was over, we headed for the South. Half of us went to Sydney and the other half to Melbourne. Sabino and I went to Sydney. We found work in construction through an employment agency. I made £48 a fortnight. I lived in Newtown in a boardinghouse and worked with Sabino and Julián Oriñuela. We stayed there for four months and then decided to try something else.

We headed back to the Far North, and, before Rockhampton, we met a Hungarian on the train. He and Sabino spoke in English and Sabino ended up making him a loan. The Hungarian talked us into getting off the train in Rockhampton. The first day we were there, he found us a job laying tracks for the railway. After a few days, the boss wanted to split us up and send us to the interior. By then, Sabino was losing his faith in the Hungarian.

We all lost our jobs when we refused to go. So, the Hungarian found us employment in construction, but then we Basques picked cotton on contract for a Russian farmer instead near Rockhampton. That pay was terrible, we were only earning about £3 per day for all of us. We quit and went to Rockhampton to find the Hungarian to ask for repayment of Sabino's loan, and he was gone.

We didn't know what to do next. But as we walked along the street, a truck stopped. The driver was an Italian and he asked where we were from. He took us to his place—it was a rundown delicatessen. He said that an Italian friend of his needed help. That man came and asked if we would like to sharecrop with him. We could grow tomatoes, onions, cabbage, and melons on his place. We were to do the planting and harvesting and pay for half of the petrol for the tractor. We would also cover our own food costs. He promised to split the profits with us and predicted that we could make £1,500 before Christmas.

So, we bought our supplies from the delicatesssan and moved to the farm. We lived with the Italian in his hut and planted 7,000 tomatoes in one field and 10,000 in another. In a couple of months, we were shipping tomatoes every day, but never saw any money. The Italian told us to be patient. Finally, one morning when we got up, he was gone. Sabino and I went to town looking for him. We were told that the Italian had gone to the police to report that we had threatened to kill him!

We went to the delicatessen to complain, and the owner took us to his lawyer. He called the other Italian's lawyer and they began to laugh and joke over the phone. They weren't going to help us.

We then went to the police station, but we were worried since our Italian partner used to send free vegetables to the constabulary. He was there along with six policemen. They shoved a paper in Sabino's pocket. It was a quitclaim to our contract and our promise to leave town. There was no contract. We never signed one; the present document had our forged signatures on it. I threw it on the table and dared them to arrest me. The Italian was afraid and slipped behind the policemen.

We were ordered to leave town in a few hours. We pooled our money and found that we didn't have enough to buy tickets as far as Brisbane. We boarded the train and stayed on it anyway, and in Brisbane the railroad confiscated our luggage.

We ran into a French guy on the street and he took us to a Catholic church. At first, the priest didn't want to become involved, but eventually gave us a meal and a bed. Next day, we found jobs in construction through an interpreter at a bank. One day, I went to the Department of Immigration to file a complaint, but was told that, without proper documentation, they couldn't do anything. I produced the address of an Italian to whom we had shipped vegetables and he denied ever receiving them.

We earned a stake to retrieve our luggage and buy tickets back to Sydney. We worked there in construction. We had a lead from a Catalan we knew in Rockhampton. We worked for four months and then headed for Griffith to pick fruit. We found work harvesting oranges and grapes through the Griffith Employment Office.

We harvested for two and a half months, and then planned to head north for the cane harvest. Sabino left a week before me. He got off the train in Rockhampton and went to the delicatessen. It was all fixed up.

He accused the owner of being in on the scam, and they got into a fistfight. Later, the Italian went through the streets of Rockhampton with a shotgun looking for Sabino. Fortunately, they didn't meet.

The next week, I stopped in Rockhampton and went to the delicatessen. I knew nothing about Sabino's fight. The Italian made a move for his weapon when I walked through the door, but then he stopped. He admitted he had cheated us and asked for an address to which he could send us our money. He later mailed me a check through my brother in Sydney, but it only covered our out-of-pocket expenses. At least it was something. I later learned that the Italian farmer had worked that same trick on Greek, Italian, and German immigrants in other years!

It was now the 1961 harvest and I worked with five Basques in a gang. That slack, Sabino and I headed back to Sydney. We worked for the Sydney Water Board for a month, and then found work in construction for fourteen months until the Company went broke. My brother Elias found me work in a factory (Bradford and Kendall) and I stayed there for the next ten years. I changed to a better factory job that I have to this day.

I met Matilde Felices in 1964, in Sydney, and we married in 1965. She is from a farming family in Abella, Huesca. She had a friend here and decided to come in 1962. She had been working as a clerk in a bakery in Zaragoza for nine years. Before we married, she lived with her girlfriend. Since entering Australia, she has worked as a janitress in Sydney for the last seventeen years. We have no children.

It took me two years to learn English. I attended night classes for a month in Newtown, and then just picked it up at work and in the street. We speak Spanish at home. At work, I use Italian, English, Spanish, and Portuguese. Since I arrived, I read *El Español* regularly and, since 1963, I get the *Sun*. I see no publications from Europe, although I used to listen to radio broadcasts on shortwave from there, but no longer. I joined the *Club Español* here in Sydney in 1962. From 1966 to 1972, I was a member and even an officer in the *Gure Txoko*. In 1973, I joined the Eastern Suburbs Club. Once, we took a fifteen-day vacation to a resort on Hayman Island off the Queensland coast. In 1967, I was naturalized in order to enjoy full rights here and give up my Spanish passport. I have belonged to the Public Workers' Union and the Amalgamated Steel Workers. I had to in order to work. I favor the Labour Party. We are Catholics, but do not attend church.

I earn A$240 weekly and Matilde makes A$250 fortnightly. We bought our house in 1967 for A$10,000 and our first car in 1974. Australia has good work conditions and poor social services, given the amount of tax you pay. Life here is boring; the people are dead. Europe has much more atmosphere. We went there for two months in 1971—to Euskadi, Zaragoza, and Huesca. We went again to the same places for four months in 1979. Matilde does not like it here. We are discriminated against—Wogs—and the language is always a challenge. Someone once threw garbage into our house. She is not naturalized.

We plan to retire in Euskadi.

José Bilbao and Marisol Luno^[30]—This couple came to Australia in 1964. They had been warned by someone who claimed that there were snakes and kangaroos in the streets. It didn't matter because they were not headed for the Far North. Rather, he worked for two months in construction in Sydney and for two years in the Morris automobile factory. He then found employment in the telegraph office, a job that he has held ever since.

They structured their lives around work. He worked a night shift at the telegraph office and got home about five a.m. She left at 5:30 a.m. for her job as a janitress. He would listen to *Radio Nacional de España* to get the news and sports from Europe, and go to bed about 6:30. She returned in the late afternoon, and he left for a part-time cleaning job at 6:30 p.m. before starting his telegraph one at 9:30. She noted that she cried many times, particularly the first years. It was all so hard, and they suffered particularly from lack of the English language. "You can't imagine what it is like to live in a country where you cannot communicate."

José described how they had no money and lived in the house of Julián Oriñuela for several months when they first came. It was when the meetings were being held there by those trying to put together *Gure Txoko*. José recalled how the call to see the potential building went out. He attended and the space was overflowing with seventy or eighty people. It was decided that each would put up A$100 as seed money to buy the place. But then, a letter went out raising the amount to A$200.

It was more than José and many others could afford. "Had they kept it to A$100 they would have had twice as many founders, fifty. That would have raised the same amount of money and provided more life to the association." Some, like José and Marisol, eventually joined when they could afford to. Others signed up to a monthly payment plan to cover their A$200. It seems that, if you left the Club for no reason, you could ask for your money back.

On the tape, Carlos said that he, as president in 1980, convened a meeting of the memberhip to revise the policy. By that time, several had gone back to Europe and asked for their A$200. Others just left it when they departed. José and Marisol told Carlos about visiting former member, Montero, in Plentzia. He complained about having received a check from the *Txoko*. Actually, he was offended. Rather than cash it, he had it framed and displayed on his living-room wall.

José has served on the board of directors of the *Txoko* and was goalie on its soccer team. He loves sport and golfs today.

Carlos, José, and Marisol all opined about the nature of return trips to Euskadi. You pine for it and keep saying "Next year…," but then you keep putting it off. This couple came in 1965, thinking of staying for a short while, and made their first trip back in 1982. They noted that they were both the youngest in their families, so that meant that your parents were likely gone to the grave, as well as some or all of your siblings. That meant that your visit was a round of visiting aged friends, that you might or might not still have something in common with, and nieces and nephews. You were unlikely to see any of them more than once, so it was "hello/goodbye." When you weren't traveling about the Basque Country complying with these obligatory visits you just hung out in bars and maybe went to soccer matches.

Neighborhoods had changed. You used to know all of your neighbors and exchange daily news and frequent house-visits with them. No longer. Today, you might not even recognize, let alone know the surname, of many of your neighbors. You might barely nod when passing each other in the hall [reminiscent of the criticism of life in Australia as expressed by many of my informants]. It is a long way to go just to experience that. Marisol noted, "We might go back to the Basque Country when we retire for an extended stay. Maybe a year. But we will come back here. Our children are all established here now."

Melbourne

Juan Zabalegui # —I was born in 1934 in Artajona [Artaxoa], Navarra, and attended eight years of school. I speak Spanish, Italian, and English. My parents were farmers from Artajona and neither ever emigrated. I am one of five siblings and the only to emigrate.

Before coming here, in 1959, I was a store clerk and worker in a *chorizo* factory in Pamplona. I saw the recruitment announcement on the bulletin board in city hall and decided to come to Australia for two years. It sounded really good, like you were going to supervise blacks or something.

I sailed on the *Montserrat* and was government-assisted. We were taken to Bonegilla like refugees and put in barracks. I thought I was coming to a good life, but it was very militaristic. I was used to city life and froze at Bonegilla. I was then sent by the government to Ingham to farmers asking for men to cut cane. I did so with five Navarrans and two from Baracaldo [Barakaldo]. I earned £22 per week. I was there for two months and hated it. I was the weakest cutter in the gang. I worked for only three months, enough to earn my fare to Melbourne. I arrived there with £6 in my pocket. I had the address of Javier Iriondo and went there, but no one was home. I then had the good luck of entering by chance the bar where ten or twelve Spaniards hung out. A Navarran and Filipino took me to their home.

I then found work in a butcher shop for a few weeks. My next job was dishwashing in the Hotel Oxford through a fellow Navarran that I met casually in the city. I then rose to be a cook. I made £25 per week. I worked with a guy from Bilbao. I did this for two years but wanted to return to my trade as butcher. Through the newspaper, I found work in a butcher shop in Elsternwick, Victoria. My fiancée joined me and we were married. I made £22 weekly. I was there for six months and then found a better butchering job in St Kilda.

I did that for two years and then had an argument with my boss. I found better employment through the newspaper in a different St Kilda butcher shop.

In 1974, we went to Spain, thinking of staying permanently. I worked in two factories in Pamplona for three months each, but then we changed our minds. We disliked the political situation and our eldest son cried and pleaded to come back to his natal Australia. I hated the violence. Spain had been much better under Franco. We spent the rest of our time in Europe just holidaying, and then returned to Australia in 1976. I am employed here in Melbourne as a butcher ever since.

It took me about a year to learn some English. I attended classes, read the newspapers, and talked to people on the street. I read the *Sun* and the *Herald*. Once in a while, I get *El Español*. Matilde likes *Women's Weekly*. I receive no publications from Spain. We joined the *Club Español* in 1961 and the *Gure Txoko* in 1964. I sometimes listen to the Spanish broadcast on ethnic radio. I maintain contact regularly with my family, mainly by telephone. At home, we speak Spanish and English—Spanish with my son and both with my daughter. I believe that they should keep up their Spanish and oblige my son to study it with a grammar. I would like them to visit Spain again. If they want to stay, that is up to them. After all, who am I to object, given that I emigrated? I won't criticize their choice of a spouse as long as the person is white.

I used to frequent a hotel in Fitzroy because my Spanish friends went there. But it is not essential for me to live around other Spaniards. I believe that you can trust Basques more than southern Spaniards. I prefer Basques as they have aspirations. North Italians are more serious than southern ones. It is like northerners versus southerners in Spain. Lower-class Australians are jealous of immigrants. I have had a few insults, but just walk away from the situation. I am sometimes frustrated when I have to tolerate insults from stupid people because my English doesn't permit me an eloquent reply. It is like Australians who are critical of the English "Pommies," but who remain silent in their presence because they know that they will be bested in any verbal exchange.

I met my wife, Gregoria Galdeano, in 1957 at the festival of *San Fermín* in Pamplona. She had been working in the city for five years as a seamstress. She was from Los Arcos, Navarra, and her father was a marble worker in Pamplona. She was twenty-four when we married in 1960.

I make A$440 weekly and Gregoria earns A$300 per week in a cigarette factory. We bought our first car in 1962 and our house in 1976 for A$40,000. We had an apartment in Pamplona, but sold it when we decided to return to Australia.

It was a mistake to emigrate. One should never leave their country unless forced to by circumstances. If I were reborn, I would never leave

Pamplona. There is more atmosphere there than here. I would consider retiring in Europe, but only if I win the lottery. Life is easier here. You can own your own home and the parks are nice. The cost of living is better than Europe. Australia is about the only place to emigrate left on the planet, even if it does let multinationals dominate its economy.

Domingo Arroquero # — I was born in Ondarroa in 1931 and went to school for eight years. I know Spanish, Italian, English, and some Basque. Father and Mother were both from Mutriku (Motrico), Gipuzkoa, and were farmers in Ondarroa before she died. Neither ever emigrated. We were eight siblings. Patxi, the eldest, lives in Chicago since 1956, after herding sheep in the American West. He is in the lumber business. The second, José María, is a truck owner in Donostia after having been in the USA for two years. None of the remainder have emigrated.

Before I came here, in 1958, I worked on my uncle's *baserri* in Mutriku and then in Ondarroa for four years in an ice factory. Threre was little work in Spain and we were a large family. I thought of coming for five years. I considered no other destination. I saw the publicity by the government for recruits and applied. I came government-assisted on the *Toscana*. I was in a migrant camp near Brisbane for two weeks, and then an old Catalan farmer came looking for workers.

I went to Ingham to his place and found life here to be very different. The language was a major barrier. I hated the work. I cut with three from Aulesti and made £400 for the season.

I then went to Melbourne where I got a job washing dishes. José Antonio Ugalde told me about that city, but I found a dishwashing job in a hotel through a friend there. I went by myself, and then stayed in a boardinghouse owned by Catalans. I made £17 weekly and hung out with Spaniards. I worked that job for two years, until the hotel was knocked down for an office building.

So, I went with some Spaniards to Mildura to pick fruit. The work was advertised in the newspaper and there was little on offer in Melbourne at that time (1961). Anyway, after two months in Mildura, I found a job through a Spanish friend in Melbourne in a television-manufacturing factory. I made £30 weekly and lived in an apartment in St Kilda. I was on the night shift, and, after a year, the factory was closed, and I was laid off. So, I went to work for an aluminum factory. I found the job through the newspaper.

I was there for nine years and was fired. By then, I was a foreman and got into an argument with the boss. I wanted a union and the boss was opposed. He blamed me for stirring up the workers.

I then went to work in a pastry factory and have been there for the last eight years.

When I came, I could not date Australian girls because of the language. I tried to go to night school but quit after a few days. It took me three or four years to learn some English, mainly by talking with fellow workers. I occasionally read the *Melbourne Herald*. My wife buys *El Español* every week. I sometimes read *La Fiamma* and *Il Globo* if I come across an issue at work. We joined the *Club Español* in 1973. I sometimes listen to ethnic radio.

My wife, Gloria Carlos, is from Liédena [Ledea], Navarra. Her deceased parents are from Estella [Lizarra]. Her father was a railway worker in Liédena. She came to Australia in 1960. She had just broken up with her fiancé in Spain and wanted to get out. She came on a government-assisted flight. I met her at Mass at Saint Patrick's cathedral. We were married that same year.

Our teenaged daughter and son are in public schools here. We use English at home and with the children. I tried to teach them Spanish but gave up. They attended lessons at the *Club Español* but quit going. I prefer that they marry Australians because this is their country. I would not want them to marry a Basque; Basques are brutish—although there are good and bad in every group. Younger Australians discriminate against us, although it is getting better. I have been insulted, but never had a fistfight over it. I think my nationality hurt my employment chances here more than once.

I earn A$200 weekly and Gloria, employed in a factory, earns A$126. I bought my first car in 1959, and we purchased our home in 1963 for £7,000. We own a holiday house on the beach that we bought in 1975 for A$29,000. We go there frequently, almost every week.

There is more atmosphere in Spain, but life is much better in Australia. You enjoy yourself more in Spain, but there is no money there. I have never been back. I hope to one day, but just for a visit. Gloria wouldn't mind retiring there. She is fine with staying here. Neither of us is naturalized. We should become citizens in order to enjoy fuller rights.

Tomás Maguregui * # & —I was born in Gizaburuaga in 1928. I completed six years of school and then studied for five with the friars in Pamplona. I know Spanish, Basque, Italian, and English.

Father was a farmer in Gizaburuaga until he died. Mother was from Oiz (Ziortza), Bizkaia. Father had been a miner in Nevada for sixteen years. We are nine siblings. The eldest, Pedro, was in the USA for six years as a sheepherder and is now a farmer in Gizaburuaga. The third, Martín, is a merchant mariner and has sailed all over the world. My sister, Carmen, lives here in Melbourne where she is a hospital worker. I am the sixth and live here and am a fruiterer. The eighth, Juana, lives in Gernika as a housewife, but was in France for two years. The youngest, Sabino, lives in Traralgon as a construction worker after living in Mexico for twenty years.

Before coming here in 1952, I was living in Gizaburuaga and had worked in commercial fishing for two years. Life was bad in Spain; no work. I wanted to spend two years here to save some money and go back. I first tried to go to the USA but couldn't get permission. I then attempted to get into Venezuela. I heard about Australia from merchant mariners in the port out of which I was fishing. I had no relations at the time here. Pascual Badiola heard of me and offered to help. He arranged my papers and advanced my passage. I sailed from Genoa to Brisbane with five other Basques. We managed to get on the train by ourselves and were met in Ingham by Rufino Mendiolea.

My first job was cutting cane through Pascual. I found the climate to be dreadful and hated the work. I earned £150 weekly. I cut with José María Jayo, several other Basques, and an Italian.

That slack, I cut sleepers in Tully. José María had the contacts there. I did that for five months until returning to the cane harvest in Ingham.

The following slack, I went to Mildura with Eulogio Churruca to pick fruit. After the harvest was over in two months, we went to Melbourne where I found work on the railroad.

Two friends and I just went to its headquarters and asked for employment. We made £12 and one shilling weekly. We did that for two months, and then I found work in a hotel as a dishwasher. I made £30 weekly there and stayed for fourteen months. I left because I had an opportunity to become a waiter in an Italian restaurant. I found that job through a Basque friend who was working there.

I have been a waiter in several Melbourne hotels for a total of twenty-three years. In 1973–1974, I returned to Spain to start a restaurant in Amorebieta. But I changed my mind and came back to Melbourne. I worked the next two years as a waiter in the St Kilda Travel Lodge. Then, in 1976, I bought a fruit shop in Mount Waverley in partnership with Alberdi, my brother-in-law. I subsequently bought out his interest. I am still there today.

When I was in Ingham, I learned no English, Italian only. Since coming to Melbourne, I took a correspondence course for a year and a half. After my third year, I was becoming conversant. Since 1955, I read the *Melbourne Age* and the *Herald* every day. Once in a while, I get *Il Globo* here and *La Gaceta del Norte* from Spain. I listen to *Radio Nacional de España* frequently on my shortwave radio. I joined the *Gure Txoko* when it was founded. I belong to no other social club. I correspond regularly with my family; weekly.

Mutual friends introduced me to my wife, Carmen Martínez, in 1958, and we were married the following year. She was twenty-nine. She is from Sevilla. Her parents were born in Lora de Rio, Sevilla. He was a farm laborer until they immigrated here. Carmen's brother, José, was in Australia first and brought out the whole family. Their father worked in a factory in Melbourne his first six months, and then for six years as a butcher before he died.

I hate unions and favor the Liberal Party. I was naturalized in 1958 for no particular reason. They just sent me the papers and I filled them out. We are Catholics, but do not practice. We have three children. We use Spanish and English at home. We make no special effort to teach the children Spanish, but they pick it up. I have no particular preference regarding their choice of a spouse. I would object to an Aborigine and a Chinese would be so-so. My sister lives here and is married to a Russian.

I see Basques here regularly. My sister lives in Melbourne, and, last night, Fidel Lizarazu came to our house to play cards. Two months ago, I attended the picnic of the ex-*Gure Txoko*.

I made A$35,000 last year. I bought my first car in 1960. We had land on a beach here but sold it when we went to Amorebieta to live in 1973. We paid A$2,000 in 1970 and sold for A$3,000. In Amorebieta, we owned a restaurant, but sold it to return to Australia. After we came back, we bought a house here in 1975 for A$37,500. I paid A$13,500 for the fruit shop in 1976. Our daughter now lives in Europe, she teaches English in Durango, and we plan to go there in two years to stay. We plan to buy a farm in Gizaburuaga. I want to be a gentleman farmer there for a while.

Fidel Lizarazu^31—I was born in Azcoitia [Azkoitia]. I was young, twenty, and didn't want to do military service for that…Franco. My sister was already here; otherwise I probably would not have come. I travelled by train from Hendaye to Genoa. I met an Extremeduran on the train and we became friends. He had been a merchant mariner for twenty years. He knew some English and was experienced. In Italy he protected me from being taken advantage of—you know how the Italians are. Anyway, he wanted me to forget Australia. "Come to sea with me; Australia is a very dry and very bad place. I've been there." He took me to the office of the Norwegian Shipping Line where he had worked, and they offered me a job.

But all of the arrangements were in place for my trip to Australia, so I declined. I was the only Basque on the ship. Well, there was one Navarran married to a Castilian woman. There were many Italians and one had cut cane with Spaniards and knew some Spanish. I learned some Italian on that trip. I arrived in Sydney speaking it, if badly.

We first landed in Fremantle and then Melbourne. I went to the Melbourne Spanish Club for a visit. Then it was on to Sydney. There I stayed for a few days with a friend of my brother-in-law, Antonio Esparza. Then I took a plane to Townsville where my sister met me in the airport.

I worked with Esparza, and it was a bad year for cutting cane. It was very difficult work in the cane. We were used to fresh water and here we drank out of canvas bags that smelled bad. The new ones gave water a horrible taste. But, by mid-afternoon, when you were dying of thirst, it tasted good!

My first slack, I went to Griffith to pick fruit. The next harvest, Antonio purchased a harvester with some Navarrans. I soon bought one of them out and became Antonio's partner. We then bought a second. But then a typhoon hit and ruined a lot of cane. We couldn't get cutting contracts, and almost lost the machines that year. In 1969, I sold my interest to a son of a Catalan farmer.

I remember one year a bunch of us went in four cars from Dimbulah to Sydney. It took us a month. We were looking for work, and, in Mackay, were told to try Emerald. So, we went there, the middle of Queensland. It was unbelievably hot. We were offered work and went to the farm, and it was so miserable we left immediately and headed for Brisbane. We applied for work at a firm that hired us—and then said we were being transferred to Emerald! So, we walked out and continued to Sydney.

It was in 1969 that I met my first wife, Carmen, in Melbourne, and we decided to go back to Spain on holiday, along with a couple of Basques and a *Santanderino*. He, like me, had not done military service, and we were afraid of landing by plane in Madrid. We wanted to cross into Spain at a border post. We decided to go to Fremantle to catch a ship to Italy and a friend of Carmen there offered me a job as a bricklayer. I told him that I knew nothing about that trade, and he said he would teach me. "Stay here and work for one year and then go to Spain."

Well, we had our tickets and boarded the ship. They wanted me to sign on as a crewman, because they were losing mariners in port and were undermanned. But we were on vacation and declined.

When we reached Italy a friend of the captain offered me work as a waiter in a restaurant that he was opening on the Swiss border. It was going to feature Spanish cuisine and he needed someone like me who knew Spanish and some English and Italian. So, on the way to my holidays in Spain, I had three different job offers outside my field!

We spent four and a half months on holiday, and then flew back to Perth to look for work.

The first day, we were offered jobs as either gardeners or cooks. We went to another place and were offered work as tire-fitters. They would train us and maybe send us up to the northwest where there was a great demand. We decided instead to go to EPT, a big electrical firm installing electricity lines. They asked us about our experience, and we said that we had just arrived from Spain. They hired us immediately.

I had a truck-driver's license from Queensland. I got it by giving the local constable a bottle of brandy. He was a nice guy and the biggest drunk in the district. He used to hang out with immigrants, and one day, when I was doing haul-out for Esparza with a tractor, he asked if I had a license? I didn't and he said that we needed one. We were crossing the highway and could be involved in an accident. It would be way worse if we didn't have a license. So, Esparza and I went to his office with a bottle of brandy, and he gave us both a license on the spot without any testing.

Anyway, EPT made me a driver. First, we transported power posts near Perth and then they sent us to the northwest where we worked for a while.

I had left a car in Queensland, so I decided to return there. My *Santanderino* friend was working there as well. I cut a little for Esparza at the end of the season and then went to the tobacco in Dimbulah, and then the fruit harvest in Griffith.

Then, my *Santanderino* friend and a Navarran and I took off for Western Australia in my car. There are straight stretches that are unbelievable. You see a light in the distance at night and it is a half hour later that you pass one another.

In Perth, we heard that John Holland was hiring steel-fitters. The secretary said that they only wanted experienced steel-fitters and it was a waste of our time to fill out the application otherwise. The *Santanderino* had a little experience; we other two had none. "We are steel-fitters." "Well, then, you are hired. Do you want a plane ticket?" "No, we have a car."

When we got there, they asked if we had tools, forceps, etc. and we didn't so they gave us some. The Navarran was pretty nervous as they were sending us to the ends of the earth. We were in Parduroo, more than a thousand workers, and there was absolutely nothing. We were opening a new iron mine. The only entertainment there was on Saturdays they set up a microphone and we sang karaoke. We had to amuse ourselves.

A Spaniard from León then contracted with us to make [unintelligible] for him. He treated us well and it was lucrative. We then went to harvest tobacco and next worked for a French Company on bridge projects and rail lines as steel-fitters. We were now professional ones! [Laughter.]

It was very hot up there and we decided to head South. When we came to a highway bridge that was under repair, while we were stopped, a farmer approached us and tried to get us to work for him. We said that we were tired of desert and more desert and kept going. After a few days in Perth, we decided to head for Melbourne. In Kalgoorlie, a

Calabrese approached us speaking Italian and asked us to work on a bridge he was building. We did that for two weeks and then continued on to Melbourne.

Our next work was constructing water tunnels on the Upper Thompson in Victoria. They were for Melbourne's municipal water supply. If, in Western Australia, it was hot, here it snowed a lot. It paid well and we came and went several times. In summers we went fruit harvesting as you paid no tax. When the weather turned bad, it was back to the tunnels. Underground the weather didn't matter, it was always the same!

I then went to work for Bascom Construction here in Melbourne on electrical lines. Then, one year, they wanted to send me to a distant project and my wife was pregnant. I refused to go and went to work for Transfield here instead. I helped install a sea platform and was then sent to a refinery that Zurich Oil has here in Victoria. I do construction and maintenance there for Transfield and have been with it nearly twenty years now. I am involved with *Gure Txoko* here and try to attend its events.

In 1980, I went to the Phillipines and married my present wife, Ledilita. I have traveled many times to the Philippines and Fiji on holiday. We have two children. My *Santanderino* friend also married and moved back to Spain.

I went back to Spain in 1969, 1980, and 1992. The last trip I took my eldest daughter to see the Summer Olympics. We traveled via America and went to Disneyland. My father died when I was thirteen and we were many children. My siblings are now all professionals. My brother, who stayed on the farm, is an engineer at the Danobat furniture cooperative factory, but you should see him scythe hay. My niece teaches English and French in a college. She sometimes emails me in English.

If I were alone, I would consider moving back to the Basque Country. It is impossible. My wife doesn't even speak Spanish, and, in Azkoitia, everyone wants to talk to you in Basque. I will stay here.

Pablo Oribe[32]—Pablo ("Paul") Oribe was born in Gallarta, Bizkaia. It was an iron-ore mining town that has all but disappeared into its open pit. Pablo's father was descended from Ayala [Aiara], Araba. He was a union organizer and city councilman with leftist political leanings. He was anticlerical and did not baptize his children. When the Spanish Civil War broke out, Gallarta was firmly anti-Fascist and most of its young men fought for Euskadi. As their defeat became imminent, many of the town's children, including Pablo and his siblings, were among the children sent abroad—to England in the case of the Oribes. The parents fled to France. The father ultimately disappeared in a Nazi concentration camp and the mother lived through the Second World War as a political refugee in France.

The Oribes descended from one of the chiefs in the Basque Country's bloody conflict of the fourteenth and fifteenth centuries between Oñacinos and Gamboinos. The Oribes were Gamboinos and were all but wiped out. Pablo's grandfather had a *baserri* in Beotegui [Beotegi] that he sold in the 1970s to move to Bizkaia, which was experiencing a mining boom. He became a transporter of the iron ore.

Gallarta was socialist, largely non-Basque-speaking, yet very pro-Basque nationalist. Pablo certainly imbided those values. He recalls in his hometown the many folkloristic manifestations of Basque culture. He sang the Basque songs of his youth throughout his life. Indeed, his limited knowledge of Basque was mostly manifested in memorized lyrics. He is quite explicit throughout his memoir that he is Basque first and foremost, and that Euskadi, not Spain, is his homeland. He uses Basque phrases, but his shaky orthography in Euskera underscores his weakness in it. He expounds a very cosmopolitan and universalistic attitude towards people everywhere, with the exception of Fascist Spaniards and, above all, Franco's loathesome *Guardias Civiles*. While not sharing religious beliefs, he is accepting of those of others—with the exception of proselytizing Catholic priests who proclaimed that he and his equally agnostic wife were doomed to go to hell for their skepticism.

In England, Pablo, a young teenager, was billeted and schooled in the Midlands in Wickham Market near Ipswich. He went to work for the English Electric Company and attended night classes at the Stafford Technical College. He thereby polished his English skills, as well as his mechanical ones. Among the refugees, French was often the *lingua franca*, and he found himself interpreting, on occasion for the English authorities in their dealings with their Spanish-speaking charges. In short, "Paul" (his newly adopted English name), was more than just a polyglot, he gradually became a semiprofessional translator. He also became an avid reader of English (and world) literature; an avocation that converted him into a bibliophile and book collector for life.

He moved to London, and, in 1943, met Mentxu, his future life companion and mother of his five children, at a gala organized by Spanish-Republican leader Azaña for the Spanish and Basque refugee community in the city. She, too, was a Basque refugee child.

As the Second World War wound down, Paul moved Mentxu and their infant son to France, where he was reunited with his mother and other family relations. He anticipated that the stay there would be brief before his eventual return to his beloved Basque Country after Francisco Franco's imminent fall from power. After living near his mother for a few years, in 1947, they settled in Bourdeaux, where Paul worked as a draftsman for a factory, designing equipment. By then he had become an accomplished toolmaker, inventor, and gunsmith. He converted the latter from a hobby into a part-time business. He also found employment as a translator and salesman who used his English skills to board ships in port to offer French goods to their crew—from foodstuffs to trinkets. He received a commission on sales, and the business was brisk and lucrative.

With his language skills, he was often commissioned to help the floating Spanish-refugee population of the day to fill out forms in English or French. He thereby became familiar with the IRO and one day decided that he might consider applying himself for emigration through it. He didn't want to select a destination that Spaniards had colonized (Latin American countries), so his choices on offer were Canada, New Zealand, or Australia. Of course, his English skills made any of them less than daunting. He chose Australia, believing that it might provide more opportunity for his family while they awaited their eventual return to Euskadi. He was accepted and departed by himself to establish a *pied-à-terre* in Victoria before sending for his family.

On the voyage aboard the *Sorrento* of the Italian Lauro Shipping Line, from Trieste to Australia, the large contingent of refugees from several countries were upset over the diet—pasta, pasta, pasta. They prevailed upon Paul to approach the captain, and he was able to convince him to vary the menu. The young man's natural leadership skills were increasing.

Paul's first job in Melbourne was as a toolmaker with Astor Radio Corporation. After his family joined him, an Australian friend offered him the position of house-sitting a property located in Boronga, NSW, near the city of Mildura in rural Victoria. The Oribes moved there and Paul went to work for Andy's Engineers—an industrial mechanics' business. He also, working out of his residence, became the famed gunsmith for the entire region; not to mention the semiofficial translator for the Southern Europeans, including Italians, confronted with legal issues. The local employment service hired him to interpret when they were allocating nomadic non-English-speaking Southen Europeans to harvesting jobs in the district. He actually taught Italian in a formal class attended by a number of prominent Aussies. He also became an official translator of books from Italian and Spanish regarding viticulture (another of Paul's interests) for publication in English by the CSRIO (Commonwealth Scientific and Industrial Research Organisation, or Australia's national science agency). Paul invented a grape press and bottling machine and began producing his own vintage that he labeled Oribetxea ("Oribe House").

The Oribes' home became a meeting place for many of the region's leading citizens and intellectuals. Their dinner parties were famed as opportunities for serious and civil discussion of any topic. All were welcome, as long as they respected the opinion of the other guests.

The Oribes' residence also became a gathering point for the nomadic Basques that passed through Mildura seasonally during the annual fruit and vegetable harvest. Paul tells us,

> Because I am a Basque my predisposition and inclination was for them; but even the farmers of this region said that never in all of the previous harvests had they ever witnessed or encountered a group of people as hardworking, accommodating, and of such good humor as the Basques. The first Sunday, they went to Mass in the local church and "took possession" of the choir. The faithful of the place had never seen or heard anything like it, it seemed like the philharmonic orchestra of London had just descended on Mildura. That was in the newspapers and it was all a great success. One of those Sunday afternoons during the harvests, I witnessed a spectacle that is worth recounting. We were seated

in front of our house on Coleman Avenue when we saw a group of thirty or forty Basques approaching, all in their twenties and thirties, and singing and laughing. Some carried cartons of beer on their shoulders as if they were "on safari." Suddenly, altogther most exclaimed "Look, it is Oribetxea and the *ikurriña*." Upon entering our property, they sat on the grass around the place as if it was their house. For them, that place was like a port in the storm, a little piece of Euskadi. Mentxu had one of her daughters with her and they went into the kitchen to prepare a meal for everyone. It was a good thing that our pantry was filled to the brim, because after they left that evening it was as if a cloud of locusts had passed over our property. They sang and danced until well into the night. The neighbors on our street had never seen anything like it. Since then, they always ask the same question, "When are we going to have that marvelous group through here again? That had to be one of the best evenings that we have ever had here." So, yes, during our lengthy stay in Mildura, we witnessed similar spectacles. At times the Basques came two by two and remained to sleep in our house, usually on the floor of my workshop, until they found a farm on which to harvest. Nothing has given me greater satisfaction than to have been stopped on the street, here in Australia or in Europe, by someone saying "*Coño*,"[33] you (some *usted*, others *tu*) are Oribe. You have to remember me from the year 57 when you found me work and housed me for several days." Inevitably, they embrace me and thank me profusely for what, for me, had seemed a normal procedure. Something that, in my youth, I would have internalized in my upbringing. I would bet that in homes throughout Australia and the world there are hundreds of photographs of me and my family, our home, and the activities in it.

The family and their dog *Beltza* (or "Blackie" in Basque) lived there for several years, and, in the early 1970s, the Oribes bought a block of land and designed and built their own house in Mildura. Paul also decided to retool his career. In 1954, he began working on an official translator certificate with an eye on becoming an interpreter during the upcoming 1956 Melbourne Olympics. He was successful and spent months in the city serving in that capacity leading up to and during the Games. He learned from a friend that the Department of Emigration had a dossier on him that described him as "a polyglot, a progressive, a radical in his thinking but a partisan of no political party, who has had relations with Communists and Anarchists."

Paul aspired to becoming an academic. In 1957, he was given a teaching appointment in Mildura High School. A school inspector then convinced him to pursue his teaching credentials. He left his family in Mildura to attend the University of Melbourne's Teaching College and was then assigned for student teaching to a school in Mornington. He considered starting his own engineering firm in Melbourne but did not do so.

After completing his studies, he had teaching positions in three schools, including Mildura College, before obtaining his final posting in Karingal College in greater Melbourne. He was given an extended leave that allowed the family to visit the Basque Country, before beginning his teaching duties in Karingal in 1973. It was his first trip back and—his words—"For the first time in my life or since leaving my country—and I don't mean Europe or Spain—I was in my homeland again" and "I have never felt anything other than Basque." The only negative was that "Franco, unfortunately, was still alive."

Back in Australia, in 1975, Paul had the opportunity to enter a program of graduate studies at Monash University, whereby he would attend classes in modern languages three of the weekdays and teach at his college the other two. He received his degree two years later and a superior posting in Cranbourne College in a Melbourne suburb. It would be his final position before early retirement for medical reasons. By that time, he was supervising thirty teachers as head of a division.

He and Mentxu then decided, in 1985, to return permanently to the Basque Country to live. First, they had an apartment in his ancestral area of Amurrio, Araba, but its climate proved inimical to Mentxu's health. So, they moved to Irun. Six years in all passed and their joyful lives in Euskadi gradually waned. They came to realize the Basque Country and family relatives that inspired their memories while residing abroad had evolved into something else—or passed away. And then there were the children. Now grown, they had remained in Australia and the pain of that separation became too much to endure. The Oribes moved back to Melbourne.

Ramón Arrien # —I was born in 1931 in Rigoitia [Errigoitia], Bizkaia, and attended school for eight years. I speak and read Spanish, Basque, Italian, and English. My parents were both from Rigoitia and lived on a *baserri*. Neither ever emigrated. I was one of seven siblings and the only to emigrate. Before coming here in 1960, I was a cabinetmaker in Rigoitia for five years. We were a large family, and someone had to leave. I thought I would stay in Australia for three years.

I had a friend, José Antonio Ugalde, in Melbourne. But it was an article in the newspaper announcing the recruitment for here that attracted my attention. I came on the *Montserrat* with government-assisted passage. My parents were happy about it. I spent a month in Bonegilla before being sent to Queensland. The language was a problem; I could only communicate with gestures.

My first job was cutting cane in Innisfail for an Italian farmer. I earned £50 weekly. I worked with José María Azpiazu (Kortezubi), Fidel Aldamiz (Ereño), and Panuelo Rojos (Bilbao). That first slack, I found work as a plasterer with the Innisfail Electric Public Commission. A Spanish hotelkeeper found me that job. I did that for six months and then went to Ingham to cut cane with the same gang as the year before. Pascual Badiola found us our contract.

That slack, I returned to work with the EPC. They sent me a telegraph offering to rehire me. They transferred me to Sydney. I worked for the Electric Commission there for four years, then in Tasmania for one and another four in Melbourne. It was then, after nine years, that I married. I no longer wanted to be shifted about, so I found a job with a construction company in Melbourne. I just went to their headquarters and asked for work. That was ten years ago, and I am still here.

Because of the language, it was very hard for me to meet Australian girls. Also, there was the discrimination against us. Australians couldn't stand us and there were many big fights. Lately, it is a little better.

After six months, I began learning some English. I had a grammar that I studied at home. I never attended classes here. I began reading the *Sun* about fifteen years ago and I get *El Español* every week. I receive no publications from Europe. I listen to *Radio Nacional* from Spain every day on my shortwave radio. I correspond with my family every week, and two months ago called my sister in Europe. In 1969, I joined the Melbourne *Gure Txoko* and have served as both an officer and its president. I was naturalized in 1978 because I had lost my Spanish passport and wanted to visit Spain. I favor Labour in politics

I met my wife, Josefina Lecende, in the *Gure Txoko*, in 1966, and we married in 1967. She is from La Coruña, Galicia. She was working as a nurse in a Melbourne hospital. She had been employed for four years in England and came to Australia on vacation, liked it, and decided to stay. We don't enjoy Australian food. At home, I cook Basque style and Josefina does Galician. We have two children. Amaya is eleven and her godfather is Tony Torrijos. Aitor is seven and his godfather is Juan Antonio Ugalde. At home, we use Spanish. I would like to teach the children Basque, but Josefina does not know it. It is very important to me to live around Basques and I see my friends regularly. I want my children to marry Basques; Basques only. We are Catholics, but I don't go to church. The rest of the family does.

I bought my first car in 1963 and my house, in 1964, for A$9,000. I make A$211 weekly, plus overtime, and Josefina works as a janitress in a hospital and earns A$80 per week. I inherited part of the family property in Rigoitia, but do not want it as my brother is the heir and should own it all.

The working conditions and wages are better here for a working man. People mind their own business and the beer is great. But there is too much discrimination against the Aborigines and New Australians. Australians are stupid in politics; they criticize and then vote for Fraser. Australians can't stand us. In the hotels you can get into big trouble—they call us "Wogs" and "bloody bastards." The Australians are bludgers and work little. All of the best buildings in this country were put up by Europeans. They are two-faced; real savages. They spend all they earn. The lower-class Australian is filthy and a drunkard.

Basques are more noble and get along together better than Spaniards. Spaniards are more hot-headed. Italians are a bit false and can't be trusted. North Italians are better than southern ones.

We visited the Basque Country and all of Spain in 1979 for four months. I don't like the congestion and the climate in Melbourne. If I had the money, I would rather own a farm. I grew up on one. One day, I would like to retire in Europe, in my *own* country.

Iker Erkoreka # & —I was born in Sopela (Sopelana) in 1933. My mother was from there and Father was from Neguri. He never emigrated. My brother, Lander, was here in Australia from 1958 until 1966. He now drives a taxi in Sopela. None of my other siblings ever emigrated, although Joseba is a merchant mariner.

Before emigrating in 1959, I worked from age thirteen for five or six years in a bakery in Plentzia and was a merchant mariner for three with the Sota[34] Shipping Company and then one with the Arzola Shipping Company. When with Sota, I jumped ship in Canada and spent six months felling timber in Ontario. I wanted out of Spain because of the politics. I shipped out again, hoping to jump ship again in Canada. But we were diverted to a Poland-to-India run. It was then I learned of Australia. I thought if I came here for four years and got my Australian citizenship, I could then go to Canada. I considered the USA, but I had my brother here, he came in *Operación Canguro*. I also had a cousin in Ingham, Ángel Vidaurrazaga from Sopela. He was in Australia from 1958 until 1972, and now lives in Algorta. My parents didn't mind my emigrating, but I had an uncle and aunt that were opposed. I came on the *Montserrat* with my passage government-assisted. I spent just one night in Bonegilla before the Australian authorities sent me to Ingham to my brother and cousin.

My first job was cutting cane for Italian farmers. Our gang included my brother Lander, Alberto Ansoleaga, my cousin, Ángel, one Italian, and one Galician. I made £700 and bought my first car.

After the harvest, I went to Sydney with Lander, Alberto, Ángel, and Raimundo Aresti from Leioa, Bizkaia. We got a job with a construction company. Raimundo had been in America and knew enough English to read the newspaper "help-wanted" ads. I stayed there for five months, making £17 weekly, and then Raimundo saw the announcement for a job cutting timber in Bairnsdale, Victoria. Four of us Basques decided to go there—Raimundo, Alberto, a man from Gernika, and me. My cousin, Ángel, joined us later. We worked on contract and made £3 per day at first but after getting the knack made up to £70 weekly each. I did that for the next six and a half years in various places, always in Victoria.

For one season (1964) during this time, I returned to Ingham to cut cane for the Galician Frank Cao. I went with Lander, Ángel, and two Asturians. I left before finishing the harvest because I got into an argument with Pascual Badiola over rates paid by farmers that year to canecutters. I had had enough with the Far North. I was tired of the bickering and competition among the canecutters.

I got bored with the woods and went to work for an Italian Construction Company as a rigger. Ramón Arrien, from Rigoitia, found me that work in Thomastown, close to Melbourne. We had been shipmates. I was there for six months but couldn't get along with my Italian fellow-workers, and so I went back to the timber.

While I was in Thomastown, I lived in the house of Miguel Amorebieta from Gernika. We had been shipmates on the *Montserrat*. He came with me when I returned to pine-felling. After six months, I had an argument with my boss and decided to leave.

I went to Melbourne and found work with the John Fox Construction Company building a bridge. I then ended up with the Swiss firm, VSL Construction Company, in bridge-construction work, and, after thirteen and a half years, continue with them to this day.

I have been assigned to many different job sites all over Australia. I worked in Brisbane for one and a half months, Canberra on two occasions—once for six months, Tasmania for ten months, Adelaide three different times, and Sydney often. I spent a month on my own in Perth, checking out the employment opportunities there. I met an old Basque who had been crayfishing there for more than thirty years. It was the 1960s so he would have come to Western Australia in the 1930s.

I once had a dispute with the Company. An Aussie and New Zealander hired after me wouldn't say how much they were earning. I became suspicious. I said that if they wouldn't reveal the numbers, I would go to Company headquarters in Sydney to file a complaint. Sure enough, I was making A$15 weekly less on the grounds that "they know English." Language had never been a problem. Anyway, I threatened to quit unless they gave me a A$30 raise and I got it.

I make A$350 per week after taxes and my wife makes A$160 as a waitress in a hospital. We own an apartment for which we paid A$30,000 four years ago. We just purchased a vacant lot here for A$9,000. I don't have a car at present. I would like to buy one and a proper house as well.

I would like a beach house. I would never like to be in business on my own because I don't like dealing with people.

I met my wife, Marcelina Pelaez, in 1971 and we were married in 1972. She was twenty. She is from Asturias. Her mother opposed our marriage as I am an atheist. I belong to no church. She was earning very low wages in Spain working in a textile factory and had a second cousin here in Melbourne. He and his wife were her godparents. They helped her to obtain government-assisted passage. She was one of eleven siblings and the only to emigrate. Her father was a miner and farmer, and wanted to keep all of his family near him.

It took me about a year to learn some English. I had no trouble dating Australian girls, I almost married one. I tried to attend English lessons but gave up. I have been reading the *Sun* and the *Herald* newspapers for the last ten years. I know English, Spanish, Italian, and a little Basque. I was naturalized in 1964, and even obtained a Canadian visa intending to emigrate there. But I delayed because I had a serious relationship with an Australian girl at the time. In politics, I favor the Labour Party and I support ETA. I joined the Melbourne *Club Español* in 1961 and was a member until 1970. In 1963, I joined the Melbourne *Gure Txoko* and served on its board. We once sent ETA A$500 from the Club.

I insist on being considered a Basque. It is on my Australian passport. I was once accused of being a Spaniard by a German engineer and I blew up. The man had insinuated that he had been a pilot and took part in the bombing of Gernika. I threatened to kill him, but some of our fellow workers separated us.

The Spaniards in Melbourne hate us Basques (one of the few exceptions being a Catalan priest who defends our cause). They despised the *Txoko* and wanted it to fail. We even received anonymous threats to burn it down. The last time I was in the *Club Español* was about 1970. I nearly got into a fistfight. Several were putting down Basques. One, in particular, irritated me. I had worked with him in the timber and helped him out on several occasions. That night, he pronounced that anyone who supported the Basque cause ought to be killed. Soon thereafter, he and four Spaniards came to the *Gure Txoko*. I told him, "You get out right now. The others can stay if they want, but you are our enemy and are not welcome here."

I have visited the Sydney *Txoko* many times and was disappointed.

More Spaniards than Basques are regulars—no political conscience, it is a scandal as a Basque organization. I could only stand to stay there for five minutes.

I recall a hilarious incident in our *Txoko*. The police raided us and were carting off the liquor when our president showed them a letter of acceptance from Calwell to visit us. The head constable huffed and said, "C'mon boys, we're in the wrong place." After that, the police would come around periodically, but never hassled us.

The dissolution of the Melbourne *Gure Txoko* was very sad. Interest was clearly waning. We called a series of meetings to save the place. Twelve showed up for the first one, seven for the second, and three for the third. The handwriting was on the wall.

Marcelina was naturalized in 1977, and the following year we went to Europe to visit Sopela, Asturias, and France. We would like to go again, but only for a visit. We both like Australia and intend to stay here. When I retire, I would like to own a house on a beach, either here or in Asturias.

There is considerable discrimination here against immigrants. They call us "Bloody Wogs" in the taverns. Maybe ten or fifteen percent of Australians are industrious. Most are not very well educated. All they talk about is cars, girls, and drinking. They gamble a lot and never save. I like the social equality and quality of life here—the fishing and the beaches. I dislike the discrimination and find Australians to be politically naïve, easily swayed. Kids here have too much freedom.

There is far too much discrimination against the Aborigines. I was once busted for buying a gallon of grog for one. In Lakes Central I was given a notice to be out of town within twelve hours for dating an Aborigine. When Gino Paris organized his famous expedition to Darwin in the middle of the desert, they came across an old Basque who had three or four Aboriginal consorts.

I have no strong feelings about who our only child marries. I would prefer a Basque, but it is up to her. At home we speak Spanish, and it is important that she learn it. I try to teach her a little Basque as well. It is important to me to be around other Basques. I work with one, and Miguel Amorebieta comes to our house at least every two weeks to visit. I think that Basques are more noble than Spaniards. We are a whole different people.

I tried to help my wife's sisters to immigrate, but it didn't work out. A merchant mariner friend of mine wrote me a few years ago asking for help and I told him to just jump ship here. He did so and lived with us for a year. He is still in Australia.

I am now happy here, but it was a mistake to emigrate. It is never a good idea to leave your home. Every emigrant loses something; leaves it behind.

Alberto Ansoleaga*#& —I was born in the Bizkaian town of Sopela (Sopelana) and grew up on the *baserri* Aldeko. Five of us from there came out on the first expedition in 1959—on the *Monte Udala*. We were all schoolmates in the Basque Country and just decided to come out together to see another world. If we made a fortune, we would return rich; if not, then poor. The Spanish *Instituto de Emigración* was announcing out of its office in Bilbao the opportunity to go to Australia. Why not? So, we filled out our papers. Our village doctor had to certify us as healthy, as did a doctor in Bilbao working for the *Instituto*. Then we had a final medical exam there from an Australian doctor. It was the first Australian we met. If we weren't healthy, no one was. If we couldn't enter Australia for physical reasons, no one could. They gave us a little pamphlet that described conditions working cane—maybe two or three pages. We didn't really care. We knew that in Australia sugar cane and kangaroos awaited us.

We disembarked in Brisbane and were sent to a government camp about thirty miles from the city. We were there for about a week, just eating and sleeping. They then sent us to the North, to Ingham, to cut cane. After our first week, had we heard that there was a boat moored in the harbor fifteen miles away, we would have made a beeline to it. We would have done anything to escape. There was no life in the town, we were always among the sugar and listening to the strange birdcalls during the night. We knew nothing but how to cut cane—no English or Italian even. Our hands were destroyed after that first week. No, had there been a boat 30 or 40 miles away, we would have walked to it. We were just there out of personal pride and because we had no escape. It was like being on an island with no life vest and with no way to swim off it. Eventually, we adjusted. We were all bachelors between twenty-two and thirty years of age.

The first year, there were the five of us from Sopelana and three *Gallegos*, two brothers and a friend of theirs we met on the boat. We all formed a gang and cut for a farmer named Cao—he was Galician and was married to a woman from Santander. The first slack season, I worked for him cleaning paddocks and fixing up the place. He was very good to me. But then he sold out and moved to Tully. Our Galician companions left as well. The two brothers were corresponding with an uncle who had lived twenty or twenty-five years in Derby in West Australia married to a black woman [Aborigine]. They went to Derby and I never heard from them again. Their friend moved to Townsville. A couple of years later, he cut cane with us again. Meanwhile, the second year another friend from Sopelana, Iker, came in the second expedition and he cut with us.

We never had any problems with our gang. There were many screwings among the cutters—in some Basque gangs and particularly Italian ones. Four or five experienced Italians might contract with a few farmers and then sign on maybe three new guys. The veterans knew that the newcomers wouldn't make it, particularly if you made their lives impossible. So, after a few weeks, the new men left, and the veterans kept all the money from the contract. We never had any of that.

Our life here was very unstable. Maybe a friend from 400 kilometers away passed through and said there was work where he came from. You just threw your old socks in a wornout suitcase and off you went. Then you get there and there was nothing. So, you moved on.

During the slack, some went to the fruit or timber in the South. I think it was in the slack season of 1961, about Christmas time, that I joined the expedition organized by the Italian contractor, Gino Paris.[35] He had a sawmill and furniture store in Ingham, and built houses as well. He got a contract in Darwin to construct part of a new suburb—chalets with swimming pools. There were about thirty of us in all. We were mainly Basques, about twenty, a few Spaniards, and seven or eight Italians. Antonio Mendiolea was our leader.

We spent a week in Ingham loading building materials and equipment onto two huge trucks that were to take us overland to Darwin. Then we set out and the trip took eleven days. In the little town of Hughenden, between Charters Towers and Mount Isa, we met a Basque who had lived there for maybe twenty years. He was about sixty and Antonio Mendiolea knew him from when he worked on the coast earlier.

He was the only Basque in town, and he knew English and Italian, but had forgotten his Basque and Spanish. He was from Mutriku, I believe. [Alberto denied Iker Erkoreka's contention that the old Basque lived with several Aborigine women.] I have heard that there is a Basque mining engineer who has lived in Alice Springs for many years.

In Darwin, we stayed in military barracks made by the Americans during the war. We were there for three or four weeks. We ate our meals every day in the best hotel in Darwin—all thirty of us. But Gino Paris had run out of money and couldn't start the work. I think he anticipated some financing coming from a partner, but then it did not. Anyway, he told us to go back to Ingham. In the empty trucks it took only half as long as the trip out. In Ingham, he gave us checks for three weeks' wages, but they did not clear. He had insufficient funds in his account. A short time later, he paid us all in cash—maybe £30 each.

I began coming South in the slack season, usually with members of our gang. We might harvest fruit and then go to Sydney or Melbourne. My last season, five of us went straight to Sydney, and the same day we arrived there had employment in the Ford Motors plant. But then, three weeks later, there were the Christmas holidays and we were all put on the street.

We read about logging work in Gippsland (Victoria) for the Australian Paper Mill. Its main factory was in Traralgon. So, for the next four slack seasons, I went straight there to work for a contractor of the Mill. Jack Ivies was Irish, or the son of Irish. He treated me very well. And then I decided to stay in the timber. I didn't go back to Queensland to the cane. After so many trips back and forth, I wanted to settle down.

Felling was piecework. We would cut logs into six-foot sections and bundle then into cubits. We were paid £3 per cubit. It was softwood for paper manufacturing. We were organized into two-man or four-man gangs. The first two years I worked near Stockdale and lived in a barrack there. Then, we moved to Mount Margaret. There, we lived in a boardinghouse and commuted into the woods each day for our work. It was about half an hour away. In Mount Margaret, we were seven Basque loggers in all, and one Italian.

For a while, we cut around Marysville, Victoria. We could work there for six or seven months of the year; but then it got too muddy during the wet season for the trucks to haul out the timber. But you could always find a lower or dryer area, and, so, it was pretty much year-round work. We cut silver tops, eucalyptus, gum, and even pines as well.

There were many factors that affected logging. We preferred trees that were about a foot in diameter. They were ideal. Around Mount Margaret there were some plantations, and they were optimal. The trees were not too crowded together. Mature trees in old-growth forests were the worst. They might be two- or three-feet around and had to be split. Some could be partitioned with an axe; others had to be blown apart with an explosive charge. That was dangerous, and some men were injured.

We would try to fell the trees so they would fall in clusters for easier trimming and bundling. The trees that grew too close together were harder to work. Their tops and branches tended to become entangled and it took more effort to clean them up. Most of the forests were on public lands and our contractors were private bidders. They would get blocks at several elevations and with different tree species. Some of a block might be steep and other parts of it less so and easier to log. The contractors always wanted us to cut some of the mature trees in difficult stands as well. They had paid for that timber. We sometimes negotiated a little bonus for cutting the stands where the going was slow.

Sometimes we clear-cut a mountain and planted pines after cleaning off the old-growth timber. If a mountain was too steep for the trucks, we might simply burn it and then plant pines—just like in the Basque Country.[36]

When we worked around Mount Margaret, we averaged three to six cubits a day. It was good money. Other places we made less. Logging is not particularly hard work; certainly not compared to cutting sugar cane. While there were some areas that suffered from bushfires, we did not experience that. We saw an occasional snake, but not many. It was pretty cool; almost too cool for snakes. I know of no one bitten by a snake in those forests; I certainly have never had a close call in all my years here. There used to be some Basque timber workers around Mount Gambier, South Australia, but no longer.

One year when I was felling timber near Lakes Central, I would go into town nightly to a hotel. There were two Basque brothers there from Bermeo in a fishing venture who put me in touch with a Yugoslav fisherman who knew Spanish. I signed on with him for room and board and 11 percent of the catch. The last three months of that season we caught small, edible sharks off the Tasman coast. I left because the shoals and currents there were so dangerous. A short while later, that Yugoslav was shipwrecked.

We were in the Melbourne *Gure Txoko*. I remember when Arthur Calwell, leader of the opposition, came there. It seems that an Irish friend of Javier Iriondo set up a meeting at which Javier planned to extend the invitation. When they entered, Calwell was amazingly abreast of Basque matters. He laughingly refered to Basques as "the Aborigines of Europe."

In general, I cannot compare the standard of living here and in Spain. You earn much more here. But there is more to life than money. In Gernika, with fifty *pesetas* in your pocket, you have a better life than here with £30 or £40. There one "lives." Here you "exist." There, when you leave your house in the morning, you strike up a conversation with the first person you meet. Here you get up at six, catch the bus, and ride to work in silence, maybe reading a newspaper. There is no conversation. If I had any means of earning a living in Spain, I would return immediately. I have friends and family there; here it takes years to even make a friend among your fellow workers. We stay in touch with Europe by telephone. One month our bill was A$400. I am a socialist and think that Australia, with all its touted democracy, is very authoritarian.

[His wife, Laura, noted that her mother was devastated when she decided to come to Australia. She and the mother worked their *baserri* alone. But she was curious and wanted to see the world. Her uncle even returned from the USA to try and dissuade her. He likened taking women to Australia to "white slavery." She bristled at that, and told him, "I am perfectly capable of making my own moral choices." Her brother, Julen, a priest, defended her, and that tipped the balance.

She also recounted how, after a month here, she heard that the *Monte Udala* was docking with Spanish immigrants. So, she and a Basque girlfriend went to the dock. There was an Andalusian man meeting the vessel as well, and he overheard their Basque conversation. He asked how long they had been in the country and was astounded. "Such a short time and you speak English so well!"]

Each voice speaks for itself, but I would now underscore some of what collectively they speak to me. The intentions of many of the newcomers regarding their emigration to Australia included avoiding military service, the search for greater freedom and better economic prospects compared with conditions in Franco's Spain, and even a degree of youthful curiosity and sense of adventure.

We have been treated to many ethnic stereotypes in these pages. Basques are different than Spaniards in many different ways—language, culture, worldview, and character (or not). Italians are trustworthy (or not) and hardworking (or not). North Italians are superior to Sicilians (or not). North Italians are just like Basques (or not) and Sicilians are like Andalusians. For most of the respondents, Australian Aborigines are beyond the pale and you certainly would not want your child to marry one. There are, however, a few exceptions, in that some of the respondents were opposed to the general discrimination against the country's indigenous population.

There is the interesting question of the perceptions of Anglo-Australians of Basque respondents and their understanding of how they are perceived by Anglo-Australians. To be plausible, an ethnic stereotype has to have some element of truth, or at least consensus among many people. Several of my respondents discussed their experiences with discrimination and/or recounted those of their fellow ethnics. Many shared the view that Aussies were incapable of either hard work or saving their money. Rather, they lived for the day and gambled and drank excessively. Some respondents distinguished between the classes and generations. On balance, the most discriminatory Australians were lower-class, and the insults and even fistfights devolved in the bars and dancehalls where immigrants commingled with fellow manual laborers.

There was a lack of consistency regarding generation; some believed that the elder generations were more prejudiced and that things were getting better, while others felt that the elders were tolerant and more appreciative of immigrants while the younger folk rejected them. A few informants underscored their view that the worst were the Australian-born offspring of former immigrants. On balance, there is a low-key discourse to the effect that immigrant workers were protected in the workplace, both legally and by the appreciation of them by their Australian supervisors. A few even opined that it was better to work for an

Australian than for a Basque or Italian former immigrant. The latter were overly demanding and more capable of taking advantage of the worker's lack of English skills.

I would also comment on the "Dagoes" and "Wogs" insult, on the one hand, and the "convicts," "drunks," and "gamblers," on the other. I believe that for many of the respondents the latter set of ethnophaulisms was a reactive antidote to the former. "We may be Wogs, you lazy convict bastards, but we Wogs made Australia what it is today!"

There is an interesting division over the issue of life in Australia. For many, daily life was privation, a kind of purgatory that one endured to save up for the triumphant return to Europe or key to an eventual secure future in Australia. Some were either incapable of such a regimen from the outset or came to the conclusion, after years of self-sacrifice, that life is for living. Throughout, there is the undercurrent that, for better or worse, the greater one's involvement with Australians, the more unlikely that one will ever realize his original goals upon entering the country. Most married. A Basque, or even Spanish, spouse helped keep the dream of eventual return to Europe alive. Marrying an Australian-born person of Italian descent complicated matters, since her family was Australia-based (and possibly Italy-oriented as well). Marrying an Anglo-Aussie meant crossing the Rubicon into a strange new world, punctuated by English, squash, golf, rugby, and possibly Protestantism.

Notes

1. I would add methodological and bibliographic notes. Regarding my methodology, in order to enhance the readership's comprehension, I have retouched and reorganized the responses into a comprehensive narrative usually told in a first-person voice. I will introduce each biographical vignette with its subject's name, adding * if the account is based exclusively upon a taped interview, # if derived from a questionnaire, & if from my personal written notes [Douglass field notes], and ^ if from tapes recorded by Carlos Orue as part of the Urazandi project [Orue Urazandi interviews]. I will give multiple symbols if I have used more than a single source. I have deposited both the tapes and interviews in the archive of the Center for Basque Studies at the University of Nevada, Reno, under the rubrics of "Douglass Australian Tapes," "Douglass Australian Questionnaires," and "Douglass field notes." I would further remark that most respondents used "Spanish" and "Basques," "Spain," "Basque Country," and "Euskadi" interchangeably.
2. These range from the short monograph by Vanda Moraes Gorecki, *The Basques of Tropical Queensland* (Surry Hills: NSW Adult Migrant English Service, 2003)

[*The Basques*], about Segunda Bereciartua of Aulesti/Murélaga, Bizkaia, who immigrated with her husband, Pedro Bengoa, and established a cane farm in Ayr to that on Conchita Mendiolea (from Lekeitio and the widow of John Mendiolea of Ingham) in the book edited by Linda White and Cameron Watson, *Amuma, Amatxi, Amona: Writings in Honor of Basque Women* (Reno: Center for Basque Studies, University of Nevada, Reno, 2003) [*Amatxi*]. It might also be noted in this regard that anthropologist Gloria Totoricagüena is sensitive to women's issues in her work *Australia: Vasconia and the Lucky Country,* and we have the several monographs and articles on the history of the sugar industry, the Herbert District, and Basques in North Queensland by Bianka Vidonja Balanzategui, married to an Ingham-born Basque, Mark Balanzategui.

3. The Zavattaros were from Milan, Italy, and owned the Commercial Hotel (later called the Belvedere) in Ingham. They had a cook from Lekeitio among their employees, and he attracted considerable Basque trade to the business.

4. It might be noted that some Basques were acquiring tobacco farms of their own, often by leasing them from the returned soldiers that the government had settled in the Atherton Tablelands. According to Secundino Laucirica, this did not always turn out well. The tobacco combine was a monopoly that set prices and in 1960 they offered one shilling a pound. It ruined many farmers. Javier Iriondo told me that he and his brother had leased tobacco land in Mareeba for two years from an Italian. The first, they made double what they could have earned on salary. The second, a big storm hit and wiped out the crop. His brother wanted to continue, but Javier was dubious. The first year, they had almost been cheated out of their crop by the Italian. Javier left. Secundino Laucirica further noted that, in 1961, several immigrants put their savings into tobacco properties near Roma, Queensland, and, when the crop was coming along well, there was a drought. The freshwater for irrigating ran out and some tried watering the plants with a saline substitute. They lost everything (Douglass field notes).

5. There is the legendary tale among Hinchinbrook Basques about Pascazio Gabiola recounted to me by Johnny Mendiolea and Floren Laucirica. He was slight in stature and was hired by a prejudiced British gang as the one they would exploit and then could rift out. He knew what was up and cut one day for them, harvesting two rows to their one. When they asked him to stay, he declined. He had just wanted to show them up (Douglass field notes).

6. She told me that she is fed up with both. The renter in Galdakano is impossible to deal with and can't be evicted under Spanish law. For that reason, the other stands empty and is not offered for rent. Consequently, she just put it up for sale (Douglass field notes).

7. I interviewed Secundino in 1980 in Millicent. He noted that fifteen years earlier, between Millicent and Mount Gambier, there were seventy to eighty Basques living in the area, most felling pines on contract. The majority were experienced, having worked in the logging industry of the Basque Country (it was common for someone farming a *baserri* to fell pines part-time for wages or on contract). At present, he calculated, fewer than ten Basques resided in the same area. Many had gone

back to Europe to live. He noted that you could make £80 to £100 fortnightly in timber, almost as much as cutting cane, and the work was year-round (Douglass field notes).

8. The daughter, Miren, sat in on the interview. She bristled when her father stated that her elder brother, Joe, was more Basque then she. Miren declared that she feels more Basque than Australian and that you had to speak Basque very slowly to Joe for him to understand it.

9. Douglass field notes.

10. Several Ingham Basques told me that the confrontation was at the end of the annual dance. John Mendiolea recounted that one of Franco's nephews came here to work. He cut cane in Innisfail. He then went to Charters Towers where he disappeared. John thought someone might have killed him (Douglass field notes).

11. He was also a noted soccer player who captained a local team that was the first to compete in Donostia's Atocha stadium. He served on the board of directors of the city's *Real Sociedad* squad. Uncle Ramón was likewise both a champion cyclist and soccer player at the national level. Uncle Javier was an outstanding *pelotari*. He was the Spanish champion in *pala* and the Olympic champion in 1924 in that game. His daughter, Matilde, was a pioneer female race-car driver in the 1960s, erasing the sport's gender line. Uncle José was a renowned cross-country runner. The Adarragas are easily Euskalherria's and Spain's most notable sports dynasty (See Dinastías deportivas, *Revista Oficial de CIHEFE*, at httpwww.cihefe.es/cuadernosdefutbol).

12. He was also a rugby and basketball player and was a notable relay runner. He won the decathlon championship of Bizkaia and Gipuzkoa on two occasions. Fernando was runner-up in pole vaulting in both the Mediterranean (Beirut) and Iberoamerican (Santiago de Chile) Games and represented Spain in the Rome Olympics. Agustín's sister, Carmen, was four times on the Spanish national women's basketball team and was the national subchampion in feminine *balonmano*. This generation of sports figures was somewhat limited in exposure by the disruptions to Spanish athletics caused by the Spanish Civil War, World War II, and the subsequent boycott of Franco's Spain by the international community.

13. Two legendary Australians who won world championships.

14. Xabier Arzalluz was the longtime head of the Basque Nationalist Party and the power behind *Eusko Jaurlaritza*.

15. Recorded mainly in October of 1990. I have included some information from earlier interviews.

16. Actually, it is likely that it began in 1968. That year, there was an article in the *La Vanguardia* newspaper of Barcelona describing the birth of a "new city" called "Barcelona Gardens" in Ayr and built by a successful Catalan, Bruno Tapiolas. He had emigrated from Creu de Barbará, Sabadell, fifty years earlier at twenty-two years of age and first cut sugar cane before acquiring his own farm. He then went into the residential construction business in Ayr and Townsville. He regularly assisted immigrants from Sabadell, like his collaborator—Benito Droguet—who was specialized in metallurgical housing construction. Droguet had entered Australia

seven years earlier with his wife and infant son. The two men conceived of Barcelona Gardens, an independent community of 1,500 residences, in its first phase. Droguet penned a letter to the *La Vanguardia* newspaper's correspondent in which he stated, "as Catalans, we want to make of "Barcelona Gardens" a piece of Catalonia, giving its streets names of prestigious Catalans like Balmes, Gaudí and Clavé." In addition to announcing the creation of the project in the autonomous Townsville suburb called Cranbrook, the letter asked for information regarding the Day of the Sardana, since Ayr's Catalans wanted to celebrate it and were unsure of the exact date! (Jaime Torrents, "Una nueva ciudad australiana: Barcelona Gardens," *La Vanguardia*, March 28, 1968, 52.)

17. I attended the 1981 *Dia de la Raza* celebration with Agustín and Mary. It was held at the Townsville International Club. There were about one hundred people, with Catalonians predominating. The only Basques were the Arrates, John and Begoña Bengoa (she is the president), Mrs. Goicoechea, the young Ymaz couple, and Elias Alcibar and his wife and son-in-law. Agustín noted that he tries to get along with everyone, but that when you call around to Basques in Ayr about attending a Spanish function like this, most people waffle and few show up.
18. Stated in 1980 interview.
19. Stated in 2002 interview.
20. Moraes Gorecki, *The Basques*, 49.
21. Inquest of Felix Arangüena, Queensland State Archives, JUS-N 235/58.
22. Douglass field notes.
23. From an interview conducted by Carlos Orue on June 15, 2001, in Brisbane.
24. When I interviewed Secundino Laucirica in Millicent (1980), he cited Juan when arguing that it is necessary to become involved in local activities. If you don't, you invite the criticism from Australians that you are clannish. Both he and Juan enter billiards competitions in the local taverns. Juan has his gun club and Secundino belongs to two golf ones. He noted that the first couple of years no immigrant is very functional or happy. But then, you have to enjoy life. You can't just save money. He recounted, critically, the story of the Italian on his deathbed who upbraided his wife for eating a meal in a café next to the hospital in order to be with him more time. The dying man told her she should have gone home to cook in order to save money (Douglass field notes).
25. Totoricagüena, *Australia*, 220–21.
26. I interviewed Javier Iriondo in Traralgon in 1981 and he recounted how he, his brother, one Bernardo (from Errenteria), and Rafael Alegría from the Sydney *Gure Txoko* brought Arriya II and two other *aizkolariak* from the Basque Country. Qantas donated the airfares. They performed in November at the Melbourne Show and then went to Perth for the city's 150th anniversary celebration. Javier traveled with them as their interpreter. He also recounted that an old Australian told him that three Australian woodchoppers heard of the Basque ones several decades ago and booked passage on a boat to Spain that was shipwrecked. Then, in 1936, Arriya II's father, Arriya I, had arranged his papers and fare to come here, but had

to cancel due to the Spanish Civil War. Javier had just forwarded ten Australian (British-made) axes to the Basque Country, as they were superior to the Basque ones (Douglass field notes).

27. During this interview, Pascual Garmendia recounted how he once played on a Mareeba team that was mainly Spanish and competed in Queensland's third division. It would travel to Ingham for spirited competition. After a while, he quit because he became tired of the constant "*Arriba España.*"

28. What follows is derived from an interview that I conducted at Ajurienea (the residence of the Basque president in Vitoria/ Gasteiz) on November 9, 1995. Carlos was attending the First Congress of Basque Collectivities in the World to be held in the Basque Country (as was I). I interviewed both Carlos and another Sydney delegate, María Asunción Lasa. She was the secretary/treasurer of the *Txoko*. There was a third Sydney delegate with them, Urbieta, who was originally from Elgoibar, but he was not present for our interview. The thrust of my queries was to update my impressions of the *Txoko* since my visit to it in 1980 (or before Carlos emigrated to Australia).

29. I now add material from my interview with Carlos in 2002 in Sydney.

30. Recorded by Carlos Orue on July 11, 2001.

31. Recorded by Carlos Orue in Melbourne on February 2, 2002.

32. The following account is derived from the manuscript that he handed me at the Melbourne *Gure Txoko* picnic in 2002. It is the account of his life that he addresses to his descendants. It is replete with a family genealogy and is entitled "Nere Zail Ibilerak. Gallartatik Munduan Zehar" ("My Difficult Wanderings: From Gallarta across the World"). It was penned, in 1996, when he was seventy-one. I provide no page numbers, since, to my knowledge, it has never been published and is not on deposit in any archive.

33. Literally means "cunt," but it is used in everyday discourse as an exclamation tantamount to "Holy crap!"

34. Alberto Urberuaga related that this company, based in Bilbo, was famed for using primarily Basque crewmen. In about 1950, a Sota (rechristened Socoa Shipping Line) vessel landed in Lucinda and the Mendioleas, Balanzateguis, and Badiolas went there to invite the Basque (but not Spanish) crewmen to a barbecue. Later, at least four anti-Franco crewmen jumped ship and were hidden on Basque-owned farms. They were provided with attorneys who managed to legalize their status by arguing that the conditions on board were intolerable [quite unlikely] (Douglass field notes).

35. According to Alberto Urberuaga, Paris's daughter was married to a Basque, from Mendata—Aranas. Paris put a sign on the last truck that said "Darwin or Bust." It turned out to be both (Douglass field notes).

36. In his native land, the deciduous endemic forests have been supplanted in the main with *pinus insignis*, a rapid-growing pine from California used primarily as paper pulp. Ironically, the Australian eucalyptus is a ubiquitous, non-endemic aboreal invader of California and the Basque Country.

CHAPTER 12

The Facilitator

Alberto Urberuaga*#&—I was raised on a *baserri* in Kortezubi, one of six siblings—two girls and four boys. As a youth I worked on the family farm but was convinced that it offered little future. So, I applied myself to my studies and eventually became a veterinarian. My sisters were the eldest and youngest in the family. My eldest brother stayed on the farm with our parents. One of my brothers became a Franciscan missionary and spent many years in Peru. Another is a merchant mariner, a chief machinist on ESSO tankers. He lives in Lekeitio, and there are many mariners in that town who work for ESSO—mainly as machinists.

Like many Basques, I was unhappy with life in Franco's Spain, and was on a waiting list for permission to emigrate to Argentina. It was in 1950, that Pascual Badiola, who was originally from Olaeta near Lekeitio, returned from Ingham to Bizkaia with his family for a visit of fourteen or fifteen months. His wife, Angela, was also born on a *baserri* near Lekeitio. I met their daughter, Miren, and we became betrothed. She had a brother named Iñaki. They were Pascual's only two children. So, it was in August of 1953 I travelled to Genoa by myself to board a ship for Australia. Pascual was my sponsor and Ingham my destination.

During the voyage, I met the Commissary Officer on board who was a dual citizen of Italy and Argentina, having been born in South America. When he was fourteen, his Italian parents returned to Italy with their family. He welcomed the opportunity to speak Spanish with me; I was the only Spanish national on the boat. We became close, and, once in Sydney, he insisted on presenting me to his friend, a Basque—a Navarran named Alberto Fernández de Viana. He was the Spanish consul in the city and his brother lived in Bilbo. So, the consul was familiar with Bizkaia, and we two Albertos became friends before I headed north.

I married Miren and we resided on Pascual's farm. I worked in farm management with Iñaki and also did some of the manual labor (plowing, planting, and even some cane cutting). He was married to Eugenia Etxabe, who was from Aulesti and the sister of Antonia, wife of Rufino, the eldest son in the Mendiolea family. Eugenia died young in an accident on the farm.

I know that, when I first arrived, there were some here who were skeptical of me because I was a veterinarian. "What is he going to do here?" I never practiced my profession, and I wasn't afraid of farmwork. I grew up on a *baserri*. I could cut cane as well as 75 percent of the men here.

The history of the farm was interesting. Pascual had gone into partnership, in the late 1930s, with the sister of an Ingham Basque pioneer named Romualda Menchaca de Iraegui. She had come in 1923 and had her own farm with her husband. However, he died in a shotgun accident, so she leased the place to three Italians. In the early 1930s, one of them left for Italy after having been threatened by the Black Hand gang. And then the other two Italians experienced considerable crop losses to the cane beetle and forfeited on their rent. She took the farm back and went into partnership with Pascual Badiola to run it. At that time, he was also in partners with his brother-in-law, Julián Araquistain, in a sugar property in Stone River that Julián had purchased from his brother-in-law, Aniceto Menchaca. Pascual sold Julián his half and concentrated on his new holding with the widow Menchaca de Iraegui. In 1940, they had a peak of 2,400 tons.

Pascual had a hired helper paid by Romualda (since she did not work on the farm). For fifteen or twenty years it was Domingo ("Txomin") Larrañaga from Aulesti. When I married and moved in, I kind of became the hired hand. By then, Pascual's son, Iñaki, was also running the farm.

The Basques were liked by the hotelkeepers here (many were Italian). On Saturday night, the cutters would go from hotel to hotel in *chiquiteo*.[1] They took turns buying drinks for everyone. They were bachelors and had quite a bit of money—contract cane cutting paid well. They would take turns "shouting" (paying for) a round for everyone in the place— maybe twenty-five in all. The British drank in their favorite hotel, maybe for hours, and then went home to bed. The Basques went from hotel to hotel after a few stubbies (beers) in each. They formed choirs and sang songs; and the hotelkeepers even learned some of them. A favorite was "La Paloma." Then the Basques might order a beef dinner, or possibly *bacalao a la vizcaina* (codfish Bizkaian style), just like back home in Lekeitio. The Italians learned to cook Basque dishes well. Unlike the aloof British growers, Pascual hung out with his men.

It was in the mid-1950s, and the Basques of Ingham began to organize themselves. At that time, ten or twelve Basques would get together on Sundays and play handball against the backwall of the Mendioleas' house, the *Villa Milano*. There were some great matches. Félix Jayo was the champion. The Mendioleas, Badiolas, and Balanzateguis rotated hosting a Sunday "smoko," or barbecue, a get-together for three or four families. But the focal point was the Mendioleas. So, most of the Basques of the Ingham area saw each other regularly.

Teresa Mendiolea was a wonderful person, very frank, and she gave a lot of good advice to young cutters. After her husband died, she was farming with her four sons, Rufino, the eldest, Antonio, Aniceto, and Johnny. It was a large farm, and she decided to give it in equal parts to her four sons. It is my understanding that she gave her daughter, Dolores, £17,000 and that she and her husband, José Larrazabal, used the money to buy the farm that they were leasing. Then, Aniceto married Rufino's widow (to keep the property "in the family") and Johnny bought out Antonio. So, now Aniceto and Johnny were equal partners in the farm.

It was about 1955 that Joe Miguel, a Catalan, suggested that there should be an annual Spanish festival held here, and it should be on Saint Ignatius Day—the Basque patron saint. We were already celebrating it among ourselves. I was asked by Joe to give a talk about Saint Ignatius at the organizational meeting. I had studied at the college named for Saint Francis Xabier, member of a prominent Navarran family from the town of Javier (Xabier). Francis was Ignatius's disciple, and one of the earliest Jesuits. So, I knew their history pretty well. Ignatius had changed Xabier's life completely with the famous question, "What does it profit a man to gain the whole world if he loses his immortal soul?" Juan María Tellería of Townsville (formerly the driver of Dr. Salinas of Lekeitio in Spain's *Vuelta de España* bicycle race) got involved. We had an Italian band here, and Tellería, who was a musician, taught it how to play "The

March of Saint Ignatius." He was an accomplished *txistulari* [pipe and tambor player] and had played for Lekeitio's famous *Espata Dantza* dance group. There were three good singers here who performed Basque songs. There was a big barbecue and we invited Ingham's mayor and the federal senator. Every Basque was welcome, as were their non-Basque spouses and even their steadies—Italians and Aussies included. That festival lasted for about six or seven years, and was organized annually by the Mendioleas, Balanzateguis, Joe Miguel, and me.

Those same years, Ingham started its annual Maraka Festival (I think it's an Aboriginal word). It is still the town's biggest event. Each of the local nationalities was asked to organize something reflecting its culture. I was athletic—I had been a soccer player and was a discus thrower in the Basque Country. I thought it would be great for Basques to exhibit their traditional stonelifting at the Maraka Festival.[2]

I had written a letter to the newspaper *El Correo Español* congratulating Garcia Ariño for winning the annual world handball championship. The letter was in the name of the Basques of Ingham. García Ariño sent an autographed photo inscribed with his thanks to the Basques of Ingham. I received a nice reply from Aitona as well, a famous columnist in the paper's Basque-language section. So, I was in correspondence with him and now asked for his advice. We needed two stones for our event. It was arranged to have Alberdi, a famous stoneworker in Markina, make them. They were then sent out with the *Montserrat* expedition, under the care of my neighbor named Bengoechea. He was from a *baserri* in Gernika next to my family farm.

But some of its immigrants disembarked in Perth and others in Adelaide. I lost track of the stones, and, after a month, I wrote Juan Ugalde in Melbourne and he finally located them in a railway station in South Australia. They were in two enormous cylindrical packages that the railway officials were afraid to fool with. I sent photos of them before they were boarded in Santurce [Santurtzi]. So, the stones were released to me. It cost £32 to send them to Ingham. For the next three years, we Basques put on a weight-lifting demonstration during the Maraka Festival.

Maraka, and festivals in other North Queensland towns, always had a cane-loading competition. Pedro Aranas from here was a phenomenal loader, and he usually came in second behind the champion, an Aussie from Innisfail.

In the early 1950s, there was a real shortage of canecutters. Some years, the growers even had to depend upon cutters from the Aboriginal reserves. It was then that Pascual, the Mendioleas, and the Balanzateguis brought in a few Basques, maybe enough to make up five or six gangs. Two Italians had gone to Italy to recruit men with some success. But the shortage continued, and the Canegrowers Association held various meetings about the problem. Roy Dickson was the chairman, and he was impressed with the Basques. They were the strongest and most reliable cutters of all. They soon had a great reputation.

Joe's brother, John Miguel, brought to one of the growers' meetings a copy of Robert Laxalt's article from the June of 1955 *National Geographic* magazine: "The Land of the Basques." He pounded it on the table and said, "these are the ones you need to bring here because they are faithful and never fail." Dickson asked me for the names of the Basque provinces in Spain to forward a request to Madrid for immigrants from them. I was concerned that Madrid would reject an appeal for only Basques, so I suggested they include Santander and Aragón. They were sturdy mountain people as well and would have good stamina for cutting. For my money, the Italians are the best immigrants of all. They help one another and have strong families. I have great admiration for them. Like all peoples, there are some good ones and some bad ones.

About that time, Joe Miguel had shown up at the *Villa Milano* Sunday gathering and he was very agitated. He held a newspaper in his hand, I think from Townsville, but maybe Brisbane. It reported a talk given by Townsville's Anglican bishop in which he called the Basques "the most bigoted Catholics in the world." He was opposed to recruiting them for the sugar industry. Joe asked how a bishop in this tolerant country could say such a thing. Some of us wanted to complain to the newspaper, but, in the end, we did nothing. It was basically a stupid article, and it wasn't even mentioned in the *Herbert River Express*. It had no impact upon Australians' opinion of us, let alone federal immigration policy.

I wrote to my friend, Fernández de Viana, about the Basque-recruitment idea, and he replied that Madrid might accept the request for Basques as a short-term contribution to help the unemployment problem in Spain, but that it would not alleviate it. Eventually, the recruitment would have to be broadened to central and southern Spain as well. Thus were born the first two recruitments that came to be known as *Operacíon Canguro* and *Operación Emu*. The recruitments were done in cooperation with the Spanish trade unions and the CIME.

The first recruitment of Basques for Queensland left Trieste on June 6 of 1958 and arrived in Brisbane on August 6. It was supposed to land in Cairns instead but was diverted. Fernández de Viana asked me to meet it on his behalf. Joe Miguel and Pascual Badiola were scheduled to go as well, but they were in the middle of the harvest and could not get away. There were 168 in all. I believe it was a Basque-surnamed *montañes* (from Santander), named Ángel Arnaiz, that suggested it be called *Operación Canguro*. This was very logical, since the animal was synonymous with Australia. I thought that he came in the first expedition, but later learned that the Arnaiz brothers were actually in the fourth—an expedition that left Santander. There was a Basque-speaking chaplain, Don Tomás Ormazabal Oyarbide from Lesaka, Navarra, in this first expedition. He got off in Cairns, and then we travelled together to Brisbane to help the immigrants disembark and head for the cane districts.

It was the second recruitment that had trouble on board. It left from Santurce and stopped in Piraeus to board Greek emigrants. On the high seas, some Greek made sexual advances to a Basque woman and there were fistfights.[3] The Basques and Greeks were kept apart for the rest of the trip. When the vessel arrived in Sydney, the Spanish and Greek consuls met it. The problems were all sorted out, but in the press the boat was referred to as the "Pirate Ship."

Félix Jayo, the baker in Trebonne, was very involved in situating the new immigrants. He was from Aulesti and came to Australia in 1950, nominated by the Mendioleas who were also originally from Aulesti. Félix delivered bread and knew everyone. He could cut cane better than anyone and taught many how to do it. He sometimes helped unemployed men with money without expecting repayment. He helped arrange contracts for both farmers and gangs. If a gang had trouble with its employer, Félix would find it a different farmer. Here in Ingham, the Aulesti connection was very strong; people from there were the key to everything.

Not all of the immigrants cut cane for long. Juan María Tellería is an example. He moved to Townsville and worked construction. Everyone knew him as Juan Txistu or Juan Zubieta. He was the one who played at our Saint Ignatius Day festival. The "Zubieta" referred to the palace of Zubieta in Lekeitio. He had grown up there because his father was its groundskeeper. Tellería went to Darwin as part of a construction crew taken from around here by a local Ingham contractor for a project. From Darwin, Tellería went to a fellow townsman in Alice Springs for a short time. I once spoke with a man who met a tall and wide-eyed Basque in Mount Isa, and I am sure it must have been Tellería. He married a Dutch woman and went to Cooberpedy, or some other famous opal town. I know he ended up with a rich claim as he made several trips back to Europe. When Dolores Mendiolea married, he sent her opal earrings as a wedding gift. The Mendioleas had sponsored him.

There was one very unusual case involving Jaime Aseguinolaza, an Araban from Salvatierra, who had been a pig buyer in Spain. Don Tomás told me this story; few have ever heard it. Jaime came here in the second expedition—the *Toscana*. He cut cane for a little while, and then got a small farm behind mine. But then he went to Wollongong to work in the steelworks. We continued to correspond.

As it turned out, there was a very wealthy livestockman, sheep and cattle, in Gilgandra, New South Wales. He had thousands of acres. He was Irish and a bachelor. He had been to Canada and Chicago, Argentina as well, travelling to see meat facilities. He read about the Basque recruitments and he wanted to hire one. He put an ad in the newspaper. That was a little ridiculous. Who among us Basques was going to read the newspaper or even could? However, he heard that some Basques were working in Wollongong, so, he went there. He knew that Basques wore berets and he ran into Jaime on the street. Jaime had a beret. He took Jaime to his farm and eventually came to treat him like a son. He even paid for Jaime's trip to Spain so he could look for a wife. They might have even travelled together.

Jaime was thinking of getting his own small livestock operation, and he was taking his wages partly in animals. Eventually, he had several hundred cows that he was running on his patron's property. There was an Australian manager there, and he and Jaime got along. But, in a letter to me, Jaime expressed his doubts over how that would all turn out. I know he married and brought his wife here. I have lost track of him. I imagined that Jaime's patron terminated the manager, and that Jaime runs the place—but I don't know.

In 1959, I was invited by the head of the *Instituto Español de Emigración* to attend the Second Congress of Spanish Overseas Emigration to be held in Galicia. My friend, the consul in Sydney, had recommended me to represent Australian immigrants (the majority of the delegates were from Latin American countries). There would be about 250 people in attendance, including representatives of the receiving countries. Australia had maybe seven or eight government officials there. They were organizing the third expedition of Basques, and asked if I would help with the recruitment as a kind of assessor. I agreed and they paid half of my plane ticket to Europe and offered me free passage back to Australia onboard ship with my recruits.

The first two recruitments had been almost exclusively bachelors; they now wanted to include some betrothed men. I was asked by the Director of Spanish Emigration, Carlos María Rodríguez de Valcárcel, to bring with me a list of men in the cane districts with fiancées in the Basque Country. He approved their reunions on an individual case basis. Those women flew to Australia rather than making the sea voyage.

I remember that a Navarran, Antonio Esparza, who came in the first expedition, gave me the name of his fiancée, Paula, from Azpeitia, who was working in Eibar. He urged me to talk her into coming. I was ambivalent about going that far. I knew of cases of women who came and hated Australia. So, the request struck me as a bit much. But I went to visit her accompanied by an elderly returnee from Ayr named Muguira. He talked to her about how Australia was a land of opportunity for a young couple, and about the great climate in North Queensland—no winter colds or need for warm clothing. And she decided to emigrate. Anyway, the idea was to recruit people who might put down roots and stay in Australia.

I called the Director of Spanish Emigration, Carlos María Rodríguez Valcárcel, to explain a special problem. The Australians wanted married couples, and I had some affianced ones who did not want to marry unless they were certain that they would be approved. I was given permission to recruit them on condition that they would marry after the approval, but before embarking. I ended up with four such couples, including a fellow veterinarian, Agustín Adarraga. The boat trip to Australia was their honeymoon. In all, there were fifty married couples in this third recruitment.

I was to sit in on the interviews and maybe serve as an interpreter between the Australians and Basque speakers. The Australians were not interested in wealthy people; they wanted workers. The questioning was thorough, and they denied many applicants. I coaxed some of the men to give good answers. I told León Vega to bring up the fact that he was an orphan (true) and that he was adopted (true) but didn't get along with his parents (untrue). He was to say that he wanted to come to Australia to make a better life for himself on his own terms.

The applicant had to pass three exams. The first was pretty general, and, if he made it to the second round, the questioning became intense. That was when many were weeded out. The third interview was a follow-up, along with a strict medical exam carried out by the Australians. The Spanish officials conducted the interviews, always in Spanish, but there was always an Australian official present. He had the final say. It helped your score if you knew a little English. The intending immigrant had to put up 5,000 *pesetas* as his contribution to the costs.[4] He had to sign an agreement to cut cane for two years. If he failed to do so, he had to repay the entire cost of his transportation. The Australians were looking for four hundred men for the expedition, and it seemed like they would have to interview four thousand.

I was sent to *Gernika zabala*[5] to recruit, but I didn't have to do much as the word spread like wildfire. The men came looking for me. I did my interviews in the *Bar Arrien* of Gernika. I explained the conditions and the work, including its seasonal nature and downtime. A man from Mundaka came and said that he had about seven or eight interested couples there and asked me to meet with them in the town. And nobody showed up! By then there were rumors flying about, false and exaggerated ones—particularly about the snakes. Sure, we had snakes, and every year or so someone died of snakebite, but we were not in constant mortal danger. It was said that the cutter worked in water up to his knees. Then, too, I had given an interview to a newspaperman in the Congress, and he inflated all of the numbers regarding wages, the value of farms, etc. That caused me some grief later.

Our voyage was uneventful. The vessel, the *Monte Udala*, was owned by the Aznar family of Bilbao. The captain and most of the crew were Basques. I was paid £125 for serving as the interpreter and teaching English to the migrants for a few hours a day. We arrived in Melbourne in

January, and it was still months until the sign-on. So, my recruits were sent to Bonegilla. From there, some went to temporary agricultural jobs and others to the steel mills in Wollongong. Most were from Bizkaia and came north for the season. Many were already in cane gangs that had come together in Europe before the departure, or on board the ship. All found work. Many already had relatives in North Queensland and were headed for a particular farmer. Some cut cane for four or five years, and then moved to another place in Australia. Others returned to Europe with their savings—a group of men from Muxika did that.

Father Ormazabal became the itinerant chaplain for the Spanish community of North Queensland. He was always on the move. Once, at night, he ran off the road into a creek. He was trapped inside and would have drowned, since the water was over his car. He didn't dare open the window or door. But his headlights were still on, and a passing driver saw them and gave the alarm. They got Ormazabal out alive and pretty much unhurt. He was a student of Basque history and the language. He knew the theories that Basque might be related to Japanese. He always dreamed of returning home to die in the Basque Country, but never made it. He had a massive stroke in Cairns.

On balance, Don Tomás was admired by everyone. I do remember, however, that a Navarran that will remain unnamed went to the South to work on the Snowy Mountains Irrigation project. While there, he took up with a prostitute. He brought her back here in a house trailer the next cane-cutting season and went from barrack to barrack selling her services. Many here were critical of that, and someone wrote an anonymous letter about it to the Navarran's fiancée who was still in Spain (while this caused trouble, the couple was eventually married). The Navarran was convinced that Don Tomás had penned the letter, and once threw him out of a barrack over it. Even after the priest's death, that Navarran continued to despise him.

We later had a non-Basque Jesuit here in North Queensland who had been in Japan, from Andalusia, I think. He tried to follow in Ormazabal's steps, but it wasn't the same. I believe that in Melbourne they had a Basque-surnamed Argentinian priest named Saldigorria. They called him the "gaucho priest." But I think his main assignment was to minister to the growing Latin American population in Victoria.

Félix Jayo and I used to nag the owner of the Trebonne Hotel, the

Italian Joe Sartoresi, to build a handball court. Félix had his bakery right across the street from there, and many Basques came to it for bread and advice. Sartoressi had many Basque customers, and so, in 1959–1960, he finally built it.[6] It had lights so it could be used at night as well. I wrote to the Basque Country to Aitona, and he sent me the dimensions of undersize courts (like ours would be) in Latin America. I remember the one from Bogotá, Colombia, in particular. I inspected the job with Félix Jayo in September of 1959, or the night before I left for the Congress in Spain. That *frontón* produced a lot of business for the hotel. It filled up with Basques every Sunday morning and afternoon. That finished off the smokos.

We organized championships, and even gave out cups to the winner and runner-up. I was once the runner-up, and still have that trophy. Félix Jayo was the best local player, but there was one memorable match on the Trebonne court. A Navarran, Pedro Ardaiz from Pamplona, brought out four *paletas* (paddles) with him. He grew up across the street from the professional handball court, and was a very intelligent and elegant player. I believe he came here in the *Toscana* expedition. I intervened to get permission for his fiancée to join him in Australia.

A professional handball player, Salvador Ruiz, or "Chiquito de Bermeo" as he was known, immigrated in the first expedition to cut cane. He had been banned from playing in Spain for some reason. When he heard of the *frontón* in Trebonne, he asked me to organize matches for him with bets on the line. I didn't think anyone would play against him for money; I told him that he might win a carton of beer or two, but not money. But then Pedro Ardaiz accepted the challenge. Both would put up £70—winner take all. Chiquito would play normal handball (hitting it with his open hand) and Pedro would play *a pedreda*, a style in which normally you catch the ball, hold it an instant, and then throw it overhand against the front wall. It is very tiring and hard on the shoulder. Chiquito thought his victory was a cinch, but Ardaiz used a different style, returning the shot underhanded and expending less energy. He was very accurate, wore Chiquito out, and won three games to love. Chiquito paid up and said, "You fooled me like I was a Chinaman."

One day, Ardaiz offered to play me for money. He would use a *cesta*, a *jai alai* wicket that I had at home. It had been sent to me by the owner of the *Bar Mendia* in Lekeitio. We were good friends and I spent a lot of time there. So, when a *pelotari* brought him a *cesta* signed by many of the players in Miami, he sent it on to me in Australia with one of the immigrants. I told Ardaiz that he would crush me, but he replied that I would have all the advantage, since the *frontón* in Trebonne was too small for a *cesta* and had no backwall. He would have a terrible time just keeping the ball in the court.

Just then Chiquito was walking by and I called him over. I asked if he would like to take the bet? He thought about it, but then remembered the earlier humiliation. He said to Ardaiz, "I don't want to have anything to do with you." Actually, it was a friendly exchange; Ardaiz was always a gentleman with everyone. Anyway, the Trebonne court was very popular for years. However, with time the cutters aged and there were no replacements—so it was abandoned.

In about 1962, Javier Iturriaga, born into a Uruguayan-Basque family and presently the Spanish Minister of Consular Affairs in Australia, came to Ingham on an inspection tour. He had heard complaints about my statistics. I had been accused of inflating the earnings of the average canecutter in order to entice men to come. I showed him the official statistics for the previous three-year period produced by the Canegrowers' Association, and they were not that far off what I had estimated. The work was highly paid, but seasonal—about 25–30 weeks. It was also very physically demanding.

Iturriaga was asked to give a talk to the Ingham Rotary Club on the subject of Spanish immigration, and it made him very nervous. He wanted to know if it would be covered by the local newspaper. I told him "probably," and he didn't want to do it. But I insisted that that invitation was a great honor, and he finally accepted. He spoke in generalities and I served as his translator.

Afterwards, we went to a bar for a drink with Bob Shepherd, the publisher of the *Herbert River Express*. Shepherd asked Iturriaga if he felt more Spanish or Basque, and Javier turned his back on him. Shepherd rephrased the question and asked what is the difference between a Spaniard and a Basque? I interrupted and asked if a Welshman was English? Shepherd replied that, no, he was British. So, I said, "Well, Basques are Iberians like Spaniards, but have an entirely different language, culture, and race. The ultimate difference was in how you feel." When the Spanish soccer team plays in the World Cup competition, I feel Spanish, but when Athletic Bilbao plays Real Madrid, I am Basque—no question.

Iturriaga spent several weeks in Ingham collecting data, since he was assigned to make recommendations to Madrid regarding policy for future Spanish emigration to Australia. He was very nervous about how his report might be received; it might even compromise his career.

Most Australians saw us all as Spaniards. I once introduced a man from Santander to an Aussie who asked him if he was a Spaniard or a Basque? Later his companion complained about the question. "Aren't we all Spaniards?" Yes and no. I read a lot about Basque history and culture.[7]

There was a certain amount of sympathy here in Ingham for Basque President Aguirre and the Basque Nationalist Party. In Ayr, the climate was different, as Basques there wanted to fit into the town's Anglo world, not stand out as "different." Then, too, some of its Basques were almost anti-nationalists. Most were from simple rural backgrounds and little educated, particularly in politics. They might dismiss a man by saying "he has been in prison, so he is a one-hundred-per-cent nationalist."

Actually, the history of Basques in the Hinchinbrook and Burdekin is quite different. Ayr was a British bastion. Most of the farmers were Anglos, as were the canecutters. Most of the sugar properties there were part of an irrigation system. The weather is drier and the water supply more reliable than in the Hinchinbrook, and the land is more expensive. It was hard for the Basques to break in, although a few did. It took more capital to get started there than in the Hinchinbrook. But then your returns were better, as the amount of cane per hectare and its sugar content were both quite a bit higher.

In 1956, President Aguirre put out an appeal to the Basque communities around the world to send money for the ambitious Second World Basque Congress that the Basque government-in-exile was organizing in Paris. Pascual received a letter from the *lehendakari* that mentioned me. My brother, a Franciscan missionary, was a good friend of Aguirre, and the president later sent me an autographed photo.

Vicente Balanzategui was the main influence here in favor of nationalism, and he sent £150, fifty in the name of each of his children. I know that when the Solano family[8] of Lekeitio had to flee Bizkaia for Iparralde,

Vicente sent them a lot of money over time. He was quiet about that, a private man. He was very well read in Basque matters, and both he and his wife spoke impeccable Basque. It was not *Euskera Batua*, of course, but it dated from before there were a lot of Spanish loan words. They taught that Basque to their children here in Australia. When their son, Bingen, took his wife to Lekeitio, he put her in a course to learn the language. At our smokos on Sundays, Vicente often gave informal lectures on Basque topics. Most of the people had little formal education, and they learned a lot from that. I consider him to have been my "father" in Basque matters.

A lot of people here donated to the Congress. I remember a recent migrant that still owed money for her passage, and, when she heard of the campaign, she committed £5 to it. She remembered, with emotion, when President Aguirre visited her hometown of Gernika when she was small. "If I don't give you more, it is because I don't have it," she said. I am sure we sent more than £200 from here. Almost everyone donated.

Pascual and I went to Ayr to try and raise money. We hoped to get £1 from each Basque there, and we only collected £6 or £7 altogether. There were rumors that Aguirre intended to use the money for himself. We disrupted a festival in Brandon with our appeal, and so we decided to leave the Burdekin. The next day, a Basque in Ayr said to Pascual, "If you needed it, I would give you the jacket off my back, but not for that." I sent Aguirre a list of all the donors with their addresses, and each one received a personal thank-you letter from the *lehendakari*.

After the three recruitments, there were many more non-Basque Spaniards here in North Queensland. Some of them resented Basques and thought we felt superior to them. Navarrans could be the worst. Most didn't speak Basque, so they put it down. They would say that all Spaniards should just speak "Christian," meaning Spanish. The obvious reply was "why not just use English, since we are all in Australia—or even Italian?"

I shut up around Spaniards that know nothing about us. They might say that Basque wasn't even a language, just a dialect. If we tried to use our Spanish, they would laugh at our mistakes. We don't have gender concordance in Basque, so we might say "*la padre*" or "*el casa*."

I once had a conversation with two Andalusians, Martínez and Rodríguez, who insisted on buying me a drink and then attacked Basques and the language. I told them I would hear them out in silence, if they would give me the same courtesy during my rebuttal. Their real question was "Why did you guys take up a collection for ETA in Ayr?" I replied that there was no such collection. I said that, had there been, I would have contributed to it gladly. I said that Franco was the real founder of ETA when he tried to commit a Basque genocide. ETA was the result of that campaign, and we should erect a monument to him in the Basque Country. Without Franco, the language would have died out. Now, if you go to Bilbao, there is great enthusiasm. Even adults are trying to learn Euskera, I am optimistic that it will survive.

The Andalusians were referring to the collection for the Basque Congress, and that was two years before ETA was even founded. I offered to show them my dated and autographed photo from Aguirre as proof, but they were not interested in evidence. Before my turn to speak, I went to the restroom and when I returned one of the Andalusians had already left. He was only interested in making his own points. Those kinds of discussions finally finished off the Festival of Saint Ignatius in Ingham. They still celebrate a Saint Ignatius Day festival in Ayr that was organized by Agustín Arrate.

Actually, I have several good Spanish friends here. Those two Andalusians apologized to me the next day, saying that they had had too much to drink. The following year, I met Martínez in the Sydney Spanish Club and invited him to go with me to the *Gure Txoko* for a drink. Antonio Esparza was always critical of the Basque language—mainly because he couldn't speak it—but I think he actually served for a time as the president of *Gure Txoko*. We have always remained close friends.

I can remember having conversations in the Basque Country with Extremadurans. I recall four who were cutting pines near Bedarona. One of them said to me, "If we had had an ETA in Extremadura, I wouldn't have to be here today doing this work." He meant that an Extremaduran ETA would have confronted the enormous class differences in his homeland, and he would have made decent money there without the need to migrate to the Basque Country to do so. They were living in Gernika and studying Basque in school. I think such people are more admirable than some of the Basques themselves—they care more about Basque culture. We Basques have been the worst enemies of our culture, because we do not take it seriously enough.

When Franco had six ETA operatives executed about 1975 for a terrorist act in Barcelona, one of the men had been born in Zarautz, but both of his parents were Extremadurans. He gave his life for the Basque cause. It is my understanding that the body was returned to Zarautz for burial. At the funeral, it was wrapped in the outlawed Basque flag. The mother of the deceased said a few words in the cemetery. She urged Basque youth to follow her son's example until the Basque people were free. So, many of the most fanatical defenders of Basque freedoms were people with non-Basque last names like González, Pérez, and Álvarez.

Until about 1975, most Basques were favorably impressed with ETA. If they weren't supporters, then at least they were sympathetic. I had my own personal history. Loren Arcocha from Ondarroa came here. He was very intelligent and learned English quickly. He went back to the Basque Country and joined ETA. He was totally involved, and then had to get out of Spain. He made it to Portugal and from there to Canada. From Vancouver he wrote me a long four- or five-page letter asking me to take up a collection for ETA here. I discussed it with several people, but it wasn't really possible. After our Ayr fiasco over a cultural event, it would have really been controversial to ask for money for ETA.

I have always admired the commitment to the Basque cause of people from Ondarroa.[9] Everyone thinks of Gernika, but it is nothing—just historical. It is full of Franquists and *Guardias Civiles*. Ondarroa has the most committed nationalists in our region, those willing to make personal sacrifices.

At one point, our friar wrote all of us siblings to suggest that we concede any claims to the *baserri* to our eldest brother. He had lived on it all his life and cared for our parents. We all agreed immediately. We were to get one-fifth each of the proceeds from the sale of the pines on the property when they were harvested, but he would retain the land and house. It would always be our sentimental home. When he decided to build a road so you could drive a car to the front door, my merchant-mariner brother and I paid most of the costs.

Our Franciscan brother spent many years as a missionary in Lima. He is now retired and lives in Bermeo. He actually works for *Viajes Altamira*, a tour company. He organized trips around Europe for people from here and accompanied them as their guide. A stay in Rome is almost obligatory, a kind of pilgrimage. My brother has been in Italy twenty-four times. He did a trip through the Mediterranean for Félix Jayo and Johnny Bengoa and their wives. He took my wife and me to Austria, Switzerland, and Germany. José Gabiola and his wife went with him to Scandinavia. When, about 1967, the Bulgarian government wanted to attract Spanish tourism, Madrid put the proposal out to several tour companies, and *Viajes Altamira* won the bid. It appointed my brother to lead the first group there. He spent several weeks and returned with a changed view (more positive) of the Communist system. They could not have treated him better. So, my brother has seen more world than most.

I worked with Iñaki for Pascual on the farm for wages until 1964. There were always differences of opinion and frictions. In 1962, I had an argument with Pascual and left the farm to cut cane in Abergowrie. But my wife kept coming to me crying and begging me to come home. Anyway, in October of 1964, I told Pascual I wanted to go out on my own. He was a little surprised and asked what I intended to do? I replied that Australia was full of many opportunities, and I wasn't worried. Actually, I was pretty involved with the four Bengoechea brothers in a mechanical-harvesting operation. They had expected that their brother-in-law was going to enter the partnership, but that fell through. So, I was cutting cane with them, and we had several British farmers who wanted to contract our services permanently. I thought I could be part of that mechanical-harvesting operation, at least for starters.

About Christmas time, I told Pascual that I was leaving for sure, and that he and Iñaki could run the farm together. I wanted to give him plenty of notice before the next harvesting season so they could find an employee to replace me if need be. I expected that the farm would go to Iñaki. I believed that my departure was a good idea, because there is always the potential for problems in farm partnerships. There are differences of opinion on what to do. Apply more fertilizer or less? Buy a piece of equipment or not? One might work harder than the other, and that can create resentment. Then, too, over time, if you had children, they might have their own disagreements with your partner.

Anyway, a week later, Pascual told me that he had decided to divide the farm in two and lease half to each of us—Iñaki and me. I told him that I was totally committed to leaving, and that he shouldn't break up his property to suit me. I would take care of his daughter; she wouldn't die of hunger. But he, too, was decided and so I stayed. We leased our separate parts until 1969, which is when we each purchased them. Pascual died that same year. He had cancer and knew that he was dying. Romualda was too old to continue without him. Besides, his death would trigger estate-tax issues. She convinced him to sell instead.

By then, we each had close to 2,500-ton sugar peaks—certainly enough to stand alone. Nevertheless, such a division has its costs, at least A$25,000. If one piece of equipment was sufficient before, you now needed two. If one shed protected your machinery, now you needed another. Still and all, it was worth it. We had different ideas on how to farm. I think that time has proven that mine were valid.

The Burgos trial in 1970 was a watershed event here. Before then, the Australians were pretty confused about the difference between Basques and Spaniards. But there was coverage of Burgos for many weeks throughout the Australian media. I would say that it created better understanding, even sympathy, for the Basque cause. We shared Australian values of freedom of speech and democracy. However, we also got a lot of good-natured kidding out of it. In the Trebonne Hotel, the Australians would say things like, "You blokes are worse than the bloody Irish." But it was really all in jest. They knew us well as individuals; they all had Basque friends by then.

I just [1980] met a couple at Wallaman Falls. They were touring. She was Catalan and he was from Tolosa. In 1945, he was arrested for putting up "vote no" signs in Donosti just before a referendum. He was released and fled to France, where he met his refugee wife. They came to Australia and ran a furniture store in Adelaide until retirement. Each year they pick grapes in Victoria for eight weeks and collect their money in cash (and thereby pay no tax on it). I asked them for details, as I might go to that harvest myself. It sounds very lucrative and I would like to see South Australia. They go lobstering as well, since they have a big boat. They said that there are two brothers, the Jaureguis, who are commercial lobstermen in Adelaide. They were in Trebonne briefly, but before my time.

Ingham was always more friendly to foreigners than, say, Ayr. People here are more relaxed. Maybe 75 percent of the population is Italian. Basques and Sicilians, for instance, migrated here with very different intentions. The Sicilians were looking for land and a permanent future. The Basques mainly wanted to earn some money and return to Europe after a few years. So, they missed out on many opportunities. "Why invest in something here if I am going back to the Basque Country next year?" The irony is that, many of the Basques who did so, found that Europe had changed during their absence. They thought they could retire on their savings, but inflation was such that their nest egg was cut in half in five or six years. The pace of life was different as well. Here, life is quiet, you can always find a free parking place for your car. There, you drive in circles endlessly, without even finding a costly one. They couldn't adapt and some came back to Australia.

If you emigrate, you become stuck between two worlds. My family moved to Lekeito and I kept the cane farm here. I commute. I come here for the season and live by myself until the harvest is over. Then I go to Lekeitio for six months with the family. I have been doing that for the last five years. Now my wife talks about moving back here; she misses her Australia. But my daughter, Amaya, plans to stay permanently in Europe. What can we do? We have a divided family and a divided country. Tony Mendiolea is in my same circumstances; he farms here and his family lives there.

I think we Spaniards get along better than the Italians. There is quite a lot of tension between North Italians and Sicilians. We do have some problems with Andalusians, but it is not as pronounced as the Italian friction.

Notes

1. Reference is to the Basque custom in their homeland of bar-hopping after work. In the Basque Country this meant drinking a short shot of wine in each place before moving on. In Australia, it was more likely to be a stubbie (a glass of beer).
2. Tony Mendiolea told me that some Basque boys brought out two weights from the Basque Country, one weighing ten *arrobas* and the other twelve. It was not clear whether they were the same stones that Alberto commissioned. Tony noted that he, himself, spent six months in his spare time collecting old car batteries and melting down their lead from which he fashioned two metal hand weights for weight-carrying contests. They were used in several competitions, but then disappeared—probably stolen and sold for scrap metal (Douglass field notes).
3. I was told by the Spaniard, Pascual Rivas García, in the Sydney *Gure Txoko* that he was on the boat and one night he pinched a Greek woman on the fanny when leaving the dining area. She yelled and a Greek man turned around and punched the wrong Basque in the face. That started a big fight. Pascual later went to the captain, confessed, and handed over his passport. He volunteered to be sent back to Europe. However, when they learned of it, the other Spanish nationals on the boat said they would go back, too, were Pascual dispatched. He also noted that there was one

Spaniard on board who was said to be an informer (*chivato*). He remained locked in his room the entire voyage for fear of being tossed overboard. Rafael Alegría reported to me that the captain of the ship, a Bizkaian, confronted the Greek rioters with a pistol in hand and backed up by other Basque crewmen with firehoses, some being French Basques. The ship was owned by the Sotos of Bilbao and called regularly at the Philippines. At sea, they flew the *ikurriña*. Indeed, many of its crewmen over the years settled there. When a Soto vessel arrived in Manila, the city's Basque *pelotariak* would board to dine and speak Basque with the crew. It was common for Soto crewmen to visit the *Txoko* in the 1970s when in Sydney (Douglass field notes).

4. This was the standard charge agreed to by the various governmental agencies and NGOs involved in the process.
5. It means "wider Gernika," the town and its hinterland.
6. Reverend Ormazabal blessed the *frontón* at its formal dedication. The ball court was touted as the only one of its kind in Australia (*Herbert River Express*, December 5, 1959, 1).
7. Much to my surprise, he had even read three of my books—*Amerikanuak, Death in Murelaga*, and *Beltran: Basque Sheepman of the American West* (Reno: University of Nevada Press, 1979).
8. Don Carlos Solano was from one of the most prominent families of Lekeitio and lived there in the Zubieta palace. He served as a member of the Bizkaian Buru Batzar, or central committee of the Basque Nationalist Party, during the Spanish Republic, and therefore had to flee to Jatsu (Jatxou), Lapurdi, when Franco took power. His family struggled financially.
9. Loren Arcocha subsequently served as the town's mayor.

CHAPTER 13

Becoming a Basque Entrepreneur

Joe (José María) Goicoechea Ugarte # & * —I was born in Lekeitio. My father, Ignacio Goicoechea Onaindia,¹ was from Aulesti and Mother (Margarita Ugarte Ugartechea) was from Markina. My father's brother, Uncle Justo, had immigrated here in 1928 and was living in the Burdekin as a labourer.

I had an elder brother, Juan María (John), and sister, María Rosario (Rose). Mother brought us out to Australia in late 1938. We had been trapped in the Basque Country by the Spanish Civil War and had managed to get to England. I was four years old. The British government transported us here because father was already in Australia.

Father was a carpenter working in Innisfail at the time. He was never in sugar cane; he was always a tradesman. He came to meet us in Fremantle where we made port the first week in 1939, and then travelled aboard ship with the family to Sydney. We continued north by train to Home Hill where we stayed with Patxi Achurra, for nine months, while our future house in Ayr was under construction. Mother did the cooking at Achurra's.

The Second World War began, and Father was in the Civil Construction Corps (CCC). His unit constructed facilities in Charters Towers for the Americans. I remember visiting him there. They were building hangars.

I attended school in Ayr until I was fifteen. At that time, we went to the Basque Country for eight months. I had to leave because, if I turned sixteen while there, I would have had to register for conscription into the military. When we came back, I passed my junior exam, but that was the highest level of schooling available in Ayr. If you wanted to do your senior level studies, a two-year program, you had to leave for boarding school, and my parents couldn't afford that. So, at sixteen I became a cadet draftsman at Inkerman Mill. But I soon left for Townsville, because I wanted to further my studies. I worked there as a cadet draftsman on the concrete foundation of a power station that the Townsville Electricity Board was constructing. From there, I moved to the cement works at Stuart, still as a cadet draftsman. I attended engineering classes at night in a technical school. There was no James Cook University then. I eventually completed three years of the four-year course in mechanical and electrical engineering. I didn't finish it because my real interest was in civil engineering, but it wasn't on offer. During that time, Father was working on the Burdekin Bridge project.

While I was in Townsville, I had an athletic career. I played on the town's semiprofessional rugby football team and was a competitive swimmer. I represented Townsville in a lifeguard competition in Brisbane. But then I was injured and had to give up football.

When I was nineteen, I applied for a job with the new John McIntyre firm. John was a young, twenty-eight-year-old consulting engineer from New Zealand. After doing some projects in West Queensland, he decided to start a consulting business here. I was his second hire, and he taught me a lot about civil engineering. I was the only Aussie (and Basque) working for him as a professional. He brought in people from New Zealand. I stayed with him for ten years.

First, I worked on the cement foundation of a hospital; I was experienced in that from my days as a cadet with the Electrical Company. Then I was in Hughenden for three or four months, where I met my first wife—Sonia Jensen. I was twenty at the time. She was raised and educated in southern Queensland, and she was a nursing assistant in the Hughenden hospital. My next assignment was Richmond, where I helped design and oversee the installation of the municipal sewer system and public swimming pool. Then John sent me to Townsville to set up an office for the firm. He moved his residence there. Over the years, I did projects for McIntyre in Cloncurry, Burketown, Mount Isa—many Queensland country shires.

Things were picking up in West Queensland. Utah Construction Company had a big dam project there, many others were working for Mount Isa Mines, and you could see a big expansion of the economy coming. We secured a lot of infrastructural work—particularly sewer and road projects. I was in Mount Isa for a couple of years. But I could see that my future with the company was limited. It was hiring engineers better qualified than I; and was then supervising them. I understood that I would be passed over when it came to promotions. I simply did not have the credentials. I was taking correspondence courses in several subjects—physics, chemistry, and trade drawing. But that was a slow process and I didn't have the time to relocate to pursue a proper degree. I had a growing family and needed to work.

Today [2002] the McIntyre firm has maybe two hundred employees and offices in Mount Isa and Brisbane, as well as Townsville. It is one of the biggest operators in all of Australia. While I was there, I hired many Basques during the slack season. They included Florén Iturraspe, Elias Alcibar and his brother Patxi, "Serenga," and "Bermeo." When Juan Azpiri had such severe asthma that he couldn't cut cane in Ingham, Teresa Mendiolea called me, and I hired him as a favor to her. I sent him to Cloncurry.

Anyway, I asked John McIntyre to transfer me out of Mount Isa and I went to Cloncurry myself. I was now about twenty-six. I spent three years in Cloncurry doing public works jobs, mainly streets. By then, I had three children—Stephen, my youngest son, was six months old. At one point I made an arbitrary decision that saved the shire maybe £5,000. It was the first time that I had taken such an initiative, and it planted in me the thought that I could be doing this on my own and pocketing the profit, rather than simply collecting a paycheck. Despite the fact that it was the right decision and saved the public money, the head of the Cloncurry Shire Council was irritated by it. So, I decided to resign to take a trip to Spain with my family. My father was in Lekeitio recuperating from an illness, and Mother had gone there to care for him before bringing him back to Australia. I borrowed money here from my uncle, Justo Goicoechea, and six months later I was in the Basque Country.

We stayed there for about eight months. Once again, my military status became an issue. The Spanish authorities were claiming that I was eligible and had not done my military service. At one point, I had to give them my passport and then couldn't get it back for several months. I think someone was looking for a bribe. Anyway, I didn't offer one and started raising a stink, so they gave it back and I left the country.

It was the year 1962 when I returned to Australia. John McIntyre hired me back immediately. He sent me to Aramac to oversee construction of an airport. While I was there, I had the chance to join a startup construction firm that had fifteen or so shareholders. I didn't have money to invest, but I was to be a supervisor, and with a chance to acquire an interest. There was to be a probationary period of about three months. During that time, I supervised a project in Mackay, but I couldn't get along with our general manager and decided to quit.

So, now I was back in Ayr with a wife, three kids, and a dog. We were living in my mother's house. My plan was to leave my family there with her while I went bidding on public tenders. I was confident that, with my contacts and experience, I would secure some, and then put together a team to do the work. At that time, Iñaki Albisu, from Gernika, came to me. He was married to Julia Muguira and was on his father-in-law's cane farm. He didn't like farming that much, and he owned a truck and wanted me to give him work. Well, I didn't have a job myself at the moment.

My wife and I decided to visit Cairns for a few days' vacation; her sister lived there. I picked up the local newspaper, and there was a classified ad in it from a Mount Isa construction company looking for an engineer. I knew its owner, Bert O'Brien, from my Mount Isa days and rang him up. He offered to hire me, but I specified one condition. He was an older man on the verge of retirement. So, I stipulated that within a couple of years I would have the opportunity to buy him out. He agreed, and I moved my family to Mount Isa and began working for him.

Well, in six weeks, Iñaki Albisu and I together bought the business. O'Brien wanted £15,000, ten thousand down and the rest from the house rentals. They were bringing in £20 each per week. When I first returned to Mount Isa, I had borrowed £1,200 from a local banker to set up my family. When I now asked him for £3,000 more the answer was no. Eventually, I borrowed that money from José "Romeo" Goicoechea, a friend that I had given a lot of work to in the past. He was like a father to me, but no relation, and lived with us in Ayr. Iñaki borrowed £6,000 from his father-in-law, Manuel. We offered to pay O'Brien £8,500 down (we needed £500 to meet payroll) and the other £1,500 out of our first proceeds, and he accepted. We renamed the business the Vasco Construction Company.

It had two houses, two vacant blocks of land, and a lot of junk—pre-war, worn-out equipment, including a 1933-vintage D4 earthmover. Iñaki didn't know anything about construction, but he was a quick learner. We had contracted work-in-progress worth £7,000.

Within six months, we paid off Bert that remaining £5,000 debt. After nine, I repaid Romeo the £3,000 loan. Almost one year to the day of the purchase, I bought Albisu out for £26,000. £6,000 went to his taxes, £6,000 to his father-in-law, Manuel Muguira, so Iñaki cleared £14,000. He went back to Gernika and bought a business there. That same banker who refused me £3,000 now lent me £40,000. I spent £15,000 on new equipment.

So, I owned everything and employed a number of Basque boys—Francisco Alcibar, my uncle Justo Goicoechea, and José Badiola from Ondarroa among them. Badiola's wife went to work for us as cook. I built a four-flat unit that they lived in. I also had Valentín Gutierrez who was from Galicia or Santander, and another Galician as well. I trained a number of them to run equipment—rollers and front-end loaders. They weren't very educated but were quick learners. After a mistake or two, they became decent operators. They banged up some equipment, but they were hard workers and made me money. Several got licensed, and that became their permanent occupation. They never went back to cane cutting.

I called my men my "Spanish euclids." "Euclid" is an Aussie word for a large mining dump truck. The machinery inspector in Mount Isa was my friend, and he was very tolerant when it came to my employees' formal credentials. He trusted our work. I was friendly with most of the shire officials in Mount Isa. I put on a weekly Friday-after-work party. I explained to the guests that their cold beer came from a "Spanish Euclid"—a wheelbarrow full of ice with a Spaniard pushing it.

We were very busy, and it was nothing for me to get up on a Sunday morning to pour bitumen when there was no traffic on the roads. By 10 a.m., I might have made a £2,000 profit. I was a subcontractor for a major construction company that had tried to hire me a few years earlier. Between Mount Isa Mines and the local shire, I could barely keep up with the demand. I was careful to price my bids properly and came out very well.

At one point, I won a tender in Burketown to build that area's first bitumen roadway, three miles long. It was a half-year contract and we completed the work in three months and two weeks. I took my Basque boys there, and we all lived in a man camp. I hired an Australian woman to cook for us.

After three years, or in the mid-1960s, I decided to move the Company to Townsville. I left a general manager, Glen Steele, in Mount Isa to continue to supervise projects there. But I could see a bright future in Townsville. They were building an Australian military base on the edge of the town, and would need installations, runways, and housing projects. At first, I wasn't successful. Others underbid me. But there was a real estate developer, John Bartlett, who was constructing residential housing. He wanted us to go into partnership. He had a 50 percent partner that I bought out, and Bartlett and I formed Goicoechea Construction Company.

We purchased 5,000 acres at Bluewater (332 miles north of Townsville) that had three or four miles of beachfront. We projected a major development there, but it did not go forward. We also bought a 3,000-acre cattle station just west of Townsville (Oak Valley). John and I didn't always agree. He didn't have a very good reputation either. I was in Spain when I got a call from Bartlett stating that we had an offer on Oak Valley from a buyer in Melbourne. He suggested we sell. In the event, he sold my half and charged me a commission, and then became the new owner's partner. It was obviously time to split up. I gave him my interest in Bluewater for his half of Goicoechea Construction Company. I kept a little acreage at Bluewater, where I had a 250-tree mango plantation and processing plant.

I formed a company with another contractor in Mount Isa, the Stubbins Brothers. We called it VSB (Vasco and Stubbins Brothers) Construction Company. I eventually gave my interest to them. For a while, Goicoechea and VSB were two of three players in the Mount Isa construction scene. The other was a large national consulting firm, and it went after the biggest projects. They had the necessary infrastructure that we lacked. We couldn't afford all the engineers and accountants that you needed for those big projects. We got along pretty well, although there were always the little incidents and envies that are natural among rivals. But we sometimes subcontracted work from them. We actually did most of the streets within Townsville over time.

I always had a close relationship with my men. I can only recall one strike. It was in Mount Isa shortly after I had moved to Townsville. I got a call about it and hopped on a plane. I went straight to where the men were assembled. It was largely six or seven Australian blokes on the crew. I had some good ones over the years, and many that weren't so good—on a bender or sleeping one off when you needed them. The Basques were the most reliable and respected, although I recall a very loyal and hard-working Aborigine and another half-breed. They both admired the Basques. Whenever a man complained, I paid him off. In fact, I might give him a little more than he had coming—just so he wouldn't come back.

Anyway, that strike was over in a few minutes. I would call upon one of them and say, "Remember the time your wife was sick in Sydney and I gave you a week off and paid your airfare to go see her?" I could pick out each of them with something like that, and they couldn't look me in the eye. The next day, they all turned out for work. It was the only time I can recall being the object of industrial action.

I now set up several holding companies for tax purposes, all with Basque names—Toki, Bizkaia, and Mendi. Actually, Mendi Proprietary Ltd and Goicoechea Construction both ended up under the holding company called Toki. We have another company, Izarra, that is involved in pine plantations in South Australia.

We developed our own kerb-and-gutter machine, patented it, and set up an equipment company to market it. There were always problems with that initiative. The machine was complicated and temperamental. You had to have well-trained men running it. It could lay down forty feet of product a minute. We once poured 50,000 feet with it in Mount Isa for the Thiess Brothers, and made a dollar-per-foot profit. We sold that machine to them at a profit. But, to be cost-effective, you had to get contracts for big projects all over Australia, or at least Queensland. We tried to sell the machine to other contractors, and only found a couple of buyers in Australia—one in Melbourne and another in Perth. About this same time, through the equipment company, I bought the Panorama Restaurant. It was wiped out in the 1971 cyclone, but it was insured, and

I later sold it at a A$20,000 profit. It was probably the only restaurant in the world that sold kerb-and-gutter machines as a sideline!

Anyway, I decided to go international. We demonstrated the machine in Las Vegas and Phoenix and licensed a manufacturer of it in North Dakota. I sold one in Winnipeg. We were also in Abu Dhabi, Crete, and Czechoslovakia. I took the machine to Europe. I transported one by airfreight from Brisbane to London. The airfreight alone cost several thousand dollars. Passing through England, I managed to make a sale to a company in Scotland. We displayed at the Hanover Fair.

I then went to Spain. Two friends in Lekeitio helped me put together a team for a demonstration in Bilbao. There was a lot of press coverage. But there were problems. The materials in Europe were a little different than those in Queensland, just enough to cause challenges figuring out the proper mix. The men we hired and tried to train really "didn't give a shit." They were just putting in time. The demonstration in Bilbao proved a failure, so I took it to England. After several months there, that didn't work out either. On that trip, I lived for three months in Lekeitio, six months in Madrid, where I put my kids into school, and nine in Surrey, England. I think that journey began in 1971, and we came back to Australia in 1972. It was Stephen's first trip to the Basque Country.

I could leave because of a faithful employee, Kevin Doyle, that I had inherited from Bartlett when we formed Goicoechea Construction. He was very capable of running the business, even though his formal schooling ended when he was fourteen. In fact, over the years I have been to Spain fifteen or twenty times, sometimes for several months, and that would never have been possible without Kevin. He is our second in command. He is now seventy-three years old and still working for Mendi.

For many years, we used the machine here on our own projects. However, its technology is now about thirty years old, and it requires too much skilled labor to operate. The machine is no longer active. By the time we retired the machine, we were only using it for twelve days a year. It didn't compensate for the cost of keeping a team together and on hold.

After twenty-three years of marriage, my wife, Sonia, died of cancer. When I returned from that sales trip to Europe, I met my second wife, Alwyn Dolan. We were introduced to one another by a mutual friend.

She had been married twice and had no children. Our marriage only lasted for four years and was a mistake. We lived near Lake Tinaroo in the Atherton Tablelands. I bought a 300–400-acre abandoned dairy farm there and ran cattle on the property. Then, I purchased a rice and peanut farm, Lotus Glen, near Mareeba. Next, I bought another obsolete dairy farm near Malanda. While I was doing that, Goicoechea Construction continued to operate in Townsville, largely under Kevin's supervision. Most of our work was subcontracting for the Kern Corporation. We did projects in Atherton, Cairns, Emerald, Bowen, Charters Towers, and Townsville.

After I divorced, I moved back to Townsville. About then, through Mendi, I bought into 1,500 acres of scrubland to the north of the city called Mount Low. There were ten partners in all, and Mendi, like each of the rest, had 10 percent. Then, three of the partners, including Mendi, bought out the others. By then, we had begun building houses and a shopping center, and Mendi was doing about 90 percent of that construction. We three partners divided up Mount Low into three parcels and then drew lots for them. But, then, one of my partners bought the other out, so I became the minority partner of a very ambitious man. Not a comfortable position to be in. He had cattle operations, hotels, and other investments in Queensland. He became overextended and went broke, so I bought his holdings in Mount Low out of bankruptcy receivership. I did that through Lotus Glen, a company with its own losses that could be carried forward for tax purposes. Mendi has improved 600 lots at Mount Low to date, and it is only about 30 percent built out—it is a totally planned community.

Curiously, we first bought Lotus Glen from Kath Mostyn, the mother of my present wife, Jenny. I had known Kath from my days in Burketown; she was a publican in Kurrumba at that time (the town with the airport that I used on trips to and from the Gulf Country). I met Jenny briefly when I purchased Lotus Glen. She was still married then. After her divorce, she moved to Townsville with her mother. Then, I happened to see her at a horse race, and we started dating. We were married a year later. So, from that Lotus Glen deal, I ended up with the Mount Low property, a mother-in-law, and a wife!

My daughter, Teresa, lives in Toronto for the last seventeen years. She is forty-eight. She was a kindergarten schoolteacher when she met her husband, a Canadian, and he now has a dry-cleaning business. Their two sons were born in Australia, and one of them came back to here. He wanted to be a military pilot, but had problems qualifying in Canada. Today, he is a member of the Royal Australian Air Force, stationed with a Herculean unit in Richmond (Sydney). They have a daughter.

My other daughter with Sonia is Maria Dolores. She was a nurse who married a doctor—Rod Martinez. He was born in Australia, but his father immigrated here from Argentina. His grandfather emigrated from Spain to Latin America. They have four children between thirteen and twenty. They live here in Townsville and host a dinner for us almost weekly.

Son Stephen was the real surprise. He had no interest in the business. I wanted him to become an engineer and then take over from me one day. He wanted to be a doctor instead but couldn't get into medical school. So, he graduated from the University of Queensland in Brisbane with a Bachelor of Science. He went into microbiology and became a pathologist technician. He worked at that for ten years here in Townsville in a public laboratory. But then, in 1991, he came to me and asked if he could take charge of my kerb-and-gutter business. I was shocked. He liked his work but felt like he was topped out in that career. He had a good feel for numbers, and he did a great job for me.

By then, Kevin's wife wanted him to retire and move to Cairns, and Stephen was just beginning. We were small, maybe only six or seven employees in all, and our future was unclear. So, I leased space for our headquarters, thinking that it might be for just a short time until we wound down the company.

In 1994, I formed a new company out of the old Mendi, also named Mendi Construction, and gave Kevin Doyle 20 percent ownership. Stephen now owns 50 percent of that remaining 80 percent. We sold the headquarters of Goicoechea Construction. We then bought 25 hectares here in Garbutt that we paid A$150,000 for when a property nearby was selling for much more. Actually, I placed about three hectares in a block owned by a Goicoechea Family Trust and leased it to Mendi Construction for its headquarters and equipment yard. We called that company Crocodile Investments, because the three hectares had once been a crocodile farm. The street that the headquarters is on is called Crocodile.

I gave each of my daughters 15 percent of that trust, so they already have ownership and an income from it.

The rest of the Garbutt land was owned by Mendi Construction, and developed by it. So, we had plenty of space for Mendi's needs (new headquarters and equipment yard) and we have been selling off the remaining parts of the property for an amazing return. We still have some parcels for sale.

So, today, I have three children from my first marriage, eleven grandchildren in all, and a sixteen-year-old daughter, Anamari, with Jenny. She is currently attending a boarding school in Brisbane (a Catholic girls' school).

We are a close family. When we were younger, we three Goicoecheas played musical instruments. My brother played the violin and I the violin, banjo, and mandolin. Rose was a pianist. We had a group, the Goicoechea Trio, and performed at many weddings throughout North Queensland. But Rose and I didn't get along. I have tried to reconcile with her, but, to this day, she won't have anything to do with me.

Today, Mendi is our main company and it employs about forty people. None of them are Basques because there aren't many left, and those still active have their own businesses—usually harvesters or cane farms. Technically, I am retired, and my son Stephen runs Mendi. But really, I am still involved a lot. In addition to our construction bidding, we now engage in our own hauling business. To be competitive today, particularly against the big players, you have to be vertically integrated. By quarrying and hauling our own materials to the jobsites we cut costs and can submit lower bids. We are working on a big development in a remote area north of Townsville—Bushland Beach (the former Mount Low). It is a planned community, anchored by a hotel project and shopping center. The hotel is owned and operated by another of our holding companies—Markina.

I have been a shareholder in the North Queensland Rugby team since 1996. Earlier, I had been president of the board of the Cloncurry Rugby team. For Townsville to challenge in the national competitions, it had to have a proper stadium. There was a defunct harness-racing facility here in Townsville that could be transformed into a rugby stadium. There was a fundraising effort and it brought the community together.

Mendi became very involved and provided considerable work for nothing and at cost. I think that I saved them about 3.5 million dollars. All of the construction companies here became involved that way (some with labor and others with machinery). Mendi moved hundreds of thousands of yards of dirt and worked on the drainage system and the turf. We did, or supervised, all of that effort. A friend, the owner of Caltex, donated 50,000 liters of fuel for the equipment. If you want to ask others to help, you had better do so yourself.

I was one of the six directors of the team. But, eventually, I didn't agree with some of the board's policies, and I resigned in 2000. The project was foundering, and, by then, I was out half a million dollars. We did get a ten-seat corporate suite for three years, valued at about A$25,000 annually. I didn't want to lose anymore. Eventually, many who leant money lost it. I still support the team and the board knows it can count on me going forward. Mendi has a corporate box for the games.

I have been active in public affairs. I was a member and founder of the Rotary Club of Cloncurry and a member of the Mount Isa and Townsville ones. I ran for councilman in Townsville but was unsuccessful. I then entered the mayoral race on three occasions. The first time, I obtained 40 percent of the vote against a very popular Labour mayor. The *Townsville Daily Bulletin*, in September of 1979, or the month before that election, asked the [rhetorical] question, "How independent is a candidate for mayor who has been supported by the local Liberal and National Party MPs against the Labour candidate?" Joe's answer was, "I am a North Queenslander of Basque descent and Basques have always been independent people." The second time he ran, he got 16,065 votes to the 16,532 for the victor. The third election was not as close. Many people said I was too ambitious, and they might have been right, too!

I was pretty well known in North Queensland, obviously, but then I made Australian national news the hard way. I always liked the water and sailing. I swim regularly in the ocean. I had three yachts over the years, mainly just to take my friends out on excursions. A couple of summers ago, two friends and I decided to take a cruise to Cape Cleveland to possibly stay overnight in a fishing shack. We went in a small roundabout. One was Jenny's brother-in-law, Graham Weir, and the other was a longtime fishing mate and fellow building contractor here, Noel Hyde. He was overweight and we nicknamed him Porky. We set out, and the prognosis was for stormy weather. We were going on a Thursday, and, between the forecast and it being a weekday, there weren't likely to be many people in the fishing shacks that dotted that country. However, we knew it intimately and intended to hug the shoreline. We weren't worried.

Along the way, we decided to put into drag some nets for prawns. We stupidly tied up to a mangrove, rather than putting out the anchor. When we returned an hour later, the boat was 300 to 400 yards out in the bay. It had slipped its moorage. I decided to swim after it, but the wind was blowing, and the roundabout had a canopy that acted like a sail. I couldn't gain on her and had to turn back.

It was then that we decided to split up. We left our mate behind and he walked to a nearby hut, while Porky and I set out overland and through the water heading for the fishing camp. It was about two miles away, we reckoned. Well, the going was rough. The tide was in and sometimes we were up to our chests in water as we mucked through. Then, we came upon a little vacant fishing shack, and it had a dinghy. We commandeered it and started rowing. We could see our boat out in the bay, and we took turns with the oars to eventually reach it. Well, we hadn't noticed that the dinghy had a leak, and, when we tried to stand on the edge to make our way on board the boat, the dinghy capsized. It hit me in the head, and, for a minute, Porky was trapped under it. I started after the roundabout, but it was floating away from us. Pretty soon, I was twenty yards from it and twenty yards from Porky, who was clinging to the dinghy. I decided to go back to him to make sure he was okay. It took us about an hour to right the dinghy and get into it, but it was swamped. We were sitting in water and had about two or three inches of freeboard. The waves were sloshing in and kept filling the dinghy about as fast as we could bail. Our aluminum oars were gone.

It was about eleven in the morning and we were adrift heading for Magnetic Island. So was the roundabout. I thought we would arrive there about six, but then the wind shifted, and we were headed out to open sea. We tried to keep our spirits up and joked a lot. It would have been a real worry in our circumstances had we missed Magnetic Island and floated out to sea. So, I said to Porky that, if that happened, in two or three weeks' time one of us would have to eat the other. There were two good reasons for me to eat him. First, his weight; he was succulent.

Second, the fact that he was an unseasoned steak-and-potatoes Aussie, and he hated my spicy "Spanish" cooking. Whenever I prepared fish for him, he complained about the garlic and olive oil. Obviously, he would find my flesh unpalatable.

Anyway, the tide shifted, and we started drifting back towards the mainland. In the middle of the night, we were almost rammed by a trawler that was travelling on autopilot. We yelled in hopes of being picked up, but no one was on deck to hear us. The next morning, we were close to Echeron Island, considerably north of Townsville; we had floated about forty kilometers. We spied a structure on top of a hill, so we maneuvered the dinghy to land. Porky was down to his underwear and I was suffering from hypothermia—my legs were black.

It turned out to be an observation tower that the Royal Australian Air Force used to direct training bombing runs on nearby islands. There was a water catchment attached to the building, and we found an old teapot and drank cold water from it. It was chilly. We spent the second night inside the tower, sleeping on a cold cement floor and covered with corrugated-tin roofing to keep the wind and rain off. By now the conditions were nearly cyclonic, and the wind was blowing sheets of rain horizontally into our shelter through the uncovered observation opening.

It turned out that the authorities had ordered an air search for us all of Friday, but then called it off due to the weather. We were essentially given up for dead. Air, Sea, and Rescue continued the search the next day with troops on land, light planes, and boats. There was a helicopter pad next to the tower, and, the next morning, we were arranging rocks on it to spell out "help." It was then that the pilot of a fixed-wing aircraft spotted us. He sent a helicopter, and we were soon in Townsville. That cost Mendi A$10,000, but it was obviously worth it. I picked up a newspaper, and the article on the front page spoke about what good fellas we had been—it was like reading our own obituary. Instead of a funeral, we immediately organized a big party for that evening and into Sunday. That Saturday night, while the celebration was on, the telephone rang, and I picked up the receiver. It was my daughter, who was at the Honolulu airport on her way from Toronto to likely attend my wake. She was checking in with Jenny to see if there were any updates. Needless to say, she was shocked to hear my voice. I told her to keep coming and join the party. She did so and stayed with us for a two or three week visit.

I always felt that the Basques of North Queensland should organize. I attended some of the Spanish fiestas that were held in Ayr. We formed the Spanish Society of North Queensland and I was its first president. We once organized Basque games and different people put up booths, some selling drinks, with signs like "Markina," "Amorebieta," etc. But that was mainly active in the Burdekin, and it seemed like something should be done on a wider scale.

We are told the following in a published account based on a 2000 interview with Joe,

> The most recent gathering of North Queensland Basques was in 1996 at Bushland Beach Hotel, Bushland Beach. With visitors from Euskal Herria staying, José María (Joe) Goicoechea (of Mendi Constructions) invited Basques from the Burdekin, Townsville, and Ingham to join him and his family and guests for lunch. Basque food and dancing and music were enjoyed and Joe, though recovering from a bout of illness, still managed to entertain the gathering with his mandolin playing. Special shirts were available for purchase at the event. These featured the flag and map of *Euskadi*, stools of cane and the words: *The Basques of North Queensland, Australia.*[2]

So, some of us met a few years ago in Agustín Adarraga's house to discuss the matter, and then I hosted an organizational meeting in the Seaview Hotel (I was part-owner of it). After that, the Spanish Society of North Queensland held its meetings at the Seaview here in Townsville. But it eventually failed.

Anyway, subsequently, I attended *Jaialdi* in Boise and was very impressed. So, in 2001, I hosted a party in my house to see what could be done here. We thought we had invited everyone. I asked Dolores Mendiolea from Ingham and Johnny Achurra from Ayr to help me. People came from Trebonne; the Arrates from the Burdekin attended. Everyone had a good time, but afterwards some people groused that they had been left out. I guess it was inevitable that a few would be overlooked. It wasn't intentional.

There had been a Polish Club in Townsville that leased a small building from the local council, but it had failed. That locale was empty, and I knew key people in the local Government. I was able to secure that lease for A$20,000. We formed the Basque Club of North Queensland Association and I loaned it the money for the lease, plus A$3,000 for startup costs. I was elected first president; Mary Arrate was the vice president; and Pedro Mendiolea, from Ingham, was our first treasurer. Gloria Totoricagüena came here about that time to finalize the research for her book, and she helped me with the organizational details.

I am very Basque and proud of it. I have been to Spain fifteen or twenty times. When I am here, I miss the Basque Country. When I am there, I miss Australia. Sometimes, I feel like a traitor to both places! I once lived in Madrid for six months, but I had never been south of it until my last trip this past July. We saw the Alhambra then, and it is magnificent. Maybe I shouldn't admit it, but I have a thing about *Maketos*. They are a different race.

Notes

1. In 1952, Ignacio Goicoechea applied for an Australian passport to be able to go to Spain (and return) with his daughter. He stated in his application that he was born in 1891 in Murélaga [Aulesti] and married to Margarita in Markina on February 11, 1929. Ignacio first entered Australia in March of 1912 on the vessel *Caledonian* that landed in Brisbane. In 1927, he went to Spain and returned to Australia in February of 1936. In 1948, he left for Marseilles and returned to Australia in 1949. He listed his occupation as carpenter. (Australian National Archives, Brisbane, Application for Passport J25 1958-479.)
2. Vidonja Balanzategui and Debono, "The Fronton," 26.

CHAPTER 14

The Wandering Basque

We met Frank Alcorta in this book's first chapter. Jan and I visited him and his wife, Arantxa Querejeta, in their home in Bicheno, Tasmania, in 2002. I interviewed them both extensively at that time. My last meeting with Frank was in 2007, and we have continued to correspond down to the present. It was my intention to use the interviews and letters as the basis for a brief sketch to be included as one more case among the several voices of Chapter 11. However, I have changed my mind for a couple of reasons.

First, Frank's account is far too rich, not to mention unique, to be shortened. In many ways, he may be regarded as the antithetical Basque Australian in this account—a loner who lived both physically and mentally far from his countrymen. He has never belonged to a Venezuelan-Basque or Australian-Basque (or Spanish) club. As much (or more) a citizen of his adopted and beloved Australia, Frank maintained, and continues to do so, relations with his Basque homeland—where he has both blood relatives and in-laws from two marriages. Over the years he has purchased property in Brisbane and Bargara, Darwin and Bicheno—but also in Gipuzkoa and Navarra.

Second, as we shall see, Frank is an accomplished writer. He has published four books in English, his nonnative language. For many years, he was both an editor and columnist in two Northern Territory newspapers owned by News Corps (the Rupert Murdoch chain), and was actually hired by a major Australian politician as his speechwriter! In short, Frank reminds me in more than one way of Joseph Conrad, that consummate ex-pat literary spokesman—albeit Alcorta has never attempted fiction.

When we last met, Frank and his second wife, herself a Basque from Donostia/San Sebastián, were living in Bargara, Queensland. They read daily issues of Madrid's *El País* and a Basque newspaper as well. They received *Noticias de Euskadi* from the Basque government, displayed a Basque flag in their living room, and a bumper sticker of it on their automobile. At my request, Frank showed me his war medals for combat service in the Australian Army. They were from four countries (Australia, Malaysia, South Vietnam, and Great Britain). Despite his evident Australian patriotism, he dislikes the Australian flag because of its British Commonwealth emblem. It connotes subservience to the British monarchy, and therefore offends his egalitarian sensibilities. I have copyedited but lightly Frank's own account of his life, and have added a few footnotes to clarify and contextualize some of his points:

Francisco Alcorta Azpiroz—I was born in Txomin-Enea, a working-class suburb of San Sebastián, Spain, on March 16, 1936, just months before that exercise in savagery called the Spanish Civil War began. I grew up with another exercise in barbarism, World War II, and my adolescence was marked by the scarcity and penury of the postwar years.

I was a Basque child speaking only Basque until I began school at six years of age, when I was introduced to Spanish. My father was from San Sebastián and my mother from Areso, a picturesque village in northern Navarra where only Basque was spoken. That is still the case today.

My parents spoke Basque at home. But from the time I commenced my primary school years, followed by high school, Spanish became dominant. I was able to complete secondary education, a high achievement in the late 1940s and early 50s, in a Catholic Brothers school, the *Sagrado Corazón*, because an aunt of mine, Juanita Alcorta, a worker in the town's Tobacco Factory, now the *Tabakalera*, paid my monthly fee of 25 *pesetas*.

My father participated in the Civil War as a truck driver, his trade for many years. I do not recall him ever mentioning the war or even talking about it with my mother. He worked for his father, Don Ignacio Alcorta, who managed a coal storage business. Father drove the delivery truck, though there was also a donkey and cart in the store to deliver coal to flats and apartments in the centre of town, a job that fell to me when I was 11 or 12 years old during every summer's school holidays. The bags weighed thirty kilos and had to be taken up the stairs because I was never allowed into a lift. It was hard physical labor.

I have two brothers—one, Ignacio, born in 1937, the other Juan José, in 1944. Both worked in banking and rose to the ranks of the well-to-do middle class raising large families and retiring comfortably in San Sebastián. We maintain occasional contact.

My parents would have liked me to go into a respectable career such as banking, but my adolescence was full of romantic, or at least I thought they were romantic, stories about Spanish conquistadors, navigators, and explorers who opened up the world in the fifteenth and sixteenth centuries, obtaining the first universal empire in the history of humanity.

So when I was 18, I believe from memory, after completing some cursory paperwork, I migrated to Venezuela in a rusty Italian tin can that left from the northwestern Spanish port of Vigo. Life on board was miserable. One meal a day, usually chickpeas, sleeping in hammocks, sharing a few toilets with a couple of hundred young men (no women on board in my first crossing of the Atlantic) and showering with a hose that pumped seawater. The young men were from all over Europe, all seeking a better life beyond the seas.

I knew no one in Venezuela, though another aunt of mine had gone there some years before, but we were not in touch. I was full of hope that I would carve out a future for myself in this new land—America.

Here I have to mention that I had met and fallen in love with a beautiful young girl when I was just 17 and she all of 14. Her name was Arantxa and she was the sister of a classmate, Juan Ignacio Querejeta, who would later become a renowned and much-respected orthopedic surgeon. They belonged to a remarkable family.

Their father, Elias, a wealthy entrepreneur, was on Franco's side during the war and was appointed governor of Murcia afterwards. He then went on to become president of the *Diputación* or Deputation (local Government) in Guipuzkoa, a Basque province bordering France, and, among other personalities, he formally received Hitler's right-hand man, Goering, in San Sebastián.

Another of his sons, also named Elias, went on to become a famous film producer who revolutionized Spanish and European cinema and won the Cannes Film Festival a couple of times, as well as the Berlin and Venetian festivals. The only award that eluded him was the Oscar, though he was nominated once.

I have put some emphasis on Arantxa's family to state the obvious: Clearly, I was not the man they would have preferred for their daughter and sister, though that never even occurred to me then as we exchanged our dreams. Teenage love, I guess, lives in a cocoon, or perhaps my indifference to what anyone thought was only a product of the arrogance of youth. There were no explicit promises made to her before I left because I believed they were not necessary with eternal love.

Venezuela was an exciting shock to this young Basque brought up in the austere environment of a region best known for its cold winters and stormy seas. In that Caribbean nation what reigned was noise, colour, and gaiety. Most people ranged from brown to black, though no one appeared to care a fig about it. The only shocking bit that struck me immediately after arrival was the poverty. Obviously, parts of Caracas were well off, but the surrounding hillocks, *cerros* in Spanish, were home to hundreds of thousands of *negritos* (Blacks) lacking the most basic facilities and services.

Still, I didn't have a lot of time to reflect about the new panorama opening up in front of my eyes because the most essential thing now was to earn some money.

I found a room, if such it could be called, in a hostel run by a Portuguese family who also helped me find a job in the construction industry.

After a few months I had saved enough money to move on to my real destination, the great swathe of land between the Orinoco and Amazon Rivers known as the *Gran Sabana* (the Grand Savanna) or Venezuelan Guyana, dominated by the heights of Mount Roraima and by rare natural geographical gems such as *Salto Ángel*, the longest waterfall in the world. The region was known for its abundance of alluvial diamonds and gold. I intended to become rich, of course, striking a vein of abundance in my first day of prospecting.

My fantasies were soon erased. Three Spaniards accompanied me. One was a Castilian, another a Catalan, and the third a Basque from Navarra called *Catire* in Venezuelan Spanish. It meant blonde. We travelled by bus to Ciudad Bolivar on the shores of the Orinoco River and from there to a penal settlement, El Dorado, some distance to the south along a dirt track. This is where the road ended, indeed where all roads ended. From there on to the interior it had to be done by canoe on navigable waters or trekking. Or, if lucky, by a single engine plane to far away settlements like Icabaru or Santa Elena del Uairen on Brazil's border.

I met the man who would be my partner for the next two years in El Dorado. He was a Negro, illiterate but strong and decent, who went by the name of Carmelo. He joined our small group in a motor-powered canoe to a small village of mostly indigenous people not far from the rundown jail. There we took up a straw-roofed hut after paying a small fee to its owner, an Indian, and hung our hammocks. We cooked our rice and other scarce supplies in an improvised wood-fired kitchen.

To our surprise we met a rather old and wizened European in the next hut. He was a Frenchman who, he informed us, had escaped from Devil's Island in French Guiana and settled here some years ago where he fathered a crew of kids with several Indian women. *Catire*, his real name was Ruben, had a camera and took a few photos, some of which have survived to this day.

We began prospecting almost immediately with Carmelo's skilled tutoring after trudging a fair way from the village, if such it could be called, until we struck a promising alluvial river. That was the beginning of a journey with disastrous consequences for my Spanish companions who, after a few weeks, started coming down with fevers and various illnesses. All three were evacuated and I lost track of them, except for Ruben, who I met again when I returned to San Sebastián after my time in the diamond fields and who would die a terrible death shortly after from one of his infections.

Time did not seem to matter in that awful emptiness. All that mattered were the bits of fine crystal that we were able to pan from time to time from the creeks which allowed us to eat. We also found some gold, which did not have the same allure, but could also be traded. Carmelo and I passed the days working tirelessly, cooking our scant meals, then sleeping in our hammocks to the sounds of the forest. We hardly spoke with each other except for the most functional things and tasks.

The bounty that I thought at the tip of my fingers now seemed unattainable, or at least so far away as to be little more than a dream. The most common of events around us was death, often violent, sometimes slow and passive. I was bitten by a snake that had taken shelter in my broad-brimmed hat one night. After I put on my hat in the morning without even looking in it, the snake managed to bite me in the left eyebrow before falling to the ground and slithering away. It was a *coralito*, Carmelo informed me, and I would be dead in a day or two at the most. He seemed indifferent mainly because those things were so common and therefore undeserving of major attention. Years later, Australians, also a product of a harsh and demanding land, taught me an expression that best-defined Carmelo's reaction: "Shit happens."

I was sick as a dog for a day or so, vomiting even after my guts had emptied, and writhing in pain in my hammock. But slowly the pain went away, the cramps disappeared, and I was back to normal in no time. Carmelo welcomed my return with a smile. I have absolutely no idea of the alchemy within my system that allowed me to survive. More likely, on reflection, the bite on the eyebrow was superficial and not enough venom had been injected.

So, it went on and on. The days had no meaning and neither did the weeks or months or indeed years. Survival was all that mattered in that savage and majestic land dominated by the massif of Mount Roraima.

Until one night in a recondite corner of the forest not far from Icabaru the wavering light of a kerosene lantern woke me up. It was approaching our camp. I dared not make any noise to awaken Carmelo because I suspected whoever was coming had a firearm, common in those parts. I got out of my hammock silently, picked up my sharp machete, and lay in ambush in low brush to wait for the intruder. When he was level with me I swung the machete so it would cut him fair in the stomach. But nothing happened. The light simply vanished. There was no one there.

In the morning, still somewhat shaken by the experience, I told Carmelo what had happened during the night. His eyes widened and lit up. "You have seen the miner!!" he exclaimed.

Carmelo was referring to a legend common among prospectors about a ghost whom they called "the miner" that roamed selected parts of the vast country and appeared from time to time to lucky diamond prospectors. Lucky because invariably the appearance of the ghost indicated a substantial find.

I am not superstitious nor much inclined to believe fairy tales, but, so help me, that is exactly what happened. Over the years I stopped telling the story because no one was inclined to even consider it a possibility. As I am certain will be the case with my readers now.

As usual we had camped near a creek in the vain hope of finding some bounty. This one proved different. In a few days we found more diamonds of all shapes and colours than in all the time we had spent in Guayana until now.

The man who bought them in a nearby settlement, probably Icabaru though my memory is quite foggy after all these years, claimed to be a Dutchman. More probably he was a South African employed by De Beers, a huge conglomerate with a near monopoly in diamond trading.

We split the money, bolivars, in two and Carmelo and I parted ways. He had enough to buy his Orinoco land and I had enough to return to the Basque Country and try to reset my life.

First thing I did in Caracas was exchange the bolivars for American dollars in the street. Then I rented my old room again in the same old Portuguese hostel where, by coincidence, I met an old acquaintance, a Galician (northwest Spain) tradesman who was embarking next day back to Spain. He told me he had saved enough to buy a flat in Bilbao where he had resided before migrating to Venezuela. His wife was still there.

On the spur of the moment I asked him whether he could take some of my money to my parents in San Sebastián? I would pay his bus or train expenses from Bilbao. The reason for my impulse was that I had been informed I would not be able to get a passage across the pond for another couple of months because ships were all booked up. I had a dire feeling that my parents were not doing well and wanted to help them. This took some mental gymnastics because my original impulse was to purchase a house in the old fishing port of San Sebastián and pursue my studies in journalism, which is what I wanted to do, in Madrid. My parents took precedence because I was 22 and therefore confident life would provide me more chances to do my own thing.

And those were the days you could actually trust people. The Galician did as promised. I was right about my parents' financial situation. My grandfather, I learned shortly, had sold his coal store (*almacén*) and my father, now in his late 40s, did not have a job. They were about to lose their rental flat in Txomin. The money helped them buy a unit in San Sebastián's newest suburb, Amara, and to get a taxi driver's licence which gave my father some breathing space.

However, it was Arantxa that was foremost in my mind and heart. And she had not forgotten me either. We resumed our entirely platonic relationship for a month or two before I returned to Venezuela, this time to work for an oil company based in Maracaibo and exploring the region bordering Colombia. I knew nothing about the mechanics of the job, but my bush experience gave me the skills to set up camps and deal with logistics. I am not sure about the name of my employer, though I believe it may have been Texaco or some other American company.

Around August or September of 1959, I made my fourth and last American sea crossing back to Spain after receiving a letter from Arantxa expressing strong doubts about our future together.

Little did I know that my return would lead to the biggest and most profound change in my life—an embrace of a land down under, Australia or *Terra Australis*, which would become not just my adopted fatherland, but the birth country of my daughters, granddaughters, and great grandkids.

The reason for my sudden decision to return to Spain had a name, Arantxa, who, I learned, was dating a young entrepreneur, a hotel owner from Getaria, a beautiful port town not far from San Sebastián and best known as the birthplace of Sebastian Elcano, the first man to navigate around the world in 1521. But she dumped her boyfriend as soon as she found out I was back, and we resumed our fraught relationship.

The question I asked myself was what next? The signs of economic recovery were everywhere in the Basque Country where tens of thousands of migrants from other parts of Spain, particularly the impoverished south, had flocked. A new and powerful Basque middle class was emerging on the back of that migration. Clearly, there was no need to leave because jobs were aplenty and opportunities abundant.

Yet something within me hankered for other shores, other horizons, and other experiences. One morning, probably in October, I read an ad in the local paper about something called Operation Emu, an Australian Government initiative to attract Basques (officially mentioned) to that country. Applicants would be interviewed and those selected could expect to leave by ship at a date not yet specified towards those far shores.

Most applicants in fact were not Basque, rather Spanish from other parts of the country. Among them were several families with children, but the bulk of us were single young men. I was selected, probably on the sole grounds of my youth, only 23, and willingness to work.

We departed from Bilbao a few days before Christmas. Arantxa accompanied me to the port city and bade me farewell from the quay. She was visibly upset and crying. My heart went out to her as I watched her while leaning on the handrail on the slowly moving vessel.

The ship, *Monte Udala*, was captained by a stern, no-nonsense Basque, as indeed were most of the crew. From day one the difference between the *Monte Udala* and the mainly Italian boats I boarded in my journeys to and from South America was stark. Here we enjoyed simple, but excellent, food, and the showers were immaculate, as indeed were our quarters. And there was order, a far cry from the normal situation in most of my Atlantic crossings.

I was surprised that we did not follow the Mediterranean route towards the Suez Canal, but instead replicated almost exactly the course taken by British Captain Arthur Phillip in 1788 with his First Fleet bringing 736 convicts to the newly founded colony of New South Wales. We touched down in the Canary Islands before heading off to Capetown in South Africa, then across the Indian Ocean to Melbourne (not to present-day Sydney as Captain Phillip had done). It was a marvellous cruise that ended on January 20, 1960.

And so was our arrival, at least in my eyes. I looked at the hazy land I was about to settle in as the ship neared the coast, all the while trying to make sense of the tumble of emotions in my heart and mind. An impossible task.

The Australian Customs officials who came on board looked at us with the same curiosity that we looked at them. This was not yet the age of globalization, uniformity, and cheap air travel. They were different to us and so were we to them. Yet, differences aside, by the time I completed the formalities of Customs and touched land I felt a tug in my heart that told me I would always be close to these people and this land, my new frontier.

We were taken by train to Bonegilla Camp in the north of the State of Victoria, where more than ten thousand immigrants from Europe (the White Australia Policy was alive and well in 1960), mainly from Holland, Germany, Italy, and now Spain, were housed in huts. Bonegilla today is formally part of Australia's historical legacy and a tourist attraction.

In theory all of us were under a bond to be employed where the various state and federal Governments believed we would be most useful. In practice the law was unenforceable and (most certainly in my case) we moved how, when, and where we pleased. The rule of thumb was jobs and money, not Government diktat.

My first job was digging trenches with a pick and shovel (you didn't need English to do that) in Mildura, a town on the border between New South Wales and Victoria, where, as luck would have it, I met another Basque, the headmaster of Mildura's secondary school married to an Australian lady. Then for a few months I worked for NSW Railways based in Narromine, a small town in outback NSW. We, meaning a dozen or so young men, lived in canvas tents on the side of the railway and cooked in a collective open fire outside. Shower and toilets were nondescript. The people in Narromine were great.

Some of us waited impatiently for June, the beginning of the cane-cutting season, to leave Narromine and move to Ingham, in North Queensland, to cut cane where the money flowed out of taps.

I used up the time in Narromine, to learn some basic English using a system invented by myself which said that language is a matter of words, not just grammatical rules and the ridiculous complexities of syntax. In my opinion (again without any supporting evidence or research) humans normally employ no more than a thousand words, and probably fewer, in their everyday intercourse. I figured therefore that learning five new words a day would make me functional in six months. Which is exactly what happened. Pronouncing the words in a non-phonetic language such as English was something else, and here is where the best schools in the country, the pubs, came in handy. Sharing a few beers with my new compatriots was a top way to learn the sounds of those new words.

In Ingham we had to join a union, the Australian Workers Union in this case, and find partners, before we could sign a contract with a farmer. I became the ganger, boss, of a group of three Spaniards (including myself), one Swede, one Austrian, and an Italian and we were contracted by a farmer, married to a beautiful young lady who happened to be the daughter of Basque farmers (I cannot recall their names), a fair way from Ingham itself.

We worked from dawn to dusk, the money was good, an average of £40 to £50 a week, compared with the £12 we earned on the railroad.

Happy as Larry, as my Australian friends taught me to say. I even contemplated buying a block of land north of Ingham on a deserted beach fringed by oyster-bearing rocks with a creek running down the middle. I would build a shack with an outside shower and toilet and write the novel of the century. Years later when I told my daughters of my dreams, they laughed. Hang on kids, I would tell them, I've been pretty good at converting dreams into reality—at least some of the time.

All that was until mid-September when I received a letter from Arantxa, who had waited all these months to write at all. In the letter she explained curtly that she had a new boyfriend with whom she had established a serious relationship. In time I learnt that the new bloke fitted to perfection her family's idea of someone suitable for their daughter. He came from a good upper-middle-class family, was a professional of some sort, serious, elegant, perfectly behaved, and reasonably good looking. More important, he did not have the slightest intention to leave the Basque Country anytime soon, if ever. (Years later, Arantxa explained to me that the cause of their breakup had been his mother, who warned him over and over that she would leave him if and when I showed up again. Fancy that.)

We still had almost two months to finish the cane-cutting season and this I intended to complete because I had given my word. But the letter made me lose my bearings; I had no idea what I would do after that. I was certain of only one thing, this time I had no intention of going back to Spain to beg for a bowl of her love.

I was told in the pub in Ingham that there were plenty of jobs to be had in the Queensland mining district of Mount Isa which I had never heard of before. My drinking mates told me that I could get there by train, first from Ingham to Townsville in the south, then from Townsville to Mount Isa, which was a long way out in the northwest of the State and close to the Gulf of Carpentaria. That was how far the train went in those days and that is how far it goes today.

The day after my arrival I got a job underground mining; first time I had ever done that. Miners were accommodated in the Mineside barracks, which had a mess where we were also fed. I learnt the use of explosives, a trade that would serve me well later in the four years of war in various Southeast Asian theatres and in my stay in Papua New Guinea.

Some three or four months after I started a massive strike was called with miners demanding a so-called lead bonus. The mine was a treasure trove of lead, zinc, and silver, and underground miners were particularly exposed to lead contamination, so their demands were undoubtedly justified. But I did not have the time or the inclination to wait around, probably for months, before the dispute was settled, so I set out towards the east with two or three others in a car.

Our first stop was Cloncurry where by chance I met the man, Alexander Holland, known as "Dutchy," who became my partner for a few months of roaming Outback Queensland doing odd jobs such as fencing, culling kangaroos, and trapping dingoes. We also prospected for opal in Opalton, south of Winton in central Queensland, but without luck. Dutchy was a drover and jackaroo (or cowboy in American parlance), but he had fallen off his horse shortly before and was convalescing, as he said—meaning drinking beer, smoking handrolled cigarettes, and doing nothing.

To me this period was full of images of an amazing geography, immense plains, eroded hillocks, and patches of forest. We travelled by car down dusty dirt roads and slept wherever we chose in our commodious sleeping bags, swags we called them, oblivious of snakes or mosquitos (mossies).

I also had a unique experience that marked my life. Aboriginal rock art was everywhere, in low-hanging caves as well as on exposed cliffs. The only rock art with which I was familiar (from seeing it in documentaries and various reports) was the Altamira Cave paintings in northern Spain, dating back 13,000 years. That date coincided with the widely held belief that Aborigines had arrived in Australia about that time, which marked the end of the last ice age.

This art that I was seeing here in Australia was surely much older than that, as well as incredibly more sophisticated than Altamira's. A seed was sown in my mind that has never abandoned me. When did Aborigines arrive in Australia and, much more important, did they come from anywhere? And where was the evidence of their origins?

More about that later. Dutchy and I had a good time working our butts off in rural Queensland. One time, while doing a fencing job, we contracted a young Aboriginal man who accompanied us to McKinley, a tiny town with a pub, where we intended to have a rest for a day or two.

We headed off to the bar on arrival and asked the Aboriginal (always called "Blackfella" then) to come in with us. The bar was half full with cattlemen who reminded us loudly, half of them looked as if they had had a drink or two too many, that Aboriginal people were not allowed into pubs. But Dutchy insisted that an exception should be made for our fellow; he was a good worker and would enjoy a beer.

A very insistent Dutchy was getting hot under the collar. I murmured quietly to him that we would probably lose any fight because there were too many of them. Dutchy would have none of it. His face red with anger, he swung a punch at his nearest opponent. The punch was the trigger for an all-out brawl in which we did our best, but without a lot of success. The Blackfella looked on with amusement from the outside while we pummeled each other merrily. A fight like this would have left some dead in the diamond fields of Venezuela. Here it was a less-than-friendly fisticuff.

Afterwards, nursing our numerous bruises, we bought a carton of beer and ambled out towards a shady tree to eat some dry meat and have a well-deserved sleep in our swags.

In early December we looked at our cash savings and decided on a month off in Brisbane, the capital, to taste booze and fun. Brisbane then was just a large country town bathed by frangipani, poincianas, jacarandas, and low homes with wide verandas. The tallest building was the Town Council, a Victorian sandstone not far from the centre, Queen Street, where trams circulated with their usual clanking.

We stayed in a large hostel, with a typical Queensland architecture, a wide veranda surrounding dingy rooms, not far from the Central Station where we arrived by train (Dutchy had sold his jalopy for peanuts). The hostel, miraculously, has survived Brisbane's astonishing urbanization.

In a week our money was pretty well gone. I recall Dutchy and I walking down Mary Street near the centre, one morning while nursing a dreadful hangover and seeing an Army Recruitment Centre. We gave each other a look and without a second thought walked in and joined the Army for a six-year period. This was not a show of patriotism, but something to do, a spur of the moment thing—simple as that.

The recruitment officer heard my accent and asked me where I was from. I told him Spain and he didn't appear to show the slightest surprise or reticence. There were lots of so-called New Australians in the Army in those happy days. After our health check, which was quite thorough, we were put in a bus with other young blokes and taken to a large Army base at Enoggera, a suburb to the west. We spent Christmas 1961 "bashing dishes" (cleaning dishes) at Enoggera Army Mess.

Shortly afterwards we were posted to the Army Recruit Training Centre at Kapooka in NSW for three months. We learned to call officers Sir and to parade, not much about guns or living in the bush that we could do at least as well as our instructors and probably better. At the end of the three months we both chose the Infantry and were sent to Ingleburn, a training camp not far from Sydney.

In mid-1962 we were off to Malaya (shortly to become Malaysia) to fight a Communist insurgency that had been going on for nearly a decade. We joined the Second Battalion, Royal Australian Regiment, as reinforcements based in Terendak Camp in Malacca. Dutchy, given his background with horses and cattle, was sent to a unit responsible for reprovisioning troops in the jungle with a train of mules. I was sent to 2 Platoon Alpha Company.

Each company consisted of three platoons of about 30–32 men each, and in turn the platoons were made up of three sections. Our battalion was part of the 28th Commonwealth Brigade that included a battalion of New Zealand soldiers and another of British troops, the Kings Own Yorkshire Light Infantry. From time to time and depending on the various operations a battalion of Gurkhas also joined us.

The brigade was engaged in a war against Communist insurgents led by Chin Peng, a hero of the Malay resistance to the Japanese during World War II. But despite Chin Peng's leadership and the resilience of his troops, the war had become a very uneven fight by 1961/62. The main reason for that was the nature of an insurgency that basically consisted of angry Chinese revolutionaries. But the majority ethnic group in Malaya were Malays. They were overwhelmingly Muslim and, despite their dislike of British colonial rule and of the presence of foreign troops, they were disinclined to support Communist Chinese insurgents.

Chin Peng was in retreat, but he kept up a stubborn fight well into the 1960s and beyond. He was never captured. I secretly admired Chin Peng. He was very courageous and intelligent. I believe that eventually he just disappeared into the Chinese community and I heard much later that he died a peaceful death. I would have liked to know him.

In any case we had all the advantage of superior weaponry, logistics, and supplies. They were on their own without any kind of outside support, a situation entirely different to what we would find in Vietnam in a few years.

Most of our operations, usually three months long in the mountainous border with Thailand, were really mopping up affairs with no standup battles or contacts with the enemy who avoided us at all costs. Certainly the operations were physically demanding. They were also stressful because we had no idea when or how the enemy might turn up and shoot back. But, in comparison with Vietnam, the Malay Emergency was a walk in the park.

Originally I was in for a two-year tour, but, about six months after arrival, I received a letter from Arantxa to tell me that she remained single after all and still loved me. She got my address from my parents who she visited often to find out any news about me.

I had never stopped loving her. I wrote back explaining where I was and what I did (it is unlikely she even knew where Malaya was) and to say that when I had saved enough money I would fly to Spain to marry her. Saving money meant not spending, an oxymoron easier said than done when you are in your mid-20s in tropical Asia and in the company of people of your own age and with the same habits.

But I did as promised by three means: I extended my two-year tour in Malaya to nearly three, did not take a single day's holiday, and volunteered for every operation so that I could live the life of a monk in the jungles and away from any earthly temptations.

A few months later I received news that my father had died of a sudden heart attack as he was taking his taxi out of the garage one morning. He was in his early 50s, my mother just 48 and now a widow. Just as well my two brothers were there to help, which they did selflessly and with unending generosity.

In 1964 I became formally an Australian citizen in a ceremony in the offices of Australia's High Commission in Kuala Lumpur. The certificate, now yellowing, is still with me. Some of my fellow soldiers accompanied me to the ceremony that ended with a great celebration in the nearest bar. The strangeness of a Basque from Txomin-Enea adopting Australian citizenship in the capital of a British colony escaped me completely.

Arantxa rarely wrote, but when she did it was to repeat her message that what had been born in our hearts in our teen years was still there. In none of the letters did she give me an explicit promise that she would marry me after I returned. Finally, in March 1965 I flew from Singapore to Barcelona where she waited for me at the airport. She looked beautiful and we fell into in each other's arms in an eternal hug. Then by train to San Sebastián.

As the train pulled up in San Sebastián's railway station after a night's journey, I had to make an effort to understand my own feelings and sort out at least some of my thoughts. Arantxa and I had not had any sleep during the trip. There was too much to talk about and too many things unsaid for too many years that now bubbled to the surface incoherently.

I think neither of us made a lot of sense in anything that was said. Adding to the emotional or spiritual confusion was the fact that I had not seen her in nearly six years, three of which I had spent as a soldier in active service in Malaya. That had left its mark as it always does on everybody who has shared the military experience. It may not be openly acknowledged, but it is there.

Then there was the shock of being suddenly back in the land of my birth and feeling a perfect stranger. I was about to turn 29 years of age and Arantxa 26. We had spent twelve years hankering for each other, we believed, and now neither of us had a clear idea of our immediate future or what lay ahead beyond that.

My mother and brothers welcomed me and a room was ready for me in the flat in Amara that I had named Icabaru in memory of the diamonds that had made things a bit easier for my parents. I had brought a small suitcase with a coat, a couple of pairs of long trousers and some three shirts, socks, and underwear that I had purchased in Malacca. The coat had been tailor-made by an Indian and was a perfect fit. Other than that I had travellers checks to cover all expenses and two passage tickets to return to Sydney, Australia, from the port of Gibraltar in May on board the *PO Oriana*, a British liner.

I could not meet Arantxa's parents as I had wished because they had left for Valencia on the eve of my arrival. No doubt they still hoped their daughter would see the light and I would go back to wherever to resume my life free of encumbrances.

To my surprise, Arantxa had not taken any practical steps to, for example, acquire a passport or enquire about the necessary preparations for a Catholic Church wedding ceremony. The Church, as had been the case for centuries in Spain, still had a monopoly on marriage in the 1960s, which involved first the formal ceremony and then the formality of notifying the nation's Civil Registry.

So, it was a case of getting down to work from day one. Applying for a passport was easy because Arantxa was 26, came from a splendid family, and had no police record or indeed anything that could be taken as an obstacle to obtain it. We travelled to the capital, Madrid, to complete the procedures and, while there, we also visited the Australian Embassy to find out what we had to do for Arantxa to travel to Australia. No problem at all. I was an Australian citizen travelling with an Australian passport. And people in the Embassy were also aware I was a serving soldier in the Australian Army. My wife, said a young public servant with a smile, would be as welcome in the country as I had been.

The real problem arose with the Church. We had intended to marry in a small side chapel of the Buen Pastor Cathedral, an unmistakeable landmark in San Sebastián. But I had not counted with the probability that Don Elias Querejeta, Arantxa's much respected father, had whispered a couple of stories into the bishop's ear about my awful unsuitability for their beautiful daughter.

I was interviewed in an office in the Cathedral itself by a tall and extremely thin priest with a rather cadaverous face on which two malevolent eyes hid above prominent cheekbones. He murmured something about postponing or delaying our decision to marry because we both needed time to think things over and over. His monotone went on and on while Arantxa and I stared at him in silence.

In the end I lost my patience and asked him to concentrate on the specifics. We wanted to marry as soon as possible because we were booked on a passenger liner in May and there were any number of things that we had to do between now and then. He did not like the interruption and took a few seconds to reply. Basically he said he couldn't authorise the wedding ceremony until provided with evidence of my marital status and that could only be affirmed by the parish priest of wherever I had been for the past few years.

I am not sure he had ever heard of Malacca or whether the place sounded like some exotic corner of hell to him, but he became adamant about obtaining a document backed by the Church about me. My passport and other Army documents, stating clearly that I was single and without any formal or informal relations, did not seem to matter a damn to this Holy Inquisitor.

In the end I grabbed his arm and banged it against the desk telling him that Arantxa and I intended to go back to Australia together, married or not. It was up to him to legalize our union in the eyes of the Church or let us go on living in sin. Ridiculous but true.

I did send a telegram to my commanding officer in Terendak Camp asking him to return a telegram to me signed by the Catholic padre in the battalion saying that I was single, but I never received it. I can imagine their reaction. They probably thought I was out of my mind.

In any case, confronted by the reality of what we planned the Church authorities finally decided to permit the wedding, which took place on April 3, 1965, in precisely the place we had chosen. Arantxa's three brothers had persuaded their parents to return from Valencia and they attended the ceremony as did my mother and two brothers. It was simple and short.

Afterwards I had booked a function room in the Orly Hotel, near the well-known La Concha Bay of the city, with some tasty finger food and drinks. My mother was dismayed. She told me that had my father been alive it would have been celebrated in a very different manner. I can just imagine. I was coldly polite to Arantxa's parents and they were frigid towards me. Such is life.

My bride and I then flew from the nearby airport of Fuenterrabia to Palma de Mallorca (Majorca) for a week's honeymoon before returning to San Sebastián and a few formal farewells.

Then we travelled on the *PO Oriana* from Gibraltar to Naples, Port Said in Egypt, Aden in Yemen, Columbus in Ceylon (now Sri Lanka), Fremantle, just south of Perth in Australia, and Sydney where we boarded a train to Brisbane.

Arantxa's first impressions of Australia were horrible. We tried to get into a pub in Fremantle where she was denied entry because women were not allowed into bars with men. They were welcome only in so-called beer gardens. The streets were empty of people, a sharp contrast with San Sebastián, and those ambling to a vague destination seemed ill-dressed and shabby. The food in a tiny restaurant was, according to her, awful. We could not drink a glass of wine because very few places were licensed though customers were sometimes welcome to bring a bottle of wine with them and pour it into tea cups. She did not see a single thing that she liked.

And worse was to come. In Brisbane we rented a room in a hotel while I looked for accomodations somewhere near Enoggera Army Base. I could have asked Defence to house us in Army compounds, but I thought that would be too much for Arantxa.

After a few days of frenetic searching, I found a single room with a small kitchen in a large bungalow with other rooms for hire in the suburb of Newmarket, a few miles from the centre of town. Toilets and showers were shared with the other tenants. There was a shopping centre within walking distance (just as well because we did not have a car) where we bought some basics to start a new life in Australia. To this day I am amazed that Arantxa did not demand an immediate return to the Basque Country where she had enjoyed an incomparably higher living standard than here.

It was an inauspicious beginning, for sure, from which she probably never really recovered. It took her 22 years to accept Australian citizenship, which she did only at my behest because I thought it rather silly that whenever we returned from holidays abroad she and the kids (born in Australia but included on her Spanish passport) would line up with foreigners to go through Customs while I whizzed in with my Aussie passport. She actually shed a couple of tears when her Australian Citizenship Certificate came through the post (she refused to attend any ceremony). One time, many years later, she commented to me: "If ever I leave you for someone else don't look for me among Australians."

The thought that I had made a terrible mistake bringing her here tormented me many times. When you love someone, I reflected often, you want their best for them and, clearly, this was not it. I could have easily stayed on in the Basque Country where a bright future beckoned to me. But I loved Australia and felt a deep sense of obligation to the Army.

Despite a less than felicitous beginning, however, we had many happy moments and it is fair to say that, if anything, our love for each other was cemented in Newmarket where we found a friendly and open community. One of our neighbors, Mrs. Payne, a widow of an Australian veteran of World War II, became Arantxa's mentor and best friend when I left for Vietnam.

Shortly Arantxa became pregnant with our first baby, a beautiful girl who she chose to name Lorena, born on April 14, 1966, in Brisbane's Mater Hospital, a private Catholic entity. This was just a few weeks before I was posted to Vietnam with an advanced party to prepare the ground for the arrival of the Sixth Battalion, Royal Australian Regiment, my own battalion. I was then platoon sergeant of 2 Platoon consisting of 32 young men, mainly conscripts, in Alpha Company.

Our training had been exhaustive and intense, and we thought we were well prepared for whatever eventuality in this new theatre of war that many of my men had never even heard of before the terrible lottery of conscription inducted them into the Army.

At the end of May I was on a flight to Manila and Saigon with a hundred or so other troops, mainly noncommissioned officers (NCOs) charged with the logistics of embedding a battalion of around 700 men into the province of Phuoc Tuoy, a key province directly in the path of the enemy to South Vietnam's capital and site of Government.

Starting from the beaches of Vung Tau, we moved to Nui Dat, a huge formerly French rubber plantation, to establish our base. The task had not yet been completed when thousands of enemy troops, both Vietcong and North Vietnamese, attacked Delta Company consisting of barely 100 Australian soldiers in the rubber plantation of Long Tan, just a few kilometers away from the base, on August 18, 1966.

The large enemy force was intending to attack the Nui Dat Base itself, which they had blanketed with mortar fire the previous night, but had encountered this tiny force of Australian soldiers, which they thought puny and easy to dispose of on their way to their main target.

With nearly half of Delta Company's soldiers dead or wounded and running low on ammunition, the remaining Delta soldiers, under the command of Major Harry Smith, fought off repeated enemy assaults in a heroic stand that later was commemorated as Long Tan Day throughout Australia in the memory of all our fallen in that war.

Well-directed artillery fire and the arrival of our seven armoured personnel carriers with mounted Alpha Company soldiers late in the afternoon, under the command of another brave soldier, Captain Charles Mollison, helped save the day. We did not have air support because of the low clouds and heavy monsoonal rain.

Our convoy of seven armoured personnel carriers came to a halt on the edge of the rubber plantation while the monsoonal rain fell in buckets. As usual I was riding on top of the carrier because that gave a wide field of vision and because, in any case, I thought the safety of the steel walls inside was illusory. A rocket-propelled grenade, or RPG, easily breached them. Just in front of me, but below, rode the APC commander, a corporal and a New Zealander I believe.

To my surprise a cloud of enemy rose from the underbrush in front of my eyes, hundreds I thought. I jumped out of the APC after shouting "fix bayonets" to the two sections of my platoon inside the APC under the command of Lieutenant Peter Dinham, a Duntroon (elite Australian military college) graduate. I thought that given the enemy's proximity close quarters combat was inevitable.

As I testified to the Honors and Awards Tribunal in Maroochydore in March 2016, with more than one hundred and fifty people in attendance, I advanced towards the milling throng of Vietcong and North Vietnamese soldiers at a steady pace until I emptied the twenty-round magazine in my Self Loading 7.62 rifle with the bayonet sticking out the end. The enemy seemed confusedly shocked while I felled a number of them. They did return fire but it was panicky and relatively inoffensive. A couple of rocket-propelled grenades exploded against the trees without causing any damage among us.

My biggest fear was that they would roam around the APCs dropping hand grenades down the open hatches. That would have been a major military catastrophe, as well as a human disaster of course.

While I fumbled in my basic pouch to replace the magazine, I saw signs that the Vietcong might be recovering their composure and discipline. Bad news. Fortunately, one of the machine gunners in the platoon, Ronnie "Dread" Brett, had come out of the hatch and joined me. In all likelihood Ronnie saved my life. I did return the favor to him in the Battle of Bribie on February 17, 1967, when one of his legs was shredded by machine gun fire from the hip down and I took him to safety on my shoulders. He was evacuated by helicopter to Vung Tao's Military Hospital, then back to Australia. Sometime later we heard that he had committed suicide, joining a long list of ex-servicemen who chose the same exit.

The APC commander, armed with a heavy 50-caliber weapon, also opened fire. Then the rest of the platoon came out of the carrier and what had been a rout became a stampede. I had a lot of respect for the Vietcong and North Vietnamese fighting ability and discipline. I still do after all these years. But on that day those virtues failed them. I guess they were human after all.

We were able to break through to Delta Coy and help write a glorious episode in Australia's military history though it did not seem like that at the moment. Rather the opposite in fact.

Next morning, we swept through the battlefield, which had become a carnage. Hundreds of broken bodies were scattered everywhere. And, judging by the blood trails that we followed afterwards, many more hundreds, perhaps thousands, had been wounded.[1]

My actions in that battle would earn me a Medal for Gallantry fifty years later after a thorough investigation by the Australian Defence Honors and Awards Tribunal. The medal is equivalent to the American Silver Star or the British Military Medal. The medal was invested on myself by Australia's Governor General, Sir Peter Cosgrove, representing the Queen of England, on October 9, 2016. Ronnie Brett, a great soldier and wonderful lad, received a posthumous Mention in Despatches.

I had also been awarded a Mention in Despatches for another action a couple of months after Long Tan when I was acting platoon commander after our Lieutenant had been evacuated back to Australia with a serious bout of malaria. My platoon fought dozens of skirmishes and battles, the most serious being the Battle of Bribie in mid-February 1967, when my already depleted force of 22 men lost seven seriously wounded, leaving us as little more than a glorified section.[2]

Vietnam was a whole other story from Malaysia. Our enemies were Communists, certainly, but Vietnamese nationalists first, even Ho Chi Minh. Not only could they bring in supplies from the Soviet Union and China, but they moved forces from North Vietnam to Laos, Cambodia, and south along the Ho Chi Minh trail. They had the support of the majority of the people. Some of the South Vietnamese might disagree with me, but there is no way that the Vietcong could have survived in their country without popular support. We were supposedly "winning the hearts and minds" of the people, but how do you do that when you are a foreigner killing them?

In June of 1967, the Battalion's commanding officer, Lieutenant Colonel Colin Townsend, acting in conjunction with Company Commanders selected my platoon and myself to conduct the 6 RAR's last patrol of the Battalion's tour of duty. A video of that patrol, in which I end up drinking a glass of champagne with Colonel Townsend, is available on the Australian War Museum website that can be accessed through Google.

Here I should mention, perhaps as a mere curiosity, that I was part of a group of Australian NCOs posted to the American 9th Infantry Division on occasions during Operations Duck 1 and Duck 2 during December 1966 and January 1967. I have often used the term "training" to describe our task but the dim recesses of my foggy mind after half a century tell me it would be more accurate to say that we were liaison soldiers sent to work with our American friends and allies to ensure the smooth embedding of the Division in the Mekong River Delta.

My first impression of the Americans was that they were green as cucumbers, a fairly normal perception for someone who had served in Malaya for three years (our group also included the odd Korean War veteran) and who had already spent more than six months in Vietnam under almost continuous engagement.

The second impression was that our approach to war was different. We were business-like, cautious when needed, very professional, and, to put it in terms that may be understood, boringly British. The Americans on the other hand were intense and passionate as well as, unfortunately in my view, too impulsive.

Finally, the Americans were clearly divided by race or ethnicity. There were white soldiers, mainly from the South, Hispanics, and Blacks and relations between them, as far as one could see, were not so much unfriendly as nonexistent. Amazing to the eyes of Australians whose infantry platoons were more like intimate families where we all knew each other, shared our problems and occasional quarrels as well as our joys and hopes, and would remain mates forever. In short, our homogeneity trumped whatever differences may exist.

This tended to make the Americans less efficient, a pity because even a cursory glance at the roll call of Congressional Medals of Honor, America's highest award, shows patently that courage was not the preserve of a single group or race but spread equally among white, black, and brown.

Also, the officer class included mainly West Point graduates who, along with Brits graduating from Sandhurst or Australians from Duntroon, had all the attributes of generational blue bloods born with the right to rule. I guess it is not very different in the armed forces of other nationalities.

Then of course there was the thorny question of the American (or Australian) hierarchy's relations with the Vietnamese. In theory we had arrived in their country to save them from Communism. In practice Americans led and the South Vietnamese did as told.

All very difficult.

After our tour of duty some of my soldiers believed I had been instrumental in saving their lives. I was very proud of them and remain so to this day. Most of them were conscripts, wrenched from their comfortable lives to fight a war that did not make any sense to them in a country most of them had never even heard of.

I am still in touch with those of the soldiers in my platoon still alive. Some years ago, in a flight of fancy, I proposed making them honorary Basques, a proposal that attracted some laughs, but, I strongly suspect, delighted them. Some even travelled to the Basque Country just to see the birthplace of their platoon sergeant and sometime leader. I am aware of six of my Australians that are still alive. We have a battalion reunion about every two years when we meet and exchange our aches and pains. And often enough our memories.

We returned to Australia from Vietnam on board of an old aircraft carrier, the *HMAS Sydney*. Arantxa and Lorena were waiting for me at the Brisbane wharf. She had endured just over a year of separation and fear. Only when she heard on the radio that I had been decorated with an MID did she find out that I might have been in danger, because in all my letters I had insisted that nothing serious was happening.

The butcher in the Newmarket shopping centre and a few other people in the close neighborhood commented to her that she must be very proud of me. Pride is not exactly what she felt. We hugged each other for a long time until the baby in her arms became alarmed and started crying. She did not know her father.

I still had a few months to serve that were spent mainly training foreign forces in jungle warfare up north near Rockhampton in Shoalwater Bay.

Also, a man to whom I shall always owe a debt of gratitude, Mauree Sheehan, my old platoon commander in Malaya, visited us in our unit in Newmarket and insisted that I should accompany him to see the dean of the Faculty of Arts in the University of Queensland. The dean encouraged me to begin a Bachelor of Arts part-time, which I did. I found tertiary education a boon to my atrophied senses that helped me put aside the bitter sequels of war.

We try to romanticize war, but it is an entirely brutalizing and unwelcome development. I think that those of us who have seen war firsthand are all pacifists. I wish there was another way to solve our big problems. I remember going through the pockets of a young Vietcong that I had just killed in the mountains of Nui Din. I found a wallet and in it two photographs. One was of an elderly couple, probably his parents, and three younger boys, his brothers I suspect. The other was a picture of a raving beauty—his wife or girlfriend. I imagined they must have shared the same dream and plans as Arantxa and I. He also had a crucifix, so he was a Christian, a Catholic. And I thought to myself, "I shot him and his family will never know how he died. It could have been me that he shot instead, and he could have been looking at my picture of Arantxa and the new baby." We buried him in a shallow grave because we didn't have time to dig deeper; a few mangy dogs or wild pigs likely ate him.

Our return from Vietnam was not warmly welcomed by Australians in general, because the war and compulsory military service introduced in 1964 had been enormously unpopular from day one. So we largely kept quiet about our service and tried to resume an appearance of normality in a society where, as we were forced to hear on occasions, we were "baby killers."

I had not taken any holidays during my campaign in Vietnam because, before my departure, we had purchased a block of land in Ferny Hills, a new leafy suburb to the west of Brisbane, where we intended to build our first home in Australia, and I was keen on saving whatever I could for it.

The block of land was now ours and, after arranging a loan from the War Service Homes federal agency, we contracted a builder to construct a house with steel, not timber, props, and girders. It was a beautiful place with views into the far distant hills of Mount Glorious. We moved in in early 1968 to enjoy some peace and tranquility for the first time since our star-crossed wedding. We also bought a secondhand car, a Mini Morris.

Arantxa was pregnant again while I served my last few months in the Army, mainly training foreign soldiers in the art of jungle warfare in the Shoalwater Bay area near Rockhampton in Central Queensland. I was offered some inducements to remain, mainly a possible promotion to lieutenant after completing a course, but Arantxa had begged me never to leave her again to fend off the phantoms and ghosts of war on her own alone. She was right, of course.

After leaving the Army I got a pen-pushing job as a public servant in the Queensland Department of Immigration in Kangaroo Point where I earned a reasonable salary. One of the main events I recall was the last arrival of a batch of Spanish immigrants who were housed at Wacol, an old Air Force training camp near Brisbane. There were no Basques among them, and I acted as translator and logistics coordinator.

It was not a successful attempt to settle more Spaniards in Australia. Within the short space of less than a year more than 90 percent of them had returned to Spain. Of course, I continued to study part-time, attending evening classes, at Queensland University.

So, everything was set to live a comfortable and predictable life in a nice suburb free of any troubles or disturbances. Neighbors would gather ever so often to share a barbecue, have a few drinks, and talk about the universe. It was a typical Australian neighborhood in a typical Australian city living typical Australian lives.

Arantxa also seemed a lot more settled while Lorena, babbling only Spanish at this early stage (brought up by her mother who spoke no English and was absolutely reluctant to learn it though she eventually did), grew by leaps and bounds into a beautiful little girl.

Our second baby, Susan, was the prettiest infant in the world, but born with fatal internal problems that had to do with her aorta vein and heart. She died in Brisbane's Royal Children Hospital some three weeks after birth, a dreadful blow to both of us. Arantxa and I knew of no case in our respective families that had ever experienced anything like

Susan's problems, so we had no idea what had brought it all about and no one in Brisbane's medical fraternity had any explanations except that those things happened from time to time.

It was only years later, when hearing of similar problems about Vietnam veterans, that I learned about the colossal damage done by Agent Orange, a defoliant, used extravagantly in Vietnam. It was then that we could begin to understand this and other health problems associated with Dioxin, a lethal byproduct of the defoliant. No Vietnam veteran in Australia was ever compensated by Monsanto, the American producer of Agent Orange. And the Australian Federal Government was equally non-committal when it came to acknowledging its effects, including higher rates of death by cancer among veterans. That remains the case to this day.

A handful of months went by when I came across a newspaper ad in the local *Brisbane Courier-Mail*, a newspaper, seeking people to serve as patrol officers in Papua New Guinea, then an Australian colony (though never called by that name—Australian administered territories sounded nicer). The job appealed to me and so did the pay, about double what I earned in the Department of Immigration.

I applied after discussing it with my wife and had to sit for an exam at Enoggera Army Base, my old fiefdom, which was exactly the same as I would have had to take for a promotion to the officer class in the Army. I passed with flying colours. I was then required to attend a course at the Australian School of Pacific Administration (ASOPA) in Mossman, a classy suburb of Sydney, before being posted to PNG.

My 16 classmates were all ex-Army and about my age. After completion of the course and a few other requirements we became commissioned police officers (only time I have been an officer and a gentleman) and, as well, had the responsibilities of magistrates when dealing with local issues in our respective postings.

By then Arantxa was pregnant again. I flew to Port Moresby, PNG's capital, some three weeks before she gave birth to our daughter Elena, this time without problems. She was taken to the hospital by one of our friendly neighbors, Gary Bowden, who, together with his wife Lorraine, also looked after Lorena for a few days until my wife returned from the hospital. Babies had to be four or five weeks old before being allowed to fly, so I did not see my family for all that time.

They came from Brisbane to Port Moresby where they changed planes to fly to Madang on the north coast and the administrative centre of the district of the same name where I waited for them. Next day we flew in a single engine plane to Saidor, the patrol post that serviced a large area known locally as the Rai Coast. Our new house was an elevated bungalow with some basic furniture that included a kerosene fridge and a wood-fired oven. We employed a domestic servant, a local girl who did a great job throughout her time with us, a couple of years. Our gardeners, to call them something, were prisoners—*calabus* [*calaboose*] *men*—serving various sentences for crimes ranging from theft to murder.

The man in charge in Saidor was an assistant district commissioner, George Bailey, an Englishman married to Beverly, an Australian lady. He was answerable to the district commissioner in Madang. There were three patrol officers in the post, including myself. The detachment of native police consisted of about nine or ten men led by a sergeant.

The job of a patrol officer consisted mainly of keeping the peace among tribes that had been at war with each other for thousands of years, while bringing them at least the beginning of something that could be called modern services such as basic health and primary education for at least a few children, those living close to Saidor. The teacher was an Italian married to an Australian.

We took long patrols to the interior of the country, often exploratory journeys into unknown territory, accompanied by dozens of bearers and always a detachment of native police armed with .303 rifles from WWII. The patrols, lasting anything from two to four weeks, were the most essential part of our administration in the wild country. Pidgin English, or Neo-Melanesian as it was pedantically called, became the common language.

It would take a book to describe my own experiences in that savage and beautiful land which enamored me. However, three or four events may suffice as examples. One was a patrol I led up the Warup River in the Finisterre Mountains late in July of 1969, just as Armstrong and Aldrin landed on the moon. The patrol made contact with 92 previously uncontacted indigenous people. It was one of the few times when I took a handgun with me and the police accompanying me actually had fully loaded magazines which, fortunately, we did not need to use.

The contact or negotiations in a jungle clearing, using a *Tanimtok* or translator, took about three days. Essentially, they consisted of exchanging gifts such as salt, knives, mirrors, and small steel axes in return for their peaceful acceptance of the new order, which had descended upon them with no warning and about whose existence they were fully aware, although they had avoided it until now.

Another time, deep in the mountains to the south, I came across a case that needed a compromise between my western values and education and local traditions. A young girl, probably all of 13 or 14, had fallen in love with a young man, but had also been sold to the tribal elder, a toothless old dwarf who had several other wives. The girl told me in Pidgin that if she was forced to comply with tribal law then: *"baimi getap dispela diwai nau brukim eskin bilong mi"* (I'll get up that tree and throw myself down to my death), a common enough form of suicide in PNG.

I consulted with my police, particularly with Kombi, a tall senior constable from the Sepik region whom I had earlier recommended for a bravery award after saving a couple of carriers from drowning in a wild river in the Nankina Valley. I told him I did not want to break the village's customary law, but could not tolerate the suicide of a young girl. They concurred. So, the girl and her boyfriend came with me to Saidor to avoid the inevitable punishment. Unfortunately, violence between the boy's family and the tribal elder broke out, causing five or six deaths and necessitating another patrol to reestablish order in the place.

Also, in my fairly frequent patrols to a place called Tapen, about 1,500 meters high above sea level, I met a couple of German Lutheran missionaries living in a mission-built bungalow on top of a hillock overlooking the Church. They were the nicest people anyone could wish to meet and I always stayed with them instead of the usual *haus kiap* (a shack with a straw roof) which all villages had for visiting patrol officers. They always met me as if, somehow, I had arrived to protect them from harm.

Their problem was that they were entirely unsuited to their environment. He would have made a top parish priest anywhere in northern Germany, and his wife, without doubt, would have helped the community with her generous heart. But here they were completely out of place and the only times they left their home was to administer their Christian rites to their less than enthusiastic congregation in the church.

Further, *Sanguma*, a dreadful type of sorcery responsible for more deaths in PNG than malaria or any other tropical disease, reigned supreme in Tapen. They could not name the sorcerer who I would have arrested and brought to trial (by me) in Saidor because no one would tell them (or me) who it was. Fear does that sort of thing.

One night when I was visiting, we heard a heartbreaking and very loud scream coming from a hut in the village. I rushed there thinking someone may have been hurt, but all I saw was a group of natives standing in front of the hut. Inside a man was still screaming. I entered and he, middle-aged and squatting terrified on the wooden floor, pointed to the straw roof outside. A small bamboo cane was hanging there. In the small tube I found some feces mixed with a tuft of hair that, the witnesses insisted, belonged to the screaming wreck of a man on the floor of the hut. He had been cursed and knew he would die shortly. That is what happened quite soon thereafter. (Incidentally, it occurred to me more than once in that amazing land, if a human mind is capable of killing, may it not be capable of other miracles, such as curing a disease?)

A couple of years later I learnt that the missionary's wife, an enormously good-hearted woman, had slit her wrists and needed evacuation by a monoplane to Lae, a larger centre in the east. The information was secondhand and I had no way to verify it. Nor could I find out what became of these two good people afterwards.

Finally, while talking about questions of faith I also met and established good relations with a native elder named Yali, the creator of the Cargo Cult in the Rai Coast that then spread to other parts of PNG. Yali had helped Australian troops against the Japanese invaders during WWII and had received high praise for his efforts. During those years he saw planes dropping supplies by parachute, which gave him the idea that Europeans (as white people were called) had the magical powers to bring in all sorts of valuable goods, cargo, from the skies. It all had to do with witchcraft and, of course, we kept our magic powers to ourselves.

After the war, Yali promoted those ideas and acquired quite a following. I jailed his right-hand man, Dui, after a violent episode in a nearby village. While in the *calabus*, Dui's first duty in the mornings was to pump water by hand from the tank under our bungalow to a small container on the roof that we then used to shower.

Papua New Guinea's splendor was a savior for me after my war experiences in Southeast Asia and I felt I could have gone on there forever. The kids grew up in utter and complete freedom, Arantxa had a colonial experience that would shortly become extinct and is unrepeatable today, and we had everything we wanted at our fingertips, including fresh lobsters that native fishermen practically picked up from the rocks on the sea, and wine brought by boat.

However, I knew we were living in a bubble during a time of rapid global change whose influences would affect the future of this country, as well as, of course, our own future. My studies through Queensland University towards a Bachelor of Arts went smoothly, mainly because the university behaved extraordinarily well and sent me the books I needed to complete my essays and assignments. I now needed to concentrate on what my future career would be because my kids were rapidly approaching school age and Arantxa and I would need some predictability to plan ahead.

In Madang's colonial circles, mainly made up of administrators, planters, and business people, the accepted doctrine was that nothing would change in the short to medium term. The country needed at least another generation, or probably two generations, to reach a stage when it could become a self-governing or independent nation.

Wishful thinking, I believed, though I agreed that Papuans and New Guineans were nowhere near the point where they could manage their own affairs. Much of the country remained unexplored, the infrastructure was pitifully poor (in Saidor for example we had no more than 10 kilometers of dirt tracks fit for vehicles), formal education was practically nonexistent in most of the country, as was health care. But for the intervention of *kiaps* (their name for us patrol officers), tribal war would have remained endemic.

Outside factors were at work, however, which took no account of those obstacles to an immediate withdrawal of Australians, the main being purely ideological—colonial rule was deplorable and it should be ended. Stuff the consequences.

In December 1972 Australians elected a Federal Labor Government under Prime Minister Gough Whitlam, some of whose first decisions were to withdraw the remaining Australian troops from Vietnam, end conscription, and grant Papua New Guinea independence by 1975.

I decided on a teaching career to ensure the family's future. It was nowhere near as attractive or exotic as being a patrol officer, but Australia needed teachers—not *kiaps*.

The Commonwealth Teaching Service, a federal agency, granted me a scholarship to obtain a Diploma of Education with the University of Queensland after I completed my Bachelor of Arts. The condition was that I would then accept a posting in a secondary school in Papua New Guinea. That suited me fine and we moved back to our home in Brisbane for the time it would take—one year.

In 1973, with a BA, Dip.Ed behind my name, I was posted to Aitape, an important settlement on the northern coast of New Guinea. I taught there for a year in a secondary boarding school where pupils from the Sepik Region as well as from as far away as Telefomin, in the Star Mountains of the country's centre, attended.

While in Aitape my wife and I were lucky to meet an extraordinary couple, Rob and Meg Parer, who ran a big copra plantation and various businesses. The Parer dynasty in Australia has a remarkable history stretching back to the gold rushes in the 1850s, when they came from Spain originally, and have made an extraordinary contribution to Australia and to PNG. Meg claimed to descend from King Bruce of Ireland.

For some three years I had been planning with Arantxa a crossing of Papua New Guinea across its widest point along the border with Iran Jaya, now West Papua, a part of Indonesia. It would be the first crossing from north to south and the very first by a solo explorer. In 1928/29, two Australian patrol officers, with the full backing of the Australian Government and accompanied by a strong detachment of native police, succeeded in their second attempt to cross the country from south to north. Both men were dead within a year of completing their feat. The physical consequences were dire.

In 1961, an American, Michael Rockefeller, an heir of the Rockefeller fortune, organized an expedition starting in the then Dutch-controlled west of PNG. But the expedition ended in disaster after Rockefeller was killed by members of the Asman, or perhaps Tugeri, tribe. They were headhunters and he was probably eaten. Cannibalism was common in the country. His body was never found and the expedition aborted.

I had long wanted to enter the region dominated by the Star Mountains to contact tribes and groups with no previous history of contact with Europeans to ask them about their migratory habits. This had to do with my belief that Man's origin is probably multiregional and that the Out-of-Africa theory, still very much the orthodoxy, is bunkum.[3]

Also, a romantic holdover of my Basque ancestry told me that it would be fitting for a Basque to conduct an expedition across the last remaining bit of unexplored territory in the South Pacific. After all, Basques had been prominent in opening up the South Seas nearly five hundred years earlier, from Elcano to Urdaneta (in my opinion the best navigator of all times), to Legazpi and Bonaeche and Retez (who had named New Guinea in 1534). They ensured that the Pacific Ocean was also known as the Spanish Lake for nearly two hundred years.

I could get no financial backing at all. Further, the administration in Port Moresby was dead set against my proposal and insisted on a large deposit to finance my possible rescue, a demand that I ignored on the basis that once I entered the forbidden land no one could possibly stop me. The sole people who helped were Rob and Meg Parer who gifted me some much-needed supplies. Also, the only time of the year I could complete the expedition was December 1973 and January 1974, to coincide with school holidays in Australia. These were the two worst monsoon months when all the rivers and creeks become huge obstacles.

The story is told in detail in my book, *A Trip to the Stone Age*,[4] and I won't repeat it here. I am still very much astonished that I was not killed in my endeavor. Lady Luck—and solely Lady Luck—was responsible for bringing me back to civilization.

Arantxa and our two daughters had flown to Brisbane in late November, where they stayed with our old friends, Gary and Lorraine, because our house on the other side of the street had been rented. They met me at the Brisbane airport when I arrived in late January 1974 after my two-month expedition. We stayed at Gary and Lorraine's place that night. Next morning the four of us flew to Darwin, the Northern Territory's capital, to begin a sojourn of 23 years.

In Darwin I had a teaching post awaiting me at Nightlife High School, in the northern suburbs. Arantxa did not like what she saw, a tumble-down hardscrabble sort of town, she thought, of about 45,000 people set in the hard tropics. She gave me three months to find a job elsewhere.

We stayed at a motel while I reported to the Department of Education that, shortly, assigned us to a Government lodging in Stuart Park, not far from the centre of town. In those days everything was owned by the Government in Darwin, meaning Federal Government, and private housing was simply not available. I also borrowed some money to buy a secondhand small Volkswagen.

It was not difficult moving our few belongings to our new house, an elevated large dwelling with three bedrooms, one bathroom, and the laundry on the ground floor. The windows were all louvered as they had been in New Guinea. It was a lovely place.

Much to my surprise I had very much enjoyed teaching in Aitape and now it was more of the same, but with renewed vigor. The classes in Nightcliff consisted of a motley crew of youngsters from everywhere. It was with pleasure that I shared their restlessness and, too often, their exuberant behavior.

Also, I accepted a part-time job as a history tutor in the Darwin Community College at Casuarina, also in the northern suburbs, to try and recover the money recklessly spent in my expedition across PNG and, now, in the purchase of a car. The college was the only tertiary institution in the entire Northern Territory and my classes consisted of adults studying by correspondence with a southern university or trying to complete their Grade 12 so they could begin tertiary studies. They were invariably keen as mustard.

And that applied to the population of Darwin, a vibrant mix of youth and enthusiasm. We would meet with friends Fridays after work at the beer garden in Nightcliff Pub on Arafura's seashore to share a few beers and discuss the wide horizons opening up on this last Australian frontier. For us, anything was possible. Several decades later I read a piece in *The Economist*, a much-respected newspaper based in London (but with a worldwide readership), that early settlers in the Northern Territory consisted of "misfits and fortune seekers." An apt description that immediately consigned my family and myself to the ranks of misfits.

This early impact that the Territory had on me never vanished and to this day it remains in my heart.

By early December of that year, through a combination of hard work and thrift, we had enough money to plan a holiday in Spain. We flew to Heathrow in London where we hired a car for six weeks in Europe and, after a night stay in a bed-and-breakfast in Dover, we crossed the Channel to Calais in France and drove leisurely to San Sebastián where we stayed with my mother. It was a trip we would repeat every couple of years.

On Christmas Day after an extended lunch at home, a neighbor knocked on the door and asked us to turn on the TV. It had news that might concern us. It sure did. The lead story was of a terrible cyclone, Tracy, that had devastated Darwin leaving dozens of people dead and many more injured. Most of the town had been turned into rubble.

Arantxa let out a small cry and adjourned to the bathroom. I think she was sick. The kids did not quite understand the extent of the disaster—just as well.

I rang the Australian Embassy in Madrid who informed me that all flights to Darwin had been cancelled and that we would have to change our return tickets to Sydney. From there, the kind person at the other end advised me to travel to Canberra to get in touch with the Commonwealth Teaching Service in the suburb of Woden.

We left immediately after changing our scheduled flights in a travel agency. It had been one of the most amazingly beautiful holidays we had ever had. Arantxa's father had passed away while we were in PNG, but her mother was very much alive and well, as were her brothers who this time seemed to welcome me.

We landed in Sydney, this would have been the first week of January, a holiday month in Australia much as is August in Europe, rented a car, and drove directly to Canberra, nearly three hundred kilometers to the southeast, where we found a cheap motel to stay for a few days until I sorted out my future.

The Department of Education, no longer the Commonwealth Teaching Service, was sympathetic to our plight and offered me an office job that I rejected because I was keen to get back to Darwin. Once again, I guess to Arantxa's despair though she never said a thing, I was disregarding a well-paid plum job in a comfortable and civilized environment to explore the remote corners of the Top End and its, in my view, endless possibilities. Sheer insanity.

Alice Springs, the Territory's second largest town with about 12,000 people in central Australia, had not been affected by Darwin's catastrophe so I had no trouble booking myself a flight the next day. After arrival I immediately got in touch with the Department of Education in the small town to tell them I wished to get back to Darwin. No trouble, I was told, in fact they needed teachers badly up there for the beginning of the school year, hopefully in the first or second week of February. Myself, along with a dozen or so other people, all men, were bundled into an Air Force supply plane to Darwin. Arantxa and the girls stayed behind at the motel in Canberra to wait for news.

After landing I could not recognize any landmarks. Wherever I looked from Berrimah Airport there was utter devastation, just as if a nuclear bomb had been dropped on Darwin. I was given a lift to our place at Stuart Park, which was still standing, though the two rooms in one of the wings had been blown away and a tree trunk poked into our lounge and kitchen. Most of our belongings were lost with the surprising exception of a few PNG memories that I kept apart in a safe metal container. Among them was the yellowing diary of my expedition across PNG. It would be the source for the book I published later, in 2010, about the experience.

The car had been peppered by thousands of what appeared to be shotgun pellets and had practically lost its blue paint. But I was absolutely thrilled when the motor whirred into life as soon as I turned the key.

I drove to the centre to see if I could get information from the Department of Education about what I could do next. Nightcliff High School was gone, as indeed was our marvelous pub where we gathered with friends on Friday afternoons. However, I would be welcome to begin the school year at Casuarina High, also in the northern suburbs.

Next, I went to the post office where I could use a phone to call Arantxa and inform her of what was happening. I told her that I thought I could arrange their return in a few days. The Department of Education paid their flight. By then I'd removed the tree trunk, cleaned up what remained of the house, placed a mattress in the living room where Arantxa and I would sleep, and prepared the sole remaining bedroom for the two girls. Also, I was able to reestablish the running water, and, with the help of a couple of Army experts (sent to Darwin to help with the recovery and who had provided me with the mattress), got one electrical connection from the ground up to the kitchen though we did not start cooking for some weeks.

Those of us returning to Darwin or who had not been evacuated in the days following the cyclone were fed at various public messes in still-standing high schools, in our case nearby Darwin High School. I always ensured that a bottle of red wine was well ensconced under my arm when queueing for our meals.

With all the frenetic preparations for the family's arrival concluded, I reported to the community college where a remarkable academic and head of Humanities, Ted Milliken, some years older than myself but keeping fit and well, welcomed me into my old part-time job. Most lecturers had fled to greener and safer pastures. Their disappearance opened up an opportunity for me.

By the end of 1975, I left the Department of Education to take up my appointment as a full-time lecturer in the faculty of Community Studies, even though my academic qualifications were still short of what was demanded, usually a PhD or at least a Masters' degree.

Also, we had to leave our Stuart Park home that was then bulldozed and rebuilt for someone else. We moved to a newly built Government house in a large block of land at Wulagi, a brand-new suburb in the north. We added a pool and a great garden to the place that, eventually, after the Northern Territory achieved self-Government on July 1, 1978, and the newly elected Legislative Assembly introduced a bill making private housing the norm, we purchased.

By then I was completing my Master of Arts with the University of Queensland and had enrolled with the University of New England in Armidale for a Master of Education. The thesis for my MA was the emergence of the Labor Movement in the Northern Territory in the early twentieth century. It was later published as my first publication.[5] My MEd (Honors) thesis was on the role of bilingual education in Aboriginal schools, something that I was very much in favor of when I started my Masters but ended up against after examining in detail the evidence.

By 1981/82, I had two Masters, a Bachelor of Arts, and Bachelor of Education Studies. I was head of the Department of Community Studies (a position that became dean of Faculty after the Community College became Charles Darwin University in the late 1980s), a long way from my unforgettable days in Outback Queensland with old Dutchy.

A few other things were happening at the speed of light. The first is that Arantxa was happy and enjoying life while our two girls had started school and made friends quickly. Second was my publication of an article in 1976 in the local newspaper, *The Northern Territory News*, about my strange theories on the origins of humans. It attracted widespread derision and at least a TV interview where I was made a fool of, as well as a humorous radio sketch. None of those things made me change my views at all nor did I retract or express any regrets. Basque stubbornness.

The upside was that the article had been widely read, and newspaper managing editors kind of like that. In this case the managing editor was a crusading New Zealander, John Hogan, a former rugby player with whom I would enjoy many good times over the next few years. John offered me a column in the Saturday edition of the paper to comment on Territory politics, economics, social issues—or any topic that tickled my fancy. My column, regarded as controversial by some, became a hit.

After a few years in Darwin there was an unwritten convention with Arantxa that we would alternate holidays in Europe every two years with my preferred vocation, exploring recondite corners of the Northern Territory sometimes with the help of Conservation Commission (now Parks and Wildlife) rangers and others by myself. This went on for a decade and a half. Whenever I entered the wild realm of practically unknown regions of the Territory I received the immense gift of coming into contact with awesome beauty, unique flora and fauna, and a fascinating historical legacy in the form of rock art and other remnants found in large middens of an astonishing Aboriginal culture, the oldest continuous culture in the history of humanity.

From Arnhem Land in the north to the angry hillocks of the MacDonnell ranges east and west of Alice Springs (in ancient times taller than the Himalayas) and to Ayers Rock and the Olgas in the south, the country spoke to me of billions of years of history. Arnhem Land particularly was to me a place of absolute wonder, not just for its natural beauty but because—judging by the sumptuous and abundant rock art—it was probably the home of the most advanced civilization in the world some forty thousand years ago. This is not balderdash or a flight of fancy but a statement based on the immense archaeological evidence found in that recondite corner of the world. The evidence is resumed in one word: Art.

It reflects two things: One was knowledge of techniques and paint-like substances to print on rocks images that would last tens of thousands of years (no one really knows exactly how many). The other was that the inhabitants of this lucky region lacked nothing. They certainly had plenty of sustenance in the form of edible bush food, fish, game that they chased with boomerangs, a superb aerodynamic tool/weapon almost certainly originated from Arnhem, and peace. Without peace and the security that it brought they would not have been able to leave their majestic legacy.

The result of my roaming was a book, *Explore Australia's Northern Territory*, commissioned by an imposing public servant and head of the Conservation Commission at the time, Col Fuller, now retired and still one of my closest friends.[6]

The book sold six printings. The various editions had an introduction by two remarkable men, Les Hiddins, a former Army Major who created the so-called *Bush Tucker* TV series, one of the most successful series in the history of Australian television. Les had been sent to my platoon in Vietnam in March 1967 as reinforcement after our bloodbath in the Battle of Bribie on February 17. He went on to rise to major and obtain a Science degree at James Cook University of Townsville.

The other man was Harry Butler, also the central figure of a television program aimed at raising awareness of environmental issues in Australia. Harry and I walked part of the great Larapinta Trail in central Australia together and were joined by Col Fuller. In his introduction Harry remarks that his bond with myself was cemented by our joint fascination with the haunting beauty that surrounded us.

I also met an incredible Aboriginal woman, Marjorie Harris, who came to see me because she had been told I might be able to help her put together a short book about her experiences as a member of the stolen generation, which referred to tens of thousands of Aboriginal children abducted by the police from their parents to be placed under the care of state or, more often, religious agencies, particularly Catholic Institutions, for their education and upbringing.

The policy was introduced between 1906 and 1910 as the result of a firm belief among Australian authorities that full-blood Aborigines were doomed to extinction after a catastrophic decline in population following the European settlement. It was not repealed until 1969 although, in the Territory, it was implemented for a little while longer. It applied mainly to so-called half-castes (mixed-blood Aborigines).

Marjorie's story was heartbreaking, as indeed was that of every other child forced to undergo that experience. Her tribe was in the Nitmiluk Cattle Station in Central Australia and one day a couple of policemen turned up and took her away. Her story was self-published by a printer in Palmerston, near Darwin.[7] I was not paid to do the job.

Finally, during this period I became one of the founders and first president (1979–1985) of the Northern Territory Vietnam Veterans Association, a fledgling organization of about six or seven members initially. We got together to try and help our fellow veterans shamefully neglected by successive Australian Governments.

You can't give a nineteen-year-old a gun and have him kill people without consequences, and those were quite visible after they returned home except that no one (certainly no one in authority) seemed keen to look, much less examine and take remedies. Our home became the *de facto* Vietnam veterans' refuge in Darwin. The police would call me when they had a problem. One time a young veteran sequestered himself in a petrol station and fired a few random shots from his .22 gun. He was asleep when I got to him and he ended up working as a gardener at Darwin Community College. Another call was when a man threatened to jump off the balcony of his room in the Travel Lodge. I broke down the door and convinced him to come out. Then there was the midnight call from the manager of the Sports Club in Nightcliff. He had a wild veteran smashing beer bottles and threatening everyone. I went there and got a bottle of rum from the bar. We drank together and talked until five or six in the morning. He came home with me and stayed in our house for the next two weeks, when he drifted off to Western Australia where he came from.

I picked up others from the streets or from the long grass (called *kunai*) where drunks and derelicts slept and brought them home to be cared for by Arantxa, who did all of the work for which I would be awarded an Order of Australia Medal in 2013.

We also lobbied the Federal Government strenuously to establish a branch of the Department of Veterans Affairs in Darwin, something that finally came about in the early 1990s, as well as purchasing a rundown house in Bagot Road which we turned into a refuge named Coral House. Today, it serves for veterans of the Iraq and Afghanistan wars.

We were able to establish August 18 as Long Tan Day to commemorate our fallen in Vietnam. The day became a national institution in the coming years. A man who provided invaluable help making Long Tan a national observance was Tim Fischer, himself a Vietnam Veteran and then leader of the Country Party (now National Party) and deputy prime minister of Australia. Tim used to fly to Darwin to meet with his Country Liberal Party colleagues and lent us enormous moral support in our endeavor. In the process he and I became good friends.

The last time I remember meeting him was in a pub in the Mall in Alice Springs with Arantxa and Tim's wife. We ate the best American spare ribs I have ever tasted washed down by Tim and me with plenty of beer and red wine, all loudly relished under the censorious looks of our wives. After his political career Tim was appointed Australian ambassador to the Vatican where he did a very competent job indeed.

In 1983 my career took yet another turn when the chief minister of the Northern Territory, Paul Everingham of the Country Liberal Party, asked me to take a year or so off from the Community College to become his speechwriter. Paul was an enormously successful politician who had steered the Territory into self-Government in 1978, and, along with his colleagues and a bunch of dedicated public servants, was responsible for the longest period of prosperity in the turbulent and short history of this last outpost of civilization. Measures such as the one-stop-shop to establish a business, thus doing away with layers of bureaucracy, 24 hours shopping, breaking the monopoly of lawyers to negotiate buying and selling real estate, and many others led to substantial improvements in productivity and thus economic growth. I accepted and had an interesting time among politicians who I learnt to respect over the year or so that my appointment lasted before, once again, moving to greener pastures.

In 1985 John Hogan founded the *Sunday Territorian* under the leadership of Gary Shipway, a brilliant editor, and myself as the senior political reporter and editorial writer. Gary and I worked together for nearly ten years without a single quarrel or major disagreement—a rare thing. I used to call him Shipwreck because of his less than orderly private life, but that is another story.

The *Sunday Territorian* became instantly popular with readers mainly because it was irreverent, profane, and bold, while always reflecting faithfully issues of concern to Territorians.

As well as reporting the news, I wrote the seventh day editorials and various comment pieces. Of course, many of my opinions were challenged and, in a society as varied, rough and tumble, young and often undisciplined as the Territory's the challenges were sometimes expressed with an invitation to share some bare knuckles. One incident remains in my mind.

In 1987 I received a letter from Galawrruy Yunupingu, an Aboriginal leader of the Northern Land Council (NLC) and member of the Gumatj, the dominant tribe of Arnhem. The NLC was one of three land councils in the Northern Territory, the other two being the Tiwi Land Council, in charge of administering the two Tiwi Islands of Bathurst and Melville about 100 kilometers north of Darwin, and the Central Land Council, in charge of the vast sprawl of central Australia with Alice Springs as its most important town. The NLC was a very important agency in charge of administering Aboriginal affairs in the Top End.

Galawrruy, named the Australian of the Year on January 26, 1978, Australia Day, didn't like some of my opinions, arguing that welfare kills people just as effectively as guns. I maintained that if the indigenous people truly wanted to recover their lost dignity and pride they needed to learn to take care of themselves rather than rely on handouts. I also said that land rights should eventually be transformed into private property rights. He didn't like any of that.

One day, during a gathering at his rambling seaside house in Arnhem, probably influenced by one too many sips, he threatened to have me killed. The silly old bugger even put out a bounty of A$3,000 on me, an amount that struck me as derisive. Two police came to see me in the newsroom to ask me how I intended to proceed? I told them not to worry because I would handle this problem myself. I went to meet Galawrruy and we had a chat. He denied that he wanted me dead saying that all he sought was "to straighten you out." I replied that what he had meant was to have me stiff and convinced him that killing me was not such a good idea. I also told him that if anyone in my family got hurt I would make him pay personally. I regarded it as a minor incident. That sort of thing happened all the time in the Northern Territory.

The newspaper became something of a phenomenon, in fact prompting a visit by our owner, Rupert Murdoch, with whom I had a photo taken before adjourning to a raucous dinner at a Greek restaurant on Cavanagh Street. In attendance were Shipwreck, John Hogan, and the then chief minister, Steve Hatton. Those were golden years for us. Our home became a gathering centre for politicians, business people, academics, and many others to debate noisily all sorts of things of importance to the Northern Territory, often well into the night and even into the next morning.

In 1988 or 1989 I was sent to Bougainville Island in Papua, New Guinea, as the foreign correspondent of News Corps to cover a rebellion of native islanders against the Rio Tinto–owned mine of Panguna, one of the largest copper deposits in the world. The spills from the mine's tailings had ruined the lives of thousands of small farmers who had depended upon their holdings for many generations. The uprising eventually claimed about 20,000 lives until it was settled when the rebels negotiated a peace deal with the PNG Government. Panguna remains shut down.

I was in Bougainville for about three weeks until the PNG Government threw me out. It didn't like my coverage. I was put on a plane and sent back to Australia.

Shortly after I started writing for the daily *Northern Territory News*, as well as for the *Sunday Territorian*, hard work but well remunerated. In addition to my previous job writing editorials and columns, I contributed a short piece at least once a week to the prestigious national newspaper—*The Australian*.

In 1991, I was commissioned to write an account of the bombing of Darwin by Marshall Perron, then chief minister. On February 18, 1942, 128 Japanese aircraft attacked the town, killing 233 and wounding 250, as well as causing widespread destruction. Marshall wanted the book published in time to commemorate the next year's 50th anniversary of the bombing. With some inestimable help from experts in the field, including amateur historians, I put together a book, *The Northern Territory at War 1939–1945*,[8] that attracted very positive reviews in various southern newspapers.

Arantxa and I also received visits from the Spanish Ambassador in Canberra, Jose Luis Pardo, and his Basque wife from San Sebastián. We became good friends and Jose Luis ushered a visit by then Prince Felipe, now King Felipe VI, to Darwin in 1990 (if my memory serves me right) where we shared a splendid lunch in the huge bungalow overlooking Darwin Harbour that was the residence of the Territory's administrator, the Honorable James Muirhead (the term administrator means that his functions were much the same as those of governors in the states; but the Northern Territory was a self-governing region, not yet a state, hence the change in terminology). I presented a copy of my book *Explore the Northern Territory* to Prince Felipe. I am not sure that he has had the time to read it. In any case I thought he was an impressive, highly educated, and intelligent young man. He was the best ambassador that Spain could have sent to our wild frontier.

Arantxa and I went back to the Basque Country several times. The first trip was in 1970 to see relatives and revisit our roots while introducing our tiny daughters to them. The next one was in December of 1974 when we missed Cyclone Tracy. In 1977 we went back and bought a block of land in Arizkun (Navarra) in the Valley of Baztan. We planned to build a cottage there and even had the plans drawn up.

As usual, we landed in London and rented a car for the duration of our visit. As we approached the Pyrenees I was overwhelmed with emotion and said: "Look at my mountains." Little Lorena sitting in the back of the car replied: "Well, the Australian mountains are my mountains." Naturally she was excommunicated on the spot. Today she even likes cricket; obviously a lost cause.

In 1977 or 78 we pondered whether we should move to Arizkun, but then Arantxa had a change of heart. She thought it would be too traumatic for the girls. She sensed better than I that they were fundamentally Australians. So was I except that I thought that Arantxa deserved what she had always hankered for, a life in the Basque Country.

In 1979 we bought another block of land in Zaldibia [Gipuzkoa] jointly with one of Arantxa's brothers, Juan Ignacio, and his wife Carmina. We thought we might build on it and move there in our retirement one day.

I have lived away from the Basque Country since 1954 and today I think of myself as Australian, although I have never renounced, and never will, my Basque roots. Those entrenched feelings about my roots have led me to follow the politics of the Basque Country with interest over the years, including of course the emergence and history of ETA, the Basque separatist terrorist organization responsible for the fracturing of Basque society and setting the region's economy back at least a generation.

This demands a short reflexion that should begin by stating the obvious: A Basque migrant of my generation always took with him an idealized image of the Basque Country as it was in the early 1950s. The image perdured and nothing could shake it. We did not take into account the inevitable changes that would occur in the years since. ETA was part of those unwelcome changes.

The thing that strikes me most to this day is that I could never debate rationally either ETA or the secessionist policies pursued by an important part of the Basque population. Whenever the topic came up, it triggered an explosion of fervor and zeal that precluded any kind of objective argument. This I found puzzling and unsettling.

It was impossible, for example, to say that ETA's story of rampaging murders damaged the reputation of Basques overseas, such as myself. We had always been regarded as hard working, honest, and reliable people, but ETA put a serious dent in that reputation. Of course my relatives and acquaintances were aware of my four years of war in Southeast Asia and argued, with some twisted logic, I admit, that maybe I should be the last person to criticize ETA's tactics.

And it was just as hard not to suggest that we Basques had been an essential factor in Spain's history, particularly its imperial past, or the bloody Carlist Wars of the nineteenth century with Basques as main participants. And so on. Whenever I rejected the exclusivist philosophy that was the foundation stone of Basque nationalism for an important segment of the population, I received a spray of harshly felt abuse. But I know of no other nation or society that has prospered and become a haven of human rights and democracy by excluding those who do not share its race, ethnicity, genome, or DNA.

Another bone of contention was that I never shied away from expressing my support for the Basque Nationalist Party (*Partido Nacionalista Vasco* or PNV) for its moderation which, particularly in these more recent times of rampant extreme populism of the right and left, is even more gratifying. Those views were peculiarly unwelcome among the more radical elements in our midst that blamed the oppressive policies of the Spanish Government for the violence. There was some undeniable truth in that, too.

As always, there are two sides to the coin and I seemed to miss both during my visits. In short, those were unpleasant experiences and I always longed to return to the vast oasis of peace and beauty of the Northern Territory.

But enough of that.

By the mid-1990s, Arantxa was beginning to feel unwell probably as a result of her long exposure to the tropics. The oppressive heat of the monsoon season was affecting her badly. We took two or three weeks off and flew to the island of Tasmania in the south, just for a driving holiday, a change of climate, and some rest.

While touring the beautiful island we came upon a little village on the east coast, Bicheno, where some waterfront land was up for sale at throwaway prices. We ended up purchasing a lot of some 16,000 square meters (close to four acres if my arithmetic is right) where we built a house. The climate was, of course, a great deal cooler than Darwin's and Bicheno was a peaceful retreat where people seemed, and were, nice and friendly. We decided that this was our future home and we sold our properties in the Basque Country to bring the money to Australia and build a kind of retirement buffer.

Our daughters were married by then and we had a granddaughter, Amaya, in Alice Springs. They were off our hands and so we were free to choose where to retire and perhaps, with some luck, begin to live a period of tranquil serenity after all the tumbles in our lives.

Alas, it was not to be. To be sure, the beginnings were auspicious. With our neighbours, the closest half a kilometer away, we formed what we called The First Settlers Club, which consisted of convivial get-togethers and exploratory walks into the hills around and beyond. I also enjoyed underwater fishing with the help of a snorkel and spear, as well as a wetsuit to cope with the cold water. We never lacked fresh fish and the whole thing was fun—so was clearing the weeds and some tea trees in the large block of land to make way for a beautiful garden stretching all the way to the rocky shore.

But things went from bad to worse with Arantxa who, in the last three years or so of her life, needed round-the-clock care after being diagnosed with cervical cancer. I had to take her to the hospital in Launceston every couple of weeks, where she undertook a variety of tests and treatments—a round-trip of nearly 500 kilometers.

I was forced to witness the waning away of a life than had meant all for me. A good man was with me in those difficult moments. He was Dr. Richard Vane Tempest, an Englishman and general practitioner in Bicheno. He was also an extremely close friend who would report after work at our home to share a couple of beers and plenty of talk with me while Arantxa rested in bed in our bedroom—an unforgettable character.

The end came at 10:43 a.m. on August 23, 2003, when she passed away peacefully in my arms. After I closed her eyes I thought that this was it for me as well. I did not want to go on living.

But my daughters were coming for the cremation and funeral and I had promised Arantxa that her ashes would be scattered on Mount Urgull, San Sebastián's landmark, where she would have an eternal view of the most beautiful bay in the world and be surrounded by eternal peace. So there were some arrangements that needed immediate attention. That allowed me some breathing space away from the grief over her loss.

I flew with her ashes to San Sebastián at the end of 2003 and scattered them just as I had promised. Elias Querejeta and his wife came all the way from Madrid by taxi and the driver was waiting for them. Elias was in mortal danger had ETA learned that he was in the Basque Country—he was on its death list. We had no dinner, or anything else, planned, so he left immediately. After a short stay of a week or so I returned to Tasmania.

Soon thereafter, as a kind of miracle, another extraordinary woman crossed my path—another Basque from San Sebastián, of course. We decided to share our lives together come what may. No one in San Sebastián or indeed among my friends in Australia gave a penny for our future. Col Fuller, my old friend, told me on the telephone that watching me was "like watching a train wreck in slow motion." But as I write this we have been together for more than fourteen years of tumbles, journeys, and adventures and have settled in a small coastal town, Bargara, in central Queensland.

I am under her strict orders to say absolutely nothing about her. She wants to maintain her privacy and I very much respect that. She is one hell of a lady to whom I am grateful for restoring the zest for a life that I thought had ended—my own.

So, it has been my destiny to share my beloved and adopted country with two wonderful women from Donostia. Both chose me and got Australia in the bargain. With both the compromise has been to share a life with alternating periods "Down Under" and in our Basque homeland. In 2015 I took my bride on an extensive tour of Australia so that she might know a continent rather than just our little country town of

Bargara. We had taken long trips up and down the country and along the eastern seaboard before, but never around it. I am not sure whether that was a turning point in her decidedly pro-Basque Country views, but it may have had some influence.

The trip, by 4WD (SUV in American parlance) car, lasted from March of 2015 until June. We took a tent that we bought at a supermarket for A$90.00 and two rubber mattresses, as well as sleeping bags, a small table, two folding chairs, a gas cooker, and some crockery and cutlery. And, of course, an Eski to cool my beer and some perishable food. It had nothing to do with the usual Australian grey nomads who travel in style with their large caravans.

We drove south towards Canberra, then to Kapooka and nearby Wagga to refresh my soldiering memories, Mildura where I'd had my first job (I could not recognize the town), and to South Australia (which I was very familiar with, but my wife was not). From Ceduna in SA we headed to the Nullabor Highway, the longest straight stretch of road in the world (147 kilometers without a single curve) and where stories about UFOs abounded though we did not see any, much to HER disappointment. The highway (in Europe it would have merited the category of secondary road) was fringed by landing strips to help land the Royal Flying Doctor in case of accidents or other emergencies.

It was beautiful all the way to Western Australia where I had been only once on a quick visit to its capital Perth. While in Perth we stayed two nights with Laury (Cheyenne) Bodey and his wife Robyn in their large home near the Swan River. Cheyenne had been a forward scout in my platoon (a sort of bait to trick the enemy in the thick jungles). Needless to say we are close mates.

We left for New Norcia, Australia's sole monastic town, about 140 kilometers north of Perth and the end destination for a well-frequented *Camino Salvado* pilgrimage. As the name indicates the town originated as a mission founded by two Spanish Benedictine monks, Rosendo Salvado and Joseph Serra, in 1846 when Perth's population consisted of just a few hundred British settlers while the rest of Western Australia was largely terra incognita. It was named after the Italian birthplace of St. Benedictine.

I was impressed by the beauty and unique elegance of the architecture that would have fitted well in any of Spain's numerous towns housing monasteries or medieval Romanic churches. Further, along the road to New Norcia we came upon two tiny sandstone chapels, Santa Ana and Santa Teresa, exactly the same as small hermitages in the Basque Country's forbidding mountains or valleys. The site where the Spanish cockleshell landed these dedicated men is now the site of Cervantes, a great little coastal town.

And these magnificent monuments looking down on us with their grandeur were all built in the mid-nineteenth century by hand and with none of the advantages of modern tools. I gawked at their majesty wondering at the faith of the missionaries and founders, a faith that unfortunately I do not share but for which I have nothing but respect and admiration. The buildings in New Norcia have been registered by the National Trust of Australia and are now a major tourist attraction.

Less well-known is that a number of monks wandered north over the following years to spread the faith, opening up the huge vastness of the country and founding Missions such as Kolumbaru on the northern coastline. Kolumbaru was bombed by the Japanese in 1942 killing a couple of Spanish monks.

My wife and I continued our wonderful trip hugging the western coast to the towns of Exmouth and Broome. From there we drove east towards Kunnunurra, on the shores of Lake Argyle and bordering the Northern Territory, my own spiritual home. Then came a litany of well-known small towns such as Timber Creek, Katherine, Tennant Creek, and so on until we turned up the Barkly Highway towards Queensland. We explored the State's Outback, so familiar and endearing, including Hughenden, Charters Towers, Townsville, and Ingham, where I learned that the *frontón* (handball court) built by Basque canecutters and farmers in the late 1950s had been turned into a car park. Time does move on.

We travelled up north all the way to Cape Tribulation where Captain Cook had repaired his sailing vessel in 1770 and where we had the opportunity to catch up with a bunch of Cassowaries, ostrich or emu-like flightless birds originally from New Guinea (but now next to extinct in that country), timid when confronting humans but extremely dangerous if provoked. An amazing journey.

One final Post Addendum.

This contribution would miss something terribly important, indeed crucial, if I did not mention my daughters, Lorena and Elena. Both are conscious of their Basque heritage but Arantxa could not speak our ancient language (neither could I after so many decades away) and were brought up with Spanish, though their English is impeccably Australian today.

Lorena completed Year 12 of her education at fifteen years of age because she was unusually bright. She received several written offers from various universities to apply for entry but Arantxa and I, in talks with Lorena, thought she was too young to start a career and asked her whether she would prefer taking a year's sabbatical in the Basque Country with her uncle Juan Ignacio and aunt Carmina in San Sebastián. She agreed immediately.

The year would shape her consciousness forever, I believe. San Sebastián and the Basque Country became very important to her, not necessarily in a spiritual or emotional sense but as places where you could have fun as well as a high-quality life. And Juan Ignacio and Carmina practically adopted her as a daughter (their own daughter is married and working in Boston).

Elena was always a rebel. After school, without consulting her parents, she got a job in Darwin and got on with her own life.

Neither of them was happy about my decision to enter another relationship after their mother's death, and this has been a turning point for all of us. For some years I tried to maintain the pretense that eventually things would return to normal and my second wife encouraged me to do everything possible to ensure that that was the case.

But to no avail, since, in July of 2010, coinciding with my battalion's reunion in Brisbane, Lorena broke her last ties with us. Shortly after, she, her husband, a geologist working for Glencore, and two beautiful daughters moved to London where they have been since. I received a letter by slow mail on occasion of my Order of Australia award in 2013, to which I replied and, in October 2016, following widespread publicity, TV appearances, and so on, about my investiture of my gallantry medal, I received an email from one of her daughters seeking to "mediate" between myself and her mother. There was no mention of my present wife who obviously remains the biggest obstacle in our relationship, so the mediation did not work. I guess I shall have to wait until the next medal before we try again.

Elena and I have maintained a close enough relationship, thank goodness, although she also maintains her distance from my wife. Elena is Australian to the marrow of her bones though, surprisingly, she is closer to the idea of Spain because in the past few years, mainly because of her fluency in Spanish but also because she is as clever as they come and knows very well the ins and outs of Australian public administration, she has been working for a couple of Spanish multinationals alongside some Spaniards. She and her English husband Steve, live in Toowoomba, Queensland at present.

Their daughter Lauren and her boyfriend visited San Sebastián last year and were enthused by it. They intend to go back at some stage.

And I now have two great grandkids in Alice Springs by my eldest granddaughter, Amaya Alcorta (she has kept the surname), who I intend to visit shortly.

Cheers to one and all.

Frank

Notes

1. Frank's commanding officer eventually published his memoir of the Vietnam War [Lieutenant Colonel Charles S. Mollison, *Long Tan and Beyond: Alpha Company 6 RAR in Vietnam 1966–67* (Woombye, Australia: Cobb's Crossing Publications, 2004)], in which he underscores on the first page his admiration for: "…the fearless Platoon Sergeant, Frank Alcorta, who always led by example" (p. iii), adding later: "Sergeant Frank Alcorta was one of the best soldiers in Alpha Company and an outstanding leader. He was certainly the bravest man I ever came across" (p. 358).
2. At the same time, in subsequent correspondence with me over the years, Frank noted that he and his platoon were never properly recognized by Australia for their action at the Battle of Long Tan. He found this absurd, particularly when the Australian forces in Iraq subsequently named two of their ground operations after him—based upon his Vietnam legendary service. It seems that, at the time, when his commanding officers nominated their men for highest honors, they were unsuccessful. There was a quota on such recognition, and it was being garnered by officers who had never even been in combat themselves. Frank and his men were subsequently put in for Long Tan medals, but it was decades after the fact and the necessary documentation had been lost or misplaced. However, retired Lieutenant Colonel Harry Smith MC, the commander of D Company at Long Tan, made proper recognition of the battle's heroes a lifelong personal mission. In 2008, the Defence Honours and Awards Appeals Tribunal of Australia's Department of Defence gave Lieutenant Colonel Smith the Star of Gallantry, but denied his requests for his troops. He continued his campaign and on November 8, 2016, Frank was one of ten men who received bravery awards at a ceremony in Canberra.

3. In other words, Frank concluded that the migration of Aborigines and Melanesians was out of Australia as far as New Guinea, rather than the reverse. In effect, he was arguing for multigenesis of human evolution (with one branch being the Australian Aborigines), rather than the predominant unigenesis view in paleoanthropology that our ancestors evolved in Africa and then migrated out of it to eventually populate the globe. He was obviously impressed by the similar phenotypes of Aborigines and Melanesians, as well as the difference in their appearance from other human populations. Frank would pay dearly for his iconoclasm, particularly given his lack of formal credentials in the matter. Ironically, he has been vindicated, in part at least, by the small but growing school of multigenesists within my discipline of anthropology. See P. J. Habgood, *Morphometric Investigation into the Origins of Anatomically Modern Humans* (Oxford: Archaeopress, 2003). It is also true that some of the new generation of Australian social anthropologists have rejected the "Out-of-Africa" thesis to be a white (read imperialist) discourse that ignores ancient indigenous founding myths that the Aborigines descended from their gods *in situ*, without migrating from anywhere; see Ibid; David Reich, *Who We Are and How We Got Here: Ancient DNA and the New Science of the Human Past* (New York: Pantheon Books, 2018).
4. Frank Alcorta, *A Trip to the Stone Age: An Account of the First Solo Expedition across Papua New Guinea at Its Widest Part in 1973/74* (Perth: Chargan My Book Publisher Pty. Ltd., 2010).
5. Frank X. Alcorta, *Darwin Rebellion, 1911–1919* (Darwin: History Unit, Northern Territory University Planning Authority, 1984).
6. Frank X. Alcorta, *Explore Australia's Northern Territory*, intro. Les Hiddins (Frenchs Forest, N.S.W.: Child and Associates, 1989).
7. Frank X. Alcorta, *Marjorie Harris: "Rainbow"* (Palmerston, N.T.: Keith Hart, 1998).
8. Frank X. Alcorta, *Australia's Frontline: The Northern Territory's War* (North Sydney: Allen & Unwin, 1991).

Conclusion (Bis)

I began my personal Australian odyssey in 1978. By then I had coauthored *Amerikanuak: Basques in the New World*, a work that was arguably the foundational text in the emergent interdisciplinary concern with Basque Diaspora Studies. When Jon Bilbao and I undertook that task, arguably the whole bibliography on Basque emigration could be listed on a single sheet of paper and, given the Franco regime, there was little interest in Basque scholarship focused upon the homeland itself—let alone its diasporas. That would change as the Basques of Hegoalde acquired their own public university systems in the post-Franco era and then academia around the world began to anticipate the quincentenary in 1992 of Colombus's first voyage. Suddenly, there were grants and conferences throughout the planet regarding European emigration and the adaptation of its immigrants in the various host countries. The Basques, as Spain's quintessential mariners and emigrants, not to mention builders of his flagship the *Santa María* and members of its crew, were at the very vortex of this development.

2015, or the fortieth anniversary of the publication of *Amerikanuak*, was a commemorative year of its influence. The new generation of Basque diaspora specialists, in the main anthropologists and historians, organized a series of conferences in the book's honor at several North and South American venues (as well as Havana) and universities throughout the Basque Country. There was even a conference dedicated to *Amerikanuak* in Iceland (regarding the massacre of 32 Basque whalers in 1615 in that country).

There is no small irony in the fact that I was a precursor of Basque Diaspora Studies in general, yet a laggard in their Australian narrative (despite having been the first to conduct both field and archival research regarding it). There are, however, certain advantages in bringing up the rear, the main one being that I have thereby had the benefit of all that has gone before. I can, and have, incorporated the insights of such competent researchers as Bianka Vidonja Balanzategui, Robert Mason, and Gloria Totoricagüena Egurrola into this text. My dear friend and colleague, Koldo San Sebastián, provided data on the late nineteenth- and early twentieth-century Basque presence in the Antipodes that I would have overlooked had I published this work thirty years ago. I have not included photographic material to this already overly lengthy text. Indeed, any attempt to do so would have fallen far short of the many illustrations in Gloria's book, particularly those documenting the activities of Australia's Basque associations.

So, if I coauthored *Amerikanuak* nearly half a century ago during the dawning of my professional career, I now present *Australianuak: Basques in the Antipodes* four decades after beginning my Australian research, in the twilight of my sojourn on this planet. In preparing this text, I have listened to dozens of tapes, some so brittle with age that they disintegrated and had to be reconstructed by my university's audiovisual technical staff. Most of the voices were echoes from the past that brought tears to my eyes as I transcribed their messages. Alberto Urberuaga, Johnny Mendiolea, Agustín Arrate, and Alberto Ansoleaga have all died. Agustín Adarraga, Frank Alcorta, and Joe Goicoechea all struggle with the shared infirmities that augur our finality. To all of them, and to the myriad of other "informants" who informed this narrative, I offer my thanks and this documentation of their stories as our collective tiny slice of immortality.

I would underscore another unique feature of the present book, namely, that it is actually three books between two covers. By that I mean that it is reflective of data collected at the beginning, mid, and terminal points (1980, 2002, and 2018) of two approximately two-decade intervals. Chapter 1 is my personal account of my 2002 excursion in Australia that implicitly bounces its reflections off impressions gleaned during my 1980 visit. The Coda does the same with respect to the 2002 trip. These are not simply way stations in a larger single journey. Rather, the truly interesting lesson for me is the extent to which my predictions of the future of the Basque-Australian experience were inaccurate, on the one hand, and the evolution of myself as their observer, on the other. While the traveler, William Anthony Douglass carried a passport bearing the same name, but each time it had a different photo. That, in itself, is reflective of official recognition of one's changing persona, however oblivious we individuals might be to that process.

Regarding the first point, I would underscore the evolution of the Sydney *Gure Txoko* as an illustration. In 1980, it was vibrant, if closed to outsiders, and composed almost exclusively of manual laborers, many of whom were ex-canecutters relocated to urban Australia. Conversely, in 2002, the Club was all but moribund. Its president, Carlos Orue, declared that it would fail once he and his wife had buried the last of the handful of elderly bachelors who still frequented the place. Its governing structure (as in board) was all but gone. I certainly had no reason to disagree with the gloomy prognosis. Hence, I was simply astounded in November of 2018 to sit across from a Board of Directors consisting mainly of European-born Basques in their twenties and thirties, all professionals and many with doctorates, as they described the "new *Txoko*" and their collective vision of its open embrace and universal mission.

As for my own evolution, I can only say that the Bill Douglass who first conceived of this research project in the 1970s was the product of the structural-functional paradigm in which he was trained at the University of Chicago, who then lived through the symbolic anthropological iconoclastic interlude, followed by postmodernist skepticism of any investigatory paradigm, and now writing in the inelegantly denominated post-postmodernist moment. My, how we academics preen with self-importance! To all of this professional scrambling, I would add life experience itself. This seventy-nine-year-old is far different from the twenty-seven-year-old who graduated in 1967, let alone the middle-aged man with the dying wife who visited Australia in 2002.

If I were to oversimplify the sum total of my professional and personal evolution, I would say that it has been movement from the belief in my ability to conduct objective scientific research regarding the collective reality (social, cultural, religious, economic, political) of my collectivity—in this case, Basques in Australia—to an appreciation of the limitations of such a "scientific" endeavor. Rather, I now regard myself to be the facilitator of the protagonists themselves as they tell their individual and collective stories.

I once gave a lecture on the Basque diasporas in the national library of Buenos Aires. When I finished, an insistent hand went up instantly, demanding to be recognized. I was then berated by a Basque who I am pretty certain was anti-Semitic. He objected to the use of a Jewish word, "diaspora," to refer to his countrymen—and himself. I explained that the term had been transformed into a sociological one from a Jewish referent; there was even an academic journal regarding migration worldwide called *Diaspora*. Heads around the room nodded in understanding, but I could see that my interlocutor was unconvinced. I half expected him to march out of the room in protest (he did not).

There is a little kernel of truth, however, in viewing the Basque emigration experience, including the formation of its various diasporas, as quite akin to that of the Jews. Both lost political control over their historical territory and became obsessed with recovering the homeland and creating a modern nation-state within it. Both peoples were scattered throughout the planet—migrating to every one of its inhabited continents. Both spoke a language that was tantamount to a secret code. Both were prone to form voluntary ethnic associations in their host societies to prolong, if not permanently at least generationally, their cultural legacy—a celebration of their uniqueness. Both encouraged ethnic group endogamy as a part of that strategy. Both tried to project a sympathetic image to the wider societies in which they were embedded. Both sought to garner economic and political influence without compromising favorable public sympathy—if not always with unqualified success. Hence, both had their detractors among the homeland's immediate neighbors and the countries of their diasporic settlements. The ethnic nationalism of each posed irritants to such arrangements as the European Union and the Middle East.

At the same time, it is an oversimplification to speak of *the* Basque emigrant even when telling such a circumscribed story as Basque emigration to Australia and its sequel of Basque-Australians. There were the "leavers" who departed their European homeland once and with the intention of never returning for anything more than a visit. There were the "stayers," those who considered emigrating to Australia either through their own volition or encouraged to do so by relatives or friends who were already settled in the Antipodes—yet who decided not to do so. There were the "sojourners," those who signed short-term contracts to live and work in a particular profession in Australia as a life's interlude in which to amass capital for improved circumstances in their ethnic homeland (retirement of a mortgage on one's *baserri*, purchase of a small business like a bar or restaurant, or a truck to engage in transportation, acquisition of a flat near urban employment, etc.). There were the "reemigrants," those who went first to Argentina where they settled for a few years before proceeding on to Australia, those who herded sheep in the American West before cutting sugar cane in North Queensland, or vice versa. There are the footprints of the "Wandering Basque" Frank Alcorta on Euskadi, Spain, Venezuela, Guyana, Australia, Malaysia, Vietnam, and New Guinea—an Australian nomad whose address might be Brisbane, Darwin, Bicheno, or Bargara. At times, both a follower of men like Dutchy Alexander and Northern Territorian Governor Paul Everingham, and, at others, their leader. Then, too, there were the hyphenated Basque-Australians, the descendants of immigrant parents or grandparents who retained an ethnic legacy filtered and fostered more through the prism of hearsay than personal experience—themselves tourists in the ancestral Basque homeland.

All of these many incarnations and faces of Basque emigration shared one thing in common. When I met them, they were half a world and hemisphere away from Europe and living full Australian lives, yet always with a piece of their brain, heart, and probably one eye cocked on a distant ethnic homeland that some had not seen for decades and others never. Each had his or her plan when interviewed—some intended to travel to Euskadi within a specified timeframe and others never—but such plans, of course, are always subject to life's vagaries, not to mention the changes within oneself. Some who told me they would never leave Australia now live in Euskadi (or died there). Others who claimed they would make that move the coming year remain in Australia (or died there).

I would conclude by placing Basque emigration to Australia within the broader context of its history of its two other key destinations—Latin America and the United States. The former, and particularly the southern cone nations (Uruguay, Argentina, and Chile), were by far the longest-standing destination of Basque emigrants, as well as their attractor of greatest magnitude. For half a millennium, Basques, particularly those from Hegoalde, formed an integral part of the Spanish colonial enterprise. Subsequently, over the past two centuries of mass European transatlantic emigration, Latin America received by far the largest number of its Basque contingent. To this day, any intending Basque emigrant cannot help but think of Latin America as his or her potential destination—where he or she is fluent in the national language, conversant with the Hispanic culture, and likely to have kinsmen (or at least acquaintances) prepared to facilitate the move.

Of greater relevance to the present study is the contrast between Australia and the United States as the two major attractors of Basque emigrants in the Anglo world, not to mention their common differences with the Hispanic one. Their obvious commonality is the extent to which most Basque immigrants entered each of these Anglo countries through the narrow window of a single occupation—sheepherding and sugar-cane cutting. Both were arguably the most disdained occupations in their respective economies. Both were centered upon remote rural areas and tended to isolate and insulate the immigrants from the dominant Anglo culture. Both occupations were seasonal, providing much of their labor force with employment for but half of the year. And, in both settings, Basques experienced considerable prejudice before attaining wide acceptance.

In the American West and Australia alike, the manual-laboring immigrant generation accomplished considerable socioeconomic mobility, but within the industry in question—becoming respected sheep ranchers and canefarmers. In both, the occupations that first attracted intending Basque immigrants were eclipsed (in the American West, by the decline of open-range sheep grazing and, in Australia, by mechanization of the harvest), and at about the same time (the 1960s and 1970s). Nevertheless, in both contexts, ironically, there was formal recruitment of Basques to an occupation that was in the twilight of its very existence—herding sheep and cutting cane.

In both contexts, Basques eventually established a group reputation for hard work, loyalty, and integrity. There emerged in both the notion that the word of a Basque was as good as a written contract. In both, the original stereotypically denigrated occupation became a point of ethnic pride for Basque descendants long removed from the activity. Urban professionals in the United States might use the expression "Not bad for a sheepherder," while their Australian counterparts invoke "I'm just a simple farmer at heart." These two overriding occupational identities mask even Basque-immigrant historical realities, since, at all times, there were a number of immigrants who were tradesmen or went into mining or logging without ever herding a single sheep or cutting a sugar stalk. Then, too, in recent years, both Australia and the United States attract Basque tourists, students, and professionals—some but brief visitors; others more-lengthy sojourners or even permanent settlers.

We might also note that in all three destinations there was a tendency to form a Basque collectivity in the port-of-entry metropolises (Buenos Aires, Montevideo, Santiago de Chile, Caracas, Bogotá, La Habana, Lima, New York, Los Angeles, San Francisco, Sydney, Melbourne). In most cases, these contained a contingent of Basque mariners and other globetrotters. It might be noted that, within the ranks of Spain's merchant mariners, there was a core of Basque culinary specialists. Unsurprisingly, then, the port-of-entry Basque collectivities tended to contain a cadre involved in the hospitality industry—primarily as chefs, bartenders, and restaurateurs.

In both settings, there was a tendency for ethnic-group endogamy in the first generation and to a lesser degree among its offspring. By the third generation, it was all but absent. Again, there was a tendency in both contexts for sons (not exclusively, but in particular) to follow in their fathers' footsteps. Daughters were more likely to marry out and pursue a non-agricultural career. Again, by the third generation, the grandchildren of the original migrants in both contexts were pursuing higher education, while prepared to accept the occupational and physical mobility that it entailed.

In Australia and the United States alike, Basques carved out a unique ethnic identity in the sense that their Anglo neighbors came to apprehend and comprehend them to be distinct from other Europeans in their midst—albeit, a bit shaky on detail. Again, outside of Queensland's Far North and the American West, in both countries there remained profound ignorance regarding the Basque people and their language.

In both, the language and many of the customs were diluted among the offspring of the immigrants and all but gone by the third generation. In both contexts, there were belated efforts to recover the past through the celebration of ethnic festivals and the establishment of social clubs. The former, as both episodic and colorful events, drew considerable attendance of both hyphenated Basques and their non-Basque neighbors. They were also highlighted in the press and touted for their folkloric properties. The clubs were more work and tended to be the projects of the dedicated few—a core of true believers and a larger passive membership of well-wishers. Many hyphenated Basques simply could not be bothered to even join, let alone volunteer.

There were also evident differences between the American West and the Far North. The entry of Basques into the former began as a mid-nineteenth-century phenomenon centered upon the California gold rush. Nevertheless, it had certain profound roots in Spanish colonial history. Basques founded the earliest European settlements in Arizona and New Mexico in the sixteenth and seventeenth centuries. Basque ship captains were instrumental in the European exploration of the Pacific coast from Baja California to Alaska.[1] Basque missionaries and administrators were prominent in Alta California during its brief Mexican period in the first half of the nineteenth century. In short, in one sense, Basque settlement in the American Southwest and Far West was the northernmost expression of a centuries-long historical complex that extended uninterruptedly to Tierra del Fuego.

Australia was on the fringe of, but marginated within, the Spanish colonial enterprise. Basques formed a part of the contingent exploring the Pacific during its centuries as "the Spanish Lake," including people like Urdaneta who believed that there was a southern continent to be discovered. Nevertheless, the actual European discovery, settlement, and administration of Australia was a late eighteenth-century Anglo endeavor. Australia did have some relations with South America and the Philippines, glimpses of which we have considered in this narrative, but they were tangential at best.

Returning to the mid-nineteenth-century California baseline for "modern" Basque settlement in the American West, within a decade after the discovery of gold there was a discernible Basque ethnic network facilitating the entry of Basques into the budding ovine industry of southern and central California. By the turn of the century, the Basque sheepherder was a ubiquitous figure throughout the American West. Its Basque-American community was already delineated and mature by the time that Basques began jumping ship or otherwise languishing in port in Sydney and Melbourne, some of whom found their way to the already established Italian (and Catalan) sugar complex in Queensland's Far North. In short, Basque emigration to the American West was highly circumscribed and purposive, a near-group phenomenon, whereas that to Australia was far more aleatory and individualistic.

Then there is the difference in scope and scale. According to the estimate predicated upon the 2000 US census, at the turn of the century there were approximately 57,000 Basques and their descendants in the United States; whereas I would estimate that the high-water mark for Australia (circa 1970) would have been fewer than 2,000 persons. Those evident differences obviously affected the capacity and need for Basque clubs (*euskal etxeak*) and cultural associations in the two venues. There are currently more than thirty in the United States, most under the umbrella of NABO (North American Basque Organizations, Inc.), whereas there have never been more than three in Australia at any one time, and they are not formally linked together.

Basque emigration to the American West played out over a vast geographical region, the thirteen western states, favoring development of that unique ethnic institution—the Basque hotel, not to mention the network tying them together. The seasonally unemployed sheepherder likely spent the off-season in a Basque hotel to await spring lambing. For the upcoming season, he might change employment, likely as an individual, from his existing location to a ranch that was a thousand miles away—a move predicated upon the information and contact given him by the Basque hotelkeeper.

Basque immigration in the Far North was much more circumscribed, limited largely to three sugar-cane districts and the Atherton Tablelands. Most canecutters knew all of the region's Basques by name—canecutters and farmers alike—and moved among employers (both Basque and non-Basque) in constituted gangs. There was really no demand for the "Basque hotel" *per se*; indeed, the many that were owned by fellow Southern Europeaner Italians provided Basques a sufficient ethnic refuge, particularly given the likely fluency of the canecutter in the Italian language that became the main non-English vernacular of the sugar industry. It is particularly telling that the only physical setting for Basque sport and festivities in the Far North (until the founding of Townsville's Basque Club of North Queensland less than two decades ago) was the *frontón* of Trebonne's Hotel, owned and operated by two Italians.

During the slack season, the unemployed canecutter was less likely to languish in some cane barrack (although a few did) and rather more prone to become a nomadic harvester—whether of tobacco, fruit, or vegetables. This practice is akin to today's seasonal Mexican harvesters in California.[2] The Queenslander slack-season migrant was more likely to travel in the company of other Basques (and Spaniards), often some or all of his cane-gang members, rather than on his own. They often moved along an established ethnic network or found employment through the advice and contacts of fellow-ethnic "veterans" of the harvesting in a particular area. At times, employment was secured by recourse to employment agencies or reading newspaper ads. It was common for the migrants to purchase (and pool) automobiles to facilitate their mobility. There was constant erosion as some became construction laborers on projects like the Snowy Mountains Hydroelectric Scheme, steel workers in Wollongong/Port Kembla, miners in Mount Isa, loggers in Victoria and South Australia, or even urban workers in places like Brisbane, Sydney, and Melbourne. Another factor was that the migrants tended to explore multiple slack-season destinations over time, thereby expanding their Australian horizon.

As a consequence, while many a sheepherder experienced but one or a few ranches in the American West, the tiny ethnic enclave of the Basque hotel in a nearby small town, and a few hours in American cities while in transit, the canecutter traversed vast stretches of the Australian continent from the tropical Far North to the temperate South. A few of the more intrepid even probed Western and South Australia and the Northern Territory. Even those who remained seasonal harvesters were likely to sojourn for a few days in Sydney and/or Melbourne. In short, the Basque emigrant canecutter in Australia was far more likely to garner a cosmopolitan overview and understanding of that continent than did his sheepherding counterpart of North America.

There were, therefore, factors in play that broadened the horizon of the canecutter while narrowing that of the sheepherder. By and large, in Australia, particularly after World War II, Basques entered a country that welcomed newcomers as one means of growing the national population. It was about that time that the United States enacted its most xenophobic immigration legislation. Consequently, the essentially indentured laborers recruited for both economies entered under differing conditions.

The post–World War II sheepherder could work in the United States for three years but was then required to leave the country; the canecutter was obliged to cut for two years but was then free to stay in both Australia and his occupation of choice.

We might also note that once the settlement of Basques in the Australian South is included, the overall geographic scale of Basque immigration in the two continents is much more comparable. The distinction is that, despite the far superior numbers of Basques in North America, they were far more insular vis-à-vis one another given the relative lack of seasonal physical mobility. The Bizkaian Basques of southern Idaho had little connection with the mainly French-Basque settlements of central California until very recently (facilitated in large measure by establishment of NABO in the 1970s). Conversely, given the seasonal ramblings of the canecutters and the erosion in their ranks of those who remained in the South, the Basque-Australian community was stitched together by an extensive network of personal ties. Canecutters passing through Sydney or Melbourne might very well visit the city's *Gure Txoko*. Even someone like Paul Oribe, present in Mildura via a very different career path, came to know and host the dozens of migratory canecutters harvesting that area's crops.

I would now truly conclude this book with the words not of its author but of one of its protagonists—Pablo (Paul) Oribe,

> It is difficult, but not impossible, to transplant anything—including human beings. At times, referring to the latter, one has to admit that this process takes one or two generations, as is the case with the Basques. There exist colonies of our countrymen in many parts of the world, and, almost without exception, as long as there exist immigrant persons, the members of the communities hold onto the possibility of returning to the "roots" of their country of origin. Their life in the adopted country seems to be of a temporary nature and their feelings are ambivalent. It gives the sensation of a suspended existence. In general, their children are born in the new habitat and many of them, due to their cultural isolation, marry persons of other ethnic groups. Many persons believe that the blood tie will be sufficient to retain their children in the new country; but no, it seems like no. I am not sure why,

however, but there always remains something inside, like an unfulfilled desire that pulls you toward the homeland and that calls to you to return. As long as this occurs, true happiness (if such exists) will be difficult to attain. After considering all of this, one never adapts completely to the new ambience, and, like the "wandering Jew" of Eugene Sue, never stops turning over doubts in his mind. But the funny thing is that you cannot cure this sentiment by returning to the womb, to one's "roots." This I know well, and, believe me, it has been a very painful lesson to learn.

Notes

1. Douglass, *Basque Explorers*.
2. Interestingly, none of the unemployed sheepherders entered the ranks of, or competed with, the Mexicans. Maybe it was because they were solitary figures rather than team members, too intimidated to travel alone great distances for seasonal piecework.

APPENDIX I

European Residence of Basque Adult Males Recruited for Queensland, 1958–1960 (n = 384)

Community of Origin	1. Vessel *Toscana* Ex Trieste-Brisbane June 27, 1958	2. Vessel *Montserrat* Ex Bilbao-Melbourne May 5, 1959	3. Vessel *Monte Udala* Ex Bilbao-Melbourne Dec. 19, 1959	4. Vessel *Monte Udala* Ex Santander-Melbourne June 20, 1960	5. Vessel *Monte Udala* Ex Santander-Melbourne Dec. 18, 1960	Totals
I. Province of Araba/Álava						
Agurain/Salvatierra	1					1
Arangiz/Aránguiz	1					1
Barajuen/Barajuén	1					1
Gasteiz/Vitoria	3		2			5
Gaubea/Valdegovia		1				1
Lagran/Villaverde		1				1
Luzkiano/Luzquiano	1					1
Pipaon/Pipaón			1			1
Ondategi/Ondátegui			1			1
Totals	7	2	4	0	0	13
II. Province of Gipuzkoa/Guipúzcoa						
Aia/Aya	1		1			2
Amezketa/Amezqueta	1		1			2
Astigarraga		1	1			2
Ataun	1					1
Azpeitia		3				3

692 APPENDIX I

Community of Origin	1. Vessel Toscana Ex Trieste-Brisbane June 27, 1958	2. Vessel Montserrat Ex Bilbao-Melbourne May 5, 1959	3. Vessel Monte Udala Ex Bilbao-Melbourne Dec. 19, 1959	4. Vessel Monte Udala Ex Santander-Melbourne June 20, 1960	5. Vessel Monte Udala Ex Santander-Melbourne Dec. 18, 1960	Totals
Beasain					1	1
Beizama		1	1			2
Berrobi		1				1
Bidania/Vidania			1			1
Deba/Deva		1				1
Donostia/ San Sebastián	2	2	5			9
Eibar		1	1			2
Elgoibar		1				1
Errezil/Régil			1			1
Hernani	1	2	1			4
Hondarribia/ Fuenterrabía					1	1
Legazpi/Legazpia	1					1
Legorreta	1					1
Mutriku/Motrico	1					1
Oñati/Oñate			2			2
Orio/Villafranca de Orio	1	2				3
Tolosa			1			1
Zarautz/Zarauz		3	2			5
Zegama/Cegama	1					1
Zumaia/Zumaya		1				1
Totals	11	19	18	0	2	50
III. Province of Navarra						
Añorbe		1				1
Agoitz/Aoiz		2				2
Araitz/Araiz		1				1
Arellano		1				1

Community of Origin	1. Vessel Toscana Ex Trieste-Brisbane June 27, 1958	2. Vessel Montserrat Ex Bilbao-Melbourne May 5, 1959	3. Vessel Monte Udala Ex Bilbao-Melbourne Dec. 19, 1959	4. Vessel Monte Udala Ex Santander-Melbourne June 20, 1960	5. Vessel Monte Udala Ex Santander-Melbourne Dec. 18, 1960	Totals
Arguedas	2		1			3
Arroitz/Arróniz		1				1
Artaxoa/Artajona	2		1			3
Artabia/Artavia			1			1
Arzotz/Arzoz			1			1
Aiegi/Ayegui			1			1
Azagra		1	3		2	6
Azantza/Azanza		1				1
Beire	1					1
Berbintzana/Berbinzana	2		1			3
Beriain/Beriáin	1					1
Caparroso		1				1
Cabanillas			1			1
Cascar			1			1
Zarrakaztelu/Carcastillo		2				2
Cascante			1			1
Castejón			1			1
Cintruénigo		3				3
Corella	2		7	1		10
Etxarri Aranatz/Echarri-Aranaz		1				1
Lizarra/Estella			2			2
Eultz/Eulz		1				1
Ezkurra/Ezcurra			1			1
Faltzes/Falces	5	6	1			12
Fitero			1			1
Fontellas			1	1		2

APPENDIX I

Community of Origin	1. Vessel *Toscana* Ex Trieste-Brisbane June 27, 1958	2. Vessel *Montserrat* Ex Bilbao-Melbourne May 5, 1959	3. Vessel *Monte Udala* Ex Bilbao-Melbourne Dec. 19, 1959	4. Vessel *Monte Udala* Ex Santander-Melbourne June 20, 1960	5. Vessel *Monte Udala* Ex Santander-Melbourne Dec. 18, 1960	Totals
Garaioa/Garayoa	1					1
Garde			1			1
Goizueta		1				1
Igari/Igal	1					1
Iturgoien/Iturgoyen		1				1
Larraga	7	3				10
Larraun/Larráun		1	1			2
Lerín			1			1
Lizaso			1			1
Lodosa			2			2
Lorca	1					1
Irunberri/Lumbier	1					1
Marcilla		1				1
Mendabia/Mendavia			1			1
Milagro		1				1
Miranda de Arga		1				1
Amunarritz/Munarriz		2				2
Obara	1					1
Iruñea/Pamplona	1		4			5
Azkoien/Peralta	4				1	5
Puiu/Pueyo	1					1
Ribaforada			1			1
Zare/Sada de Sangüesa			1			1
Santacara	1					1
Tafalla			1			1

European Residence of Basque Adult Males

Community of Origin	1. Vessel Toscana Ex Trieste-Brisbane June 27, 1958	2. Vessel Montserrat Ex Bilbao-Melbourne May 5, 1959	3. Vessel Monte Udala Ex Bilbao-Melbourne Dec. 19, 1959	4. Vessel Monte Udala Ex Santander-Melbourne June 20, 1960	5. Vessel Monte Udala Ex Santander-Melbourne Dec. 18, 1960	Totals
Tutera/Tudela	1		7			8
Uxue/Ujué		1				1
Urdanotz/Urdanoz	2	1				3
Urritza/Urriza	2					2
Usotz/Usoz			1			1
Valtierra	3		2		1	6
Viana	2	2	1			5
Villafranca	1	4	2			7
Totals	45	41	53	2	4	145

IV. Province of Bizkaia/Vizcaya

Community of Origin	1. Vessel Toscana	2. Vessel Montserrat	3. Vessel Monte Udala	4. Vessel Monte Udala	5. Vessel Monte Udala	Totals
Abadiño/Abadiano	1					1
Ajangiz/Ajanguiz	1	1				2
Amorebieta	1		1		1	3
Amoroto	3		1			4
Arbatzegi-Gerrikaitz Munitibar/Arbácegui	1		1			2
Arrieta		1				1
Aulesti/Murélaga	1	1				2
Bakio/Baquio			2			2
Barakaldo/Baracaldo		1	1		1	3
Bermeo	7	7	10	1		25
Bilbo/Bilbao	3	4	9	2	3	21
Durango			3			3
Erandio		1				1
Ereño		2	5			7

APPENDIX I

Community of Origin	1. Vessel Toscana Ex Trieste-Brisbane June 27, 1958	2. Vessel Montserrat Ex Bilbao-Melbourne May 5, 1959	3. Vessel Monte Udala Ex Bilbao-Melbourne Dec. 19, 1959	4. Vessel Monte Udala Ex Santander-Melbourne June 20, 1960	5. Vessel Monte Udala Ex Santander-Melbourne Dec. 18, 1960	Totals
Ermua					1	1
Errigoiti/Rigoitia	2	2				4
Forua	2	2	1			5
Galdakao/ Galdacano	1		1			2
Gamiz/Gámiz					1	1
Gautegiz-Arteaga/ Gauteguiz de Arteaga		1		1		2
Gordexola/ Gordejuela		1				1
Getxo-Areeta/ Guecho-Las Arenas	1		1	1		3
Gernika-Lumo/ Guernica y Luno	6	6	10			22
Güeñes			1			1
Ispaster		1				1
Iurreta/Yurreta	1					1
Kortezubi/ Cortézubi	2	6				8
Leioa/Lejona		1				1
Lekeitio/Lequeitio			1	1		2
Markina-Xemein/ Marquina-Jeméin	2					2
Mendata		2	3			5
Morga	1	3				4
Muxika/Múgica	4	1	7			12
Mundaka/ Mundaca		1			2	3
Mungia/Munguía			1			1

Community of Origin	1. Vessel Toscana Ex Trieste- Brisbane June 27, 1958	2. Vessel Montserrat Ex Bilbao- Melbourne May 5, 1959	3. Vessel Monte Udala Ex Bilbao- Melbourne Dec. 19, 1959	4. Vessel Monte Udala Ex Santander- Melbourne June 20, 1960	5. Vessel Monte Udala Ex Santander- Melbourne Dec. 18, 1960	Totals
Nabarniz/ Navarniz		1				1
Ondarroa	3					3
Portugalete		1	1			2
Sestao		2		1		3
Sopela/Sopelana	3	1				4
Sukarrieta/ Pedernales	1					1
Zaratamo		1				1
Ziortza-Bolibar/ Cenarruza- Bolívar		1				1
Zugaztieta/ La Arboleda					1	1
Totals	47	52	60	7	10	176
Totals: I-II-III-IV Combined	110	114	135	9	16	384

Source:
1. "Nominal Roll of Approved Migrants Embarked on S.S. "Toscana" on June 27, 1958 from Trieste to Brisbane." Australian Archives: Accession File BT 613/1, item 58/7548, Department of Immigration, Correspondence File: '"Toscana" ex-Trieste," 28.6.58. 1958–1964.
2. "Nominal Roll of Approved Migrants Embarked on S.S. "Montserrat" on May 5, 1959 from Bilbao to Melbourne." Australian Archives: Accession BT 567/1, item 59/5368, Department of Immigration, Correspondence File: '"Montserrat," Nominal roll' 1959.'
3. "Nominal Roll of Approved Migrants Embarked on S.S. "Monte Udala" on December 19th, 1959 from Bilbao to Melbourne. Australian Archives: Accession BT 541/1, item 60/307. Department of Immigration, Correspondence File: '"Monte Udala" Assisted Passage Scheme,' 1959–1963.
4. "Nominal Roll of Approved Migrants Embarked on S.S. "Monte Udala" on June 20th, 1960 from Santander to Melbourne." Australian Archives: Accession BT 541/1, item 60/7021. Department of Immigration, Correspondence File: '"Monte Udala," at Melbourne 22/7/60,' 1960–1962.
5. "Nominal Roll of Approved Migrants Embarked on S.S. "Monte Udala" on December 18, 1960 from Santander to Melbourne." Australian Archives: Accession BT 583/1, item 61/242. Department of Immigration, Correspondence File: '"Monte Udala," ex-Santander 18.12.60,' 1961–1962.

APPENDIX II

Queensland Basques Entering Australia between 1900 and 1930 (inclusive) Who Became Naturalized Citizens (Listed Chronologically by Earliest Date of Entry)

Name	Residence	Place of Origen	Year of Birth	Year of Entry	Year of Application	Occupation
1. Aniceto Menchaca	Stone River (Ingham)	Bilbo	1889	1907	1909	Carpenter
2. John Ugarte	South Johnstone	Ereño Bizkaia	1888	1909	1923	Miner and Farmer
3. Tomas Ugarte	Innisfail	Kortezubi Bizkaia	1878	1910	1914	Labourer
4. Elvig Ugarte	Innisfail	Ereño Bizkaia	1892	1911	1914	Labourer
5. Julio Arana	Jarvisfield (Ayr)	Portugalete Bizkaia	1887	1911	1925	Labourer
6. Johan Menchaca	Beeva (Ingham)	Bilbo Bizkaia	1892	1911	1914	Labourer
7. Santos Villacian	Ingham	Bilbo Bizkaia	1887	1911	1914	Labourer
8. Valentin Ypinazar	Jarvisfield (Ayr)	Bilbo Bizkaia	1884	1912	1923	Farmer
9. Angel Lazcano	Innisfail	Bergara Gipuzkoa	1890	1912	1914	Labourer
10. Gabriel Sesma	Ayr	Lekeitio Bizkaia	1890	1912	1926	Canefarmer
11. Angel Alberdi	Jarvisfield (Ayr)	Murélaga Bizkaia	1890	1912	1915	Labourer
12. Domingo Plaza	Ayr	Bizkaia	1888	1912	1938	Farm Labourer
13. Juan Astorquia	South Johnstone	Murélaga Bizkaia	1898	1914	1926	Labourer

APPENDIX II

Name	Residence	Place of Origen	Year of Birth	Year of Entry	Year of Application	Occupation
14. Pio Iturriga	Ayr	Abadiano Bizkaia	1891	1914	1931	Labourer
15. Gerardo Alonso	Ayr	Andoain Gipuzkoa	1889	1914	1932	Farm Labourer
16. Daniel Martinez	Mourilyan	Los Arcos Navarra	1896	1915	1920	Canefarmer
17. Pedro Bengoa	Ayr	Murelaga Bizkaia	1895	1915	1942	Canefarmer
18. Francisco Aspiri	Tully	Ibarrengelua Bizkaia	1889	1915	1936	Canefarmer
19. Vicente Balanzategui	Ingham	Lekeitio Bizkaia	1893	1915	1923	Canefarmer
20. Jose San Vicente	Innisfail	Sestao Bizkaia	1893	1915	1924	Labourer
21. Pascasio Gabiola	Innisfail	Amoroto Bizkaia	1897	1915	1924	Labourer
22. Agustin Villanueva	Innisfail	Bizkaia	1897	1915	1924	Labourer
23. Pedro Elortegui	Lannercost (Ingham)	Mungia Bizkaia	1890	1917	1924	Cane Planter
24. Norberto Balanzategui	Ingham	Lekeitio Bizkaia	1901	1921	1928	Labourer
25. Claudio Bilbao	Home Hill (Ayr)	Ea Bizkaia	1903	1923	1933	Farmer
26. Blas Gainza	Home Hill (Ayr)	Bilbo Bizkaia	1901	1923	1930	Farmer
27. Benito Achurra	Ayr	Berriatua Bizkaia	1903	1924	1935	Canegrower
28. Candido Malaxechevarria	Jarvisfield (Ayr)	Markina Bizkaia	1899	1924	1945	Canecutter
29. Santiago Mendenzona	Ayr	Gizaburuaga Bizkaia	1899	1924	1940	Labourer
30. Yrinio Bilbao	Ingham	Mañaria Bizkaia	1903	1924	1932	Labourer
31. Leon Muguira	Mackanade (Ingham)	Nabarniz Bizkaia	1897	1924	1932	Canefarmer
32. Martin Uberuaga	Ayr	Gizaburuaga Bizkaia	1903	1924	1929	Labourer

Name	Residence	Place of Origen	Year of Birth	Year of Entry	Year of Application	Occupation
33. Manuel Goicoechea	Ayr	Mendexa Bizkaia	1898	1924	1937	Labourer
34. Gregorio Totorica	Ayr	Munitibar Bizkaia	1891	1925	1941	Farmer
35. Jose Domingo Totoricaguena	Ayr	Murélaga Bizkaia	1906	1925	1937	Canefarmer
36. Jose Gabiola	Home Hill (Ayr)	Amoroto Bizkaia	1897	1925	1933	Canefarmer
37. Gregorio Odorica	Home Hill (Ayr)	Kortezubi Bizkaia	1903	1925	1932	Farmer
38. Raimundo Berricua	Home Hill (Ayr)	Ea Bizkaia	1908	1925	1938	Canefarmer
39. Ceferino Oar	Jarvisfield (Ayr)	Arrieta Bizkaia	1884	1925	1937	Canefarmer
40. Felix Plaza	Ayr	Nabarniz Bizkaia	1893	1925	1935	Canefarmer
41. Antonio Alberdi	Stone River (Ingham)	Bizkaia	1898	1925	1936	Canegrower
42. Valentin Madariaga	Ayr	Mungia Bizkaia	1907	1925	1938	Canecutter
43. Juan Muguira	Macknade (Ingham)	Nabarniz Bizkaia	1890	1925	1934	Labourer
44. Bonifacio Bilbao	Ayr	Bedarona Bizkaia	1905	1925	1934	Labourer
45. Pablo Ocamica	South Johnstone	Mendexa Bizkaia	1904	1925	1933	Labourer
46. Pascual Badiola	Ingham	Lekeitio Bizkaia	1905	1925	1934	Labourer
47. Luciano Mugaregui	Ayr	Murélaga Bizkaia	1898	1925	1932	Labourer
48. Pedro Zubizarreta	Ayr	Ea Bizkaia	1904	1925	1932	Labourer
49. Victoriano Foruria	Home Hill (Ayr)	Ispaster Bizkaia	1908	1926	1936	Canefarmer
50. Juan Izzaguirre	South Johnstone	Mallavia Bizkaia	1901	1926	1940	Carrier
51. Francisco Larruscain	Ayr	Markina Bizkaia	1906	1926	1937	Labourer

Name	Residence	Place of Origen	Year of Birth	Year of Entry	Year of Application	Occupation
52. Vicente Muguira	Ayr	Murélaga Bizkaia	1902	1026	1935	Canefarmer
53. Cecilio Bazurco	Ingham	Mutriku Gipuzkoa	1907	1927	1936	Farmer
54. Francisco Trojaola	Ingham	Araba	1903	1927	1934	Canecutter
55. Cristobal Eguiguren	Ayr	Ondarroa Bizkaia	1902	1027	1932	Farmer
56. Jose F. Churruca	Home Hill (Ayr)	Mutriku Gipuzkoa	1907	1927	1936	Canefarmer
57. Justo Goicoechea	Home Hill (Ayr)	Murélaga Bizkaia	1909	1028	1942	Labourer
58. ? Guerricabeitia	Home Hill (Ayr)	Munitibar Bizkaia	1905	1928	1941	Farmer
59. Jose Espilla	Ingham	Etxebarria Bizkaia	1902	1929	1945	Canecutter
60. Santos Alberdi	Stone River (Ingham)	Bizkaia	1909	1929	1936	Canegrower
61. Jose Ybarlucea	Ayr	Murélaga Bizkaia	1906	1930	1937	Labourer
62. Vicente Asumendi	Macknade (Ingham)	Xemein Bizkaia	1901	1930	1936	Labourer
63. Ambrosio Sandumbide	Ayr	Murélaga Bizkaia	1910	1930	1938	Labourer
64. Antonio Landa	Ayr	Ispaster Bizkaia	1905	1930	1938	Labourer
65. Telesforo Zarragoicoechea	Home Hill (Ayr)	Munitibar Bizkaia	1907	1930	1938	Canefarmer

APPENDIX III

Australian Poem in Basque[1]

(1927)

MOTRIKU'TIK AUSTRALIA'RA

Milla urte ta bederatzireun	In the year of nineteen-hundred
ogei ta zazpigarrena,	and twenty-seven,
Kristo zerutik jetxi zanetik	the one we are living after
orain pasatzen gaudena;	Christ descended from heaven;
Australia'ra sartu ezkero	the first time I am telling this story
au kontzaten det aurrena,	since I came to Australia
mundu onetan nik ezagutu	the worst year that
dedanik urte txarrena.	I have experienced in my life.
Pentsamentu bat orain artu det	I have taken the decision
bertso batzuek jartzeko,	to write a few bertso,
plaza batian kantatziarren	so that they can be sung
jentiak aditutzeko;	and heard by people;
Australia'tik bialtzen ditut	I am sending them from Australia
España'n inprentatzeko,	to be printed in Spain,
lagun zar bati agintzen diot	I am telling an old friend
nire errian saltzeko.	to sell them in my town.
Ortik onera pasatu ditut	Traveling from home
lur ta itxaso luziak,	through many lands and seas
prantzes barkuak ekarri nundun	a French boat carried me
irugarrengo klasian;	in third class;
gutxi jan eta padezituaz	with little food and
egarri eta gosiak,	suffering thirst and hunger,
nunbait merezi izango nitun	I must have deserved
kastigu oiek guztiak.	all those penances.

Geroko penak ekartzen ditu	It provokes future pain
aita ta amak uztiak,	to leave father and mother;
bizi-modua zer dan guk emen	what life is young folks
ikasten degu gaztiak;	we learn it here;
denpora onekin padezituaz	enduring it all in these times
pasako dira guztiak,	everything will pass;
oraindañoko urtiak baiño	it is better to start anew
erosuago dek aztia.	than continue these last years.
Ogei ta bat urte artian	Raised by mother and father
aita to amak azita,	until I was twenty one,
onera sertan etorri giñan	why did we come here
Españ'n ondo bizita?	when we had a good life in Spain?
au dek mutillen abildadia	this is the capacity of boys
osasun ona eukita,	who enjoy good health,
jango badegu lana egin bear	we have to work if we want to eat
goizean goizo jaikita.	after arising early in the morning.
Jaun Zerukoak orain eman dit	The Lord of the heavens just granted me
akordatzeko grazia,	the grace to remember,
nola naguan aita ta amak	how I was raised with a lot of sacrifice
ondo kostata azia;	by mother and father;
egun batian pentsatu nuan	one day I thought
Australia ikustia,	of seeing Australia,
neronen faltaz badaukat orain	it is only my fault now
emen bizitza tristia.	this sad life of mine here.
Gu emen nola bizi geraden	I will tell everyone
esango diet danari:	how we do live here:
arrazoi txarrak aditu bear	we have to hear bad arguments
ta gogor eldu lanari;	and work heavily;
kalabazia tomatiakin	calabash with tomato
dirade gure janari,	is all we have to eat,
eta errekan geldi daguan	and on top of it water
ura gañetik edari.	that is motionless in the creek.

Ondo kostia da emen orain irabatzen dan dirua, egun luzia lanerako ta beti eguzki berua; lendik ez nitzan listua baiño ia galdu zait burua, txerriai ere ez diot opa olako bizi modua.	It is the result of much effort the money we earn here, long days of work and always a hot sun; I wasn't clever before but now I have almost lost my mind, I don't wish this life even for a pig.
Nere ideaz etorri nitzan Australia'ra igesi, egin nulako ondo bizi ta diru asko irabazi; ez etortzeko esanagaitik ez dirate galerazi, entzun txarreko pizti gaiztuak ez du besterik merezi.	It was my own thought to escape to Australia, for I had a good life and my earnings were solid, even if they told me not to leave they didn't forbid me, a wretched animal who doesn't listen doesn't deserve anything else.
Au ere esan egin bear dut daukadan arte buruan: zapai batian biok lo eiten degu ijituaren moduan; satisfazio guztiz onekin biok alkarren onduan, "au baiño mutil oberik ez dek -pentsatzen dala- munduan".	This also I have to say as long as it is on my mind, we both sleep in a sheet as do the gypsies; with all this satisfaction both next to each other, thinking, "there is no better boy than this one in the world."
Orain jendiak pentsatzen badu esana guzurra dala, etorri eta proba dezala gusto duanikan bada; biajeko lain egingo al degu iñoiz nola edo ala, ortakoz lana egin bearko egunez ezer ez dala.	If someone thinks that what I say is a lie, let him come here and try it on his own if he so desires, let us hope we somehow earn enough for the journey back, for that we will need to work beyond our daily tasks.

Nungua naizen ez det ukatzen,	I will not deny where I am from,
ni naiz Gipuzko'kua,	I am from Gipuzkoa,
da nere lagun maite dedan au	and this my dear friend of mine
Bizkaia'n bataiatua;	was baptized in Bizkaia;
onek esan dit amairu bertso	he told me thirteen bertso
badiradela naikua,	are already enough,
orain beste bat ipini eta	now I will write one more
akabatzera nijua.	and I am going to finish.
Amairu bertso atera ditut	I have come with thirteen bertso
nai dizkienak ikasi,	whoever wants let him learn them,
etorri gabe obe dezute	it's better you are attentive to these news
emengo berri ikusi;	without having to come here;
enteratzeko paper au artu,	take this bertso-paper to learn from it,
ez da batere gaezti,	it's not expensive at all,
nere lagunak salduko ditu	my friend will sell it
iñok nai badu erosi.	if anyone cares to buy.

Bertso auek, bigarren bertsoan esaten danez, emen inprentatzeko bialduak dira. Bañan ez dakigu ola egin ote ziran. Bertso-papera ez baitegu iñondik jaso al izan.

> These bertsos, as stated in the second strophe, were sent to be printed here. But we do not know if they actually were. We have not been able to find any copy of the bertso-paper.

Guri, Ondarroa'ko Agustin Zubikarai adiskideak bialdu zizkigun, makinaz idatzita eta bukaeran onako oar au erantsita:
  "Bertso oneik Matzuri baserriko etxekoandreak abestu-ala kopiatuak dira."

> The acquainted Agustin Zubikarai from Ondarroa sent them to us, typewritten and with this additional note:
>   "These bertsos are copied as the lady of the *baserri* Matzuri sang them."

Aurretik, berriz, beste argibide auek ematen ditu: "1927'garren urtean Motriku'tik Australia'ra joan ziran, desertore, lau mutil: Frantzisko

Txurruka, Maixa'kua; Arrieta, Langa-Etxebarri'kua, "Pikua", Pikua baserrikua; eta Zezilio Basurko, Aategi'kua."
Azken onek bialdu zitun bertso oneik Australia'tik.

Earlier he provides this information: "In the year 1927 four boys, army deserters, went to Australia: Frantzisko Txurruka, from Maixa; Arrieta from Langa-Etxebarri; "Pikua," from the baserria Pikua; and Zezilio Basurko, from Aategi."
This last one sent these bertsos from Australia.

Notes

1. Antonio Zavala, *Ameriketako Bertsoak* (Tolosa: Auspoa Liburutegia, 1984), 103–8.

APPENDIX IV

Original Membership List of the Spanish Society of North Queensland, 1970–1971 (n = 161).

Name	Number in Family	Community of Residence
1. Bruno Tapiolas	2	Brandon
2. Agustín Adarraga	7	Townsville
3. Jorge Salles	3	Townsville
4. Wilfred Tapiolas	4	Townsville
5. Ted Slingsley	4	Townsville
6. Benito Droguet	3	Ayr
7. Rosa Droguet	2	Ayr
8. Steve Comas	3	Ayr
9. Joe Coicoechea	5	Townsville
10. José Ignacio Gabiola	2	Ayr
11. Isaac Oar	5	Ayr
12. Justo Arroita	3	Ayr
13. Teresa Gabiola	1	Ayr
14. Juan Comas	4	Brandon
15. Agustín Ymaz	3	Ayr
16. Serapio Torotica	4	Ayr
17. Pedro Morato	2	Home Hill
18. Arthur Comas	1	Ayr
19. Agustín Arrate	5	Clare
20. Rafael Ferrando	5	Home Hill
21. Rev. Tomás Ormazabal	1	Tully
22. Joe Tapiolas	5	Ayr
23. Bruno S. Tapiolas	6	Ayr

Name	Number in Family	Community of Residence
24. Juan Bengoa	4	Ayr
25. Salvador Fortuny	2	Townsville
26. Frank Oar	10	Ayr
27. Agustín Castrejana	4	Ayr
28. Ramón Pla	2	Ingham
29. Margarita Goicoechea	1	Ayr
30. Juan Fernandez	4	Townsville
31. Antonio Llamas	4	Townsville
32. Leo Aguirresarobe	1	Dalbeg
33. Lorenzo Pellizer	1	Dalbeg
34. Nino Gnessotta	2	Dalbeg
35. Miguel Diez	5	Townsville
36. Manuel Castello	4	Ayr
37. Iñaki Navaran	6	Halifax
38. José Luis Echeandia	1	Halifax
39. Martin Echeandia	1	Halifax
40. Robert Milne	3	Ingham
41. Manuel Arnaiz	3	Ingham
42. John Mendiolea	5	Ingham
43. Sabino Balantzategui	6	Ingham
44. Umberto Zamaran	2	Townsville
45. Ignacio Badiola	2	Trebonne
46. José Larrazabal	5	Ingham
47. Noel Craig	3	Townsville

Coda

As the Air New Zealand flight descended into Sydney, I was awash with intermingled memories and feelings. Jan died in 2005 and I had not been back to Australia since her farewell journey here in 2002. My best intentions of finishing this book at that time had gone a glimmering through a combination of life circumstances that included several more years of caregiving, my heart attack while fishing in Mongolia, a failed third marriage and divorce, etc. I had even come to doubt that I would ever complete this project.

Then, too, in the interim, Gloria Totoricagüena had published her tome on Australian Basques and a number of related articles had come out as well. Many of my former key informants were now dead—including people like Eusebio Illarmendi, Rafael Alegría, Carlos Orue, Agustín Arrate, both Johnny and Conchi Mendiolea, etc. So, there was new leadership among Basque Australians (most unknown to me) and/or those who were children when I began this intellectual journey in the late 1970s, and their collective story was now nearly two decades older than my last exposure to it. In short, I felt that I needed to update my manuscript before remanding it to a publisher.

For the next four days, my routine was to open and close the microfilming reading area of the New South Wales State Library. In my previous research I had neglected the country's Spanish-language newspaper—*El Español en Australia*—founded in 1965 and still publishing today. I thought I could cover the entire run but was confronted with over fifty rolls of microfilm and therefore became selective. That actually turned out reasonably well, given the newspaper's evolution over time. I read the first nine rolls, or up to 1981, and then the periods 1998–2003 and 2007–2009. So, of course, I covered the issues that came out during the Burgos trial and the transition from Franco to the current Spanish democracy.

One morning, over my coffee and muffin, I read an issue of the *Financial Review* (November 15) with a story regarding Australia's threat to take India to the World Court for dumping sugar on the world market and thereby causing the world price to collapse by half. It was such a big deal that Australian Prime Minister Morrison took aside India's leader Narendra Modi at the APEC meeting in Singapore that both were attending. The world price now stood at A$400 a ton when the Australian grower needed A$450 to break even. *Déjà vu* and *plus ça change*!

I was scheduled for two dinners during my Sydney stay. The first was with Tommy Mendiolea and the second was with the Board of Directors of the Sydney *Gure Txoko*. Tommy and his significant other, Darren, picked me up at my hotel and we dined in a trendy restaurant on the waterfront. I recorded him through the music and din. I had many questions regarding his retention of his Basque identity.

Tommy and Darren had just returned from Townsville after wrapping up Conchi's affairs. She had died of cancer a few months earlier. Both Tommy and Darren had arranged their work lives to move to Townsville to care for her the last few months of her life when she was on chemotherapy and in and out of hospital.

The whole Mendiolea clan loved Darren, and Conchi wanted to attend his and Tommy's wedding before she died. It didn't happen because, while they had been a couple since 2004 and owned a house in Sydney together, they felt no particular need to formalize the relationship. All of this was our first topic of conversation, because both Conchi and Johnny Mendiolea struggled with the news when Tommy came out. He noted that it was a real problem for him as well. Raised in a conservative Catholic family, he was in denial throughout much of his youth. In fact, Jan and I had had numerous conversations with his parents during the initial period when they were torn between their love for their son and their religious beliefs. As with most things, the passing of time proved to be the palliative. Conchi and Johnny began to make trips to Sydney to visit Tommy and his (former) partner.

In 2002, Johnny and Conchi moved to San Sebastián for an extended break, following many years of caring for Fermina, Conchi's mother, who had been suffering from Alzheimer's disease and who had recently passed away. Conchi owned an apartment in the city, but, under Spanish law, the longterm tenant was paying less rent than the property taxes and would have to be bought out of the lease. I arranged for a lawyer for her in San Sebastián and the only alternative to a buyout was for her to occupy the space. So, once their many years of caregiving were over, Conchi and Johnny made the move. Given the Mendiolea family's medical history and his recent heart bypass, he was in delicate health.

Johnny began remodeling the essentially trashed property, and after just a few weeks in Donostia, while on a run to the hardware store, he dropped dead in the street, aged seventy-one. Conchi needed to remain in the apartment for a couple of years in order to qualify as rightful occupant of it, so she remained in San Sebastián until 2006.

After she sold her apartment and moved back to Townsville, Conchi bought a house there and fixed it up. She began taking classes at James Cook University in the art program and became an accomplished painter. She ultimately sold several of her works and gave many to friends and relatives. Just before her terminal illness, she had enrolled at JCU in creative writing classes and was penning poetry. She and I maintained a constant correspondence by internet over all these years, and she solicited my opinion of her work. She sent me images and then her first poems (always with self-deprecating asides asking if I thought she was just wasting her time).

In 1992, Tommy studied for a semester in San Sebastián on the USAC program there along with his brother Johnny and Amaya Arrate from Ayr. Tommy and Amaya, both schoolteachers in the Hinchinbrook at the time, were actually housemates before and after their sojourn in Europe. I had some influence on their lives, since I encouraged their parents to send them to our UNR-based program. Eldest brother, Johnny Mendiolea, also a schoolteacher (in Townsville), joined them on the San Sebastián program. I was curious how all three now viewed that experience and their subsequent involvement (if any) with their Basque identity.

All three had returned to their teaching appointments after the USAC semester and a year later, or in 1994, Tommy decided to try his luck in Sydney. By then, he was more accepting of his sexuality and felt increasingly uncomfortable in North Queensland—particularly his hometown. In the big city he first worked in a pub before qualifying as a flight attendant for Qantas Airlines. His language skills no doubt helped. In the event, he held that position for two decades, flying regularly to London and Frankfurt.

Tommy has made literally dozens of trips to the Basque Country. Since his mother lived alone in Donostia, he made numerous trips to see her when on vacation or on work trips to England and Germany. He could come down for two or three days between flights. He feels a particular affinity for San Sebastián after USAC and so many visits to Conchi.

Tommy's brother, Johnny, has never been back to the Basque Country since the USAC program. However, his younger brother Stephen went once to see their mother when Conchi was living in San Sebastián. On one visit, when the brothers happened to coincide in the Basque Country, they attended a family reunion of sorts in Aulesti along with the Trebonne Jayos, their aunt, Dolores Mendiolea, and her husband, José Larrazabal, and Tomás and Mari Ibañez (all of whom were otherwise visiting the Basque Country at the time).

Then there is the friendship he formed with Maite Manterola from Orio. She is connected to the Jayos in Trebonne. She came to Trebonne in 1997 on a working vacation and then spent time with Johnny and Conchi in their Townsville home. She wanted to experience Sydney, so they put her in contact with Tommy. While she was there, they became quite friendly and would attend the *Gure Txoko* together for the lunches. He met José Goicoechea of Sydney that way and they are friends to the present. Maite comes to Sydney still every couple of years to visit her friends—she has a great love for Australia. Also, when Conchi was living in San Sebastián she was visited there often by Maite and her parents, becoming close friends.

Tommy remains in touch with Maite regularly by WhatsApp. He also now stays in contact with several of his relatives in Europe. He has a cousin in Lekeitio, the son of his paternal uncle, Antonio Mendiolea. Antonio moved permanently from Ingham to the Basque Country in 1974. Tommy has no other relatives there that he remains in contact with any longer. Tony Mendiolea came to Australia for Conchi's funeral. Conchi was not close to her own brother until a few years ago. But they reconciled and he came to Australia for her graduation from James Cook University.

When Conchi knew she was dying, she arranged her possessions into lots that she intended for different relatives and friends. After the funeral, Tommy and Darren traveled to the Basque Country for a month of relaxation and to deliver some of Conchi's bequests to European relatives. Tommy met some of his maternal relatives for the first time in Torrelavega, Salamanca. They visited Conchi's brother (who subsequently passed away from cancer) and his family in Salamanca, and also his maternal cousins in Bilbao.

Tommy has been in the Sydney *Club Español* when taken there once by Tony Esparza. Tony and his father, Antonio, now reside in Spain. Tommy has not been back to the Spanish Club. He does not follow Basque affairs that much nor does he read the Basque or Spanish press, including *El Español en Australia*. He still goes once in a while to the Sunday lunch at the *Gure Txoko* but is not a member. Darren has been in the *Gure Txoko* with him. When he was in Townsville caring for Conchi, Tommy was too busy to attend the monthly lunch at the Basque Club of North Queensland.

All of my leading questions along these lines caused him to speculate about his Basque feelings. He noted that there was a longstanding tension in the Mendiolea family over Conchi's mixed Basque and Spanish heritage. She was only part Basque and felt like she was never fully accepted. Their grandmother, Fermina, moved into their home for most of the years they were growing up, and she spoke no Basque—only Spanish and almost no English. So, his Mendiolea household used Spanish rather than Basque as its vernacular. While he attended grammar school in Lekeitio during 1974, Franco was still alive, and Basque was suppressed. Also, his Basque was the Bizkaian dialect rather than the *Batua* being taught in school. To this day, while he understands (if cannot speak) Bizkaian, *Batua* is unintelligible to him. In short, the ambivalence in their upbringing regarding the two cultures carried over into the adult lives of Tommy and his three siblings when it comes to joining Basque collective activities like the *Gure Txoko* or the Basque Club of North Queensland. He didn't want to overly emphasize the point, as he regards it to be but a low-key reality, but background noise, nevertheless.

About ten years ago, Tommy began studying psychology in his spare time. He picked up a few university credits in it along the way. Then, a couple years ago he felt burned out at Qantas and decided to go back to school to get a degree in psychology. He completed his final full-time registration just a few months before diagnosis of Conchi's terminal illness. By then, he had graduated and had a job as a school psychologist in the NSW Department of Education. He loves his work and our dinner doubled as a celebration, since he had just finished his trial period and had been awarded a permanent position.

Tommy noted that his Basque is rusty, and he would like to study it again one day. He needs to learn *Batua* and has an audio course in it. With his new field and job, he has no time for it now. He might take conversational Basque courses later at the *Gure Txoko* here. He would like to spend quality time in San Sebastián after his retirement. It is then that he intends reading his Basque culture and history books that he stores today in boxes in his garage. When dividing up his mother's things, he kept most of her art books and Basque-related ones as well.

When I asked him to sum up his Basque feelings today, he became contemplative and replied that he loves the culture and language, but not the politics. He is saddened when Basques his age deny they are Spanish, yet carry a Spanish passport, as it continues a long enmity between people who are often biologically and culturally entwined. The denial of their historical connection to Spain is both wrong and naïve. He is more universalist and noted that Basque exclusiveness and nationalism in general have caused much suffering to many people worldwide. He concluded,

> I am proud of being Basque, but also of my heritage from something larger—Spain. I don't have eight Basque surnames in my ancestry, through Mom we are Spanish as well. I am Australian first and of Basque-Spanish extraction. I think most descendants here are Australian first and proud of it. With my nephews, there is some awareness of their Basque-Spanish roots, but no comprehension of the Spanish or Basque languages. They may visit the Basque Country one day out of curiosity, but they will do so as tourists.

My second evening out in Sydney was for a dinner triggered by my visit with the board members of the Sydney *Gure Txoko*. My main contact was Manu Martín, longstanding board member and Australia-born. When I arrived, the other board members were busily preparing our meal. Manu noted that the language situation in the Club is a real blend of Basque, Spanish, and English. He and Joe Goicoechea were born here and had learned a Basque dialect. They are both enrolled in the Txoko's language class trying to acquire *Batua*. They can follow a conversation, but not respond to it. Everyone knows Spanish and varying degrees of English. So, a conversation may go on five minutes in one of the languages and then switch to another. Or all three might appear in a single sentence. A little French might creep in as well, since most of the board members understand it.

Manu insisted on taking me to the second floor for a brief show-and-tell. Everything looked much the same as on my last visit in 2002, including the seldom-used Basque library ensconced behind glass. Manu pointed to the more recent wall mural that had been painted by the Zornotza (Amorebieta) illustrator and storyteller, Eider Eibar, in May 2011. Eider was on a tour of Australia and offered, pro bono, to prepare the exposition of a mural in the *Gure Txoko*. The afternoon was a great success, with about eighteen children of all ages sharing the stories in Euskera and English. At the time, the upstairs' space was used as a play area for children of members attending the *Txoko*'s monthly lunch, so the idea was to make the room more child-friendly. The mural is a delightful rendering of several Basque legendary figures with cartoon-like welcoming smiles.

Manu also pointed out a photograph on the wall of a Philippine girl breaking a bottle of champagne on the bow of a sailing boat. It was at the launching of the *Pakea* of yachtsman Unai Basurto. It was built in New South Wales and then fitted out in Sydney. *Pakea* was then sailed to Bilbao for the start of the Velux 5 Oceans, a 30,000-mile, round-the-world, solo-yacht regatta begun in October of 2006.

The Philippine girl is Amaia Lasa, daughter of the then caretaker of the *Gure Txoko*, José Lasa, from Gipuzkoa. She is flanked by Carlos Orue, the then *lehendakari* of the Club.

We observed a portrait of Carlos, president of *Gure Txoko* from 1993 to 2009, by Enrike "Misha" del Val. The Bilbao artist had come to Sydney with an Australian significant other to study for a Masters of Art. After stepping down as president, Carlos was soon diagnosed with cancer and went back to the Basque Country. After a few months there, he returned to Sydney and died shortly thereafter. His wife, Miren, donated the portrait to the *Txoko*, retaining a copy for herself. She returned to the Basque Country in late 2018, and two days later, was attending the funeral of her brother-in-law, who had just died of cancer. Then, her sister was diagnosed with the disease. Manu stated that, "if it weren't for Carlos Orue, the *Txoko* would have failed"—a comment that would become the evening's mantra.

The third innovation was the framed enormous *txapela* commemorating the fiftieth anniversary (2016) of the founding of *Gure Txoko*. Under the *boina*, there were plaques with the names of the twenty-five original founders, all men excepting one woman (Teodora Torrontegui), as Manu pointed out. Four still survived in 2016: two here in Sydney, one in Newcastle, and one in Navarra. All were given a copy of the commemorative-beret ensemble. The *txapela* for Ramón Peñagaricano was delivered to the ninety-one-year-old founder, and first *lehendakari*, in his home in Ciriza (Ziritza), Navarra, about 15 kilometers west of Pamplona. It was presented by Estefanía Martino Echarri, current president of the *Txoko*, who was on a visit to the Basque Country, and Mari Asun Salazar, the *Txoko*'s winner of that year's *mus* tournament and its representative in the world championship competition. He became very emotional.[1]

Manu then told me about their new constitution. It needed updating and was not in compliance with changes in the 1990s of Australian law regarding such associations. It also created a closed *Txoko* with a quota on non-Basque members. So, the board took three years rewriting the constitution and soliciting thoughts along the way from the membership. The new document was approved in December of 2015, or right before the 50th anniversary commemoration. It created a new class of "members" open to anyone. Social members get a discount on the annual fee and can participate in any club activity, but they cannot serve on the board or vote. Since approval, and particularly stimulated by the anniversary celebration, membership in the *Txoko* has grown by 20 percent. There are currently 112 ordinary members and 22 social ones.

A serious source of the latter are "sympathizers," such as the Catalans, who join out of a sense of reciprocal obligation. The Catalans of Sydney have a small club without a premise of their own. They teach Catalan classes here at the *Txoko* and use the *frontón* to practice for their famous *castells*, or human tower spectacle, that they perform throughout the greater Sydney area. The Irish also use the *Txoko* for social events. Manu showed me a gift from them which was a framed pronouncement of their gratitude written in both the Gaelic and Basque languages.

Manu spoke about the *Txoko*'s own Basque-language classes. It seems that it was always a hassle to keep the Sydney-born members' children attending. Manu and Joe Goicoechea are enrolled, along with their respective children. The teacher would usually be an enthusiastic volunteer passing through Sydney on a tourist visa or a short-term visit. The instructor might stay for three or six months, and then move to Melbourne or return to Europe. There was no continuity.

But now they have Nekane Reta Murua from Lazkao, Gipuzkoa. She is a godsend. She has about eleven students at present, the majority adults. The parents of the four or five kids have trouble getting them there by the usual 6:30 class time. Many others live too far away to even consider enrolling their child. Then there is Nekane's hectic schedule as well. She is often on work-related trips (like tonight) to places such as Melbourne and Canberra. Before settling in Sydney, she completed a doctoral degree in nanoparticles at the University of South Australia in Adelaide and worked as a lab researcher in a Sydney-based paint company developing the paint products of the future. She is partnered with Jon Urrejola, a member of the current board. They share a house with current board member Beñat Oliveira Bravo.

The logistics of attendance at *Gure Txoko*, given the widespread dispersal of its membership throughout the metropolitan area, are challenging. Nevertheless, there is the European-born, Basque-speaking member who is a lecturer in the Visual Arts Department at Charles Stuart University in Bathurst, three hours' drive on the western side of the Blue Mountains, who is a regular. It becomes a matter of level of fundamental interest that orders one's personal priorities. Both Manu and Joe Goicoechea are dependable regulars; their spouses and children come infrequently.

I asked if any of the members here belong to the Spanish Club as well? He thought that a couple might; but was unsure. He noted that it experienced a major crisis seven or so years ago. The Board of Directors sold the building to a developer at a bargain price. They did so illegally and lost litigation for alleged malfeasance initiated by some of the members. At one time, many *Txoko* members belonged to the Spanish Club as well. During the 1960s and 1970s, it had one of the few *expresso* machines in Sydney, and an after-hours' liquor license that kept open its bar after the pubs closed. It also held dances that attracted both Spanish nationals and Latin Americans.

Manu was uncertain of the whole story regarding the closure; but believed that the board had to make restitution. By then, it was too late to save the building. It has been converted into a hotel. So, the Spanish Club limps along. While it has money in the bank, it has no facility and has to rent premises for its occasional event. It would have fewer than two hundred members today and their average age would be in the seventies. The younger ones would be Latin American. In short, the *Club Español* was dying out, literally. There might be a handful of *Txoko* members who still pay their annual dues out of habit—he wasn't certain.

He knows of no one in the club who reads *El Español en Australia*. It is mainly about Latin American affairs, both here and in the home countries of Australia's Latin American population. The editor of the newspaper for the last ten or fifteen years is Nelson Cabrera. He comes around the *Txoko* once in a while looking for news stories. He published several articles during the 50th anniversary celebration. That probably helps attendance—a least a little. Cabrera distinguishes this as a "Basque" association and not a "Spanish" one.

We were summoned downstairs to dinner. There was a lively crowd seated around the table bantering back and forth amidst much laughter and camaraderie. Two board members remained in the kitchen putting on finishing touches to our meal. The current president of the *Txoko* is Estefanía Martino Echarri, born in Navarra and a non-Basque speaker. She followed Rubén Álvaro, another Navarran and non-Basque speaker, in the presidency.

Rubén was born in Pamplona and his mother is Scottish. His parents brought him to Australia when he was three or four years old; they now live back in Europe. Rubén is married to an Aussie and has children and grandchildren here. He is the sole director of a successful insurance brokerage. His educational background is in finances and economics.

All of the other board members are products of the *ikastola* system and therefore know *Batua*. Estefanía is the first female president.

Joe Goicoechea spoke about the "new" *Txoko*. He reminded me that he was present, in 2002, when I met with Carlos Orue, and the then president was very pessimistic about the future. Joe had recently joined what was a nonactive board. In fact, in those days, a "meeting was a call from Carlos to ask Joe's opinion about a decision that Carlos and his wife Miren had already made." The average age of members would have been more than fifty. Now there is a youth movement, and he and Manu are the only old-timers on the board. The committee now meets the first Tuesday of every month. That is also a function of the new law regarding associations, which requires more formality and accountability.

There is no longer a newsletter. Joe commented that, with the internet and Facebook, it is not necessary. I asked specifically if they circulated news about ETA's announcement last May 2 that it was disbanding? Beñat jumped in and said he is the one who puts out internet news for the club, and that it was a delicate matter,

> The *Txoko* is a gathering place for people from other parts of Spain, the Catalans for example, and we all have our personal opinions. I tried to put out an as objective message as possible. We didn't write our own article or take one from any Spanish or Basque newspaper. Rather, I reprinted an international one— from the BBC. We had the Catalan referendum and the sexual assaults in Pamplona during San Fermín this year, as well. We were very cautious about what you put, what you don't put, and how you put something.

Having agreed with Beñat, it then became obvious that the committee members shared the view regarding ETA that it was time to put the violence behind us, but that ETA's existence was convenient to the Spanish government as a whipping boy for political ends. Estefanía brought up the case of the six young men who have been in prison for three years for a bar fight in Alsasua (Altsasu) in which a couple of off-duty *guardias civiles*, dressed in civilian clothes, were injured. The defendants were tried and convicted under terrorism laws. This was absurd and has converted them into a *cause célèbre* in Spain and the European Union. Estefanía noted that the government uses the turmoil in the Middle East and Arab terrorism as an excuse to leave Spain's laws in place to be used at its discretion against anyone—like the Alsasua prisoners and Catalan nationalists. Joe Goicoechea weighed in with the opinion that the lack of political debate within the precincts of *Gure Txoko* was probably a big factor in the Club's survival for more than fifty years.

Estefanía opined on the difference between the old and new Basque migration in Australia, and their differing impact upon the *Txoko*. In the old days, the founders were looking to provide a context where Australian Basques could gather and indulge in, and preserve, their language and heritage. They might intend to go back to Europe or not, but their regular contacts with it were infrequent and it was a major undertaking to return permanently or even for a visit. Now the contacts are constant, and the new migrants are adventurers. Many arrive as part of "seeing the world." Others come for employment or educational opportunities. Most are indecisive about remaining. That is its own challenge, since some become involved enthusiastically in the *Txoko*, but then their interest and participation wanes. They may return to Europe or continue on with their globe-trotting. So, the challenge now is to strike a balance—remaining open to them and their contingencies, but without depending excessively on them for the Club's future. It remains a work in progress and maybe always will be.

There was then discussion about the history of the weekly Sunday lunch. They can accommodate thirty to forty easily. Until about five years ago, it was on a first-come basis, but many times they ended up throwing away food. So, you now have to reserve your space in advance, usually over the internet or telephone. Now, the lunch is a better money-maker.

There was general discussion about the commemorative event in 2016. All treated it as a watershed one in transitioning the old club into the new one. Manu, as chairman of the events' subcommittee, described the organization of the many events crammed into about a two-week period (Basque film festival, in-house banquet, street dance, a *soka-tira* exhibition, a woodchopping performance, a pub-crawl or *txikiteo* here in the neighborhood, and a handball match). They also brought a music group out from the Basque Country. Manu proclaimed it to be by far the most demanding undertaking he has ever managed. It was all announced in the Sydney media, with an open invitation to everyone. They went through this neighborhood and left notices on doorsteps. Several came, particularly to the banquet.

Manu recounted the case of a Swiss neighbor who paused at the open door that day while passing by walking his dog. He peeked in and Manu greeted him. The man commented that he was always curious what went on in the building, since, in thirty years, he had never seen the door open before. Manu invited him to enter and he returned for lunch after taking his dog home. He brought one of his paintings—a panoramic view of the Sydney Opera House. He was documenting "Old Sydney." Manu asked him if he remembered the shop on the corner that was now closed? The Swiss recalled when a woman of some migrant extraction opened it, and he had become her regular customer. He didn't know where she was from; and the store closed a couple of years before. Manu said, "follow me," and he led him to the table where the proprietor, Mari Asun Salazar, was sitting. They ate together totally engrossed in memories. The Swiss neighbor is a semi-regular at the Sunday lunches.

Joe noted that they now might get a reservation from eight Australians at a time. Also, a pair of Australian couples might book a reservation independently and then meet up here, start chatting, become friends, and maybe come back as a foursome. Attendance has gone way up since the commemorative celebration.

Manu stated that they now receive considerable local and national media attention. A few months ago, the *Txoko* was featured on a television program, and, last month, Australian National Radio did a broadcast from the premises. During *San Fermín*, they were interviewed by newspapers regarding the significance of the event. Two weeks from now, their Sunday lunch is scheduled to be featured in the Sydney Food Guide.

I asked if they paid salaries to anyone, and they laughed and joked about it. Beñat emphasized that volunteerism is what made the *Txoko* work. It gave you a good feeling that you were doing something worthwhile. When he arrived here, he was astounded to see Basques on the other side of the world trying to preserve their heritage, and he wanted to be a part of it. Estefanía seconded the notion, while qualifying her statement with, "I am not even Basque, but.... " She noted, however, that they might be reaching their outer limits. If the number you are cooking for as a volunteer gets to be forty, that is quite a burden. To do it week after week, for nothing more tangible than a "good feeling," may not be viable indefinitely. It is just another issue that the *Txoko* will have to face in the future.

The *frontón* is hardly ever used for *pelota* any longer. During the commemoration, two Basques, including Beñat, played a match against two players from the New South Wales Handball Association, and lost. "We lost on purpose since to win would have been inhospitable!" Beñat observed. [Laughter.]

Every two years, the *Txoko* holds a *korrika*, that is about one mile long, in conjunction with the event in Euskalherria. It is more of a walk than a run, so the elderly and children can participate. Afterwards, they take a photo against a landmark background, like that of the Opera House. They then have a lunch.

Last year, the Club bought a kilometer in the famous annual *korrika* in the Basque Country that raises funds for language preservation. As luck would have it, they got sponsorship of the first kilometer that begins in Gernika. They put up their banner and several Queensland returnees showed up for the start. The Sydney *Txoko* received considerable coverage in all of the Basque media—including ETB (Basque Television).

The Club is trying to decide on its next event. Maybe in November or December, they will do a combined *San Ignacio* and *Olentzero* Christmas event outside in one of the parks. You need to keep in mind that July is the middle of the winter here, and it is risky to schedule anything outside at that time of year. It is likely to be cold and dreary. So, for the last couple of years they have clustered their annual events into an outdoor one in November to make them more user-friendly.

I then asked each of the persons present at the dinner for a short biographical sketch. I started with Manu. He is of Navarran descent through his mother's side, although she was born in Cuenca. His mother was working in the emergency room of a Madrid hospital, when Manny's father, a *Madridleño*, was admitted for an operation. They came to Australia in 1959 in one of the recruitments, Operation Emu, on the *Monte Udala*. They landed in Melbourne and went to the migrant camp Bonegilla. His father picked grapes and fruit for about a year with the womenfolk still residing in the camp. Then he got a job at the steelworks in Port Kembla and moved to Wollongong, about 80 kilometers south of Sydney. They lived in a suburb called Wombarra. That is where Manu grew up. His father was injured on the job and received very little by way of compensation. His legal team skimmed off the majority and, eventually, after many years of legal and medical battles, he was pensioned. So, his mother was commuting to a job in Sydney weekly to support the family. That was a burden, and they moved to the inner city.

Later in life, as an adult, Manu went backpacking around the world. After a short period in the Basque Country, and other parts of Spain and Portugal, he went to London where he put himself through engineering school for four years at Southbank University. He worked in a wine cellar/liquor store to meet his expenses. Manu then moved to the Basque Country for an extended stay to "explore my roots." He met his partner, Edurne Bengoetxea, in Barasoain, Navarra. She is originally from Tolosa, and is "prepared to list her eight Basque surnames!"

Together, they moved to Sydney. Today, he is self-employed with an engineering consultancy, concentrating on projects with social or environmental benefits (schools, libraries, recycling centers, composting facilities, and the like). After raising their children, Edurne has now returned to university part-time to complete her degree in Early-childhood Studies. She works three days per week as a self-employed preschool teacher. They have two boys—Aidan (an Irish name) and Unai. Both come here to the *Txoko* for language classes, although the logistics are sometimes difficult. Manu has been on the board of the *Txoko* since about 2006 or 2007.

Next came the president, Estefanía Martino Echarri. She was born and raised in Pamplona (her maternal family being from Vidaurreta/Bidaurreta). She has a PhD in Cell Biology from the University of Granada. She began her graduate studies at the University of Barcelona and followed her mentor when he transferred to the Andalusian institution. Her dissertation is on "The Implications of ADAMTS1 Protease in Angiogenesis and Cancer." Her significant other is Miquel Guisado Moriones who has a career consulting with the German software company SAP. His company transferred them to Australia and paid their moving expenses.

Estefanía joined *Gure Txoko* in 2013 and became a board member in 2015. She organized the Basque-dance classes and found a teacher for them. She enrolled herself but had to discontinue when she became pregnant. She also reactivated the Basque-language classes. She now has a two-year-old toddler named Irati Guisado Martino. Estefanía works for a biotech company here engaged in cancer therapy. When I asked her how she became president, she replied, "I was tricked." [Laughter.]

I then turned to Usue Garmendia Olano. She lives upstairs as one of the Club's two custodians. She said that she came to Australia looking for an adventure. Usue is fluent in Basque, English, and Spanish, and has an intermediate-level knowledge of Italian and French. She holds a Bachelors' degree in Human Resources Management from George Brown College in Sydney. She has just enrolled in a year-long course regarding administration of migrant affairs. She is unemployed and has held a number of part-time jobs. Her visa status prevents her from securing regular full-time employment. She is working to change that, but it takes many months. She first intended staying here for only a short time, maybe three months, but she liked Sydney and has now been here for a year.

Her roommate, Iruñe Peñagaricano, was born in Navarra, but heard a great deal about Australia from her father. She is the youngest child of Ramón Peñagaricano. When she graduated, she came out of curiosity. She knows English well and has Australian citizenship. She is fluent in Spanish, German, French, and Basque, having obtained a joint Masters' degree in Sociology from Institutions and Regional Governance—University of Paris-Descartes, in France, and the University of Ingolstadt, Germany; as well as a Human and Social Sciences degree in the Sociology of Contemporary Societies from the University Paris-Descartes. Prior to those studies, she had a degree in Economic and Business Sciences from the University of Navarra. She has done her custodial work until recently and has just she landed employment in social management administration here in Sydney.

Next was Joe Goicoechea Gangoiti. There was considerable banter and laughter over his name: "Joe," "José," "Josu," "Joseba." His parents were from Bermeo. His father was a fisherman from the age of fourteen, and his mother worked in fish processing. His father was tired of the lengthy absences and hard work that were the fisherman's lot. He would sometimes be as far away as Sierra Leone.

So, in 1966, he decided to move to Sydney. They only knew one word in English—"yes"—and they answered everything with it at first. His mother's sister was here with a fish-and-chips shop. His father worked most of his career at Kellogg's Cereals, but also was a handyman at a

Sydney grammar school and a car factory. His father was very Basque. He told Joe, "Inside the door of this house you speak only *Euskera*; outside of it you speak anything you want." His parents joined the *Txoko* in the 1980s and brought him here a lot when he was a kid.

Joe was born in the year 1973. He is in IT/Finance and holds a degree in Physics and Computer Science. He is married to an Australian Greek. He has two children and tries to use Euskera with them. They used to come more often to the *Txoko*, but the daughter is now fifteen and the son fourteen, and they both have their own friends and activities.

He first went back to the Basque Country when he was one—and has been back about every five years since. It was unusual in those days for whole families to make the trip. It was quite expensive. They would travel with Air India because it was the cheapest carrier. They went from here to Bombay and from there to London. There wasn't even a terminal in Bombay—just a hut with vending machines and rats everywhere. He has taken his own children to the Basque Country on three occasions.

His sister, Miren, married a Catalan from Barcelona. They lived in Turkey for five years and then Vitoria-Gasteiz for another five—all related to his work. Their two boys attended an *ikastola* in Vitoria-Gasteiz and studied *Batua*. They came back to Australia two or three years ago and are members of the *Txoko*.

Joe noted that when he first remembers going back to Bermeo, he would talk to the kids in his Basque and they would answer in Spanish. Then the *ikastolak* reinforced Basque, but it was *Batua*, not the local dialect. His last visit he noticed that the youth were communicating among themselves more in Spanish than Basque—not a promising sign.

Beñat Oliveira Bravo was born in Donostia. His father was in IT. Beñat attended the *Santo Tomás Ikastola* in Donostia. He studied civil engineering in Barcelona at the *Universitat de Catalunya*. He therefore speaks Catalan. He finished the equivalent of his Masters' degree and wanted to go abroad to get a doctorate in something. He applied and was accepted to Cal Tech in aeronautical engineering—but was not given a scholarship and therefore could not afford to study in the States. One of his professors in Barcelona knew that he wanted to go abroad and that he loved surfing. His mentor had a close colleague at Macquarie University in Sydney and contacted him. The Barcelona professor announced to Beñat one day that it was all arranged, and so Beñat came here in 2013 to get a PhD in Geophysics. He brought his surfboard and in two years never went surfing. [Laughter.] Today, he is doing a post-doc with the Macquarie professor who was the graduate advisor for his doctorate. So, he remains in academia as a researcher.

I asked if he was married? "No-o-o-o!" [Laughter.] When he first came to Sydney, he stayed in a boardinghouse near the university that was mainly for Asians. So, he felt like he was not even getting any exposure to Australian culture. When he left Spain, he was resolved not to have anything to do with Spanish nationals and Basques in Sydney, in order to experience real Australian life.

After about a year and a half, he felt very isolated and lonely—without friends. So, he went to the *Txoko* and immediately felt the vibrant social life that he had left behind in Europe. It was there that he made his first real friends. He was amazed to find people on the other side of the world working so hard to preserve their Basque language and culture and wanted to be a part of it. He served on a subcommittee during the commemoration events, and then came on the board in 2017. It was obvious that everyone liked him, and Manu remarked that Beñat always brings a positive view to any problem and is a great board member.

It seems that Beñat (along with Zaloa de Arrieta) was instrumental in bringing to Australia the performer Fermin Muguruza and his band's "No More Tour." They were playing on the Asian mainland and in Japan.

Zaloa was the secretary of the *Txoko* from 2010 to 2013 and vice president in 2014. She stepped down from office as she was expecting her first child. Originally from Hondarribia, Gipuzkoa, Zaloa was instrumental during the transition phase of the Club as she was its first officer ever able to correspond with the Basque government in Euskera. She had come to Australia, with her partner, prior to the recent exodus of Basque youth from Euskalherria.

It was thanks to her contacts in the Basque Country that *Gure Txoko* was able to contact Fermin Muguruza and his band while they were on their world tour. Somewhat on the fly, they agreed to add Australia. There was a very successful concert held here in Sydney. Some of the band members were billeted in homes. Beñat and Zaloa put out a call to the membership for spare mattresses and blankets, and part of the band's entourage slept on the floor in the *Txoko*. Subsequently, *Gure*

Txoko has been approached by several other Basque musical groups asking for assistance in arranging an Australian tour. Some, like Berri Txarrak ("Bad News"), have done so.

Izaskun de Allende Muriedas was up next. Her father was from Sopelana (Sopela) and her mother and grandmother from Bakio—although descended from Asturias. Her parents are now retired. Her father was a bank employee and her mother a travel agent. Isazkun was raised and educated in Bilbao. She wanted to study environmental sciences at the University of the Basque Country and had to go to the Vitoria-Gasteiz campus for that. She finished her last year at the Leioa campus outside of Bilbao.

She came to Australia in January of 2014. Her Basque partner at the time was working for a Sydney-based company that had a factory in Asturias. The Company manufactured "green walls" and had a patented system to collect, store, and reuse rainwater through plants. They met in Bilbao a year before emigrating to Australia. He was studying Business Administration there and was making frequent trips to Australia. The Company asked him to relocate to Sydney for two years, and they did so with their expenses paid. She looked at it as a life experience, an adventure.

Her first three months, she took an English Advanced Cambridge Certificate course and worked in a coffee shop part-time, while awaiting her visa that would permit her to work full-time. When she got it, her first employment was with the Cervantes Institute in Sydney. She was one of its Science and Cultural Programs coordinators for two years, before moving to Macquarie University. She just got a very interesting job as the Workplace Diversity & Inclusion Coordinator in its Human Resources Department. She is in charge of issues like gender equity, LBGTIQ inclusion, cultural intelligence, Indigenous affairs, etc. I asked if she was married and she said, "No. Like Beñat I am a little scared of that!" [Laughter.]

Jagoba Landa Quincoces then spoke. He is from Azpeitia, Gipuzkoa, and studied at Mondragon University, graduating with a Bachelors' degree in Business Administration and Human Resources. He had an aunt here in Sydney who invited him to come to Australia to learn English. He arrived on October 31, 2003. He spent his entire first year traveling throughout the country until his money ran out. So, he returned to Sydney to take classes for a postgrad degree in IT, and to finalize his visa situation so that he could work full-time.

He first visited the *Txoko* almost immediately after arriving in Australia, but began coming regularly the second year, or after his return to Sydney. He ended up becoming the live-in caretaker and serving for about five years on the board. He went off it a couple of years ago. "I saw so many enthusiastic young new members and thought they should have to chance to lead." But then, about six months ago, they asked him to come back on the board and he agreed.

He is employed by an Italian manufacturer of white goods and kitchen cabinetry. He is the manager of the spare-parts' department. He speaks no Italian. He is not married but has a Colombian partner. They have no children.

Finally, there is Aitor Aramburu Iztueta from Donostia. His father was from Zumarraga and worked for Elkar (Basque book and discography publisher and distributor). His mother is from Ataun and was a high school teacher. Aitor came to Australia four and a half years ago. He studied engineering in Donostia and then moved to Edinburgh for the last two years of his degree. He met his partner (now spouse) there. She was studying Spanish literature and history. She had spent a year in Spain and written her thesis on the troubled Basque transition (ETA, GAL, etc.) to democracy. She would ask him many questions; they became close.

Her sister was about to marry in Australia, and they decided to come here for the wedding. Since it was such a long and costly journey, they bought one-way tickets thinking that they would see if there were opportunities for them here. Today, they both have good jobs and are married (for one year) and without children as yet. He works for the Mondragón-based Fagor kitchenware company as an e-commerce and digital marketing director. He trains maintenance technicians. He got the job because he could speak both English and Basque. His wife works for Universal Music as an e-commerce specialist. She manages the website and the online marketing.

When they first came to Sydney, they were the caretakers of the *Txoko* and lived upstairs for six or eight months. They came to realize that it was too much to do in addition to their full-time jobs. It really hadn't been his intention to become involved with Basques here, but the director of HABE (a Basque government institution coordinating adult literacy in Basque) was a friend of his and urged him to check out the Sydney Basque Club. He probably came for the first time about three weeks after arriving here. He became the Basque teacher for a while and went on the board about three years ago. His wife is attending the language class. They are thinking of returning to Donostia in a year or two, and she wants to know the Basque language.

There was one board member missing from the dinner, Jon Urrejola Eguren, from Durango, Bizkaia. He graduated from Mondragon University with a degree in organizational engineering and came to Australia in 2012. His father, Juan Mari, was born in Berriz, Bizkaia, and his mother, Irene, was born in Angiozar (Bergara). She runs the lottery shop in Durango. Jon is married to Nekane Reta Murua, the current teacher of Euskera at the *Txoko*. He presently works as a researcher for a high-tech medical startup company developing a micro-device for implantation in the back to block pain signals to the brain. It is still in the design phase and is not yet produced economically on an industrial scale.

The evening's conversation concluded with a free-ranging discussion. Manu stated that the collective effort by everyone around the table was successful because it was "a labor of love." The *Txoko* is a kind of Basque ambassador to the wider world. It also provides assistance to Basques passing through Sydney. It receives requests from the Old Country from young people seeking advice on relocating here or visiting. Maybe one a week. They always try to answer and assist. They have helped several people prepare and file their visa application and then find employment in Sydney. Jon was critical to the *Txoko* in its interaction with the Old Country. He had many contacts there and was a great communicator. He answers most of the correspondence and queries from Europe.

Joe added that everyone had personal reasons for being here, but there was a collective purpose as well. There was also a disposition to work through any minor friction in the best interest of the *Txoko*. He opined that possibly it had to do with something unique in the Basque character. There is a kind of cooperative spirit and tolerance that is not found in every group. His Greek wife can tell that a person from Madrid is not from the Basque Country the minute she meets her or him.

Estafanía noted that, "For us, the new migrants, the *euskal etxea* (she used that term) is a place where we can display our culture to the wider community." Manu weighed in with the expression, "waving the *ikurriña*." "But," she added, "we must always respect the need of the older members to have their ethnic refuge."

I was now off to my next port of call—Townsville. I had contacted Bianka Vidonja Balanzategui to set up a meeting and she insisted on preparing a lunch for me instead. She was particularly interested in my meeting her son Javier. He had done an Honour's thesis on ETA while studying for a Bachelor of Arts at the University of Queensland in Brisbane. We were scheduled to eat at Javier's house in the suburbs.

I was picked up at my hotel by his sister, Keziah, and her significant other, Johannes Inoke. He is of Fijian extraction on his father's side and his mother is from Amsterdam. Johannes was raised in Innisfail. Keziah was about to have a baby and they planned to marry next April. They met while working at the same hotel in Brisbane six years ago. They both studied at the University of Queensland; he graduated with an Engineering degree and she with a Master's in Business. He now works at BMD Urban (a construction company) here, one of Mendi Constructions competitors. He specializes in drainage systems. She works for Regis Aged Care Facility as its manager.

Her brother Javier had changed careers to work for Townsville's James Cook University after a decade working for the government. He originally had moved to Canberra to undertake a graduate internship with the Australian Capital Territory (ACT) government. He also later worked for the Australian government and pursued a Masters' degree in Public Administration. It was there that he met his wife, New Zealand–born and Gladstone-raised Alicia. She had also moved from Queensland to work as a graduate intern with the ACT government, and also later with the Australian government, while undertaking a Masters' degree in Human Resource Management. Javier and Alicia were in Canberra for six years before moving to Brisbane in 2016 to continue their public service careers. After the birth of their daughter, Alegra, they resettled in Townsville to be closer to family and be able raise their child in a less hectic environment.

After finishing high school, Javier had spent a year in Pucallpa, Peru, as a Rotary International exchange student, where he learned fluent Spanish. He and Alicia have been to Europe on several occasions, traveling widely throughout the continent; but have only visited the Basque Country once. Keziah and Johannes have also made one recent trip to Europe, along with Keziah's sister Viktoria. They spent five days in all in the Basque Country—beginning in Bilbao, then San Sebastián, and finishing in Lekeitio, where the girls contemplated their grandparents' graves. They then toured other parts of Europe, including visiting Amsterdam.

Victoria has a Masters' degree in Media Relations from Brisbane's Griffith University. She also did a Rotary Exchange, spending her year in Rio Neginhos, Brazil, where she learned Portuguese. She works in Sydney for a television station: Special Broadcasting Service—National Indigenous Television (SBS—NITV). Her partner, Jean, is of Japanese and French descent. They have no children.

There is another sister, Petra (unmarried), who has an undergraduate degree in Archeology from the University of Queensland and has undertaken further study in her field at Flinders University, Adelaide. She has recently moved to Sydney to further her career in cultural-heritage management. She visited the Basque Country as part of a trip to Spain to attend the Catholic World Youth Day in Madrid. She plans to return to Spain soon in order to learn Spanish.

Twenty-one-year-old Sabin is the youngest in the family. He is named after his grandfather, Sabin Berbix Balanzategui, whose parents emigrated to Australia from the Basque Country in the early twentieth century. He lives at home in Ingham with his parents and works as a trainee with TELSTRA, a telecommunications company. He was absent today due to other commitments, but he had said: "Tell Professor Douglass that I am very Basque." He has yet to go to the Basque Country.

Keziah noted that her father, Mark Balanzategui, had never been to the Basque Country. Mark has not even been to Europe as yet, unlike Bianka, whose family relocated from Slovenia to Graz, Austria, after World War II. She has been to Graz numerous times to visit relatives; but never to the Basque Country, despite her publications regarding Basque topics here in the Far North. Keziah noted that she and her siblings all hope to accompany or facilitate her parents' travel to the Basque Country in the near future.

When we arrived at Javier's and Alicia's house, Bianka was well engrossed in preparing a Basque meal. Mark was wearing an Ingham Italian Festival tee-shirt. The event had just celebrated its 25th anniversary. In recent years Mark and Bianka had both volunteered at the Festival. We reminisced about the first one. I had attended to give a public lecture as part of the proceedings and sign my new book at the time: *From Italy to Ingham: Italians in North Queensland*. He and Bianka continue to volunteer for the Italian Festival every year.

As we dined, the uniqueness of the Basques came up several times. During a discussion of the language, Johannes compared the Basque Country to his father's island, Rotuma, in the Fijis. It seems that its people are Polynesian, unlike the Melanesians of the neighboring islands, and their language is unique even within the panorama of Polynesian ones. The island only has a few thousand inhabitants and is the object of a concerted effort to save not only the culture and language but the sovereignty of the island for the Rotuman people. He thought the situation to be not unlike that of *Euskera* and its speakers in Europe.

Bianka and I discussed her current activities. She has just finished her PhD work at James Cook University and won a six-month postdoctoral internship in industry. It will be her task to enhance school groups' experiences when they visit Paronella Park. Opened in 1935, its attractions are a castle (now in ruins) and gardens built in the Moorish style by Catalan immigrant José Paronella. Bianka has surveyed nearly three hundred schools in the North Queensland region, soliciting their reasons for visiting the Park and requesting suggestions on how their field trips could be made more relevant to their study units. Bianka will then compile task sheets that conform to the National Curriculum.

As for language retention, since Mark's mother was not Basque, the language was not spoken in his household, although his father, Sabin, used it with fellow Basques. Javier knows the odd expression, but is more fluent in Spanish, given his Peruvian experience and association with Spanish and Latin American immigrants here. He has made some attempts to impart Spanish to his daughter but noted that it is difficult in a predominantly English-speaking environment.

Bianka and Mark and their children go to the monthly lunches at the Basque Club in Townsville whenever they can. However, she is skeptical of its future, given that with each successive generation the language is spoken less and the links with the Basque Country become more tenuous.

I interviewed Johnny Mendiolea that afternoon. He first went to the Basque Country with his parents, Michael, and Tommy in 1974. They lived in Lekeitio for twelve months and he attended primary school, completing his grades four and five. Franco was still alive, so all instruction was in Spanish. After he graduated from grade twelve in Ingham, he gained employment as an apprentice electrician at Victoria Sugar Mill for a period of four years. After his first year, he went to Spain by himself and stayed in both Lekeitio and Salamanca with his uncle and aunt for about six weeks. On his return to Australia, he completed his trade qualifications and then enrolled at James Cook University to complete a teaching degree. His next trip was in about 1992 or 1993 with his brother Tommy and friend Amaya. He thought the USAC program in San Sebastián was fun,

> A good little holiday with a bit of study and self-reflection on the side. We took it seriously, but not too seriously. The academic courses were very enlightening and well delivered. The cultural excursions were appropriate and well organized. Not that I participated in many of these excursions. They were usually on Saturdays and Sundays and I had indulged in too much "Cuba Libre" on Friday night. Actually, I knew the Basque Country pretty well by then, so I didn't really need them. It is a regret though that I did not totally immerse myself in the cultural aspects of the course.

Before going on the USAC program, he had completed two years of teaching at a Catholic high school in Townsville. He had taken an unpaid six-months' leave of absence. After the four months in Donostia, his then girlfriend joined him, as well as his brother Michael and one of his mates. They all did a two-month "Kon-Tiki" (i.e., whirlwind) tour of Europe.

He returned to his teaching job and has worked for Townsville Catholic Education ever since. Today he teaches some mathematics and is in charge of trade and vocational training. He was a pastoral coordinator for a number of years. He noted that, "despite the name, it is not just about religion. Of course, being a parish school, religion is certainly a significant part of the role. But the pastoral side highlights the importance of forming the student's entire character within the general framework of Christian morality. If you don't achieve this, the curriculum *per se* is irrelevant."

After he had completed ten years in the pastoral role and also serving as a curriculum leader for three, he was exhausted and ready for a change. His principal knew that and called him in and suggested that he consider administration. They needed a vice principal for their school in Mount Isa for about two years; would he accept the position? He agreed to do so. But his father had just died and his grandmother had passed away the year before. He did not want to stay in Mount Isa indefinitely and it was resolved that he would serve the two years and then return to his old position at his old school.

In the event, six months after he arrived in Mount Isa, his principal took leave and John was made the acting principal of the school. It was stressful, but he enjoyed the challenge. Mount Isa is far inland and has a climate much like Reno—hot summers and cold winters. The ochre-colored landscape is spectacular. He tried to find some Basques there, but was unsuccessful.

There had been many working in Mount Isa earlier, during the development phase of the mine. They did all the hard work then, along with other migrant groups like the Italians and Slavs. But mining was now mature, the city a little in the doldrums, and those migrants that had made their money were forty or fifty and perhaps had returned to their homelands, the coast, or the capital cities. "I didn't find any Basques at all in Mount Isa."

He was offered a permanent position in Mount Isa and/or the possibility of becoming the principal of a school in Ingham, but he wanted to go back to his old position in Townsville. Conchi was completing her two-year stay in Spain and was coming back to Townsville alone. Her boys needed to set her up in a house and look after her. So, John returned to his old post and has subsequently done a little administration, pastoral guidance, and vocational training. He noted the importance of the latter since the reality is that only forty to fifty percent of their students continue on to higher education, and they need to develop alternative career pathways for the others.

John married Allison, a Tasmanian woman, in 1999, and they have two sons, Ethan and Macauley. He has never gone back to the Basque Country and neither she nor the boys have ever been there. Whenever they could afford a vacation, about every two years, they would go to Tasmania to see Allison's parents and family. His boys are now eighteen and fifteen, and last year was the first time they had ever been to Sydney, Melbourne, and Canberra. They loved it and want to go back. His wife and the boys would like to go to Spain and see the place that he has told them about. He hopes to make a family trip there in the next two or three years. "I want the boys to be able to say that at least I took them once. If they want to return after that, it is their concern."

John speaks Spanish, but it is getting rusty. He is unsure how it will persist now that Conchi is gone. He used it with her, but now has no one to talk to. His Basque is much poorer. He can understand it, and come up with short questions and replies, but is no longer really a Basque speaker. He said that it is his fault that his boys don't know the languages or more about their culture. Conchi used to speak with them about Basques, but now she is gone. "Amuma taught them a lot about their heritage and they loved their grandmother very much. But their mom and dad have not really exposed them to the richness of Basque culture."

I asked if he follows Basque affairs or interacts with anyone in the Basque Country on the internet? He laughed and replied, "I follow you. I have read nearly all of the books you gave to Mom and the *Basque History of the World* one too. I remember when you came to our farm when I was a little boy. I remember Jan fondly." He added,

> I am very proud of my heritage and particularly my father and his parents, Tomás and Teresa, and the path that they and others laid for other migrants to follow. I have witnessed the books and the signatures of the many hundreds of Basque migrants who came to Australia that were assisted by my dad and his family. From a young age, Dad was immensely proud of his Basque heritage, shared the stories of migrant hardship, perseverance, ingenuity, success, and, at times, failure. I know firsthand the incredible contribution that the Basques have made to this country and am very proud of it. I have my own little story, but I am part of a bigger, richer, and diverse Basque migrant story. The evidence is everywhere throughout the canefields and the social and cultural

fabric of North Queensland. You just need to know where to look. The time has to be right to engage with that story, and I plan to do so if I am still around.

We then spoke of his brothers. Michael lives in Ingham and is an elementary schoolteacher there. When he got his degree, his parents still had their cane farm. His wife, Tricia, is also from Ingham, the daughter of a canefarmer of Anglo descent. Her sister, Trina, also married an Ingham canefarmer of Italian descent. So, after teaching in Mount Isa for two years, Tricia responded to the call of home and took a teaching job in Ingham as well. Today she teaches a little and oversees curriculum from kindergarten through year six.

Stephen, fourteen years younger than John, came to Townsville with his parents and grandmother after they sold the cane farm. He attended Ignatius Park Catholic High College, but was not academically oriented. He completed an apprenticeship as a motor mechanic at Pickering Motors here in Townsville. He spent a number of years as workshop supervisor in the luxury car department. He grew tired of the work and became a driver for RACQ, the automobile club, providing roadside assistance to needy motorists. He then worked a few years in the RACQ roadworthy division. If you want to sell a used car it has to be certified as roadworthy through a RACQ inspection. About five years ago, Stephen bought a business that services and cares for hydraulic struts in automobiles and general industry. On the side, he repairs and builds custom-made cricket bats.

Stephen is married to Anne and they have two girls. She is from Townsville and of Anglo descent. Townsville never had agriculture, so unlike the Burdekin and Ingham with their Southern European migrant influence, Townsville has always been very British. Today, if you hear a foreign language in the street it is likely to be Asian and spoken by a tourist. It would not be Italian or Spanish. Anne's parent probably got a real shock when she first took up with Stephen.

Neither John nor Michael have been back to Spain since the USAC trip, but Stephen went a few times with Conchi. Also, three years ago, he went with her and Mari Ibañez to look after them and serve as their chauffeur.

None of the three Mendiolea boys living here in the Far North are members of the Basque Club of North Queensland. Michael really lives too far away. Also, all are married to non-Basque Anglo women who feel out of place in the Club environment. When it first started, John and Allison attended a few times. They have not gone in the last three years. His Aunt Dolores is very involved and always asks him to come whenever they meet. He noted that the distancing of the Mendiolea boys is not out of disdain for their heritage.

He admires what his aunt and uncle (José and Dolores Larrazabal) have done for the Club and speculated that when he retires and has more time, he might get involved in it again. It has become very cosmopolitan—there are now a lot of Latin Americans at events—and he thinks that that is a good thing.

He brought up his relative, Joe Iturraspe. It seems that the Iturraspes were related to the Mendioleas through Conchi's father, Julio. Joe's parents lived in the Burdekin and fell upon hard times. They were in poor health. Johnny and Conchi brought them to Ingham and cared for them. Joe never forgot that. He later went to Vancouver with two other friends from the Burdekin to cut timber in British Columbia and stayed on when the other two returned here. He has visited Australia several times since and always stopped off to see the Mendioleas. Joe has a son in Melbourne. Last Christmas, when Conchi was very unwell, Joe came to Townsville to see her. He was in the country to visit Melbourne where his son's companion had just given birth. Joe wanted to see his new grandson.

John noted that when he retires, he wants to travel to North America. He has no interest whatsoever in California or Florida. Rather, he is fascinated by the bright lights of New York, and, of course, Idaho, with its historical Basque sheepherding influence. His other destination is Vancouver—to visit Joe.

I remarked that John looked like his father and he became emotional and agitated. He was pleased by my comment and spoke of how selfless his father was. "Even after he retired to Townsville, once a week he drove to Ingham to help illiterate elderly migrants of all nationalities fill out forms for medical care and retirement benefits. He received no compensation—it cost him his time and money."

John is convinced that the intense caregiving for twelve years of his incontinent and dementia-stricken grandmother had a significant and negative impact on his health. "Dad would have to hold her aloft for several minutes while mum bathed her and soothed her bedsores."

John noted,

> I did that a few times when I was a fit twenty-five-year-old and I could barely manage it. Dad was much older and had a bad heart, yet he did it twice a day every day without a single complaint. I, to this day, do not know how he managed it. He was the glue that held us all together. Our Basque identity was forged through him. It was after he died that all three of us drifted away from the Basque community. That is a big part of the explanation. When I think of who he was and all the good that he achieved and how selflessly he contributed to society and those in most need, I often think that I have accomplished little in my own life.

John reached out and placed his hand on my arm. "It's time for me to go now before I tear up."

The next morning, I drove to Ayr to spend the day and night at the home of Mary (Bengoa) Arrate. I wanted to clean up my earlier interviews with her deceased husband, Agustín. When she showed me to my room, Mary noted that my bedspread had been knitted by Conchi Mendiolea's mother, Fermina. Tommy had included it in the box of her things that Conchi had designated for Mary.

We began to review each of her children's background. Son Johnny went to the Basque Country when he was in his early twenties after losing his best friend in an accident. He stayed for more than a year in Markina with his father's mother and in Gernika with Mary's sister, Tere.

John married Danielle, a Home Hill girl of Italian descent (non-Sicilian). Her father was born in Home Hill as well and her mother is Anglo. John is now fifty-one and Danielle is forty-five. She worked as an assistant to a solicitor in Home Hill when they married and still does. They have three children—Lily seventeen, Julen fifteen, and Dominic thirteen. John had a haul-out business and a small cane farm. After giving up the former, he went to work for Kensington Mine as a mechanic and he flies back and forth to it. The mine is inland from Mackay, near Conclurry. He alternates weeks there, which gives him time to work his cane.

Daughter Amaya became a schoolteacher and taught in Ingham. She was rooming with Tommy Mendiolea there when the USAC opportunity came up and they went to Donosti. She returned to Ingham to her teaching job and was renting a large house in Trebonne owned by Ramón Balanzategui. It was then that Mark Kelly, from Sydney, showed up as the new paid director of the Ingham Italian Festival. Amaya showed him space in the extensive property. He later reminisced that he liked the atmosphere and thought he literally saw an aura around her head. In short, it was love at first sight. He rented the room. Later, Mark and Amaya became flatmates in new quarters in Ingham.

Amaya's cousin, Bego, was teaching in a Catholic school in Townsville. Amaya wanted out of the public education system and applied to the parochial one. The diocese offered her a post at its Palm Island school in the roughest part of Townsville. It was a Black neighborhood, where, when a police officer had killed an inebriated Black, the Aborigines burned down the police station. Amaya knew that her father would have a heart attack had she accepted employment there. She reapplied and was offered a post about twenty miles from Townsville that she accepted. Eventually, she ended up at her cousin's school.

Meanwhile, she bought a house at auction in Townsville. She had some money; her grandmother had bequeathed a small inheritance to each of her grandchildren. The house had four bedrooms and she decided to rent out three of them. Mark Kelly rented one of them and a few weeks later he came to Gus and Mary to ask for Amaya's hand in marriage.

Daughter Idoya is a certified cardiac nurse in Townsville. She is married to a non-Basque Aussie, David Phillips. David is the equivalent of a dean at a local private secondary school. Mary isn't sure of his ethnic origin. "Like Mark Kelly, he is just Australian." David is a rugby coach and takes his kids to the British Isles every other year for a tournament. Both Mark and David treat Mary's daughters like princesses.

Idoya and David purchased an apartment in Markina from Gus. He owned two; the third and second floors of the same building. One of Agustin's brothers lived in the second-floor one (the apartment their mother once occupied). Agustín's two nephews still run the family's mechanics business.

So, Idoya and David began taking Patxi to Markina. He attended kindergarten in Markina when the family went there for six months to remodel the property; he was three or four and learned Basque. They take him back about every two years. Mary considers his Basque to be better than hers, certainly his *Batua*. Idoya always speaks Basque with him no matter where or whoever is present. David is very supportive.

A *jai-alai* player in the United States nicknamed "Txapo" lives across the street. His parents are in Markina and he returns with his family to visit. His son, about Patxi's age, knows only English. Txapo now calls David to coordinate their visits so Patxi can hang out with the other boy and translate for him as needed. Patxi is worried about losing his Basque and so David plans to take Patxi to Markina over this coming Christmas. Idoya can't make it due to work obligations.

Mary's sister, Tere, still lives in Gernika with her husband, Luis. Her father, Ignacio Gabiola, brought them out to Australia when their son turned one; no doubt hopeful that they would stay. But Luis missed Gernika, so they returned. He is an electrician there. They make regular trips to Australia—she came for her father's and mother's funerals and Idoya's and Johnny's weddings. They both attended Mary's seventieth birthday celebration and Peter's eightieth. Mary goes to the Basque Country nearly every year and stays with Tere in Gernika and in Idoya's apartment in Markina.

Mary's brother Peter is married to Marian Malaxecheverria from Lekeitio. They have two children—Cristina and Luis (Louis). Cristina is a masseuse in Townsville. She was a nurse before that. She married a Colombian, but it didn't work out. Her eighteen-year-old daughter, Layla, speaks Basque. Cristina is close to her cousins, Amaya and Idoya.

Louis lives on his parents' cane farm. His marriage to an Australian ended in divorce. They have three children that live with him and his parents here on the farm.

Brother John married a woman from Aulesti, Begoña Martiartu. He met her while spending twenty months in the Basque Country, mainly Lekeitio. He had traveled there with Johnny, Dolores, and Teresa Mendiolea. Johnny Mendiolea met his future wife, Conchi, on that trip. John died in 2009. He had three daughters—Rosemary, Elizabeth, and Begoña—all of whom speak perfect Basque. Rosemary works in the front office of the Townsville hospital. [Begoña is a schoolteacher in Townsville—at Amaya's school. Elizabeth sells cars for the Toyota agency in Ayr.]

Mary gave me several "artifacts." These included two kitchen aprons with "The Basque Club of Nth. Qld." emblazoned on them, along with a map of Australia with a Basque flag in its center and a *lauburu* emblem below it. There was also a coffee cup with the words "Basque in Australia" and two crossed flags (Australian and Basque). She laughingly asked if I recognized it. I did not, and she said that it was her idea and she copied it from a pin from the Boise *Jaialdi* with crossed American and Basque flags. I had given it to her in 2002 on my last visit to North Queensland.

She then showed me a framed photo of her deceased husband, Agustín Arrate, against the backdrop of a Basque flag and with two verses in Basque along the side. It seems that they were written by the Markina *bertsolari* (and professional clown), Eneko Arrate, Agustín's nephew and sung by his father, Javier, at the burial of Agustín's ashes in the Markina cemetery. Copies of the photo with verses were given to Mary and each of her three children. The verses read:

Euskal Herritik Australiara	From the Basque Country to Australia
bidaia luzea dago	it is a long journey
gazte-gaztetan joan ziñen zu	you were very young when you went
kañaberaren abaro	to the place of the sugar cane
eta geroztik uste ez harren	never believing that you would
han geratu luzaro	stay for so long
Australiako bizi modua	you loved completely
maita zenuen zeharo	the Australian way of life
hala to ere Euskal Herri zaharra	but you loved even more
maite zenuen gehiago.	the old Basque Country.
Orain barriro, agur esanez	Now, again, saying goodbye
itzuli zara etxera	You returned home
joan baitzara goxo-goxoki	For you went ever so sweetly
jainkoaren besapera	to God's promised land
gure bizitzak, nola ez, Agustin	our lives, how could it be otherwise,
jarraituko du aurrera	Agustin, will proceed forward
baña goazen danok batera	but let's all go together
esker onak ematera	to give our thanks
eta egon trankil, noiz bait zeruan	and be in peace, one day in heaven
danok goaz alkartzera.	we will all be together.

Mary's son, John, and his sons arrived to have dinner with us. He had injured his shoulder and was going through some rehabilitation. His wife is currently in Fiji with their daughter. Lily just graduated from high school and the custom is to take a graduation trip abroad. Danielle had just been named Queensland's mother of the year, which accorded her a week's trip to Fiji. Mother and daughter are currently there.

Johnny noted that he was probably remiss in transferring Basque culture to his children. It was hard, in part, because his wife was not Basque. They didn't frequent the Townsville Basque Club. Between his job at the mine and farming on his cane property, there was also little time. Mary plans to take his daughter to the Basque Country next month and Lily has expressed interest in returning there in 2020 with school friends. John plans to return to Markina as well, after many years' absence, "when the time is right."

He has become very interested in the local and national cane-cutting competitions. The national one began at a farm in Dalbeg and is now held in Home Hill. It is becoming a tourist attraction—this year's event attracted 5,000 spectators. The competition is, of course, about nostalgia, since no one cuts manually any longer. It is usually won by elderly Italians, several of whom are mentoring younger aspirants like Johnny—none of whom had ever cut before. His mentor is a Basque named Lorenzo Zumarán who lives in Home Hill. Zumarán has actually won the championship in the past. Johnny didn't realize that the man was Basque until Mary told him so. She put him in touch with his mentor. Each year he gives Johnny a few more tips and last year he lost to his protégé in the local competition. He remarked to the press that maybe he had taught Arrate "too much." The man, in his late seventies,[2] now has serious cancer and is unlikely to enter future competitions. Johnny came in first in his age bracket in this year's national competition and aspires to winning it all one day.

The competition's sponsors grow about two hectares of cane intended specifically for the trials. Each competitor is given a section of cane to cut within about fifteen minutes. The winner is the one with the shortest time. When the event was transferred to Home Hill, the sponsors wanted to find some Badilla cane—a variety no longer grown. Johnny is involved as a volunteer for the Canegrowers' Association at their local experimental plot where they develop and test new varieties.

Johnny knew of a patch at the station and was able to get some cuttings for the competition's plot. It is used to demarcate the sections that will be assigned to each contestant.

From Ayr I drove to Ingham to meet with Hinchinbrook Shire mayor Ramón Jayo. I first visited his parents in Trebonne. Félix is now bedridden. Pilar told me that they closed the bakery thirty years ago. When her son, Ramón, told her of his plans to run for mayor she replied, "Why on earth do you want to do that? That job makes for enemies and headaches. I won't vote for you." But, of course, she did.

Her daughter, Miriam, is married to an Aussie who is a mechanic. They live around the corner here in Trebonne with their two sons. So, Félix and Pilar often babysat the two grandsons, just about every day. They are now twenty-five and seventeen or eighteen. They have never been to the Basque Country. The eldest is a mechanic with his father and the younger is in his final year of a boilermaking apprenticeship at one of the local sugar mills. They speak Basque because their grandparents always used it with them. Their Aussie father is supportive. Their daughter also speaks it, since she has regular interaction with her parents and has been to the Basque Country three times—first when she was seven, then when eighteen, and more recently after Pilar recovered from breast surgery for cancer. All were extended stays with relatives in Aulesti. The mother and daughter want to go to the Basque Country next year, but the two grandsons and their father have no interest in coming along.

Mayor Jayo received me at the shire hall. When he learned that I was from Reno, he said that he had relatives in Nevada, Astorquias—they grow corn. When I said that he might have meant Boise, Idaho, he concurred. "Yes, yes, it must be Idaho." Ramón is the first Basque mayor of Ingham. "Of all Australia, I believe," he added with a laugh. He received 58 percent of the vote in a field of five candidates, so he didn't face a second round. "The community was looking for a change; not much happened here under the previous administration."

He brought considerable experience to the office. He studied family law for three years at the University of Queensland but was turned off by "progressive" new Australian family law legislation in the late eighties that he regarded to be "bullshit and quite unjust and unequitable." He went into local government, first at Dalrymple Shire council and then at Charters Towers Regional Council, where, since 2008, he has been the director of planning and development. His wife, Sharon, also a local of Ingham, was adamant that their eldest child, Rachel, commence her senior year of schooling in Ingham. So, in 2010, they bought a small cane farm at Macknade, and returned to live in the Hinchinbrook Shire. From 2010 until 2015, Ramón continued to work for Charters Towers Regional Council, commuting from Ingham weekly. It is not a long drive—a little over two hours. He noted that today you need proper credentials for the work he did in government, but then you interviewed, and, if appointed, it was your job performance that counted.

He speaks some Basque—enough to communicate with his parents in it. When he was ten, they took him to the Basque Country for eighteen months. He attended school in Aulesti. It was there that he learned Spanish. He has lost much of it and regards his Basque to be better. His wife is a "fair-dinkum" Aussie—Adams. She was born here to a cane-farming family. He has two daughters and a son. When he takes his kids to visit their grandparents, they can't understand a word that is being spoken. "I make it worse by telling them we are talking about them." His daughter is now studying at James Cook University to be an early childhood schoolteacher. The son is only twelve. They have never been to the Basque Country and have no desire to go. The daughter has been to Italy once on a school excursion and they spent time in England as well, but not Spain. Next year she intends to go to the United States.

Ramón has never been back to Spain since the one trip and has no desire to return.

His sister and parents used to ask him to go, but he declined, even before he was married to a non-Basque. "I don't like travel. I would rather stay home sitting on a tractor in my cane field." Were he to travel it would be somewhere like Iceland or Africa. There, he would leave the city and go out into the countryside to see how people grow things. But he then mused, "Maybe in a few years I'll take my wife to the Basque Country, just so she can understand what my parents and me talk about. By then, the kids will be gone. They have no interest in Spain."

He thinks he may still be a member of the Basque Club in Townsville but was not certain. He was a charter member, and even reviewed some of the early documents that needed to be filed to create the Club, but he hasn't been to any of the lunches for a very long time. The Larrazabals invite him regularly, but he has his heavy work schedule (the consultancy and mayoral duties) during the week and spends weekends with his aged parents and on his tractor. Then, too, his wife and children don't really relate to Basque identity. He did, however, express a little remorse. "I should make a bigger effort to attend once in a while. Maybe, I will when things settle down."

I asked if he has ever been in the Sydney *Txoko*? He has not and added that when he has to go there, he conducts his business and heads straight for the airport. "I hate cities; I'm just a country boy at heart."

There was a Basque *cesta* on the wall of his office that was given to Ramón by a Basque who owns a Gold Coast restaurant. The man is an avid angler and he comes here to Forest Beach to fish with an Australian buddy. On one trip, he read about Ramón's election to mayor and called him up to congratulate him on the victory. The man was born somewhere in the Basque Country and speaks Basque. Ramón called him a "real character." He sent the *cesta*. When I asked if he had any other Basque things, he spoke about his weight-lifting stones. It seems that he bought a house from Alberto Urberuaga in Trebonne to use as a rental and these two stones were there. One now holds up a flowerpot at his sister's house and the other at that of his parents. He thinks they must be worth a fair bit. The Sydney Club heard about them and offered to buy the stones, but he did not want to sell.

I asked if he had further political aspirations and Ramón laughed at the question. He had an agenda when he ran for mayor. He wanted to foment economic development here so the youth wouldn't have to keep migrating out. He wants to be a canefarmer full-time,

> I love to see stuff coming out of the ground. I love to work in the dirt. It probably comes from my grandparents over in the Old Country. As a kid, I was always at the Badiolas. I didn't spend much time in the bakery. I loved farming and they taught me all about it. I stayed with them for weeks at a time. My father cut cane and then timber for the mills, but he was never a farmer.

When I asked how things were going with his agenda, he replied that he was pleased most of the time, adding, "You can't please everybody. Some people should just have never been born."

The next morning, I met with Amaya Arrate at her house in Townsville. We started by discussing the genesis of the Basque Club of North

Queensland. One morning, Joe Goicoechea called her and asked if he could stop by. Her mother, Mary Arrate, and some other Basque ladies happened to be having tea with Amaya. It would have been about a year before the Basque Club of North Queensland was founded, or 2002, since the Club just celebrated its fifteenth anniversary this year. Joe said that his idea was to start a Basque Club in Townsville, halfway between the major Basque settlements in the Herbert and Burdekin.

A steering committee was formed to discuss the potential Club. There was also a follow-up lunch/meeting organized, to which all identified Basque families were invited. A few months later, Joe Goicoechea identified a closed building that had once been the Polish Club here. He was prepared to put up the money for the lease and repairs as a loan. He said, "As it stands, we only see each other at funerals; it used to be only at weddings. We need to meet without it being a sad affair."

Joe served as the first president and Mary Arrate was the first vice president. The building needed work and the idea was to give it a "Basque flair." Jon Larrazabal, son of José and Dolores Mendiolea, is an architect and he drew up plans. Many people donated their labor—several were in the construction trades.

The Basque Club has a steering committee that Amaya has served on from the beginning. The main activity is a monthly Sunday lunch that is hosted by volunteer groups. Mary puts on two annually, including one held in the Burdekin. José and Dolores, despite their advanced ages and poor health, continue to sponsor. There is also a men's group, headed by Amaya's husband, Mark Kelly, that hosts two annually. Phil Zumarán learned from Joe Goicoechea how to cook an excellent *paella*, and Phil has now initiated Idoya's husband, David Phillips, in that art as well.

In all, there are eleven hosted luncheons (none in January). The event's volunteer group does everything. It publicizes, takes reservations, does the setting up, operates the door, bar, and raffle, and cooks, serves, and cleans up. Usually, each of its members brings a dish.

Amaya is in a cooking group organized by her cousins, Diana Gabiola and Rosemary Bengoa. Amaya ran the bar at their last event, along with an Italian friend, granddaughter of the owners of the Trebonne Hotel who built North Queensland's only *frontón*.

The December lunch is held at the clubhouse and prepared by local caterers so that no one has to work over the holiday. At that time, there is an *Olentzero*, or the Basque equivalent of Santa Claus, for the children. It is usually Jon Larrazabal; or David Phillips in his stead. The *Olentzero* listens to their Christmas wishes, and gives out a traditional lump of coal to the naughty ones and a bag of lollies to all.

The lunches are open to anyone on a reservation basis. Attendance varies according to the time of the year and venue. It ranges between fifty and one hundred. Many journey to Townsville from either the Herbert or the Burdekin. Pedro Aranas, from Ingham, is a regular and Ramón Balanzategui from there belongs to the men's cooking group. There are no other special events during the year comparable to the Saint Ignatius Day festivities of yore. If someone happens to be coming through from the South or from the Old Country, there may be a potluck dinner for those interested in an encounter. One was being organized for tomorrow night in my honor. The lunches provide most of the operating income of the association.

Amaya began a cooking class initiative as another fund-raiser, but mainly to introduce the wider pubic to Basque cuisine. Some were skeptical that anyone would show, but she was persistent. She wanted to charge A$15 for a two- or three-hour class. Mari Ibañez, the non-Basque wife of the deceased Tomás Ibañez, agreed to teach the first class that imparted recipes for the *tortilla española* (egg and potato omelet) and *croquetas*. It was a great success and netted A$210, including a donation of fifty dollars by Joe Goicoechea toward food costs.[3] Cooking class posters and lunch photos are posted regularly on the Club's Facebook page. The monthly menu can vary, and, at times, includes Italian dishes. However, it is the traditional Basque cooking that appeals most. Elderly members often remember their childhood fare nostalgically. When served pigs' feet or tripe they are likely to say, "I haven't tasted this since my mother died."

To celebrate its tenth anniversary, the Club sponsored a mini-*Jaialdi* inspired by the Boise event. There were about 150 people in attendance. An Australian woman, Robin, married to Phil Zumarán and versed in dance, taught about eight kids how to do several Basque dances. These included her two grandchildren and Amaya's children as well.

Amaya received her education degree from James Cook University and then taught for two years in Ingham in a primary public school.

While there, she roomed with Tommy Mendiolea. "The Basque community of North Queensland is small and intimate. Tommy is like a cousin to me."[4] In February of 1992 she went overseas to Japan to visit Tommy Mendiolea. He taught English there for eighteen months. From Japan, she visited Greece, Turkey, and Egypt. In September, she met the group from the University Studies Abroad Consortium for orientation before proceeding by bus to Donostia where they were to live for a semester. Tommy was part of that program, as was his brother Johnny. Tommy suggested that they all get an apartment together. The Mendioleas were pretty fluent Spanish speakers and that was a distraction for Amaya. She used either her poor Spanish or English with them most of the time. Actually, the semester they spent there together improved her Spanish more than her Basque. The two boys could wing it, but Amaya had to study pretty hard.

Tommy had a friend, Asun, who worked at a radio station. It had promoted a program that was sending student volunteers to help war refugees in Bosnia. Amaya interviewed and was accepted. She spent three weeks there and then went to London to work for a year as a substitute teacher. She visited Morocco, Scotland, Spain, and Holland from there, always returning to London to earn money for her next trip. In all, she spent two and a half years abroad before returning to Australia in May of 1994. She did so to be a bridesmaid at her best friend's wedding. While here, she was a substitute teacher for two days a week and then packed rock melons in a shed in Clare for the other five. She was saving for more travel and, in September, she went to Mexico, Colombia, Ecuador, Peru, and Bolivia for four months with two friends, including a girl from Ayr (of Italian descent).

By January of 1995, Amaya was back in Australia. She returned to Ingham to teach for two years. She was disenchanted by then with the public education system and was exploring the possibility of an appointment with a Catholic school in Townsville. It was about then that she met Mark Kelly. He was hired to run Ingham's Italian Festival beginning with about the third one. He and Amaya ended up as housemates. In 1998, she moved to a new job in a new parochial school in Townsville and bought a house there. Mark followed and they were married soon thereafter. He went to work for the mining company, BHP. It had a nickel refinery in Townsville.

Amaya taught for five years before going on maternity leave to start her family. Her son, Joseba, now sixteen, was the result. They had a daughter shortly thereafter, Maite, now fourteen. Mark was offered a promotion if he would move to BHP headquarters in Perth for two years. Amaya was ambivalent. It was far from her family and they were considering spending time in Markina. But he was really motivated so she agreed on condition that the move would be for two years only. They rented out the Townsville house and went to Perth. Their daughter, Ainara, now twelve, was born in Perth.

The Basques in Perth were few in number and had no club or even an occasional get-together. Amaya did encounter a tiny Basque network that linked Western Australia with the Burdekin and the Basque Country. Luis Lequerica was a successful contractor to mining companies. Amaya thought (without being sure) that he was born in the Burdekin and raised in Gernika, and that his family had a tavern in Lekeitio. He met his future wife, Marisol, there. But he wanted to return to Australia. He came back to Ayr where he had an uncle. A short time later he had an opportunity to move to Perth and did so. First, he traveled to the Basque Country for Marisol, married, and brought her to Perth with him.

Then there was Mari Louise Arroiti from Ayr. She was orphaned and went to Perth to live. Another Burdekin family, the Alcibars, lived in Perth as well. Iñaki Sesma, who had also lived in Ayr at one time, married Marian Alcibar from Ayr. He recently retired from his work in Perth and is planning a visit to Lekeitio this year.

Last June or July, Iñaki and Elena Sesma, along with Elena's mother, Julie Alcibar, came here from Perth. It was a regular Sunday lunch day at the Basque Club and about a dozen extended family members came to be with Iñaki and Elena. The old men enjoyed playing *mus* and talking in Basque.

Amaya and Mark lived for two years in Perth and then returned to Townsville. But then, BHP sold its Townsville operations to another company, owned by Clive Palmer. He ultimately shut down the nickel refinery here, putting 800 people out of work. Mark was an early termination. He was able to secure a job in media communications with the shire council—a post that he occupies to this day.

While Amaya was on maternity leave, she received a call from her assistant principal to the effect that changes in national education policy mandated that primary-school-aged children receive foreign language instruction. They needed extra Italian instructors and offered to pay her educational expenses for the training. She agreed and took the year-long program offered through Brisbane's Australian Catholic University, which ran an extension service for the group here in Townsville. Her cousin, Begoña Bengoa, also completed the same course. It was mainly by correspondence, although periodically an Italian instructor from Brisbane traveled to Townsville for intensive immersion classes. Given her history with foreign languages, and particularly Spanish, Amaya found learning Italian to be easy. The biggest problem was not confounding the two Romance languages.

Amaya is therefore now an Italian language teacher at her school. She teaches students between five and twelve years of age. Her two daughters have excelled at Italian as well. The eldest, Maite, opted for it as her language elective when she was in eighth grade and has studied it ever since. Ainara studies both Italian and Japanese. There are two Italian-language competitions for students here annually. The Italian government sends two or three judges from Brisbane from the Italian Learning Centre that it funds there.

Maite won this year's competition for the elder group (sixth grade and beyond) and Ainara came in first for the younger one (called the Maria di Marzio Award and funded by an Ayr family as a memorial to their daughter who died prematurely). John Mendiolea's son was the runner-up. So, Basques beat out descendants of Italians in their own language. Amaya kidded some of her Italian friends about it, but the joke fell flat. "Italians don't find things like that to be funny. It's like telling them that we can cook better than them."

Ironically, none of Amaya's children speak Basque or Spanish. They can understand some of both, having been around them with their grandparents. Amaya even tried to speak Basque with them when they were little, claiming that she knew no English. But they saw right through that since she used English with Mark. He has been studying Spanish of late and they try to speak it some at home. But his skills are rudimentary so they lapse easily into English. "I think we have done a good job in preserving the Basque culture with the children, but not the languages." Amaya speaks to her children in Basque and they are able to understand very easily, although they answer her in English. Amaya noted that her own Basque is more the Bizkaian of her parents than *Batua*. When she returned here after USAC and tried it on some of the elderly, they could not understand her. So she reverted.

Amaya has been to the Basque Country at least ten times. The children have only been twice. The first time was when they took Agustín's ashes to be buried in the family crypt in Markina. They spent about four weeks in the town, and by the end of the stay the children were starting to say a few simple things in Basque. Amaya has since thought that it would be wonderful to take them for an extended period so they could have real immersion, like their cousin Patxi.

They are planning another trip to Europe in December of this year. It will begin in Italy so the children can experience the history and monuments first hand. They will visit Pompeii and Sicily, since Amaya has never been there. They will then spend two or three weeks in the Basque Country. "We stick close to our village [Markina]. We might go to Vitoria on a day trip." She has only been once (1992) to the festival of *San Fermín* in Pamplona. "The first thing that we do is go to the cemetery where my father's ashes are buried."

Mary Arrate had shown me a copy of a short manuscript that Amaya had written based upon her upbringing in Ayr. It is called "Footprints in the Pig-Pen. A Basque Memoir." Reference is to the footprints that she and her siblings made in the freshly poured cement of the floor of a pig-pen that her parents were building at the Clare farm. They still survive. She self-published just six copies for her siblings and cousins. I had asked if she would give me a photocopy for our Basque Library at UNR? She handed it over. She then showed me an album in which she had collected multiple newspaper articles on Basque activities here in Australia and Europe as well. She agreed to photocopy for me several that I selected.

We reviewed her book collection. It had many Basque titles, including University of Nevada Press and Center for Basque Studies ones. Mark Kurlansky's work on Basque history of the world, Vanda Moraes Gorecki's work on her grandmother, and the book *Amatxi, Amuma, Amona: Writings in Honor of Basque Women*, edited by Linda White and Cameron Watson and containing Bianka Vidonja Balanzategui's chapter on Conchi Mendiolea, were also present. Then, too, there were several works on Italian culture and history in both Queensland and Europe.

We ended the interview with Amaya questioning me regarding my opinion of the future of Basque culture in Australia. She was not very optimistic. She works with her kids and Idoya's son, Patxi, is extraordinarily involved in his Basque heritage. Both David Phillips and Mark Kelly are supportive; indeed, proud to see the legacy retained within their families. But the forces of time and intermarriage are inexorable. She could only think of two cases in the Club membership in which a Basque was married to a Basque—and, in both of them, there is Italian admixture. The reality is that there is constant mixing (read dilution) of this sort, and it was likely to result at some juncture in the loss of Australia's Basque legacy.

I arrived at the Basque Club of North Queensland building half an hour before dinner in order to interview its president, Pedro Mendiolea. We were interrupted by the visit of three members of the local Somali Club who were renting the premises the following weekend and needed to discuss some details. After they left, Pedro noted that they sometimes sublet the premises to other groups for the income. They charge A$15 an hour or a A$150 fixed fee for a full day and night. It happens only sporadically, maybe six times annually, and they are not particularly aggressive in finding clients. The Somalis have no locale of their own and have rented the Basque Club four times over the past three years. The location is actually owned by the Townsville municipal council and is part of a city park. There is another building next door that is rented by a police-managed youth sporting organization and the Bridge Club. The facilities share parking.

I asked if the Basque Club is for rent to individuals, particular members, for family celebrations. He replied that there are sometimes birthdays or reunions, but that the space is too small for most weddings, for instance. It seats a maximum of between forty and fifty people comfortably—particularly if there is music and room needed for dancing.

The exterior of the building has a bit of the feel of a Basque *baserri* and the interior is highly Basque themed. There are images of the escutcheons of the four provinces and an impressive tree of Gernika. Picasso's famous painting is exhibited on one wall. There are several uses of the Basque *ikurriña* and its colors. Lekeitio, home and/or Old World focal point of many Club members, is prominent. There is both a poster and two photos of the town and its signature harbor. There is the image of a Basque *baserri* with dancers in folk costume performing in front of it. There is a pair of *jai alai cestas*, or wickers, on one wall.

The escutcheons of all four Hegoalde soccer squads (Pamplona's *Osasuna*, Vitoria's *Deportivo Alavés*, the *Athletic* of Bilbao, and Donostia's *Real Sociedad*) are all on display. And, finally, there are two photos of individuals, the Club's founder and first president, Joe Goikoetxea, and Basque president Juan José Ibarrtexe, the latter with a greeting to Basque Australians.

Pedro recalls attending an organizational meeting convened by Joe Goikoetxea in his home in 2003. "I was aware that there were a few Basque clubs in Argentina and the United States but was not nearly as informed as Joe." There were about twenty-five in attendance, including Mary Arrate and John Achurra from the Burdekin and some others from the Herbert. It was agreed that there should be a club and we developed lists of known Basques. A group of volunteers even went through telephone directories to identify Basque-sounding surnames in towns where Basques had settled traditionally. Pedro thought that telephone calls were made to ascertain interest and there was a general mailing to the master list.

In any event, on August 10th of 2003, there was a formal meeting of the Club at the Wulguru Community Centre. Joe was elected first president, Mary Arrate was vice president, and Pedro became treasurer. A Board of Directors was also named. There was a lawyer present, married to a Jayo in Trebonne. He had drawn up the draft constitution and, after the meeting, the necessary application for formal recognition under Australian law was submitted for approval. The Club was recognized formally as an "incorporated organization" on November 13th of 2003, hence the present celebration of its fifteenth anniversary.

For the first year and a half, meetings (with dinners) were held in the municipal community center in the Townsville suburb called Wulguru. It was then that Joe secured the lease on the old Polish Club and leant A$20,000 to the Basque Club to purchase it. Shortly thereafter, the Club applied for a grant to the Queensland government funded by a tax on casinos designated to support worthwhile social and cultural projects. The Basque Club received A$30,000 to remodel the kitchen and bar. Mark Balanzategui's cousin, Tony, here in Townsville, is a builder, and he supervised the volunteer workers.

Pedro served as treasurer for about seven years before assuming the presidency that he has held for the past eight years. His treasurer is currently Begoña (Bego) Bengoa.

Since its inception, the key activity of the Club is the monthly lunch. It is the main source of income beyond membership fees. The annual quota of the latter is A$20. There are approximately 150 dues-paying members. Membership is open to interested non-Basques as well, and there are several Latin Americans. The Club does not always[5] celebrate specific holidays or holydays—such as the feast day of Saint Ignatius. Outside of its eleven monthly lunches (none is held in January), there is the occasional *ad hoc* dinner when someone from the Basque Country (usually a journalist) or tour group is passing through. It can occasion a potluck get-together. There was one a couple of months ago for a reporter from the Basque Country, and the dinner for me tonight was another example.

The Club organized a miniature *Jai-aldi* to celebrate its tenth anniversary. There were displays of Basque sport, including soccer and *txingas*, dancing and music, as well as lots of traditional food. About 250 were in attendance, including 100 at a cocktail party, and the festivities lasted for three days. The bishop and mayor came.

Pedro indicated a framed *boina* on the wall and told me its story. It seems that an Aussie in Euskadi, whose companion is Basque, has a travel agency there. He specializes in organizing trips to "Basque Australia" for interested people in the Old Country. Some have relatives here; others are just curious after learning of Basques in Australia from the media. He rents a fifteen-seat van and a trailer for luggage. So, in early 2015, he called to see if the Basque Club was open as he had a group from Vitoria-Gasteiz that wanted to visit it. Pedro put out the news and enough members responded to warrant holding a special potluck dinner for the group. About twenty or thirty came and "it was a special night." Nine months later, Pedro and Bego were in Vitoria-Gasteiz representing the Club at the Sixth Congress of Basque Collectivities in the World, and the entire traveling group invited them to dinner in appreciation of their earlier one in Townsville. At that time, they were presented with the *txapela* in commemoration of the Townsville event.

Pedro recounted a similar initiative by Carlos Orue of the Sydney *Txoko*. He wanted to bring ten or fifteen interested *Txoko* members (several had relatives who had cut cane in the Far North). They were here for four days, witnessing cane-burning in the Burdekin and visiting Ingham. They came to a dinner at the Basque Club here in Townsville and presented it with a commemorative plaque (now hanging on a wall in the premises). Pedro tried to organize a trip to Sydney by Club members, but there was insufficient interest in it here. Pedro and Bego attended the Sydney *Txoko*'s celebration of its fiftieth anniversary. They did so at their own expense, but as representatives of the Basque Club of North Queensland. They presented the *Txoko*'s directors with a photograph of a burning of cane in the Far North (displayed on a wall today in the *Gure Txoko*).

Pedro is a civil engineer. He graduated from James Cook University and is married to a Townsville woman that he met while attending school. She is a couple of generations removed from her English and Irish ancestors who immigrated here.

Pedro was born in Ingham, son of Antonia Etxabe, wife of two of Teresa Mendiolea's sons. Antonia was one of nine sisters, four of whom reside still in Lekeitio. So, Pedro has many cousins there and it is his first port of call and base of operations on his frequent trips to the Basque Country. He has taken six or seven trips of about four weeks duration each, and numerous shorter ones. "Even if we Mendioleas were originally from Aulesti, Lekeitio is our hometown now."

He has three sons and they have been to the Basque Country as a family on three occasions. Their last trip was about five years ago. One of his sons lives in Melbourne and is a schoolteacher. The youngest is a pharmacist and lives here in Townsville. The middle son lives in Brisbane where he is a civil engineer. He lived for two years in Scotland and made several trips on his own to the Basque Country during that time. One of those years he went to Lekeitio to spend Christmas break with his relatives. None of Pedro's sons is married.

Pedro has a brother, Joe, who lives in Cairns and works as an accountant. Joe is married to a woman of Italian descent (Leonardi) from Ingham. Joe has been to the Basque Country at least a dozen times. He has walked parts of the *Camino de Santiago* on four occasions. They also have a sister, Ana, with Down syndrome who lives here in Townsville in a supervised group house. She spends alternate weekends with her mother, Antonia, who has lived in Townsville for the past twelve years.

Pedro moved her here because of her poor health as she became older. Ana has been to the Basque Country on one occasion when she was about two. Her parents took her to Pamplona at that time to get a second opinion from a specialist in Down syndrome.

Pedro goes to Brisbane frequently, but rarely sees any Basques there. He struggled to remember any and came up with a son of Dolores Larrazabal and Javier Balanzategui, while noting that the latter now lives here in Townsville. Pedro goes to Sydney once in a while and does visit the *Txoko* on occasion. He mentioned Joe Goicoechea and Manu Martin as his acquaintances there. He also mentioned his cousin Tommy Mendiolea. I asked if he had ever been in the Sydney Spanish Club and he replied, "once or twice—just out of curiosity."

Pedro noted that none of his sons speak Spanish or Basque. Maybe they can count to ten in each. "I didn't really carry on the tradition," he noted apologetically. He concluded by saying that the four of them plan to walk part of the *Camino de Santiago* next April. Brother Joe is providing them with his *Camino* hiking gear and advice.

Notes

1. As of March of 2019, the only surviving founders were Peñagaricano and Benito Bañuelos of Sydney.
2. Matt Sherrington, "Cane History Celebrated," *North Queensland Register*, June 2, 2015.
3. She remarked that Joe is always quite generous when it comes to displaying the Basque heritage. Amaya's husband, Mark, was the paid director of Ingham's Italian Festival and, when he told Joe that he wanted to include in it a Basque *txingas* (weight-carrying) competition, Joe handed him A$100 towards the prize.
4. She recalled that she never knew that Tommy was gay. "People have said to me, 'you must have suspected when he didn't date girls,' but I didn't date anyone at that time, either. It was years later that he called one day to alert me. I think he had to leave here to find more space to work out his life. North Queensland was very confining for him."
5. In 1911, it did celebrate *Aberri Eguna* (or Day of the Country) on which its first *Korrika* (marathon) was held. (*Euskalkultura*, May 9, 2011.)

Bibliography

"'Al Capone' of the Canefields." *Parade*, no. 348 (November 1979): 23–25.
Alcorta, Frank X. *Darwin Rebellion, 1911–1919*. Darwin: History Unit, Northern Territory University Planning Authority, 1984.
———. *Explore Australia's Northern Territory*. Introduction by Les Hiddins. Frenchs Forest, N.S.W.: Child and Associates, 1989.
———. *Australia's Frontline: the Northern Territory's War*. North Sydney: Allen & Unwin, 1991.
———. *Marjorie Harris: "Rainbow."* Palmerston, N.T.: Keith Hart, 1998.
———. *A Trip to the Stone Age: An Account of the First Solo Expedition across Papua New Guinea at Its Widest Part in 1973/74*. Perth: Chargan My Book Publisher Pty. Ltd., 2010.
Aulestia, Gorka. *Improvisational Poetry from the Basque Country*. Reno and Las Vegas: University of Nevada Press, 1995.
Bakaikoa, Baleren, and Eneka Albizu, eds. *Basque Cooperativism*. Reno: Center for Basque Studies, University of Nevada, Reno, 2012.
Ballyn, Susan. "Jean Baptiste Lehimas de Arrieta, the First Spanish Settler?" *The La Trobe Journal* 68 (Spring 2001): 42–50.
Baume, F. E. *Burnt Sugar*. Sydney: Macquarie Head Press, 1934.
Bernard, William S., ed. *American Immigration Policy, A Reappraisal*. Port Washington, New York and London: Kennikat Press, 1969.
Bertei, J. M. "Innisfail." B.A. thesis, University of Queensland, 1959.
Birch, Alan. "The Implementation of the White Australia Policy in the Queensland Sugar Industry 1901–12." *Australian Journal of Politics and History* 11, no. 2 (1965): 198–210.
Blainey, Geoffrey. *The Tyranny of Distance*. Melbourne: Sun Books, 1966.
———. *All for Australia*. North Ryde, New South Wales: Methuen Haynes, 1984.
Bodnar, John. *The Transplanted: A History of Immigrants in Urban America*. Bloomington: University of Indiana Press, 1985.
Bolton, G. C. *A Thousand Miles Away: A History of North Queensland to 1920*. Canberra: Australian National University Press, 1972.
Borin, V. L. *The Uprooted Survive: A Tale of Two Continents*. London: Allen and Unwin, 1959.
Borja, Marciano R. de. *Basques in the Philippines*. Reno and Las Vegas: University of Nevada Press, 2005.
Borrie, W. D. *Italians and Germans in Australia*. Melbourne: F. W. Cheshire, 1954.
Briani, Vittorio. *Il lavoro italiano oltremare*. Roma: N.p., 1975.
Bruer, Jeremy, and John Power. "The Changing Role of the Department of Immigration." In *The Politics of Australian Immigration*, edited by James Jupp and Marie Kabala. Canberra: Australian Government Publishing Service, 1993.

Burrows, Geoff, and Clive Morton. *The Canecutters*. Melbourne: Melbourne University Press, 1986.
Campion, Edmond. *Rockchoppers: Growing Up Catholic in Australia*. Blackburn, Vict.: Penguin Books, 1982.
Canals, Josephine. "The Catalans and Their Place in Melbourne's History." In *The Spanish Experience in Australia*, edited by Carmen Castelo. Jamison Centre, ACT: The Spanish Heritage Foundation, 2000.
Caro Baroja, Julio. *The Basques*. Translation by Kristin Addis and Introduction by William A. Douglass. Reno: Center for Basque Studies, University of Nevada, Reno, 2009.
Cerezo Martínez, Ricardo. *La Expedición Malaspina 1789–1794*. Volume 1. *Circunstancia Histórica del Viaje*. Madrid: Ministerio de Defensa, Museo Naval, and Lunwerg Editores, 1987.
Cervantes Saavedra, Miguel de. *The Adventures of Don Quixote*. Translated by J. M. Cohen. Harmondsworth, Middlesex: Penguin Books, 1950.
Chapman, Peter, ed. *The Diaries and Letters of G.T.W.B. Boyes. Volume I, 1820–1832*. Melbourne: Oxford University Press, 1985.
Chidell, Fleetwood. *Australia—White or Yellow?* London: Heinemann, 1926.
Cilento, Raphael. *Triumph in the Tropics: An Historical Sketch of Queensland*. Brisbane: Smith and Patterson, 1959.
Clark, Manning. *A Short History of Australia*. New York: Mentor Books, 1969.
Cohen, Joel S. "Economic Growth." In *Modern Italy: A Topical History since 1861*, edited by Edward R. Tannenbaum and Emiliana P. Noether. New York: New York University Press, 1974.
Commonwealth of Australia. *Census of the Commonwealth of Australia*. Volume 2. Melbourne: Government Printer, 1911.
———. *Census of the Commonwealth of Australia: Taken for the Night between the 3rd and the 4th of April, 1921*. Volume 1. Melbourne: Government Printing Office, 1921.
———. *Commonwealth Parliamentary Debates*. Canberra: Government Printer, 1924.
———. *Commonwealth Parliamentary Debates, 1925*. Canberra: Government Printer, 1925.
———. *Commonwealth Parliamentary Debates*. Volume 116. Canberra: Government Printer, 1927.
———. *Commonwealth Parliamentary Debates*. Volume 120. Canberra: Government Printer, 1929.
———. *Census of the Commonwealth of Australia, 30th June, 1933*. Volume 1. Canberra: Commonwealth Government Printer, 1933.
———. *Census of the Commonwealth of Australia, 30th June, 1947*. Volume 1. Canberra: Commonwealth Government Printer, 1947.
Commonwealth of Australia Committee of Inquiry into the Sugar Industry, 1930. *Reports of the Sugar Inquiry Committee*. Canberra: Government Printer, 1931.
Commonwealth of Australia, Department of Immigration and Border Protection. *The People of Australia: Statistics from the 2011 Census*. Canberra: Australian Government Printing Service, 2014.

———. *The People of Queensland: Statistics from the 2011 Census*. Brisbane: The Queensland Government, 2014.
Connolly, Roy. *John Drysdale and the Burdekin*. Sydney: Ure Smith, 1964.
"Contract Immigrants, Queensland: Permits to Introduce." Broadsheet. Melbourne: The Parliament of the Commonwealth of Australia, 1907.
Cordasco, Francesco. *Italian Mass Emigration: The Exodus of Latin People. A Bibliographical Guide to the Bollettino dell'Emigrazione 1902–1927*. Totowa, N.J.: Rowman and Littlefield, 1980.
Corris, Peter. *Passage, Port and Plantation: A History of Solomon Islands Labour Migration 1870–1914*. Melbourne: Melbourne University Press, 1973.
Cortes, J. "Spanish." In *The Australian People: An Encyclopedia of the Nation, Its People and Their Origins*, edited by James Jupp. North Ryde, N.S.W.: Angus and Robertson, 1988.
Courtenay, P. P. "The White Man and the Australian Tropics—A Review of Some Opinions and Prejudices of the pre-War Years." In *Lectures on North Queensland History*, Second Series, edited by B. J. Dalton. Townsville: History Department, James Cook University of North Queensland, 1975.
Cresciani, Gianfranco. "Italian Anti-Fascism in Australia (1922–1945)." In *Affari Sociali Internazionali*, numero unico. Milan: Franco Angeli Editore, 1978.
———. "The Proletarian Migrants: Fascism and Italian Anarchists in Australia." *The Australian Quarterly* 51, no. 1 (March 1979): 4–19.
———. *Fascism, Anti-Fascism and Italians in Australia*. Canberra: Australian National University Press, 1980.
———. "The Bogey of the Italian Fifth Column: Internment and the Making of Italo-Australia." In *War, Internment and Mass Migration: The Italo-Australian Experience 1940–1990*, edited by Richard Bosworth and Romano Ugolini. Roma: Gruppo Editoriale Internazionale, 1992.
Cunningham, Peter. *Two Years in New South Wales*. Sydney: Angus and Robertson, 1966.
Denoon, Donald. *Settler Capitalism: The Dynamics of Dependent Development in the Southern Hemisphere*. Oxford: Clarendon Press, 1983.
Department of Manpower and Immigration. *Immigration and Population Statistics*. Ottawa: Federal Publications, 1974.
Devanney, Jean. *Sugar Heaven*. Sydney: Modern Publishers, 1936.
———. *By Tropic Sea and Jungle*. Sydney: Angus and Robertson, 1944.
Dignan, Don[ald]. "Archbishop James Duhig and Italians and Italy." In *Altro Polo: Studies in Contemporary Italy*, edited by Ian Grosart and Silvio Trambaiolo. Sydney: Frederick May Foundation, University of Sydney, 1988.
———. "The Internment of Italians in Queensand." In *War, Internment and Mass Migration: The Italo-Australian Experience 1940–1990*, edited by Richard Bosworth and Romno Ugolini. Roma: Gruppo Editoriale Internazionale, 1992.
Donaldson, Robert, and Michael Joseph. *Cane!* London: Sphere Books Limited, 1967.
Doran, Christine. *Separatism in Townsville*. Townsville: History Department, James Cook University of North Queensland, 1981.

Douglass, William A. *Death in Murelaga: The Social Significance of Funerary Ritual in a Spanish Basque Village*. American Ethnological Society Monograph No. 49. Seattle: University of Washington Press, 1969.

———. "Rural Exodus in Two Spanish Basque Villages: A Cultural Explanation." *American Anthropologist* 73 (1971): 1100–14.

———. *Echalar and Murelaga: Opportunity and Rural Depopulation in Two Spanish Basque Villages*. London: C. Hurst and Co.; New York: St. Martin's Press, 1975.

———. *Beltran: Basque Sheepman of the American West*. Reno: University of Nevada Press, 1979.

———. *Emigration in a South Italian Town: An Anthropological History*. New Brunswick: Rutgers University Press, 1984.

———. "Sheep Ranchers and Sugar Growers: Property Transmission in the Basque Immigrant Family of the American West and Australia." In *Households: Comparative and Historical Studies of the Domestic Group*, edited by Robert M. Netting, Richard R. Wilk, and Eric J. Arnould. Berkeley and Los Angeles: University of California Press, 1984.

———. "Basques," in *The Australian People, An Encyclopedia of the Nation, Its People and Their Origins*, edited by James Jupp. North Ryde, N.S.W.: Angus and Robertson, 1988.

———. "The Basque Stem Family Household: Myth or Reality?" *Journal of Family History* 13, no. 1 (1988): 75–90.

———. "The Basques of North Queensland, Australia." In *Homenaje a Francisco de Abrisketa/Frantzisko Abrisketa'ri Omenaldia*, edited by Román Basurto Larrañaga. Bolibar, Bizkaia: Sociedad Bolivariana del País Vasco, 1993.

———. "The Famille Souche and Its Interpreters." *Continuity and Change* 8, no. 1 (1993): 87–102.

———. *From Italy to Ingham: Italians in North Queensland*. Brisbane: University of Queensland Press, 1995.

———. *Azúcar amargo: vida y fortuna de los cortadores de caña italianos y vascos en la Australia tropical*. Bilbao: Servicio Editorial de la Universidad del País Vasco, 1996.

———. "Los vascos de North Queensland, Australia." In *Los otros vascos. Las migraciones vascas en el s. XX*, edited by F. Xavier Medina. Madrid: Editorial Fundamentos, 1997.

———. "Speech Delivered by Professor William A. Douglass." In *Euskadi munduan eraikitzen. World Congress on Basque Communities, 1999*. Vitoria-Gasteiz: Servicio Editorial del Gobierno Vasco, 2000.

———. "Basque Immigration in the United States." *Boga: Basque Studies Consortium Journal* 1, no. 1 (2013): 1–13.

———. *Basque Explorers in the Pacific Ocean*. Reno: Center for Basque Studies, University of Nevada, Reno, 2015.

Douglass, William A., and Jon Bilbao, *Amerikanuak: Basques in the New World*. Reno: University of Nevada Press, 1975.

Douglass, William A., and Joseba Zulaika. *Basque Culture: Anthropological Perspectives*. Reno: Center for Basque Studies, University of Nevada, Reno, 2007.

Easterby, Harry T. *The Queensland Sugar Industry*. Brisbane: Frederik Phillips, Queensland Government Printer, 1931.

Fernández Albaladejo, Pablo. *La Crisis del Antiguo Régimen en Guipúzcoa, 1766–1883: Cambio Económico e Historia.* Madrid: Akal, 1975.

Fernández-Shaw, Carlos M. *España y Australia. Quinientos años de relaciones.* Madrid: Ministerio de Asuntos Exteriores de Espana, 2000.

Finch, M.H.J. *A Political Economy of Uruguay since 1870.* New York: St. Martin's Press, 1981.

Fitzgerald, Alan. *The Italian Farming Soldiers: Prisoners of War in Australia, 1941–1947.* Melbourne: Melbourne University Press, 1981.

Foley, Larry. "The Basques—Strongmen of the Canefields." *People Magazine* (October 18, 1967): 12–17.

"From Two to Two Million Tons of Sugar." *Producer's Review* (July 1964): 17–91.

García, Ignacio. *Operación Canguro: The Spanish Migration Scheme, 1958–1963.* Sydney: Spanish Heritage Foundation, 2002.

Gómez-Piñeiro, Francisco Javier, et al. *Geografía de Euskal Herria.* Volume 7. *Euskal Herria.* San Sebastián/Donostia: Luis Haranburu, 1979.

Grassby, Al. *The Spanish in Australia.* Melbourne: AE Press, 1983.

Grattan, Michelle. "Immigration and the Australian Labour Party." In *The Politics of Australian Immigration*, edited by James Jupp and Marie Kabala. Canberra: Australian Government Publishing Service, 1993.

Greenwood, Davydd. *Unrewarding Wealth: The Commercialization and Collapse of Agriculture in a Spanish Basque Town.* Cambridge, London, New York, Melbourne: Cambridge University Press, 1976.

Grenfell Price, A. "The White Man in the Tropics and the Problem of North Australia." Manuscript in the Edward Leo Hayes Collection, Fryer Library, University of Queensland.

Gurdon, Michael A. "Australian Attitudes to Italy and Italians, 1922–1936: With Special Reference to Queensland." B.A. thesis, University of Queensland, 1970.

Habgood, P.J. *Morphometric Investigation into the Origins of Anatomically Modern Humans.* Oxford: Archaeopress, 2003.

Harris, Stuart. "Immigration and Australian Foreign Policy." In *The Politics of Australian Immigration*, edited by James Jupp and Marie Kabala. Canberra: Australian Government Publishing Service, 1993.

Harvey, John R. *Black Hand Vengeance.* Sydney: Invincible Press, 1943.

Hempel, J.A. *Italians in Queensland: Some Aspects of Post-war Settlement of Italian Migrants.* Canberra: Australian National University, Department of Demography, 1959.

Henderson, L.D. "Italians in the Hinchinbrook Shire, 1921–1939." B.A. thesis, James Cook University of North Queensland, 1978.

Holborn, Louise W. *The International Refugee Organization: A Specialized Agency of the United Nations: Its History and Work 1946–1952.* London, New York, Toronto: Oxford University Press, 1956.

Horne, Donald. *The Lucky Country.* Blackburn, Victoria: Penguin Books, 1976.

Huber, Rina. *From Pasta to Pavlova: A Comparative Study of Italian Settlers in Sydney and Griffith.* St. Lucia: University of Queensland Press, 1977.

Hughes, Robert. *The Fatal Shore: The Epic of Australia's Founding*. New York: Vintage Books, 1988.
Ibañez de Aldecoa, Excm. Sr. D. Zoilo. "Apuntes Necrológicos." *Euskal-Erria* 33 (1895): 378–80.
Inchausti, Manuel. "Los Vascos en el Mundo." *Anuario de Eusko-Folklore* 29 (1980): 91–94.
Ispizua, Segundo de. *Historia de los vascos en el descubrimiento, conquista y civilización de America*. Volume 3. Bilbao: J. A. Lerchundi, 1917.
Jenkins, J. T. *A History of the Whale Fisheries from the Basque Fisheries of the Tenth Century to the Hunting of the Finner Whale at the Present Date*. Port Washington, N.Y. and London: Kennikat Press, 1921.
Kabala, Marie. "Immigration as Public Policy." In *The Politics of Australian Immigration*, edited by James Jupp and Marie Kabala. Canberra: Australian Government Publishing Service, 1993.
Keene, Judith. "A Symbolic Crusade: Australians and the Spanish Civil War." In *La Mistica Spagnola: Spagna America Latina*, edited by Gaetano Massa. Rome: Centro di Studi Americanistici, 1989.
———. "Surviving the Peninsular War in Australia: Juan D'Arrieta—Spanish Free Settler and Colonial Gentleman." *Journal of the Royal Australian Historical Society* 84, no. 2 (June 1999): 36–47.
Kendrick, John. *Alejandro Malaspina: Portrait of a Visionary*. Montreal: McGill-Queen's University Press, 1999.
Kerr, John. *Northern Outpost*. Mossman: Mossman Central Mill Company Limited, 1979.
Kurlansky, Mark. *The Basque History of the World*. New York: Penguin Publishing Company, 1999.
La Expedición Malaspina 1789–1794. Volume 9. *Diario General del Viaje, Corbeta Atrevida, por José Bustamante y Guerra*, edited by María Dolores Higueras Rodríguez. Madrid: Ministerio de Defensa, Museo Naval and Lunwerg Editores, 1999.
Lamidey, N. W. *Aliens Control in Australia, 1939–46*. Sydney: N. W. Lamidey, 1988.
Robert Langdon. *The Lost Caravel*. Sydney: Pacific Publications, 1975.
———. *The Lost Caravel Re-explored*. Canberra: Brolga Press, 1988.
Langfield, Michele, and Peta Roberts. *Welsh Patagonians: The Australian Connection*. Darlinghurst, NSW: Crossing Press, 2005.
Lawler, Ray. *Summer of the Seventeenth Doll*. Sydney: Currency Press, 1957.
Lawson, Rosemary. "Immigration into Queensland 1870–1890." B.A. thesis, University of Queensland, 1963.
Le Play, Frédéric. *L'Organisation de la famille selon le vrai modèle signalé par l'histoire de toutes les races et de tous les temps*. Paris: Téqui, 1871.
Levick, B. B. "Origin and Development of the Central Mill and Small Farm System in Queensland," ms. Copy in Colonial Sugar Refining Company Archive (Sydney). Box n.1.0, Folder 3.
Lizzio, Santina. *Basilisk: Township of South Johnstone*. Cairns: Bolton Print, 2006.
Lloyd, Peter. "The Political Economy of Immigration." In *The Politics of Australian*

Immigration, edited by James Jupp and Marie Kabala. Canberra: Australian Government Publishing Service, 1993.

Luciano, Giuseppe. *La guida annuale per gli Italiani del Queensland*. Brisbane: N.p., 1931.

Luzuriaga, Juan Carlos. "Francisco Xavier de Viana y Alzáybar." *Euskonews & Media* (online journal) 302. At http://www.euskonews.eus/0302zbk/kosmo30201.html.

Lynch, John. *Spain under the Hapsburgs*. Volume 1. *Empire and Absolutism (1516–1598)*. Oxford and New York: Oxford University Press, 1964.

Lyng, J. *Non-Britishers in Australia: Influence on Population and Progress*. Melbourne: Macmillan and Co., 1927.

Martin, Jean I. *Refugee Settlers: A Study of Displaced Persons in Australia*. Canberra: Australian National University Press, 1978.

Mason, Robert James David. "Agitators and Patriots: Cultural and Political Identity in Queensland's Spanish Communities, 1900–1975." PhD dissertation, University of Queensland, 2008.

———. "Repositioning Resistance: Basque Separatism, Religion and Cultural Security in Regional Queensland, 1945–70." *Queensland Review* 20, no. 1 (2013): 37–51.

Maxwell, Walter. *Sugar Industry of Australia*. Melbourne: Government Printer, 1912.

Melchiore, C. *Il divinismo ossia la civile convivenza per tutti. Opuscolo progetto per la fondazione de una colonia italiana agraria e industriale in Australia*. Melbourne: N.p., 1878.

Menghetti, Diane. *The Red North*. Studies in North Queensland History, No. 3. Townsville: History Department, James Cook University, 1981.

———. "The Internment of Italians in North Queensland." In *Australia, the Australians and the Italian Migration*, edited by Gianfranco Cresciani. Milano: Franco Angeli Editore, 1983.

Mercer, P. M. "Pacific Islanders in Colonial Queensland 1863–1906." In *Lectures on North Queensland History*, edited by B. J. Dalton. Townsville: History Department, James Cook University of North Queensland, 1974.

Merrick, Thomas W., and Douglas H. Graham. *Population and Economic Development in Brazil, 1800 to the Present*. Baltimore: The Johns Hopkins University Press, 1979.

Mollison, Lieutenant Colonel Charles S. *Long Tan and Beyond: Alpha Company 6 RAR in Vietnam 1966–67*. Woombye, Australia: Cobb's Crossing Publications, 2004.

Monaghan, Jay. *Australians and the Gold Rush: California and Down Under 1849–1854*. Berkeley and Los Angeles: University of California Press, 1966.

Moraes Gorecki, Vanda. *The Basques of Tropical Queensland*. Surry Hills: NSW Adult Migrant English Service, 2003.

Morrissey, G. C. "The Occurrence of Leptospirosis (Weil's Disease) in Australia." *The Medical Journal of Australasia* 2, no. 1 (1934): 496–97.

Moses, John A. "Attitudes to the Question of New Settlers in Queensland during the Twentieth Century." B.A. thesis, University of Queensland, 1959.

Naipaul, Shiva. *A Hot Country*. London: Hamish Hamilton Ltd., 1983.

Naish, John. *The Cruel Field*. London: Hutchinson & Co., 1962.

———. *That Men Should Fear*. London: Hutchinson & Co., 1963.

Okrent, Daniel. *The Guarded Gate: Bigotry, Eugenics, and the Law That Kept Two Generations of Jews, Italians, and Other European Immigrants Out of America.* New York: Simon & Shuster, 2019.

Ott, Sandra. "Indarra: Some Reflections on a Basque Concept." In *Honour and Grace in Anthropology*, edited by J. G. Peristiany and Julian Pitt Rivers. Cambridge, New York, and Melbourne: Cambridge University Press, 1992.

———. *The Circle of Mountains: A Basque Shepherding Community.* Reno and Las Vegas: University of Nevada Press, 1993.

Palmer, George. *Kidnapping in the South Seas Being a Narrative of a Three Months' Cruise of the H. M. Ship Rosario.* Edinburgh: Edmonston and Douglas, 1871.

Panettieri, José. *Inmigración en la Argentina.* Buenos Aires: Ediciones Macchi, 1970.

Pares, Luis Amadeo. *I Fiddled the Years Away.* Brisbane?: N.p., 1943?

Parliament of the Commonwealth of Australia, The. *Commonwealth Parliamentary Debates, First Parliament, First Session.* Volume 5. Melbourne: Government Printer of the State of Victoria, 1901.

———. *Report of the Royal Commission on the Sugar Industry Together with Minutes of Evidence and Appendices.* Melbourne: Government Printer for the State of Victoria, 1912.

———. *Commonwealth Parliamentary Debates.* Volume 1. Canberra: Government Printer, 1929.

Payne, Stanley G. *Basque Nationalism.* Reno: University of Nevada Press, 1975.

Price, Charles A. *Southern Europeans in Australia.* Melbourne: Oxford University Press, 1963.

———. *The Great White Walls Are Built: Restrictive Immigration to North America and Australasia 1836–1888.* Canberra: Australian National University Press, 1974.

———. "The Ethnic Character of the Australian Population." In *The Australian People: An Encyclopedia of the Nation, Its People and Their Origins*, edited by James Jupp. North Ryde, N.S.W.: Angus and Robertson, 1988.

Quaife, G. R. *Gold and Colonial Society 1851–1870.* Stanmore: Cassel Australia Ltd., 1975.

Queensland Royal Commission. *Minutes of Evidence Taken before the Royal Commission to Inquire into the General Condition of the Sugar Industry of Queensland.* Brisbane: Government Printer, 1889.

Reich, David. *Who We Are and How We Got Here: Ancient DNA and the New Science of the Human Past.* New York: Pantheon Books, 2018.

Report of the Royal Commission Appointed to Investigate Certain Aspects of the Sugar Industry. Brisbane: Government Printer, 1943.

Salvado, Dom Rosendo. *The Salvado Memoirs: Historical Memoirs of Australia and Particularly of the Benedictine Mission of New Norcia and of the Habits and Customs of the Australian Natives.* Translated and edited by E. J. Stormon. Nedlands: University of Western Australia Press, 1977.

San Sebastián, Koldo. *Basques in the United States.* Reno: Center for Basque Studies, University of Nevada, Reno, 2016.

———. "Vascos en Australia: los marinos." Euskonews & Media (online journal) 724 (2017). At http://www.euskonews.eus/0724zbk/kosmo72401es.html.

———. "Basques in Australia," unpublished document, n.d.

Solberg, Carl. *Immigration and Nationalism: Argentina and Chile, 1890–1914*. Austin: University of Texas Press, 1970.

Sugar Industry Labour Commission. *Report of the Royal Commission Appointed to Inquire into and Report regarding the Number of Pacific Islanders to be Deported from Queensland at the end of the Current Year, the most efficient manner of Repatriating them, with the probable cost thereof; whether there are in Queensland any Pacific Islanders whose Compulsory Deportation would be inconsistent with humanity or with good faith; and whether sufficient Labour for carrying on the Queensland Sugar Industry is likely to be available when Pacific Islanders can no longer be lawfully employed; and if sufficient labour for such purpose is not likely to be locally obtainable, the best means of supplying the deficiency; together with the Minutes of Proceedings. Minutes of Evidence taken before the Commission, and Appendices.* Brisbane: Government Printer, 1906.

Tavan, Gwenda. *The Long, Slow Death of White Australia*. Melbourne: Scribe Publications, 2005.

Thernstrom, Stephen B., ed. *Harvard Encyclopedia of American Ethnic Groups*. Cambridge: Harvard University Press, 1980.

Thompson, Anne-Gabrielle. *Turmoil—Tragedy to Triumph: The Story of New Italy*. Stanthorpe, Qld.: International Colour Productions, 1980.

Torrents, Jaime. "Una nueva ciudad australiana: Barcelona Gardens." *La Vanguardia*, March 28, 1968, 52.

Totoricagüena Egurrola, Gloria. *Australia: Vasconia and the Lucky Country*. Vitoria-Gasteiz: Servicio Central de Publicaciones del Gobierno Vasco, 2008.

U.S. Department of Labor. *Annual Report of the Commissioner General of Immigration to the Secretary of Labor, Fiscal Year Ended June 30, 1925*. Washington, D.C.: Government Printer, 1925.

Valentine, James. *Then and Now: Historic Roads Around Sydney*. Sydney: Angus and Robertson, 1937.

Veyrin, Philippe. *The Basques of Lapurdi, Zuberoa, and Lower Navarre: Their History and Their Traditions*. Translated by Andrew Brown and Introduction by Sandra Ott. Reno: Center for Basque Studies, University of Nevada, Reno, 2011.

Vidonja Balanzategui, Bianka. *Gentlemen of the Flashing Blade*. 1st ed. (Townsville: James Cook University, 1990); 2nd ed. (Brisbane: Boolarong Press, 2015).

———. *The Tropical Queensland Sugar Cane Industry: A Structural and Material Survey, 1872 to 1955*. Townsville: Material Culture Unit, James Cook University, 1994.

Vidonja Balanzategui, Bianka, and Barbara Debono. "The Fronton: A Basque Legacy in Tropical Queensland." *Journal of the Society of Basque Studies in America* 21 (2001): 17–34.

Villaamil, Don Fernando. *Viaje de circunnavegación de la corbeta Nautilus*. Madrid: Sucesores de Rivadeneyra, 1895.

Warhurst, John. "The Growth Lobby and Its Opponents: Business, Unions, Environmentalists and Other Interest Groups." In *The Politics of Australian Immigration*, edited by James Jupp and Marie Kabala. Canberra: Australian Government Publishing Service, 1993.
Waring, Lola. "Lola's Memories of the Catalans in Melbourne." In *The Spanish Experience in Australia*, edited by Carmen Castelo. Jamison Centre, ACT: The Spanish Heritage Foundation, 2000.
Wawn, William T. *The South Sea Islanders and the Queensland Labour Trade*. Canberra: Australian National University Press, 1973.
White, Linda, and Cameron Watson, eds. *Amuma, Amatxi, Amona: Writings in Honor of Basque Women*. Reno: Center for Basque Studies, University of Nevada, Reno, 2003.
Whitfield, Teresa. *Endgame for ETA: Elusive Peace in the Basque Country*. Oxford and New York: Oxford University Press, 2014.
Zavala, Antonio. *Ameriketako bertsoak*. Tolosa: Auspoa, 1984.
Zulaika, Joseba. *Basque Violence: Metaphor and Sacrament*. Reno and Las Vegas: University of Nevada Press, 1988.

Journals, Newspapers, and Official Publications
The Australian Sugar Journal
Brisbane Courier
Cairns Post
Census of the Commonwealth of Australia
Commonwealth Parliamentary Debates
Courier-Mail
Cultura Proletaria
The Daily Standard
El Español en Australia
Euskal Etxeak
Evening Star
Herbert River Express
Home Hill Observer
Italo-Australian
L'Italo-Australiano
Johnstone River Advocate
Melbourne Age
New Zealand Tablet
North Queensland Herald
North Queensland Register
Otago Daily Times
El País
Queensland Parliamentary Papers
Queensland Votes and Proceedings
The Queenslander

The Record
La Riscossa
Smith's Weekly
Sydney Morning Herald
The Telegraph
Townsville Daily Bulletin
The Townsville Herald
Tuapeka Times
La Vanguardia
Warwick Daily News
The West Australian
The Worker

Archives
Australian Archives
Australian National Archives
Charles A. Price, Collection of Naturalisation Records
Colonial Sugar Refining Co. Archive (Sydney)
Colonial Sugar Refining Co. Collection, Archives of Business and Labour, Australian National University
Mitchell Library
National Archives of Australia (Brisbane)
Queensland State Archives

Index

Page numbers followed by n indicate endnotes. Numbers in italics indicate maps.

ABC, 550
Aberasturi, Jaime, 428
Abergowrie district, 238
Aberri Eguna (Fatherland Day) celebrations, 13, 16, 18, 346, 350–51, 355–56, 758n5
abertzale (Basque patriotic), 14
Aboitiz, Milagros, 29, 370, 519–20
Aborigines, 59, 741; Basque views of, 416, 454, 486, 638, 677–78n3; discrimination against, 575, 579, 585, 639; in labor force, 251–52; rock art, 638, 664–65; stolen generation, 665
Abyssinia, 207, 209
Acha, Fernando, 449
Acha, Pedro, 427–28, 431, 449–52
Achabal, Imanol, 441
Achurra, Elisabeth, 270n143
Achurra, Hilario, 487, 511
Achurra, John (Johnny), 625, 755
Achurra, José, 497
Achurra, José Francisco ("Patxi"), 270n143, 611
Achurra, José María, 270n143
Achurra, Saturnino, 332n32, 410, 414
Achurra, T. M., 332n33
Achurra Calzacorta, Benito, 270n143, 319–20, 332n29, 332n33, 700
Achurra family, 262–63, 487
activism, 321
Adarraga, Agustín, 36–37, 360, 363, 454–60, 598, 625, 680, 709
Adarraga, Austin, 458
Adarraga, Ignacio, 37
Adarraga, Juan Bautista, 459

Adarraga, María, 36, 455–57
Adarraga, Xavier, 37
Adarraga family, 588n11
Adarraga Gorrochategui, Luis, 454
Adelaide, Australia, 90, 202, 215
Adelaide Advertiser, 516
Adelaide News, 366
Adey, A. H., 165
Afghanis, 385
African Americans, 263n21
age differences, 585–86
Agent Orange, 653
Agote, Manuel, 77
agricultural jobs, 55–64, 155, 473, 600
Aguirre, Antonio, 332n33, 483
Aguirre, Benedicto, 431
Aguirre, Carmen, 481–82
Aguirre, Franco, 530
Aguirre, Inmaculada, 480
Aguirre, José, 481
Aguirre, José María, 399–409, 431, 434–36, 446, 479
Aguirre, Juan Pedro, 83–84
Aguirre, Ramón, 487
Aguirre, Ventura, 480
Aguirre Fernández, Karlos, 373–74
Aguirresarobe, Jesús, 493
Aguirresarobe, Leo, 710
Aguirresarobe, León, 493–94
Aguirresarobe, Lorenzo, 493–95
AIDS, 457
aitonak (grandparents), 355
aizkolariak (woodchoppers), 354, 365–66, 410–11, 530, 537–38, 589n26
Ajurienea, 590n28

Alabama, 80
Alberdi, Ángel, 316*t*, 358, 699
Alberdi, Antonio, 462, 701
Alberdi, Josefina, 462
Alberdi, Juanita, 462
Alberdi, Santos, 462, 702
Alberdi farm, 518
Albisu, Iñaki, 614–15
Alcántara, Julián, 347
Alcibar, Elias, 486–89, 498, 589n17, 613
Alcibar, Francisco, 615
Alcibar, Julie, 751
Alcibar, Marian, 751
Alcibar, Patxi, 613
Alcorta, Amaya, 677
Alcorta, Ignacio, 628–29
Alcorta, Juanita, 628
Alcorta, Juan José, 629
Alcorta Azpiroz, Francisco (Frank), 31–33, 627–77, 680, 683
Aldamiz, Ángel, 547
Aldamiz, Fidel, 547–48, 574
Aldecoa & Co, 92
Alegría, Rafael, 23, 357, 530–33, 589n26, 610n3, 711
Alice Springs, 661
alien internment, 218–25
Aliens' Registration Bill, 218
Aliens Restriction Act, 67n59
Allica, Juan Francisco, 91
Almería, Spain, 279
Alonso, Gerardo, 700
Alsasua (Altsasu), 721–22
Altamira Cave, 638
Altuna, Pedro, 28–29
Álvarez, Gorka, 357
Álvaro, Rubén, 720
Amalgamated Steel Workers, 556
Amezaga, Rosa María de, 355
Amonarriyz, Joseph, 95
Amorebieta, Javier, 346
Amorebieta, Miguel, 577, 579
Amoroto, 323
anarchists, 126, 142, 205, 210–11, 232n233, 308

Anbeko, 13, 345–46
Anchia Bastarrechea, Claudio, 332n29
Anchochoury, Gregopire, 95
Ancibero, Antoine, 95
Andalusia, 279, 310
Andueza, Paula, 546
Andy's Engineers, 571
Anglicans, 94, 208
Anglo-Australians, 104, 327–29, 328*t*, 330*t*, 585
Anglos, 66n46
Ansoleaga, Abel, 349
Ansoleaga, Alberto, 349, 580–84, 680
Ansotequi, A., 332n33
anticlericalism, 337
Anti-Fascist Committee of the Herbert River (*Comitato Anti-Fascista dell'Herbert River*), 205–6
anti-Fascists, 210, 337
anti-Franquism, 324–25
anti-intellectualism, 8
Antipodes, 305–33
anti-Spaniards, 360
ANZAC (Australia and New Zealand Army Corps) Day, 13, 16, 21, 37n2
Apraix, José, 478–79
Araba/Álava, 281, 318, 691
Arabs, 63
Aramburu Iztueta, Aitor, 730–31
Arana, Julio, 699
Aranas, Badiola, 465
Aranas, Pedro, 429, 594, 749
Aranas, Pete, 465
Aranas, Sabino, 430–31
Arandi, Pierre, 95
Arando, Andrés, 422
Arando, Jesús, 422
Arangüena, Félix, 497–98
Arangüena, Pedro, 316*t*
Araquistain, Angela, 332n32
Araquistain, Julián, 419, 486, 518, 592
Araquistain, Leandra, 419
Arcocha, Loren, 606, 610n9
Ardaiz, 396
Ardaiz, Pedro, 601–2

Arenas, Josefa, 79
Arenas, Martín, 94, 102n112
Aresti, Raimundo, 520, 524, 576
Argentina: Basque immigrants, 683–84; foreign-born population, 43–44; immigration policy, 43–47, 146, 307–8; Italian immigrants, 106; *Primer Congreso Mundial de Centros Vascos* (First World Congress of Basque Centers), 355; Spanish immigrants, 263n12, 307–8, 312
Argote, Agustín, 14
Ariño, Garcia, 594
Aristi, Ignacio, 414
Arizona, 686
Arlendi, Cedro, 90
Arluciaga, Imanol, 526
Armand Béhie, 94–95
Armando Diaz, 206
Armaolea, Tomás, 503
Armati, P. V., 156n3
Armstrong, J., 240
Armstrong, John Ignatius, 272
Armstrong, R. E., 272, 274, 277–79, 283
Arnaiz, Ángel, 596
Arnaiz, Manuel, 710
Arrate, Agustín (Gus), 26, 35, 364, 383, 430, 461–75, 481, 485, 605, 680, 709–11, 740–43, 753
Arrate, Amaya, 35, 374, 383, 466, 472–73, 713, 741, 747–54
Arrate, Eneko, 743
Arrate, Idoya, 35, 383, 741–42, 754
Arrate, Iñaki, 462–63
Arrate, Javier, 743
Arrate, John (Johnny), 35, 383, 466–67, 740, 744–45
Arrate, José, 476
Arrate, Laureano, 476
Arrate, Mary (Bengoa), 361, 383, 467, 471–74, 626, 740, 743, 748, 753, 755
Arregui, Domingo, 369–70
Arregui, José, 350, 524, 533
Arresuvieta, José, 100n94
Arriaga, Juan Cruz, 363

Arrien, Ramón, 346–47, 574–77
Arrieta (surname), 99n72
Arrieta, Nicolás, 322
Arrillaga, Frank, 418
Arrillaga, Pedro María, 418
Arrillaga, Rosaria, 418
Arrilliaga, Frank, 365
Arriola, Manuel, 90
Arriya I, 589n26
Arriya II, 365–66, 589n26
Arrizubieta, Belinda, 508
Arrizubieta, Eusebio, 420, 506–9
Arrizubieta, Nieves, 420
Arroita, Justo, 709
Arroiti, Luis, 492
Arroiti, Mari Louise, 751
Arrom de Ayala, Antonio, 66n34, 80
Arroquero, Domingo, 561–63
Arroquero, José María, 561
Arroquero, Patxi, 561
art: chainsaw, 14; rock art, 638, 664–65
Artajo, Martín, 255
Artaro, Manuel, 514
Artiach, Frank, 484
Artozano, Pedro, 90
Arzalluz, Xabier, 588n14
Arzola Shipping Company, 576
Aseguinolaza, Jaime, 597
Ashley Brothers, 93
Asian immigration, 53–54, 63, 64n2, 104
Asman tribe, 658
Asociación Navarra Boomerang (Navarran Boomerang Association), 361
Aspiri, Francisco, 700
Asselin, J. C., 75
Assisted Migrant Program, 271–304
Assisted Nominated Dependents' Scheme, 294
L'Associazione dei Produttori Italiani nell'Industria dello Zucchero (The Association of Italian Producers in the Sugar Industry), 189
Astoreca, Isaac, 551–53
Astoreca, Pilar, 552
Astorquia, Félix, 411, 420–26

774   Index

Astorquia, Joaquín, 491
Astorquia, Juan, 423, 699
Astorquia, María Pilar, 383, 411–12, 422, 745
Astorquia, Valentín, 491–93
Astor Radio Corporation, 571
Astrea, 77, 84
Asturi, Eusebio, 481
Asturian Club. *see Centro Asturiano de Sydney*
Astuy, Sabino, 548–50
Astuy, Valentín, 513, 550
Asumendi, Vicente, 702
atheism, 209, 453, 578
Atherton Tablelands, 34, 284, 322, 326t, 327, 359–60, 687
Athletic, 25
Atrevida, 78, 97n41
Aulesti, Bizkaia, 13, 35, 318, 323, 596
Aulestia, Gorka, 37n1
Aurelia, 260, 272, 296
Ausejo, Ramiro, 312
Australia: 19th-century, 51–52, 66n40, 69–102, 305; Age of the Bourgeoisie, 51; agricultural history, 55–64, 155; alien internment, 218–25; Aliens' Registration Bill, 218; Aliens Restriction Act, 67n59; Basque place names, 65n24; Basque population, 4, 46–47, 65n24, 69–102, 334–90, 679–90, 754; Basque press, 367–68; call for immigrants, x, 8, 14, 23, 40–68, 103, 106–9, 119–29, 133, 140, 151–53, 241–42, 245–56, 258–62, 267n110, 268n112, 268nn119–20, 271–305, 311, 314, 363, 388, 493–94, 520, 523, 595–99, 634, 691–97; Catalans in, 387; demographics, 384–88; Department of Education, 661–62; Department of Immigration, 235, 252–54, 261, 286, 385–86, 555, 573; Department of Veterans Affairs, 666; economy, 49; ethnic groups, 46; federation, 110–17; foreign-born population, 43–44, 65n21, 69, 384–85; foreign capital, 49, 65n28; gold, 38n12; immigration history, 42–55, 59, 216–17, 390n22; immigration policy, 41–45, 49–50, 146–47, 165–75, 243, 267n110, 386–87; immigration quotas, 174, 189, 386; Italian population, 70–71, 103–10, 146, 173, 175, 387, 390n22; labor history, 49–52, 57, 76, 82, 293–94, 309–10; Leases of Aliens Restrictions Act, 198; liquor laws, 352–53; Nepal-born population, 384; Non-Intervention Policy, 209–10; plantation system, 55, 58–63, 75–76, 107, 115; population growth, 50, 66n34, 69; Queensland Aliens Act, 199; Racial Discrimination Act 1975, 385–86; rehabilitation and renewal, 235–70; relations with Italy, 296; relations with Spain, 298; Southern Europeans in, 69–77; Spanish Assisted Migrant Program, 271–304; Spanish population, 81, 145, 286, 327, 334–80, 387; sugar cane districts, 156–57n21; sugar consumption, 67n62; sugar industry, 55–64, 110–17, 245–46, 291–94, 314; Treaty of Peace, 241; unemployment, 228n113; White Australia policy, 53–55, 61, 63–64, 69–70, 104, 110–11, 132–33, 140–41, 165, 171–72, 384–86, 635. *see also specific states*
Australia and New Zealand Army Corps (ANZAC) Day, 13, 16, 21, 37n2
Australian, 547
Australian Accordion Society, 429
Australian Armed Forces, 319–21, 628, 639–40, 643
Australian Broadcasting Commission, 231n222
Australian Canegrower, 492
Australian Catholic Church, 271, 289
Australian Citizenship Act 1973, 385–86
Australian Citizenship Convention, 280
Australian Communist Party, 316–17

Australian National Radio, 723
Australian Natives' Association, 167, 174
Australian Paper Mill, 582
Australians, 416
Australian Sugar Journal, 273–74
Australian Sugar Journal, and the Australian Canegrower, 492
Australian Sugar Producers' Association, 135, 183–84, 240–41
Australian Sugar Review, 495
Australian Workers' Union (AWU), 112, 125, 129–31, 138, 144, 154, 157n22, 175–79, 182, 184, 191–92, 202, 229nn136–37, 275–76, 292, 446, 636; Patriotic War Fund, 308–9
Austrians, 124, 136–37, 262, 275–76
Autonomous Basque Community (*Euskadi*), 2–4, 22, 38n13, 210, 500, 520, 558
auzoak (neighborhoods), 5
AWU. *see* Australian Workers' Union
Ayo, Félix, 332n30
Ayr, Australia, 130, 161n113, 182–83; Barcelona Gardens, 588–89n16; Basque population, 317–19, 467, 516, 603, 606, 611; Italian population, 146, 174, 326t, 516; landownership, 327–29, 328t; Saint Ignatius Day festival, 605; Sicilian population, 516; Spanish population, 287; sugar industry, 310, 501, 509
Ayr Advocate, 477, 479, 482–83, 485, 488, 490, 492, 495
Ayr District Canegrowers' Executive, 274
Ayr International Club, 361, 477
Ayr Lion's Club, 475
Ayr Spanish Club, 471
Azaguirre, Juan, 448–49
Azcarate, Ramón, 489
Azcarraga, G., 315, 316t
Azcona, Jesús, 540–43
Azkarate, Miren, 28
Azkue, José Antonio, 20, 501
Azkue Azkue, Jugatx, 373–74

Azpiazu, Antonio, 332n33, 425, 433, 436, 439, 442
Azpiazu, José María, 547, 574
Azpiri, Antolín, 416, 481
Azpiri, Antonio, 481
Azpiri, John, 417
Azpiri, Juan, 276, 410, 416–18, 423, 613

Babinda Italian Club, 203
Babinda Mill, 175–78, 183, 191, 223, 287
Badilla cane, 744
Badiola, Carmen, 415
Badiola, Edurne, 415
Badiola, Esteban, 415
Badiola, Ignacio, 710
Badiola, Iñaki, 329, 442–43, 592
Badiola, Jesús, 415
Badiola, José, 415, 499, 615
Badiola, León, 332n32
Badiola, Loren, 415
Badiola, Pascual, 262–63, 273–75, 285, 363, 375, 392, 419, 468, 486, 489, 498–99, 563, 574, 577, 591–92, 596, 701
Bagatella, Ann, 502
Bailey, George, 654
Balanzategui, Bingen, 363
Balanzategui, Elizabeth, 448
Balanzategui, Javier, 732–34, 758
Balanzategui, Jesús, 484, 507
Balanzategui, Juan, 418–21, 427, 507
Balanzategui, Keziah, 732–33
Balanzategui, María, 263
Balanzategui, Mark, 587n2, 733–35, 755
Balanzategui, Miguel, 420
Balanzategui, Miren, 394, 420
Balanzategui, Norberto, 316–17, 700
Balanzategui, Petra, 733
Balanzategui, Ramón, 749
Balanzategui, Sabin, 733–34
Balanzategui, Sabino, 518, 710
Balanzategui, Victoria, 733
Balanzategui family, 263, 310, 505
Balanzategui Loyola, Vicente, 319–21, 603–4, 700

776 INDEX

Ballyn, Susan, 89
balonmano (handball), 457, 588n12, 593
Balts (Lithuanians), 237, 240–41, 243–44
bananas, 161n119
Bank of New South Wales, 350
Bañuelos, Benito, 350, 358–59, 543, 547
Bañuelos, Sylvino, 543–44
Banyan, Australia, 177
Baptists, 208
Barcelona, Spain, 125–26, 291
Barcelona Club (Melbourne), 305, 336
Barcelona Gardens, 588–89n16
Barcs, Emery, 231n222
Bargara, Australia, 673
Baroja, Pío, 381
Bartlett, John, 616
Basarte, Isildro Goñi, 296
Bascom Construction, 568
baserriak (farmsteads), 4–9
Basque Americans, 301n31, 320, 375n1, 413, 418, 683–87, 689
Basque Argentinians, 10
Basque Australia, 756
Basque Australians, 683, 689
Basque Chileans, 10
Basque Club (Sydney), 731
Basque Club (Townsville), 687
Basque Club (*txoko*), 334. see also Gure Txoko
Basque Club of North Queensland, 361, 625–26, 747–49, 754–56
Basque clubs (*euskal etxeak*), 354, 687
Basque Country (*Euskalherria*), 1, 2, 3, 278–79, 734
Basque cuisine, 749
Basque dance, 354, 725–26, 749, 755
Basque Diaspora Studies, 679–80, 682
Basque language. *see Euskera*
Basque Nationalist Party (*Partido Nacionalista Vasco*, PNV), 25, 38n13, 603, 671
Basque place names, 65n24
Basque press, 367–68, 378n102
Basques, 416; *aitonak* (grandparents), 355; in Americas, 78; anti-Franquism, 324–25; in Antipodes, 305–33; in Argentina, 683–84; in Australia, 46–47, 69, 77, 83–95, 161n113, 310–11, 322, 334–80, 516, 679–90; in Australian Armed Forces, 319; background, 1–12; *Caledonien*, 315, 316t; chain migration, 299n12, 388; copper gougers, 200; cultural life, 324–25, 345–46; cultural preservation, 752–54; diaspora, 10–11, 682–83; discrimination against, 557, 562, 574–75, 586, 604–5, 608; emigration to Australia, 387–88, 683–84; emigration to US, 687; entrepreneurs, 611–26; ethnic identity, 685; ethnic stereotypes, 585; European residences, 290–91, 691–97; facilitator, 591–610; female immigrants, 318–19; generational differences, 585–86; history of, 753; integration of, 329; musical groups, 728–29; nationalism, 1–3, 24, 324–25, 337, 351, 468, 488, 504, 520, 716; naturalization of, 219, 318–19; in New Australia, 381–90; in North Queensland, 271; occupational identity, 685; preference for, 279–80; press coverage of, 369–72; in Queensland, 327, 699–702; recruitment of, x, 253, 262, 271–304, 363, 595–99, 634, 692–97; religiosity, 337–38; sheepherders, 301n31, 320, 373, 413, 418, 524, 683–89; single-adult-women, 318; soccer teams, 25; sojourners vs settlers, 381–84; Spanish alternative, 271–304; Spanish Euclids, 615; sponsorship of, 262–63, 319–20, 395–96, 422, 440–43, 449–50, 462, 478, 501, 505; in sugar industry, 193, 271–304, 310, 316–17, 319; uniqueness of, 734; voices, 391–677; wandering, 627–78; workers, 422; work scouts, 284
Basque sports, 362–66
Basque Television (*Euskal Telebista*, ETB), 372, 538, 724

Basque Week, 355–56
Bastos de Ávila, Fernando, 267n110
Basurco, Cecilio (Zezilio), 322, 374, 702–7
Basurto, Unai, 717
Batasuna (Union), 19, 22, 24, 38n5
Battle of the Solomons, 223
Batua, 727
Baume, F. E., 193–96
Bazurco, Cecilio, 702
BBC, 421, 721
Beeva, Australia, 317–18
Belvedere Hotel, 429, 587n3
Benedictine monks, 312–13
Bengoa, Begoña (Bego), 357, 589n17, 741, 752, 756–57
Bengoa, John (Johnny), 466, 473–74, 515, 607, 742–43
Bengoa, Juan, 710
Bengoa, Mary, 35, 465, 469, 740, 743
Bengoa, Pedro, 587n2, 700
Bengoa, Peter, 473–74, 481, 742
Bengoa, Rosemary, 748
Bengoa, Tere, 742
Bengoa farm, 515–16
Bengoechea, Jesús, 478–79, 607
Bengoetxea, Edurne, 725
Bennier (Benier), Frank, 366
Berbix Balanzategui, Sabin, 733
Bereciartua, Segunda, 462, 473–74, 587n2
Bereicua, Domingo, 516
Bereicua, Fabián, 508–10
Bereicua, Juan, 509
Bereicua, Julia, 487–88
Bermeo, Bizkaia, 91
Bermeo restaurant (Carrum), 101n97
Berricua, Raimundo, 701
bertsolaritza, 37n1, 460
Betos, Joseph, 311
Bhutanese, 385
Bicheno, Tasmania, 671
Bilbao, Bonifacio, 701
Bilbao, Claudio, 476, 700

Bilbao, Frank, 321–22
Bilbao, H. L., 90
Bilbao, Iban, xiin3, 391
Bilbao, Jon, 679
Bilbao, José, 527–28, 557–58
Bilbao, Spain, 280–81, 311
Bilbao, Y., 370
Bilbao, Yrinio, 700
bilingualism, 511
bioscience, 456
Bizkaia Proprietary Ltd, 617
Bizkaia/Vizcaya, 4; alternative immigrants from, 281, 290–91, 318, 322–23, 695–97; Old Law (*fuero*), 1
blackbirders, 57
black-fellows agreement, 127–28
Black Hand gang, 213–17, 232n240, 592
Black Shirts, 200–212
Black Swan Hotel (Sydney), 94
Blainey, Geoffrey, 48–49
Blainey debate, 386–87
Blake, Damian, 355
Blanco, Miguel Angel, 24–25
Blanco y Negro, 503
Blucher, Heather, 514–15
Bluewater, Queensland, 616
BMC (British Motors Company), 524
BMD Urban, 732
Bodey, Laury (Cheyenne), 674
Bodnar, John, 64n3
Bogotá, Colombia, 685
Boletín del Banco de Vizcaya, 488
Bolshevism, 201, 336–37
Bombala, 315
Bonanno, Joe, 474
Bonegilla Camp, 250–51, 559, 635
Bonegilla Migrant Centre, 285
Borin, V. L., 264n29
Borrie, W. D., 229n138
Bosnian Australians, 16
bounty system, 49–50
bourgeoisie, 51
Bowden, Gary, 653
Bowen Independent, 477

bowls, 500
boxing, 365, 368
Boyes, G. T. W. B., 86–88
Boy Scouts, 236
Brandon Progress Association, 182
Brazil, 43–44, 47
Bresciani Motors, 461–62
Brett, Ronnie "Dread," 647–48
Briani, Vittorio, 70
Brigando, Mario, 119
Brisbane, Queensland, 317; Basque population, 319, 498–500, 639, 645; Italian population, 71, 215, 327
Brisbane, Thomas, 85–86
Brisbane Courier, 125
Brisbane Courier Mail, 446, 653
Brisbane Golf Club, 500
Brisbane Spanish Club, 360
British Isles: immigrants from, 43–44, 66n46, 69–70, 121–24, 193, 241, 245–46, 264n36. *see also* Great Britain
British Motors Company (BMC), 524
British Preference Committee (Burdekin), 182–83
British Preference League, 181, 183–87, 189, 196–97
British Preference movement, 165, 175–200, 229n138
Broadwater Mill, 72
Bronco, Tony (Antonio Onaindia Laca), 321, 373–74
Bubé, José, 462, 465
Buenos Aires, Argentina, 685
Buhot, John, 57–58
Building Labourers' Union, 552
Bulgaria, 607
Bulow, 122
Bundaberg, Australia, 107, 117
Burdekin Bridge, 612
Burdekin Community Club, 491
Burdekin Hotel, 467, 477, 480, 482, 485, 491, 495–96
Burdekin International Club, 472, 482–83, 491

Burdekin Shire: Basque population, 34–35, 161n113, 262–63, 274, 316–19, 322–23, 388, 461–98, 603, 611, 625; British Preference Committee, 182–83; Catalan population, 35–36, 324; Italian population, 107, 110, 117; labor history, 148, 178; Spanish population, 327; sugar industry, 182, 191, 274, 329, 330*t*, 463, 509, 511, 518
Burdekin Soccer Club, 483
Burdekin Squash Club, 488
Burke, T. M., 171
Burmese, 385
Burnt Sugar (Baume), 193–96
Buruaga, Martín, 332n29
Bushland Beach, 621
Bustamante y Guerra, José, 77, 83
Butler, Harry, 665

Cabarrús, François, 77
cabinetry, 500
Cabrera, Nelson, 720
CAC (Civilian Alien Corps), 221–23
Cadiz, Spain, 291
Cairns, Queensland, 310; Basque population, 319, 322–23; Italian population, 118, 146, 148, 174, 325, 326*t*; Spanish population, 287, 307
Cairns Migrant Center, 268n119
Cairns Post, 450
Caja Rural de Navarra, 361
Calabrians, 213, 215–16
Caledonian, 626n1
Caledonie, 315, 316*t*, 320
California, 10, 50, 378n102, 686, 689
California Café, 542
California-ko Eskual Herria, 378n102
Caltex, 622
Calwell, Arthur, 235, 243–44, 347–48, 584
Camarero, Mariano, 392
Cambodians, 385
Camerero family, 310
Camino de Santiago, 757–58

Camino Salvado Pilgrimage, 674
Campion, Edmund, 281
Canada, 41, 43–44, 526
Canadians, 385
Canals, Josee (Josephine), 305–6
Canary Islands, 279
Canberra, 315
Canberra, Australia, 221, 340
Canberra Hotel (Paddington), 550
canecutters and canecutting, 16–17, 34, 111–14, 129–56, 358, 400–406, 438, 446, 478–81, 684; Americans' gang, 554; Basques, 323, 374, 388, 396, 479, 487–92, 496–99, 501, 505–7, 511–16, 544–45, 551, 554–56, 559, 563, 567, 576, 581, 595–96, 600, 637, 683, 689; competitions, 594, 744–45; displaced persons (DPs), 113; gangers and gangs (*see* gangers and gangs); immigrant recruitment for, x, 14, 47, 113–16, 119–20, 241–42, 245–47, 253, 257–60, 268nn119–20, 271–304, 363, 520, 544–45, 561, 598–99; Italians, 135–36, 157n22, 241–42; labor force, 140, 192, 239–42, 251, 264n36, 268n119, 272, 287, 297, 414, 442, 449–50, 524; mateship, 113; mechanization, 291–92, 403–8, 414, 424, 431–32, 435–38, 441–43, 479, 487, 493, 545–46, 565–66; shortage, 595; Spanish, 128, 136, 271–304, 327; wages, 114, 130, 190, 401, 413–14, 439, 462–63, 476, 484, 489, 504, 509, 514, 518, 524, 549, 559, 577, 637; work conditions, 112, 119, 190, 413–14, 430–31, 434, 463, 468, 482, 486, 494, 565; work stoppages, 129–30. *see also* sugar industry
Canefarmers' Association of North Queensland, 120–21
Canegrowers' Association, 190, 449, 595, 602, 744
cannibalism, 658
Cantamessa, Giuseppe, 219
Cao, Frank, 577

Cao, Paco, 478
Caracas, Venezuela, 685
Carboni, Raffaello, 70, 95n8, 389n13
Cardwell, Australia, 135, 174, 326*t*
Careaga, Cornelio, 35, 410
Careaga, Pedro, 232n233, 316*t*
Carega, Cornelio, 487
Cargo Cult, 656
Caritas and Acción Católica (Catholic Action), 267n110
Carlist Wars, 9, 92
Carlos, Gloria, 562–63
Carlton and United Breweries, 306
Carmagnola, Frank, 205–6
Caroline, 85
Carrero Blanco, Luis, 369
Carroll, P. J., 470
Carrum Progress Association, 101n97
Casa de España (Whyalla), 340
Casal Català (Catalan House), 306
Castello, Manuel, 710
castells, 718–19
Castrejana, Agustín, 440, 481, 710
Casuarina High (Darwin), 662
Catalan, Anselmo, 312
Catalans, 35–36, 124–25, 210, 412, 718–19; 19th-century, 94; in Australia, 69, 79, 82, 130, 219, 271, 305–6, 309–10, 321–24, 337, 387; identification as Spaniards, 390n22; nationalism, 721–22; naturalization of, 219; recruitment of, 123, 126–28, 305
Catalonia, 470
Catalunya, 327
Catholic Club (Sydney), 340–41
Catholic Immigration in Queensland, 294
Catholic Leader (Queensland), 370
Catholics and Catholicism, 46, 207–9, 231n211, 236, 297, 337–38, 370; missionaries, 79; priests, 312–13
Cavallaro, Pearl, 398–99
Cavallaro, Sam, 398–99
Cazzulino, Mario, 205

CCC (Civilian Construction Corps), 221–23, 611
CCEM (*Comisión Cátolica Española de Migración*, Spanish Catholic Migration Commission), 255, 267n110, 294
celebrities, 366–67
cement, 518
Centennial Park (Sydney), 532, 537
Center for Basque Studies, 32, 753
Central Land Council, 668
Central Region, 157n21
Centro Asturiano de Sydney, 345, 348, 368
Centro Español (Melbourne), 339–45
Centro Español (Sydney), 339–45, 359, 368, 528, 543, 758
Centro Español (Victoria), 339–45
Centro Español de Queensland, 163n153
Cephee, 320
Cerezo Martínez, Ricardo, 97n41
Cervantes Institute, 729
Chacartegui, Juan Estanislao, 320–21
chain migration, 299n12, 388
chainsaw art, 14
Challis, Christine, 30, 98n71, 99n73, 100n91
Charles Darwin University, 663
Chevron Hotel, 521
Chidell, Fleetwood, 169–70
Chile, 43–44, 47, 683–84
Chilibots, Jean Baptiste, 95
Chinese immigrants, 53, 69–70, 148, 155, 161n119, 168–69, 171–72; in Australia, 384–85; opium smokers, 67n59; pioneers, 67n59; settlers, 58, 62–63
Chin Peng, 640–41
Chiquito de Bermeo (Salvador Ruiz), 601
Christ Church, New Zealand, 83
Christianity, 209
Church of Christ, 208
Churruca, Eulogio, 563
Churruca, Francisco, 322
Churruca, Jose F., 702
CIME (*Comité Intergubernamental para las Migraciones Europeas*), 249–50, 256–59, 268n112, 268n118, 271, 274, 279–80, 294, 543
Cincunegui, Ángel, 316t
Ciriaco & Company, 438–39
citizenship, 417
Civilian Alien Corps (CAC), 221–23
Civilian Construction Corps (CCC), 221–23, 611
Clare Club, 475
Clare Spanish Club, 475
class differences, 114, 137–38, 161n113
Clemençot, Prudencio, 93
climate, 279
Cloncurry Rugby, 621
Club Español (Melbourne), 560, 562, 565, 578
Club Español (Mount Druitt), 524–25
Club Español (Sydney), 24, 347, 359, 404, 433, 522–24, 530–33, 537, 544–50, 553, 556, 719–20
Club Gallego, 345, 347
Club Hispano-Australiano, 339–40
Club Ibérica, 360–61
Club Italiano, 205
Club of Franco, 360
code-switching, 33
Cold War, 271, 324
Colonial Sugar Refining (CSR) Company, 60–63, 116–29, 139, 201, 414, 428
colonization, 305–25
Columbus, 78
Comas, Arthur, 709
Comas, Juan, 709
Comas, Steve, 709
Comas family, 472
Comisión Cátolica Española de Migración (CCEM, Spanish Catholic Migration Commission), 255, 267n110, 294
Comitato Anti-Fascista dell'Herbert River (The Anti-Fascist Committee of the Herbert River), 205
Comité Intergubernamental para las

Migraciones Europeas (CIME) or Intergovernmental Committee for European Migrations (ICEM), 249–50, 256–59, 268n112, 268n118, 271, 274, 279–80, 294, 543
commercial fishing, 516, 608
Commodore Hotel (later called the Belvedere), 587n3
Commonwealth of Australia. *see* Australia
Commonwealth Serum Laboratories (CSL), 455
Commonwealth Teaching Service, 658
Communists and Communism, 190–92, 209–10, 321–22, 331n16, 337
computer technology, 19, 27
Congregationalists, 208
Consolidated Pneumatic Tool, 14
construction industry, 350, 358; Basques in, 398, 425, 482–84, 521, 543–45, 554–55, 567–68, 576, 581, 615–17; wages, 543
controversy and confrontation (1925–1945), 165–234
Cook, James, 45, 77
Coolgardi, Australia, 306
coolies, 53, 57
copper, 200
Coral House, 666
Correo Español, 513
Corriere della Sera, 169, 421
Corris, Peter, 67n56
Corta, Eugenio, 422
Corta, Pedro, 422
Corta, Sabino, 422
Cortes, J., 80
Cosgrove, Peter, 648
Costa Brava restaurant, 522, 533, 550
Country Liberal Party, 667
Country Life, 485
Country Party (now National Party), 244, 477, 667
Country Womens' Association, 220, 222
Courier Mail, 173, 216, 426, 488
Craig, Noel, 710

Cranbourne College, 573
crayfishing, 490
crime: ethnic, 200, 212–17; organized, 215–17; petty, 369–70
Crocodile Investments, 620
croquetas, 749
Crown Hotel, 513
CSL (Commonwealth Serum Laboratories), 455
CSR (Colonial Sugar Refining) Company, 60–63, 116–29, 139, 201, 414, 428
CSRIO (Commonwealth Scientific and Industrial Research Organisation), 571
cultural genocide, 278–79
cultural preservation, 752–54
Cultura Proletaria, 232n233

D'Agostino, Vicenzo, 215–16, 232n240
Daily Mail, 143–44
Daily Mirror, 522
Daily Telegraph, 547, 551
Dall'Osto, Cris, 157n22, 161n113, 229n137, 329, 397–99
dance, 354, 378n79, 472, 749, 755
Danesi, Carlo, 185, 211
Danesi, L., 185
Darling Downs, 327
D'Arrietta, Stewart, 366–67
Darwin, Australia, 309, 582, 659–62
Darwin, Cynthia, 477
Darwin Community College, 660, 666
Davies, John Richard, 310
d'Azeglio, Massimo, 384
de Allende Muriedas, Izaskun, 729
Dean, William, 459
de Arrieta, Jean Baptiste Lehimas, 30, 84–90, 98nn71–72, 100n85, 100nn89–90, 366, 707
de Arrieta, Zaloa, 728
De Beers, 633
Debono, Barbara, 365
Decalzara, José, 100n94
Deia, 375, 421, 428, 488, 513, 519

de Inchausti, Manuel, 322–23
de Inciarte, Juan, 97n41
Delaraga, José, 100n94
de la Riva, Ramón, 297–99
de la Thorezia de la Vega, Adelaide, 89
de los Angeles Ribero, María Victoria, 508
del Val, Enrike "Misha," 717
de Miguel, Alfonso, 377n53
demographics, 384–88, 413
Denmark, 77
Denoon, Donald, 43, 64n3
depression, 497–98
de Rays, Marquis, 72
De Román, Margarita, 550
Descubierta, 78, 84, 97n41
deserters, 322
de Tovar Arredondo, Antonio, 97n41
Devanny, Jean, 229n136
de Viana, Leoncio, 84
de Viana, Melchor, 84
de Vita, Angelo, xiin3
Día de la Hispanidad, 360, 471
Diario Vasco, 375
Diaz, Eusebio, 441
Díaz, José Luis, 295, 297
Dickson, Roy, 595
Dickson Award, 138–40, 144
Diez, Miguel, 710
Dinham, Peter, 647
Dioxin, 653
dirigistes, 61
discrimination: against Aborigines, 575, 579, 585, 639; against Basques, 557, 562, 574–75, 586, 604–5, 608; Basque voices on, 422, 447–48, 477–78, 488, 491–95, 499–503, 506, 510, 523–26, 542, 548, 552, 560; against immigrants, 163n154, 169, 171–72, 177, 184–87, 579; against Italians, 177, 184–87, 242–43; racial or ethnic, 46, 53–55, 58, 61, 385–86, 408, 412, 433, 440, 443, 446, 450; religious, 46; against women, 644–45

displaced persons (DPs), 113–14, 236–37, 240–44, 264n29, 266n80, 541
Do, Chingo, 67n59
dock workers, 319, 436, 439
Dodin, Bernard, 432
Dodin, Christien, 432
Dodin, Françoise, 432–33
Dolan, Alwyn, 618–19
Doltheguy, Pierre, 90
Domanovicé, Branko (fictional protagonist), 113–14
domestic service, 289
Donaldson, Robert, 112
Donatiu, José María (Catalan Joe), 336
Donelly, Bridget, 94
Douglass, Jan, xi, 710
Douglass, William Anthony, 65n23, 681
Douglas Shire, 174, 326*t*
Doyle, Kevin, 618, 620
DPs (displaced persons), 113–14, 236–37, 240–44, 264n29, 266n80, 541
Droguet, Benito, 35, 469, 472, 588n16, 709
Droguet, Rosa, 709
Drysdale Mission, Western Australia, 313
Duch, Juan, 122
Duchess of York, 85
Dui, 656
Duñabeitia, Angel, 435
Duñabeitia, Lorenzo, 437
Dunedin, New Zealand, 94
Dunlop Hotel, 450
Dunstan, W. J., 179
Durán, Lorenzo, 309–10
Durán family, 310
Dutch immigrants, 245–46, 635

Easterby, Harry T., 61
Eastern Suburbs Club, 556
Eastern Suburbs League, 522, 552
Eastern Suburbs Rugby League Club, 550
Echabe, Julián, 91
Echalar, John, 90, 100n93

Echarri, Fernando, 508
Echart, Henri, 90
Echeandia, Domingo, 478
Echeandia, José Luis, 405, 478–80, 710
Echeandia, José Martín, 478
Echeandia, María Angeles, 478
Echeandia, Martin, 710
Echebarri, Fernando, 420
Echebarri, Milagros, 420
Echeberry, Arnaud, 90
Echevarria, Consuelo, 504, 506
Echevarria, Fernando, 504–6, 508
Echevarria, Pedro, 100n94
The Economist, 660
egalitarianism, 7, 49, 161n113, 308, 523
Egaña, Julián, 489
Egiguren, Jesús, 346–47
Eguia, José, 100n94
Eguia, Julian, 417
Eguia, Luis, 477
Eguiguren, Cristobal, 702
Egyptians, 384
Eibar, Eider, 717
Eizaguirre, Jaime, 490, 511
Eizaguirre, Juan, 490, 510–12, 516
Eizaguirre, León, 511
Eizaguirre, María Pilar, 490–91, 511
El Caso, 450
El Correo Español, 519, 594
Electric Public Commission (EPC), 574
El Español en Australia, 367–69, 389n13;
  Basque readership, 411, 415, 421,
  426, 428, 433, 436, 439, 446, 450,
  479, 482–83, 502–3, 506, 508–9, 519,
  522, 525, 547, 550, 556, 560, 562, 574,
  711–12, 715, 720
El Gol, 428
Elisabe, Vincent, 95
elitism, 161n113
Elkano, 9
Elkar, 730
El Mundo Deportivo, 550
Elordieta, Andoni, 19–20, 23–24
Elordieta, Isaias, 517
Elordieta, Jesús, 20, 517–20
Elorduy, Enrique, 332n31
Elortegui, B., 332n32
Elortegui, Joaquín, 332n32
Elortegui Azcorra, Pedro, 319–20, 332n32, 700
Elosseguy, François, 95
El País, 628
El Pueblo Vasco, 433
embargo, sugar, 181, 184, 186, 189
Emerson, Roy, 344
Emigrantes Trasplante de Catolicismo (Catholicism's Transplanted Emigrants), 267n110
England, 69
English language, 557
English language classes, 487, 492, 599–600
entrepreneurs, 611–26
EPC (Electric Public Commission), 574
Epelde, José, 332n29
EPT, 566–67
equipment companies, 617–18
Equity Trustees, 306
Ercoreca, Iker, 349
Ereño, Bizkaia, 13
Erezuma, A., 332n32
Erkoreka, Iker, 576–80
Erkoreka, Lander, 576
Eroski, 361
Erviti, Victor Moizes, 211
Escribano, Mariano, 341
Escualdun Gazeta, 378n102
Escuela de Naútica (Nautical School), 93
Esparza, Antonio (Tony), 353–55, 425, 446, 544–47, 565–67, 598, 605, 715
Espata Dantza, 500
Espilla, Jose, 702
ETA, 3, 11n2, 19, 24, 368–69, 460–61, 520, 578, 605–6, 671, 721–22
ETB (*Euskal Telebista*, Basque Television), 372, 538, 724
ethnic crime, 200, 212–17

ethnic differences, 137–38, 181, 446, 585
ethnic discrimination, 46. *see also* discrimination
ethnic festivals or feast days, 350–52, 594, 605, 685–86. *see also specific festivals*
ethnic groups, 46. *see also specific groups*
Etxabe, Antonia, 757
Etxabe, Eugenia, 592
Etxarri, Joseba, 372
Etxetxu, 36
Eureka Stockade, 70
Europe, 122; emigration to Australia, 42–55, 144–45, 235, 691–97; Mediterranean, 64; Northern, 69–70; refugee camps, 240; Southern, 64, 69–77
European labor, 62–63
Euskadi (Autonomous Basque Community), 2–4, 22, 38n13, 210, 500, 520, 558
Euskal Artzainak Ameriketan (Basque Sheepherders in America), 373
Euskal Australiar Alkartea (Basque Australians Together), 373–74
euskal etxeak (Basque clubs), 354, 687
Euskalherria (Basque Country), 1, 2, 3, 278–79, 346, 734
Euskalkutura.com, 372
Euskal Presoak Etxera, 24–25
Euskal Telebista (ETB, Basque Television), 372, 538, 724
Euskera (Basque language), 11n9, 33, 324–25, 448–49, 473, 604–5, 727, 734; at home, 411, 415, 429, 480, 488, 519; learning, 347, 352, 719, 725–26
Euskera Batua, 459
Eusko Deya, 347
Eusko Jaurlaritza, 18–19, 23–27, 539
Euskonews, 101n97
Everingham, Paul, 667, 683
excise taxes, 110–11
exploration, 48
Express, 91
Extra, 550
Ezquerra, Manuel, 97n41

Facebook, 721, 749
facilitator Basques, 591–610
Fagor, 730
fair play, 104
famille souche (stem family), 5–6
Far East Asians, 384
farmers' associations, 121, 475
farms, 4–5, 137
Far North Queensland: Basque population, 322–24, 551, 686–88; Catalan population, 324; colonization of, 305–25; labor history, 181; settlement of, 106; Spanish population, 145, 305–10, 359; sugar industry, 145
Fascism and Fascists, 200–212, 222, 319, 336–37, 375n8, 526
FCIC (Federal Catholic Immigration Committee), 244–45, 255
feast days, 350–52, 605. *see also specific festivals*
Federal Catholic Immigration Committee (FCIC), 244–45, 255
federation, 110–17
Federazione Lucana, 15
Felices, Matilde, 556–57
Felipe VI, 669–70
Fenoglio, P., 178
Ferdinand, 9
Fermín, 351
Fernández, Ester, 513
Fernandez, Juan, 710
Fernández, María, 420
Fernández, Saturnino, 336
Fernández de Viana, Alberto, 332n31, 591, 595–96
Fernández-Shaw, Carlos M., 66n34, 209
Ferny Hills, 651
Ferrando, Rafael, 709
Ferry, Thomas A., 153–56
Ferry Commission, 165
Fiat Tractor, 462
Filipinos, 375n8, 384–85
Financial Review, 712
Finns, 193, 241, 264n36, 287

First Settlers Club, 672
First World Congress of Basque Centers (*Primer Congreso Mundial de Centros Vascos*), 355
Fischer, Tim, 666–67
fishing, commercial, 516, 608
Five Ways Hotel (Paddington), 341
Flaminia, 259, 261
Flanders, 79
Foley, Larry, 370–72
football (soccer), 21–22, 25, 344, 347, 353, 362, 438, 440, 454, 512, 525, 553, 588n11, 755
foral tradition, 1–2
Ford Motors, 582
foreign capital, 49, 65n28
foreigners, 24, 216
Fortuny, Salvador, 710
Foruria, Victoriano, 701
Fosterson, Maureen, 516–17
Foxwood Club, 417
Fraire, Chiaffredo Venerano, 104, 106–9, 117–18, 154, 156n3
France, 72, 180
Francis Xavier, 39n22
Franco, Francisco, 2–3, 8, 14, 209, 271, 319, 348, 471, 606; media coverage, 368–69; political action against, 351–52; support for, 448, 560, 605
French, 526–27
French Basque Country (*Iparralde*), 1, 232n227
French immigrants, 69
frontón (handball court), 5, 356–57, 364–65, 371, 600–601, 748
Frost, David, 354
fruit horticulture, 200, 555, 561, 565, 581–82, 608, 688; Basques in, 404, 419, 421–24, 432, 435–38, 441–46, 450, 476, 479, 481, 489–90, 499, 501–7, 509, 516, 518, 521, 549, 567
fuero (Old Law), 1–2
Fuller, Col, 673
Furor, 98n66

Gabiola, Diana, 748
Gabiola, Ignacio, 740
Gabiola, Joe, 481
Gabiola, José, 607, 701
Gabiola, José Ignacio, 709
Gabiola, Pascazio, 587n5, 700
Gabiola Bereciartua, Teresa, 373–74, 709
Gainza, Blas, 700
Galdeano, Gregoria, 560
gangers and gangs, 112–16, 131–32, 400–402, 410–14, 486; alien gangs, 193; Americans' gang, 554; Basque, 410, 424, 430–31, 441, 444–46, 501–2, 507, 551, 556, 576, 581, 595, 636, 687; ethnic lines, 181; Finnish, 193; foreign gangs, 181; Italian, 117–18, 128, 581; labor force, 447, 463; Spanish, 126, 128
Garaizar, Irati, 30
Gárate, Cosme, 440
Gárate, Gregorio, 440
Gárate, Iñaki, 446, 502
Gárate, Jesús, 410, 414
Gárate, Ramona, 437
Gárate, Tomás, 432, 437–40, 442, 446, 502
Garay, José M., 284
Garcia, Ignacio, 244–45
Garcia, Ildefonso, 312
García, Luis, 358–59
García, Trini, 309–10
García family, 310
Garizoai, Manuel, 26
Garmendia, Lorenzo, 514–15
Garmendia, Pascual, 494, 521, 532, 539, 590n27
Garmendia Olano, Usue, 726
Garramiola, María, 332n28
Gatton College, 276
Gavazzi, Mario, 263
gender differences, 308, 337–38
gender discrimination, 644–45. *see also* discrimination
General Sturgis, 541
generational differences, 585–86

Gentlemen's Agreement, 183–84, 186, 190, 199
George III, 45
George IV, 85
Geraldton, Australia, 128, 202
Germans: alien internment, 218–25; in Australia, 44, 65n21, 390n22; in Chile, 44; immigrants, 43–44, 64, 69, 76–77, 105–6, 246, 252, 295, 635; in sugar industry, 136–37, 287
Gernika, 599
Gil, Iñaki, 354
Gil, Thomas, 312
Giménez, Urbano, 312
Gippsland Times, 519
Gipuzkoa/Guipúzcoa, 98n72; immigrants from, 281, 290–91, 318, 323, 691–92
Girl Scouts, 236
Gnessotta, Nino, 710
Goby, Charles Arthur, 90
Goicoechea, Jenny, 374
Goicoechea, José "Romeo," 614
Goicoechea, Justo, 332n31, 615, 702
Goicoechea, Manuel, 701
Goicoechea, Margarita, 710
Goicoechea Construction Company, 417, 435, 441, 485, 616–17, 619–20
Goicoechea Family Trust, 620
Goicoechea Onaindia, Ignacio, 316t, 611, 626n1
Goicoechea Trio, 621
Goicoechea Ugarte, Joe (José María), 361, 383, 460, 471, 496, 538, 611–26, 680, 709
Goicoechea Ugarte, Juan María (John), 611
Goicoechea Ugarte, María Rosario (Rose), 611
Goikoetxea (Goicoechea) Gangoiti, José (Joe or Josu), 23–25, 28, 36, 210, 332n28, 332n30, 360, 714, 717–23, 726–27, 731, 748–49, 755, 758, 758n3
Goikola, 35
Goirigolzarri, José Ignacio, 501, 503
Goirigolzarri, José Luis, 446, 501–2
Goirigolzarri, Juan Manuel, 501, 503–4
Goirigolzarri, Leire, 373
Goirigolzarri, Luis, 438
Goirigolzarri, Ramón, 438, 446, 501–3, 508
Goirigolzarri Etxeandia, Leire, 373–74
Goitiandia, 34
Goitiandia, Sebastián, 332n31
Goitiandia, Vicente, 363, 476, 487, 496
Gojeascoa, 34
gold, 38n12, 50, 53–54, 80, 95n8, 686
golf, 523
Golf Digest, 522
Goñi, Carlos Arturo, 101n96
Goñi, José Luis, 341, 343, 349, 523–26
Goñi, Peter, 336
González, Gustavo, 453
Goondi Mill, 62, 125–28, 175, 181–83, 191
Gordonvale, Australia, 310
Gorri, 15
go-slow, 309
Grace Brothers Construction Company, 547
Gráficas Ipar, 361
Granada, Spain, 279
Grand Hotel, 511
grandparents (*aitonak*), 355
Gras-i-Fort, Peter, 79
Grassby, Al, 368, 386, 389n13, 475
Great Britain, 47–48; immigration from, 43–44, 105–6; Treaty of Commerce and Navigation, 197. see also British Isles
Great Depression, 173–75, 187, 189, 329, 448
Greater Brisbane, 326t
Great White Industry, 151
Greeks, 69, 104, 148, 155; in Australia, 65n21, 174, 390n22; immigrants, 168–69, 252, 286, 596, 609n3; naturalization of, 173; in sugar industry, 136–37
green walls, 729

Griffith, Samuel Walker, 61–63, 107
Griffith-Yenda, 501–10
Grose, Francis, 99n82
Grossardi, Donna, 202
guardias civiles, 721–22
Guerricadbetia (Guerricabeitia), José, 370, 702
Guisado Martino, Irati, 725
Guisado Moriones, Miquel, 725
Gumatj tribe, 668
Gumguya Park (Melbourne), 15–16
Gure Txoko (Melbourne), 17–19, 27, 345–48, 404, 513, 560, 564, 568, 575, 578–79, 584
Gure Txoko (Sydney), 17, 24–29, 348–59, 368, 404, 446, 521, 524–33, 538, 544–46, 578–79, 605, 689, 712–24, 728–32, 756–57; *Aberri Eguna* celebration, 355–56, 530, 532, 537; anniversary celebrations, 356, 718, 722–24, 728, 757; Basque cultural week, 354–55; Basque-dance classes, 725–26; Basque-language classes, 352, 719, 725–26; Board of Directors, 16, 536–37, 558, 720–21, 725–26, 728; computerization, 19, 27; dues, 537; feast days, 350–52; founders, 522, 529, 557–58; *frontón*, 26–27, 349–50, 362–63, 530, 532, 724; history of, 531–32, 681; *korrika*, 724; MacTxoko, 29; meetings, 16, 721; membership, 16–18, 24, 378n101, 529, 536–37, 539, 543, 548, 551–52, 556, 718–23, 727; *muslariak* (*mus* players) ambassadors, 26, 353, 530; *mus* tournament, 350, 525–26, 530, 532–33, 718; new *Txoko*, 681; *Noche Buena* celebration, 532; *pelota* tournament, 350, 352, 525–26, 529–30, 532; picnics, 29, 353, 532; political factions, 359, 553; press coverage, 375; *la rana* tournaments, 532; Saint Ignatius Day festivities, 356–57; soccer games, 26, 353, 529–32, 553, 558; subsidy, 539; weekly dinner, 22, 352, 537
Gutierrez, Valentín, 615

La Habana, Cuba, 685
Habana Plantation, 61
HABE, 731
Habgood, P. J., 678n3
Halifax, North Queensland, 133
halo effects, 161n113
Hambledon Mill, 125, 191, 223
handball (*balonmano*), 457, 588n12, 593. *see also pelota*
handball clubs, 363–65, 371, 601–2
handball court (*frontón*), 5, 356–57, 364–65, 371, 600–601, 748
Hanwick Social Club, 508
harrijasozaile (weightlifting), 364, 371, 471, 594, 609n2
Harris, Marjorie, 665–66
Harris, Robert, 21–22
Hatton, Steve, 668
Hawkins, Geoff, 31
Hazon, Roberto, 71
HB (*Herri Batasuna*), 38n5
Hegoalde (Spanish Basque Country), 1–4, 2
Henderson, L. D., 196, 199
Herald, 560, 564, 578
heralds, 367–75
Herbert District, 587n2
Herbert River, 107
Herbert River Angling Club, 429
Herbert River Canegrowers' Association, 241–42, 291
Herbert River Canegrowers' Council, 295
Herbert River district, 161n113; alien internment, 221–22; Basque population, 317–19, 322–23, 388; Italian population, 110, 117–18, 148, 174–75, 177, 198–99, 205–8, 214–15, 225n22; labor force, 193, 294; land ownership, 199; Southern European population, 135; Spanish population, 327; sugar industry, 131–33, 136–37, 162n153, 193, 223, 238, 241, 287, 294, 297, 329, 330t
Herbert River Express, x, 119, 215, 218–19, 259–60, 274, 283–86, 411, 415–17, 421,

426–28, 433, 439, 442, 446, 595; "The Outpost," 206
Herbert River News, 436
Hernández, Theodore, 312
Hernani, 38n12
Hernani Kronika, 37
herri (Basque village), 5
Herri Batasuna (HB), 38n5
Heyes, Tasman, 256, 268n115, 277–78
Hickey, Lancelot, 343
hidalguía, 6
Hiddins, Les, 665
Hilaro, Pedro, 316*t*
Hinchinbrook International Club, 411, 417–18, 421, 429, 437
Hinchinbrook Shire: alien internment, 222–23; Basque population, 392–446, 603; Basque sports, 364; demographics, 412; Italian population, 146, 174, 199, 219, 325, 326*t*; landownership, 327–29, 328*t*; Maraka Festival, 364; recruitment of immigrants, 253; sugar industry, 196, 496; tobacco industry, 199
Hispanic Center of Far North Queensland, 451
history: 19th-century Australia, 69–102; 1891 (Fraire Expedition) to 1925 (Ferry Exposition), 103–64; 1925–1945 (controversy and confrontation), 165–234; Age of the Bourgeoisie, 51; agricultural, 55–64; rehabilitation and renewal, 235–70
HMAS Sydney, 650
Hogan, John, 664, 667–68
Hogar Español ("Spanish Home"), 339–40
Hola, 417, 428, 506
Holden Migrant Accommodation Centre, 296
holidays, 471
Holland, 635
Holland, Alexander "Dutchy," 638–40, 683
Holt, Harold, 279–81

Home Hill, Queensland, 489–90; Basque population, 317–19, 463–65, 478–79, 611; Spanish population, 287
Home Hill Observer, 477, 485, 490
homosexuality, 712, 758n4
Honeybrook Electrical Company, 403
Hong Kong, 385
hospitality industry, 685
Hotel Oxford, 559
Howard, John, 459
Huesca, Spain, 281, 302n52
Hughes, Robert, 45
Hughes, Thomas, 122, 124, 126, 311
Hughes, William, 171–72
Hungarians, 287
Hunt, Atlee, 121
Hunt, Geoff, 458
Hyde, Noel, 622

Iantzi, Julian, 372–73
Iantzi, Mitxelena, Julian, 373–74
Ibañez, Mari, 378n79, 420, 714, 738, 749
Ibañez, María, 378n79, 421–22
Ibañez, Tomás, 378n79, 418–22, 424–25, 427, 486, 496, 507–8, 714, 749
Ibañez de Aldecoa, Zolio, 92
Ibar Azpiazu, José Manuel (Urtain), 365, 368
Ibarra, 92
Ibarra, Domingo, 419
Ibarrtexe, Juan José, 755
Ibarruengoitia, Jenaro, 435
Iberia, 10, 81
Iberian Club, 418, 421, 429, 433, 440, 443, 446
Icabaru, 642
ICEM (Intergovernmental Committee for European Migration), 249–50, 256–59, 268n112, 268n118, 271, 274, 279–80, 294, 543
ICI (Imperial Chemicals Industries), 527
ICMC (International Catholic Migration Commission), 249, 255, 266n80, 267n110
Idaho, 10, 19, 320, 689

Idoeta, Alberto, 411, 423–24
IEE. *see Instituto Español de Emigración*
Ignatius of Loyola, 21, 35, 39n22, 346, 350–51
ikastola school movement, 368–69
Ikurriña, 26, 346, 732, 754
Il Globo, 421, 450, 508, 519, 562, 564
Illarmendi, Eusebio, 23, 349–50, 355, 370, 524, 526–30, 711
Il Popolo d'Italia, 186
immigrants and immigration, 9–10, 53, 560–61; air vs boat, 303n107; assimilation, 475; Basque preference, 279–80; Blainey debate, 386–87; British preference, 165, 175–200; causes of, 153; chain migration, 299n12, 388; debate over, 165–75, 235–36; discrimination against immigrants, 163n154, 169–72, 177, 184–87, 579; from Europe, 42–43; exploitation of, 157n22; land ownership, 165; *Operación Canguro* (Operation Kangaroo), 281, 283, 290, 576, 595–96; *Operación Emu* (Operation Emu), 285, 455, 595–96, 634, 724–25; *Operación Eucalipto* (Operation Eucalyptus), 284, 523; *Plan Marta* (Martha Plan), 286–87, 289–90, 341, 525; quotas, 165, 172, 174, 318, 386; recruitment call, x, 8, 14, 23, 40–68, 103, 106–9, 119–29, 133, 140, 151–53, 241–42, 245–55, 258–62, 267n110, 268n112, 268nn119–20, 271–305, 311, 314, 363, 388, 493–94, 520, 523, 595–99, 691–97; renewed, 235–70, 266n80; sojourn vs settlement, 381–84; Spanish Assisted Migrant Program, 271–304, 602–3; sponsorship, 262–63, 319–20, 395–96, 422, 440–43, 449–50, 462, 478, 501, 505; treatment of, 542
Immigration Act (US), 318
Immigration Restriction Act, 123
Inchausti, José, 316*t*
Inchausti, Máximo, 521
indarra, 8

India, 53, 57, 385, 712
Indonesians, 385
Indus, 76, 103
industrialization, 3, 10
Ingham, Queensland, ix, 13, 34, 130; Basque community, 262–63, 299, 317–18, 467, 496, 505, 592–93; cane-cutter demands over pay and procedures, 190; Italian community, 161n113, 204–6, 219, 238, 325; Italian Festival, 364, 734, 758n3; Little Guernica, 388; Maraka Festival, 594; Saint Ignatius celebrations, 593–94, 605; Spanish community, 287–88, 359; sugar industry, 190–91, 467–68, 500, 505, 507, 545, 554, 561, 636
Iñigo, Plácido, 362
Inkerman Mill, 129, 190, 329, 330*t*, 612
Innisfail, Queensland, 130; Basque population, 317–23, 446–49, 574; immigration debate, 168; Italian population, 177, 185, 204–5, 325; Spanish population, 287, 310, 332n34, 336; sugar industry, 191, 211, 317, 551; Weil's disease, 191; work stoppages, 177
Inoke, Johannes, 732
Institute for Credit to Italian Workers Abroad, 266n94
Instituto Español de Emigración (IEE, Spanish Institute of Emigration), 255, 277–78, 281, 580, 598; *Operación Canguro* (Operation Kangaroo), 281, 283, 290, 576, 595–96; *Operación Emu* (Operation Emu), 285, 455, 595–96, 634, 724–25; *Operación Eucalipto* (Operation Eucalyptus), 284, 523; "Report on the Areas of Recruitment of Canecutters to Migrate to Australia," 278–79
Intergovernmental Committee for European Migrations (ICEM) or *Comité Intergubernamental para las Migraciones Europeas* (CIME), 249–50, 256–59, 268n112, 268n118, 271, 274, 279–80, 294, 543

International Anti-Fascist Solidarity (*Solidaridad Internacional Antifascista*), 211
International Brigade, 210
International Catholic Migration Commission (ICMC), 249, 255, 266n80, 267n110
International Club, 361, 477
International Congress of Basque Collectivities, 19
International *Mus* Federation, 530
International Refugee Organization (IRO), 236, 267n110, 541
International Society of Basque Studies (*Sociedad Internacional de Estudios Vascos*), 322
International Workers of the World (IWW), 201
Internet, 32, 375, 721
internment, alien, 218–25
Interviu, 513
Inunciaga, José María, 430–34, 441–42
Invicta Mill, 475
Iparralde (French Basque Country), 1, 2, 4
Iraqis, 384
Iriondo, Dionisio, 494
Iriondo, Javier, 20, 345, 347, 519, 559, 584, 587n4, 589n26
Irisarri, Susana (Susie), 21
Irish Australians, 137–38
Irish Catholics, 345
Irish Club, 282
Irish immigrants, 44, 69, 105–6, 245–46, 719
IRO (International Refugee Organization), 236, 541, 570
Isasi, José Manuel, 504
isolationism, 209
Italia Libera, 239
Italian, 415, 436, 448, 752
Italian Bulletin in Australia, 202
Italian Club (Babinda), 203
Italian Club (Melbourne), 347

Italian Colonial Committee, 71–72
Italian Festival (Ingham), 364, 734, 758n3
Italian Miracle, 288
Italian Producers' Club, 228n108
Italian Progressive Club, 185, 211
Italians, 277, 308; assimilation of, 161n113; in Australia, 43–46, 65n21, 69–76, 73*t*, 90, 103–10, 143–45, 154, 174–75, 387, 390n22; Basque views of, 412, 416–18, 433, 440, 443, 446, 453, 477–78, 485, 491, 503, 508, 512, 552, 560, 609; Black Hand, 213–17, 232n240, 592; Bolshevists, 201; and British preference movement, 178–79; crime, 200, 212–17; debate over, 168–72; discrimination against, 177, 184–87, 242–43; displaced persons (DPs), 237; ethnic stereotypes, 585; farmers, 144; Fascists, 200–212; in France, 180; immigrants, xi, 105–6, 110, 148–52, 161n113, 165, 170–72, 175, 241, 288, 635; internment of, 218–25; land ownership, 179, 197, 199, 327–29, 328*t*; land speculation, 149; "Manifesto Against War," 208; *metayer* (sharecropping) arrangements, 106; naturalization of, 173, 186–87, 207; in New Zealand, 75; in North America, 201; in North Queensland, 148–49, 184–85, 198, 287; in Oceania, 146, 173, 201; POWs, 220; in Queensland, 201, 325–27, 326*t*; recruitment of, x, 103, 106–9, 119–22, 133, 140, 151–53, 241–42, 245–53, 258–59, 275–76, 295; renewed acceptance of, 235–70, 266n94; rural workers, 284, 293; socioeconomic mobility, 144; in South America, 44, 201; in sugar industry, x, 117–28, 131–44, 154, 190, 193, 196, 199–200, 241, 252, 264n36, 287, 294, 297, 329, 330*t*; in tobacco industry, 199–200; unemployment, 250–51, 284; in US, 44

Italo-Australian Club, 453
Italo-Australiano, 127, 133, 202
Italo-Australians, 140, 174–75
Italo-Australian Union, 169
Italy, 70, 197, 241, 288, 296
Ituarte, Félix, 431–33, 435–36, 439, 441–43
Ituarte, Gregorio, 431, 433, 442
Ituarte, Martín, 433
Ituraspe, Floren, 486–87
Ituraspe, Francisco, 486
Ituraspe, Frank, 487
Iturbe, Iñaki, 489–91
Iturraga, Félix, 288
Iturraga, Florén, 496, 613
Iturraga, Javier, 602–3
Iturraspe, Joe, 739
Iturriaga, Félix, 255
Iturriaga, José María, 423
Iturriaga, Pio, 315
Iturriga, Pio, 700
Ivies, Jack, 582
IWW (International Workers of the World), 201
Izarra Proprietary Ltd, 617
Izzaguirre, Juan, 701

jai alai, 5, 321, 362, 376n36, 458, 742, 749, 755
Jaialdi, 39n20
Japanese immigrants, 63, 147–48, 163n162, 168–69, 385
Jarvisfield, Queensland, 317–18
Jauregui, Dionisio, 515
Jauregui, Felipe, 515–16
Jauregui, Félix, 517
Jauregui, Javier, 515
Jauregui, Juan, 516
Jauregui, Luis, 515, 517
Jauregui, Miguel, 515–17
Jauregui brothers, 608
Java, 67n62
Javanese, 63
Jayo, Félix, 35, 362–63, 378n79, 383, 410–14, 417, 422–24, 462, 505, 551, 593, 596, 600–601, 607, 745
Jayo, Fernando, 478
Jayo, José Luis, 411, 423–24
Jayo, José María, 35, 363, 410–11, 414, 563
Jayo, Ramón, 366, 383, 745–47
Jayo family, 714
Jensen, Sonia, 612, 618
Jesuits, 600
Jiménez, William, 313
John Fox Construction Company, 577
John Holland Construction Company, 481, 567
John Manners & Co., 341–42
Johnstone District, 327
Johnstone River, 128
Johnstone Shire, 162n153; Italian population, 146, 174, 198, 325, 326t; Spanish population, 136, 146
Jones, Ignatius, 367
Jordana, Juan, 332n34
Joseph, Michael, 112
jota, 378n79
judo, 453
Julia Creek-to-Darwin highway project, 496
Jumna, 107
Juventud Obrera Católica (Catholic Worker Youth), 267n110

Kalamia Mill, 189–90, 329, 330t, 479
Kalamia Mill Suppliers' Committee, 274
kaletarrak (street people), 7
Kalgoorlie, Australia, 306
Kanakas, 53, 57–63, 69–70, 105, 110–11, 119–20, 139, 151
Karingal College, 573
Keene, Judith, 86, 99n76
Kelly, Ainara, 751–52
Kelly, Joseba, 751
Kelly, Maite, 752
Kelly, Mark, 35, 741, 750, 752–54, 758n3
Kely, 748
Kennedy district, 222

kerb-and-gutter machines, 617–18
Keriri, 375n8
Kern Corporation, 619
Khan, Jansher, 458
Kings Cross Hotel (Sydney), 340–41, 524
Knox, Ronald, 231n211
Kolumbaru, 674
Korcula, Yugoslavia, 253
korrika (marathon), 724, 758n5
Korta Gabiola, Esther, 373–74
Kurlansky, Mark, 21, 32, 753
Kwantu Maru, 308, 375n6, 551

labor history, 49–58, 61–63, 75–76, 111–12, 309–10; 19th-century, 82; alien internment and, 223; immigrant recruitment, x, 8, 14, 23, 40–68, 103, 106–9, 119–29, 133, 140, 151–53, 241–42, 245–55, 258–62, 271–305, 311, 314, 363, 388, 493–94, 520, 523, 595–99, 691–97; manual labor, 298; shortage, 287, 595; strikes, 180–81, 190–92, 229n136, 437, 519, 638; unemployment, 228n113, 248–51, 284; unions, 52, 209, 437, 492, 556–57, 562; work stoppages, 129–30, 177, 309; WWII, 224–25. *see also specific industry*
Labour Party, 51–53, 105, 144, 152–53, 182, 209, 224; Basque support for, 450, 453, 485, 488, 502, 522, 525, 550, 557, 575, 578
Laburdi, 232n227
Lacaze farm, 126
La Fiamma, 417, 421, 433, 450, 479, 482, 485, 508, 546–47, 550, 562
La Gaceta del Norte, 433, 519, 564
La Gazzetta Illustrata, 450
Lahiguera, García, 288
Lalli, Piero, 206, 256–58
Lamiquiz, Juan, 431–34, 436, 441
Lamiquiz, Sancho, 408–9, 442
Landa, Antonio, 319–20, 702
Landaburu, Mateo, 489
Landa Quincoces, Jagoba, 729–30

land grants, 74, 85–86
Lando, A., 256–58, 260
land ownership, 136, 165, 179, 182, 197–99, 220–21, 327–29, 328*t*
land rights, 668
land speculation, 149, 196
land use, 493
Langdon, Robert, 372
language issues, 433–36, 450, 453, 479, 499–500, 507–8, 528, 557, 561–62, 577, 636, 685–86
language preservation, 724
Lannercost, Queensland, 317–18
Lanzon, Alfred, 337
Laotins, 385
La Región, 488
Largo, Fernando, 341–42
La Riscossa, 205–6
Larragan, Francisco Javier (Frank), 161n113, 407, 438, 443–46, 502
Larragan, Jesús, 443
Larragan, María Teresa, 443
Larramendy, Jean, 95
Larrañaga, Domingo ("Txomin"), 592
Larrazabal, Dolores, 714, 739, 758
Larrazabal, Fernando, 450
Larrazabal, Jon, 748–49
Larrazabal, José, 274, 378n79, 450, 593, 710, 714, 739
Larrazabal, Patxi, 452
Larruscain, Francisco, 701
Lasa, Amaia, 717
Lasa, José, 717
Lasa, Koke, 26
Lasa, María Asunción, 590n28
Lasala, Roberto López de, 341–44
La Semana, 417, 421, 426, 428, 450, 506, 508
La Spina, Rosa Norma, 436
Lasserre, Clement, 95
Latin America, 41, 268n112, 683–84
Laucirica, Floren, 360–61, 426–30, 587n5
Laucirica, Gregoria, 426–27, 450–51
Laucirica, Jesús, 427

Laucirica, Joe, 428–29
Laucirica, José, 427
Laucirica, Joseba, 449
Laucirica, Mary, 428
Laucirica, Secundino, 427, 587n4, 589n24
La Vanguardia, 588–89n16
Laxalt, Robert, 374, 448, 595
Lazcano, Ángel, 447, 699
Lazzarini, Gloria, 35–36
lead bonus, 638
League of Australian Friends of Italian Freedom, 202
League of Catholic Women, 341
Leases to Aliens Restriction Act, 136, 198
Lebanese, 384
Lecende, Josefina, 575
Lecube, Alejandro, 321
Lecuona, José, 35
Lecuona, José Domingo, 35
Lee's Hotel, 363, 500
leftists, 316–17, 321
Legarra, Joseba, 478
Legarreta, Josu, 353–57, 375
Leguineche, Manuel, 374–75
Leisure and Allied Industries, 29
Lejarcegui, Ciriaco, 404–5, 431–37, 441–42
Lejarcegui, Juan Pedro, 434
Lejarraga, Celestino, 482
Lejarraga, Enrique, 482–83
Lekeito, 314, 318, 323, 754
León, Joe, 457
Le Play, Frédéric, 5–6
leptospirosis (Weil's disease), 190–92, 375n6
Lequerica, Jenaro, 473
Lequerica, Luis, 751
Letamendi Zabala, Esteban, 98n65
Leunda, Joaquín, 95
Lezamiz, José Luis, 449
Liberal Party, 480, 495, 517, 564
Lima, Peru, 685
Lion's Club, 466

liquor, 542
liquor laws, 352–53, 579
literacy, 269n122
Lithuanians (Balts), 237, 240
Little Guernica (Ingham), 388
Little Italy, 242
Liverpool, England, 93
Lizarazu, Fidel, 564–68
Lizarralde, Manuela, 552
Lizasoain Echegia, José María, 91
Llamas, Antonio, 710
Llera, Pepe, 449–50
Lloyd Sabaudo Shipping Line, 150–51
lobster, 516, 608
local activities, 589n24
Lodore, 91
logging, 425, 582–83, 587n7, 688
Longarte, José Antonio (Tony), 35, 431–32, 435, 440–43
Long Tan Day, 666–67
López, Ángel, 343–44
Lopez, Latxi, 38n13
López, Lidia, 548
Los Angeles, California, 685
Lotus Glen, 619
Lower Burdekin, 150
loyalty oath, 218, 520
loyalty tests, 236
Lucinda Hotel, 429
Lujanbio, Maialen, 460
lumbar, 414, 490
Luno, Marisol, 557–58
Lyde, L. W., 132–33
Lyng, J., 71

MacAlister, A., 76
Macarthur, John, 85–86, 89, 99–100n82
Mackay, Heather, 458
Mackay Mill, 62, 136, 178–79
Macknade Mill, 117–19, 125, 131–32; growers and peak tonnage, 329, 330*t*; labor force, 181–84, 223, 283, 295, 317–18, 414, 428, 442; mechanization, 297; suppliers, 149

Macrossan, 106
MacTxoko, 29
Macussi, Oreste, 428
Madariaga, Serafin, 442
Madariaga, Valentín, 332n30, 701
Madrid, Camilo, 451, 489
Madrid Restaurant (Fremantle), 336
Magellan, 9
Magnetic, 622
Magueregui, José, 321
Maguregui, Carmen, 563
Maguregui, Juana, 563
Maguregui, Martín, 563
Maguregui, Pedro, 563
Maguregui, Sabino, 563
Maguregui, Tomás, 563–65
Maketos, 626
Malaga, Spain, 279
Malaspina, Alessandro, 70, 77–78, 97n44
Malaxechevarria, Candido, 700
Malaxechevarria, Ignacio, 410, 417
Malaxechevarria, Luis (Louis), 742
Malaxechevarria, María Angela, 466
Malaxechevarria, Marian, 742
Malaxechevarria, Mateo, 519
Malay Emergency, 640–41
Malays, 148, 385
Malbon, 200
Maldonado, Antonio, 469
Maltese immigrants, 69, 106, 155, 181, 241, 245, 264n36
Manchester Empire News, 217
"Manifesto Against War," 208
Manini, Gino and Maria, 363
Manners, John, 341–42
Manpower, 247
Manterola, Maite, 714
manual labor, 298. *see also* labor history
manufacturing, 3
Maraka Festival, 364, 500, 594
Marcos, Ricardo (Bolita), 339
Mareeba, Australia, 449–54, 587n4
Mareeba International Club, 450, 453
Mareeba Spanish Club, 472
Maria di Marzio award, 752

mariners, 92–95, 319, 566
Markina-Xemein, 323
Marloo, 123–24
Marqués, Hilario, 423
Marqués, Marcos, 489
Marqués, Matilde, 522
Marshall Plan, 244
Martha Plan (*Plan Marta*), 286–87, 289–90, 341, 525
Martín, Manu (Manny), 357, 716–20, 722–25, 728, 731–32, 758
Martínez, Antonio, 308
Martínez, Carmen, 564
Martínez, Daniel, 375n6, 700
Martínez, Faustino, 317
Martínez, Francisco, 211
Martínez, Miguel, 336
Martínez family, 310
Martino Echarri, Estefanía, 718, 721–26, 732
Marxism, 308
Mascot Social Golf Club, 522
Masino, Lidia, 14–15
Mason, Robert James David, 125–26, 130, 142–43, 322–25, 327, 336, 382, 680
Massey Ferguson mechanical harvesters, 291
Masters and Servants Act, 127–28
Masterton Hotel, 453
Mataró, Catalunya, 332n34
mateship, 49, 51, 113, 303n107, 402, 408, 486
Mauritius, 67n62
McCarthy, J. B., 186
McIntyre, John, 612–14
McIlwraith, Thomas, 62
Meabe, Pedro, 547
meat pies, 80
Meaurio, Manu, 357
mechanization, 291–97; kerb-and-gutter machines, 617–18; mechanical harvesters, 291–92, 403–8, 414, 424, 431–32, 435–38, 441–43, 479, 487, 493, 545–46, 565–66
Mediterranean crops, 83

Mediterranean Europe, 64
Mediterraneans, 70, 104
Melanesians, 677n3, 734
Melano, Mario, 187, 205–6
Melbourne, Australia, 685–87; 19th-century, 95, 102n112; Basque cultural life, 345–46, 404; Basque population, 90, 95, 102n112, 559–86; *Centro Español*, 339–45; Fascists, 202; *Gure Txoko*, 17–19, 27, 345–48, 404, 513, 560, 564, 568, 575, 578–79, 584; *Hogar Español* ("Spanish Home"), 339–40; Italian celebration, 201–2; Italian population, 70–71, 215; Parer Empire, 80, 306; population growth, 50; Spanish population, 80, 82–83, 305
Melbourne Age, 201, 564
Melbourne Argus, 123
Melbourne Barcelona Club, 305, 336
Melbourne Cooperative Brewery, 306
Melbourne Cricket Club, 306
Melbourne Exhibition (1881), 80
Melbourne Herald, 562
Melbourne Italian Club, 347
Melbourne Philharmonic Society, 71
Melbourne Tramways Trust, 306
Menchaca, Aniceto, 314, 392, 419, 592, 699
Menchaca, Johan, 314, 699
Menchaca, Romualda, 332n28
Menchaca de Iraegui, Romualda, 323, 592
Mendenzona, Santiago, 700
Mendi Construction Company, 36, 619–22, 624
Mendicute, Fabián, 424
Mendieta, David, 26, 30
Mendiolea, Ana, 757–58
Mendiolea, Aniceto (Ceto), 392–95, 422, 469, 593
Mendiolea, Antonia, 757–58
Mendiolea, Antonio (Tony), 392–95, 410–11, 416, 430, 441, 518, 551, 581, 593, 609, 609n2, 714
Mendiolea, Conchita (Conchi), 33, 378n79, 383, 397, 587n2, 711–15, 736–40, 742, 753
Mendiolea, Dolores, 378n79, 392–94, 500, 593, 597, 625, 714, 739, 748
Mendiolea, Fermina, 715, 740
Mendiolea, Joe, 757–58
Mendiolea, John (Johnny), 33–35, 262, 365, 371, 378n79, 383, 392–99, 410, 413–15, 431, 441, 460, 472–73, 478, 587n5, 588n10, 593, 680, 710–14, 735–42, 750–52
Mendiolea, Juan, 363
Mendiolea, Matias, 358, 416
Mendiolea, Michael, 33, 383, 738–39
Mendiolea, Pedro, 754–58
Mendiolea, Rufino, 364, 392–97, 506, 563, 593
Mendiolea, Stephen, 33, 357, 361, 383, 626, 714, 738
Mendiolea, Teresa, 33–34, 299n12, 336, 375, 392–94, 398–99, 410–11, 413–15, 448, 468–69, 505, 593, 613, 737, 757
Mendiolea, Tomás (Tommy), 33–35, 383, 392, 712–16, 735–37, 740–41, 750, 758, 758n4
Mendiolea family, 273–75, 362–63, 415, 424, 434, 472, 496; application for immigration, 262; farm, 441, 446, 518, 546; nominations, 294; *Villa Milano*, 593
Mendiolea Memorial Cup, 364
Mendi Proprietary Ltd, 617
Mendizona, Jaime, 431
Menghetti, Diane, 221, 229n136
Menzies Hotel, 524
Mercantil Rowing Club, 306
merchant mariners, 314–15, 563, 576, 580, 685
Metalworkers Union, 525
metayer (sharecropping) arrangements, 106
Methodists, 208
Mexico, 686, 690n2
Mezo, Luis, 346
Middle East, 240

migration patterns. *see* immigrants and immigration
Miguel, Henry, 545
Miguel, Joe, 593–96
Miguel, John, 595
Mildura College, 573
Millicent, South Australia, 510–20
Millicent Gun Club, 511
Milliken, Ted, 663
Milne, Robert, 710
Mindegia, Mikel, 354
miners and mining, 319, 323, 637–38, 669, 688
Minvielle, Jules, 376n36–376n37
Mirani, Australia, 326t
Mirror, 525, 550–51
Mitchell, Thomas, 38n12
Modi, Narendra, 712
Moe, Victoria, 518
Mohammedi, 114
Molina Restaurant (Melbourne), 346
Mollison, Charles, 647
Monash University, 573
Monasterio, Pedro, 420–21, 424–25, 428
Monasterio, Tomás, 363
Monsanto, 653
Montero, Francisco, 350
Montero, Francisco Javier, 533
Montero, J. de, 167
Monte Udala, 599–600; Basque cohort, 114, 285–91, 293, 580, 584, 635, 691–97; Operation Emu, 724–25
Montevideo, Uruguay, 44, 685
Montini, Giovanni Battista, 249
Montserrat, 284, 358; Basques who arrived on, 514, 520, 524, 547–51, 554, 559, 574–77, 594; European residence of adult males recruited for Queensland who arrived on (1958–1960), 691–97
Moraes Gorecki, Vanda, 586n2, 753
Morales, Sol, 410
Morato, Pedro, 709
Morell, Esteban, 305–6
Morell, Stephen, 305–6
Moreno, Henry, 312
Moreno, Stephen, 312
Morgan, Mary, 91
Morris, Carol Ann, 446
Morris automobile factory, 557
Morton Park, 86, 88–89, 100n89–100n90
Mossman Central Mill, 120–21, 130, 223, 524
Mostyn, Kath, 619
Mount Cuthbert, 200
Mount Druitt *Club Español*, 524–25
Mount Fox, 414
Mount Fox Timber Company, 423
Mount Gambier, 516
Mount Isa, 319, 358, 388, 482, 597, 637, 736
Mount Isa Mines, 612–13
Mount Low, 619
Mount Margaret, 582–83
Mount Morgan, 200
Mount Urgull, 673
Mount Waverley, 564
Mourilyan Mill, 175, 179–84, 191, 211, 215–16, 317–18
Moyano, Ana, 525
Mugaregui, Luciano, 701
Mugica, José, 440
Mugica, José María, 498–500
Mugica, Juan María, 438, 440, 444, 446
Mugica, Miguel, 440, 444
Mugica, Santiago, 430
Mugira, Johnny, 444
Muguira, George, 484
Muguira, John (Johnny), 444, 476
Muguira, Juan, 502, 701
Muguira, Julia, 614
Muguira, Leon, 700
Muguira, Manuel, 614–15
Muguira, Vicente, 702
Muguruza, Fermin, 728–29
Muir, R., 239–41, 260
Muirhead, James, 669
Mulgrave Mill, 122, 223

Mulgrave Shire, 325, 326t
multiculturalism, 22, 412–13, 426, 475, 561, 649
multigenesis, 677–78n3
multilingualism, 443, 447, 556
Mundara, 518
Muñoz, Florencio, 545
Murdoch, Rupert, 668
Murelaga, Domingo, 369–70, 429
Murua, Nekane Reta, 719
mus, 25–26, 344, 353, 356, 360–61, 448, 530, 751
music, 346
musical groups, 728–29
Muslims, 236
Mussolini, Arnoldo, 186
Mussolini, Benito, 200–201, 203, 207, 218
mutil/neska (boy/girl) dolls, 15
Mutriku, 323
"Mutriku'tik Australia'ra" (From Mutriku to Australia) (Basurco), 322, 374, 702–7

Nabarniz, 323
NABO (North American Basque Organizations, Inc.), 687
Nanango, Queensland, 317
National Farmer, 492, 495
National Geographic, 421, 595
nationalism: Basque, 1–3, 24, 324–25, 337, 351, 468, 488, 504, 520, 716; Catalan, 721–22; Spanish, 2; ultranationalism, 18–19
National Political Party, 492
nation building, 9
naturalization, 98n60, 98n62, 101n97, 186; in 19th-century Australia, 90; of Basque immigrants, 219, 318–19, 411, 415, 422, 426, 429, 443, 477, 483–85, 509–10, 513, 525, 556, 564, 578; of Catalan immigrants, 219; of Italian immigrants, 187, 207; of Southern European immigrants, 173
naturalized citizens, 82, 699–702

Nautical School (*Escuela de Naútica*), 93
Nautilus, 83
Navarán, Ignacio, 478
Navaran, Iñaki, 710
Navarra, 3, 9, 11n1, 21, 210; immigrants from, 8, 281, 291, 312–13, 318, 323, 327, 604, 692–95
Navarra Boomerang Australia Alkartea (Navarran Boomerang Australians Together), 373–74
Navarran Boomerang Association (*Asociación Navarra Boomerang*), 361
Navarro, Gregorio, 313
Nazis, 222
Neapolitans, 70, 167
neighborhoods (*auzoak*), 5
Neo-Melanesian, 654
Nepalese, 385
neutrality, 24
Nevada, 10
New Australians, 93–94, 381–90, 575, 640
New Caledonia, 72, 526–27
Newcastle, Australia, 154
The New Guard, 203
New Guinea, 658
New Ireland, 72
New Italy, 72–74, 105, 154
New Lombardy, 179
New Mexico, 686
New Norcia, 79, 312–13, 674
News Corps, 669
New Settlers' League, 149, 259–60
New South Wales, 47, 261–62; Basque place names, 65n24; Basque population, 90–91, 319, 547; drinking laws, 340–41; Fascism, 203; fruit horticulture, 200; immigration history, 53; Italian population, 70; Italians, 72, 154; labor force, 505; seasonal work, 113; Spanish population, 81–82; sugar industry, 57, 60, 62, 67n62, 260–62
New South Wales Corps, 99n82
New South Wales Handball Association, 724

New South Wales Spanish Club, 340–41
New South Wales Sugar Millowners, 241
newspapers, 367–68, 378n102
New World, 9–10, 42
New York City, New York, 685
New Zealand: Basque place names, 65n24; construction industry, 543–44; demographic expansion, 66n34; Fascists, 202; immigration policy, 41, 43; Italian population, 71, 75
New Zealanders, 385
nickel, 405
Nielson farm, 481
Nieto, Samuel, 340
Nightcliff High School (Darwin), 659–60, 662
Nightcliff Sports Club, 666
NLC (Northern Land Council), 668
"No-Bull-Shit-Monkey" *peña*, 26
Non-Intervention Policy, 209–10
Noorla Bowling Club, 417, 437, 439–40, 443, 446
Noorla Hotel (Ingham), 204–6
North America, 201
North American Basque Organizations, Inc. (NABO), 687
Northern European immigrants, 69–70
Northern Italians: Basque views of, 422, 488, 495, 517, 523, 585, 609; immigrants, 154–56, 213–14
Northern Land Council (NLC), 668
Northern Region, 114, 156–57n21
Northern Territory, 31, 307–9, 660, 663–64, 688
The Northern Territory News, 663–64, 669
Northern Territory Vietnam Veterans Association, 666
North Italy, 69, 76
North Queensland: alien internment, 222–23; banana industry, 161n119; Basque population, 34, 273, 317, 320, 348, 473, 538, 587n2, 594, 625; Fascism, 203; *frontón*, 748; immigrant centers, 254; immigration debate, 167; Italian population, 110, 148–49, 151, 177, 184–86, 198, 214–17, 220, 224–25, 238–39, 287; labor force, 148; population, 140–41; Reign of Terror, 212; renewed immigration, 247; Southern European population, 135, 144–45, 327–29; Spanish population, 124, 128, 271, 285–88, 294, 338–39, 604; sugar industry, 14, 56, 60–62, 116, 125, 133, 145, 186, 191–92, 196–97, 223, 273, 285, 290, 293–95, 317–18, 329, 683; US military presence, 223; Weil's disease, 191; WWII, 221, 223; Yugoslav population, 124
North Queensland Herald, 107–8
North Queensland Register, 141–42, 152, 216–17, 229n136
North Queensland Rugby, 621
North Queensland Spanish Society. *see* Spanish Society of North Queensland
Norwegian Shipping Line, 565
nostalgia, 361–62
Noticias de Euskadi, 628
Noticias de Navarra, 362
Nouvelle France, 72
Novelli, Maria, 442–43
novels, 374
NSW Railway, 542, 636
Nullabor Highway, 674

Oak Valley, 616
Oar, Ceferino, 701
Oar, Frank, 710
Oar, Isaac, 709
O'Brien, Bert, 614
Ocamica, Pablo, 701
Ochoa, Juan, 91
Odorica, Gregorio, 701
O'Grady, John, 366
Olabarriaga, José Luis, 349
Olazabal, María Dolores, 495
Olazabal, María Pilar, 495
Old Law (*fuero*), 1–2

Old Peoples' Home, 475
Olentzero, 16, 749
Oliveira Bravo, Beñat, 719–24, 727–28
Olympic Games (2000), 25
Onaindia, Saturnino, 332n28, 446–49
Onaindia Laca, Antonio (Tony Bronco), 321, 373–74
opals, 597, 638
Operación Canguro (Operation Kangaroo), 281, 283, 290, 576, 595–96
Operación Emu (Operation Emu), 285, 455, 595–96, 634, 724–25
Operación Eucalipto (Operation Eucalyptus), 284, 523
Operación Marta, 286–87, 289–90, 341, 525
Operation Duck 1, 649
Operation Duck 2, 649
Operation Karry, 290
Operation Torres, 290
opium, 67n59
Oregon, 10
Oribe, Pablo (Paul), 19, 348, 568–74, 689–90
Oribetxea (Oribe House), 571–72
Oriñuela, Julián, 344, 349–52, 355, 520–23, 554, 557
Ormaechea, Luis, 484
Ormaechea, Tomás, 14
Ormazabal, Tomás, 250, 281–83, 338, 469, 545, 596, 600, 709
Orontes, 320
Orsova, 320
Orue, Carlos, 22–31, 270n143, 355, 533–40, 558, 586n1, 681, 711, 717–18, 721, 756–57
Orue, Miren, 22–25, 30, 534–36, 539, 717–18, 721
Orvieto, 332n32
Osa, Imanol, 441
Osasuna, 25
O'Toole, Jack, 366
O'Toole, Martin, 366

Our Lady of Montserrat celebration (*Sardana* Day), 360, 460, 469–71
"The Outpost," *Herbert River Express*, 206
Overseas Fascist Party, 203

Pacific Islanders, 57, 76, 104, 107. *see also* Kanakas
Pacific Islanders Act, 61
paella, 748
Pakea, 717
Pakistanis, 385
pala, 588n11
Palace Hotel (Melbourne), 94
Palace Hotel (Sydney), 94
Palmer, Clive, 751
Palmer, George, 67n56
Pane, Caesare, 365
Panguna, 669
Panorama Restaurant, 617–18
paper-pulp industry, 442, 513, 590n36
Papua New Guinea (PNG), 653–58, 669
Parade magazine, 232n240
Pardo, Jose Luis, 669
Parer, Anton, 79
Parer, Antonio, 79–80
Parer, Damien, 306
Parer, Felipe, 80
Parer, Francisco, 80
Parer, Josep (José), 79–80
Parer, Juan, 80
Parer, Meg, 658–59
Parer, Pau, 79
Parer, Ray, 306
Parer, Rob, 658–59
Parer, Stephan (Esteban), 80–81, 83
Parer, Warwick, 306
Parer Empire, 80, 306
Pares, Luis, 81, 162n153
Pares, Luis Amadeo, 336
Paris, Gino, 411, 414, 417, 439, 579, 581–82
Parke, Edward, 38n12
Park Hyatt Hotel (Melbourne), 13
Paronella, José, 338–39, 734

Partido Nacionalista Vasco (PNV, Basque Nationalist Party), 25, 38n13, 603, 671
pastoralism, 53, 55
Patagonia, 310
pathology, 456–57
Patrick, Jon, 28
patriotism, 137–38, 236, 628
Pavetto, F. M. "Nando," 256–58, 260
peanut industry, 245
Pelaez, Marcelina, 578
Pellizer, Lorenzo, 710
pelota, 5, 15, 26, 345, 362–65, 371, 423, 434, 446–47, 457–58, 588n11, 724. *see also balonmano* (handball)
pelotaris, 528
Pena, Antonio, 311
Peñagaricano, Iruñe, 726
Peñagaricano, Ramón, 349–50, 529, 718, 726
Peninsular War, 65n24, 87, 99n72
People, 370–71, 417, 439
Perdella, Norma, 439–40
Perea, José, 538
Pérez, Eugenio, 271
Perron, Marshall, 669
Perrot, Eugene, 90
Perry, Maude, 94
Perth, Australia, 71, 674, 751
Philippine Company, 77–78, 92
Philippines, 92
Phillip, Arthur, 635
Phillips, David, 741–42, 748–49, 754
Phillips, Patxi, 35, 742, 753–54
PICMME (Provisional InterGovernmental Committee for the Movement of Migrants from Europe), 249–50
Pidgin English, 654
Pikua, 322, 707
Pilarica (Aragón's Virgen de Pilar Day), 460
Pine Creek, 309
pine harvesting, 490
Piñerena, Francisco, 91

pinus insignis, 590n36
Pioneer Mill, 190, 497; growers and peak tonnage, 329, 330*t*; labor force, 509, 516
Pioneer River Farmers' and Graziers' Association, 120
Pitt, William Morton, 85–87, 89
Pius IX, 231n211
Pius XII, 249–50
Pla, Ramón, 364–65, 435–36, 441–42, 710
Plan Marta (Martha Plan), 286–87, 289–90, 341
plantation system, 55, 58–63, 75–76, 107, 115
Plaza, Domingo, 316*t*, 699
Plaza, Félix, 332n30, 484, 701
Plaza, J., 319–20
Plaza, Jesús, 484–85
Plaza, Juan, 484
Plaza, Venancia, 484
Plaza, Victor, 484
PNV (*Partido Nacionalista Vasco*, Basque Nationalist Party), 25, 38n13, 603, 671
poetry, 374, 703–8
Poles, 241, 243–44
political action, 351
political egalitarianism, 49
politics, 18–19, 24, 32–33, 321–22, 449, 474
Polynesians, 734
Polynesien, 95
PO *Oriana*, 644
portero, 525
Port McDonald Football Club, 511
Portuguese immigrants, 44, 69
Post, 439
POWs (prisoners of war), 236, 263n5
Pratt, Mary, 512
Preciosa, 93
prejudice, 429, 440, 443, 447, 450, 475, 517
Presbyterians, 208
Price, Charles A., 64n2, 69, 97n59, 311

Primer Congreso Mundial de Centros Vascos (First World Congress of Basque Centers), 355
Prince of Wales Hotel (Dunedin, New Zealand), 94
Princes Bridge Hotel (Melbourne), 306
prisoners of war (POWs), 236, 263n5
Proserpine, Queensland, 130, 154, 174, 543
prostitution, 600
Protestants, 46, 161n113, 207–8, 236, 280–81, 297
Provisional InterGovernmental Committee for the Movement of Migrants from Europe (PICMME), 249–50
Public Workers' Union, 556

quality of life, 489
Quantas, 589n26
Queen Hotel, 467
Queensland, 54, 55, 56; alien internment, 221; Austrian population, 124; Basque population, 250, 299, 313–14, 317–19, 322–24, 538, 612, 691–702; Catalan population, 124–25, 323–24; climate, 279; Department of Immigration, 652; European-born population, 145; foreign-born population, 69–70, 73, 73t, 74, 174; Great White Industry, 151; Iberian population, 81; immigration debate, 165, 167, 169; immigration laws, 74; Italian population, 75–76, 103–9, 134–35, 145–53, 174–75, 201, 207, 221, 246, 266n94, 325–27, 326t, 387; Kanaka population, 110–11; labor history, 57, 106, 278–79, 325–29; land ownership, 74, 197; naturalization, 98n62; *Plan Marta* (Martha Plan), 286–87; recruitment of immigrants for, 106, 122, 314, 691–97; Southern European population, 76–77, 134–35, 325–29; Spanish population, 82, 134–35, 142, 145–46, 162n152, 200, 306, 321–22, 327, 652; sugar industry,

56, 57–62, 67n62, 111, 115–17, 132, 140, 147–51, 165, 183, 196–97, 238–40, 243, 260, 272, 277–79, 305, 311, 317–18, 388; tobacco industry, 119; Trades and Labour Council, 251; White Australia policy, 64
Queensland Aliens Act, 199
Queensland Canegrowers' Association, 183–84, 239–41, 249, 293
Queensland Canegrowers' Council, 191, 220, 274–75
Queensland Country Party, 236
The Queenslander, 110, 123–24, 127–28
Queensland Guardian, 210
Queensland Spanish Club, 336
Queensland Sugar Growers' Council, 192
Querejeta, Arantxa, 627–30, 634–37, 641–46, 650–53, 657–64, 667, 670, 672–73
Querejeta, Elias, 629–30, 643, 673
Querejeta, Juan Ignacio, 629, 670, 674
Quigg, George, 354
Quinn, James, 81
Quintana, Bilbo, 553
Quintana, Eduardo, 521, 553–57
Quintana, Elias, 556
Quintana, Ester, 553
Quintana, Julián, 349–50

race relations: Basque views on, 482, 485, 488, 491, 542, 604–5, 626, 649; black-fellows agreement, 127–28; discrimination, 53–55, 58, 61, 385–86, 408, 412, 433, 440, 443, 446, 450; prejudice, 429, 440, 443, 447, 450, 475, 517; segregation, 263n21; White Australia policy, 53–55, 61–64, 69–70, 104, 110–11, 132–33, 140–41, 165, 171–72, 384–86, 635; White Australia Sugar League, 149; white bounty, 110–11, 129–30; white slavery, 584
Racial Discrimination Act 1975, 385–86
RACQ, 738
radical politics, 321–22

radio, 231n222, 232n227, 453
Radio Euskadi (Basque Radio), 372
Radio Independiente Pirenaica, 513
Radio Nacional de España, 421, 433, 511, 557, 564, 575
railway, 505, 507, 509, 542, 554, 636
rana, 532
Randwick Golf Club, 522
Rangers Soccer Club, 439
Rank-and-File movement, 191–92
Reader's Digest, 453, 522
Real Sociedad, 25
Red Cross, 456, 536
refugees, 235, 240, 386, 542. *see also* immigrants and immigration
Regazzoli, E., 133
Regazzoli Hotel, 134
rehabilitation and renewal, 235–70
Reitano, Felix, 133–34, 138
religiosity, 337–38
religious discrimination, 46. *see also* discrimination
Renteria, José, 316t, 370
"Report on the Areas of Recruitment of Canecutters to Migrate to Australia" (IEE), 278–79
restaurants, 336
Reta Murua, Nekane, 731
retention money, 112–13
Returned Sailors' and Soldiers' Imperial League of Australia (RSSILA), 148
Returned & Services League (RSL), 147, 182, 196–97, 220–24, 236–42, 245–46, 266n94; Basques in, 482–83, 506, 509, 548, 552
Rice Journal, 495
Rios, Roman, 312
Rio Tinto, 669
Ripple Creek Plantation, 107–8
Rivas García, Pascual, 609n3
road work, 485
rock art, 638, 664–65
Rockchoppers, 281
Rockefeller, Michael, 658

Rockhampton, Queensland, 76
Rodríguez de Valcárcel, Carlos María, 598
Rojos, Panuelo, 574
Roma, 498
Roma, Queensland, 154, 587n4
Roman Catholic Church, 46, 200, 203, 209, 249
Rose Hotel (Sydney), 94
Ross, Emiliano, 313
Rotary Club, 276, 285, 602, 622
Rotondo, Agostino, 364
Rotondo, Janet, 425–26
Rotuma, 734
Royal Philippine Company, 77
RSL. *see* Returned & Services League
RSSILA (Returned Sailors' and Soldiers' Imperial League of Australia), 148
rugby, 462, 502, 550, 621–22
Ruiz, Isidore, 312
Ruiz, Salvador ("Chiquito de Bermeo"), 601
Ruiz de Gordejuela, Milagros, 506
rural Basque life, 4, 6–7
rural workers, 260, 284, 293
Russian immigrants, 44, 58, 136–37, 201, 308

Saenz, Ciriaco, 545
Saenz family, 310
Sailors', Soldiers' and Airmens' Fathers' Association, 220
Saint George Club, 546
Saint Ignatius Day celebrations, 16, 346, 350–51, 356–60, 448, 460, 472, 500, 593–94, 605
Saint Joseph's Day, 471
Salazar, Mariasun, 350, 355–56, 718, 723
Saldigorria, 600
Sallais, George, 470, 472
Salles, Jorge, 709
Salvado, Rosendo, 79, 674
Salvation Army, 208
Sandumbide, Ambrosio, 702

San Fermín, 723
San Francisco, California, 685
San Gil, Victoria, 15–16
Sanguma, 656
San Just Torner, Eduardo, 66n34, 81
San Lesmes, 379n125
San Sebastián, Koldo, 102n113, 315, 319–21, 680
Santamaría, Tomás, 95
Santana, Manuel, 344
Santander, Spain, 281, 302n52
Santiago, Chile, 685
Santiñan, 341
San Vicente, Jose, 700
Sanz, Serafín, 313
SAP, 725
Sardana Day (Virgin of Montserrat's feast day), 360, 460, 469–71
Sardinia, 214, 258–59
Sartoresi, Joe, 362–63, 601
Saviane, Tom, 206
sawmills, 518
SBS (Special Broadcasting Service), 375
Scandinavian immigrants, 43–44, 64, 76–77, 105–6, 124
Sceusa, Francesco, 133
Schipper Steamship Company, 122
Schlink, Mark, 26
Schuette, Abram, 90
Scottish immigrants, 69
seasonal work, 113, 302n78, 688
Seaview Hotel, 625
Second World Congress, 285
separatists, 500
Serra, José María, 79
Serra, Joseph, 674
Sesma, Ángel, 545
Sesma, Aquilino, 315–16, 316t
Sesma, Brígida, 315–17
Sesma, Elena, 751
Sesma, Iñaki, 751
Sesma, José Gabriel, 315–17, 316t, 319–20, 699
Sesma, Plácido, 312

Sesma family, 315
settler societies, 43
Sgoi, Santina, 485
sharecropping, 106, 554
Sheehan, Mauree, 651
sheepherders and sheepherding, 301n31, 320, 373, 413, 418, 524, 683–89
Shepherd, Robert (Bob), 161n113, 602
Shipway, Gary, 667
SIA, 232n233
Sicilians, 123–24, 155, 180–81, 213–16, 243, 257–58, 516; Basque views of, 416, 429, 443, 446, 486, 488, 495, 609; immigration debate, 167, 171–72, 217; recruitment of, 133; stereotypes of, 585
Silkwood, 180
Singaporeans, 385
skilled workers, 296–98
Slavs, 69
Slingsley, Ted, 709
Smith, Forgan, 198
Smith, Harry, 646, 677n2
Smith's Weekly, 185, 203, 207
snakes, 119
Snowy Mountains Hydroelectric Scheme, 48, 527, 600, 688
soccer (football), 21–22, 344, 347, 353, 362, 438, 440, 454, 512, 525, 553, 588n11, 755
soccer teams, 25
social clubs, 334–37, 354, 359–60, 685–87. *see also specific clubs*
Socialism, 205, 209
Sociedad Internacional de Estudios Vascos (International Society of Basque Studies), 322
Socoa Shipping Line, 590n34
sokatira (tug of war), 20–21, 364, 467, 471
Solano, Carlos, 610n8
Solidaridad Internacional Antifascista (International Anti-Fascist Solidarity), 211
Somali Club, 754

Sorli, Gabriel, 210, 336
Sorrento, 570
Sota Shipping Company, 576, 590n34
South Africa, 41, 43, 385
South America, 43–44, 47, 201, 357–58
South Asians, 385
South Australia, 55, 82, 319, 688
Southeast Asians, 384
Southern Europeans, 64, 150, 297; Basque precursors, 69–77; immigration debate, 167, 174; in North Queensland, 140–41, 144–45, 327–29; in Queensland, 145–46, 325–29; in sugar industry, 138, 145–46, 151, 177, 329
Southern French, 69
Southern Italians, 213–14
Southern Region, 157n21
South Johnstone mill, 175–77, 181, 191, 317–18
South Koreans, 385
Spain, 142, 173; anarcho-syndicalism, 125–26; historical territory, 2–3; post-WWII, 271; relations with Australia, 66n34, 298, 716
Spaniard's Hill, 86
Spanish-American War, 98n66
Spanish Assisted Migrant Program, 271–304
Spanish-Australian Club of Canberra, 340
Spanish Basque Country (*Hegoalde*), 1–4, 2
Spanish Catholic Migration Commission (*Comisión Cátolica Española de Migración*, CCEM), 255, 267n110
Spanish Chamber of Commerce, 343–44
Spanish Civil War, 207–10, 317, 337, 370, 468
Spanish Club (New South Wales), 340–41
Spanish Club (Queensland), 336
Spanish Clubs, 344–45
Spanish Euclids, 615

Spanish Handball Club, 363–64
Spanish Herald, 506
Spanish immigrants: in Argentina, 263n12, 307–8, 312; in Australia, 23, 43–44, 69, 77–83, 104, 122–26, 135–37, 241, 268n112, 271–308, 321–22, 387, 602–4, 609n3, 635, 652; Basque views of, 416–18, 429, 433, 440, 477–78, 493, 503, 512, 517, 523, 579, 609; collectivities, 334–80; land ownership, 327–29, 328t; in Latin America, 268n112, 297; naturalization of, 173; Operation Karry, 290; Operation Torres, 290; in Queensland, 142, 162n152, 174; recruitment of, 126–27, 253–55, 262, 267n110, 268n112, 271–304; refugees, 237; in sugar industry, 119, 123–28, 136–37, 149, 180, 193, 201, 241, 252, 264n36, 271–304, 309–10, 329, 330t; in tobacco industry, 200; in Venezuela, 263n12; WWII, 218. see also Basques; Catalans
Spanish Institute of Emigration. see Instituto Español de Emigración
Spanish language, 33, 344, 422, 477
Spanish nationalism, 2
Spanish Relief Committee (SRC), 210–11, 232n233, 331n16
Spanish Restaurant (Dunedin, New Zealand), 94
Spanish restaurants, 336
Spanish Society (Atherton Tablelands), 359–60
Spanish Society of North Queensland, 324, 356–61, 460, 471–72, 625; membership, 35–36, 709–10
Spartan, 79
Spearing, James, 89
Spearing, Sophie, 89
Special Broadcasting Service (SBS), 375
Special Broadcasting Service (SBS)—National Indigenous Television (SBS—NITV), 733
Special Olympics (2000), 25

sponsorship, 262–63, 319–20, 395–96, 422, 440–43, 449–50, 462, 478, 501, 505
sports, 362–66, 439–40, 503, 588n11–588n12
squash, 36–37, 457–58
SRC (Spanish Relief Committee), 210–11, 232n233, 331n16
Sri Lankans, 385
St. Mary, 91
St. Mary's Cathedral, 341
St. Patrick's (Ingham), 204
Stanthorpe, Queensland, 326t, 327
Station Hotel, 429
Steelcon Company, 452
Steele, Glen, 616
steel industry, 600, 688
stem family (*famille souche*), 5–6
stereotypes, 161n113, 504, 506, 517, 523, 585
St Kilda Travel Lodge, 564
Stone River, 317–18
Storich, Edgar, 255, 288
Stott, Sydney, 343
Stubbins Brothers, 616–17
Suez Canal, 71
sugar consumption, 67n62
Sugar Cultivation Act, 163n162
Sugar Heaven (Devanny), 229n136
sugar industry, 55–64, 56, 110–17, 129–56, 712; Basques in, 316–17, 319, 323, 358, 466–67, 477, 485, 636, 687; British preference movement, 175–200; cane districts, 156–57n21; embargo, 181, 184, 186, 189; excise taxes, 110–11; expansion of, 129, 162n153, 182, 196; history of, 587n2; immigrant recruitment for, x, 8, 14, 121–29, 153, 241, 248–55, 260–62, 271–305, 311, 314, 363, 388, 493–94, 520, 595–96; Italian penetration, 110, 117–28, 133, 140, 143–44, 152–53, 190; labor force, 295, 309–10, 323, 404–5, 430, 447, 455; labor history, 14, 131, 138–41, 147–48, 152–53, 163n162, 223, 238–44, 247, 251, 261–62, 268n119, 271–304; labor strikes, 180–81, 190–92; mechanization, 291–97; socioeconomic mobility in, 324; Southern Europeans in, 329; Spanish alternative for, 271–304, 310, 327, 332n34; work stoppages, 129–30. *see also* canecutters and canecutting; gangers and gangs
Sugar Inquiry Committee, 188
sugar peaks, 115, 199–200
Sugar Producers' Association, 199
Sugar Workers Act, 136
Sugar Workers' Union, 191
suicide, 497–98
Sun, 513–14, 519, 546, 549, 560, 574, 578
Sunday Mail, 222–23, 490
Sunday Sun, 477
Sunday Territorian, 667, 669
surnames, 100n93
Sydney, Australia, 542, 685–87; 19th-century, 94–95; Basque population, 90, 94–95, 348, 354, 520–58; Catalan population, 718–19; Fascists, 202; foreign-born population, 79; Italian population, 71, 154, 215, 251; MacDonald's fad, 29; Old Sydney, 723; Spanish Chamber of Commerce, 343–44
Sydney Basque Club, 731
Sydney Catholic Club, 340–41
Sydney Electricity, 536
Sydney Food Guide, 723
Sydney Gazette, 85
Sydney Hispanic Society, 343
Sydney Morning Herald, 351, 421, 508, 522, 549
Sydney Opera House, 521
Sydney Spanish Club. *see Centro Español* (Sydney); *Club Español* (Sydney)
Sydney Telegraph, 502
sympathizers, 718–19

Tabanera, Santiago Ruiz, 255, 283
Taiwanese, 385

Talleres Echevarria, 14
Tapiolas, Bruno, 310, 324, 460, 472, 484–85, 588n16, 709
Tapiolas, Joe, 709
Tapiolas, Wilfred, 709
tariffs, 117
Tasmania, 31, 489–90, 507, 519, 549; Basque place names, 65n24; Basque population, 574, 671; Italian population, 70–71
Tavan, Gwenda, 388n3
taxes, 110–11, 436
technology: computer, 19, 27. *see also* mechanization
Tejada, Celedonio Moreno, 346
Tejada, Lucía, 346
Telediario, 32
The Telegraph, 216–17, 525, 546
television, 372, 375, 724
Tellechea, John Hulian, 312
Tellechea, Pedro, 91
Telleria, José, 332n29
Telleria, José Ignacio, 480
Tellería, Juan María (Juan Txistu or Juan Zubieta), 593–97
Telleria, Juan Tomás, 480–82
TELSTRA, 733
terrorism, 216, 721–22
Terry, Samuel, 89, 100n89
Teruel, Spain, 281, 302n52
Texaco, 634
Thais, 385
Thiess Brothers, 617
timber, 410–11, 414, 423, 490, 511–16, 581–84
Tinaroo, 326t
Tiwi Land Council, 668
tobacco farms, 587n4
tobacco industry, 119, 199–200, 245, 284; Basques in, 399–403, 432–34, 438–39, 441, 445, 449–53, 463, 476–78, 481, 489–90, 494, 499, 504, 514, 518, 567, 688; risks associated with, 452; wages, 502

Toki Proprietary Ltd, 617
Tony & Company, 439, 442
Torotica, Serapio, 709
Torrente, Miguel, 232n234
Torrents, Salvador, 332n34, 336
Torrijos, Antonio (Tony), 346–47, 575
Torrontegui, Teodora, 377n53, 718
tortilla española (egg and potato omelet), 749
Toscana, 277, 281, 284, 358; Basques who arrived on, 413, 494, 511–12, 544–45, 561, 597, 601; European residence of adult males recruited for Queensland who arrived on (1958–1960), 691–97
Toscanelli, 260
Toscano, 103
Toscano colony, 76
Totorica, Gregorio, 701
Totoricagüena, José, 332n30
Totoricaguena, Jose Domingo, 701
Totoricagüena, Serafina, 483
Totoricagüena Egurrola, Gloria, 28, 90, 268n110, 374–75, 587n2, 626, 680, 711
Totorico (Totorica), Gregoria (Gregorio), 370
Townley, Athol, 280
Townsend, Colin, 649
Townsville, Queensland, 107, 125, 128, 181, 221, 454–60, 738
Townsville Basque Club, 687
Townsville Catholic News, 469–70
Townsville Daily Bulletin, 417, 421, 436, 439, 442, 446, 477, 483, 485, 488, 492, 622
Townsville Electricity Board, 612
Townsville General Hospital, 456–57
Townsville International Club, 589n17
Townsville Migrant Center, 268n119
Townsville Pathology Lab, 457
trainera (rowing), 345
Transfield, 568
Transport Workers Union, 522
Trans-Tasman relations, 389n8
Trápaga, Juan Ignacio, 367, 378n101

Trápaga, Monica Maria, 367
Traralgon, Victoria, 510–20
Treaty of Commerce and Navigation, 197, 240
Treaty of Peace, 241
Treaty of Tordesillas, 77
Trebonne Handball Club, 363–65, 371, 601–2
Trebonne Hotel, 363–65, 419, 600–601, 608, 687, 748
Tree of Gernika, 532, 537
Triple Entente, 137–38
Trojaola, Francisco, 702
Tueros, Gotzon, 354
Tugeri tribe, 658
tug of war (*sokatira*), 20–21, 364, 467, 471
Tully, Queensland, 181–82, 191, 287, 317–18
TV Week, 417, 439
txapela (beret), 39n23
Txapo, 742
Txarrak, Berri, 729
txingas (weight-carrying), 364, 471, 609n2
Txistu, Juan. *see* Tellería, Juan María
txistu music, 346
txoko (Basque Club), 334; MacTxoko, 29. *see also* Gure Txoko
Txori Alai (Happy Bird), 356
Txurruka, Frantzisko, 707

Uberuaga, Martin, 700
Ugalde, Amaia, 15
Ugalde, John (Johnny), 21–22
Ugalde, José Antonio, 561, 574
Ugalde, Juan, 345, 594
Ugalde, Juan Antonio, 13–15, 17–21, 345, 347–48
Ugalde, Sabino, 521, 554–56
Ugalde, Tomás, 345
Ugali Catholic Club, 502
Ugali Club, 433, 446
Ugarte, Anastasio, 316t
Ugarte, Elvig, 699

Ugarte, John, 699
Ugarte, Tomas, 699
Ugarte, Valentín, 341
Ugarte, Xavier, 29
Ugartemendi, José, 95
Ugartemendia, Jean, 95
Ugartemendia, Jean Baptiste, 95
Ugarte Ugartechea, Justo, 611
Ugarte Ugartechea, Margarita, 611
Ugarte Ynchaurraga, Eloy (Elvig), 315
Ugarte Ynchaurraga, Juan (John), 314–15
Ugarte Ynchaurraga, Tomás, 315
Ugartiburu, Vincente, 369–70
Ukrainians, 44
ultranationalists, 18–19
ultrapatriotism, 236
Unamuno, Ignacio, 413
Unamuno, José, 413
Unamuno, Juan, 410–11, 413–17, 496
Unamuno, Juanito, 35
unemployment, 228n113, 248–51, 284
United Nations (UN), 271
United Nations Convention on the Elimination of All Forms of Racial Discrimination, 385–86
United Nations Relief and Rehabilitation Administration (UNRRA), 236
United Protestants' Association, 209
United States: American West, 10, 46, 301n31, 373–74, 524, 531, 561, 683–88; Basque Americans, 301n31, 320, 375n1, 413, 418, 683–87, 689; Basque-language publications, 378n102; Cold War, 271; discrimination against immigrants, 163n154; foreign-born population, 43–44; immigrant population, 66n34, 153; Immigration Act, 318; immigration policy, 41, 43, 47, 146, 165; immigration quotas, 165, 318; Italian immigration, 146; Johnson Act, 165; Marshall Plan, 244; military presence in North Queensland, 223; race relations, 263n21, 649
United States Army, 649–50

808 INDEX

University of Melbourne, 573
University of Nevada Press, 753
University of New England, 663
University of Queensland, 651, 657, 663
University of the Basque Country (UPV), 39n19
University Studies Abroad Consortium (USAC), 39n19
UPV (University of the Basque Country), 39n19
Urazandi project, 28, 586n1
urbanization, 48
urban sprawl, 25
Urberuaga, Alberto, 232n227, 276, 285, 362–65, 371, 375, 424, 455, 590n34, 591–610, 680, 747
Urberuaga, Andrés, 489, 496
Urberuaga, José, 487
Urberuaga, José María, 495–97
Urberuaga, Victor, 487, 496
Urberuaga Badiola, Amaia, 373–74
Urbieta, José Antonio, 355
Urdaneta, 686
Urdangarín, Miguel, 355
Uriarte, Ángel, 444
Uriarte, Antonio, 512
Uriarte, Cornelio, 512–14, 519
Uriarte, Francisco, 438, 444
Uriarte, José, 438, 444, 446, 452–53
Uriarte, José Luis, 446
Uriarte, Juan, 401
Uriarte, Miren, 512
Uriarte, Pedro, 438, 512
Uribe, Juan, 28–30
Urigüen, Jesús, 411
Urigüen, José, 410
Uriona, Félix, 431
Uriona, José María, 431
Uriona, Juan, 431
Urionabarrenchea, Jenaro, 286
Urizar, José Maria, 316*t*
Urizar, Pedro Martín, 398
Urkullu, Iñigo, 38n13
Urquidi, A., 332n33

Urquidi, Joseba, 346
Urquijo, Miguel, 91
Urquijo, Vicente, 91
Urquiza, Isidoro, 452
Urquiza, Juan José, 452
Urquiza, María del Carmen, 452
Urquiza, Roberto, 451–54
Urrejola, Juan Mari, 731
Urrejola Eguren, Jon, 719, 731
Urrutia, Javier, 355–56
Urtain (José Manuel Ibar Azpiazu), 365, 368
Urtubi, Juan, 484
Uruguay, 43–44, 47, 683–84
Urzaa, Esteban, 484
Urzaa, Juan, 484
Urzaa, María Jesus, 484
Urzaa, Santiago, 483–86
USAC (University Studies Abroad Consortium), 39n19
Utah Construction Company, 543, 545, 612–13
Uzcudun, Paolino, 365, 368
Uzin, Sabino, 434–35

Vacca family, 310
Vane Tempest, Richard, 672–73
Vasco and Stubbins Brothers (VSB) Construction Company, 616–17
Vasco Construction Company, 614–15
Vasconia, 25
Vasquez, Joseph Merrey, 81
Vega, León, 599
vegetable farms, 450, 476
Velux 5 Oceans race, 717
Vendrell, Antonio, 308
Venezuela, 263n12, 267n110, 629–34
Vestey, William, 309, 331n14
Vestey Group, 312, 331n14
Viajes Altamire, 606–7
Viana, Francisco Javier, 77, 83–84, 97n41
Victoria, Australia: Asian population, 53–54; Basque population, 90–91, 317–19; call for immigrants, 81;

foreign-born population, 53–54; gold, 50; Italian population, 70–71; labor history, 181, 183–84, 285; seasonal work, 113; Spanish population, 81–82; sugar industry, 125
Victoria Insurance Co., 306
Victoria Mill, 119, 121, 131–32, 397; growers and peak tonnage, 329, 330t, 392; labor force, 132, 163n162, 223, 283, 295, 410–11, 414, 439, 446; mechanization, 293, 297
Victorian Rowing Association, 306
Victory Café (Ingham), 417, 545
Vidaurrazaga, Ángel, 576
Vidonja Balanzategui, Bianka, 67n60, 113–14, 157n35, 365, 587n2, 680, 732–35, 753
Vietnamese, 384–85
Vietnam War, 646–51, 653, 677nn1–2
Vigo, Spain, 291
Villacian, Santos, 699
Villalba, Antonio, 309–10
Villalba, Marina, 375n6
Villa Milano, 34, 593, 595
Villanueva, Agustin, 700
Ville de Metz, 320
Ville de Strasbourg, 320
virtual friendships, 24
voluntary associations, 335
volunteerism, 17, 25, 723–24
VSB (Vasco and Stubbins Brothers) Construction Company, 616–17
VSI Construction Company, 577

Wacol, 652
Wagga Wagga, New South Wales, 91
Wakefield, 125
Wales, 69, 307–8
wandering Basques, 627–78
War Emergency Organization, 220
Waring (nee Sans), Lola, 306
War Museum (Canberra), 384
war veterans, 141–42, 147
Waterman, C. I., 280–81

Watson, Cameron, 587n2, 753
Wawn, William T., 67n56
Weekly Times, 513
weight-carrying (*txingas*), 364, 471, 609n2
weightlifting (*harrijasozaile*), 364, 371, 471, 594, 609n2
Weil's disease (leptospirosis), 190–92, 375n6
Weir, Graham, 622
welding, 490, 492
Wellington, New Zealand, 202
Welsh colonists, 69, 307–8
Western Australia, 55, 66n33, 82, 98n59, 688, 751
whaling, 92–93
WhatsApp, 714
White, Linda, 587n2, 753
White Australia policy, 53–55, 61–64, 69–70, 104, 110–11, 132–33, 140–41, 165, 171–72, 384–86, 635
White Australia Sugar League, 149
white bounty, 110–11, 129–30
white-collar labor, 296–98
white slavery, 584
Whitlam, Gough, 368, 657
Whyalla, South Australia, 340
Wickham, Henry, 58
Williamstown, Victoria, 91
Windsor Pictures Co., 306
W & J Tyrer, 93
Wollongong, Australia, 285, 597, 600
Woman's Weekly, 417, 482, 506, 513, 560
women, 391, 584, 587n2; Basque immigrants, 318, 323; discrimination against, 644–45; in domestic service, 289; *Plan Marta* (Martha Plan), 286–87, 289–90, 341; prostitution, 600; Spanish immigrants, 286, 294, 303n102
woodchoppers (*aizkolariak*) and woodchopping, 354, 365–66, 410–11, 530, 537–38, 589n26
woodwork, 500

Woolworth's, 506
Woothakata, 326t
The Worker, 178, 180–81, 201–2
work ethic, 429, 437, 440, 443, 447–48, 476, 480–82, 488, 502–3, 520, 523, 548, 552
work scouts, 284
work stoppages, 129–30, 177, 309
World Congress of Basque Centers (*Congreso Mundial de Centros Vascos*), 355–57, 756
World Migration Congress, 363
World War I, 137–38, 140–42, 319, 384
World War II, 211, 218–25, 319, 640
Wroite, Doroteo, 311
Wyreema, 315

xenophobia, 143, 152–53

Yali, 656
Yarbayo, Jose, 312
Yarra River, 306
Ybarlucea, Andrés, 492
Ybarlucea, José, 492, 702
Ybarrolaburu, Esperanza, 290
Yenda Diggers Club, 502, 506
Yenda Hotel, 502
Yenda Rugby League, 502
Ymaz, Agustín, 709
Ynchausti, Santiago, 332n30
Ypiñazar, Valentín, 315–16, 316t, 699
Ypiñazar Co., 316
Ypiñazar Sesma, Juanita, 316–17
Yribar, Begoña, 428–29
Yribar, Belen, 428
Yribar, Luz María, 428

Yugoslavs, 124, 193, 241, 262, 277, 287, 295
Yunupingu, Galawrruy, 668

Zabala, Alberto, 475–76
Zabala, Antonio, 476–77
Zabala, José María, 475–78
Zabala, Josu, 34
Zabala, Lucia, 510
Zabalegui, Juan, 559–61
Zabaleta, Pedro, 494
Zalapa, Carlos, 343
Zamaran, Umberto, 710
Zárate, Rufino, 417, 489
Zarauz, Victorino, 524
Zarragoicoechea, Telesforo, 702
Zavattaro, Camillo, 394
Zavattaros, 587fn3
Zazpiak Bat escutcheon, 26
Zelman, Alberto, 71
Zimbabwe, 385
Zobella, Mario (fictional protagonist), 193–96
Zozaya, Andrés, 95
Zozaya, José, 95
Zozaya, Nicolás, 95
Zuazo, Francisco, 312
Zubieta, Juan. *see* Tellería, Juan María
Zubikarai, Agustin, 706
Zubiri Ibarrondo, Ilari, 28
Zubizarreta, Pedro, 701
Zumarán, Lorenzo, 744
Zumarán, Phil, 748–49
Zumarán, Robin, 749
Zurbano, Bonifacio, 93–94
Zurich Oil, 568